Rochelle Young

Jess M___
8-22-99

2/2
330
2500 Milvia
Alta Bates

2/4 — Fri* — SAN FRANCISCO *
12   10²⁵pm
Tower Air #154
Bday 11ᵗʰ: 32 yr.
Nina

D0166517

Also by Jess Mowry

WAY PAST COOL

RATS IN THE TREES

CHILDREN OF THE NIGHT

SIX OUT SEVEN

SIX OUT

ANCHOR BOOKS
DOUBLEDAY
New York London Toronto Sydney Auckland

SEVEN

JESS MOWRY

An Anchor Book

PUBLISHED BY DOUBLEDAY

a division of Bantam Doubleday Dell
Publishing Group, Inc.
1540 Broadway, New York, New York 10036

Anchor Books, Doubleday, and the portrayal of
an anchor are trademarks of Doubleday, a division of
Bantam Doubleday Dell Publishing Group, Inc.

Six Out Seven was originally published in hardcover
by Farrar, Straus & Giroux in 1993. The Anchor
Books edition is published by arrangement with
Farrar, Straus & Giroux.

Library of Congress Cataloging-in-Publication Data

Mowry, Jess, 1960–
Six out seven / Jess Mowry.—1st Anchor Books ed.
p.   cm.
1. Afro-American teenage boys—California—
Oakland—Fiction.
2. Oakland (Calif.)—Fiction.   I. Title.
PS3563.0934S58   1994
813'.54—dc20   94-20252
CIP

ISBN 0-385-47534-9

Copyright © 1993 by Jess Mowry

All Rights Reserved

Printed in the United States of America

First Anchor Books Edition: October 1994

10   9   8   7   6   5

TO BLANCHE RICHARDSON
of Marcus Books in Oaktown:
a sister who's there for us all

FOR WEYLEN

AND FOR ALL MY YOUNG
BROTHERS AND SISTERS
who ain't having no more of
whitey's great big new video game

Special thanks to Ras and Yolanda,
keepers of the magic.
And to my editor, Phyllida Burlingame,
for curving along to Corvus

PART ONE

There's something sad about a prison bus.

Seeing one on the road, most people look only once and then turn away: word to the mothers and fathers that life doesn't always flow like a child's summer dreams. Young bloods hanging together or cruising in cars might snicker and joke, but they'd do the same thing in a graveyard at night, denying that coffins could wait in their future. A prison bus is a concept gone wrong, like worms in a Big Mac or Mickey Mouse in KKK robes. Maybe it's because a bus is such a harmless, friendly thing . . . a bright yellow one carries kids full of dreams, and a Greyhound is silver and gleaming and going somewhere.

A prison bus goes nowhere. Its route is a sideslip in time, like a wrong turn down a dead-end road, leaving its travelers confused and angry and late for their true destinations.

Corbitt Wainwright thought these things as he sat in a tree. His legs were drawn up in the broad, spreading fork, his arms crossed over his knees and his chin dropped on top. His eyes were slitted against the hot Mississippi sun, concealing what could have been anger as the prison bus passed. The bus was a faded, gray, nothing kind of color, like the weather-worn asphalt of the narrow old road. The fierce sunlight glinting on massive window bars made Corbitt think of his father's ancient shotgun, the black so worn on its barrels that sometimes they seemed to be silver.

Buses were trucks in a way, and trucks fascinated Corbitt

like trains had captured the hearts of restless country boys a century before; big beasts of burden, snorting smoke, sweating heat, and smelling of the man-strength of hot iron and oil. Trucks, like trains, never seemed to rest; always moving on to faraway places, and never a part of the land they passed through.

Schoolday afternoons, weekends, and the long days of summer vacation usually found Corbitt at the truckstop a mile west of his home. The huge machines were familiar to him: he could tell a Freightliner from a Kenworth while it was still just a blur in the distant heat-haze, a Cummins engine from a Caterpillar when it was only a faraway moan, and was almost always right, running to wake a dozing pump-jockey as the trucks began downshifting whenever they were going to pull in.

Buses stopped too; the Greyhounds only for passengers because they fueled and serviced down in Jackson. They seldom needed anything the truckstop could provide, never seeming to have breakdowns, and even flat tires were rare. But most of the drivers would let Corbitt wash the windshields. He always did a good job, using sun-hot water from a black plastic bucket. A couple of jockeys had been fired for splashing a hot windshield with cold water and cracking it. Corbitt's formula was a dash of ammonia in the water, just enough to crinkle his nose as he balanced on one of the pump-island ladders. The jockeys let Corbitt borrow their ladders because washing a Greyhound's windshield wasn't expected of them. Corbitt had noticed a long time ago that a lot of people never did much more than what was expected of them. The Greyhounds' glass collected amazing yellow mosaics of splattered bugs from the trip through the valley, and it was hard work scrubbing off those sticky, sun-fried messes. Corbitt always cleaned the mirrors too; carefully, because the drivers had them adjusted with scientific precision and would pitch the furies if they were moved. That the Greyhound drivers, princes of the road, trusted Corbitt to wash their mirrors was an honor of sorts. Corbitt liked the way the big buses trembled, their engines loping in that impatient idle that marked a Detroit Diesel. The drivers usually paid him a dollar, though Corbitt had to split it with the jockey whose ladder he'd used. That was just a business-thing.

There were local buses too, and Corbitt knew their names like he recognized the trucks: GMs, Carpenters, Waynes, Superiors, and Bluebirds. But whatever company had built the prison bus hadn't put their name on it.

Maybe, Corbitt wondered, they'd been ashamed to?

Now he sat hidden by the tree's lush leaves and the denser, twisting vines that were slowly strangling it to death. Earlier that morning as he'd crossed the steamy fields, he'd thought of sitting on the roadside fence to watch the bus pass. But when he'd seen it coming, far down the shimmering ribbon of road, with sun-struck hellfire reflecting off thick glass and bars, he'd run back and climbed the tree instead. You didn't wave to a prison bus any more than you'd wave to a funeral car. That might make the people inside even sadder.

Corbitt didn't want to make his father sad.

His eyes blurred with tears. All he could see were shadowy profiles behind the bars and glass, as if nobody inside even cared to look out because they were no longer a part of the land they passed through.

The nothing-colored bus dwindled into the greens and browns of the valley on its journey to nowhere. The moan of its engine faded to a murmur as it slowed for the New Crossing bridge. Corbitt heard the deck planks rattle, and then the bus was gone. Blue exhaust-haze ghosting above the road, and the scents of hot iron and oil, were all that remained. It was mid-morning, Sunday, the highway stretched empty now, and only the sleepy drone of insects stirred the steamy silence. A crow flapped past, following the road in the hope that the bus had killed something.

A feeling came to Corbitt, new yet strangely familiar, as if he were in a place between future and past, alone in the tree, looking both ways. It was as if the past had ended when the bus rolled by. So, what was the next-thing? It seemed for all his thirteen years Corbitt had been hearing people talk of the next-thing; as if everything here was just temporary and they were really waiting for the next and better thing to appear. Was that why so many never did more than what was expected of them? But *how* would it come, Corbitt wondered, and how would you know it? Would there be a sign, like in magic? Could you hear it in the distance, downshifting just for you?

Corbitt listened to people a lot. It wasn't really eavesdropping because most folks acted like he wasn't there anyway. His dad had always said that even a mule could pass for smart if it kept its mouth shut. But Corbitt wasn't sure he believed that anymore. Even though he listened hard and didn't talk much . . . at least to white people . . . he still seemed to get treated like a jackass. Lately he'd started to wonder if all he was doing was sideslipping in time. Maybe there was no next-thing coming for him? And, if this was as good as it got, maybe he was stupid for thinking it wasn't good enough?

Corbitt sighed and closed his eyes. Maybe his next-thing had *already* come by, slowed, and then gone on without him because he'd been too stupid or lazy to run out and flag it down?

Despite the tree's shade, it was hot; hot even for Mississippi in July. It was wet, sticky heat and the northern truckdrivers hated it. One had told Corbitt that it made you slow and lazy. Maybe it did? Northern people always seemed smarter and faster-talking. Maybe that was why a lot of southern whites didn't like them? If that was true, then it seemed unfair as hell he'd been born here. Most of the northern whites were friendly. Sometimes they told him jokes. Corbitt usually tried them out on his brothers, Lamar Sampson and Toby Barlow. Sometimes on Sherry Cooper, too. Toby got them all right off. Lamar, you sometimes never knew for a week. And, naturally, Corbitt didn't tell the really dirty ones to Sherry.

One time, a young white lady with big pink sunglasses, who had gotten off the Greyhound to buy a Pepsi, had asked Corbitt a lot of questions about who he was and what life was like for him. She was going to college in California and studying Social Anthropology. She had seemed surprised that Corbitt knew what anthropology was, even if he'd never heard of the social kind. Anyway, he'd felt as if she was trying to be nice, but she was too serious about everything. She'd asked if he knew any folk-tales, so he told her a joke. Not a dirty one, naturally, but a plain old little niggerboy joke. A lot of white people relaxed if you did that, but she'd only gotten more serious. She'd even written the joke down, word for word in a notebook. Anyhow, the lady had asked permission to take his picture and had made him stand in front of the battered row of rusty oil-drum garbage cans around back of the building to do it. Having to pose like a poor little niggerboy bothered him. He'd read that primitive people in Africa thought you captured a piece of somebody's soul when you took their picture; like something that could be used against you in Voodoo. Corbitt thought that was a lot of shit. Besides, Mrs. Griffin said the idea was pure nonsense, and *she* of all people should know. Then too, he got his picture taken every year at school so that it was in the yearbook, and if some asshole white-trash kid wanted to go and stick pins in it, nothing had jabbed Corbitt yet. Still, the thought of his picture in California being studied by Social Anthropologists . . . he'd looked it up at the New Crossing library . . . was sort of strange. But the lady had given him a five-dollar bill and bought him a bottle of Pepsi. He'd traded the Pepsi back to the truckstop store for a Coke after the Greyhound pulled out, and buried the fiver with his other secret money in a Prince Albert can beneath the old bridge.

Corbitt ran over the joke again in his mind . . . *little nig-gerboy goes to the sawmill, tells the man his daddy needs some two-by-fours. Man asks how long he wants them. Little nigger-boy thinks a minute, then says he's gonna want 'em a long time cause they buildin a house.* Funny to figure that going to college in California. Well, if the lady wanted to call it a negro folktale, that was her problem.

Damn it was hot! Corbitt's good clothes were put away for school in the fall, and as usual he wore only his ragged summer jeans, which were threadbare and faded the color of weak powdered milk. Two seasons ago they'd been overalls, but he'd gotten too tall for the straps since then and the front flap hardly reached halfway up his chest anymore, so now he wore them like jeans, held at his waist by a wide brown belt with a big square brass buckle that some trucker had thrown away. Both knees were ripped open, one back pocket was gone, and the cuffs were frayed to ribbons and reached only partway down his shins. The front flap hung like an indian boy's loincloth. They rode so low on his narrow hips that a few curls of hair usually showed. Only the lady on the Greyhound had ever looked twice at them; nobody around here thought that worn-out rags looked out of place on a blackboy.

Corbitt considered a moment, then shucked his jeans and relaxed back naked in the wide tree fork. No one could see him concealed by the curtain of leaves so he might as well be comfortable. He dug an almost empty pack of Top tobacco from his remaining pocket and carefully rolled a cigarette. His fingers were thin, and very long. They were also quick and sure and full of smooth moves, and he didn't waste a speck of tobacco. Corbitt was amazingly tall for thirteen, straight and slender without being skinny, his long body tapering from wide shoulders to lean hips that made keeping his jeans on a perpetual problem. It was as if he hadn't been born to wear clothes. His bones were slim and fine beneath tightly defined muscles, like something built to crouch for hours in wait and then leap out and run for miles in chase. He might have looked fragile if he hadn't been so tall.

And he wasn't just black: he was so totally black that even other blacks made jokes about it. His smooth midnight skin seemed to absorb light instead of reflecting it. Like space. He might have looked delicate if he hadn't been so black.

Corbitt Wainwright, born to live naked and run, liked to read more than just about anything else. There was a tiny branch library in New Crossing, a bigger one up in Starkville, and the number of his dog-eared library card was stamped between the covers of an amazing amount of their books. Corbitt had received several awards for reading, but he didn't really give a shit. To his mind that was like getting a prize for eating. His dad read a lot, too, and was always bringing home paperbacks. Corbitt liked best to read about starships and space and alternate universes, where sideslipping in time could get you someplace . . . usually better. He'd probably spent half his life naked, but he didn't run much, and then almost never when it was expected of him. His grades in P.E. reflected that. Often in the hot summer nights he'd lie on his back by the river, gazing up at the stars and dreaming that they would be his next-thing.

His eyes were clear and black and as shiny as obsidian, seeming large in his long narrow face. He had prominent cheekbones, a nose like a small snub of nothing, and hair as bushy as an ebony dandelion puff. His lips never quite met over big white teeth, and turned up at the corners, giving him a sort of V smile even when there was nothing much to smile about. He didn't know it but his face was the face of a prince. His people had been warriors and rulers in a faraway land a long time ago. Because they were fierce fighters, and smart, few had ever been captured and chained. It was probably an accident or a betrayal that caused Corbitt to exist where he was today. But his people had also been kind, and had had no word in their language for greed, so maybe it wasn't surprising that not many were left anywhere in the world. Those few would have recognized Corbitt in an instant, but that was a story he'd never read, in a book that would never be written. In this time it was a nice face, and about the only part of him to reflect his true age. But it was so black that most people couldn't seem to see the real boy behind it, though almost everyone liked his smile.

Today, Corbitt didn't feel much like smiling.

The gray bus to nowhere had been his father's next-thing. Not all next-things were better. That was a new thought for Corbitt.

Corbitt's mind didn't so much wander as flick about like something darting from tree to tree through a sun-dappled forest in search of prey. Now came an image of Sherry Cooper by the river, poised naked with the water flowing at her feet. He felt a stirring in his loins, a sensation that had become familiar in the past few seasons. He glanced down, watching his dick rise between his legs.

There was a rustle of feathers overhead; a dry sound like dead leaves. Corbitt looked up to see a crow land on a branch. Maybe it was the same one that had been following the prison bus. But then all crows looked alike . . . though probably not to other crows. The bird's feathers gleamed like oiled gunmetal, and it seemed to stare down at Corbitt with slyness in eyes of frozen gold. It gave a croak that sounded too much like a smart-ass chuckle to Corbitt.

"Oh, go to hell," Corbitt told it. His loins cooled.

Corbitt ignored the crow and considered getting drunk. But what good would that do? He couldn't stay that way until his father came home, so it would just be a waste of time and money. Corbitt didn't have much money, and he wasn't exactly sure how important time was.

He pulled a blue Bic lighter from his jeans and held it up to a sunbeam, squinting at the fluid level. Butane was a liquid under pressure, he knew; a captive liquid sort of serving time until it got released and became a free vapor once more. He'd read the term *free vapor* in a book. Somehow it had a nice sound. Besides, a vapor was almost nothing, and nobody expected much from a nothing. The lighter was almost empty. Corbitt turned the tiny valve all the way down before firing his cigarette with the briefest flicker of flame. The lighter was one of his treasures; a thousand times more meaningful than any old award for book-reading. A truckdriver had given it to him that spring . . . a whiteman from the north who'd bummed a hand-rolled Top cigarette from Corbitt as if white men asking for spit-licked cigarettes from thirteen-year-old Mississippi blackboys was the most natural thing in the world. The gleaming blue Marmon-Herrington the man drove had OAKLAND, CALIFOR-NIA painted in small letters on the doors below the company name. Corbitt knew that California was technically in the west, but when you were black in the south most everywhere better was always north.

Inside the truckstop building, behind the counter in the little room where Mrs. Rudd sold bus tickets and passengers waited, was a huge map showing all of the places where Grey-hounds went. Corbitt had gone in and studied it. Oakland was a long, long ways away.

The white truckdriver had called him son . . . not boy, the way most whites except that bastard Shilo Bates were always careful *not* to do . . . or even kid, the way most whites did. They had sat in the shade of the truck in the dusty back lot and talked about engines and truck stuff while smoking Corbitt's cigarettes. The man had bought Corbitt a beer, like the most natural thing in the world, and hadn't once asked what life was like for him. Corbitt had caught a glimpse of a picture in the man's wallet: it showed a pretty black woman and two gold-colored boys in swimsuits on a bright green lawn. It was only an accident that Corbitt had seen, and he was happy about that. He wasn't sure why, but it wouldn't have meant as much if the man had intentionally showed it to him. Corbitt watched all the time for the shiny blue Marmon-Herrington but it never passed through again . . . or maybe it had but he'd missed it. The lighter was almost empty now, but Corbitt planned to keep it anyway.

Naked in the tree, his thoughts darting through the sunlight and shadows of his mind, Corbitt smoked his cigarette with the same casual grace that he did everything. Besides, his father had always said that if you were going to take the time to roll a good cigarette you should also take the time to sit back and appreciate what you'd done. Corbitt never smoked and worked at the same time. Of course, Lamar Sampson never did either, but that was mostly because he got whopped if his mom or dad caught him. Now, as he smoked, Corbitt's eyes gazed out through the curtain of leaves, across the shimmering road and the hazy green-and-brown fields to the faint purple hills in the west. A feeling stirred inside him, close to but different from the restlessness between his legs. A next-thing was coming. He could sense it like faraway thunder or the eerie hollowness in the air just before a tornado touched down. The signs were all around, and yet there was no definite one to guide him. Not all next-things were good: he knew that now. And, if you sometimes had to help them happen by doing more than what was expected of you, then maybe you could also hide from a bad one just as he'd hidden from the prison bus?

He glanced up at the crow, but it also seemed to be searching the western distance. Corbitt wished that he'd asked his dad more questions. Man-questions. It was sad to realize all he should have asked now that it was too late. His mother didn't always understand his questions . . . she got the words right but sometimes not the real question *behind* the question. It was sort of like, if he went and got good and drunk today, so fucked-up that Toby and Lamar would have to carry him home, his mom would think he'd done it because he was sad about his father. She wouldn't understand that all he really wanted to do was break the hateful continuity of these recent days. But then, getting drunk would almost be what was expected of him. Corbitt wanted to do something besides what was expected of him; especially for his mother. There were already too many problems, and most were caused by money. And now, with his dad gone, there would be hardly any money at all. Maybe, he thought, that's what it was . . . the scary hollowness in the air he wanted to hide from. Maybe it wasn't a next-thing at all but only the fear that he'd never be able to do any more than just what was expected of him.

Corbitt's eyes caught a tiny movement at the edge of the road: a field mouse. He tried to imagine what that vast empty grayness ahead looked like to a mouse. Could it even see the other side? The mouse wanted to cross over, but Corbitt could sense its fear; so small to him but so huge to the mouse. Yet he could see what the mouse could not . . . through different eyes and higher perspective . . . that the narrow country road stretched clear for miles and was perfectly safe to cross. Corbitt's V of a smile touched his lips. He whispered, "Go for it, little brother. Just over there be your own next-thing, an a good one, all soft an green an waitin for you."

The mouse hesitated, made a short darting run, but then scampered back to refuge in the roadside weeds once again. Its sides were heaving in fear as it stared across to the tall grass ripe with seeds.

"Go for it," Corbitt urged in a whisper once more. "Listen, I know for my ownself how that ole empty gray be so scary to you. But it be only so much of nuthin. Gonna go an waste your life stayin scared of some little nuthin? Keepin yourself here be just what spected of you. So, go an do somethin more."

A smile sparked in Corbitt's eyes as the mouse hurried straight across for its next-thing. Suddenly, a gunmetal blur fell from the sky and the crow caught the mouse in its beak. It beat the tiny body on the pavement then began to rip it apart. The frozen-gold eyes seemed to find Corbitt's, and the bird gave its croaking chuckle again.

"Bastard!" bawled Corbitt. He had nothing to throw except his lighter, and that he wouldn't do. Dropping from the tree, he dashed through fierce sunlight to the fence. The crow glanced at him, but only chuckled again and went right on ripping at the mouse. Corbitt could have leaped the fence as if it were so much of nothing. Instead he slumped against it, sobbing, and pounding his fists on the splintery top rail. "You bastard! You goddamn little black bastard!"

The crow kept eating. After a minute, Corbitt straightened his long back and wiped at his eyes. It was only a mouse. Who gave a shit what happened to one goddamn Mississippi mouse? Returning to the tree, Corbitt slipped his jeans on and began walking slowly back across the field.

Two boys lay together on dry, yellow grass in the skeletal shade of a dying oak tree. Both were half-naked; one clad in cutoffs, ragged and dirty, with a toe poking through a hole in his Nikes. The other wore wash-faded Levi's, and his Nikes were newer, though shapeless and squashed with the soles almost gone. White males their age would never have lain down together that way . . . like children or brothers . . . and that made these two look savage and wild. One was the color of old city soot or the satiny shade of brand-new truck tires. And he wasn't just fat, he looked almost helpless flat on his back; a small-boned boy buried in a huge, sloppy mass of black blubber. His jeans couldn't be buttoned more than halfway, and had slipped down his thighs so his butt was sunk bare in the grass. A band of bright sunlight striped over his middle, and another boy's dick might have stirred in its warmth, but his lay unseen in the shade of his belly.

The second boy lay at a quarter past three, with his head on the first boy's soft spill of stomach, so his coffee-brown face seemed to float on a big sooty pillow. A pack of Kools lay near his ear, half-sunk in the funnel of the fat boy's belly button. The fat kid's head was propped against the tree trunk, and he held an open paperback book between the twin rolly masses that passed for his chest. He was reading aloud in a voice that was husky but splintered by squeaks. A cigarette smoldered in pudgy fingers, and the smoke spiraled skyward in the motionless air. A second chin padded his jawline a little, and his cheeks were chubby and round, but his face remained free of the blubbery fat that had swallowed the rest of his body. It was a face like an African cherub's: wide-mouthed with a flat, bridgeless nose, and full lips that rested in a half-open pout to reveal the glitter of strong white teeth. His black eyes were bright and thick-lashed, and looked like the kind that could take in everything while nobody noticed. His hair was an Afro-ish bush that had probably never seen scissors. Instead of an earring or fake golden chain, he wore an ancient Pukka-shell necklace, bone-white with two turquoise beads. The book on his chest was a cheap sci-fi novel with black cats in space suits pictured on the cover. The title was *Space Panthers*. He turned the last page, and an inch of ash fell from his cigarette and landed on a nipple so deep-sunk in fat that it formed a tiny cup. He flicked the ash away with a finger and went on reading. Four empty Coke cans lay by his side on the grass. A fifth can balanced midway between his chest and belly button, rocking to the rhythm of his breath. Picking it up, he gulped the last swallow, then dropped it among the others. His hand searched the grass in a scatter of Twinkie wrappers, but found only sticky cellophane. "Yo, Beamer. That all there is, man?"

The other boy sat up instantly. Near his knee was a well-worn backpack and a street-scarred Steadham skateboard. The pack had to be his because its straps would never have fit the fat boy. The board must have been his too because it barely looked rideable for a normal-size kid. Digging through the pack, Beamer pulled out a Twinkie; single-wrapped like they came when you bought a whole boxful. A little more searching turned up a sixth can of Coke. "They yours, Tam. Shit, I ain't hungry."

The fat boy studied Beamer with that knowing look of for-ever homeys, but took the last Coke, which Beamer popped for him, and watched the Twinkie being unwrapped. Beamer hes-itated, looking suddenly shy, holding the Twinkie in thin, dirty fingers. "Um . . . Tam? Member when I used to feed ya, man?"

The fat boy gulped Coke, and burped, sending ripples through his body, and slowly shook his head. "Jeeze, Beamer, that was fuckin *years* ago. When we was *little*, man."

Beamer's face was hard to describe. Though he was thirteen, and the same age as the fat boy, he had the innocent face of a child. His wide amber eyes held no calculation. The best word was *unfinished;* like an uncompleted plan. His thin, lanky frame seemed the same way; chest muscles sketched but never filled out. It was basically a little boy's body, stretched instead of grown, coffee-colored and darkened by dirt. His cutoffs and Nikes were the same he'd been wearing for most of the summer, and his hair looked like dreadlocks baled up in burlap. He probably smelled worse than he looked, though the fat boy seemed immune to his scent.

Beamer's face turned bashful. "Yeah. But . . . ain't nobody peekin us. Ain't nobody gonna see an figure us homos, Tam."

The fat boy sighed, but smiled. "Oh, what the fuck. Go for it." He closed his eyes and opened his mouth, taking the Twinkie in one messy bite from the other boy's fingers. "Spose you been pickin your nose," he muttered through a mouthful of cream filling.

"Nuh-uh!"

"Well then, bet you didn't wash your hands last time you pissed, man."

"Um . . . did you, Tam?"

"Like, where?"

"What I sayin."

The fat boy opened one eye. "So, why you used to feed me anyways, man?"

Beamer looked even shyer and dropped his eyes.

The fat boy smiled. "Aw, hey, homey, you was the one come runnin to me with your dick in your hand first time it got hard. Shit, just never no tellin what gonna 'barrass your ass."

Beamer giggled and flopped down, his head plopping onto the fat boy's belly and making it wobble like Jell-O. For a few minutes he just stared at the sky beyond the tree branches. The fat boy shut his eyes and waited. Finally, Beamer murmured, "Um . . . maybe I kinda figure I get you so fat you can't climb them stairs no more. Then you stay with me forever."

The fat boy laughed. "Jeeze, Beamer, I know you all my fuckin life, an times I still don't believe what come out your mouth."

Beamer turned his head, meeting the fat boy's eyes. "Um . . . what I say stupid, Tam?"

"Naw. You past cool, homey. Fuck, I hate climbin stairs, man."

"Well then, most work, huh?"

The fat boy dropped a hand on Beamer's shoulder. "Shit, you never *had* nuthin down there to eat anyways, man. For sure shouldn't wasted your food on me."

"Shit, I not need much." Beamer patted the fat boy's belly like he was proud of it.

The fat boy's eyes scanned quickly around. "Jeeze, Beamer! Don't *do* that! It look way fuckin queer, man!"

"Um, sorry." Beamer tapped a finger on the dog-eared paperback. "Um . . . what there in that book, Tam . . . that word, void, at the end where all them space cats flew off to? Um, what it mean?"

"Mmm." The fat boy struggled a little like he wanted to sit up, but then gave it up. "Well, that time it mean space . . . like they all went explorin to find a new planet for their people. But, void usually mean nuthin." He waved a hand toward grimy brick buildings showing through the little park's scraggly trees. "Like this motherfuckin hood, man."

"Oh." Beamer sat up and looked around as if seeing something new. "Um . . . I always kinda figure nuthin all black."

The fat boy killed the Coke, and snickered. "So, what the hood, man?"

A tawny light sparked behind Beamer's eyes. For once in his life he'd gotten a joke. "Thanks, Tam."

"Huh? For what, man? Readin to your ass?"

Beamer ran dirty fingers through his hair. "Um . . . yeah. For that. But most for bein my homey." Sitting cross-legged, Beamer scratched at his armpit. "Um . . . cause I a motherfuckin crack baby, man."

The fat boy frowned. "Yo! I tell ya a b'zillion fuckin times stop sayin that shit, man! It just . . . well, it just make it worse, what it is! I don't know how, but it does! An nobody give a shit anyways!"

Beamer dropped his chin in his hands. "I just wish I not. That all."

The fat boy sitting up was like some old movie of a submarine surfacing. Fat seemed to cascade down his body to slop around his waist in a blubbery wave that filled his lap and spilled over his thighs. He counted on chubby fingers. "Yo! Listen up! You gots yourself two good arms, two good legs, an from one dude who ain't fuckin gay to another who ain't, you don't look half-stupid. Fact is, most time you got least six out seven, an you way good at smokin the suckers when you ain't."

Beamer's eyes widened. "No shit, Tam?"

"Word, man. Just don't fuckin hug my ass here, okay?"

Beamer nodded solemnly. "Uh-huh. But . . . um . . . I wish I could read, man. Even a little. An really be cool, like . . . um, you, Tam. Shit, you really the coolest dude in Oaktown! All seven! Chill over Hobbes, even."

The fat boy snorted. "Cool, chill, ice, fuck all that, man!" His belly button had squished shut, and he pulled the Kool pack out of it. "Sides, man, chill factor in this hood be directly proportional to the long of your green."

Beamer laughed. He had a way cool laugh. Just like his smile he put everything he had into it. He studied the fat boy a moment. "Um, Tam? Um . . . fat good for babies, ain't it? What I sayin is, mean they gonna live an get strong, uh-huh?"

"Mmm. Well, I spose, man. It always sayin in them old books how African people make big fat healthy babies . . . cept in Somalia an poor places like that."

Beamer nodded. "What I figure."

The fat boy shook a Kool from the pack for Beamer and then another for himself. Beamer fired both with a Bic. The fat boy blew smoke and glanced toward the street. "Talkin bout Hobbes, sometime it seem like he the M.C. of cool in this hood, even if he a dealer. So, how you like workin for him, man?"

Beamer's face darkened a little. "Um . . . well, it okay. He put me on sellin to little kids. Call me a natural." Beamer also glanced toward the street. "Um, I need the green, Tam."

The fat boy nodded. "Mmm. Your dad takin most of it, ain't he?"

"Um . . . well . . . yeah. Course, his job not pay nuthin worth shit. But I keepin some back . . . um, for myself. There . . . um . . . 'portant shit I gots to buy." Beamer's face darkened further. "Hobbes straight up with me. It that goddamn Akeem, always backstabbin."

"Yeah? So, who this Akeem sucker, man?"

"Y'know? Hobbeses's bodyguard."

"Oh. You mean Sebastian. He was in two of my classes last year right after he moved here."

"Uh-huh. Cept now all the time he tellin the dudes call him Akeem. Say, Sebastian a fuckin slave name. Um, so what a slave name, Tam?"

"It somethin you sposed to be shamed of. A name white people give ya a way long time ago."

Beamer scratched his hair again. "Um . . . but I not know no white people, Tam. Never ever did." He poked a thumb against his chest. "Yo! My name Calvin Willis Brown! My own dad gimme that name, an I fuckin for sure ain't shamed!" He looked down at himself and spread his arms wide. "An I *am* fuckin brown!"

The fat boy blew a smoke ring. "Well, technically you black, man."

"Well, duh!"

"Well, what I sayin is, you proud of it?"

"Well, I guess. Shit, only thing I not proud over be bein a motherfuckin crack baby."

The fat boy sighed. "Oh, don't fuckin start, man. Anyways, what I tryin to tell ya is that some brothers an sisters take 'em a African name cause they proud bein Africans."

Beamer flicked ashes from his Kool, and scowled. "Shit, man! Sabby ain't no fuckin African! Shit, he ain't even *all* fuckin black! An, anyways, he a goddamn 'merican just same's me!"

The morning sun was climbing, stealing away the small patch of shade under the tree. The fat boy, now full in the sunlight, wiped sweat from his forehead. "Forget it, man. Shit, a name don't signify nuthin if you don't know the fuck who you are to begin with. An you gots no probs with that, homey."

Beamer smiled once more. "Um, so what kinda name be Lactameon, man?"

The fat boy shrugged. "Fuck I know. A goddamn hard one for people to spell! I think it somethin my mom dug up out some way old book."

Beamer touched Lactameon's arm. "Um, Tam? Um, if you was to go an have a kid . . . a boy-kid . . . you name him somethin African?"

"Mmm. Well, I don't know, man. I think I go an name him whatever fit . . . somethin he be proud of, what I sayin. Like, a strong name for a strong little black dude." Lactameon considered, crushing out his cigarette in the grass. "Funny as hell when you think about Sabby gettin into that sorta shit."

Beamer spat. "Not funny when he go an shove his motherfuckin Uzi in your face over it, man!"

"Mmm. Guess not, huh." Lactameon brushed more sweat from his body. Puddles of it formed in his fat rolls and squeezed out in trickles when he moved. He heaved himself back into what little shade remained by the tree trunk. "Spose that all the Cokes, huh?"

Beamer nodded. "I can cruise to the market an score somethin else."

Lactameon slumped against the tree, gazing up through dusty leaves at the sky. "Naw. Save your buck, Beamer. Shit, you shouldn't wasted it on them Twinkies an Cokes anyways."

"But you like 'em, Tam."

Lactameon shook his head. "Yo. Listen up, man. I gots a real lunchtime comin, you don't. An, that buck you keepin back from your dad? You usin it for food, right? What I sayin is, you ain't wastin it on somethin stupid like a goddamn gold earring or some other showtime bullshit like most them other dealer dudes do?"

"No, Tam. Fuckin swear to God! I total careful with it, man! Shit, I gots to be now!"

"Well, good, man. Like I sayin, you gots it down six."

Beamer watched the fat boy wipe more sweat from his face. "Um, Tam? Gots some milk here. You can have one, you want, only they not cold."

"Huh?" Lactameon looked as Beamer dug a small can from his pack. "Yo, the fuck you doin with condensed milk, man? That kinda baby food."

"Um . . . well, it fuckin good for your ass, huh? Make you strong?"

Lactameon smiled. "Course it does, homey. An you keep on drinkin it." He glanced at the sun. "Yo! Cruise home with me, man. I make us up a whole big motherfuckin mess of Beefaroni. Like, all you can eat."

Beamer looked sad. "Gots no time. Gots to work. I workin right now cause it Sunday an little kids be comin in soon."

Lactameon blew out a sigh. "Shit, Beamer, you know what

you doin to them little suckers, don't ya? What I sayin is, *you* know for a fact what it like with a fucked-up crack brain. Don't it make you sad to see 'em burnin out theirs?"

Beamer pulled up his legs and hugged them to his chest. "*Course* it fuckin make me sad! Figure I not feel shit? But, how the fuck else I make me money, man? Shit, all them goddamn kid-project things gots probs scorin work for regular kids! Sure the fuck not gots time for no crack babies! Shit, man, there just too many motherfuckin black kids, an not nobody want none of 'em! Shit, I used to wonder why people make babies they not gots no motherfuckin time for!" Beamer dropped his face on his knees. "Shit!"

With an effort, Lactameon scooted over to the boy and patted his back. "Don't cry, homey, it ain't fuckin cool."

"Don't give a fuck! Anyways, *you* don't care bout no god-damn cool!"

Lactameon stroked the thin boy's back, not caring if anyone saw him or not. "Okay, man. I hear ya. Just chill a little, huh?"

Beamer raised his head and wiped at his face. "Um, Tam? I hear it say on TV where you gots to read to your kids. It make 'em way smart. Um . . . you teach me some readin, man?" Beamer grabbed up the paperback. "Check it, Tam! I already read me some of them words!" He pointed. "Space Panthers. There a S, an a P, an . . ."

Lactameon smiled. Grunting, he dug underneath himself and pulled out a faded red tank-top that he'd stuffed in his back pocket. "Here, homey-mine. Wipe your face. Anyways, I been readin to your ass all week, man. Sure you just don't member from that?"

"Nuh-uh, Tam! Listen up! This here a S, an it make a ssss sound. Shit, all them letters make different sounds! You figure out that shit, your ass be readin!"

"For sure, Beamer! Jeeze, I think you gettin better, man! Shit, maybe it that milk."

"Well . . . I fuckin for sure tryin to get better." Beamer met Lactameon's eyes. "But . . . guess you gots no time for me learnin readin, huh?"

Lactameon considered that. Truth was, he seemed to have nothing but time, especially now that Beamer had a job. Up to this year he'd spent most of his summers at the old public pool,

practically living in the water, not so much swimming as just
floating peacefully in the deep corner away from the diving board
or stretched out on sun-warm concrete with a book. He'd had
a lot of friends there; mostly other fat boys. Of course, he'd been
the fattest and that got respect . . . being the best at anything
did. Every year there'd be a few new dudes, some so ashamed
of their bodies that they wore shirts in the water. He gave them
the full 411 on that: it looked lame and just let the other kids
know where to stick the knife. Not even the big, hard-bodied
dudes hassled Lactameon because they knew he had pride.
Sometimes the big dudes would stuff him with hot dogs and bet
on how many he could eat. And then there were always the
dudes who'd pay him to do a cannonball and splash their girl-
friends. Shit, how could summers be better than that . . . no
hassles, free food, friends, and respect.

    And even protection the few times he'd needed it.

    One of the Collectors had been a self-conscious fat boy two
summers ago. Really, he wasn't much more than terminal
chubbs, but had big bouncy boobs and wouldn't take off his shirt
with his homeys. That spelled probs for a gang kid. Lactameon
had handled that, and Stacy had graduated to in-your-face fat,
and these days you wouldn't even figure he owned a shirt. The
Collectors had made Lactameon their mascot, and that was as
good as a Gold Card. Being a gang mascot wasn't much work;
sometimes he went to a meet, but mostly it meant he could
hang with the dudes whenever he wanted and otherwise people
left him alone. Most gang mascots weren't fighters, though they
were targets just the same, and occasionally got kidnapped or
traded. The Leopards had a whiteboy named Winfield, skinny
and small with long hair so light it looked almost silver. He
wasn't good for much besides being a whiteboy, but then there
seemed to be no straight word on what mascots were supposed
to be for anyhow. Maybe they were just to prove that a gang
was rich enough to afford something useless. Winfield had spent
a lot of time hanging at the pool last year with Lactameon. He
was always hungry and seldom had cigarettes, but Lactameon
fed him and they had gotten to be homeys in sort of a way.
Winfield talked like a normal brother, and probably got more
respect as a curiosity than as a gang member.

    But that had been last year, and now the goddamn pool

was closed. The paper talked about too many drugs and too much gang activity, but that was total bullshit. The pool was just in a poor black hood so the white assholes took it away. If anything, the drugs and violence and gang activity had increased afterward, because the kids had nothing to do and nobody wanted them. Were white people really that stupid? Lactameon didn't think so.

Anyway, this summer there hadn't been a goddamn thing for Lactameon to do. His mom had customers all day long in the tiny apartment, so he couldn't kick back on the couch and watch daytime TV. His own little room turned into a furnace when the sun beat the building's backside. He could sprawl naked on his bed and sweat and listen to his blaster, or sweat and read a book. If his mom had a good week and scored extra food he could do any of the above, plus eat. Opening the window for air also brought in b'zillions of flies and sometimes a rat. He could hang at the Collectors' clubhouse, but that meant a three-story stair-climb through an abandoned building and then up a ladder in the elevator shaft to the machinery shed on the roof. The Collectors weren't rich, they didn't deal drugs, and despite what the papers and TV all said, there wasn't much chance of black kids stealing anything outside the ghetto, and there sure wasn't a hell of a lot worth stealing inside it. Whatever was stashed in the clubhouse for eating and drinking had to be replaced by whatever dude whose belly it filled. This also applied to batteries for their blaster. Lactameon wouldn't have minded some sort of job, but there weren't even any for older kids, much less for him or poor burned-out Beamer.

Except what Beamer was doing right now.

"Well," said Lactameon. "You come over tonight when it cool. Shit, come sleep over an take a bath. Maybe I can teach you some readin then."

"Um . . . but I sorta work nights, Tam."

"Shit, I didn't know any little kids with money stayed out that late."

Beamer stared at the grass. "I . . . gots other shit to handle at night, man."

"Well, maybe we could go to that kid-center place? They gots lots of books an magazines there. Even feed ya."

Beamer looked miserable. "I can't go there no more, Tam.

They know I a dealer now. Not want me around. Shit, Hobbes only one ever gimme a chance at doin somethin!" Beamer yanked a handful of grass from the ground and tore it to pieces. Finally he looked up again and searched Lactameon's face. "Um . . . I gots this . . . well . . . it sorta a secret, what it is, man. Even from you. It kinda like a wrong thing . . . no, maybe a right thing I done an it go wrong . . . Shit! I wish I could think, man!"

Little-kid voices carried from the street. Beamer's head jerked up, alert, as four small boys, all shirtless, in jeans and huge high-tops, came pushing through the bushes instead of using the pathway . . . a kid thing to do. The youngest was maybe six, the oldest probably eight. The three smaller boys were all shades of black, and had that sway-backed, round-tummied look of fairly well fed and healthy little dudes. But the oldest was miserably thin and looked fragile as a feather; not really that sickening skin-over-bone look like the TV pictures of kids in Somalia . . . but maybe kids starved better in America. His body was a brassy-bronze color the shade of polished water pipes, that almost looked metallic. Lactameon thought of a little toy robot, worn-out and thrown out but somehow still going. His hair was amazing; a woolly-wild jungle of yellow-brown dreadlocks that hung to his waist.

Beamer got to his feet. Lactameon sighed and began his own struggle to stand, using the tree trunk to pull himself up. He watched with Beamer as the small boys headed across the grass toward the slimy duck pond. Spitting at ducks was an old summer favorite, Lactameon remembered. Sometimes a kid, crazy in the heat, would try to cool off in the water . . . until he discovered the bottom was all broken glass.

Beamer looked like a predator scenting the wind, but then relaxed once again. "None of 'em do nuthin," he murmured.

"Too bad. Jeeze, that little half-white dude don't even look like he do food."

Beamer glanced at the fat boy, his eyes saddening. "I know him, Tam. Live in my buildin. He got done a real wrong thing. Times I give him money or somethin to eat."

"To help you?"

Beamer frowned slightly. "No, man. To help him."

"Oh." Lactameon touched the other boy's arm. "You a way cool dude, homey. Even if you don't think so."

Beamer's eyes tracked the little brass-colored kid. "He die soon. Um . . . I can sorta always tell. Maybe like your mom with her fortune-tellin shit."

Lactameon studied his friend for a moment. "Mmm. Well, my mom never tell people them kinda things, man. She say the future should always oughta be somethin people can look forward to."

"Um . . . maybe sometime you tell my fortune, Tam?"

Lactameon looked away. "Shit, I ain't really no good at it, man."

Something rustled the air overhead. Lactameon looked up to see a big black bird land on a branch. "Yo, Beamer! Check it out, man! There somethin ya don't see every day."

Beamer stared upward. "Shit, man, the fuck that?"

"Mmm. Crow, I think. Maybe a raven. But, shit, Beamer, check what it gots in its beak!"

"Fuck yeah, man! That somebody's gold chain!"

Lactameon squinted into the sunlight. "Mmm. I read bout them birds, man. They down with stealin shiny shit."

"Huh? Why, Tam?"

"The fuck I know, man. But, yo! That goddamn chain gots to be worth least a half buck if it real!"

"Fuck yeah, Tam! But . . . um . . . so how we gonna get it from way down here?"

"Mmm. You *would* gotta ask that, huh?"

"Yo, Tam! I climb on your shoulders, man! Reach that first branch!"

The big bird cocked its head and made a sound like a smart-ass snicker, then flew away. Lactameon sighed. "Dream on, homey-mine." He watched the bird's shape disappear in the distance. "Little black bastard!"

Beamer touched Lactameon's shoulder. "Um . . . please don't say that, man."

The row of eight little board-and-bat cabins looked like ancient slave quarters. And the friendly white family, lost down Bridge-end Road that spring in their big new stationwagon with California plates, probably figured, after asking Mrs. Griffin's permission, that that's what they were taking pictures of. For sure there were enough naked little kids running around—and nearly naked bigger ones since Corbitt, Toby, and Lamar were there —to fill a whole album with Old South shots. Corbitt could have sworn they expected to find a souvenir shop, maybe stocked with bullwhips and leg irons made in Taiwan like the bogus indian junk sold at the Starkville dime store. He hadn't missed how the white girl, fourteen or so, had gone all gooey at the sight of Lamar in nothing but cutoffs. Toby had said later that she'd have probably bought him to take home and cuddle if they could still do that. Toby himself seemed to confuse the whole family something awful, though they were much too polite to stare.

Really, the sag-roofed row of weather-warped wood and cracked, curling tarpaper had been built in the twenties when the narrow strip of concrete along the river had been the main highway and motels were a new invention called motor courts. If you looked hard at the rusted tin sign atop a tall iron post in front of the first cabin you could still make out the words MAG-NOLIA MOTOR COURT. The road hadn't been tended since the fifties, after the new highway was cut through from Starkville straight across the fields. Corbitt had always figured the new road was laid like that because modern people no longer had time to wander slow beside a cool, tree-lined riverbank. Most of the old highway's paving had cracked into a mosaic of cockeyed slabs, and there were many places where it had crumbled completely away. These were usually mud when it rained and dust when it didn't. It no longer had a name, and wasn't on the truckstop's Sinclair maps, but everybody called it Bridge-end Road. Just beyond the last cabin it dead-ended at the rust-scabbed skeleton of an iron truss bridge that had been a one-laner even back when American cars were as skinny as today's Subarus. The bridge had been built to last, with huge round-headed rivets and old-fashioned detail, and its massive lattice-box beams still stood straight, though they cried and creaked during flood season. Whoever had designed the bridge had planned for the future, but they couldn't have known it would just be bypassed and forgotten. The wooden deck planks were rotted soft as mush, and more than a few were missing. The road on the opposite bank still showed in places, broken and bone-white through the fields downriver, but where it hugged the shoreline on the far side of the bridge new trees and overgrowth were burying it from sight. A heavy board blocked the entrance on Corbitt's side. The word CONDEMNED could still be seen, faded as faint as the small letters on the motor court sign that said KITCHENETTES AND MODERN FACILITIES.

"Kitchenettes" meant a stove and sink and refrigerator in one corner, while "Modern Facilities" were inside bathrooms. The toilets still worked in five of the cabins, and the showers in six. Corbitt's cabin, at the end of the row closest the bridge, wasn't one of them. Water would still come from the shower head, and fill the toilet tank, but it wouldn't go anywhere except on the floor if you expected anything else. The motor court builders may have planned for the future too, because there was an older kind of facility in a shed up by Number One cabin. On its door was a chipped enamel sign that said COLORED WASH-ROOM. The white family had clucked their tongues and looked shamefaced while taking a picture of it but it was just one of Mrs. Griffin's jokes. She had another sign on her chicken coop that said COLORED WAITING ROOM. Both Corbitt's father and Lucas Sampson, Lamar's dad, had tried to fix the bathrooms lots of times, but the pipes were full of roots and new ones were too expensive. Corbitt sometimes kept catfish in the toilet tank until they were needed for supper.

In summer, Corbitt swam in the river to keep clean and in winter he washed at the kitchenette sink. His dad had run its drain out through the wall with PVC pipe and then dug a little ditch so the water went down the riverbank. It was a nigger-rig. Only Number One cabin, biggest because it had been the office, boasted a working water heater, but the lights and most of the electric plugs still worked in all. Corbitt's parents had a radio and a TV—a little black-and-white Sony that pulled in two snowy channels. Corbitt knew about satellite dishes—the truck-stop had one—but figured his mom would have liked an inside toilet better than a clear picture of the *Cosby Show*.

Two Bridge-end families had cars—trucks, actually. A truck was a useful thing, while a car would have been sort of like a satellite dish. The Coopers in Number Three owned a 1955 International pickup, and Lucas Sampson had a 1963 White Compact three-ton cabover with a steel-plated stake-bed for hauling scrap iron. Corbitt loved to ride in it. Sometimes Lucas would even let him drive along deserted backroads. Corbitt's long legs easily reached the pedals, and his natural grace never showed itself more than when he was handling and double-clutching the big old truck, though there were times when Corbitt wished for some of Lamar's muscle to wrestle the steering wheel over ruts. Lamar, Lucas's oldest son, was fourteen and strong as a mule, but not tall enough for comfortable driving. He and his father worked hard hauling scrap, but they just didn't make enough money to pay Corbitt. Corbitt often went with them anyway, partly for a chance to drive but mostly because Lamar was one of his two best brothers. Once in a great while Lucas would get a good load and have some extra money. Then he'd take Corbitt along with Lamar and his two younger sons for a movie and a pizza in Starkville. Of course, Toby Barlow, Corbitt's other best brother, would come too, but he usually managed to pay his own way with the money he made from his chores at home.

The White mounted a huge winch behind the cab, and Lucas had a cutting torch. He often eyed the old bridge. Corbitt's dad had said that Lucas wrote to the state about every six months but they wouldn't let him take down the condemned bridge. Lucas would mutter about it being a wasteful shame . . . all that fine heavy iron right there and rusting to dust. Corbitt's dad had said once that the government would just as soon forget that the bridge had ever belonged to them in the first place and, while they didn't have a notion in hell what to do with it, they hated to be reminded that it still existed. But they weren't about to give it away to niggers. Corbitt never said so to Lucas but he was glad of that: the forgotten old bridge to nowhere had a lot of uses for the Bridge-end kids.

Now, Corbitt stopped under the leaning motor court sign and studied the bridge, wondering why he didn't feel differently about it today. If it hadn't been still spanning the river, his dad wouldn't have been on that sad gray bus going nowhere.

The stark white sun was climbing toward noon, and the fields across from the cabin row shimmered and steamed beneath it. But the cabins themselves were shaded by the big river trees, and a friendly coolness came up from the slow green water. The shouts and laughter of children at play carried from behind the cabin row, along with an occasional splash when one of the kids dove off the bridge. None of their parents worried; the older kids watched the younger ones with a lot more care than might have been expected of them, and all could swim like fish by the time they could toddle down the riverbank. No Bridge-end child in Corbitt's memory had ever been hurt beyond the normal bumps and bruises of kid-life . . . except for what Shilo Bates had done.

The sounds of the children meant that all of the families were home from church. Corbitt's mom still went, but he had stopped going the year before. Corbitt's dad had gone only on special days like Easter and Christmas, maintaining that if God wasn't everywhere He wasn't anywhere. Corbitt's mom might have been a little sad when Corbitt stopped going, but she never tried to force him. Until these last few weeks, he could have easily believed that God rested between Sundays at Bridge-end.

Sundays were long, do-nothing sorts of days, and today seemed no different. Saturday's washing, fresh-smelling and clean even if faded and patched, still hung from lines between the cabins to be taken in that evening. There were the scents of Sunday dinners cooking that made Corbitt's stomach growl when he recalled he hadn't had any breakfast. Somebody had their TV tuned to a baseball game.

Lamar Sampson, who had to go to church whether he wanted or no . . . because it was "healthy" for him, according to his mom . . . was gleaming with sweat out on the sunbaked road with his old skateboard. Toby Barlow, who'd probably never been inside a church in his life but was healthy as hell anyway, stood by the battered BMX that he rode almost daily the two miles from town. He was encouraging Lamar's moves with taunting and shouts. Corbitt skated the board too, as did most of the Bridge-end kids, but there was only one solid strip of roadway remaining and even that was buckled and rough. Toby could have afforded a board of his own, but the village of New Crossing wasn't much more than the Barlows' gas station and store, a garage, a farm and feed supply, and a few other shops among a cluster of houses, and it boasted no sidewalks at all. So Toby shared the Bridge-end board.

Lamar had a faded *Transworld Skateboarding* magazine his father had fetched back for him from Jackson last year. It had pictures of ramps like kids in California practiced on. Corbitt, Lamar, and Toby had built themselves a small one from scrap wood. It was a nigger-rig, and full of splinters, but it worked. Corbitt's mind flicked from shadow to sunlight as Lamar caught air off the ramp but landed on his ass in the road. The board skittered away while Toby snickered.

"Bastard!" bawled Lamar.

"Say it loud an proud, jack," giggled Toby.

From the cool vine-covered shade of Number One's little railed porch came a stern voice. "Lamar Sampson! I swear I'll wash out that filthy mouth of yours with my yellow soap! Yes I will!"

Toby snickered again behind his hand until the voice added. "Spect you bout due for another taste your ownself, Toby Barlow."

Toby changed his snicker into a cough.

Lamar scrambled up, rubbing his butt and grinning at Corbitt, who'd snagged the skateboard. Then Lamar turned quickly to face Number One. "Oh, I sorry, Miz Griffin." He gave Toby a jab in the ribs and the other boy echoed him.

Behind the row of flowers in coffee cans a big round face

nodded solemnly from the shade. "I should say. Such talk on a Sunday!" But Corbitt sensed a smile in the old woman's words. "Not even your daddy go talkin like that when he drop a whole hunk of iron on his foot."

"Hell he don't!" Lamar whispered to the other boys. "Ain't none of us standin here ain't heard him bust out with a whole helluva lot more'n one little ole bastard, sho nuff!"

"I hear that, brother," agreed Toby. "Shitfire, y'all oughta hear my own daddy cuss when he feelin the need!"

Lamar considered. "Well, we best us be careful just the same. Fo sho I ain't one to be wantin ole Miz Griffin mad at me!"

Toby grinned. "Say that again, jack! Hell, she just might go an magic you into a big green toad-frog or somethin. Rivet, rivet!"

Lamar's eyes widened. "You shut your mouth, burrhead! She gots enough spooky ole notions already, out you givin her no new ones!" He cast an uneasy glance toward Number One, then turned to Corbitt again. "Um, she couldn't *really* do that, huh?"

Corbitt dropped the ancient flat Variflex and decked, his long toes gripping the splintery rails. He walked the board expertly end for end, and grinned. "Well, y'all wanna go an find out, dodo? Just you be doin yourself some more of that loud cussin an we all see what happen. Rivet, rivet!"

"Uh-uh! No way! Y'all ain't gonna catch *me* messin with none of that there Voodoo shit, jack!"

Corbitt frowned slightly while cutting tight eights across the road's dim white center-line. "Miz Griffin's magic gots nuthin in hell to do with Voodoo! Swear, them Friday-Fright TV shows must be soakin into your woolly little heads! Hey, y'all figure a Voodoo lady go an play the church organ? Or you think she get to be a real certified midwife with a whole stack of 'ficial birthin papers by callin up ole bones? Hell, Lamar, she slap your black butt on your bornin day. Only logical she want to be turnin you into somethin unnatural, seem like she already had her ownself a 'bundance of time for doin it. Sho nuff!"

"Well, I never say she *could*," said Lamar. "But she do bake up the most *unnaturally* goddamn good cookies in Bridge-end. Sides, she slap your black ass too, boy. An my own daddy's for that matter. Guess we all turn out just fine without no magic, huh?"

Corbitt tailed the board and balanced that way. "Sho nuff, I spose. Hell, she prob'ly slap half the asses in this county, come to that. Likely whack Toby's too, he been here for it. Alls I sayin is, use your goddamn brains more to figure out stuff you don't understand. Shit, there be more logic an science to magic than you two field-bucks ever dream."

"There he go again," said Toby. "Bein a *logical* nigga-boy."

The skateboard's wheels, first-series Santa Cruz Bullets worn half away, rattled over the rough concrete as Corbitt took a run at the ramp, aired with a graceful three-sixty, and lightly touched down. Toby clapped and raised a thumb. "Corbitt skate logical enough, don't he, Lamar?"

Lamar dropped his hands to his hips and frowned. "Logic my ass!" he muttered, flicking his eyes toward Number One. "Ain't nuthin to them slick moves but a few goddamn little ole tricks, an I gonna learn 'em or kill my ownself tryin!"

"*Fool*-self more like it," said Toby. "Anyways, what Corbitt do be magic. He a genuine Voodoo chile. Borned under a black moon. Sho nuff!"

"Oh, shut your mouth, fool!" hissed Lamar. "Ain't nobody in they right mind be believin that ole booger shit no more. But it still best to walk careful . . . so's you don't go callin up somethin out the ground, not knowin."

"Fool, your ownself," said Toby. "Say this, wish I could go an raise us up a pizza right now! Sides, all that spirit-callin stuff just ain't logical. Huh, Corbitt?"

"Mmm," said Corbitt, rolling back. "Magic still ain't nuthin to be messin with, not knowin. What I sayin is a lot of spells be just simple words an doins. Spose you could even call up somethin pretty powerful by accident." He tailed again, then smiled and pointed. "But the onliest trick to powerful skateboard moves be practice. Lots! Sides, you two burrheads done over-dressed yourselfs . . . what they callin 'poser-gear' out there in California, like it say in Lamar's magazine. Try ridin on your own natural God-give feet stead of smotherin 'em in them show-time foot-coffins."

The other boys looked down; Lamar at his big battered

Pumas, sliced and scarred from kicking scrap iron, and Toby at his black-and-white B.K.s, almost new but already scuffed and dirty. Lamar wore sun-bleached cutoffs, streaked with rust and grease, though they had been real 501s once and were still in better shape than Corbitt's. Toby was clad in ragged gym shorts, once red, now faded pink, their side seams split from being a year too small.

Lamar had just turned fourteen. Corbitt had read a lot of books in which characters were called solid muscle, but words on paper could never describe the reality that was Lamar Sampson. His shoulders were massive, his upper arms huge, and his chest muscles jutted a full inch out from his frame, as stark and squared as if they'd been chiseled from honey-brown bronze. His washboard belly looked hard enough to bark knuckles on. The only softness about him was his eyes, deep coffee-colored and tending to shyness in a wide, flat-nosed face that turned serious only when he had to think much. Lamar didn't have the slightest notion how strong he was, and often broke things without meaning to . . . toys, tape players, and Toby's arm the summer before when they'd been wrestling on the riverbank. He was always sorry as hell about it . . . he'd spent a month in misery while Toby wore a cast. Once, when they'd been drinking, Corbitt and Toby had wrapped Lamar's chest with clothesline rope to test his strength. They hadn't noticed the wire core inside the cotton. Lamar had snapped it on the second try, but he still bore the stripes on his skin. Though outweighing Corbitt once over, Lamar stood just shoulder-high to the slender boy. Toby said he looked clumsy alongside of Corbitt, like a lion cub next to a cheetah.

Thirteen, Toby Barlow was a little taller than Lamar, and might have been called either chubby or husky depending on which of the other boys you compared him to. His hair was pale blond—or would have been but for the brown dust—and was sweat-shaded now to a creamed-coffee color. He wore it long and shaggy so that he reminded Corbitt of a page boy in King Arthur's court. He had an open, friendly face, a perpetual buck-toothed grin, and eyes of a deep smoky blue like the sky before a thunderstorm. The summer sun tanned him each year to almost the tone of a real Bridge-end kid. His parents had moved down from Wisconsin five years before, when his father had bought

the old Citgo gas station in New Crossing. They'd converted it
into a mini-mart and branch post office as well. Toby and Corbitt
had become instant friends at school, like the most natural thing
in the world, though neither could have explained why, or would
have tried to. Lamar had stayed shy of the blond boy a long
time before deciding to be friends . . . could lions and tigers be
brothers? . . . but when Lamar decided something, it was final,
full-throttle, and forever. Corbitt still caught himself sometimes
trying to imagine what Bridge-end looked like through Toby's
blue eyes.

"Aw," said Lamar. "Ain't nobody skate barefoot in California. Wouldn't be *cool*. Y'all never seen none of them kids doin
it in that magazine of mine."

"Sho nuff," agreed Toby. "Sides, I member them city
streets bein all full of dogshit an busted glass."

Corbitt stomped the board's tail, flipping it into his hand
like magic. "Well, couldn't be no worse'n cowflops an scrap iron.
Anyways, that magazine be over a whole year old. Things change
fast in them cities. Everbody know that where black cool be
comin from."

Toby laughed. "Shit. Hear that boy, Lamar? Like he gots
any more idea what be California cool than you an me!"

Corbitt's mind darted back into shadow. He crossed long
arms over his slim chest and looked sulky. "Yeah? Well, you
burrheads best be believin the day might come soon when I go
checkin that out for my ownself."

Lamar frowned, studied Toby's face to see what he thought,
then chuckled and dropped a massive arm over the blond boy's
shoulders. "Sho, my man. An I spose y'all gonna go flyin your
black ass out there on one of them seven-fo-sevens too? Just like
rich whitefolks?"

"Naw," snickered Toby. "What it is, he gonna get ole Miz
Griffin to magic him right through the air with ass-travel."

"*Astral*, asshole," muttered Corbitt, still looking sulky.

Lamar's eyes softened. "Mmm. Well, like my daddy always
sayin, dream real pretty dreams, blackboy, cause them's all what
you gonna get in this world."

Toby nodded and slid his arm over Lamar's. "Sho nuff!"

Corbitt frowned and fingered the skateboard. "Oh, ain't you
two a fine pair for cheerin folks up."

Toby slapped his forehead. "Oh, shit! Jesus, Corbitt, I forgot bout your dad. Shit, we sorry, brother."

Lamar nodded hard. "Sho nuff, man. We sorry."

Corbitt's smile slowly lit once more. He suddenly wanted to hug both boys. Instead, he said, "Well, shit, I know that. Never spected y'all to go walkin on eggs round me."

Lamar suddenly grabbed Corbitt and crushed him in a Sampson-style hug. Corbitt's rib cage creaked. Lamar grinned. "Hey, man, we gots you a present surprise!"

"Lamar! Damn your ass!" cried Toby. "It was sposed to be a fuckin surprise present!"

"Oh. Yeah. I forgot. Sorry."

Toby shook his head. "Times I wonder y'all gots both oars in the water, boy. Well, it still a present anyways. Hey, Corbitt, c'mon down to the bridge an we give it ya."

Corbitt's eyes shifted past the other boys as there came a happy yell and a small glistening shadow burst from between Number Six and Seven and ran toward them. It was Trevor Sampson, Lamar's littlest brother, nicknamed Guppy. He was eight, naked and dripping just out of the river, still with a prominent little kid's tummy though muscle was showing most everywhere else. Corbitt noted that the boy's bruises were almost gone and he wasn't limping anymore.

"My turn!" panted Guppy, running up. "I gets to ride it now!"

Lamar glanced slyly at Corbitt and Toby. "Spose there ain't no better time for givin Corbitt his surprise present, then."

Toby nodded. "Yeah. Even if it ain't but a halfway one no more, thanks to you, burrhead." He whacked Lamar's broad back. "Ow! SHIT!"

"Shut up, dodo!" hissed Lamar. "Miz Griffin hear you!"

Corbitt gave Toby a grin. "Hell, boy, ain't you got it through that skull of yours by now that Lamar be hazardous to your health?"

"Oh, *boy* your ownself! Gots me this here big ole bitch of a splinter off that goddamn ramp an just now ram it up my finger a motherfuckin mile!"

Guppy's eyes went wide with delight. "Oh, maaaan! Hear that niggaboy *cussin*! I gonna tell ole Miz Griffin! She wash out that dirty ole mouth of yours for a fact, Toby Barlow! Sho nuff!"

"Yeah? Well, y'all just go an do that, you little picaninny, an best believe you ain't gonna be ridin my BMX no more, cept in your dreams."

"Picaninny your ownself, fool! I rubber, you glue, bounce off me an stick to *your* black ass, best believe!"

"Shush, you stupid little dodo!" said Corbitt. "Fore we *all* end up gettin our goddamn mouths washed! Here now, take this goddamn board an go ride your little ass off!" Corbitt took Toby's hand and spread the fingers. "Mmm. That fo sho be one mean little bastard, brother-mine. Suck it awhile, then I take it out."

Lamar peered at Toby's finger, and winced. "Too bad you just can't go an magic it out, man. That gonna hurt like a bitch, Tobe."

"Well, thanks for cheerin *me* up, burrhead!" said Toby. "Anyways, c'mon, brothers, we gots stuff to do."

"Yeah?" piped Guppy. "An I knows what! Y'all goin down neath the bridge an smoke cigarettes! Can't fool me! I tellin Mom, Lamar!"

Lamar squatted in front of the little boy. "Listen here, dodo. You do that, you ain't gonna be ridin my skateboard no more this side of your grave!"

"Oh! Oh! I scared, nigga! Sides, who die an make it *your* goddamn board anyways? Gimme a smoke an then I not tell. Done deal, dude?"

Lamar frowned. "Where he be gettin that dealin talk lately, I don't know."

"Prob'ly from school," said Corbitt. "All kinds of that dealin stuff goin on there last year. Even for the little ones."

Toby squatted beside Lamar. "Well, best believe Guppy here be too smart to fall for none of that drug shit. Hey, Gup-man, y'all be cool an I give you a smoke tomorrow. Okay?"

"Nuh-uh! What I look like, a fool? You play, you pay or I ice your black ass!"

Toby stood and spread his arms. "You see any smokes on me, Gup?"

"Spose them's square balls in them rag-ass shorts of yours, sucka?"

Lamar sighed, standing and ruffling Guppy's hair. "Aw, best give him one, Tobe. Else he be pesterin us all goddamn day."

Guppy grinned, puffing his little chest and strutting. "An *that* a fact an a half, homes! Ice be cool, an I rule!"

"Stop that stupid niggerboy shit!" said Corbitt. "Make you sound like a goddamn *fool* an a half! You been raised up better!"

Toby pulled a Kool pack from the crotch of his shorts. The other boys clustered around him so Mrs. Griffin wouldn't see, though Corbitt suspected she knew exactly what was going on. Then the three older boys left Guppy with the skateboard and walked toward the bridge. Corbitt saw that both the Sampsons' flatbed and the Coopers' pickup were gone. Lamar noted his look. "Daddy be over the truckstop tryin to hunt up a new set of generator bearins for the White. Oh, an he say he pay you five dollars for puttin 'em in. You most as good with tools as your dad. Spect your mom gone shoppin with Mr. an Miz Cooper up in Starkville."

Toby gave Corbitt a nudge. "An po little Sherry gots to ride in back, man. All alone." He heaved a huge sigh and rolled his eyes.

Corbitt ignored that. "Sho I do your generator, Lamar. Mmm. Don't know what my mom be shoppin with, for a fact. Just last night she tellin me most our food stamps this month be already spent. Social office gettin tighter an tighter with 'em. Always talkin bout government cutbacks in spendin."

"So?" asked Toby. "Then how come it sayin on TV just the other night that we gonna be sendin b'zillions of dollars to help hungry people in Russia?"

Corbitt shrugged. "Damn if I know, man. Seem like, more I learn bout the world, less I understand it. But I tellin you this for a fact, weren't for Miz Griffin always bakin up more bread she can't never eat, Lamar's mom makin us soup, an your own folks findin that whole mess of cans got wet an lost their labels, what we done for suppers this last week I don't even know."

Toby grinned. "Good thing you like Beefaroni, huh?"

Corbitt cocked an eyebrow. "Now how you know them cans be Beefaronis, man? Swear you tole me your mom up an throwed 'em out cause she didn't know if they was dog food or people food." He smiled. "Shit, Tobe, you oughta know you can't lie to your brothers."

Toby laughed. "Spose so. Just like lion-breath Lamar here can't keep no secrets from 'em, neither."

They stopped at Corbitt's cabin so Toby and Lamar could take off their shoes. One of Lamar's was solidly double-knotted. Toby watched the big boy struggle with the laces, then knelt and slapped his hands away. "Jesus, Lion-bro, you gonna bust 'em! Use your mind stead of your goddamn muscles once in a while!"

Corbitt nudged Toby in the butt with his toe. "An *you* stop thinkin with your goddamn dick, Tiger-bro. Don't be troublin me with none of that Sherry Cooper stuff when I be needin all the best of my mind right now. Don't matter a fart in the breeze to me if she ride in back that there truck or go flyin round on little ole wings like a crow-bird."

"Uh-huh," said Lamar. "Sho it don't, Cheetah-bro. An I a big green toad-frog too! Shit, here you be just now tellin Tobe he can't lie to his brothers, an yet you standin right there in broad daylight tryin to say it don't matter to you when Sherry go swimmin an that there ole T-shirt of hers get all wet an tight over her . . . you-knows."

"*Breasts*," sighed Toby. "Sherry be givin a whole *world* of meanin to that word."

"Oh, damn both your black asses," growled Corbitt. "Like, the pair of you don't go round half the time like y'all gots hydraulic jacks in your jeans!"

Lamar and Toby exchanged glances. "Shit," said Toby. "You figure she notice stuff like that, Corbitt?"

Corbitt frowned. "Gots herself two good eyes, don't she?"

"Um?" asked Lamar, resting his hands on Toby's head as the blond boy fought with the shoelaces. "She tell you stuff, Corbitt?"

"Stuff like what?"

Toby got the laces undone, and stood, sucking his finger. "Stuff like what you just now sayin, man. Girl feelins bout boys."

"You gots a tongue in that head of yours, ask her your ownself."

"Did you?"

"Course not!"

Lamar set the two pairs of shoes on the porch rail. "Um, well, then how y'all know what Sherry Cooper feelin over us?"

Seeing Corbitt hesitate, Toby grinned again. "Aw, know what, Lamar? I bet she tell him on that day we was playin the slave game."

Corbitt scowled. "You shut up your goddamn mouth, Toby Barlow! An you too, Lamar! I know cause . . . cause, I read it in a goddamn book. That how!"

Toby nudged Lamar. "Uh-huh. Well, we gots us a whole passel of magazines at the store that show what girls be showin, but don't never tell what they thinkin."

"Yeah?" said Corbitt. "An, s'prise me your folks can still sell 'em after you gone an got the pages all sticky! Anyways, I just got done tellin you two horny bastards I don't wanna be talkin bout none of that stuff today. Gots 'portant things on my mind for a fact!"

Toby and Lamar exchanged glances once more, then shrugged. The boys started for the bridge. Corbitt jammed his hands in his pockets and shuffled along through the dust. "Wish I be ole enough for gettin me a real job," he muttered. "Doin me somethin what be makin a difference."

"Well," said Lamar. "My daddy say it don't matter how ole you be round here, jobs be scarce as hen's teeth. That why he run his own business. Say he gonna starve, it be by his own hand."

Toby nodded. "Sho nuff, brother. My own daddy say, this here a repressed area."

"De-pressed," said Corbitt.

"Oh. Well, I always thought that was somethin what happen to people."

Corbitt sighed. "It does. Might say, you be repressed, you get de-pressed."

They reached the bridge. Corbitt cocked his head toward the laughter and splashing. "Shit! Them goddamn kids gonna scare all the fish from here to hell's kitchen!"

"Mmm," said Toby. "Guess when you be repressed, and get depressed, it don't take much to piss you off, huh?"

"Spose it don't."

"Well," said Lamar. "You gots yourself that good idea bout startin up your own business, Corbitt. Y'all still thinkin on it, ain't you?"

Corbitt nodded. "Sho I am. Fact is, that one of the main

things I tryin to get straight in my mind fore I go an see Mr.
Rudd."

"Sound logical to me," said Toby. "Be your own man. Just
like Mr. Sampson. What I sayin is, lookit how hard your daddy
try an find himself a job since he been back." Toby thought a
moment. "Hey, Corbitt, how come he never start up his *own*
mechanic shop?"

"Take capital for business startin, that why," said Corbitt.
"Gots to have money fore you can make money. Why you figure
I be savin back ever dime of my own this summer stead of smokin
pack cigarettes an buyin beer?"

Lamar muttered, "Seem a goddamn shame when just bein
smart can't get you nowhere."

Corbitt raised his eyes to the bridge. "That a'zactly what
bein a smart nigga get you, man. Nowhere. All expenses paid
on a free bus ride."

Lamar traced a toe through the dirt. "Um, how come he
just not stay in the Army, Corbitt? I mean, he was sendin money
home regular an all."

Corbitt shook his head. "Say he done enough fightin for
other people, special after that ole Gulf War. Say he wanna be
home an fight for me an my mom."

The other boys laid hands on Corbitt's shoulders. "We help
you fish tonight, brother," said Lamar. "Catch us up a whole
mess of cats for your mom."

"Sho nuff, man," said Toby. "Hey, Corbitt, can I spend the
night?"

"Since when you gotta ask? Long's it okay by my mom,
course."

"Oh, I already ask her, fore she leave out with the Coopers.
I even brung my toothbrush this time so's I don't gotta go an
use yours again."

Corbitt smiled. "Make me no nevermind, man, even you
do gots a dirty mouth. Um, Tobe? How my mom look to you?
What I askin is, she seem sad an all?"

"Well . . . it gotta be natural for her bein sad, y'know. But
she kiss me, an . . ." Toby smiled. "She say I a fine young man
an a good friend to you."

"Mmm. Spose you are, Tiger-bro. But don't go gettin all
high-toned over it."

They descended the steep-sloping bank to the cool shaded flat of summer-dry mud beneath the bridge. Something big and round and golden brown dropped the fifteen feet from the bridge deck out over the midstream pier and made a huge splash in the deep pool below. Corbitt's hands clenched to fists. "Goddammit to hell! Them motherfuckin fish *never* come back by tonight!"

Scowling, Lamar ran the few steps to the water's edge. He cupped his hands to his mouth as a grinning face surfaced under a sparkling bush of hair. "Hayes!" bellowed Lamar. "Get your little ass out there this minute!" Dropping his hands to his hips, Lamar glared up at the faces of a small boy and girl who were peering down through gaps in the planking. "You! Get your butts off that goddamn bridge right now! Ain't gonna be no more divin today. We us be fishin here come sundown, so's y'all can just go an do your playin upstream."

Hayes Sampson, Lamar's middle brother, came wading up onto the mudflat, plowing through the water like a little tank wrapped in foam rubber. He was ten, and huge, though his padding was backed by Sampson muscle and he carried his big round belly outthrust and proud. Like all the younger children he was naked, and seemed as at home between the green-and-brown riverbanks as any rightful water creature. "See my cannonball?" he giggled.

"Onliest cannonball I see be the one stuck on your shoulders!" growled Lamar. "Here Corbitt gotta go fishin for to try an help his mom, an you little burrheads be spookin 'em all away with your noise. Y'all go an keep them other kids upriver. You the biggest by half so's that make you the 'sponsible one. Go an pump up some air in one of them ole tubes offen the White. That keep your asses all 'mused till suppertime."

Hayes stood dripping beside his big brother. "Well, I spose I could go an do that . . . cept then they all wantin to be towed round like I they goddamn tugboat or somethin."

Lamar grinned, hefting the chubby boy under the arms and holding him up in the air; something it would have taken both Corbitt and Toby to do. "Well, what in hell you figure God go an make y'all so fine an strong for?"

Hayes giggled as Lamar set him down, and flexed his arm to make a muscle. "Mmm. Spose I is, huh?" Then he looked at

Corbitt and his round happy face turned serious. "We all sorry bout your dad, brother."

"Thanks, Hayes. I know you be."

"So," said Lamar. "That why we all us gots to be helpin Corbitt. Know what I sayin?"

The little boy nodded solemnly. "Sho nuff! Hey, Lamar, why not we 'vite Corbitt for supper tonight? Mom be cookin special anyways cause of Toby comin. Hell, she not mind settin a extra place."

Toby frowned at that. "Oh shit, Lamar. You mean your mom settin me up a goddamn special place again? How many time I tell ya I don't *want* me no goddamn special place?"

Lamar shrugged. "Well, damn my ass if I be seein why she fuss over you, man. Best believe I gots *my* say, y'all be eatin right out on the porch with Guppy an Hayes an me."

"That a'zactly what I meanin, goddammit! You an your brothers always eat out on the porch . . . cept when I come, an then you an me gotta go sit at the goddamn table inside, wear our shirts, an can't even talk normal. So, this here time I wanna eat on the goddamn porch. Okay?"

"Well, you can't."

"Well, why in hell not?"

"How in hell I know? Cause . . . cause, you be our goddamn *guest*, I spose."

"*Listen* to this shit! Five years ago I was your goddamn guest. *Now* I your goddamn brother!"

"An don't I know it, niggaboy! Only a real brother be such a piss-makin pain in my ass! Hey, Tiger-breath, y'all figure it some sorta special treat for *me*? Sittin at the table . . . gotta say *please* pass the gravy an thank-you, goddammit? Sides, y'all eat at the table at Corbitt's, don't you?"

"Corbitt ain't gots two other brothers takin up room, all that signify. Sides, him an me, we eat out on the goddamn porch whenever we goddamn please!"

Lamar crossed his arms over his chest in a gesture of finality. "Well, my mom wanna go an treat some dumb-ass niggaboy like a guest, she gots that right, ain't she? So just shut up your mouth an be my goddamn guest, fool! Sides which, she be bakin up peach pie all special on account of your ass."

Toby spread his hands helplessly at Corbitt. "Ain't I said bout a b'zillion times I like sweet-potato pie? Corbitt, you knowin for a fact Miz Sampson bake the best goddamn sweet-potato pie in all creation. So, what she make for dessert when *I* come? Goddamn peach! What you think of this shit, Corbitt?"

Corbitt grinned. "Askin me, I think y'all both be makin more noise than a couple skeletons pitchin a fit on a tin roof."

Hayes had been swiveling his head back and forth as the older boys argued. Now he piped, "Well, Tobe, *I* sho nuff take your goddamn piece, y'all ain't wantin it."

"Shush, you," said Lamar. "An don't you go tellin Mom none of this. Hear?" He spun Hayes around and slapped his bottom. "Daddy gonna be bringin home Twinkies for everbody like he do ever Sunday. Y'all go mind them little ones. Tow 'em all round like a big, mighty tugboat an I give you mine. Okay?"

"Sho nuff!" Then Hayes considered. "Course . . . if Toby ain't gonna be eatin *his* pie . . ."

"*Course* Toby gonna eat his goddamn pie!"

"*Course* Toby gonna eat his goddamn pie!" Toby echoed. He made a face at Lamar, then turned once more to Corbitt. "I didn't ask bout havin supper with you, cause . . . well, cause of the troubles an all."

Corbitt smiled. "Sides, y'all hates barfaroni."

"Smart-ass nigga. *Slinky* cheetah."

"Oh, stick that there finger back in your mouth an suck it, Tiger-ass."

Toby grinned. "Even better, I get your present, bro!" He dashed off around the shoreward pier.

Lamar sat down and Corbitt settled beside him, their backs against the pier's base. Lamar studied Corbitt a moment, then spoke carefully. "I, um, ain't wantin to make y'all no sadder, Corbitt, but I hear my folks talkin last night, wonderin how you an your mom gonna manage now."

Toby had returned, one hand hidden behind his back. His grin faded when he heard Lamar's words. He sat next to Corbitt. "Yeah, brother, my own folks been talkin bout that selfsame thing."

Corbitt was silent a time because this was a next-thing he'd been wondering about himself. He looked up at the rotted planking where sunlight stabbed down through the gaps. Finally, he said, "Maybe it was a foolish thing my daddy went an done."

Lamar's wide face went thoughtful. Toby pulled the Kool pack from his shorts and passed out cigarettes. Corbitt fired his and Toby's with his Bic, then Toby took the lighter and leaned over to Lamar so there wouldn't be three on a flame. All the boys blew out gray clouds that drifted in the sunbeams like lazy little ghosts. Lamar's big voice came gentle. "My daddy say it were a good an rightful thing, Corbitt. Say, if he knowed what happen then an there, he'd laid Bates out cold stone dead with his own bare hands. Y'all know for a fact my daddy most never get mad, but when he do the whole goddamn world best run. Could just be your daddy save mine, Corbitt."

Corbitt sighed smoke and slowly nodded. "Mmm. I never think on it like that, Lamar. Well, your daddy weren't home, an somebody had to do somethin. Spose it weren't no more'n what spected."

"Now, what you sayin?" said Toby. "Shit, brother, it was a *lot* more'n what spected! Fact is, my own mom say she'd a gone after Bates her ownself, with a gun!"

Lamar nodded. "Toby right, man. Was a whole hell of a lot more'n spected. Weren't nobody round that day but the women-folks an little ones. My own mom be scared of Bates like he Lucifer right up from hell. An the law wouldn't done a goddamn thing . . . not bein just Guppy's word 'gainst Bates."

Corbitt gazed at the gentle green water flowing past. "Well, y'all seen what the goddamn law up an done. Nobody take my daddy's word 'gainst Bates neither."

Lamar's face hardened. "Well, Guppy don't lie. No Samp-son lie . . . not even to whitefolks! Hell, you brothers figure I makin it up when I tole y'all bout that time when I round Hayes's age an Bates call me over cross the bridge bout sundown? Swear to God that old bastard feel me ever which way just like he buyin side-meat!"

"Course we believe you, man," said Toby.

"Mmm. Well, I know for a fact that Bates try that selfsame dirt on Guppy. Then, when the boy try to run an holler for help, Bates beat him up! An you brothers know it the God's honest truth that if Guppy weren't Sampson-strong Bates coulda killed him!"

"My mom say Bates a sick ole man," said Toby. "She tell

some townfolks that. Maybe it why they wouldn't let her or my dad on the jury."

Corbitt blew smoke. "Spect that logical, Tobe. My mom say even the jury they did pick prob'ly think close the same. But the truth don't always seem to matter. Maybe Bates ain't all that rich an powerful no more, but he the last of a ole-time family what settle the land round here, an I spose some folks figure ole things best not be messed with. Sides, Bates go swearin up an down on a whole stack of Bibles he catch Guppy trespassin his land for fishin his pool."

"Goddamn liar," muttered Toby.

"Got that right, brother," said Lamar. "Everbody know there ain't nuthin on Bates's land worth trespassin for, an you ain't gonna catch no Sampson goin anywhere's near that river-bend pool, not after we done raise up that spooky ole bone-cage last summer!"

"Aw shit, Lamar," said Toby. "That weren't nuthin but some ole drowned-dog ribs. Only a ignorant field-nigga be ascared of the ghost of a dog. Huh, Corbitt?"

Corbitt shrugged. "Look more bout the size of a sheep's to me. Course, the fishline went an busted fore we could get us a good look at it."

Lamar seemed to shiver. "An I be goddamn glad of that, for a fact! Just seein that spooky thing risin up out the dark make me feel like somebody walkin over my grave!"

Toby snorted. "Shit, man. The ghost of a sheep be even more no-account!"

Lamar sucked a deep breath of smoke. "Well, best leave *any* ole bones sleep in peace, say my mom. Anyways, Bates gots nuthin else on that busted-down ole farm of his cept weeds. All that there good bottomland, growin nuthin. Hell, my daddy say that there lower field down by the pool ain't even been so much as plowed for most thirty year."

Toby flipped away his Kool. "Well, ain't no secret my folks don't like the ole peckerwood bastard. He used to buy gas an come in our store when we first move here, but one day he got in some kinda big argument with my dad and never come back no more."

"Bout what?" asked Lamar.

"Don't right know. Or maybe I don't member . . . I only
bout Guppy's age my ownself then. But, I tell you this, bro, my
daddy cuss Bates up and down with words make your own daddy
blush, best believe! I think it was Bates who try makin trouble
for us gettin the post office after that."

Lamar flipped his cigarette into the river, then pulled up
his knees and rested his chin on top. "Bates gots himself a long
history of makin trouble for us kind, brother. Shit! An now
Corbitt's daddy be gettin a prison year cause of him! Times I
like to kill that ole son of a bitch!"

Corbitt put a hand on Lamar's shoulder. "Judge say maybe
my dad only serve six months if he be a good man in prison . . .
pay his debt to society." He frowned and flicked his cigarette
far out on the water. "I always wonder why they call it that.
What I sayin is, man pay his debt at the truckstop or Toby's
store, it only be membered as a good thing. Mr. Rudd or Mr.
Barlow smile an say, he a good man, give him credit. Debt my
daddy be payin ain't like that at all. Piece of goddamn paper
gonna be followin him round the rest of his natural life. They
put him in a 'puter too, so's any cop in the country can call up
his ole debt at the speed of light. Stead of givin him credit, debt
he payin make him out a bad man! Deserve no credit! Mom tell
me it prob'ly not go so hard on him if he been workin steady.
But, he gots himself no job, even if he out lookin most everday,
law figure he just another lazy nigga goin wild. Now his name
be in some goddamn 'puter sayin he a *bad* lazy nigga! Ain't true,
but nobody argue with 'puters!" Corbitt snatched up a pebble
and flung it across the river. There was a startled croak from a
crow that had probably been sleeping on a branch. Corbitt
watched it take wing. For an instant it seemed to give him an
accusing look, but then it swooped low across Bates's field, calling or cursing . . . it was hard to tell with crows. Several more
suddenly rose from the wild weeds to join it, then all disappeared
into the hazy distance.

"Little black bastards," muttered Toby. "Y'know, I had one
of 'em chase me the other day, bout sundown, when I was ridin
home. Swear it try an peck my ass."

Corbitt smiled. "Spect it just after that reflector y'all gots
on back your bike seat, man. Crows forever tryin to steal pretty

things. Maybe cause they only come in black they ownselfs."

"Mmm," said Lamar. "Didn't Miz Griffin tell us a story a long time ago bout a silver crow?"

"That be just one of them sayins, man. Like, think bout all the polishin you gots to do till a crow shine like silver."

Toby brightened. Reaching behind him, he pulled out what he'd been hiding. "Hell, most forgot! Here be your present, Cheetah-bro."

"Lord, lookit that!" said Corbitt. "A whole fuckin quart of Jack D.!"

Lamar grinned. "Me an Tobe figure it might help polish off some of your sad."

Corbitt took the bottle and held it reverently up to a sunbeam. "Mmm. I polish off all this, I fo sho not be sad cause I wake up in heaven for real! Well, here be a lion an a tiger bro for sharin with."

"Thought you never ask," said Toby. "Maybe we drink it tonight when we fishin?"

"Course," added Lamar. "We *could* take us a little taste now."

Corbitt laughed. "Mighta knowed you two gots ready-made plans. Sho, we have us a sip, but not too much. I still be thinkin out my business idea." He twisted off the cap, took a swallow, and passed it to Lamar. The big boy drank, then handed it to Toby.

Toby gulped and smacked his lips. "*That* throw a little polish on your crow, best believe! Know? I member my daddy done a lot of readin up on runnin a business fore we move down here . . . bout capital an all that other stuff y'all was talkin."

Lamar fingered his jaw. "Um, Corbitt? Y'all ever figure you might just be doin a little *too* much of that readin? I mean, it even piss off the teacher last year when you went readin on ahead of the rest of us in your books so you knowed ever next thing fore anybody else. Know? Mr. Rudd tell me one time that havin too much in your head ain't necessarily good for you. Ruin your peace of mind, he say."

Toby gave the bottle to Corbitt. "Hey, dodo! Corbitt gots himself a *whole* goddamn mind, not just a little ole piece! Sides, I never hear Mr. Rudd sayin no such thing."

Lamar frowned. "Well, he sho nuff take the time to tell me that one day."

Corbitt took a small sip of whiskey, and shrugged. "Aw, just cause I like readin don't mean I lettin no book-stuff high-tone my head." He passed the bottle to Lamar, then his eyes narrowed toward the far side of the bridge. "Know? Times I wonder if my own daddy read a little too much. Course, maybe him bein in the Army an all put more stuff in his mind. One time I hear my mom tellin Miz Griffin that he got too used to bein a regular person in the Army. Like, it go an give him ideas he can be more'n what spected of him. She say maybe it were wrong for him even tryin to settle back round here after that." Corbitt considered, his eyes on the slow-moving water. "Know? There be times when I think he think that too . . . inside-like, I mean. I'd hear him talkin to Mom sometimes in the night when they figured I was sleepin. He had him this kinda dream bout savin back enough money for buyin a good-runnin ole pickup-truck an movin us all out to California where everthin be better for everbody."

Lamar drank, then nodded. "Mmm. Times I member when your daddy do seem a little restless, man. Know? Maybe that what Mr. Rudd mean by fillin up your head with too many ideas? Like, other folks might think you tryin to polish a crow."

"What you sayin, man?" demanded Toby. "Hell, your own daddy be smart as a goddamn whip, for a fact! Shit, you just lookit how good he be runnin his very own business. An, I bet he never even need to read up no books bout it. Sides, bet he still ain't happy *all* the time."

Corbitt nodded. "Spect nobody happy all the time. Else, how you know?"

"Know what?" asked Lamar.

"If you happy, dodo," said Toby. "Sides, it *your* crow, so polish its ass off."

"Oh. Yeah, I spose that . . . logical. Well, listen here, if my daddy ain't happy sometimes, he get over it quick as he get over bein pissed-off bout somethin." Lamar studied Corbitt. "Damn your ass, nigga. Times you don't trouble me with words."

Toby snickered. "That what called *thinkin*, burrhead." He yawned and stretched. "Hey, let's us go natural. Okay?"

Corbitt glanced upstream. "Mmm. Spect we could. Sherry be gone, an ain't nobody else round but the little ones."

The three boys stood and stripped then sat back down once more. Toby's skin was pale where his shorts normally covered, though two years ago it wouldn't have been. Lamar was a little lighter there too. Only Corbitt's slender body was unchanged, as if the sun had no power over midnight.

Corbitt took another sip from the bottle, the whiskey warm and soothing like the feel of a sunbeam on his face. Here with his brothers by the river, their shoulders touching his and their scents comforting and familiar, it would be so easy to sideslip in time, so tempting today to just do what was expected of him. Lamar's voice brought him back.

"Anyways, can't see no reason my daddy gots for bein un-happy."

Toby gave Corbitt a lazy grin. "See, brother, y'all start him in thinkin. What I tell ya?"

Lamar frowned. "Oh, shush yourself, dodo. Hell, y'all hear Miz Griffin tell how much better it be for us now than back in her days. An, shit, she oughta know, on account her bein maid here when Bridge-end was a real motel for whitefolks. She always tellin stories to the little ones bout how we gotta ride in the backs of buses an not be 'lowed in the same cafes an schools with whites, nor even get to use the same bathrooms. Them ole joke signs she put up used to be for real, y'know."

"I know," said Toby. He studied his finger before slipping it back in his mouth. "That musta sucked," he added around it.

"No you don't," Corbitt said suddenly. "You can't."

Toby's blue eyes went puzzled. "Huh?"

"Ain't none of us sittin here know," Corbitt went on. "Not for real, an that a fact. We ain't gots nuthin to go by cept them ole stories Miz Griffin tell us on her porch at night when *we* was the little ones." He pointed a long finger upstream where Hayes was trudging mightily through the shallows with a piece of frayed rope over his shoulder, towing three smaller children on a big truck tube. "Know? Times I wonder if *they* be believin but half bout them days as even us did."

"Well, could we buy us a pizza back then?" asked Toby.

"It had to be at a black pizza place," said Lamar. "Huh, Corbitt?"

"Sho nuff."

"Prob'ly better," said Toby. "Like, soul-pizza."

"I think soul-food come along later," said Corbitt. "In the sixties."

Lamar shot a sudden glare across the river. "Well, some things never change, for a fact! Like that ole bastard Bates over there! Seem all he ever done be strut round his end of the bridge, watchin all us kids like he figure he still own us or somethin!" Lamar lowered his voice even though no one else was near. "What I sayin is, if this here thing with Bates an Corbitt's dad happened back in them ole days, the KKK woulda come in the night an burn all Bridge-end to the ground! There talk say Bates used to be one . . . and that he maybe still is!"

"Well," said Toby. "He sho nuff sick in the head for bein a 'perial lizard!"

"Wizard," said Corbitt.

"Yeah, I know. But my dad call him lizard. Sound better, you askin me."

"Mmm. That a fact, bro." Corbitt's eyes drifted across the river, narrowing. "Know? Times I wonder if it even matter we member what happen back then. Hell, onliest thing I can figure is life must been *really* hard for us in them days to get us thinkin it be a lot better now. There my daddy fix all them big, 'spensive trucks in the Army, yet all Mr. Rudd can find for him at the truckstop be part-time pumpin diesel. Shit, any us man-childs sittin right here could be doin that, but it be all what growed-up men can get!"

Corbitt's voice had risen, and he found his brothers looking at him a little worried. Finally Lamar spread his big work-callused palms. "But, you know Mr. Rudd doin all he can to help us, Corbitt? My daddy say he be one of the finest white men in the county that way. Ain't that so, Toby?"

Toby took a huge swallow from the bottle, then shifted his eyes to the river. "My folks don't like him much."

Lamar's mouth dropped open. *"What?"*

Toby took an even bigger gulp. He shuddered and sucked air, then gave a helpless shrug. "Shit, man, I don't know why. Hey, want I should try an make y'all happy by lyin?"

Corbitt turned to the blond boy and laid a hand on his shoulder. "Listen, Tiger-bro, you be makin *nobody* happy by lyin to 'em. Cause one day they wake up an find they been lied to. An then they ain't your brothers no more."

Toby nodded. "Sound like somethin Miz Griffin say."

"Is." Corbitt thought a moment, then shrugged. "Well, look at it like this, Tobe. Here Mr. Rudd be sellin gas a couple cents cheaper than your daddy can. Spose it only be a natural business-thing they not get along." Corbitt smiled. "Here now, boy, you gimme that bottle fore you go an get yourself field-nigga drunk in the middle of the goddamn day. Suck on that finger a little while more, it most ready."

Corbitt recapped the bottle and set it down on the dry mud, then turned to Lamar. "An I know for a fact Mr. Rudd be a good man. Hell, just lookit how he been lettin me wash all them Greyhound windshields over a year now an never once take a cent of my profits. Fact is, that why I ain't gonna drink no more . . . gonna go over in a little while an lay my idea out to the man." Corbitt slipped his arms around the other boys. "An it all cause I gots me two fine cat-bros care enough to polish my crow."

Lamar and Toby grinned at each other, then Toby nodded happily to Corbitt. "An it fo sho one smart idea too, Corbitt! Best believe! Hey, an like I tell you the other day, y'all start in makin piss-pots of money an figure you can afford yourself a niggaboy, I yours, brother. Whip me, beat me, make me write bad checks."

Lamar also nodded. "An, maybe now . . . with your daddy gone . . . Mr. Rudd be extra good to you for startin your business."

A shadow crossed Corbitt's face. "I ain't wantin him to like my idea just cause he feel sorry for me, man. I want him to like it cause it good . . . or, even *not* to like it if it ain't."

"Well," said Lamar. "Me an Tobe can't see no logical reason for it not workin out. Fact is, seem like that there idea of yours be way overdue round here. Course, you can't never tell what a white person gonna think sometimes. But Mr. Rudd, he always talk straight so's you can understand."

Toby cocked his head. "An my daddy don't? Hey, *he* white, member?"

"Huh?" Lamar looked at Toby. "Oh, shit, man, nobody who know your daddy take him for white."

"Oh." Toby turned to Corbitt. "Figure you gots yourself enough of that capital saved back?"

"Most of thirty dollars. I figure that oughta be enough for gettin started."

"Well, I might could 'vest some. Still gots a little birthday money saved back my ownself."

Corbitt smiled. "That a fact, jack? So how much it cost you two po niggas for this here J.D.?"

"Shit," said Lamar. "Y'all don't wanna know."

"Mmm. I figure me as much. Seem like you two done 'vested all I gonna let you in me already. An, best believe I pay y'all back when I start in makin money." Corbitt pulled his knife from his jeans pocket; an Army knife his father had given him, something like a Boy Scout model but all stainless steel. "Okay, Tobe. Spect we ready for the operation. Gimme that finger."

Toby held out his hand. Corbitt opened the knife blade. "This gonna hurt some, brother. That little bastard be in you mighty goddamn deep for easy cuttin out now."

"Yo. When you see a big black bird cruisin the hood with some-body's gold it either some sorta sign, or it ain't. Course, neither way there not a fuck of a lot you can do about it."

Lactameon leaned against grimy brick in the shade of an alley and watched Beamer's face as the boy worked that out. Finally, Beamer nodded. "Um . . . sound like somethin your mom say, Tam. Like, to one of her customers. Um, so, it true, man?"

"Mmm. Hard to say, homey. Her customers mostly girls an ole ladies. Pay my mom a dime to hold their hands, look deeeep in their eyes, an then rattle some bones on the table."

Beamer scratched at his crotch. "Um . . . so, you believe that shit, man? Bout them signs, what I sayin."

The fat boy shrugged. "Shit, don't much matter to me, man. Them customers mostly leave lookin happy . . . least, happier'n when they come in . . . and there always plenty of food on that table after my mom put them bones away." Lactameon frowned, watching Beamer scratch. "Yo! Don't do that, man! Shit, look like you gots goddamn crabs or somethin! Um . . . you don't, do ya?"

"Naw. Balls always itch. Um . . . don't yours, Tam?"

"Mmm. Well, sometimes. Toni White come in for another readin last week. I watch her from inside my room. My goddamn balls itched all motherfuckin night, man!"

Beamer's eyes widened. "Was that some sorta sign?"

Lactameon laughed. "You way cool, homey-mine!"

Beamer's unfinished face turned suddenly serious. "Not funny, man! Fuckin a . . . a . . . well, it a goddamn *serious* thing, what it is! You . . . you gots to love her, man! For real! An . . . an . . . if you do, then you goddamn for sure best wear a rubber!"

"Well, Jeeze, Beamer, chill the fuck out, man! Shit, I know all that!" Lactameon dragged a toe on the concrete. "Sides, Toni used to like me, but not that way."

Strangely, Beamer looked furious. "She . . . she *still* like you, stupid!" Scowling, he yanked out his ragged nylon wallet, ripped a top-line Trojan from inside, and slapped it into Lactameon's hand. "Fuckin use this, Tam! If you an her ever . . . do."

Lactameon shrugged, but slipped the foil packet into his own wallet. "Fat chance, dude."

"Oh, ha, ha, Tam make a motherfuckin funny!" Beamer looked disgusted for a minute, but then his face slowly cleared. "Um . . . you sayin you still like Toni, man? I mean, even after . . . after, what happen?"

"Huh? Oh. You talkin bout her gettin pregnant last year? Shit, man, so what? She still the same person. Word say she went to one of them clinics. That all ancient history to me. Shit, even what she doin now don't bother me. Everybody gots to eat."

Beamer studied the fat boy a time, then nodded. "You pretty goddamn way cool yourself, Tam. Most dudes just say she a ho."

Lactameon smiled. "Well, I ain't most dudes, case you ain't noticed by now."

Beamer smiled too. "No, man, you ain't. Um . . . so, what them signs you talkin say to people anyways?"

"Well, my mom say signs only advise. They don't make you do nuthin. Course, if you can't read 'em, then you gots no business lookin for 'em in the first place. Like, magic is cool, but leave it the fuck alone if you don't know your ass from your elbow." Lactameon looked down and scuffed his toe again. "Say the same thing bout fuckin, I guess. Fact is, I never."

Beamer grinned. "Shit, I know that, man."

"Hey!"

"Cause, if you done it, you tell me. Cause we homeys."

"Oh. Well, course, man. An you do the same."

Beamer looked away. "Um . . . course, man."

Lactameon squinted upward. "Well, sign or not, it fuckin for sure don't look like we gonna score us no gold chain today." He pulled his tank-top from his pocket and mopped his face. "Swear to God this the hottest motherfuckin summer I ever seen! Maybe it the greenhouse effect."

"Um, what that?"

"Somethin that makin the whole world go hot."

"Um . . . so why not they paint them houses some other color, Tam?"

Lactameon grinned. "I like your mind, man."

"Yeah? Wanna trade?"

"Shit, Beamer, you on a roll today, man. Maybe it all that milk you been drinkin. So, Beam, how come kids do crack an shit like that?"

"Well, shit, Tam, you not needin no retard to figure that out. Kids not wanted. Kids not happy. Kids do crack. I . . . see their eyes, Tam. Maybe it somethin special I gots . . . like your magic shit. Some kids gots somethin missin out their eyes. I see that, know I gots me a sucka."

Lactameon considered. "Mmm. Well, seem like to me, that little Rasta dude we seen in the park oughta be your best customer, man."

"Naw. You not see his eyes, Tam. He die for sure, but not with a pipe in his mouth."

From a scrapyard across the street came a crash of steel against steel. Both boys turned to watch a rusty old dumptruck with bars bolted to its front bumper butt the corpse of a car within reach of a big, battle-scarred crawler crane. The truck farted smoke and scuttled away as the crane's bucket smashed down and snatched up the car in tooth-studded jaws. Black smoke billowing, turntable squealing, the crane swung the car through the air and dropped it in a crusher. Another engine throttled up with a roar and there came a last scream of steel as the crusher lids closed.

"This place a lot like that for kids," Lactameon murmured.

Beamer nodded sadly. "Yeah." He glanced back down the

street. "Shit. Guess I best go on back to the park, Tam. Um
. . . you gonna come back after lunch?"

"Sure. Yo, I bring another book. Maybe we start on that
readin shit, huh?"

Beamer lowered his head a little. "Um . . . best you not
be hangin with me when I workin, Tam. Um, y'know?"

"Oh. Um, yeah, sure, Beamer."

"Um . . . maybe you come over tonight, Tam? After bout
eight, so's my dad leave us chill. I . . . um . . . need to show
you somethin, man. But I can't talk no more bout it now. Okay?"

"For sure, Beam. I be there."

"Thanks, Tam. You the best fuckin homey ever." Tugging
his pack straps, Beamer decked his old board and rolled back
toward the park. Lactameon could hear the cans of condensed
milk clinking among the little rock bottles.

Lactameon sighed, and slumped against the sooty wall.
There was still shade here, so why not make use of it? There
were three fucking blocks between him and lunch, plus a goddamn steep staircase that seemed to get higher every day. He
had a bus pass, but the bus didn't run in this hood. For sure
he'd survive without lunch, but there was nothing else to do.
Besides, he had to snag another book to make it through the
long afternoon until dinner. Lactameon used to wonder how kids
could go crazy: he didn't wonder anymore. Closing his eyes, he
thought of all the Burger King food, KFC buckets, and pizza
that goddamn gold chain would have covered. Well, Beamer
would have gotten half, but that still left enough for a couple
good meals. Or, was he technically supposed to share that with
the gang? Sometimes gang shit could wear.

He glanced up: where had that bird gotten the chain to
begin with? And, where had it gone with it? Lactameon tried
to recall what he'd read about birds. Crows were supposed to
live in the country, weren't they? Lucky little black bastards!
Lactameon tried to picture a clean, open countryside . . . the
kind where kids played on TV . . . lots of fresh green wherever
you looked, trees that weren't dying or already dead, and maybe
a clear, rocky stream like those beer commercials showed. No:
order up for a river! You could swim in a river. Lactameon
opened his mind like his mom said she did when she rattled the

bones. An open mind was free to pick up all sorts of signals. Yeah, there it was, a friendly green river, cool, and slow enough where you didn't have to swim your ass off. Something to do a way-killer cannonball from . . .

Another crash came from the scrapyard as the old truck shoved another car-corpse toward its last ride like a six-wheeled Grim Reaper. The green river image faded from Lactameon's mind. Too bad kids couldn't be recycled. Well, that mother-fucking bird was probably way out in the country by now telling niggerboy jokes to its homeys. The sun flared wickedly bright as it cleared the roofline above. Slowly the hot light came creeping down the wall, sucking up Lactameon's shade. Sighing once more, he yanked at his jeans and turned for the street. Something caught his eye, glinting in the dusty air over the scrapyard. Shit! There was the crow: a small black shape with a gleam of gold in its beak! Shit, was the stupid bird going to drop that chain in the crusher?

Behind him, voices came from the alley's opposite end. A dumpster lid slammed, but Lactameon only kept watching the crow.

Mid-afternoons were the hottest part of the long summer days. The little valley shimmered under the stark white sun, and the air seemed thick as molasses in Corbitt's lungs as he trudged the two miles through steamy fields toward the truckstop. His jeans were soaked with sweat. He stopped to pull a blue bandana handkerchief from his pocket and tie it around his head. He wished for a moment that he was back at Bridge-end swimming with his brothers. Toby had offered his bike, but riding the road would have taken longer than walking straight across country. Both other boys had wanted to come with him, but Corbitt knew he'd only have one chance to tell Mr. Rudd his idea, so all of the words had to be arranged exactly right, like any good business proposal. Besides, Mr. Rudd didn't seem to care much for Toby for some reason, and trying to think about serious stuff with Lamar around was like having a friendly bull helping you set out your Sunday dishes.

Corbitt emerged from the field path between the creeper-covered trees and bushes that formed a long narrow thicket and separated the truckstop parking area from the fields surrounding it on three sides. He paused in the last patch of shade and squinted into the yellow-brown glare wavering over the vast dusty lot. The smells of hot engine oil and diesel fumes filled his nostrils, mixed with the scents of steel and sunbaked dirt.

He noticed a half-dozen crows on a tree branch above him. They looked lazy and arrogant drowsing in the shade, and kept giving him glances from their molten-gold eyes as if considering whether it was worth the energy to curse him. Corbitt caught himself wishing he hadn't thrown that pebble across the river and woken them, but in the next instant decided that was foolish . . . these couldn't be the same crows that had risen from Bates's field. Corbitt's slender body glistened like the crows' gunmetal feathers: maybe that was what made them stare so? They were all big, bad-looking birds, and those sharp beaks were no joke. Corbitt turned away a little uneasily, remembering what Toby had said about one trying to peck him. Nobody had polished these crows.

The long walk had given Corbitt time to think, and he wasn't sure anymore if he should bother Mr. Rudd with his idea today. Mrs. Griffin maintained that it wasn't proper to talk business on Sunday. But Corbitt's dad had said such thinking was old-fashioned: work was hard enough to come by without standing on outdated conventions. Corbitt kicked his toes in the hot dust and considered. While Mr. Rudd was always at the truckstop, even he seemed to take things a little easier on Sunday, usually allowing himself a beer or two by this time in the afternoon. Corbitt hadn't seen the man since the trial was over on Friday morning. Though Mr. Rudd had spoken as a character witness for Corbitt's father—and everyone at Bridge-end agreed that had helped—he hadn't stayed on for the sentencing. Corbitt was glad of that because they'd led his father away in chains like an old-time slave.

Everybody around New Crossing said that Mr. Rudd was one of the best businessmen in the county. Corbitt wondered now whether it might be better business to wait and see him tomorrow. Corbitt had never asked him about a real job before because most anything he could do was already being done by grown men to feed their families. He'd always sort of hoped that Mr. Rudd would see he was a good willing worker and think of something, even if it turned out to be just a kid-job. Mrs. Griffin had said more than once that everything came to those who had patience and waited . . . it was supposed to be in the Bible. But then there was another saying about God helping those who helped themselves. Sometimes it was confusing what to believe. Corbitt gazed across the lot toward the cinder-block station building. Maybe this was a next-thing that had to be helped to happen? Then Corbitt wondered if he was just scared and stalling. He'd been shaping this idea since spring, and it was a little frightening to realize that a single shake of Mr. Rudd's head would make it all worthless.

He suddenly felt watched. He spun around, but it was only the crows in the tree. They had their heads slyly cocked like the cartoon birds in the old Disney *Dumbo* movie who'd never seen an elephant fly. The biggest one seemed to glance first toward the station building and then down at Corbitt. Finally it puffed and ruffled its feathers like a shrug. Corbitt stared up into the golden eyes, but if there was a sign meant for him he couldn't read it. He shrugged his own slim shoulders and turned his back on the birds. If they wanted to fly down and peck his ass they'd have done it by now.

The trucks seemed to be the only things with enough energy to keep working in the heat. A Kenworth conventional pulling a set of tankers was just leaving the pumps around front while a cabover Freightliner with a van was swinging in off the highway, its Jake-brake snorting loud in the hot stillness. Here behind the building, about a dozen rigs stood neatly aligned while their drivers ate or showered or relaxed playing video games and trading truck tales in the air-conditioned lounge. The lounge was separated from the cafe by a door with a sign that said PROFESSIONAL DRIVERS ONLY. You didn't have to be white to go in there . . . Mrs. Rudd and her waitresses smiled and joked all the same . . . but you had to be a truckdriver.

On cooler days or in the evenings a few drivers would always be gathered around one of the rigs in the back lot swapping lies. Corbitt was fascinated by the truck stories, always trying to hang close and listen. The drivers didn't mind. They'd smile and give him winks and sometimes even ask his opinion on local road conditions. Corbitt knew a lot from his trips with Lucas and Lamar. Often the drivers would send him running to the cafe or trucker's store for Cokes or cigarettes or beer. Mrs. Rudd always let him take the things out because Mr. Rudd said he was a good boy who could be trusted. Corbitt usually got to keep the change. The stories were about snow-choked mountain passes or miles of sun-blasted desert, narrow city streets with not an inch to spare, and certain state troopers and weigh-station operators that were assholes. Trucking sounded like a hard life sometimes, but a free one.

Today, three of the parked rigs stood patiently idling, their AC units purring to keep cabs and sleepers cool, either awaiting their drivers' return or letting them nap in comfort. The huge machines were loyal to their masters, cooling them in summer, warming them in winter, singing with their radios or talking with their CBs over long, empty highways or through dark, lonely nights, while all the time feeding the men's families. In another way Corbitt could imagine them like spaceships: self-contained worlds for braving the nothingness between stars. As always, Corbitt looked for the blue Marmon-Herrington but it wasn't there. If it had been he'd have taken it as a sign for sure.

Scattered among the trees in the thicket, half-covered in creepers, were the big rusty corpses of old dead trucks. Most were without wheels, and long ago stripped of their engine-hearts and useful parts to keep other, luckier trucks alive. But there was one, a ten-wheeled tractor with faded green paint, that from a distance still looked as if it might be able to fire up and tear itself free of the strangling vines. Corbitt studied it a moment, then glanced back at the station building. Maybe it would be better to wait until the day got just a little cooler before seeing Mr. Rudd? He looked up at the crows again, remembering back a few months when Mr. Rudd had let a driver dump a dead cow off a cattle truck, and how the crows had stripped it to stark gleaming bones in just a few days. Mrs. Griffin said that animals and birds gave you signs sometimes, but that crows never took life seriously enough to trust.

Corbitt walked toward the dusty green truck, imagining as always that its cloudy headlight-eyes saw him coming like some half-blind old mule put to pasture whose master still brought it a sugar lump now and then. Up close you saw that its tires were all worn smooth, some showing fabric down their centers, gray and cracked with age, and sunk deep in the dirt. It always surprised Corbitt that they still held air. He'd used to play in the truck years before, thumping each tire with a stick the way real drivers did with their special iron-tipped clubs. He smiled now, recalling how he'd always do a complete professional walk-around before "driving" away; pretending to check all the lights and turn-signals . . . though the four big batteries were bone-dry and covered with corrosion . . . struggling to raise the heavy hood panels to gauge the engine oil, black and tarry but full, and never failing to take off the cap and peer into the radiator even though it was as parched and empty as the battery cells.

Chrome letters on the grille spelled CORBITT. They looked polished because Corbitt always traced them with his finger. Mr. Rudd had said that Corbitts used to be the hardest-working trucks on the road. But they were obsolete now and no more had been built since about the time the new highway was cut through. Mr. Rudd said there had been a lot of faithful trucks in those days—Sterlings, Fageols, Browns—but they were now only names in old drivers' memories. Corbitts had been the best, he'd said; you could trust them to do an honest job even though they weren't pretty, were a handful to handle, and often gave you a royal pain in the rear. Owning one was more like a partnership than an easy ride.

This Corbitt belonged to Mr. Rudd. He'd bought it brand new right after what he called The War, when there were no Interstate freeways, Bridge-end was still a motor court, and New Crossing was called Bates Ferry. Years ago he'd caught Corbitt playing in the truck, sitting behind the huge steering wheel making motor sounds and shifting the twin gear levers. The man had been madder than hell at first, cussing Corbitt up and down and ready to run him off into the fields, until he'd demanded Corbitt's name. That had seemed to tickle the big man no end. He'd laughed then and called Corbitt close to ruffle his hair the way grownups did, and his blue eyes had crinkled at the corners like he'd heard a good joke. He'd given Corbitt a gulp of his beer and told him he could play in the truck any time as long as he was responsible and didn't break anything.

Now, Corbitt came around to the driver's side, climbed the wide running board and opened the door. The hinges were silent because he kept them oiled. The seats and interior were dust-free and clean. Corbitt settled his slender body behind the big wheel and gazed out over the long hood, past the baking yellow-brown of the parking lot, to the distant blue hills in the west. Next to the old bridge this was Corbitt's best thinking-place . . . sometimes even better because he could be alone.

Mr. Rudd had said that this Corbitt had been to California

more times than he could remember. Corbitt could feel the vast distances that had passed beneath the wheels. Sometimes at dusk he swore he could catch hazy images of faraway places trapped in the windshield the way they used to make old-time photographs on glass plates.

Once more Corbitt scanned the idea in his mind, picking through it for flaws. Cattle and chicken trucks were always dirty and other drivers didn't like to park next to them. Lucas had said that the nearest truck-wash was clear down near Jackson and that they charged upwards of fifty dollars to clean a cattle or chicken truck. Corbitt had noticed a water faucet over to one side of the lot in an out-of-the-way spot. There was a ditch nearby for good drainage. He'd carefully figured the equipment he'd need: a good heavy-gauge hose with a pistol-grip nozzle, rags and soap and a bucket, a long-handled brush, and an aluminum ladder. He'd priced everything up in Starkville: with his own money he could just about afford them all. The truckstop had its own well, so water was free. Corbitt figured to wash trucks for half what they charged in Jackson and split his profits fifty-fifty with Mr. Rudd. A partnership. It would be hard and dirty work, but he didn't have to be all muscle like Lamar or even husky like Toby to do it. Surely a good businessman like Mr. Rudd would give him a chance to prove the worth of his idea?

Maybe just a little later he'd ask, when the day cooled down. Corbitt's eyes went far away, almost seeing gray asphalt and bone-white concrete rolling under the truck's long hood while imagining how those hills might look from the other side when fading in the mirrors. The two men were almost across the lot before he noticed them. One was Mr. Rudd, in tan workpants and shirt as usual, his good-natured, well-used face shaded by a battered brown fedora. There was an old picture on the wall in his little office showing him beside his Corbitt. In it he wore one of those brown horsehide jackets that old-time truckers favored and kids today called bomber jackets. Up until the trouble with Bates, Corbitt had been saving for one, though now it seemed like a satellite dish. But then, if he ran his own successful business, who knew? Neither Mr. Rudd nor his truck looked much different in the picture, except that the man's hair was dark instead of gray while the Corbitt looked shiny and proud yoked to a round-nosed stainless-steel Fruehauf van. There were seven license plates on the truck's massive front bumper, and the driver's door was half covered with other states' permits. Today the plates were all gone and most of the permit stickers had weathered away. The truck was rusty now, and Mr. Rudd a little heavier and weather-worn himself. He wore a modern nylon jacket whenever it was cold.

The man with him was younger and smaller, but Corbitt had no problem telling that he was a driver. He wore Wrangler jeans, a Willie Nelson T-shirt, and lizard-skin cowboy boots. Old trucker jokes passed through Corbitt's mind: one was about a cowboy who wore tennis shoes so people wouldn't think him a truckdriver. Another was a riddle: *What has a total I.Q. of forty-seven, and three front teeth . . . The entire first row at a Willie Nelson concert.*

The young driver's hair was long and oily-brown under a bright yellow Cummins cap. He carried a can of Lone Star. Mr. Rudd had his customary Sunday afternoon quart bottle of Budweiser and chewed his unlit and perpetually half-smoked cigar. Corbitt jumped down from the truck and closed the door, its latch clicking smooth and solid. He noted the younger man narrow his eyes and dart a glance from him to Mr. Rudd as if searching out the older man's reaction.

Mr. Rudd's drawl carried gentle to Corbitt's ears. "Well, son," he was telling the driver. "Y'all more'n welcome to look all you like, but there a few things in this here world still ain't for sale, an that Corbitt's one of 'em."

Corbitt smiled. That's what Mr. Rudd always said.

The younger man laughed. "Hell, boss, we all got our price. Maybe just nobody found yours yet?"

Corbitt hesitated, his hand on the truck's fender. Mr. Rudd was about as even-tempered as Lucas Sampson, but he didn't take to smart-mouth from black nor white. He'd run off a couple of drivers for saying fuck in the cafe where women could hear, and he'd knocked another man flat on his ass for calling one of his pump-jockeys a niggerboy. Corbitt watched as Mr. Rudd casually slipped the cigar from his mouth and studied it.

"Well, son, I always figured the best way to keep the devil from buyin your soul was to set your price so high he says the hell with it an goes shoppin for bargains elsewhere. No shortage of folks sellin cheap these days."

This seemed to confuse the young driver. Corbitt couldn't help smiling as the man tried to read Mr. Rudd's face for a sign of his meaning. Then the driver's eyes shifted to Corbitt and narrowed again. But Mr. Rudd winked and beckoned Corbitt over, pulling him close in a rough-gentle way and dropping a huge scarred hand on his shoulder.

"This here's a Corbitt too," said Mr. Rudd. "An I reckon you'd have yourself one helluva time tryin to meet his price."

The driver gave Corbitt a one-sided grin. "Got yourself one helluva tan there, don't ya . . . kid?" He raised his eyes to Mr. Rudd as if still searching for some sort of sign. "Shoot, boss, even back in them good ole days he wouldn't have fetched much."

Mr. Rudd patted Corbitt's head. "He's bout the smartest boy around these parts, son. Top of his class in school, 'cordin to his daddy. Won him enough book-readin awards to paper a wall."

The driver shrugged and glanced briefly at Corbitt. "Bet you one helluva basketball player, huh . . . kid?"

"No, sir," Corbitt answered. "Don't much care for it."

The driver shrugged again and looked back at Mr. Rudd. "Weren't their brains anybody used to be interested in." He bent close to Corbitt. "You ain't sayin you a lazy one . . . kid? Show me some muscle."

Corbitt didn't mind jokes. They were a lot like Mrs. Griffin's signs. He smiled and flexed a long arm. The driver gave it a hard squeeze then shook his head and brushed his fingers on his jeans. "No offense, kid, but back in them ole days you'd prob'ly been in the house. Smart, good-lookin boy like you prob'ly been a 'panion to play with your owner's son. But hell, that ain't nuthin but history now. Most all forgot. Your people tell you them ole stories?"

Corbitt's lips closed over his teeth. His obsidian eyes met the driver's brown ones until they shifted away. "I read about 'em, sir."

The driver took a swallow of beer as if it were sour. "Well . . . kid, don't you go believin everthing you read. Them books wrote by folks who never knowed how things really was. Fact is, most of them owners took pretty damn good care of you people."

Mr. Rudd's voice was mild. "Oh? *Your* folks tell you them ole stories, son?"

Instead of facing Mr. Rudd, the driver shot Corbitt a sudden glare. Corbitt sensed the new tension between the two men, knowing he was the reason and sorry he'd caused it, but not understanding why. A strange helpless feeling came over him. Mr. Rudd's hand still rested on his shoulder but he felt alone.

"Ah, well," said Mr. Rudd in a lazy kind of voice. "Let's just drag it right out in the middle of the floor so's the dog can sniff it. Weren't no shame in bein a slave . . . for the slave."

The young driver's eyes locked on Corbitt's. Something like an old memory whispered in Corbitt's mind, telling him that if he just looked down at the ground everything would be all right. But then something far older made him meet the man's stare. Corbitt realized suddenly that he'd made the man look like a fool without even doing a thing, and that the man hated him for it. Corbitt stood in the hot dusty sunlight while his heart seemed to pump icewater. And the man wasn't seeing him anymore . . . was looking at the truck instead. Corbitt shivered.

The man's voice faded in like a movie soundtrack. "Times change," he was saying. "Spose you gotta go along with 'em if you wanna survive. Hell, I been city places where jokin a kid like that woulda got me shot." The man's eyes drifted past Corbitt, not seeing. "Hell, kid, I *like* you people here in the country. You got real good natures." He spat in the dust off to one side, then jerked a thumb at the truck. "Y'know, boss, I always kinda figured that's what happened to them Corbitts, if you follow me? Factory took that design as far as they could go, but then just give it up. Like there weren't no way to bring it any further along. Now, I ain't sayin they wasn't rugged ole animals . . . had to be for the life they meant to live." He gave Mr. Rudd a grudging nod. "An it took a real man to handle one."

The young driver gave Corbitt a pat on the head, then took another swallow of beer. "Anyhow, boss, like I was tellin you awhile ago, got me a Sterlin' an a Federal down home in Mobile. Keep 'em all covered up with tarps in my backyard. Give 'em a good comfortable home, you might say." He rocked back on his bootheels and jammed his thumbs in his belt. "Always heard them Corbitts was underpowered an slow. Okay for short-haul stuff, but no heart in 'em for a long hard pull."

Mr. Rudd laughed. He squeezed Corbitt's shoulder, then handed him the bottle. Going to the truck, Mr. Rudd lifted a hood panel. "You musta heard that from your daddy after he got his doors blowed off by one." Reaching in, Mr. Rudd patted the dusty engine. "Here's all the heart anybody needs, son. Cummins 262. Just about the biggest in its day, an still a right fair number of 'em out there bringin home the bacon. With that five, four, an 4:11 rears behind her she'll still show taillights to a lot of what's runnin the freeways today. Used to roll the big seven cross most of Texas, bucked snow through the Rockies, an left them Jimmys pantin for breath up the Grapevine out of L.A." He smiled, his eyes going distant. "The good ole Grapevine, son, not that there castrated six-laner they call a grade nowadays."

The young man studied the engine. "Hell, boss, that there ole steamer ain't fired in a coon's age. I can tell right from here the way the belt's rusted in them pulleys. Gotta be froze solid by now." He tilted back his cap. "Tell you what, boss. I'll up my offer to an even two-grand if you'll get some of your boys to drag it up on my trailer."

Mr. Rudd smiled and gave Corbitt a slow wink before looking the young driver up and down. "Now, would you figure me for a liar, son?"

The driver seemed surprised. "Well, course not, Mr. Rudd. Everbody knows your reputation. Hell, you might not be in the busiest corner of the country, but I heard this here place of yours mentioned clear up in Seattle one time."

Mr. Rudd dropped a hand on Corbitt's shoulder once more as if sharing a secret. "Well, son, would you believe me then if I was to tell you that this here Come-along ain't even been so much as cranked for most of twenty year?"

The driver glanced at the engine again. "I got me no trouble with that, boss."

Mr. Rudd gazed at his cigar. "Tell you what, son. You're so dead set on ownin this Corbitt, I won't sell it for love nor money, but I'll wager it up against that there shiny new Pete of yours that I can jump the batteries, squirt in some ether, an have it purrin like a mama-cat inside fifteen minutes. If I don't, it's all yours, title signed over, an chained down to your satisfaction." He glanced at the battered square Hamilton on his wrist. "We can start the time right now if you like."

The young driver chewed his lip and studied the dirt-caked engine. Corbitt drew a breath, readying himself to run for the shop and the jumper-battery cart at Mr. Rudd's sign. Pushing those two huge 8D batteries across the baking dust of the lot would be pure hell, but he'd have willingly chained himself to the cart and dragged it all the way to Starkville just to hear the old Corbitt run. He even dared hope that Mr. Rudd might let him drive it out of the vines.

But the young driver only shrugged. "Aw, hell, I believe you, boss. Anyway, look like to me I'd be a damn fool to risk my hundred-grand Pete up against this here sorry ole mule."

Corbitt sighed. Mr. Rudd smiled and closed the panel, carefully fastening the latches. He fired his cigar with an ancient Zippo. "Get no argument from me on that, son."

The driver pulled off his cap and scratched his head. "Well, tell me this, Mr. Rudd. If that there Corbitt mean so much to you, why's it just sittin there doin nuthin? I can't be the only one ever offer to buy it."

Corbitt moved close to Mr. Rudd and handed him the bottle. The big man took a sip and ruffled Corbitt's hair. "Maybe I figure it's happy right where it is? Got itself no worries, you might say." He turned to the driver. "Ain't a month go by when somebody don't come to me wantin to buy it. No offense, son, but they almost always folks like you . . . most don't even care if it run or not, just want to chain it down an haul it home to look at. Or maybe dress it up all pretty an take it to truck shows where everybody stand around talkin bout how much better things was in the ole days."

The driver laughed. "Well, Gawd almighty, boss, what in hell else could you do with such a thing? You can't be talkin bout ever puttin it to work again? Ain't sayin it couldn't be done, and I seen me a few folks what done it, but you gotta have a awful lot of love, never mind the time an money, to make somethin like that useful again." He jammed the cap back on his head and offered his hand to Mr. Rudd, who shook it briefly. "Well, hell, boss, I gotta get rollin if I spect to make Jackson by sundown. Uh . . . I up my offer to twenty-five hundred?"

Corbitt tensed: that was almost more money than his father had made in the year he'd been out of the Army.

But Mr. Rudd only smiled and glanced at his watch again. "Still got yourself ten whole minutes, son."

"You a hard man, Mr. Rudd. But I'll be passin this way now an then, an that offer still hold. Sides, you serve up the best coffee in three states." The young man's eyes drifted past Corbitt once more. "An you keep them jockeys of yours jumpin to please."

The driver gulped the last of his beer and clunked the can down on the fender. He turned and walked back toward the station building. Corbitt took the can and threw it into the thicket. He looked up at the big man, but Mr. Rudd's eyes had gone distant. Corbitt knew what a sideslip in time looked like. Once more something inside whispered a warning, but Corbitt asked anyway. "Mr. Rudd, sir? How come that man hate me so?"

"Eh?" Mr. Rudd's eyes cleared, then narrowed slightly, but didn't seem too surprised. He stayed quiet a few moments, leaning on the fender while smoke curled up from his forgotten cigar. Finally he shook his head. "Spect it bout the selfsame reason he just now gone away hatin me an this here ole truck."

Corbitt considered that. "Um, cause he can't . . . buy us, sir?"

Mr. Rudd's eyes narrowed again. "Mmm. Close enough, maybe. You got a right sharp way of seein things, son. But it ain't really all that simple. Buyin machines ain't the same's buyin people." He seemed to think a moment before adding, "Least, nowadays." He took a swallow of beer and stroked the fender. "Hell, son, I'll wager he prob'ly don't even know himself. Oh, I'm sure he could come up with a lot of reasons if you asked him outright, like you just now done me. But they wouldn't be his." He chuckled softly. "Doubt that boy ever had a 'riginal idea in his life. Seem like most people nowadays don't." Mr. Rudd gazed after the young man. "Ain't never wanted nothin bad enough to risk his own behind for it, neither."

Corbitt stared after the young driver, too. "Not even when he a kid, sir?"

Mr. Rudd gave Corbitt another thoughtful glance. "Here, son, you look thirsty." He handed Corbitt the bottle. Corbitt tilted it up with both hands and took several big gulps of warm beer before handing it back. "Thank you, sir."

Mr. Rudd was looking into nowhere. "I spect when he was a boy an come up with a real idea of his own, his folks prob'ly give him a big healthy dose of ipecac." He sighed and sat down on the running board, setting the bottle beside him, then took Corbitt's shoulders and turned him gently so they faced each other. Corbitt saw concern in the man's blue eyes. "Son, you be damn careful who you ever ask a question like that of again. Hear?"

Corbitt's eyebrows went up, but he nodded. "Yes, sir."

Still, the man didn't seem satisfied. "See, Corbitt, it tends to . . . well, upset some folks when you ask 'em questions they can't come up with no logical answers for. Now you always impress me as havin a logical turn of mind, so I spect you understand what I'm sayin here?"

Corbitt wasn't sure, but he nodded again. "Yes, sir."

"Mmm. Questions like that make them sorta folks sweat, you might say. Worse, they make 'em look foolish . . . specially when they *are* . . . like you tellin him bout readin that ole stuff in books." Mr. Rudd sucked his cigar and blew out a gray cloud of smoke. "I hear you say you don't much care for basketball?"

"Yes sir. Never much did. Seem . . . seem a foolish idea to me."

Mr. Rudd studied Corbitt up and down, and looked unhappy. "Didn't your own folks never tell you this kinda stuff, son?"

"Mean, questions, sir? My dad tell me, onliest way for learnin be to ask questions of them what sposed to know."

"Mmm. Well, I can't say he weren't right in that, son. But he should've warned you to be a mite more careful *who* you ask."

"Mr. Rudd, sir? How come you don't . . . well, seem to hate us like so many whitefolks do?"

The man chewed his cigar, which had gone out again. "An that's another one right there, son." He sighed once more and patted the running board. "Sit down here, Corbitt. Your daddy's a good man, but he should've knowed better than to come back an try settlin round here. Seem to me like you lost him just bout the time you need him most."

Corbitt sat beside the man. "Times I get to thinkin that my ownself, sir."

Mr. Rudd flicked his cigar away and stared into the thicket while seeming to gather his thoughts. A crow flapped down in a nearby tree and cocked first one golden eye and then the other at Corbitt. Like the Disney crow it wouldn't have looked out of place with a cigar in its beak. Others joined it, five, six. Finally, Mr. Rudd spoke, "Corbitt, I left school when I was just about your age. Reckon I wanted to see me some of the world, an they didn't have all these damn fool rules and reg'lations for drivers back then. But what I'm sayin is, I ain't what modern folks would call an educated man, so I can't always make my words come out gentle an exactly the way I want 'em to. Now, I *like* you, son, an I sure don't mean to hurt your feelins if I up an say somethin seem rough round the edges. Understand?"

"Yes, sir." Corbitt couldn't ever recall hearing Mr. Rudd sound or look uncomfortable the way he did now. Corbitt added, "I spect I can understand a lot of things, sir. Seem like I gots to."

Mr. Rudd nodded. "Yes, Corbitt, I spect you do. But I still want you to know that the only reason I'm tellin you this is cause I don't figure your daddy ever would. Not cause he don't love you, mind . . . just cause maybe he got himself a little too much pride. Pride can be a dangerous thing, son. It can make your life a lot harder than it ought to be. An that ain't fair to you. You got a right to be happy, Corbitt, an there ain't nothin in this here world make a person more *unhappy* than wastin life wishin for things that can't never come true. Now, you're smart, Corbitt. Trouble is, the smarter you are the more unhappy you gonna be in that kind of situation. Unhappy people get frustrated an mean. Pretty soon they go forgettin their place an up an do something without thinkin first. Like your own daddy done."

The surprise and hurt must have shone plain to Mr. Rudd even on Corbitt's ebony face because the big man laid a hand on his shoulder. "Listen to me, son, while it's open an raw in your mind. Your daddy done the right thing, no question bout that, but he was the wrong color for doin it. Hell, if Bates had tried that filthy stuff on a white child, even your friend the Barlow boy, *he'd* be the one on board that prison bus this mornin. Understand?"

Corbitt almost thought he did. But it was more like understanding how a thing worked though logic didn't give a reason
why it did. When railroads were a new invention logical people
had maintained that a fragile human body couldn't survive a
sustained speed of twenty-five miles an hour. And, by all the
logical laws of aerodynamics, a bumblebee couldn't fly. Corbitt
looked up into Mr. Rudd's blue eyes and saw only kindness
there.

"I'm answerin your questions, son," the man said gently.
"An I hope for your sake you never have to ask 'em again. See,
Corbitt, you people are *children*, an only a fool would hate
children. Many's the time I've envied you . . . that's right, son,
envied. You're so lucky that way because it takes so little to make
you happy. You just don't *need* all the things we do. If you get
'em, you don't know how to take care of 'em, an that makes you
sad. You just look at how hard Lucas Sampson works to keep
that there ole White Compact of his on the road. Hell, son, the
Compact was a city design, heavy an slow, hardly enough power
to get out of its own way, no ground clearance . . . never intended
for this kind of life. Lucas treats that truck like a high-school
boy's first Chevrolet, an yet he just barely scratches a livin with
it. Now, if he wanted to be a driver, everybody knows he could
go to work runnin one of them company-owned poultry trucks
any time he pleased. But he's tryin to be like *us*, can't you see
. . . pretendin he's a real independent operator. Now, in a way
that really ain't too far above you sittin here in this Corbitt makin
believe, is it? But Lucas is a full-growed man, with a family he
should be supportin better. Trouble is, he can't think no other
way than like a child. Ain't his fault, son, he just weren't *designed*
for it. Understand?"

For just an instant Corbitt almost did. There was almost
logic in the idea. Accepting that logic would explain away so
much that seemed wrong lately. It would almost be a relief. His
mind struggled like a starship's computer under attack in hy-
perspace. Mr. Rudd wouldn't lie. Everybody said he was as
honest as a summer day was long. He might not be an educated
man, but his thriving business proved he knew how the world
worked. And he *cared* about black people . . . everybody said
that too. All of his pump-jockeys were black, as were his cooks,
waitresses, and tire-men. There were even mutters sometimes

in New Crossing and among the kids at school that he'd hire a black over a white. Rumor told of Bates calling him a nigger-lover . . . though never to his face. Bates had his flatbed Ford, Jeep, and ancient Massey-Ferguson serviced and repaired up in Starkville rather than trade with Mr. Rudd. Another rumor said that Bates had even threatened Mr. Rudd for appearing at the trial. Toby had told about hearing Mr. Rudd laugh in Bates's face right on the courthouse steps, calling him an old dinosaur and chuckling that he was a wizard under a sheet too, according to his wife. Suddenly everything seemed to fall logically into place; like an hour or so before when Corbitt had been sitting beneath the bridge with his brothers and it had been so tempting to just let go and get drunk. He was only a kid, after all. A child. A *black* child. Nothing much was expected of him. And now this wise, respected white man had said that he was free to live his whole life that way. It would be so easy!

Maybe that was why it didn't feel right.

Corbitt saw that Mr. Rudd was watching him closely, but there was only kindness in the man's blue eyes. Another old joke drifted through Corbitt's mind; about a black man at the Pearly Gates telling Saint Peter that the happiest time of his life had been when he'd gotten his civil rights and gone to be baptized in a beautiful, all-white church . . . how all the whitefolks had been smiling, and the preacher had looked so *kind* as he'd dunked his head under the water. *But, y'know, Saint Pete, I be damned if I member ANYTHING after that!*

Corbitt felt Mr. Rudd's eyes. He recalled something his dad had once said about the Army—that the sign of a good sergeant was the ability to come up with quick answers. If they turned out later to be the right ones, so much the better. Corbitt nodded slowly. "Yes, suh."

Mr. Rudd smiled and gave Corbitt a rough hug. "There now. I always knowed you was a smart one, son. See, that's why you people always have such a miserable time in our cities. You just wasn't designed to understand complicated matters. You try so hard to be like us . . . imitate us on the outside like kids playin dress-up in their elders' clothes. But you just can't grasp how our world really works. Then, when the goin gets rough, y'all up an blow your tops like frustrated children, an break things. Your *own* things, likely as not, the way y'all done years past up there in Harlem, or Watts, or after that Rodney King trial. Why, I read just the other day that the average life expectancy for a black man in a city was only about forty years. That's plain awful, son! Barely half of ours, an most of you built so fine and strong . . . like you was custom-made for a long, hard haul!" Mr. Rudd looked sad.

And he *was* sad, thought Corbitt. Why? Because he cared!

Mr. Rudd offered the bottle. "Here, son, go an have yourself a nice healthy taste."

"Um . . . no thank you, suh. Bout had my fill today."

Mr. Rudd set the bottle back on the running board and laid a gentle hand on Corbitt's shoulder. "Now, son, I want you to understand that it ain't your fault. It's ours. We went an turned you out in a world that's just too fast for your minds. What we done to you in years past was wrong, dead wrong, an I'd be the first to admit that. We shortchanged you by bringin y'all here to begin with. We was greedy, and shamefully cruel, uprootin you from your simple, happy lives in Africa. It was like tryin to transplant little trees in the wrong kind of climate, or raisin baby wild things . . . you just can't up an turn 'em loose afterward an expect 'em to fend for themselves. It's sad, Corbitt, cause all you can ever be is like . . . well, like picture negatives of us. Nothin you can ever do is ever gonna be original or your own, an y'all just killin your poor selves tryin."

Mr. Rudd had turned away, but not before Corbitt saw tears in the big man's eyes. Despite himself Corbitt felt his own throat tighten in sadness. He touched Mr. Rudd's arm. "I . . . sorry."

Mr. Rudd wiped at his cheeks, then smiled and took Corbitt's shoulders once more. "Bless you, son. Bible say somethin about not troublin the simple, happy lives of the beasts an the children. An I'm the one who's sorry, Corbitt. See, we should be takin better *care* of you. But, you got pride, too, an it's awful hard to care for you without hurtin your feelins. An yet we *owe* you that, son. Why, y'all helped build this country for us!"

Still holding Corbitt's shoulders, Mr. Rudd smiled again. "Bet they taught you that in school?"

"Yes, suh."

Mr. Rudd patted Corbitt. "Well, son, that's why I always give you people jobs whenever I can. I'm tryin in my own poor little way to repay some of that debt, an ain't nothin give me greater joy than seein you folks happy."

Corbitt was very unhappy. He glanced up at the crows. If birds could smirk then they were doing it. Goddamn stupid smart-ass things! Crows were lazy and shiftless and stole anything they thought was pretty, even if they couldn't ever use it . . . could never *learn* how to use it! Again, Corbitt thought of the cartoon crows: lazy black birds in hats and vests, smoking cigars . . . playing dress-up. What a joke! He looked down at his body, so black it almost glowed under the sun. He remembered a few years back; reading a sci-fi story called *Space Cadet*, about boys in the future whose schooling included travel in space. The words on paper had made him cry because he realized even then that he'd been born in the wrong time to reach the stars. And now he felt the same; somehow cheated by something he could do nothing about, wanting to cry once more because this good white man who cared had just told him in a kind and gentle way that he'd never be good enough.

Above, one of the crows fixed Corbitt with a golden stare as if to pass a sign. But Corbitt didn't want any signs from crows! Yet he turned to Mr. Rudd before he thought about it, and said, "My dad was a diesel mechanic, sir. Run a whole motor-pool in the Army."

The man seemed a little confused. "Well, I know that, son. An I tried to find a place for him in my shop. But, hell, Corbitt, you know we get so many of them ignorant rednecks come through here . . . mighty particular about who touches their truck. An, can you really blame 'em, son? After all, their livins depend on them machines."

Corbitt's eyes drifted back to the crows. The sweat had dried on him and he didn't shine anymore. So why were they still watching him? Corbitt thought about how, in the Army, *lives* sometimes depended on the machines.

"You know that for a fact, son," Mr. Rudd went on in a voice of logic and reason. "Your daddy just wasn't happy washin parts. That there was *pride*, Corbitt . . . gettin in the way." Once again he took Corbitt's shoulders, searching his eyes; though what he expected to find Corbitt didn't know.

"Corbitt, son, you got to be growed-up enough for under-standin this."

Corbitt turned from the man and looked toward the western hills. "Yes, suh. I spect I is."

Mr. Rudd smiled again. "Well, like I was sayin, I knowed you was a right smart boy." He considered a moment. "Sometimes, hearin the truth is like takin a big ole nasty dose of medicine . . . best to get it all over an done with once so you can be feelin better later on. So I'll tell you somethin else, son, lest you go to gettin discouraged. We ain't no kind of super-race our ownselves. Had my fill of fightin 'gainst ole Hitler an his ideas on that subject. An we got our share of culls too. I spect you realize now that I'm in complete favor of friendliness 'tween our races, but I'd advise you to be a little suspicious of any whites that . . . well, tend to gravitate towards you. Some are just lookin for a cause, you might say . . . somethin they figure might give their own messed-up lives a meanin. Only, they ain't really about to risk their own behinds for you when the goin gets rough. Oh, they'll fire you up with all sorts of high-soundin ideas, but best you believe they know all the time that *they* ain't the ones gotta go through life wearin your color skin. They always got an *option*, what I sayin. Others, well, I spect you come to find they a pretty inferior lot."

Corbitt's eyes narrowed ever so slightly. Somewhere he felt a wrongness in all this logic . . . a flaw in the computer program, spreading a virus that would ultimately crash the whole system. Without thinking, he murmured, "Like water seekin its own level, sir?"

Mr. Rudd looked puzzled. "What do you mean by that, son?"

Corbitt wasn't sure himself. "Nuthin, suh. Just maybe some ole thing I hear."

Again, Mr. Rudd smiled. "Well, you can't always believe everything you hear, son. An even *your* mind can 'ventually sift out the truth if you work it hard enough. That's why I told it to you now, so you won't go an make yourself unhappy later on trying to figure it all out on your own." The man's smile brightened. "Corbitt, I been doin some thinkin about you. I 'magine your mother could use some extra money these days. Fact is, she stopped by just a while ago an had a word with Mrs. Rudd. Ain't no openins right at the moment for a waitress or kitchen help, but I know how much *you* like bein around trucks. Come to me yesterday, this idea. Some driver rolled in snortin fire about that checkpoint down near Jackson gettin all uppity over no-account little stuff like dirty or busted reflectors an clearance lights. Well, Corbitt, maybe you could do a walkaround on every truck pull into my pumps? Check all that piddly-ass stuff . . . mudflaps too for rips or holes. Carry yourself a rag an a bucket an wipe all them lights an reflectors clean. Tell the driver when you spot somethin busted. Likely as not he'll buy a new one at my store, the shop can put it on, an you'll prob'ly find yourself with a tip for savin the man a big fine down the road. I'll pay you five dollars a day, an you keep all them tips for your very own, just like them Greyhound windshields. How's that for a opportunity, Corbitt?"

Corbitt slid down from the running board. "Thank you, suh," he said, his voice coming husky. "I gots to ask my mom." He wanted to get away fast because he knew he was going to cry. Crying was a childish thing and he didn't want Mr. Rudd to see . . . even if it wasn't any more than what was expected of him.

Lactameon watched the black bird spiral upward into the yellow-tinged city sky. The sun struck a last glitter off the gold in its beak before the crusher doors clanked shut and a big billow of dust clouded the air. Smoke poured from a pipe as an engine thundered. Steel swallowed steel. Below on the ground the rusty old dumptruck was already shoving another car-corpse toward the crane.

"Shit!" Lactameon muttered again. Somebody, somewhere, was probably making a whole bundle of bucks from all that dirt and noise, but they probably didn't live anywhere near it. The dust cloud spread in a menacing mushroom shape, and Lactameon could almost feel the particles settle on his body. No wonder all the hood kids seemed to sweat rust. Then he tensed once more as the voices up the alley came closer. They were kid-voices, casually savage. Nobody who knew Lactameon hassled him much, though he still watched for carfuls of cruising gangbangers who might recognize him as the Collectors' mascot. But there was something about these hot summer days that drove any kid crazy. Lactameon swung around, standing his ground and squinting into the sunlight as four figures rolled toward him on rattling skateboards. There was damn little else he could do.

"Yo, Tam!"

Lactameon relaxed as four boys, all between twelve and fourteen, came ripping down to surround him. All were shirtless, wearing just jeans and big high-tops. Gold earrings and a fighting bracelet glittered fierce on dark skins, and the blackest boy's little snub nose was pierced with a circle of silver. All had yellow bandanas tied around their heads. Lactameon carried one in his pocket, but seldom wore it except for meets or defying school rules. The oldest boy was the blackest of browns and so beautifully muscled he looked like a Levi's magazine ad. He tailed his Caballero in the slick, sloppy way that said you were too good to showtime. Above his bandana was flat-razored hair that sparkled. Like the other boys, his body was sweat-sheened and gleaming, and the top of his jeans was darkened with wet. An ancient .38 revolver was stuck down the waistband in back.

Lactameon smiled and flashed the Collector sign: a thumb and the first three fingers. "S'up, brothers?"

The second boy tailed an old Sword and Skull. Dark as midnight, with large, long-lashed eyes to match, he was almost more pretty than handsome. Slender and tall, his muscle showed only as smooth rounded shapes. White fire flashed from his silver nose ring and sweat droplets flew like crystals as he shook them from his soft puff of hair. He grinned with big teeth at Lactameon. "S'the 411, brother-mine?"

"Yeah. Give us the seven, Tam," said the third boy, skidding to a stop on a splintery Slasher. Like light and dark chocolate melted together, he seemed all shades of brown. He was built about average, some muscle, some chub, and knife scars shone pale on his body and arms. The Collector sign came natural for him: he'd been caught by another gang, and among other things done to him that didn't show, they'd cut off his right little finger and made him watch rats eat it. He had caramel-colored eyes that looked warm at first glance, but always made Lactameon think of furnace-door glasses. Like those little windows, they gave only a glimpse of the heat and fury within. He drank way too much, even for a kid, but crack would have been a death sentence for him, and he would have taken a lot of company along. He seemed to know that . . . at least Lactameon hoped so. Of course all the dudes carried box knives, but the caramel-eyed boy packed a special one that used replaceable blades. Even when drunk he was way past fast in a fight, but seemed to play with his enemy as long as he could, slashing and slicing as if each razor cut was one point in a six-figure game. He hadn't wasted anyone yet, probably because only a fool or a crack-head would fight him, but he also carried a good Italian switchblade because it was over three inches to most people's hearts.

The last Collector was the same lusterless soot-shade as Lactameon . . . Stacy, the former self-conscious fat kid. While the other gang members dripped sweat, he practically poured it, panting, and dragging a foot to stop his curb-ground Chris Miller. He gave Lactameon a secret grin, signifying they belonged to a gang of their own. "Yo, Tam! Cruise up the clubhouse for sure tonight, man! Shit, we gonna total parr-tee! All your ass can eat, *guaranteed*, man! An forty-ouncers till you floatin!"

The first boy spun around with a snarl. "Shut the fuck up, you stupid shit!"

Stacy rolled back a pace, surprise on his face, and spread his arms. "But, shit, Bilal. Tam here our brother, man."

The slim, dark boy spoke quietly. "Word, Bilal. No secrets from your brothers."

"Yeah!" agreed the caramel-eyed boy. He gave Bilal a sulky scowl, but smiled at Lactameon. "Shit. Bet he already know anyways!"

Bilal frowned. "We travel faster'n word, T.K. Chill out, man."

The dark boy grinned, tapping his forehead with a long, slender finger. "Not faster'n the speed of Tam's mind."

Bilal poked the dark boy in the chest. "Oh, shut up, Silver. Seem like I can't unnerstand nuthin you say no more, an ain't hard figurin why!" Bilal shifted his gaze to T.K.'s eyes, as if trying to measure their rage. "An I ain't havin no more of you today, man! Swear to God I gonna put you on a chain!"

T.K. looked sullen, dropping his eyes as if he didn't want to burn Bilal with them, yet. His scarred bracelet flashed as he lifted a hand to brush sweat from his face. He was wearing a green nylon backpack, and Lactameon noticed the straps were too loose as if set for a bigger-chested boy.

"Um . . . cool pack, T.K.," said Lactameon.

Bilal stiffened. T.K. gave the muscled boy a smirk. "Told ya, man."

Bilal switched his suspicious look to Lactameon for a second. "Well, *course* Tam gonna know! He gonna know cause I gonna tell him, that why. But I don't need you suckas *tellin* me to tell him what I gonna tell him anyways."

Silver snickered and hopped atop a dumpster, kicking his Cons against its side. "Times I can't unnerstand nuthin *you* say, man."

"Shut up." Bilal faced Lactameon again. "*Do* you know, man?"

Lactameon spread his palms. "Know what, Bilal?"

Silver grinned. "Tam gots precision magic vision like a magnifyin prism, sees the colors of his brothers an ices all the others."

Lactameon grinned back at the dark boy. "Fuck, you way past chill, Silver! Wish to hell I could do that."

T.K. frowned. "So, what a magnifyin prison, man?"

"Shut up, dammit, T.K.," said Bilal. "Shit! The fuck I gots to work with here . . . a goddamn rappin crack-sucker, an a dude what can't hardly skate no more, an . . . an, I swear I don't know what the fuck gone wrong with you, T.K., cept it like scare the shit out me sometimes!" He glanced at Lactameon once more. "An I ain't even sure I know *you*, man . . . special, this summer. Leastways, that whiteboy belong to the Leopards hang with his brothers!"

Lactameon spread his hands wider. "Well, Jeeze, Bilal, you dudes always cruisin."

T.K. snorted. "Oh yeah, Bilal. Somethin wrong with everbody but *you*, man. So, why you still hangin with us hood niggas anyhow, you so motherfuckin fly?"

Bilal's big chest hardened. "It comin man, you an me."

T.K. shrugged. "Any time, any place . . . but prob'ly when I sleepin."

Lactameon pulled the yellow bandana from his pocket and slipped it around his head. "Oh, all you shut up! Jeeze! This just the way we sounded back in third fuckin grade, man! Bilal! You gots somethin to tell me, the fuck do it!"

Bilal spun to face the fat boy. Silver snickered again. "Watch it, man, that one of them African Sumo dudes there."

Bilal seemed to consider that. Though not an inch taller, Lactameon probably outweighed him twice. "Well, you still hangin with Beamer, Tam?"

"Jeeze, Bilal, he my goddamn for-life homey . . . since before we all was in school even!"

Bilal frowned. "Signify nuthin, man. Shit, we all little kids, one time. But not no more. This serious shit now. Best you think what been happenin in this hood since Hobbes start that house, man. To them same little third-graders we used to be. Shit, see 'em suckin them motherfuckin pipes all over hell! Scope that out, man, then you think bout choosin your life-homeys!" Bilal lifted his eyes to Lactameon's forehead. "Maybe you just ain't been wearin that enough, man. Know what I sayin? I ain't keepin no secrets from my brothers, but brothers be dudes I *know*. Word, man, you wear that. All day. Maybe it 'mind you ain't none of us in third grade no more. We see you tonight at the clubhouse, man. Bout nine."

Meeting Bilal's eyes, Lactameon nodded. Bilal held his gaze a moment more, then decked his board, but turned to Lactameon again. "Yo, man. You see T.K. wearin a pack?"

"No."

"What I figure." Bilal kicked away toward the street. The other boys followed in file. T.K. muttered, "What a motherfuckin escapade!" as he rolled past Lactameon, but the fury in his eyes was for somebody else. Silver winked slyly, and Stacy grinned, slapping his own stomach and mouthing, "Parr-tee." Then the gang cut around the corner, and the rattle of their wheels was lost in a crash from the scrapyard.

Lactameon slumped against the wall. His hand went to wipe sweat from his forehead and found the bandana. He could picture how its yellow color stood out on his dark sooty skin. Well, it would keep the sweat out of his eyes anyway. Somehow, he'd been expecting this ever since school ended. Too many things had changed since those laid-back summers at the pool. And the kids he'd known since kindergarten had changed too. He shared a couple of classes with both Hobbes and Sebastian. Hobbes read a book now and then and liked to talk about them when he had time. Other kids either feared or respected Hobbes, and that rubbed off on whoever he chilled with. Sebastian never hung with anyone but Hobbes, but then he was the bodyguard. Still, he treated Lactameon with casual respect.

Lactameon sighed. Being Hobbes's friend and the Collectors' mascot had been the best of both worlds while it lasted; but how long could you balance on the blade of a box knife?

His jeans had slipped low. He yanked them partway up. Goddamn motherfuckin clothes anyhow! Why the hell couldn't he have been born someplace where a black kid was free to be a real kid? Like the country. Shit, what could black country kids have to worry about? Well, now this day was totally fucked-over! Making sure the book and tank-top were still in his back pockets, he started up the alley for home. Shit, maybe he'd just stay in his motherfucking room . . . forever!

And, shit, he'd promised to cruise by Beamer's tonight . . . something was goin on with that dude . . . but he might just as well stick a gun in his own ear if he didn't show up at the clubhouse. He trudged along, head lowered. One of his shoes was untied, but he sure the fuck wasn't going to go through the hassle of sitting down to tie it and then getting up again . . . should have had Beamer check it. Well, at least it sounded like the gang had finally scored some real party-stuffing for a change, the way Stacy was up for it. Lactameon raised his head a little. Hell, so what was there to get all hyper about? He'd have lunch at home, bail back to the park and chill with a new book, then dinner at home, and Beamer would always scrape up something to chow on, and then a whole night ahead full of food and forty-ouncers with the gang. So, what was the prob?

But, how had the Collectors fallen in so much shit? T.K.'s eyes had been too goddamn bright. They only got like that when he'd slashed the shit out somebody. He was way good at kicking too . . . the kind you did with your feet . . . when Bilal wouldn't let him cut.

Something caught Lactameon's eye: a small dark shape ahead. He stopped. The crow was perched on a dumpster about a bus-length away. On the lid at its feet lay the glittering little chain! The bird cocked its head, then picked at the links with its beak as if trying to figure why something so pretty couldn't be eaten. Lactameon sucked a breath and held it. His jeans were slipping again, but he was scared to move and frighten the bird away. The crow looked at him and snatched up the chain.

Oh, you stupid little black bastard!

One of the lids was open and cocked back against the sooty brick wall. Still holding the chain, the crow hopped to the edge and peered down inside. Lactameon held his breath and dripped sweat. How long an attention span could a goddamn crow have . . . no longer than Beamer's? The bird hopped down and disappeared into the dumpster. Lactameon hesitated a moment,

then grabbed his jeans with one hand and began to edge closer
. . . if he could get there in time and slam down the lid the crow
would probably freak and forget all about the gold. The bandana
started to slip. Lactameon eyebrowed it up while stretching out
his free hand to grab the lid the second he got there. He was
just steps away when the bird popped back out to perch again
on the rim. Lactameon stared, then busted into laughter: the
stupid birdbrain had traded the chain for a shiny tin top off a
Night Train bottle!

"Yaaa!" Waving his arms, Lactameon lumbered forward.
For just an instant it looked like the crow would take him on;
and that beak was its own sort of box knife. But it just gave a
croak and took off with the bottletop . . . to hell for the shit
Lactameon gave. Reaching the dumpster, he peered eagerly
in. It was almost empty. A few inches of stinking wet garbage
covered the bottom. Laying on it, downside up, was a skateboard. The curb-scarred graphic showed a Rasta skull and skeleton hand holding the ace of spades. The little chain gleamed
on the skull's dreadlocks like golden gang-colors. Lactameon's
bandana slipped over his eyes.

"Shit!" He jerked up a hand to tear it off, but stopped.
Carefully, not taking it loose from his head, he retied the knot
tightly. Then, leaning his arms on the dumpster's rim, he
grinned back down at the skull. If that wasn't a sign, he'd eat
it! Shit, and here he'd been figuring that today had turned total
toilet-time! Shit, a short side-trip to the pawnshop, and then
back home with at least half a buck in his pocket! Shit, why even
go home . . . a bus ride to Burger King was what was goin on!
Lactameon shot quick glances both ways: the alley was empty.
Sighing happily, he relaxed against the dumpster to chill on the
whole thing awhile. Well, he supposed that half of that half buck
should still go to Beamer, though he wasn't sure why, and a big
quarter still covered a couple of trips to the King. But, what
about the gang's treasury?

Lactameon considered: there had been Colt 45 on T.K.'s
breath when the dude had rolled by. Maybe his whole pack was
full of forty-ouncers, maybe padded with the dudes' shirts to
keep them from clanking together or breaking? Shit, a whole
packful of Colt, and all Lactameon had gotten was an order and

an invitation to something that he was rightfully a part of anyway!
Well . . . maybe just lunch at Burger King today . . . but a big
one . . . and the rest of the buck turned over to T.K. tonight.

Lactameon had forgotten the skateboard. He studied it now:
an old Steadham Street, hard-ridden but expertly cared for. Why
would anyone throw it away? Even if the deck had been cracked,
a kid would have salvaged those expensive Indy 169's with their
almost new Rat Bones. Lactameon shifted uneasily: a board was
more individual than most dudes' hairstyles or clothes. And he'd
seen that board before. Straining and grunting, he tried to reach
it but it was just too far down. Hooking his arms on the rim, he
tried halfheartedly to hoist himself, already knowing he couldn't.
His jeans slid to his knees and the paperback fell out of his
pocket.

"Shit!" Jerking his jeans up once more, he recovered the
book, then gazed back down at the board. There weren't many
Steadhams left on the streets; Beamer had one but it was worn-
out shit, a dumpster deck that he'd found and transferred his
own hardware to. Lactameon wasn't even sure Steadhams like
that were made anymore, and a seriously ridden deck was lucky
to last half a year no matter how good, and who in this hood
was rich enough to score deuce decks at a time of an obsolete
model he happened to like?

"Shit." An idea came. Pulling the tank-top from his pocket,
Lactameon cast its strap over the board's rear truck, pulling
gently until the loop tightened. The board tilted up and the
chain slipped down to catch on the front truck's pivot. Carefully,
Lactameon fished the board out, then balanced it deck-down on
the dumpster's rim and took the gold chain. It was heavy and
real, but he'd known that it would be. Without another glance,
he stuffed it into a hip pocket. Both the board and the chain
were Sebastian's.

Lactameon felt watched. He scanned the alley again: nobody. He looked upward, but saw only the strip of hazy Oaktown
sky. He recalled now the bang of a dumpster lid just before
hearing the gang's voices . . . *his* gang's voices. A hand strayed
up and fingered the bandana. The dudes had been sweating
buckets from a long, fast ride. And now they were rich enough
for an ass-kickin party. Sebastian sometimes ran green for

Hobbes, and the kid-money Hobbes collected would be all small bills. It was probably enough to fill a pack. T.K. had been wearing a pack . . . he was the treasurer because Stacy was too slow, and Silver had gotten into crack, so who could trust him. Sebastian was built like Bilal; big-shouldered and bulky-chested, and those pack straps had been too loose for T.K.

Lactameon shivered in the hot, stagnant air. City-sound surrounded him: the steely crashes from the scrapyard, traffic in the streets, and the scream of distant sirens. But he felt all alone in an empty universe. The board still balanced on the dumpster rim. A touch of his finger would drop it back in and bury it from sight. Balanced on a box knife. How had the crow scored Sebastian's chain? Crows ate dead bodies . . . pecked out corpses' eyes. Sebastian could probably have taken Bilal with his fists, and Sebastian packed one of Hobbes's deuce Uzis. Bilal had the .38, but that was a worn-out piece of shit that sometimes misfired. Four dudes with just knives, fists, and a piece-of-shit gun against a gangstuh-type like Sebastian with a full-auto Uzi . . . and they'd come out on top? A picture like that usually left somebody terminally chill.

"Shit." It came out a sigh. So his gang had finally kicked someone. Lactameon touched the bandana again. No wonder you had to totally trust your brothers: your own ass was part of everything they did whether you were with them or not. Of course that meant whatever you did alone had to be the right thing for their asses too. He thought once more of his room, miserable, but probably the safest place he could be today . . . for all his brothers. Then he pictured Sebastian in his mind, at the desk next to his in fifth period. Most of Sebastian's casual friendliness was probably because of Hobbes. Like most dudes with hard muscles, Sebastian had those same dumb ideas about fat kids. For sure, Sebastian was a long way from being a homey, even forgetting the fact that he wasn't from the hood in the first place. But he'd probably be a better dude if he wasn't dead. Well, suppose he was laying somewhere hurt bad enough that a goddamn crow could steal his chain and maybe go back to eat out his eyes?

"Shit." A whisper of breeze drifted down the hot alley as if it was bored. The skateboard rocked gently. Lactameon watched, wondering which way it would fall. He held his breath, hoping he was reading the signs the right way. The breeze died. The skateboard stayed balanced.

Lactameon checked his bandana to make sure it was tight, then snagged the board by its front truck and headed for the street.

Brown dust betrayed the tear streaks on Corbitt's face, but he
didn't know that as he slipped between strands of rusty barbed
wire and back onto Bridge-end Road. He was about a quarter
mile up from the cabins, after taking a longer route from the
truckstop to get his crying done. Mrs. Griffin said that a good
cry every so often was healthy for everyone, but Corbitt didn't
feel any better. His eyes itched, his cheeks were puffy, and the
goddamn world hadn't changed a bit. He reached up to pull off
his bandana to wipe his eyes, but it was so sodden with sweat
he just left it alone.

   He began walking home. Any other time he would have
kept to the tree-shaded river side of the road, but now he trudged
along under the full force of the late-afternoon sun; his head
down, his hands jammed in his pockets, while he kicked his
bare feet at anything in his way. The dust he raised soon coated
him cocoa-brown all over. Then he heard a tinny clatter from
down around a bend. Looking up, he saw Toby and Lamar
bucking toward him over the broken pavement on Toby's BMX.
Both boys were wearing red bandanas, and Toby was pedaling,
standing up, while Lamar balanced on the seat, his huge arms
crossed over his massive chest. It made a funny picture for the
chubby blond boy to be panting and pouring sweat on the battered little bike while big solid Lamar rode in cool majesty like
some mega-muscled maharaja's kid behind his rickshaw driver.
Corbitt recalled how, years ago when Toby had first started

coming to Bridge-end, Lamar's parents seemed somehow upset by that picture. Corbitt's own dad, home on leave, had busted out laughing the first time he'd seen it, calling it Bates's worst nightmare. The simple truth was that Lamar rode a bike like he did everything else: straight ahead and over or through anything in his way. Not that Toby didn't ride like he was running in a motocross with a fifty-dollar prize most times, but at least he usually remembered he wasn't commanding a tank. The bike's worn knobbies plowed through a dusthole, billowing brown powder all over both boys, so they emerged from the cloud about the same color. When Toby spotted Corbitt, his usual grin went even wider. "Yo, Cheetah-bro!" he bawled, side-skidding to a stop and dusting Corbitt too.

"So, how it go, man?" Toby demanded eagerly. "Like tits, huh?"

"Yeah," said Lamar. "Mr. Rudd, he jump on your idea fo sho?"

Corbitt frowned, knuckling grit from his eyes while searching for an answer. He hadn't even considered what he was going to tell his brothers. He thought of all the time they'd spent together under the bridge talking about the idea. Something new flicked across his mind: he caught himself wondering just how much of the plan had been his own, or whether Toby's suggestions had polished it. Lamar hadn't been a lot of help.

"Maybe," murmured Corbitt at last, turning away.

"Huh?" said Lamar.

Toby cocked his head, his eyes startlingly blue in his dusty brown face. "So what in hell *that* sposed to mean, nigga?"

"*Nigger*, your ownself!" Corbitt suddenly snarled. He hunched his shoulders, and the sullen look clouding his face would never have fit it before. "Maybe mean . . . mean, *maybe*, that what!"

Lamar looked puzzled but then, Corbitt realized, he often did. Toby just grinned. "Hey, c'mon, boy. Maybe don't mean nuthin. Maybe's what your folks tell ya when they ain't really listenin."

Corbitt's head jerked up. "Got beans in your ears . . . BOY? I say maybe, *mean* maybe! Mean . . . maybe I go an change my own mind. Maybe I don't even wanna work . . . don't got to, an . . . an who gonna make me? Mean . . . mean . . . mean, maybe my goddamn idea just ain't *original*!"

Toby and Lamar exchanged wondering glances, then both got off the bike. Toby dropped it in the dust and came close to Corbitt. Lamar followed. "Hey," said Lamar, peering over Toby's shoulder. "Corbitt been cryin."

"Sho nuff has," said Toby. "What wrong, Corbitt?"

Corbitt's hands clenched to delicate-looking fists. Ignoring Lamar, he faced the blond boy. "Maybe nuthin. Maybe a lot. Gots me a right to cry, ain't I? Gots me goddamn little else, but I gots me that! Even . . . even growed-up white men cry!"

"WHAT?" both the other boys demanded together.

Corbitt shot Lamar a glare. "Ain't no concern of yours, man. It just . . . just go an make you unhappy." He shifted his eyes to Toby. "So, why in hell *you* care . . . boy? Ain't . . . ain't *your* daddy never gonna get drug off to prison just cause he black!"

Toby's mouth dropped open, mirroring Lamar's. Then Lamar gripped Toby's shoulder as if seeking reassurance. "What in hell you talkin, Corbitt?" boomed Lamar. "Toby an me, we just figure . . ."

"We figure . . . well . . . that y'all cepted that already," Toby finished.

An old trucker's joke crossed Corbitt's mind . . . *Lone Ranger and Tonto riding through a valley. Suddenly the hills to their left swarm with a thousand hostile Apaches. Then a thousand more appear on their right. Lone Ranger says to Tonto, "Looks like we're in a lot of trouble, faithful companion." Tonto answers, "What you mean, WE, white man?"*

"Cepted it?" Corbitt's voice broke. "What you mean, *cepted* it? What in hell ever make you think I cept a thing like that? Cause . . . cause I only gots me a simple nigger-mind?"

Toby's eyes went almost as wide as Lamar's. But then Lamar scowled and stepped between the other boys. "You been drinkin, Corbitt? Why in hell you talkin all foolish like this?"

Corbitt squeezed his eyes tight shut to fight the threat of tears. "ME? You callin *me* foolish, you goddamn stupid ignorant niggaboy!" He raised both fists to the sky, and his slender body trembled like a machine throttled full-ahead with the brakes locked. Suddenly, he shoved past Lamar and slammed his fists into Toby's chest, knocking the blond boy backwards over the bike so he sprawled in the hot dust. "God DAMN you!" Corbitt raged. "You can't skate better, swim better, fish better, nor get better grades than me!" Leaping the bike, he landed spread-legged over Toby and stabbed a long finger down at the blond boy's face. "You . . . you ain't even a nigga! Y'all just a . . . a . . . goddamn dirty whiteboy! What make you better'n me?"

"But, I ain't."

Corbitt searched the smoky blue. He didn't know what he expected to find there; a mirror of his own rage, or maybe a buried secret suddenly revealed. But not the hurt and confusion he saw. "You . . . y'all just sayin that."

"Why I do that, Corbitt?"

"Well . . . well, goddammit, what in hell *you* ever know bout ceptin stuff, nig . . . BOY? Go anywheres you want. Be any goddamn ole thing you want. You gots a . . . a *option!*"

Toby blinked dust from his eyes. "What's a option?"

Corbitt hadn't expected that either. He felt his rage leaking away like air from the patched old truck tubes the children played with. It suddenly seemed important not to lose any more. There was power in anger. It gave a kind of strength. "A option mean a thing you gots an I don't! Why . . . why you even come round here for anyhow? It fun, y'all 'tend bein a nigga? You too stupid for your own kind? Cause . . . cause you figure y'all makin us HAPPY?"

"CORBITT!" Lamar's roar was a lion's. Grabbing Corbitt by the upper arms, Lamar yanked him off of Toby and held him effortlessly in the air. "You shut your goddamn mouth, fool! Toby is too a nigga! Y'all gone crazy, talkin to your own brother like that?"

Corbitt struggled in Lamar's iron grip, his feet kicking empty space. "*Brother?* YOU who a fool, nigga! LOOK at him! What he ever know it cost to be black?"

Lamar gave Corbitt a savage shaking. "Fool your ownself! How many time Toby got the livin shit kicked outa him by whiteboys? What *that* cost, FOOL?"

"Shit! Make him nuthin but a little white-trash!"

Toby sat up. His eyes narrowed to indigo slits. "I ain't white! Not like you mean! An . . . an, only a *ignorant* nigga say a thing like that!"

"Goddamn right!" rumbled Lamar. "Here! Y'all whop him a good one, Tobe! He gots it comin! Slap some sense into that woolly little head!" Lamar gave Corbitt another shake. "Who in hell you been talkin to, boy? Bates?"

Corbitt felt a chill under the burning sun. He stopped struggling and looked down into Toby's eyes, waiting for the hurt and confusion to change into hate, almost wanting it to happen. Instead, the smoky blue clouded with tears that overflowed down the blond boy's dusty cheeks.

"What's wrong, brother?" Toby sobbed. "Did somebody hurt you, man?"

More of Corbitt's rage was leaking away. He was no longer sure why he wanted it . . . unless it was because it gave an intense sort of pleasure, half-familiar like some other sensation he couldn't quite call to mind. Power? In a way; but there was nothing magic in this kind of power, just a sort of tense expectancy, like a promise of release if he just kept on.

Corbitt found he couldn't meet Toby's eyes anymore. He already felt shame before he said the next thing. "Don't never call me brother again."

Toby winced, cut, just as when Corbitt had dug into his finger with the knife that morning. That little wound would heal up fast and leave no scar. But, if he'd been careless, and cut deeper . . .

Corbitt stomped hard on Lamar's bare foot. The big boy grunted in pain. His grip loosened and Corbitt tore free. Spinning around, Corbitt jammed a fragile finger between the jutting slabs of Lamar's chest. The big boy backed a step and Corbitt followed.

"YOU the ignorant nigger!" Corbitt bawled. He remembered when Lucas had to shoot his old dog. One bullet hadn't been enough. The amazement now in Lamar's eyes reminded him of how that dog had looked up at Lucas. Lamar thought these ideas came from Bates! How was he going to feel when told they were *nice* Mr. Rudd's?

Corbitt's breath came hard and fast. He'd never known that hurting people gave power. Behind him, Toby moved uncertainly as if to protect the big boy. Corbitt's nostrils were filled with the scents of his brothers. The sun burned hot on his back.

Suddenly he knew why this mounting surge of power seemed so familiar.

It had been last spring; a month before school let out. He and Lamar had spent a Saturday night sleeping over at Toby's. The Barlows' business was closed on Sundays, and Toby's parents had left early for Starkville. Toby's big bed with its soft white sheets seemed the finest of luxuries. Staying in it as long as they pleased was another. Toby had raided the store for a big bag of Chee•tos, a six-pack of beer, and a *Playboy*. They'd been lying on their backs, the sheet around their waists, and mid-morning sun streamed golden through the window while bees buzzed drowsily in the bushes beyond. Knowing that a whole, long, do-nothing day stretched ahead of them made the pleasure almost unbearable. As far as Corbitt was concerned they were the luckiest brothers in the world. Naturally all were naked: neither Corbitt nor Lamar had owned a pair of undershorts in their lives, and Toby, after battling his mother for months, had quit wearing them the first year he'd discovered Bridge-end. Corbitt's mom always made a fuss whenever he stayed at the Barlows', insisting he scrub head to toe before going . . . though nothing compared to Lamar, who grumbled that his own parents sterilized him something awful . . . and Corbitt's skin felt fresh and new against the soft linen. Pressed between his brothers, surrounded by their scents, lazy and warm with ice-cold beer inside him and Chee•to crumbs everywhere else, he'd been studying the centerfold and soon felt his dick stirring between his legs.

There was no way to hide it under the single thin sheet, but a cautious flick of his eyes left and right showed that he wasn't alone. Toby caught his glance, and giggled, "Shit, bro, it bout half-past time! Me an Lamar was startin to wonder if y'all was one of them homos or somethin." Toby pointed at the picture. "Mmm, MM! Don't she just gots her *everthin*, man?"

Corbitt relaxed . . . at least his mind did. "Well, she be pretty as hell for a fact. Course, wanna get technical, she kinda ole for us, an it be most like too much of a good thing she showin there, if you know what I sayin."

Toby considered. "Yeah. I hear that. Kinda like lookin at a super-jumbo pizza an knowin you can't never eat it all."

"But, *wishin* you could," added Lamar.

Toby pointed to a part of the picture. "Could y'all eat *that*?"

Lamar looked serious. "Well . . . I done *heard* bout it. Cept, it don't do nuthin for *my* appetite when it be starin me right smack in the face like that."

"Yeah," agreed Corbitt. "Times I hear some of the truckers talkin bout that. Black ones be called brown sugar."

Toby giggled again. "So, what they be callin white ones? Twinkies?"

"Well," said Lamar. "Goddamn if I see how that there ever be sugar-tastin. Make no matter what color, y'all askin me."

Toby nodded. "Yeah. It kinda gross when you gets to thinkin bout it. I mean, y'all stick your dick in there."

"I spect you sposed to eat it *first*," said Corbitt.

They'd talked like that awhile, and then Toby had raised another subject. Lamar went shy and wouldn't venture an opinion. Naturally, Corbitt had heard about beating off. There were lots of jokes and hand gestures at school . . . to which you listened and looked knowingly . . . but he wasn't quite sure of the actual mechanics involved. It was like that other thing . . . the *big* thing of putting your dick in *there*. Then what? Well, you fucked. But that word meant a lot of things that had nothing to do with sex. Humped? Camels had humps, and Snortin Horton "humped to please," but it couldn't mean *that* or it wouldn't be painted in letters two feet high on the sides of trucks. Dogs fucked for sure, but they also got stuck together and that didn't look like too much fun. While Toby talked like an expert, Corbitt suspected that beating off was only a recent discovery for him. Corbitt didn't believe the hairy palms and blindness bullshit that Lamar's dad had once solemnly hinted about . . . nothing logical in that . . . but he still wasn't sure it was a right thing to do. But Toby had described in glowing detail how *good* it would feel until even Lamar's shyness melted. So, shoving off the sheet and scooting back against the pillows, Corbitt and Lamar had followed Toby's lead. Toby told them to think of a beautiful girl, a real one, not a picture. It turned out that all were envisioning Sherry Cooper.

Now, standing between his brothers in the road, Corbitt recalled that first-time, next-thing feeling; how it had built within him to an almost frightening intensity. He remembered the uncertainty of waking sensations in what seemed a whole new part of himself. He'd almost been afraid of this wild force inside his own body, especially when it began to get out of control. But there was also a desperate yearning that mounted into a need for the next-thing about to happen. It was power; in a way the same sort of power he'd felt just now by hurting his brothers. But this time nothing good waited at the end.

Corbitt remembered how it had happened together for all of them that morning: and then the moments after; the twinges of guilt and uncertain shame when they wouldn't meet one another's eyes. There had been the wet results of course, lots, with Corbitt and Lamar ashamed because of Toby's fine bed. Yet there had been fascination too, realizing that this was the stuff that made life. And the most amazing thing of all was that this life-stuff from Lamar's bronze, Corbitt's ebony, and Toby's ivory was exactly the same. It had been a magical sharing that had brought them even closer together and made them feel like real brothers ever after. The guilt hadn't lasted long. They'd done it again, twice, until sweat-slicked and sore. Then they'd wrestled, Toby and Corbitt against Lamar, who won anyway, had a huge pillow fight, and lounged like naked savages on the living-room furniture, watching cartoons, smoking Tiparillos, and sharing another six-pack. Later, they'd put the sheets through the Barlows' washer and dryer and remade Toby's bed. Finally, they'd all crammed together in the shower before returning to Bridge-end. They still often did it beneath the old bridge, and the river bore their life-stuff downstream.

It had been a next-thing for all of them, thought Corbitt now. Maybe even a test that they'd come through together, all equal. But what had happened here in the road was different . . . a hurtful thing. He hadn't scarred his brothers: he hadn't cut deep enough. But he *could* have, and knowing that frightened him. It was a terrible kind of power to have to hold back a secret. Truth would always rise sooner or later, Mrs. Griffin had said. But Corbitt didn't know if his secret was a truth or a lie.

Corbitt took a deep breath of the hot dusty air and shook his head. "I . . . I sorry, cat-bros. I mean none of what I say just now. I . . . I spect it come out me cause I hurtin over my dad." It was funny how lies and secrets so quickly gave birth to new ones.

Toby smiled and smeared his cheeks with swipes of his

hands. "Aw, hell, man, we already done figure it was cause of that. Huh, Lamar?"

The big boy nodded, eyes solemn. "Sho, brother. Shit, that all what it is, Corbitt. Even my own daddy say that sometime you gots to kick a dog to make your ownself feel better."

"Woof!" said Toby, grinning again. "Well, wherever Corbitt been, he come back to us now."

"Where that?" asked Lamar.

Corbitt made a smile. "Best believe, brothers, y'all don't wanna know."

Lamar suddenly grabbed both boys and gave them a crushing Sampson hug, just laughing when they tried to crush him back. Toby wiggled free and rubbed his rib cage. "Shit, Lamar, swear I hear somethin creak in there!"

Corbitt ran his hands over his own sides. "Lamar love somethin, he like to love it to death."

Lamar looked confused. "Mean, you can love too much?"

"No," Corbitt said firmly. "Even if it kill you."

"Huh?"

Toby considered. "Y'all spect we need to get ourselfs laid, Corbitt?"

Corbitt frowned slightly. "Your fist a lot cheaper, niggaboy. Some driver tell me one time you don't gots to buy it flowers an candy an say you still love it in the mornin."

"Well," said Lamar. "The real thing sposed to be a lot better. Huh, Corbitt?"

Corbitt's frown deepened. "Now, how in hell I sposed to know?" He turned and nudged Toby's bike with his toe. "So, where was you two dodos headed?"

"Up the crossroads to meet Daddy," said Lamar. "He sayin he maybe gots himself a good scrappin job just outside Starkville, startin tomorrow. We was gonna ride back with him in the truck an ask if Tobe can come along an help. You too, if you ain't gonna be startin with Mr. Rudd right away."

Corbitt toed the bike wheel, spinning it slowly. "Not right away."

"Well," said Toby. "Y'all just come along with us then, Corbitt. You can ride the handlebars."

Corbitt's smile returned. "Onliest way that work's if Lamar do the pedalin. That mean he also be steerin, an that make a right frightenin picture in my mind. Now, you two just go on. I gots me more thinkin to do."

Toby picked up his bike. "Well, we see you later for that fishin, Cheetah-bro."

Lamar took his place on the seat. "An y'all just be careful bout thinkin, Corbitt. Get you in more trouble than it worth sometimes."

Maybe, thought Corbitt. He watched the other boys until they rounded the next bend, then began walking home once more. The thought of Toby spending the night was comforting, and yet also a little frightening; as if in being that close to the tiger he'd betray the secret. Their minds were too much alike . . . tuned to the same wavelength. Once they'd even shared a dream. Mrs. Griffin had said that that's what soul-brother meant.

It still surprised Corbitt sometimes that Toby would rather sleep on the floor with him than in his own big bed and private room. If Toby could have things his way he'd probably move to Bridge-end tomorrow, but Corbitt had long since stopped trying to understand why. Though Corbitt and Lamar always stayed at the Barlows' together, Toby usually spent the night with Corbitt at Bridge-end. That wasn't hard to figure considering how crowded things were in the Sampson cabin. Toby had stayed with them a few times; squeezing in among Lamar and Hayes and Guppy, but his presence seemed to make Mr. and Mrs. Sampson uneasy. Toby complained that they always fussed over him something awful; apologizing for the "mess," though Mrs. Sampson kept the cabin as neat as a pin, and constantly asking if he was comfortable or what he wanted to watch on TV. The elder Sampsons had been horrified when Lamar broke Toby's arm, rushing to the Barlows and offering to pay the doctor bills, even though Mr. and Mrs. Barlow wouldn't hear of it. Toby had come back the next day wearing a cast, and squirmed under the Sampsons' attentions until Corbitt had rigged his arm with a garbage bag and electric tape so he could escape to the river.

Corbitt's mom, on the other hand, had stopped treating Toby any different from other kids after the first few times he had stayed over. And Corbitt's dad had bawled Toby out more than once for stuff like burping without saying excuse-me, not washing his hands and face enough, or for picking a tick off Corbitt's back at the supper table and calling it a little bastard.

He'd told Toby to take out the garbage and help with the dishes too, quoting what he called an old African proverb that said you treated a guest like a guest for three days but then handed him a hoe.

Corbitt recalled the very first time he and Lamar had spent the night with Toby. Then it had seemed as if everyone in Bridge-end was fussing up a storm. But Toby's parents had acted like it was the most natural thing in the world. The Barlow house, in back of their store, had seemed a palace at first. Lamar was almost afraid to sit on the furniture, even though dressed in his Sunday best. There had been spaghetti and meatballs for supper, and Mr. and Mrs. Barlow had laughed and talked through the meal just like anybody else's parents. Toby's room had been the most amazing thing, along with all his toys, books, and a whole closetful of clothes. Later, undressing for bed, Corbitt and Lamar had been a little upset by Toby having shorts while they didn't . . . until Toby had stripped buck-bare too so that all were equal under the sheets. Mrs. Barlow had come in and kissed them all goodnight. Toby had lifted the snowy sheet to assure his mother that his new friends weren't rubbing off—Corbitt in particular. Mrs. Barlow had only laughed and winked at Corbitt as if they were sharing a joke on Toby.

Corbitt sighed now as he trudged along the road. Why did everything seem to be getting so complicated lately? Sideslipping in time, he didn't even look up as the Coopers' pickup clattered past, kicking back clouds of dust. He didn't see Sherry Cooper vault over the tailgate, and it was a total surprise when her arms went around him and her lips pressed his cheek in a sisterly kiss. The fine dust swirled, momentarily hiding the truck, and Sherry took quick advantage to give him a second kiss on the lips. Corbitt's mouth opened, his eyes widened, and his arms were pinned helpless at his sides in Sherry's sudden embrace. He was instantly aware of her breasts against his chest, and that only her thin cotton T-shirt separated their bodies. His dick woke so fast it almost hurt.

"Mmmffft!" he managed.

The shabby little truck rolled on another fifty feet or so, then stopped in front of Number Three with a gritty squeal of brakes. Sherry grasped Corbitt's long hands in her smaller ones and stepped back as the dust settled. Corbitt's eyes narrowed and flicked to the truck, but Mr. Cooper couldn't have seen much in the tiny rearview mirror.

"Oh, Corbitt," said Sherry. "I sorry bout your dad."

Corbitt felt his loins cooling. He wished everybody would just stop saying they were sorry. He knew they were but what good did it do? His eyes came back to the girl. Sherry Cooper was fourteen and only an inch or so shorter than he. She had almost the same slender build and delicate bones, but there was nothing boyish about her except her grin. Even in a white T-shirt, cutoff jeans, and big old Pumas, she was all young woman from any angle. Her skin was a smooth dusky satin, and her long-lashed eyes were tawny and bright like a fox's. They looked large in her fine oval face. Her nose was small, snubbed, and almost bridgeless like Corbitt's. Her hair fluffed the same but floated in an ebony halo of soft ringlets compared to his coarser curls. It was pretty, even powdered with road dust.

Corbitt sensed Sherry's sorrow for him and saw the concern in her eyes. "Thanks, Sherry."

"Times when a good ole-fashioned cry seem to help, don't it?"

"Huh?"

Foxiness shone in Sherry's eyes once more. "Your face, boy."

"Oh . . . shoot! Wish everbody stop quotin Miz Griffin at me, chapter an verse."

"Shit," Sherry corrected. "This be *me* y'all talkin to, member? Wanna go all high-toned, you can say *merde, dreck,* or *caga.*" She lifted her shirt and wet a corner with her tongue, then dabbed at Corbitt's cheeks.

Corbitt submitted for a moment, his eyes lowering to Sherry's bared middle. The T-shirt she wore, an old one of his that she'd practically begged for, was tantalizingly tight over breasts which were large, high, and proud. Her cutoffs clung low to the curve of her hips, showing a lot of her long legs sculpted with muscle from swimming. Corbitt's eyes shifted reluctantly away. He noted Mr. Cooper standing on the pickup's running board and giving them both a considering gaze. The man frowned thoughtfully, chewed his lip a moment, then turned as the passenger door creaked open and Mrs. Cooper and Corbitt's mother got out. They also gave Corbitt and Sherry what seemed to be looks of speculation while patting the dust from their dresses. Then they went around to the back of the truck for their groceries. Corbitt stepped away from Sherry and knuckled his eyes. Things were still unsettled between his legs.

He scowled as Sherry made another move with her shirttail. "Stop that, goddammit! Washin me like a little ole child for all the world to see! What in hell y'all figure you 'complishin, anyways? It like tryin to polish a crow!"

"I didn't know you could do that."

"You can't! Waste of your time, an piss off the crow!" Corbitt's flash of anger faded. He suddenly wished he could tell Sherry the real reason for his tears. He thought again of that stupid space story and how the stars were forever beyond his reach.

"Sher-reee!" called Mrs. Cooper, louder than necessary. "Y'all come help with this now!"

"Pooh!" said Sherry, as if she hadn't heard her mother. "Bridge-end ain't the world, boy." She made to tweak Corbitt's nose but there wasn't much to grab.

Corbitt slapped her hand. "Don't I know it, girl!"

"Oh. Excuuuuuuuse me! But sugar melt when it wet, y'know."

Corbitt made a face. "So do shit! An merdly, an *caga*. Pooh too, for a fact! Just you git now, an go help your momma like you sposed."

"At once, my cheetah-prince. Allow me." Sherry straightened Corbitt's bandana.

"Oh, shut up, girl. It be way after midnight an y'all just a ole punkin again." Corbitt walked with Sherry to the truck. He picked up the two Piggly-Wiggly bags his mother indicated. Neither was very heavy.

Sherry took two others—full, Corbitt noted—then faced him. "Y'all gonna go swimmin?" she asked. "I need to wash this ole dust off me too."

Corbitt shrugged. It was hard to stay sad with Sherry around, and it didn't seem very logical to work at it. "Maybe."

Mrs. Cooper, standing near, gave her daughter a long glance. "You just member to put on that ole shirt of your daddy's fore you go paradin round all wet to the skin, little missy."

Sherry's head came up, her eyes bright with foxfire.

"Mother! In Starkville they give out prizes for the best-filled wet T-shirts!"

Corbitt fumbled with the bags, almost dropping one.

"Sherry Cooper! You git them groceries in that there house this minute or I give you a right proper prize!"

Sherry tossed her head and grinned at Corbitt. "What Mom really—*technically*—talkin bout is all my new developments."

Mrs. Cooper's mouth dropped open. "SHERRY!"

Sherry's father coughed and covered his mouth, then ambled to the cabin. Corbitt's own mother might have smiled but she turned away before Corbitt could be sure. Corbitt started to follow her, but paused to whisper back at Sherry, "Sugar melt when it wet, y'know? But you be a prize worth fightin a dragon for, an no mistake. Wanna try some of that there mud-wrestlin?"

Sherry was still staring indignantly at her mother, but dropped one eyelid and whispered in return, "You just wish on a star, boy. Sides, I beat your skinny butt any ole day, best believe."

Corbitt waited until Sherry's mother headed for the cabin, then fell to one knee. "Oh, *please*, missy! Beat me, whip me, make me write bad checks!"

Sherry giggled. "Arise, Prince Cheetah."

"I already done that."

Sherry's mouth opened in delight. "Why . . . y'all ain't no prince! Just a nasty, dirty slave-boy in disguise! Go from me an cool thyself, crow without polish."

Corbitt stood and bowed. "Flatter thyself not, inflated one. I knew thee as a eater of chitlins."

Sherry sniffed. "*Flatter* ain't no longer in my vocabulary, Corbitt Wainwright, case y'all half-blind, sides bein a ignorant field-buck."

"Mmm. 'Flated still come to my mind, though. Meanin, airhead. You an that Milissa Taylor."

"That high-toned little *cow*? Don't you even say her name in the selfsame breath . . ."

"Sher-REEE!" Mrs. Cooper called from the porch. "You do your dawdlin with Corbitt later on! Right now you git that milk in this house fore it curdle out in that sun!"

Sherry sniffed again. "Shit," she whispered. "Anything go curdly fast as this here bargain-brand milk can't be too far off to begin with! Once you gone an bought it, you find out right quick y'all got yourself a'zactly what you paid for. Spect Milissa Taylor be a lot like that." She smiled a foxy smile. "See you neath the bridge, my prince?"

"Mmm. 'Pends. You gonna come wearin that ole tent of your daddy's?"

"Suffer, not knowin, boy. Sides . . ." Sherry fingered her shirt. "Just might be I love me this here one so much I don't wanna go gettin it all wet. Have y'all know I never even wash it till my mom make me. Slept it neath my pillow cause I simply *dote* on the smell of field-buck."

"Uh-huh. 'Mind me to get you one of Toby's for dotin on."

Sherry blinked her long lashes. "Oh, I already got me one of his."

"*What?*"

"That there ole black one. What he order clear from California out Lamar's skate magazine last summer. Say, don't die wonderin, on the front. You member?"

Corbitt's eyebrows went up, then he frowned. "Well . . . s'prised you ain't gots yourself one of Lamar's too . . . do you?"

"Royalty gots their secrets, boy."

A shadow crossed Corbitt's face. He shifted the grocery bags and turned away. "That don't signify nuthin, girl. Even field-niggas got secrets." He started walking down the cabin row toward Number Eight.

"See you later, Corbitt?" called Sherry.

"Maybe," Corbitt answered, not looking back.

Like the others, the Wainwright cabin was shaded by the river trees and its interior was shadowy and cool. The windows were all open, and a few bluebottle flies bumped the rusty screens trying to get in. One, smarter or luckier, lazily circled the small room, flashing metallic iridescence when it passed through a sunbeam. Corbitt stood in the doorway, his shadow stretching across the floor like an elongated African image. He watched the fly and scanned the room. Talking with Sherry had cheered him a little, still he seemed to see his home through different eyes.

It was funny how small the cabin looked: shabby and mean and just plain worn-out. Strange that he'd never noticed the warped walls, or the way the floorboards were all scooped and hollowed with their nailheads sticking up shiny and high. There was his parents' iron-framed bed, lately painted gold to imitate brass, but the effort looked childish and cheap. The quilt Mrs. Griffin had made for his mom was clean and neatly spread, but its patchwork squares had been faded castoffs from the start. The oval of rag carpet gave new meaning to the name, while Corbitt's own narrow mattress on the floor that Toby found so wonderful now seemed makeshift and temporary until something better came along. On one wall were the rows of pine book-shelves his father had built, but the battered old hardcovers and dog-eared paperbacks gave off a musty scent like obsolete knowl-edge and outdated dreams. The whole room was spotless yet somehow seemed dirty, and even the little TV should have had something better to sit on than an ancient wooden dynamite box. It was a surprise to see that the chrome was scabbing from the legs of the table where he'd had most of his meals and done years of homework.

For what?

He'd never given much thought to what he wanted to be when he grew up, but now he found himself wondering if, like the old truckers' joke, he could ever get *there* from *here*. Corbitt walked to the table and set the bags down, then sprang up and batted the fly out the doorway with his palm. Spinning like a dancer, he kicked the door shut. Turning again, he saw his mother smile.

"Ain't no wonder your coach keep sayin you a natural, son."

Corbitt jammed his hands in his pockets. "Ain't no coach of mine. An, natural *what*, I don't know." Then he searched his mother's eyes. "You . . . okay, Mom? I mean, bout Dad an all?"

Brandi Wainwright, though fine-boned and slim like her son, had honey-brown skin and soft amber eyes. Her hair was more wavy than curly, and she was hardly a head taller than Corbitt. Seeing her now through these different eyes, he couldn't find much of this woman in himself. His gaze shifted to the framed photo of his mom and dad on the bedside table. It seemed strange to have to look at a picture to remember what his father was like. The man was tall, but not strikingly so—not like Corbitt would probably be—and built a lot more sturdily. The nose, and maybe a hint of a V in the man's smile, formed the only real resemblance Corbitt could see. Toby had once said that Corbitt had his father's moves and laugh. Corbitt had read about genes, and throwbacks, but he almost asked anyhow.

Almost. He caught the question on his tongue while watching his mother put the few groceries away. No, he thought, poor black people had enough problems without adopting them. He also recalled reading that most kids asked that question sooner or later. It was supposed to be normal, probably even for nigger children. His mother turned to smile at him again and he had no more doubts. Maybe love wasn't gold, but only a fool wouldn't recognize the real thing when it shone.

"Yes, son. I spect I be all right. Your dad was . . . well, gone a lot in the Army. It ain't somethin you ever really get used to, but you an me, we manage till he home with us again. Huh, son?"

Manage on what? Corbitt thought. Since when did love buy food and pay rent?

"You look hungry, son. Can I fix you somethin?"

Corbitt had slouched, his hands in his pockets and his tummy out like a child's, something he seldom did. Now he straightened his long back. "Naw. Thanks, Mom. I manage till suppertime." He suddenly wanted to hug his mother and be hugged in return. But then he might cry. Little children cried. He watched his mom go back to fussing as if there were a million things to be tidied up and put away.

"Got us a nice big bag of rice today," said Brandi. "On special. We put some of that together with the last of Miz Griffin's stew an what be left of that soup bone for tonight. Spect you gettin a little tired of Beefaroni. An I spose you already seen Toby? I 'vited him to supper, but he tell me Lamar ask him over first. Lord, an here be that boy's toothbrush right here side yours . . . can't hardly tell 'em apart." She held up two identical green brushes that had been lying on the sink counter.

Corbitt shrugged. "Don't matter none. We was gonna go an catch rabies off each other, it happen a long time ago."

Brandi smiled once more. "Well, I be proud, I was you, havin me a good friend like Toby."

Corbitt's eyes narrowed. "Why? Cause he white?"

Brandi stood on tiptoes to slip a few cans onto a high shelf. She didn't seem to hear Corbitt's half-suspicious tone. "Tell you the honest truth, son, funny as it sound, it's got so's I don't hardly notice that no more. Fact is, I had me this dream bout you two the other night an couldn't for the life of me tell which of you was which." She folded the grocery bags to be used later for trash. "He do got the prettiest hair, though, don't he?"

Corbitt came to his mother and kissed her cheek. "Spose so. I never notice." Then he smiled. "Bein white never done him no good when Miz Griffin go an soap out his mouth, huh?"

"Mmm. Bein black never done *you* no good bout that, neither. Huh?"

"Mom? I never think bout it before, but y'all spose there be a lot of whitefolks somewheres like the Barlows?"

Brandi was quiet for a moment. Finally she sighed. "Son, you got to realize I ain't never been no further in this world than down to Jackson on my honeymoon. Spect things be a whole lot different up north . . . least that what everbody always sayin. But I got to admit I seen scant few like the Barlows in my life. They just . . . well . . . just . . ."

"People?"

"Mmm. That say it all, son." Brandi moved to the fridge, an ancient GE with its motor and cooling coils on top, and peered inside. " 'Mind me of that ole Mother Hubbard's cupboard in there. Price of meat seem to get higher ever week." She smiled back at her son. "You the one do all that readin, spect there any truth to that vegetarian healthy stuff?"

Corbitt smiled back. "Herbivores spend half their lifes eatin, Mom. Only carnivores gots time to have fun. Sides, how much 'telligence it take to sneak up on a leaf?"

"Mmm. You do got yourself a way of cuttin right to the bone, don't you, son."

Corbitt glanced at his father's old shotgun on pegs above the bed. "Maybe I go rabbit huntin again. That help."

Brandi turned quickly. "Not on Bates's land!"

"Well, course not. Though that fo sho be the best place around, all wild an overgrowed like it is." Corbitt reached past his mother and grabbed the big beef bone out of the fridge. "Bet even crow be tastier than gnawin this ole fossil! An, sho nuff be one passel of 'em hangin round here today." He twirled the bone like a baton.

Brandi laughed. She snatched the bone and swung it at her

son, who ducked. "Don't be playin with your food, boy. An I don't think I could eat me a crow to save my life. Fossil! Swear you knowin half them big words in the dictionary."

"Well, more words you know sometime seem to make it easier to say what you thinkin. Course, I don't wanna go round talkin high-toned." Corbitt pointed to a lizard clinging to the outside of a window screen. "Like callin that a sauroid."

"Sauroid, huh? Well, I member me that, even if I wouldn't dare use it in polite company. Still look like a plain ole blue-belly to me. I member when you an Toby an Lamar used to rub their tummies an put 'em to sleep."

Corbitt's smile faded. "That when we was little children, Mom." He pulled one of the chairs from the table and sat backwards in it, crossing his arms on top and dropping his chin on them. "Sides, lizards be slow an stupid. Gots only primitive little brains even though they be descended from dinosaurs what used to rule the whole earth. Times went an change on 'em. An they couldn't change with the times. Now they ain't even smart enough to know they bein tricked." Corbitt laid his forehead on his arms and stared at the floor. "Like negroids," he whispered.

Brandi put the bone on the counter and pulled a big butcher knife from a drawer to scrape off what was left of the meat. "Hmmm? Didn't catch all of that, son."

"Nuthin. Mr. Rudd offer me a job today."

Brandi turned and patted Corbitt's dusty hair. "Why, that's wonderful, son! Fact is, I seen Mrs. Rudd just this mornin bout a waitressin job. She tell me there ain't nuthin right now, but she be watchin this one girl of hers mighty close. Seem there some food thievery goin on."

The smell of meat made Corbitt's stomach growl. He glanced up sharply. "GIRL, Mom? Now, just how ole this *girl* be?"

"Well . . . hear she gots herself three little ones."

Corbitt dropped his head back on his arms. "Yeah. Bout what I figure."

"But, I been tellin you all along how Mr. Rudd gonna like your smart new idea."

Corbitt hunched his shoulders. His mouth made words as if they tasted bad. "I never even tell him *my* idea! He gots his own plan for me!" Corbitt looked up at his mother once more, his eyes glittering cold like the knife blade. "Oh, he gonna be takin real good care of us, best believe!"

Brandi's hand went to her son's shoulder. She seemed confused by his tone. "Well, son . . . if it mean doin somethin you don't like . . . or a thing what too hard for you . . ."

Corbitt snorted. "A little ole *child* could do it!"

"Well . . . I don't want you to be takin no job you don't like, son. Not at your age."

At what age then, thought Corbitt. He looked up and saw his reflection in the knife blade. He sighed and made a smile. "Course I do it, Mom. I gots to help us. I only tell him I need to ask you first, is all."

Brandi stroked the tense muscles in her son's back. "Well . . . y'all just be sure it somethin you really want, Corbitt. Say, bad as you been wantin one of them leather jackets, if you get my meanin. Just bout any kinda money be a blessin to us now . . . special cause we gonna be makin them visits to the prison once a week."

Corbitt nodded slowly. "Spect that help Dad, huh?"

"Yes, son. It awful hard bein punished for what no crime at all in the eyes of God."

Were God's eyes colorblind? Corbitt wondered. That didn't seem very logical considering all the pretty colors He'd put in the world for people to see . . . his mother's honey-toned complexion, Sherry's warm dusky brown, and Toby's golden hair. He glanced at his own ebony arm. Black wasn't a color—technically. But then, neither was white. "Guess I go for a swim an get myself cleaned up." Corbitt rose and walked to the door. Out on the porch he paused to brush some dust from his body. Frowning, he wet a finger with his tongue and rubbed it hard on his arm. At least the dust would wash off.

Hobbes's crack house was a small tin shed down a dirty little street that dead-ended at some railroad tracks. The building had once been some sort of truck shop, and faded letters still spelled FAGEOL above the boarded-up window. Lactameon wouldn't have known what that meant if there hadn't been a faint graphic showing what looked like a cross between a Model A Ford and some sort of Super Tonka. The rest of the building was layered at kid-level with spray-painted pictures, symbols, and gang marks. Some were so ancient that the gangs were long forgotten and their surviving members probably had kids in gangs of their own. The Collectors' mark was a warning, but then so was the Leopards', and both were ignored by most of the customers. The front door was heavily planked; perfect protection against gangstuhs and pigs. Until today . . .

From where Lactameon stood on the corner, cautiously scanning the short, narrow street, he could see the door standing open to darkness. Shifting Sebastian's board to his other hand, he concentrated on getting his breath back after the long, hot walk from the alley. The yellow bandana had at least kept his eyes free of sweat, but it also drew too many stares. Lactameon was used to being stared at, but a lot of those looks had been aimed at his headband instead of his body. No one had done more than stare, but then this was still Collectors' ground. Prob was, a carful of gangbangers wouldn't give a good shit about that. More than once on his way he'd felt a chill trace his spine when a car had cruised past at just that right speed. It was one thing to wear colors with your brothers, but something way else to show them alone. Two small dudes coming up the sidewalk on a battered old bike had made a one-eighty and rode away fast. Little Leopards, probably. Lactameon didn't much care.

He wasn't sure what he'd expected to find at Hobbes's house: business as usual, or a lot of dead kids in the gutter . . . including Sebastian. But this total desertion made him uneasy. By this time on a Sunday there should have been lots of kids coming and going: some walking, some on bikes like those Leopard boys, some on skateboards, and maybe even a couple of cars. Whatever had happened, word had gone out.

Hobbes had only opened the place a week or so before school ended. He'd come up from running to street-corner dealing, but had chilled with his green instead of showtiming with boomers and clothes. Lactameon recalled how proud Hobbes the third-grader had been of his first board and job as a runner. Word was in seventh grade that he'd wasted his sixteen-year-old supplier, but only to save his own ass. Lactameon wasn't sure he believed that. Hobbes had invited him to his fourteenth-birthday party in June. He'd seemed the same Hobbes as always while serving up pizza and Colt 45.

Lactameon looked around. Traffic was light on the main street, but then this was Sunday. Still, there were enough people and cars to be reassuring. Yet the absence of kids and that open front door meant some serious shit had come down. Lactameon could believe that his gang had shit-kicked Sebastian, one way or another, but for Bilal and the dudes to have gone up against Hobbes's house with only that old .38 would have taken industrial-strength balls. And yet, somebody had.

Maybe the gang had used Sebastian's Uzi after they'd kicked him? Lactameon looked for bullet holes, but found no more than usual. Maybe they'd done all the wet work inside? Shit, maybe Hobbes, Sebastian, and Hobbes's other boy, Lizard, were laying in there on the floor right now? Kids were harder to kill than most people thought—at least, black kids were.

Lactameon frowned. He was wasting time. It was either go in there and scope out the bodies, or go pawn the gold and score some cheeseburgers. Sucking a breath, he started to step around the corner.

A hand dropped on his shoulder. "I wouldn't, sweetheart."

For all his weight, Lactameon spun around fast, dropping the skateboard and grabbing for his box knife. Hobbes stood behind him. "SHIT!"

Hobbes was one of those dudes who had looked funny enough to be cute as a little kid, but now seemed like some white asshole's idea of Sambo. Lanky and lean, bony and awkward, he had slick skate moves, but Lactameon could picture himself dancing before imagining Hobbes doing it. Hobbes's hands were like big, grisly skeleton paws, and his feet seemed huge in purple-striped Cons. He was about the color of mud, with eyes to match, dribble-lipped, buck-toothed, and Lactameon had never been able to figure if he wore baby-dreads on purpose or just didn't take care of his hair. Mostly, he looked like one of those kids who could live all their lives in the worst part of Oaktown and still never learn to be bad. Today he wore faded 501s with one knee ripped and revealing a grimy kneecap, and an old denim jacket that about matched his jeans. It was just partly buttoned and showed no shirt underneath. A fine-linked gold chain gleamed on his chest, but it somehow looked like something somebody had given him that he hadn't known what else to do with. His watch was a drugstore Timex, and as usual a Kool hung from his lips.

Hobbes leaned his old Dogtown against the wall and gave Lactameon a lazy smile. "Mmm. Sorry, Tam. Y'all needin to go change your shorts?"

"Um, I don't wear none, man."

"Shit, me neither. Lotta goddamn trouble over nuthin, y'all askin me. Sabby wear black ones. Ain't that a bitch!"

"Oh, shit, Hobbes, is Sabby okay?"

"Well, he been better, for a fact. Wasn't kisses your dudes give him, man."

"Jeeze, Hobbes, I didn't even know till bout a half hour ago."

Hobbes shrugged. "Shit, man, I know you wasn't part of that party. Ain't even a mascot's job. Is it?"

"Well, I spose that 'pend on the situation. The Leopards' mascot fight sometimes, he just ain't no good at it."

Hobbes looked thoughtful. "The sit-u-ation," he repeated slowly. "Mmm. Spect it cause he a whiteboy?"

"I think it more cause he ain't a very big whiteboy."

Hobbes nodded, then glanced down at Sebastian's skate-board lying wheels-up like a dead thing. "Must be a bitch." His eyes lifted to Lactameon's forehead. "Mmm. Spose y'all know I gots to kick you, man?"

The sweat on Lactameon's body suddenly turned to ice. Shit! He'd just *known* something like this was going to happen! He swallowed. "You . . . do?"

"Well, course, Tam. Shit, if somebody was to write a rule book, that be in it somewheres. Ain't that a bitch?"

"Oh. Shit." Lactameon stared in fascinated horror as Hobbes casually reached into his jacket. Besides the two Uzis he owned, one carbine, one pistol, he carried a huge .44 auto. It was plain black. Hobbes never showtimed.

"Course," Hobbes went on. "Ain't nuthin personal, man. Shit, you an me, we used to play in that fuckin sandbox. But, you the color jump my boy an shit all over my house."

Lactameon saw only the vanishing hand that would reappear in a moment holding his death. Why the fuck didn't he *do* something. What?

"Course," added Hobbes. "Y'all could take that off."

Lactameon's hands jerked. His fingers twitched. What the fuck was wrong with him? Why in hell couldn't he just rip that stupid rag off his head and save his stupid black ass? His hands clenched to fists. Buried muscle tensed in his chest. His arms pressed deep into his sides. Swallowing dry, he rasped. "I . . . can't, man." He closed his eyes.

Hobbes's voice came from far away, slightly puzzled. "Well, why the hell not? Shit, it stuck on there with Super Glue or somethin? Want me to take it off for you?"

Lactameon kept his eyes tight shut. He wondered how long he could stand this shit before he started to bawl. "Wouldn't . . . signify," he whispered.

"So, who gonna know, man?"

Lactameon knew the answer, but then Hobbes would too. Lactameon waited. Strangely, he wished Hobbes would shut the fuck up and just do it! At least he hadn't pissed his fucking jeans . . . but nobody would ever know that. Something nudged his chest. His eyes popped open. A hardpack of Kools in Hobbes's mud-colored hand tapped his chest again. He raised his eyes to the other boy's. Hobbes only looked thoughtful. "Ain't that a bitch."

"SHIT! Hobbes, you motherfucker! You never used to play stupid-ass games, man! Shit! That sucks, man! Hard!"

Hobbes looked surprised. "Well shit, man, who playin games? What I sayin was, I *gots* to kick ya. Teacher sayin I *gots* to do my homework. Pig sayin I *gots* to respect his ass, white-man sayin I *gots* to kiss his, an now some goddamn niggaboys sayin I *gots* to kick yours. Fuck 'em. Yo, man, y'all wanna blow one or not? My arm gettin tired."

"Oh." Lactameon took a cigarette, watching while Hobbes slipped the pack back inside his jacket. A flash of the .44's butt showed for a second as Hobbes produced a lighter. He fired Lactameon's Kool, then shrugged. "Anyways, man, why you raggin on me for? Shit, it *you* standin there all black an proud an ready to die for somethin made in Taiwan. Look good on ya, gots to say. Go fly with your necklace. Yo. Know your shoe untied, man?"

Lactameon sighed smoke, surprised to find that his hand holding the cigarette was dead-steady. "Yeah. Fuck it."

Hobbes knelt and tied the laces. "Mmm. Shady under here."

"Shit, Hobbes! What you makin jokes for, man? Sabby gots his ass smoked, and your house got toasted, an . . . Jeeze, Hobbes, my dudes shoot you too?"

Hobbes stood up, glancing at the faded purple bandana tied around his jacket sleeve midway between his wrist and elbow. Lactameon had been too busy watching Hobbes's hand to notice his sleeve, soaked in places with blood. Hobbes grinned. "Just a flesh wound, sweetheart."

"Um, so whose colors is them?"

"Mmm. The red mine, the purple K mart's."

"Goddammit, Hobbes! Yo! I almost get my motherfuckin ass shot off cause I give a shit, man! Get the fuck down with that! Ain't you a little bit pissed, man?"

Hobbes flipped his cigarette away and blew out the last puff of smoke. "Oh, I pissed for sure, man. Fact is, I been with Sabby when your dudes jump his ass, they all be dirt-nappin right now. Your ass too, you been runnin with 'em." Hobbes grinned. "Sides, man, all you dudes gonna be in your clubhouse tonight, drinkin till you can't stand up. Seem like to me, ain't no better time or place for a payback . . . *if* I was gonna do one."

"Um, so you sayin you ain't?"

Hobbes shrugged. "All I sayin, right here an right now, my mind tellin me it ain't worth my time. Sides, I already plan it, man."

"Huh?"

Hobbes sighed. "Listen up, Tam. I gots to kick all you dudes, right?"

"Well . . . yeah."

"Well, five dead kids even in this hood gonna rate a *little* heat, man. For sure I could hire it out to some big dudes I know, but the pigs start in drillin the Leopards cause they *want* it to be the Leopards. So, the Leopards get pissed-off at me, an here we go with another great big motherfuckin donkey show! Sides, man, Bilal the same ole dude I know from first grade. He didn't shoot Sabby, an he didn't let T.K. loose on him neither . . . least not with his blade. That the same ole Bilal." Hobbes smiled. "An the same ole Bilal prob'ly raggin his ass off right now cause all he score was bout a buck in small change an a bucket of buffalo wings. Now, ain't *that* a bitch?"

Lactameon could picture Bilal and the dudes opening the pack. "Mmm. Well, don't a crack house make better'n that?"

Hobbes made a face. "This one been payin expenses. Don't know bout no others. Shit change since we little, Tam. Used to hear all them stories bout dudes our age walkin round with five-, ten-thousand bills in their Calvins. Shit, member way back when nobody wanna get stuffed in a dumpster, out wearin a gold chain size to collar a motherfuckin lion? So, when the last time y'all see one of them, cept on a pimp? Shit, I member my very first runnin job, man. Half buck a trip, an three, four, ever fuckin day. Now I gots me one skinny-ass little sucka on a Freddie Smith creamin his jeans he make twenty dollars. Fact is, business here be gettin any worse, I fuckin start eatin my capital, man."

Lactameon flicked ashes from his Kool. "But, jeeze, Hobbes, crack all over the hood! Shit, seem like half the kids either smokin or sellin, or both. An, they *little* kids too."

"Mmm. Ain't makin front page with me, man. Shit, Beamer been bringin in more trollin the sandbox than Lizard do cruisin the courts." Hobbes reached for his Kools again. "An, *course* they want little kids, man. Specially the dudes."

"Huh? Who you talkin bout, man?"

Hobbes fired a cigarette and blew smoke. "I talkin bout who really makin the profit, man." He raised his eyes past Lactameon toward the distant hills where big houses separated by plenty of space looked down on Oakland. Lactameon turned for a moment, then nodded. "Oh."

Some things in life were just there . . . understood . . . and you didn't need to see or think about them. Lactameon had seen little kids at the Center, clustered around the TV, laughing and giggling at the shows and cartoons. Yet most of them didn't look hostile or hurt when a commercial came on for toys or food or any other of the ten million things they didn't have. And they'd look at you like a fool if you asked them why. White people lived beautiful lives inside a glass-fronted box. So, why shouldn't golden-haired Billy or Jennifer fill shopping carts up with Pudding Snacks? And why shouldn't their mother just smile at how mall-wise her kids had become? Black kids on TV were really just white because they acted and talked just as clueless. No kids in the hood looked like that. About the only time you saw real black kids they were dressed in jail jumpsuits and chains. At least those kids looked like they had a clue.

It was the same with those houses up there. If somebody was talking about white people, or money, or the pigs beating the shit out of them, they usually glanced toward those houses. Even the Leopards' whiteboy did that. Of course, it wasn't the houses that meant anything, but it wasn't a K mart bandana you were willing to die for either. A lot of those people living in those houses probably didn't know much more about the world than what the TV told them. But then, neither did a lot of black kids in bandanas.

Hobbes sucked another hit off his Kool. "*Course* rock all over hell, man. An gettin easier to score everday. Cheaper'n a big pack of bubble gum. Lotta strange new shit too . . . like somebody doin spearmints. White motherfuckas can't pour it in fast enough. An who need a crack house no more? Score from any eight-year-old in the park, an then go suck some on the swing-set. Pigs love seein that . . . hood ain't nuthin but a great big ole self-cleanin oven, an all them cocksuckas gots to do is hold the door shut long enough. An why y'all figure ain't no crack in them pretty white hoods, man? Shit, them kids gots money out the asshole, an pigs too polite to swat their behinds. White kids been trained too good, man . . . no more *think* bout suckin rock than slammin down some Train. That shit for *niggers*, man. Ain't that a bitch!"

Hobbes spat on the sidewalk, then shrugged. "Aw, this location suck anyways, man. No help from you dudes, an them Leopards cross the tracks be dissin the suckas on their side. Shit. Motherfuckin slick-boy come cruisin last week. Either he tryin to figure if I rate a pop an a watermelon slice for him, else he scopin I long enough for makin his monthlies. Shit, man, could just be you dudes done me a favor. Ain't that a bitch."

Lactameon flipped his cigarette away. "Jeeze, Hobbes, you tellin me you gonna retire, man?"

"Shit, I dunno, Tam. Tell y'all this much, way I feelin right this minute, I could for a fact. An ain't no reason I couldn't, neither. Take my ass right out this sorry motherfucka for good, man! Shit, used to figure, I work on a garbage truck, I wanna be the driver. But I never gonna *own* that truck, man. An sure as shit I ain't never gonna own the company. *They* own the company, man. Always did, always will. Shit, I let some other sucka be the big-ass blackboy drivin the whitefolks' garbage. I gonna be a black *man* somewheres where all the black faces smile!"

"Um . . . but a lotta little suckers been payin your way up, Hobbes."

Hobbes laughed. "Oh shit, Tam, get with the motherfuckin program, man! Some boy like me *always* gonna be sellin, long's them little suckas keep on buyin an them white motherfuckas keep on pourin it in till we all kill each other. An don't y'all go dissin me, little gangstuh, you up to your ass in the mix."

"Huh? The fuck you talkin bout, Hobbes?"

Hobbes rolled his eyes. "Why I waste my time. Yo, listen up, man. Y'all be workin for the white motherfucka cause you can't take your ass cross them tracks cause you wearin that rag on your head. Yours be yellow, an that be the magic kingdom of green over there. Best goddamn pizza in Oaktown right up that street, an y'all might's well be a Mississippi niggaboy tryin to strut through a KKK march to score some. I scope you comin here, man . . . seen them two little Leopards bailin their butts for home-turf when all they wanted was a motherfuckin ice-cream cone up on *your* corner. Tell y'all this much, man, only time them stupid rags gonna be worth dyin for is when we all wearin the *same* color, an start *showin* them white motherfuckas we ain't havin no more of their shit!"

Lactameon sighed. Winfield had brought him one of those pizzas, once. They were almost worth dying for. "Well shit, Hobbes, I know all that. But I gots to live here, man. An I gots to make it through this motherfuckin summer."

"Yeah. Ain't it a bitch." Hobbes dropped his Kool and crushed it under his shoe. "Aw, shit, maybe I scope around an have me one more grand openin somewheres with a better view. But it gonna be my last, man. Word. I too fuckin old to be playin with toys in the hood." He smiled. "I leave you suckas chillin with Sabby. Shit, he already figure he drive better'n me, but your dudes best get off the sidewalk when he come down the boulevard. Course, maybe he cut *you* some slack, seein y'all returnin his ride."

Lactameon glanced down at the Steadham. "Um, so how Sabby anyways, man?"

"Mmm. Nuthin major. Course, that easy for me to say, man. Wasn't *my* balls meetin up with T.K.'s foot."

"Well, T.K. just got a little strange after what happen to him. Cuttin off his finger wasn't all them dudes done."

"Mmm. Ever figure why it happen, man?"

"Just some cruisin gangstuhs in a car."

"Yeah. Cracker-asses used to do that sorta shit to us a long time ago, man. Guess they learn their lesson, huh?" Hobbes sighed, and glanced toward the hills once more. "Why I waste my time. Seem like a motherfuckin miracle we ain't all gone crazy an ate each other or somethin. Sabby gettin some faded spots. I figure he smokin, an I lose his ass fast if that what it is. Never was much of a bodyguard, but he been a good best-boy. Stupid sucka wasn't even packin his Uzi today . . . why it *his* blood on the sidewalk stead of your dudes. Say he hate skatin with it. Ain't that a bitch. Spect he gots a new 'tude about that."

Lactameon turned toward the empty crack house. "But how they take *you*, man?"

"Shit, y'all make me fuckin blush, man. What can I say? Too much shit on my mind. Shoulda taken me a business course or somethin. Had me this password for what pass for big buyers in this hood . . . dudes I let in the back to sample the product. Bilal get hold of it somehow . . . I think I know how, an maybe I gots to do a payback after all, but not on you. Um, hang cool with that, huh?"

"Word, man."

"Anyways, Lizard was doin the door with the big Uzi, an I was passin the product, but we wasn't that busy . . . maybe six, seven suckas on the floor who prob'ly just hangin cause it still cooler inside than out on the street." Hobbes smiled. "Couple Collectors, three Leopards, an two little suckas prob'ly come down the tracks. Yo. Who the trains belong to, man?"

"Jeeze, Hobbes!"

"Anyways, I readin a book . . . ain't that a bitch . . . an somebody come thumpin the back door, an like a goddamn fool I let Lizard go for it. Sun hit that side in the mornin, can't see shit out that hole. Bilal come up with a X cap down over his eyes an give Lizard the word. I still readin bout Rasta in Jamaica . . . don't wanna be bothered. Next I know, Bilal inside with your pussy little .38 in Lizard's face! Then here come T.K. like he gots rabies or somethin, gonna own him a Uzi, cept it still on the sling an the sling still on Lizard. Maaaan, you never *seen* such a motherfuckin donkey show! T.K. in Bilal's way, Lizard ain't havin none of that drop-your-gun shit, Bilal puts a hole in the wall, an the suckas all freak! An then here come Stacy an Silver. Silver gots enough brains to keep out the way, but Stacy try for a grip on the Uzi . . . yank the clip out the motherfucka! Lizard get off his one chamber shot, pop a Leopard in the leg, then bail his butt out the front door. Two little suckas right behind his ass, an the rest of 'em so fucked they don't know whether to shit or go blind. My ass on the floor, 'hind the counter by now. Bilal doin the two-handed pig thing with gun, scopin for somebody over eleven to shoot, T.K. an Stacy trippin over the suckas, an I swear to God, Silver laughin his ass off!"

"Shit, Hobbes! What about your gun, man?"

Hobbes grinned. "So, whose side y'all on, Tam?" He glanced again toward the hills, and shrugged. "Shit, man, I dunno. Maybe I figure everbody so down with the gangstuh-thing they don't need my ass in the mix. Maybe, like I sayin, I wanna die a black *man* stead a nigger *boy.* Anyways, why I wanna kick a bunch of kids over a few bucks worth of whitey's shit? I bail my butt for the front door, man! Silver see me . . . swear that sucka smile! Ain't that a bitch!"

Lactameon nodded. "Yeah. He prob'ly would, man. Even he wasn't fucked-up."

Hobbes glanced at his bloodstained sleeve. "Well, Bilal playin for keeps, man, even he don't know it yet. Gimme a size-.38 road-rash when I dive out that door."

"Um, so what happen to the little Leopard?"

"Mmm. Ain't many dudes give a shit. Last I seen, one of yours an the other one of his was helpin him back cross the tracks. Course, your boy couldn't go no further than that. Spect they all come away with some product. Silver too." Hobbes lifted his eyes to Lactameon's bandana. "So, why y'all wearin that thing all by yourself, man? Shit, never figure *you* for a showtimin fool."

"Aw, I figure it some sorta test-thing Bilal doin on me cause I still hangin with Beamer. We never had none of that 'nitiation shit goin on. Seem stupid when you all know each other since kindergarten. Course, sometimes this summer it been like I don't know nobody no more."

Hobbes nodded. "Yeah, man. Ain't that a bitch. So, y'all eat yet, Tam?"

"Uh-uh. I was cruisin home for lunch when I found Sabby's board in a dumpster. T.K. prob'ly snag it for a trophy, but maybe Bilal didn't want nobody seein 'em with it, case Sabby kick or somethin."

"Mmm. Well, your mom always good at fixin people, man. Any that ever rub off on you?"

"Huh? Oh. You talkin like first-aid an that kinda fixin. Well, I watch her a lot. She done bullets before to keep people from gettin drilled by the pigs."

"Well, I gots me a full fridge, man, not even countin the forty-ouncers. Y'all up for cruisin back with me an maybe checkin out my boy for somethin I mighta missed?"

"For sure, Hobbes."

Hobbes grinned. "So, c'mon, man. Yo, y'all ride Sabby's board, you want."

Lactameon bent down with a grunt and flipped over the Steadham. Tailing, he hopped on top, a foot squarely over each truck, then kicked off down the sidewalk. He glanced back. Hobbes was still standing there, looking surprised. A moment later, Hobbes decked and rolled up alongside Lactameon.

"Shit, Tam! I never knew y'all could ride, man! Ain't that a bitch!"

"Well, I ain't very good. Used to have a Roskopp a long time ago, an sometimes Beamer or the dudes let me cruise theirs. But I can't ride very far."

"Mmm. Yeah. I guess y'all get tired real fast, huh?"

"No. But the boards do."

The iron-throated growl of a Super 400 carried through the late-afternoon air. Fainter came the creak and chitter of heavy springs. Corbitt stopped, halfway to the bridge, and glanced over his shoulder. The glint of sunlight on glass flickered among the riverbank trees as Lucas Sampson's White came slowly home to Bridge-end. Swirls of dust trailed the truck, rising in places above the treetops like cocoa-colored ghosts. Normally Corbitt would have dashed to meet it like the other kids who were already streaming up the bank, shouting and laughing, teeth flashing brightly, while their black and brown bodies glistened against the green foliage. Lucas always brought back some sort of treat for everyone. But now Corbitt considered how childlike that was. Funny he'd never noticed before, but the Bridge-end kids stampeded to meet *any* vehicle . . . the butane tanker that arrived once a month, and even the power company pickup when it came to read the meter. The tanker driver was black, and always brought gum. The electric man was white, but carried a huge supply of LifeSavers. And the children's parents would stand smiling in their doorways or lining the porch rails. It was like some primitive village in Africa!

Corbitt's lips curled in disgust. He glanced at the big silver starship shape of the butane tank by Number One, and then to the power lines that brought in electricity to pump water and run refrigerators, lights, and the Coopers' new microwave oven. All of the cabins boasted TV antennas. Mrs. Griffin had a telephone. This was the goddamn U.S.A., not Somalia! Why did everyone have to act so goddamn backward? There were Toby and Lamar, standing in the bed of the White, waving and cheering like the battered old truck was some sort of parade float. Their red bandanas made them look wild, and neither would have seemed out of place wearing a lion skin. Corbitt ripped his own blue bandana off his head and jammed it into his pocket, then dropped his hands to his hips and scowled as Hayes came puffing up the riverbank. He stepped suddenly in front of the smaller boy.

Hayes giggled and started to dodge around, but Corbitt grabbed his shoulders. Surprised, Hayes didn't even try to wiggle free. "What, Corbitt?"

"Why for you always runnin to meet that truck like a goddamn little ole child?"

Hayes's mouth dropped open. "Huh? That my daddy, man! An, I *is* a goddamn child! An, everbody do. Y'all do too!"

"Well . . . gettin bout time everbody *don't*! Specially them what too ole for child shit no more."

Hayes's round face went serious. "Don't matter I be a manchile now, that still my dad. Hey, c'mon, Corbitt, Daddy gots a pack of Twinkies for your ass too! Always do!"

Corbitt felt a flash of anger but released the boy. Hayes looked anxiously at the dusty truck, but then turned back to Corbitt. "Hey, y'all be needin me for somethin, man? Lamar an Tobe say to be extra 'siderate to you. Whatever you want, I do."

Corbitt sighed. "Forget it." He watched the little boy dash for the truck, then stared up into the clear blue sky and kicked his toes in the dirt. "Twinkies, my ass!"

"Now, what put Twinkies on your shit-list, boy?"

Corbitt turned to see Sherry coming up the bank. She was barefoot and still wearing his old T-shirt. She wasn't wet, and Corbitt knew she'd been waiting for him under the bridge. She had a confident kind of walk, as if always sure where she was going. Watching her, Corbitt felt his dick awakening. Then he saw a glint of gold on one of her fingers. He frowned. "Little-child shit," he muttered.

Sherry grinned. "Best be smilin when y'all say that to Lamar the lion. Twinkies his favorite food next to pizza."

Corbitt jammed his hands in his pockets and looked sullen. "Ain't scared of Lamar . . . he bout as hard to outsmart as a mule. Jump on his back, dangle a Twinkie front of his face, an he carry y'all off to Timbuktu!" Corbitt pointed. "An, why y'all wearin that?"

Sherry glanced at the golden ring on her finger. "Spect cause I like it. You winnin it for me at Libertyland last year might gots somethin to do with it, too."

Corbitt scowled. "Just no-account brass. S'prised it ain't gone all green by now."

Sherry held her hand toward the sun. "Ever bit pretty as gold. Just gots to keep it polished, is all. Gold for people too lazy to take care of their things."

The White growled to a stop with a swirl of dust and a hissing of brakes . . . just like a *real* truck. Corbitt jerked his jaw toward it. "Best hurry, fore y'all miss your Sunday treat, girl."

Sherry's hand went to Corbitt's shoulder. "I spected my Sunday treat be comin to me neath the bridge."

Corbitt shrugged off Sherry's hand. "S'prised y'all don't go an order me bathed an brung to your room, like they done in the ole days."

"They?"

"Nuthin."

Sherry searched Corbitt's face. "I'm sorry. I forgot bout your dad an all. Wanna talk?"

"No. Already had me a 'bundance of bein talked at today!"

"Well, how bout we just walk then?"

"Maybe. Sho. Why not." Corbitt gave Sherry a sidelong glance. "An don't be sayin you sorry no more bout my dad. That done. That past. An it only one little part of what wrong with everthin."

Sherry looked around and spread her hands. "Well, it still summertime, Corbitt. An it sho be a beautiful day . . ."

"Oh yeah. Whole goddamn world positively stink of summer! Smell just like nigger-sweat, y'all askin me!"

Sherry nibbled her lip. "Oh. Sorry. I forgot. No talkin."

They started for the bridge. Sherry put her hand back on Corbitt's shoulder but it soon slipped naturally down to his waist. Corbitt felt the warmth of her palm on his skin, and the nearness of her body. Her own special woodsy-clean scent filled his nostrils, mingled with that of the black river mud on her feet. Normally this would have been a pleasurable thing, but now he felt a small pride that his unfocused anger could keep even Sherry from affecting him. They stopped at the bridge entrance, both gazing at the faded letters on the plank, CONDEMNED, but Corbitt suspected only he saw the word.

They climbed the barrier, stepping from leaf-dappled shade into sunlight, and walked out on the bridge. Sherry slipped her hands into her own pockets, and Corbitt told himself he didn't miss her touch. They reached midstream and stopped. That was automatic, Corbitt realized. The little kids would often dare each other to venture on toward Bates's land: a child's game of tempting terror, like dancing on a tombstone when you still half believed something down there might wake up. The sun was drifting westward, lowering, lengthening the shadows of the bridge beams, but Corbitt knew how hot the iron rail would still be. He dropped his arms on it and forced them to stay. The burning seemed to bring a coolness over the rest of him.

Sherry saw, and winced. "What's the logic in hurtin your ownself over somethin ain't your fault?"

Corbitt said nothing to that, just leaning on the rail and pressing his chest to the hot iron. He gazed downriver to where the green water disappeared around the bend at Bates's overgrown field. He spat; his eyes never leaving the river. "They used to brand us, y'know? So's to make goddamn sure we never forget who we was."

A crease appeared in Sherry's smooth forehead. "You just now tellin me bout things what done an past. Well, all them what done that stuff to us been dead an buried ages ago. All's left is ole stories."

"Ole stories bein forgot." Corbitt spat again. The burning in his arms and chest had faded to no more than a fierce itch. The iron wasn't hot enough to scar him. He wondered why people couldn't remember pain . . . oh, you could recall that something had hurt, maybe terribly, but you could never actually *feel* it again. He sighed and pointed with his jaw. "River go west from that bend, y'know? Flow neath the new bridge where the prison bus cross, then on past the town an down to where them hills finally end. Maybe run clean to the Mississippi for all I know. Spose I could look on a map, but seem somehow like all rivers go back to the Mississippi sooner or later."

Sherry moved close to Corbitt. She lifted the bottom of her T-shirt to the rail and rested her own arms on it. Her shoulder touched Corbitt's as she leaned beside him. She spit into the water, every bit as far as Corbitt had. "There be that Great Divide, member? Like we learn in school. Rivers in the west go somewheres else."

"Mm. You right. Times I forget stuff like that."

"Well, the Mississippi go south, y'know? To the Gulf of Mexico down by New Orleans." Sherry smiled. "Where they used to have all them slave auctions. You boys figurin on buildin yourselves a raft?"

There was a rustle in the air overhead; a sound Corbitt suddenly felt he knew too well. He didn't have to look up to know what was coming to roost on the girders above. For an instant his teeth flashed in a bright silent snarl. But then he forced a long breath and a shrug. "Yeah, girl. An I flip me a coin to see who be my very own Nigger Jim, Toby or Lamar."

Hesitantly at first, then with increasing confidence, Sherry began stroking Corbitt's back. "I'm sorry. I know I ain't sposed to say this, but I know your dad bein gone them six months gonna feel like forever."

Corbitt didn't know what to say. Sherry's hand felt soft and soothing. Her touch seemed to draw some of the tenseness from his muscles. It brought memories too, but he didn't want memories . . . or to be soothed. He twisted away. "Stop that pettin me, girl! Like I was just a goddamn *child*!" He saw the surprise and hurt on Sherry's face . . . just like on Toby's . . . and felt that strange sense of power once more. "Goddammit! Is everybody round here half-blind?"

Sherry looked confused now. Corbitt turned back to the river. "What in hell be the good of a headful of books when the only next-thing comin my way be wipin 'flectors an lookin for holes in somebody else's mudflaps? Shit, that all they ever gonna let me do!"

Sherry's hand returned to Corbitt's shoulder as if drawn there. "*They?* Who this *they* you keepin on about?"

Corbitt gave the girl a pitying glance. "Shit. Smart like you be, an y'all still don't know who *they* is? You figurin *they* all be-dead an buried an gone to bones like the dinosaurs? Well, best believe *they* still with us, girl! Just got a little smaller an change their outsides some."

Sherry frowned. She took both Corbitt's shoulders and forced him to face her. He resisted at first, and muscle showed beneath Sherry's smooth skin as she held him fast. "I wanna know what all this *they* shit be about, Corbitt! An . . . an the way you sayin nigga today don't sound right . . . it ain't the way *we* say it! So, I wanna know what happen with you today . . . an right this here minute! Did you an Toby get in a fight?" She shook Corbitt as easily as she would have shaken Guppy.

Corbitt felt a laugh bubbling up inside him. It would come hollow, he knew, like something from a graveyard. He threw back his head to get rid of it and saw the crows lining the girders above . . . a lot of them. They had their heads cocked and seemed to be watching. The laugh died in Corbitt's throat. He forced his eyes from the crows and back to Sherry. "*Toby?* Now, what I just go an tell you bout the raft, girl? Toby a nigger same's us."

Corbitt did laugh then, but gently. "Hell, he don't even know he gots himself a option. Fact is, that boy don't go an wake up pretty soon, he ain't gonna know what to do with his option if it kick him in the ass. Maybe I oughta help him . . . cause I *care*. I mean, what future a blond-headed blackboy got? White kids at school won't have nuthin to do with him no more. Member a couple years back when them whiteboys went an throwed shoe polish all over him?" Corbitt suddenly burst into helpless laughter. "Man, he gonna have a worse life than US!"

Sherry gave Corbitt a furious shaking. "You just stop all this stupid talk! Right NOW! Toby gots US, fool! What he need whitefolks for? Shit, you askin me, I think you just gone jealous!"

"JEALOUS? Of what? That you sleepin his smelly ole shirt neath your goddamn pillow?"

Then it was Sherry who laughed. Holding Corbitt tightly, she pressed close and kissed him full on the lips. "Seem like Toby ain't the only one who don't know a option when it kick his own butt."

"What you mean?"

Sherry laughed again. "I mean, of all the things you could be jealous over bout Toby."

"Oh." Corbitt was quiet a moment, then he scowled. "Well, I ain't jealous of nobody for nuthin! It ain't like that!" He started to struggle free when he caught the scent of Lucky Strike smoke. He stiffened and looked past Sherry to the far end of the bridge, already knowing who it would be. Overhead, the black birds stirred and fretted and made low sounds to each other. Corbitt wondered if they were remembering the double-barreled ten-gauge Bates always carried.

Sherry's hand slipped from Corbitt's body. She turned slowly, her eyes following his. Shilo Bates leaned against a tree that had broken through the concrete and grown up in the middle of the old road. The man was in shadow. Corbitt couldn't see his face but he sensed a mocking smile. For an instant he felt naked. Then he wondered why that should bother him when all the Bridge-end children had grown up feeling the man's gaze as they played in the river. But it was different today; as if Bates knew exactly who Corbitt was . . . and *what* he was . . . and that only some words on paper somewhere prevented him from crossing the bridge and claiming Corbitt as his rightful property.

The shotgun hung carelessly in the man's hand, its muzzle almost dragging the dirt. Bates was never without it, whether patrolling his forgotten fields or racking it in the rear window of his truck when driving to town. Everyone in the county knew that one barrel packed a rock-salt charge for the butts of tres-passers while the other held bird shot for crows and other ver-min. Yet it wasn't the gun that gave Bates his aura of fear; it was his arrogant confidence, as if he knew exactly how the world worked and was only waiting for the next-thing . . . and maybe he thought he already heard it downshifting for him in the distance.

Bates was older than Mr. Rudd, and not as tall. He was potbellied, in tan pleated pants, and sag-jowled like a lazy old hound. Corbitt remembered Lucas Sampson's old Bluetick, the dog's teeth yellow and rotting. It stank, and never did anything but defend its little corner of porch. Even then it would only snap and snarl at the smaller children, slinking away from anyone big enough to stand up to it. One day it had bitten Guppy for trespassing too near. The little boy's arm had gotten infected, and Mrs. Griffin had treated it for a week with herbs and yellow sulphur salve. Lamar had been furious. He would have strangled the dog himself, but Lucas had shot it and buried the body in a corner of a field. Lamar had wanted to dig it up and leave it for the crows to pick, but Corbitt and Toby had talked him out of it. What good was vengeance on a dead dog?

Sherry was watching Corbitt's face now as he stared at the old man. Her hand went to Corbitt's upper arm and gripped it tight. "Ignore him!" she whispered.

Corbitt's eyes lifted to the crows. They seemed to have sensed the fear-aura too. Their own golden gazes were fixed down on Corbitt as if he could protect them. What a joke, Corbitt thought. As if he could!

He looked back at Sherry. "Yeah, girl. Just like everbody always be tellin their little children . . . ignore this here evil ole thing an it 'ventually crawl off all by its ownself an die. Well, I ain't a goddamn child no more, an I don't believe that shit."

Corbitt's voice came low and husky, though not by choice. He knew that Bates was hard of hearing, but he didn't care if the old man heard him or not. Corbitt's eyes glittered like ice on a wintertime road. They leveled at the man's shadowed face like X-ray lasers beaming invisible death. He wished he could burn through Bates's skull and kill the thing that lived within. His voice rumbled in his throat like a cheetah's warning growl. "I never hate me nobody afore in my whole life, Sherry. Maybe cause I never knowed a reason to. But I hate *him* an all them whites like him. You askin who THEY is? Well, there stand one in the bright light of day, an you gots to be blind not see him!"

Sherry tried to pull Corbitt away, back toward Bridge-end. "Shhh! You only go an make things worse with talkin like that! He know who you are!"

Corbitt stood proud, facing the unseen blue eyes. His toes gripped the rotted deck planks so savagely that they sank into the wood. He remembered a story Mrs. Griffin had told: of the old days when there was a line painted on the floors of bus stations to divide black and white, and how she used to sit smiling with her toes over that line. Corbitt glanced down; he was standing just past the bridge's midpoint, his own toes across the invisible line that only children dared cross . . . children, and his father. Bates had power: Corbitt could feel it like the solar wind of space stories. It seemed both fire and ice . . . the power of arrogant confidence. Corbitt had no confidence, but he'd discovered the power of hate. The hot iron had left no mark on him, but now a stripe seemed to burn across his chest. He shifted his eyes to Sherry once more and held out his free arm.

"Course he know who I be! How could he not, me black as sin in the sunlight? So, how he gonna make things worse, girl? By tellin me a secret? Shit, I never even start to believe the secret comin from him! I see him clear in the shadows for what he really be . . . just a ignorant ole fool what never had a 'riginal idea in his life!"

Sherry pulled on Corbitt's arm, trying to lead him back. "Shut up!" she hissed. "You gone crazy, boy?" Then her eyes narrowed and searched his. "What secret?"

Corbitt suddenly shivered under the hot sun. The words were on his tongue before he knew it . . . Mr. Rudd's kind words. He almost let them out. Again, he felt the power of a dangerous secret. He wondered how many other whites thought like "nice" Mr. Rudd. Not the Barlows, but the Barlows were . . . were just *people*. Corbitt didn't know any other whites. For the first time in his life he wondered why. Had he missed some sort of option, or was there an invisible Great Divide that just couldn't be crossed?

Sherry's hand clenched on his arm. Bates was raising his shotgun. Confidently. Corbitt stood, a slender column of ebony, his eyes locked on Bates's unseen face. He felt no fear. He didn't flinch when the big gun roared and shot-pellets rang off the iron beams above to spatter the river below. Rust flakes rained down. The crows scattered through the air. It seemed impossible that not a one of them fell. Their harsh voices cursed as they flew. For all Corbitt knew it was him they were cursing and not Bates. A single black feather floated slowly down to Corbitt's feet.

With his ears numbed from the gun-blast, it took Corbitt a moment to hear Sherry sobbing. The sound seemed to reach him from far away. But her grip on his arm was still strong. It took all of his own power to resist. He knelt and picked up the feather, not knowing why. Like a foolish child he stuck it behind his ear. Then, as if drunk or helpless, he felt Sherry leading him home.

There was a word Mrs. Griffin sometimes used. *Déjà vu*. It meant a feeling of having been somewhere before. Corbitt felt that now, like being caught in a slip of time going backwards.

How far back, he wondered? Sherry led him. The sun glared from the water and blinded him. Not long, he realized, not far back at all.

It had begun as a game . . . a children's game.

A hot Sunday afternoon, not two months before, beginning to shade toward cooler evening. Bridge-end had been strangely silent without the shouts and laughter of children at play. Four families including Corbitt's parents had ridden up to Starkville with the Sampsons, and the Coopers had driven into New Crossing to visit friends. Even Mrs. Griffin was gone, playing the organ for choir practice at church. For Corbitt, Toby, and Lamar, naked under the bridge with a full bottle of Jack Daniel's and a fresh pack of Kools, it was every bit as wonderful as being alone in Toby's private room . . . even better because they had the river.

Corbitt's father had found two solid weeks of work building a chicken house for a white man upriver. Corbitt and Toby had helped—Corbitt good at carpentry as with anything he could do with his hands, and Toby doing the nigger-work. Even Lamar had come on those days when he wasn't loading scrap, mostly getting in the way when there was nothing for him to lift or carry. There had been more money than Corbitt's mom and dad had seen in a year. As a sort of celebration that Sunday, Corbitt's mom had cooked up a massive midday meal and the three boys had feasted in splendor out on the porch until they were so stuffed with food they were already half drunk. They'd practically staggered down beneath the bridge, their arms over one another's shoulders and their bellies round and bulging; so full it hurt, but a good kind of pain. The whiskey and cigarettes provided by Toby seemed a luxury of pure sin on top of it all. Maybe it had been a strange idea, but sprawled between his brothers, passing the bottle and blowing smoke rings, Corbitt decided he could have died right then with no regrets.

They'd been drowsy and lazy and definitely drunk, talking about serious stuff that none would remember afterward, turning earnest gazes into each other's eyes, sometimes bumping noses while breathing whiskey fumes into one another's faces, and heaving huge sighs and small moans of pleasure in between. As always they sat on the dry flat of mud, their backs to the base of the pier and their legs spread wide because of the fullness inside them. A single bar of sunlight, golden in late afternoon, slanted down through a gap in the planking above and sparkled on the water.

The sun-bar flickered as a shadow passed through it, and Corbitt became aware of a shape silhouetted in the gold. Neither Toby or Lamar seemed to notice. Corbitt wasn't sure himself it was real, but blinked anyway to bring it into focus. Slowly a grin spread over his face. "Well, 'lo, Sherry Cooper."

"Huh?" the other boys said in unison. They swiveled their heads to look at the girl, then both made halfhearted efforts to draw up their legs. But Corbitt only grinned wider and draped his arms over their shoulders. "Aw, hell, brothers. That be like shuttin the gate after the mule done gone. Spect Sherry already seen anything what interest her."

Lamar and Toby exchanged glances, then shrugs, and relaxed once more.

Sherry was barefoot, her long legs bare in short cutoff jeans. She wore a T-shirt two years too small. Corbitt's grin changed to his usual V of a smile. "Girl, yo mammy gonna pitch a fit, she catch you dressin like that."

Toby nodded. "Paddle yo ole behind till you can't sit fo a whole solid week."

"Sho nuff," added Lamar.

Corbitt chuckled. "That there be her Milissa Taylor imitation."

Sherry dropped her hands to her hips and scowled. "What my momma don't know ain't never gonna hurt nobody. An how I dress myself be no concern of none of *you!*" She stared down at the boys until Toby and Lamar lowered their eyes. "Well, what y'all figure YOU lookin at, Corbitt Wainwright?"

"Damn if I know. Seem like somethin 'tirely new under this here sun."

Sherry sniffed. "Well, don't this just beat all to hell in a handbasket! Three lazy field-niggas lyin on their asses, stuffed so full of fried chicken an watermelon they can't hardly move, an drunk as skunks on top of it all!"

Lamar yawned as he nestled more comfortably against Corbitt. "Oh, hell, girl. Y'all don't favor the company, just you take your bouncy little behind on home."

"What you tellin me, Lamar Sampson? This here ain't your goddamn bridge, nor your goddamn river, neither! Fact is, it be your 'sponsibility to keep decent, stead of showin yourself off like a buck-naked . . . *beast*, for all the world to see!"

"Aw, shit," said Toby. "Who in hell 'vite the world down here? Next you be tryin to order us round like we was your own personal slave-boys or somethin."

"I be shamed to own myself three no-account slave-boys like you!"

"So?" muttered Lamar. "Sell us the hell downriver, an go away! I tired. Wanna sleep awhile."

Sherry was quiet a moment. There was calculation in her tawny eyes. "Well . . . I wish me it was them ole days. I have me a auction right here this minute, best believe."

Corbitt snickered. "Uh-oh, brothers. Here come the big-house missy, an we be caught in the watermelon patch."

Sherry glanced up along the riverbank. There was a short length of old hemp rope that the children used to tow the truck tubes. She walked over and picked it up. One end was frayed like a miniature ponytail. She gave it an experimental flick like a whip but it was too fine and soft to snap. Returning to the boys, she stood above them, curling the rope in her hands. "On your feet, you lazy niggaboys!"

"Don't start shit," muttered Lamar.

Sherry flicked the big boy with the rope. "Don't you back-talk *me*, you big buck! Up! All you! Or I bare your bones to the sun!"

A slow smile came to Corbitt's face. He gently shook Lamar. "Hark. I hear the missy-massa's voice."

"Oh, hark your ownself! I wanna go to sleep!"

"Shut up!" ordered Sherry. "You gots no choice, boy!"

Lamar half opened his eyes. "If *you* was a boy, I stick that there rope where the sun never see it!"

Toby grinned and leaned over to shake Lamar. "Hey, c'mon, bro. This might be fun." Getting clumsily up, Toby grabbed one of Lamar's arms and pulled. Grinning too, Corbitt rose and took the other. Together they managed to haul the big boy to his feet. He swayed and would have fallen, but they flanked him and draped his arms over their shoulders.

Lamar heaved a resigned sigh. "Oh, all right. I play, god-

dammit. But just don't go tyin me up again, huh?" He blinked
to focus his eyes on the girl. "Lotta silly-ass shit, y'all askin me."

"Nobody ask you nuthin, nigga," Sherry snapped. "An nobody give a goddamn what you think, or even if you think at
all. Ain't your mind I interested in." She coiled the rope tighter
and considered. "Now, I just buy you bucks for my plantation
an . . ."

"What kinda plantation?" asked Lamar. "Cotton?"

"Tobacco?" suggested Toby.

"Dalmatian," said Corbitt.

Sherry's whip lashed across the boys' chests. The old rope
was too soft to hurt, but Toby dropped his free hand over his
crotch. "Y'all just be careful with that thing, girl!"

"I say, shut up! You gots no right tellin me nuthin, nigga!
Slaves gots no rights at all!" Sherry tossed her head and ran her
eyes over the boys. "Fact is, I think that there ole slave-trader
done cheated me. What a sorry-lookin bunch y'all be!" She
flicked the whip at Toby. "You musta been kitchen help . . .
stealin food off your own master's table! 'Mind me of somethin
squeak when you squeeze it! Few weeks in my fields harden
you up, best believe."

"But I don't know how to pick dalmatians."

"Shut up!" The whip trailed across Corbitt's body. "An,
you! Prob'ly ain't even a week's honest work in that there skinny
butt! You housebroke, boy?"

" 'Pend," said Corbitt. "You gots HBO?"

Sherry ignored that and turned to Lamar. "An, you. By
God, look to me like this here nigga already been worked half
to death."

"Ain't that the truth," said Lamar.

"Hey, missy," said Toby. "You gots Nintendo in the slave
quarters?"

"Bet the big house gots a big screen," said Corbitt. "I be
watchin me the Playboy Channel while y'all be out pluckin
dalmatians."

"Wouldn't you skin 'em?" asked Lamar.

Sherry flailed her whip once more. "I warn you the last
time, niggas. Shut up! There be no TV where you goin!"

"So, what for supper, missy?" asked Toby.

"Candied swill," said Corbitt. "A ole Southern fav-o-rite."

"You gots a mouth on you, boy," Sherry warned. "Gonna get you in a whole heap of trouble right fast!" She turned, peering downriver and shading her eyes with her hand. "That ole paddle-wheeler be here with the tide. Best be sayin goodby to your picaninnies."

Corbitt stepped away from Lamar, leaving Toby to hold the big boy, and planted loud kisses on both their foreheads. "Bye, my cat-bros. I done been sold away."

Lamar lowered his head. Tears ran down his cheeks, dropping silently in the mud at Corbitt's feet.

Corbitt stared. "Shit. What the matter, man?"

Lamar sniffled and wiped his nose with the back of a hand. "Make me sad, what it is."

Toby lay his head against Lamar's. "Yeah. It is, ain't it?" He began to sniffle too.

Corbitt turned and gave the girl a scowl. "Now see what you gone an done! Shit, you whitefolks gots no hearts at all! Cold like the land of ice an snow you come from, all you be!"

Sherry looked uncertain. "It just a goddamn *game*."

Corbitt snorted. "You ignorant too! Bout a lot of things. Us blackfolks gots hearts an feelins an . . . an . . . ain't no goddamn tide on a river! Just how in hell you manage to run a dalmatian plantation, bein so stupid?"

Toby wiped his eyes. "Cheap labor."

Sherry stamped her foot again and flicked the whip. "You two niggas stop that bawlin!" She moved close and wrinkled her nose. "An y'all gonna need bathin fore they let you on the riverboat."

"Spose we just travel tourist class?" said Corbitt.

"Oh, shut up!" Sherry coiled her whip and pointed. "All you! Into the water! Ain't no mammy round, so's it look like I gotta bath you my ownself."

Corbitt's eyes glinted with new light. "Mmm. I start to see where *this* game be goin." Smiling, he moved to the water's edge.

But Lamar shook his head. "Just might be I gonna throw up. I think."

Toby slipped behind the big boy, clasping him around the chest to keep him on his feet. "That mean fo sho! Set your goddamn watch by it!"

Corbitt frowned. "Well, not right in our own special place. See if you can get him upstream a little, Tobe. Fast!"

"Not where the kids play!" cried Sherry.

"Hell!" muttered Toby. He started to move Lamar toward the water.

"Not in the river!" said Corbitt, silly as that sounded in his own ears.

"Then *where*, goddammit!" bawled Toby. "He's heavy!"

"Y'all better make up your minds," Lamar muttered, head down.

Corbitt pointed up the bank. "See if you get him to the road, Tobe. Ain't likely my folks get back till late. After he done, y'all can put him in my bed so's he sleep for a while. *After* he done!"

"Okay," said Toby. He draped Lamar's arm over his shoulder once more. "C'mon, bro, let's us go do the livin-color yawn."

"You a good brother," mumbled Lamar. "I love you."

"Yeah. I love you too, man. Just don't leggo your Eggo on me!"

The two boys staggered together up the bank. But Toby stopped halfway and looked back. "Spose I gonna lay down my ownself awhile. Ain't you comin too, Corbitt?"

Corbitt hadn't thought that far ahead. Sudden images of Sherry bare by the river drifted through his mind. There was a quaver in his voice when he called to Toby, "I be up in a little while, man."

Was there a wistful look in those smoky blue eyes? Corbitt wasn't sure. Toby nodded and helped Lamar the rest of the way up the bank. Corbitt watched them stumble past the bridge entrance and disappear, then Sherry's whip curled over his shoulder and wrapped around his neck. She pulled him to face her. "That paddle-wheeler still on its way, boy. You gots yourself a bath comin."

Sherry stood with her feet in the water. Sunlit ripples played on her body. Her tawny eyes ran over Corbitt once more, and again he could feel the warmth of her gaze. Sherry drew the rope slowly back. It uncoiled from Corbitt's neck, its soft strands slipping down his chest to tickle the curls below his belly before falling limply to the mud. Sherry pulled it to her, loosely looping it around one hand.

"You mine," she murmured. "My slave-prince. Caught you naked an wild in the jungle an brung you here all wrapped in silver chains. Now I gonna tame you."

Corbitt smiled. "You do skip around, don't you, girl?" The tip of his tongue moved over his lips. "Thought you was gonna bath me for that riverboat ride?"

Sherry wrinkled her little nose. "Ain't no doubt in my mind your buck-musk 'fend the whitefolks." She fingered the soft old rope. "But, I sorta favor your natural smell."

Another scent seemed to drift in the air. Corbitt felt heat spreading through his body. He swallowed, his throat dry and tight, and made the words come carefully. "Spect y'all favor gettin comfortable . . . just you an your slave-boy?"

Sherry's long lashes lowered over a quick flash of foxiness. "Now, just what you tellin me, nigga?"

Corbitt sank to his knees and bowed his head. "I just a ignorant niggaboy, missy. Don't even know my own mind. Spect I deserve me a good whippin for forgettin my place."

Head down, Corbitt could see only Sherry's feet. Black mud feathered their delicate duskiness. He saw the coil of rope drop beside them. The white folds of Sherry's T-shirt followed. Corbitt kept his head bowed, pulling in air and trying to prepare himself for the sight of her. He remembered when he was about five, balancing naked on the bridge rail, readying himself for that first frightening dive. Sherry's scent flared his nostrils. He watched her feet step nearer . . . small toenails, neatly trimmed, showing pinkly through the mud. He could have kissed them. Sherry knelt in front of him. He saw the supple strength in her thighs. The heat was mounting fast between his legs but he didn't care that it showed. Sherry's hand slipped under his arms, sliding in sweat as she urged him to his feet. There was a fragile edge in her voice.

"I *never* whip my slave-prince. Couldn't stand seein him scarred. Arise, boy. I dub thee Prince Cheetah."

Corbitt stood, and Sherry's breasts touched his chest, their warm brown nipples lightly brushing his own tiny black buds. It was like an electric arc. Boy and girl flinched back from each other.

Sherry forced a small laugh. She kept her eyes on Corbitt's, not looking down. "Did they have dragons to slay in Africa?"

Corbitt swallowed again. He held Sherry's eyes in return, not daring to let his own see Sherry's body because his dick thrust out straight and solid. He ached with a throbbing pressure ten times more intense than anything he'd ever felt with his brothers. The magic scent clung thick in his lungs. His voice was only a husky whisper. "Spose . . . spose everbody gots dragons, one kind or another."

Sherry nodded solemnly as if Corbitt had just spoken some powerful truth. She too seemed to have trouble drawing breath. Her palms glistened wet with Corbitt's sweat. She lifted one to her nose. "You smell good to me, Corbitt. Can I look at you?"

Corbitt didn't know whether to be proud or ashamed. Never had he felt so hard and huge. Muscles he hadn't used before hurt with the pulsing weight of his shaft. His blood beat hot through his body, pounding in his ears like distant drums, seeming to shake him right down to his bones. He wondered if he could ease the ache by holding himself, but despite his solidness he felt dangerously sensitive. A touch of breeze sent a shiver through him. He feared what might happen should he grip himself. The pulsing spread to his hips, moving them to a drumbeat of blood. He wanted to thrust them. His stomach muscles quivered with the strain of holding back. He tried to swallow, but couldn't. He managed a whisper through cotton-dry lips. "O . . . okay."

And now he felt Sherry's eyes moving over him again. A whimper welled in his throat. Slowly, cautiously, he took hold of himself with one hand, far back from the tip of his unsheathed dagger. Easing the weight helped . . . some, but he rasped, "Don't! Please!"

Sherry's eyes came back to his, wide and curious. "Don't, what? I just lookin. Does it hurt you to be like that?"

Corbitt squeezed his eyes tight shut. The plates of his slender chest stood out stark like Lamar's. They trembled as he sucked air. Sweat gleamed on him, running down his body. "I don't wanna play no more."

"Are you proud, Corbitt?"

It took him a moment to get Sherry's meaning. Mercifully, his mind started working again, shunting off some of the power that pulsed in his palm. He stayed rigid as steel, but the need to move and thrust faded a little. He kept his grip carefully loose, not daring to shift his sweat-slicked hand. "S . . . spose so." Hesitantly, he raised his free hand and pointed. "But I spect you every bit as proud . . . of them."

Sherry glanced down at herself. "But they don't hurt me." She cupped a breast in her palm as if to offer it.

A shiver ran through Corbitt's frame. Words came through clenched teeth. "*Please* don't!"

"Oh." Sherry took her hand away. A new light shone in her eyes. "It a kinda power, ain't it? Mine?"

Corbitt's sigh sounded like a Greyhound setting its brakes. "Oh, goddamn, yessss!" He risked a look at Sherry's body, noting that her rib structure was strong, stronger than his own. But then that was logical, so she could carry her breasts so high and proud above a waist so slim. A powerful backbone she had. A hint of babyness padded her stomach, softening and defining her navel. Corbitt's eyes drifted down to the swell of her hips and the muscle there. And there were more secrets concealed beneath faded denim.

Sherry took his free hand. "Please, Corbitt, let's play some more . . . like we used to. Seem so long since we done us any pure playin. I most forgot what you really like on the insides."

"I don't know, Sherry. It hurt me to play like this."

Sherry pointed. "Well, seem to me it *that* part of you what gettin in the way. Mean to say you can't control it at all?"

Corbitt hung his head like a little boy. "Uh-uh."

Sherry stepped ankle-deep into the river and tugged on Corbitt's hand. "Maybe a nice cool bath help."

Corbitt followed Sherry waist-deep into the river. He let go of himself and the water supported him, easing the strain on his muscles. He wondered if his pulse could be sensed in the depths, stirring whatever dwelt down there. He crossed his arms over his chest.

Sherry was watching him. "You 'mind me of a pitcher I seen one time in a book . . . original boy gettin ready for some kinda rite."

"AB-riginal. In Australia. Africans ain't the only black folks in the world."

Sherry stood in shallower water, thigh-deep. She reached to her cutoffs and touched the top button.

Corbitt's eyes widened. "What you doin?"

"Gettin myself comfortable. You naked. I oughta be too."

Corbitt suddenly scowled. "Goddammit, girl! Now you be actin cheap an slutty! Tantalizin me with your power!"

"I doin no such thing!"

"Yes you are! You be playin with your power, girl. An power ain't a thing to play with, just like Miz Griffin always say. Even if you ain't doin it on purpose it just as bad . . . maybe worse, cause power a dangerous thing to play with, not knowin."

Sherry hesitated with her fingertips on the second brass button. "Well, tell me what ole Miz Griffin be doin when she make them bones dance, if not playin?"

Corbitt made an exasperated noise. "She just gots her such a 'bundance of power she can play when she want, but she never go round tantalizin people with it."

Sherry giggled. "Somehow I just can't vision ole Miz Griffin tantalizin nobody."

Corbitt had been watching Sherry's fingers as they toyed with her jeans button. The brass glittered like gold, and sun-ripples off the river danced over the girl's beautiful body. The light was behind her, but he thought he saw a trace of uncertainty in her eyes. The part of Corbitt throbbing beneath the water wanted her to go on. The part of him bathed in sun and sweat wasn't so sure. Both parts, he realized, were love. "Well," said Corbitt. "She weren't always *ole* Miz Griffin, y'know? She married one time. An she musta loved one whole hell of a lot never to get herself married again."

Sherry's eyes met Corbitt's across the few feet of water. She smiled as if he'd just said a wonderful thing. Her fingers moved swiftly, and she stepped from her cutoffs, then tossed them up on the riverbank.

No secrets anymore, Corbitt thought. Despite the pain beneath the water, he felt that this was a good next-thing. He scanned the dusky triangle between Sherry's thighs; small velvety curls not quite concealing the soft little shape of his dreams. He thought of the things Mrs. Griffin baked, tender brown treats with a cleft of sweet butter your tongue might explore.

And then, as if in a dream, he saw her coming to him, the water sliding up her thighs, surging around her, droplets sparkling in her ebony curls. The water rippled out from her body in small gentle waves. Her hips glistened, moving with a motion

that was suddenly sure. And now his own moved. He felt his
chest tighten. He heard his heart pumping harder and harder
until even the river must have pulsed with his life. Almost, he
backed away, wanting to plunge into the water to swim from
this dangerous moment. His lips moved, trying to form words
that would warn Sherry away before he hurt her. But no sound
came out. He watched as the water covered her waist, concealing
that secret once more. But hiding it didn't help. It was like what
Mrs. Griffin had said about magic: that one look changed you
forever. His arms hung helpless at his sides. There was a new
light in Sherry's eyes as she came to him. Her hands went first
to his shoulders then slipped down his arms. She wanted this
next-thing, and he wanted it too, more than anything else in his
life. His hips began jerking to his own throbbing rhythm. The
magic scent surrounded him, honey-sweet and thick. His arms
opened to take her softness against him.

Then, Sherry's own hands clasped Corbitt's waist. Panther-
quick she tried to pull his thrusting body to her. Suddenly Corbitt found himself fighting it. A scream tore from his throat,
"NOOOO!" His back arced savagely and a silent explosion
burst from him below the water. His knees buckled and he fell,
slipping from Sherry's grasp, choking and crying and clutching
himself while his body jerked again and again, pumping his life-
power into the river. Cool, green light surrounded him. He
tried to breathe but this soft silent world was not for his kind.

Then, Sherry's hands were under his arms, surprisingly
strong, raising him even while his hips still weakly thrust. He
sucked a breath, then another, but tears streamed down his face.
Sherry clasped Corbitt against her, but like she would comfort
a child as he sobbed, his face pressed to her shoulder while she
stroked his back. Again he recalled his first dive from the bridge,
looking now upward to the old iron above. He felt once more
the shock of his five-year-old body smashing emerald green from
fifteen feet up, and the colder world below trying to strangle
him as he fought back toward sunlight and air. But there had
been Lamar, only six but already a mighty brown rock . . .
Lamar swimming him back to the warm black mud, and their
hugs on the riverbank, boyish and awkward but unashamed.

Corbitt felt lips on his own, soft and warm and tasting of
river water. Slowly, his arms encircled Sherry, and they were

together, wet and slick. Corbitt felt the beat of her heart so close to his.

Sherry whispered, "I'm sorry. I didn't know I could do that to you."

Corbitt had no words to tell her it was all right. Instead, his tongue quested, seeking her sweetness. Their first kiss lasted long. They whispered things . . . childish things about princes and dragons and castles. Then they parted a moment, still holding hands, to look at one another unashamed. Sherry bathed Corbitt's face with cool water and again they kissed, slower, exploring with tongues, tasting each other, touching here, and there. Sherry took Corbitt's shaft in her hands as it awakened again beneath the water, and her breasts were his to cup and to hold. He bowed his head, almost shyly at first, brushing his lips to a nipple. He licked the firm little bud, feeling it tighten. He formed his lips around it, then not knowing why, nipped it with his teeth, and felt Sherry shiver with pleasure. Her own hands moved under the water, stroking him until he moaned.

"How many times can you do that?" she whispered.

"Lots an lots," he murmured back. It was like sinking into a dream, a beautiful sideslip in time. And then he felt her guiding him into her most secret place.

"No!" He jerked free, splashing a silver sheet of water as he stumbled back a pace. "We can't do that!" he panted. Tears slipped down his cheeks, dropping into the river. They would drift downstream with his life-power.

Sherry's hands clasped Corbitt's waist again and tried to pull him to her. "It's all right. I want to."

But there was iron in his back and he wouldn't be moved. "Don't matter what we want. We gots to be 'sponsible. We ain't little kids playin no more. This be real power. Changes it make last forever."

Still, Sherry wouldn't let him go. "It okay, Corbitt. It . . . it be the first time. Nuthin forever gonna happen."

Corbitt's eyes cooled even as he cooled in Sherry's hands. "You read them books, same as me. You be knowin better. Wanna be like that girl in school last year . . . only twelve, an everbody smirkin an shakin their heads cause she got to go up to the Starkville clinic? Goddammit, Sherry, I LOVE you!"

Sherry released him and stepped back. Waterdrops sparkled in her hair. She sighed. "I guess you right, Corbitt. Seem like it so damn easy to forget them things when somethin like this happen." She moved against him once more, but gently. His arms slipped around her, but carefully. She kissed him again, then smiled into his eyes. "I could do it for you. I know how."

Corbitt sighed too. "That okay. I spect I live . . ." Then his eyes narrowed slightly. "So, how you know how?"

Another foxy flicker lit Sherry's eyes. "Promise you won't get wrathful, my prince?"

"Mmm. Spose not."

Sherry walked back to the shore and sat down on the mud-bank with her feet in the water. She patted a place beside her. "Come, boy."

"Mmm. Spect I just done me enough of that to wake up the dead."

Sherry giggled. "Nasty, dirty boy!" She glanced down and fingered a nipple. "An here y'all go an nip me like a wild animal, almost hard enough for drawin blood."

Corbitt waded to shore. He sat beside Sherry, then leaned over and lightly kissed her breast. "There. All better. Now, bout what you say?"

"Well, fact is, I seen y'all."

Corbitt shifted uneasily. "You, what?"

"Now you just say you wasn't gonna go an get mad, member? It was last month. Your folks was gone. I sorta peeked in your window. There was you and Toby an Lamar. I . . . sorta watched."

"Oh." Corbitt tried to decide how he felt about that. It didn't really seem important anymore.

"So?" Sherry asked. "Y'all mad at me?"

"Mmm. Spose not." Corbitt smiled a little. "Spect I shoulda pulled down the shade, cept you don't never think bout secrets in Bridge-end."

Sherry nodded, then smiled. "Ain't none of you scared of turnin into one of them homo-boys?"

Corbitt shrugged. "Never give it much thought." He smiled too. "Fact is, it mostly you we be thinkin bout. Don't get mad, now."

"Mmm. Spose I should be flattered."

"Mmm. Spose y'all should."

Sherry's long lashes lowered. "Spose you boys never once give a thought bout Milissa Taylor?"

"Oh, shut yourself up, girl." Then Corbitt smiled. "Course, she do gots herself a fine pair, don't she?"

"Corbitt Wainwright!" Sherry scooped up a handful of mud to throw at Corbitt, but he leaned over quick and kissed her. She let the mud drop into the river. "Spect we could do us some more of that? Careful-like?"

Corbitt's arms went around her. "Careful-like."

They kissed once more, but with care, knowing where it could lead. Both were breathing hard again when they pulled away from each other. Sherry nuzzled Corbitt's cheek. "My daddy got him a pack of . . ." She seemed to sift various names. ". . . rubbers, in his dresser drawer."

Corbitt cocked his head. "Your *daddy* do?"

Sherry giggled. "Course he do! I know he pushin forty, but that don't mean him an mom still don't."

Corbitt looked innocent. "Don't, what?"

"Nasty boy!" Sherry lay her cheek against Corbitt's. "I want my first time to be with you."

Corbitt looked around. "Here?"

"Course. Ain't this your special place?"

"Well, yeah. Only . . . well, I figure you be deservin of a lot better'n just sky over your head an river mud neath you."

"Oh?" Sherry let her eyelashes droop. "Like Toby Barlow's nice big bed?"

Corbitt's mouth opened, then he shut it with a snap. "What a thing to be sayin!"

Sherry examined her fingernails. "Why? Cause he so light black?"

Corbitt frowned. "Ain't no such color in creation, girl! It either black or it ain't . . . an he is."

Sherry smiled. "Make me a cigarette, boy."

"Huh? Now, y'all don't smoke."

"Please."

Corbitt pulled up his legs, dropped his chin to his knees, and looked stubborn. He waved a hand. "Poof, y'all a cigarette."

Sherry giggled and stood up, tugging on Corbitt's arm. "Pretty please? With sugar?"

"Oh, shush." Still frowning, Corbitt rose and let himself be led back to the bridge pier. He dug in his jeans pocket for his tobacco and papers. "You wouldn't."

Sherry cuddled close to him. "Not the first time. That's for you. I wait long as it takes."

Corbitt gave the girl a sulky glance as he handed her a cigarette and started another for himself. "Goddammit, Sherry Cooper. That sposed to be some sorta funny joke or somethin?"

Sherry bent forward for the lighter's flame, her breasts brushing Corbitt's arm. She smiled. "Lamar the lion-child be cuddly too."

"Sherry Cooper! What you wanna be anyways? A . . . a . . ."

"Ho?" Sherry suggested.

"Somebody oughta wash out your mouth, girl!"

"Course not." Sherry took a delicate puff of smoke. "You all be fine boys. Why is it there ain't all kinds of nasty names for when boys . . . well, check things out? How come you always spect us girls to be wide-eyed on our honeymoon night?"

Corbitt fired his cigarette and sucked smoke deep with a scowl. "Wanna know what I think, girl? I think you been hangin round that Milissa Taylor too much!" He considered, then suddenly looked triumphant. "Sides, they'd talk, an, poof, there go your reputation!"

Sherry rolled her eyes. "Oh, Lord! Corbitt, my cheetah-prince, would *you* talk?"

"Well, course not!"

"Mmm? Not even to Toby the tiger nor Lamar the lion?"

"Well . . . that be a entirely different color horse."

"Don't y'all trust your own brothers?"

"Course I do!" Corbitt dropped his chin on his knees again and gazed at the river. "Just don't seem right, hearin you talk like that, is all."

Sherry flipped her cigarette into the water and pressed close to Corbitt once more. "We still got time," she whispered.

Then there came a clumsy crackling from the woods across the river, like some big awkward animal pushing through the underbrush, though Corbitt and Sherry both knew it was Bates. The sunlight off the water hurt Corbitt's eyes. He couldn't see the man, but leaped to his feet, furious, about to scream curses. But Sherry rose and took his arm to calm him. Then, they deliberately left their clothes on the riverbank as Sherry led Corbitt away. They carried their heads high.

Now, on the bridge, with the sun glaring in his eyes, Corbitt found himself being led away once more. The shotgun blast still rang in his head and Bates's mocking smile burned in his mind. The crow feather tickled his ear. "Ain't you gonna let me slay you a dragon, girl?" Corbitt asked.

Sherry tugged harder on his arm. "Don't talk foolish, boy! Ain't nuthin that simple no more! Think about your mom, an all the little kids. Think about all Bridge-end, and don't go stirrin up ole trouble!"

Corbitt let himself be led back to his picture-negative world.

Even Hobbes was breathing hard from the three-story climb up steep creaky steps. Lactameon was panting and pouring sweat, but he had stayed at Hobbes's heels all the way. Wiping his forehead with the back of a hand, Hobbes turned and gave Lactameon a grin. "Sorry bout all them motherfuckin stairs, man." He glanced around the dim-lit hallway, where heaps of trash lined the spray-painted walls. "This one sorry motherfucka for a crib, man. Do me a lot better, for a fact, cept it close on the action an the man never gimme no shit bout rentin to a kid, long's the green in his hand on time."

Lactameon hauled himself up the last step and leaned on the banister, looking around. His bandana was soaked and his hair gave off gold-colored glints from the single small bulb in the ceiling. "Shit, man, 'pared to Beamer's place, you gots you a palace."

Hobbes watched Lactameon jerk up his jeans, studying the fat boy. "Mmm. There a lot to y'all, man, an I ain't talkin what show on the outside."

Lactameon glanced down at Sebastian's board in his hand. "You mean, like ridin?"

"Mmm. Well, that for sure, man. An then I get to thinkin bout what kinda muscle it take for haulin all that up three floors. I sure as shit couldn't do it. Ain't likely Sabby could, neither."

"Well, most dudes never think like that, Hobbes."

"Word on that, brother. What I sayin is, everthin gots it a

deep part . . . shit that most dudes don't see, else they been
trained not to look. Like, most dudes gonna spend their whole
goddamn lives beatin their heads 'gainst some sorta wall. What
'maze the shit outa me is that they never even *think* bout steppin
back for five fuckin minutes an scopin that motherfucka out.
Shit, man, least *four* other ways of gettin your ass to the other
side of that wall sides tryin to bust through it." Hobbes tapped
his forehead with a finger. "I see somethin, man, I always try
an figure least four things about it most other dudes ain't seein."

Lactameon looked down at himself for a moment. "Oh, um,
you mean like, my skatin . . . an maybe I stronger than most
people think?" He smiled. "Well, that two today."

"Nuh-uh, Tam. Three. An I already know you gots a brain."
Turning, Hobbes walked a short way to a plywood-sheathed
door, pausing to dig keys from his pocket. "I leave Sabby a quart
of J.D. for company, cause he hurtin so bad. But I figure we
both way up for a forty-ounce Green. Gots half a Leopard pizza
ready for the reactor too."

The cool of Hobbes's apartment was like a dream come true
as Lactameon stepped through the door behind the other boy.
Tingling fingers of chill caressed his body. His dick even stirred,
and he swore he felt the nipples on his chest trying to poke out.
The apartment was small, half kitchen, with a narrow door standing open to show a tiny bathroom. It was about as clean as you
would expect any normal fourteen-year-old boy to keep it, but
it contained almost everything a normal American boy would
want in his room . . . except something with prettier breasts
than Lactameon's. Two tall, grimy windows overlooked the
street, with a big, new AC unit pouring pure pleasure from one
of them. The floor was bare boards, their varnish long gone, and
dust bunnies lurked thickly under a ratty old sofa and an overstuffed chair that bled cotton. They faced a huge big-screen TV
with a new VCR that seemed straight from the starship *Enter-
prise*. Tapes were piled on top of it, mixed among what looked
like every Super Nintendo game ever made. A Pioneer stereo
sat on the floor surrounded by scattered CDs, and the speakers
in opposite corners of the room seemed big as shower stalls. An
old double bed without head- or footboards stood beneath the
windows. It had probably never been made up, but the rumpled
sheets looked fairly clean except for the fresh bloodstains.

A boy lay naked on the bed, as if bathing his bruises in cool AC breath. Streaks of dried blood showed on his body. He might have been asleep because he didn't move . . . though a darker thought flicked through Lactameon's mind . . . but the stereo was muttering an old Ice T song that spit low-thunder studio fury against the soothing murmur of air. The boy had a half-empty bottle of J.D. clutched in the crook of an arm like a teddy bear. Even bloody and bruised, Lactameon thought, he was beautiful.

For sure you could never *say* that word to another dude . . . except maybe to Silver . . . but Sebastian was beautiful just like Hobbes's room. It was hard to say why; or maybe just hard to admit why. There were bigger dudes than Sebastian going on to eighth grade, even forgetting the ones who'd stayed back several years. And, there were dudes with twice as much muscle, or handsomer faces, and a lot cooler haircuts. Bilal probably came closest to combining them all in the ultimate African mix. But Bilal was only a beautiful ghetto-boy, while Sebastian could have been on some Beverly Hills show. Even dipped in gold, Bilal would only have resembled Sebastian the way a wild junk-yard dog bathed and brushed would compare to a pedigreed prize winner. But, if you weren't going to bullshit yourself, you had to admit you admired the black-and-white mix of Sebastian's face. Lactameon's mom had once said that there were very few "pure" Africans left in America, not counting the newly arrived. If you *could* trace your family tree, you'd likely find a whiteboy in the woodpile somewhere. With his own sooty blackness and "African" face, Lactameon had never given that much thought. Once, when drunk at the clubhouse, the dudes had chilled with that program awhile. T.K. had rated a possible, Bilal a chump's-chance, Stacy an I-don't-think-so, and Silver a unanimous no-way. Lactameon had scored a tie with Stacy. Then the subject had shifted to girls, but had nothing to do with their ancestry.

There were several "mulattos" at school. A dirty-sounding word like the label high-yellow, which implied low-black and which nobody used. But they were just other hood kids, and nobody gave a good shit. Or, maybe the translation was: they couldn't pass to save their own asses. The little brass-colored boy in the park only stood out because of his waist-length yellow-brown dreads. But, admit it or not, Sebastian was beautiful

because he *could* pass. Somehow that rated him way above
Winfield too; as if there was something suspect about a "pure"
whiteboy wanting to hang with the homeys. Lactameon supposed you could spend a whole lifetime denying the subliminal
shit the TV had taught you, but he had better things to do.
Though he'd only have admitted it when drunk, if some Voodoo
spell had given him the choice between the bodies of Bilal or
Sebastian, he'd have gone for the gold. And he suspected Bilal
would have, too. Yet Lactameon's gang had really disrespected
that thing of strange beauty.

On the stereo, Ice T—rapper, rocker, or whatever the hell
he wanted to be—was naming himself a nigger in no uncertain
terms. Silver had once suggested that if he did that long enough
maybe the whitefolks would believe him. Actually, technically,
he was a mulatto, but Lactameon for sure wasn't going to suck
his dick like Ice-boy wanted anyone not down with that to do.
Fact was, the dude seemed to have a real thing about getting
his jimmy sucked-off, and Lactameon wasn't having any of it.
Even Hobbes looked surprised, cocking an ear while he untied
the bloodstained bandana from his sleeve and laid the huge .44
on the VCR before slipping off his jacket. "Mmm. Don't know
bout you, Tam. But, talkin personal, I like *my* dick goin where
the good Jah make a proper place for."

"Um . . . yeah, man. Me too."

The boy on the bed stirred painfully, maybe hearing the
voices or feeling hot breath from the hallway. He sat slowly up
like it hurt him, almost spilling the uncapped J.D. A purple-
black bruise showed stark on his golden face as he struggled to
focus on the figures at the door. Suddenly, his whole body jerked
rigid as if hit by a pig's prod.

"HAAAWBBS!"

It was a scream of pure terror. Lactameon jumped back,
slamming his bulk into the doorframe. All he seemed to see of
Sebastian were two wide-open steel-colored eyes staring with
horror at his forehead. Then, his own eyes went wide as the
golden boy grabbed a big ugly pistol from the sheets and whipped
it into a two-handed aim.

"Chill!" Hobbes leaped in front of Lactameon, spreading
his arms, but still hardly covering half of the fat boy. The shot
sounded flat; the spurt of orange fire from the Uzi's muzzle

seemed ten times more evil. The bullet hissed past an inch from Lactameon's ear. Hobbes cursed, grabbing his own gun and straight-arming it at Sebastian. "I shoot your ass, sucka! Swear to God, man! PUT IT DOWN!"

Sebastian's eyes went amazed. His mouth opened, but he still clutched the gun. "Hobbes! That one of 'em, man! Kill him, kill him!"

Hobbes's voice dropped to something more dangerous than anything Ice T could have made up. "Put. It. Down. Sabby! One. Two . . ."

"But . . ."

"Two an a half, man . . ."

Expression confused, Sebastian slowly lowered the Uzi. He looked about ready to cry. Hobbes's .44 never wavered. "On the floor, man. Just drop it. It break, I buy you a new one."

Lactameon winced as the gun hit the boards, almost expecting it to go off. Then the door across the hall whipped open, crashing back against the wall inside. Hobbes spun around, gun ready, its muzzle just missing Lactameon's nose. A red-eyed man in dirty shorts lurched halfway out of the other apartment's door. A bottle of Bird dangled from his fist. "You goddamn little shit-eatin sons of bitches! Cocksuckin motherless little niggas!"

Lactameon slipped back from the doorframe. There was a new bullet hole in the hallway's opposite wall, about a foot from the winehead's door. Remembering Sebastian, he darted a glance over his shoulder, but the golden boy hadn't recovered the Uzi. Hobbes stepped into the hall, the .44 ready. "Shut the fuck up, you sorry-ass ole motherfucka! Get the fuck back in your shithole an go fuck your mammy some more!"

The man looked about to explode, until his eyes slowly focused on the .44's muzzle, which probably seemed the size of a sewer-pipe. He hesitated a second more, then spat something pink on the floor. *"Animals!"*

Hobbes's voice broke. *"What?"* The .44's blast sounded like a movie gun in Dolby. Plaster popped from the wall near the man's head. Hobbes fired again, the big gun slamming his wrist. The man leaped back inside and crashed the door shut, tearing splinters from the frame where the second bullet had ripped through. Locks clattered.

Hobbes stayed frozen for a moment. Lactameon wondered

if he was going to shoot again. Then the boy's lanky body relaxed. Turning to Lactameon, he grinned and blew smoke from the .44's muzzle. "Take *that*, you dirty rat. Shit, man, don't ya hate 'em?" Then, remembering Sebastian, he spun around again, gun half-aimed.

Sebastian was sitting as stiff as a dick. Ice T was still bitching he wanted his sucked. Hobbes glanced at Lactameon. "Shut the door, man. Okay?" Then Hobbes crossed to the bed, shoving the .44 in back of his jeans and snagging the Uzi off the floor. "So, the fuck *your* prob, Sabby? You drunk?"

For a moment the golden boy looked like he'd just woken up. "Um . . . kinda." He started to relax, but tensed again when Lactameon shut the door and fastened the bolts. "Hobbes! He one of 'em, man! You fuckin crazy lettin one in here? Man, he come to *kick* me!"

Sebastian's voice finished on a high squeak. Hobbes frowned. "Yeah, man. He gonna fuckin beat your ass to death with your own ride. Ain't that a bitch."

"Shit! He gots my *board*, Hobbes!"

Hobbes waved the Uzi toward the J.D. bottle. "Take a chill, Sabby. A big one. Tam here know nuthin bout what come down on you, man. Brung your ride back all on his own. Seem like to me, y'all could do with a few homeys like that . . . or any homeys at all, what I sayin."

Lactameon turned from locking the door, not sure it was safe to approach the bed and offer Sebastian his board. The sharp scent of gunpowder drifted through the air, mingling with boy-sweat, dirty socks, spilled beer, and the warm, woody aroma of J.D. For a moment he thought he caught the dry, dusty bite of crack smoke, but then that might just have been what had soaked into Hobbes's jacket at the house. Hobbes turned and tossed the pistol. Surprised, Lactameon caught it one-handed, still holding the board in the other. Sebastian's mouth dropped open. "Hobbes! You crazy, man?"

Shaking his head, Hobbes grabbed the bottle and shoved it into the golden boy's hands. "Why I waste my time! Yo, Tam. Lose Ice-brain, huh? There some ole Bobby B in that pile some-wheres. Then drive-by the fridge an score us them Mickeys. Shit!" He glanced at his arm, the gash from Bilal's bullet dripping blood. "Ain't that a bitch!" Passing Lactameon to rinse his arm under the sink faucet, he muttered, "It just you an me, kid!"

It took Lactameon a few moments to figure out the CD and get the Bobby Brown goin on. Hobbes wrapped a paper towel around his arm and disappeared into the bathroom. Lactameon glanced at the fridge, ancient but big, thinking about that first icy swallow of malt, but then glanced at the golden boy, who was watching every move like a wary animal. Slowly, the way you handled a bad-looking dog, Lactameon eased toward the bed, the Uzi held muzzle-down in one hand while the other offered the board. "Um . . . yo, Sabby."

"Don't call me that, you fat-ass cocksucka! I fuckin *hate* that!"

Lactameon frowned. "Well, don't go callin me no cock-sucker, man . . . or *cocksucka*, neither. An I already heard all that other shit a b'zillion times before. An just like Hobbes sayin, I didn't know nuthin bout what happen to your ass today. Found this in a goddamn dumpster, man. Word."

When Lactameon was near enough, Sebastian reached out and snatched the board from his grip. He stared at it suspiciously, turning it over in his hands. Lactameon decided not to say he'd cruised it. "You welcome, Sebastian."

The golden boy's head jerked up, eyes like new steel. "Akeem!"

"Huh? Oh. Yeah, man. Akeem. Sorry."

"My ass!"

Just for a second Lactameon wanted to raise the Uzi and check out Sebastian's reaction to that. But, like Bobby B was saying, *don't be cruel*, and Sebastian did look like he'd been sucked through a street-sweeper. Sighing, Lactameon walked to the fridge and put the pistol carefully on top. Beautiful green bottles sweating chill met his eyes when he opened the door. Taking out two, he set one on the sink counter and twisted the cap from the other. Leaning way back, he tilted the bottle sky-ward and gulped. Fuck, it was good! Trickles leaked from the corners of his mouth, dribbling from his chin to run down his chest and drip from his belly. Hobbes's laugh came from beside him.

"*That* the way to slam a forty, man! Twenty say y'all can't kick it."

Lactameon's lips twisted in a smile around the bottle, and

he finished the whole thing. Grinning and nodding, Hobbes dug out a roll from his jeans and slapped a twenty on the counter. "One dead whiteboy for the black man!" He picked up his own bottle. "Score yourself a chaser. Pizza on the second shelf, nuke that motherfucka three. Yo, Sabby, you up for some food, man?"

Sebastian had slumped back against a window. He took a swallow of J.D. and made a face. "I ain't fuckin hungry, man. An *you* wouldn't be neither!" He stabbed out a finger like a switchblade. "An least tell him to take that cocksuckin thing off, man! Make me wanna puke just lookin at it!"

Hobbes gulped Green, and grinned. "Done my best, man. For a fact! This here one serious-shit gangstuh-boy. Death fore whitey's dishonor!"

Lactameon frowned, slipping the half-pizza into the micro-wave. "Dammit, Hobbes, stop that shit, will ya?"

Still grinning, Hobbes shrugged and took another hit from the Mickeys. "Why I waste my time. Yo, Sabby, I brung Tam up here to give y'all a scopin . . . make sure your ass gonna live. Word say he one way-slick witchdoctor."

"Shit, what I look like, a fool? Think I gonna let *him* touch me? Man, I can smell him from here! Goddamn motherfuckin *garbage* Collector, all he is!"

Lactameon twisted the cap from a second bottle. "Yeah? Well, just member that next year when you needin to copy somebody's English homework, homeboy!" He glanced at Hobbes. "Shit, this ain't never gonna work, man. If that pizza didn't smell so goddamn good, I be outa here."

"Mmm. Well, hang chilly, Tam. Sabby been through a lotta changes today. Leopards smoke *your* ass, y'all prob'ly wouldn't want their mascot gettin up close an personal neither." Hobbes took another gulp, then his face turned thoughtful. "What it is, man, Sabby *my* boy. I scope them four things bout him nobody else see. But he wearin *my* clothes, an cruisin *my* board, packin *my* piece, an right now he bleedin all over *my* goddamn bed. Yo! Y'all writin this shit down, Sabby? Cause there gonna be a popquiz, man. I *guaran-fuckin-tee* y'all that right now, this minute, there least *one* little sucka in this sorry motherfucka stretched out on some hot sidewalk bleedin his little ass off in the sun! An all he gots him for company is the rats an the flies. Best you believe *he* ain't kicked-back under some three-bill AC on clean fuckin sheets suckin J.D. an feelin sorry for *his*-self cause nobody love him!"

The microwave beeped, but Hobbes took Lactameon's wrist. "C'mon, man. I ain't havin no more of this shit today. Sabby! You lay your ass down there an let Tam give you a scopin or you can drag it home cross the hood an let your mommy kiss it all better!"

Hobbes led Lactameon across the small room. Scowling, Sebastian lay reluctantly down and crossed his arms over his chest. Hobbes frowned. "One, man! Get your motherfuckin arms down an spread your goddamn legs! Tam ain't gonna rape your pretty little ass . . . wrong fuckin side up anyways."

Glaring, Sebastian flopped his arms out on the bed. Wincing, he opened his legs. "Shit! Fat-ass cocksucka couldn't rape nobody, man! Couldn't find his own dick with both hands an a flashlight!"

Lactameon reached the bed. "You gonna find my dick in your *ear*, man, keep up that shit!" Ignoring the icy steel gaze, Lactameon bent down and ran his eyes over the boy's hard body. The bruises looked a lot worse than they were because of Sebastian's color. The cuts and scrapes were probably from kicks and the broken glass scattered all over the sidewalks. T.K. had kept his knife in his pocket anyway. Nothing looked long or deep enough to need stitches.

"Get your goddamn belly off my arm, man!"

"Shit, get your goddamn arm out my belly, asshole!" Gently, Lactameon pressed a palm to one side of Sebastian's rib cage. "That hurt, man?"

"No!"

Lactameon tried the other side. "How bout there?"

"No, asshole!"

Scowling, Lactameon lifted his hand and smacked it down. "How bout *that*, man?"

"Ow! You cocksucker!"

Lactameon straightened, yanked up his jeans, and turned to Hobbes. "I don't figure there nuthin major, cept his 'tude suckin hard. Balls pretty swelled. Best ice 'em."

"Shit, no!"

Hobbes frowned. "Oh, shut up, Sabby. Man know what he talkin bout. Take another hit. A big one. So, Tam, you figure

we should give him somethin else stead just that J.D. to chill
on? I can score just bout anythin put him out awhile."

"Mmm. That bottle full when he start?"

"Right out the store."

"Well, then just let him finish that. Can't never tell what
a mix gonna do."

Sebastian's eyes slitted. "What you talkin *mix*, cocksucka?"

"Shut up, Sabby," said Hobbes.

Lactameon scented the pizza. "Guess I could make up a ice
pack for him."

"Shit, that be way cool, Tam. Now, y'all sure ain't nuthin
more we can do? Some them cuts lookin deep an dirty."

"Well, you gots any peroxide? Maybe some cotton an gauze
an bandages?"

"Mmm. Well, it Sunday, man. Your store gots that kinda
shit be closed. But, I cruise on over to Leopard land. Back in
bout a half hour."

Sebastian's eyes got big. "Shit, Hobbes! The fuck you talkin
bout, man? You can't go leavin me alone with *him*!"

Hobbes frowned again. "Yo! Here come that popquiz,
Sabby. I ain't wastin no more of my time babysittin your high-
yellow ass! Special when you technically bein paid to watch mine.
Swear to God, man, Tam here lookin real good to me for a whole
lotta reasons you wouldn't gots a clue about."

At the fridge, pulling the ice tray, Lactameon looked over
at Hobbes. "Yo! I can't do that, man!"

Hobbes only smiled. "Y'all be fuckin s'prised what you can
do when you gots the right reasons for doin it."

Sebastian scowled. "Aw, stop tryin to smoke me, Hobbes!
Shit, he so goddamn fat he couldn't get out his own way!"

"Mmm. But, wouldn't mind bein behind him in a drive-
by. Just chill the fuck out, Sabby. You get with the fuckin program, an you an me gots us a big, bright future ahead." He
glanced at his watch. "I be back in thirty, man. Y'all do like Tam
say an drink your medicine." Unwrapping the bloody paper
towel from his arm, Hobbes went to the TV and picked up the
purple bandana. Lactameon came over. "Here, man, I do that
for ya . . . hard tyin it one-handed. Jeeze, that pretty deep,
Hobbes . . . ripped right across there. Even my mom say that
prob'ly need stitchin."

"Mmm. Well, y'all ever done stitchin, Tam?"

"No. But I watch her a lot. She done T.K. Don't look hard . . . like sewin."

"Mmm. Well, just tie it tight for now. Maybe we talk needles an thread later." Hobbes slipped into his jacket and slid the .44 back inside while Lactameon snagged a T-shirt that was draped on the back of the couch and made up an ice pack in the sink. Hobbes came over and gulped the rest of his Mickeys, then lowered his voice and flicked his eyes toward the bed. "Yo. Y'all figure he gonna be okay, man? I send Beamer by to chill his mom, case he can't make it home for a couple days. Y'all don't figure he gots somethin busted inside . . . somethin what ain't showin yet?"

"Well . . . T.K. pissed some blood at first . . . not a lot, but I could tell it sorta worry my mom. But he got better by himself."

"Mmm. Well, Sabby ain't took a piss yet, I know of. Damn! Shoulda thought about that myself, man! Course, all he been drinkin's that J.D."

"Well, if he gots to go while you're gone I ask him to watch for it. Course, that might freak him . . ." Lactameon dropped his own voice to a whisper. "Shit, Hobbes, you scope his eyes when he first seen me?"

"Mmm. Wasn't his eyes I was watchin, man. Somebody gots a gun in your face, pay more attention to a'zactly where it pointed an how steady that hand is. Twitchy trigger finger most times mean the opposite of all them ole movies . . . that the dude really *don't* wanna shoot your ass. Course, could just mean he fucked-up too. But, it them rock-steady grips tell y'all to say your prayers, sweetheart. Gots nuthin to do with balls, neither . . . just signify he *want* to kick your ass. Watch a pig sometime, man. That ain't a sit-u-ation of bein trained for the job, it just doin somethin they like doin." Hobbes's eyes shifted to the golden boy again, who was taking another drink. "Course, your dudes thump his head pretty good, man. Anyways, he chillin now, an he be a hard boy to replace, for a fact . . . gots a way-steady grip, case y'all didn't notice." Hobbes smiled. "Spect you do too."

"Aw, get out my face, Hobbes. I don't wanna kick nobody."

"Mmm. Maybe y'all just ain't found the right reason to,

man. Yo, you just do some chillin with what I sayin bout big black *boys*, Tam. An, bout them little suckas layin on the sidewalk cause they was playin whitey's great big new video game . . . fun for the whole fuckin family . . . if that family happen to be white an live in them hills."

Lactameon made a face. "Shit, man, all you askin is I play it with you."

"Mmm. Cept I just bout gots all the bonus points I need." Hobbes waved his bloodstained hand toward the bill still lying on the counter. "An there twenty for you already, homes." Grinning, he slapped Lactameon's shoulder. "Yo. Just consider my fridge your fridge. Fact is, I score us a couple fresh Leopard pizzas on my way back. Y'all gots the Uzi . . . just try not an use it on Sabby. Beamer or Lizard the only ones get in while I gone, but no reason they come around anyways. Ain't spectin y'all to kiss Sabby's ass, but maybe you could try an bring him up a little . . . maybe play him a game or somethin." Hobbes crossed back to the door and snagged his board. Opening the door, he paused a moment with a hand inside his jacket to scopeout the hall. "Here lookin at ya, kid." The door closed behind him, its locks snapping solidly into place with gunbolt clicks.

An here lookin at the kid who just try an kick my ass! Sebastian was scoping Lactameon too. He'd sucked the bottle down to a third; maybe that was why he seemed slightly more chilled now.

"Um, yo, Sabby, up for some pizza, man?"

"*Akeem*, goddammit!"

"Oh. Yeah. Sorry, man."

Sebastian took another swallow. "Well . . . Was you gonna do that ice shit or not, man? Fuck, feels like I gots basketballs down there!"

Lactameon glanced at the pizza through the microwave's window and sighed, but he got the ice pack out of the sink and went back to the bed. Sebastian's gray eyes tracked him steadily.

"Um, that gonna hurt, Tam?"

"Well, maybe feel a little weird at first, but it really help. Trust me."

"Yeah. Right, man. FUCK!"

Lactameon jerked the pack away. "Hurt?"

"*Cold!*"

"Well, jeeze, Sa . . . Akeem. What you spect ice to be? Here, kinda hold it on like that, man. Push your dick out the way. Anyhow, like I sayin, I didn't have nuthin to do with that shit."

Sebastian relaxed a little. "Mmm. That does kinda feel better. Well, you still one of 'em, man. An, shit, can't you take that cocksuckin rag off?"

"No."

Sebastian took another hit of whiskey, then relaxed a little more. "Um, can you kinda puff up this pillow, man?"

"Sure."

"An, um, there's a pack of Kools in my jacket there, Tam. Right pocket."

Lactameon glanced at the floor. Sebastian's clothes lay in a heap where Hobbes had probably helped undress him. The gangstuh look . . . everything black; Levi's, T-shirt, socks, and Cons. Lactameon smiled slightly, seeing a little black pair of jockey briefs too. The golden boy's jacket was expensive black leather, buttery soft, and sort of a cross between a biker and bomber . . . like something Michael Jackson might wear but without as many zippers.

"*Right* pocket, goddammit!"

"Huh? Oh. Well, I ain't wearin it, man." Lactameon unzipped the opposite pocket from the one he'd first gone for. He frowned a little, taking out the squashed hardpack of Kools, because he'd felt the shapes of two rock bottles and what might have been a pipe through the leather of the left pocket. Well, Sebastian was in the business, and if he was smoking the product like Hobbes suspected, that was a mix to stay out of for sure.

"You can have one, you want, Tam."

"Thanks, man. That cool." Lactameon slipped a cigarette between the boy's lips because it seemed expected, then fired it with Sebastian's Cricket. Sebastian sucked deep and let the smoke out slowly. "Um, thanks, Tam . . . an for bringin back my board . . . an, I'm sorry I called you fat."

Lactameon shrugged. "S'cool . . . Akeem. Sure you don't want some pizza? It gettin cold."

"Naw. Maybe I have me some fresh when Hobbes get back. Yo. Feel my head, man. It seem a little hot?"

Lactameon put a palm to Sebastian's forehead. "Naw. You

chilly, man." He walked back to the kitchen and opened the oven. The pizza could have used another minute of rays, but Lactameon didn't want to wait anymore. Slice in one hand, Mickeys in the other, he crossed to the TV and checked out the tapes: *Boyz N the Hood, New Jack City, Who Framed Roger Rabbit* . . . "Yo! Shit, Sa . . . Akeem! Hobbes gots him *Casablanca*, an *African Queen* . . ."

"Shit. Hobbes gots all that ole white sucka's movies, man! Like, he's Hobbes's cocksuckin hero or somethin! Chill with that . . . a black dude with a white hero! I tried watchin that African one . . . shit, ain't even no Africans in the cocksucka! An, yo! Lose that cocksuckin Bobby B! Put my Ice T disc back in."

"Well, shit, man, can't we chill with somethin else? I can hear all that gangbangin, cocksuckin bullshit any time I open my window."

"Hey! Fuck you, man! Ice T down with *us*!"

"Mmm. Too bad he wasn't down with you today, homes."

"Oh, shut the fuck up, Tam! You don't know what it is! Just do it!"

Lactameon walked back for another slice of pizza, taking a gulp of Green and leaning against the counter. "You want it changed, get up an change it yourself, SnoCone."

Sebastian squirmed up on one elbow. "Yo, goddammit! I heard Hobbes sayin you sposed to take care of me while he gone!"

"So? Wanna play a game?"

"No! I feel like shit, goddammit!"

"Well, want some pizza, man? Last chance. One, two . . ."

"Aw, suck my dick, man!"

Lactameon sighed. "Why I waste my time?"

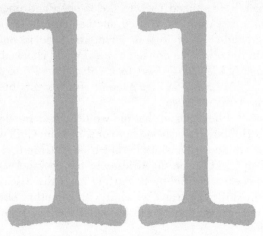

Corbitt stepped out into the cool blue glow of the rising moon and eased the cabin door closed, lifting it a little on its loose hinges until the latch caught and held. From inside he heard Jessica Fletcher on an old *Murder, She Wrote* episode, explaining to Doc Seth how she'd deduced the killer and where he'd buried the bodies because of his fight to stop a beautification project on a vacant neighborhood lot. Corbitt smiled: he'd figured it out himself by the first half of the show, but hadn't wanted to spoil the ending for his mom.

He stood for a moment on the worn porch boards and stretched his long body in the warm night air. He held his mother's butcher knife in one hand, and its blade glittered in a stray moonbeam. Friendly yellow light fanned from windows along the cabin row, and the shifting shadows of other TVs flickered across the dirt. The Browns in Number Seven, the Coopers in Two, and the Sampsons in Four had color sets and their patterns were prettier. Corbitt stepped off the porch, the soft dust sifting between his toes, and gazed up at a sky that looked like zillions of diamonds and sapphires scattered across black velvet. There was the Big Dipper. If you followed the arc of its handle you could locate the star Arcturus. Corbitt raised his eyes higher. Keep on with that arc and you came to Spica. There was even a formula for finding your way around up there: arc to Arcturus, spin on to Spica, and then curve over to . . . Corbitt frowned and dropped his eyes to Earth once more. Curve over to Corvus. That was about the last goddamn place in the universe he wanted to go!

The moon's rim was just climbing above the eastern hills, glowing like polished old bone. Corbitt glanced toward Number One. The cabin was dark, but he knew that Mrs. Griffin was sitting on the porch in her rocking chair. She'd be looking at the night sky too, and maybe thinking magic things. Then he felt her eyes sweep past him like a scanning laser before returning to infinite space once again. It wasn't frightening to know that she'd seen him, black as he was in the night. It was even comforting in a way . . . how a pilot might feel on a long, lonely flight when his radio came to life and acknowledged that he showed on someone's radar.

Mingled with the murmur of TVs, all tuned the same for the late world news, were the quiet voices of parents and the soft laughter and chatter of children. They were small sounds, sleepy and subdued. Corbitt pictured each family together in their single rooms; like safe little worlds in a huge dark universe. Another day's problems had been handled somehow, leaving this short time of peace till tomorrow. Bridge-end was beautiful at this hour, under forgiving moonlight. A vision of Sherry snuggling into her own bed came unbidden to Corbitt's mind. He felt a stirring between his legs and thought about what they'd almost done that day beneath the bridge. He'd thought about it a lot and often regretted that next-thing he'd missed. He wondered what might have happened there in the river if Sherry had been with Toby or Lamar. Would either of his brothers have held back? *Could* they have? Toby could have; Corbitt was almost sure. Lamar would have been sorry afterward; sorry with all his huge heart, but that might have been too late. At least he and Sherry would have had beautiful children.

Like the flick of a whip Corbitt's mind dropped that idea. He studied his home once again. He knew that his dad had been happy in Bridge-end on peaceful nights such as this. Sometimes he'd take Corbitt's mom for a walk along the road through the river trees. And sometimes they'd taken a blanket with them. Corbitt remembered when he was little; how he'd used to wonder why they'd go on a picnic at night and without any food. Wrapped in his own blanket on the floor, he'd pretend to be sleeping when they finally returned, though he liked to see them come in holding hands, their faces glowing with childlike light. They would bring an earthy riverland scent with them that filled the small room. Corbitt's dreams were always best on those nights.

Now, Corbitt thought of Sherry once more. He idly cut a notch in the porch rail with the knife before he realized what he was doing. "Mmm," he murmured, his face thoughtful. Kneeling, he pushed the knife up to its hilt in the soft earth near the steps. Mrs. Griffin said that a knife rested that way and stayed sharp a lot longer. Corbitt stood and looked down at the knife: there was probably a logical reason for that. He turned to scan the cabins again: it seemed suddenly important to see them through the right sort of eyes. They looked safe beneath the sheltering trees. A little of the quiet-time peace spread through him. But it wasn't enough; like a child-feeling he'd outgrown.

Three little rubies shone from the Sampson porch. That would be Lucas Sampson, Franklin Cooper, and Otis Brown smoking and sharing a Sunday six-pack of beer while talking man-stuff. Only three rubies now that Corbitt's dad wasn't there. The moon, mirrored in the windshield of Lucas's truck, looked like the smooth ivory dome of a skull. Corbitt thought of the lucky-skull sitting atop Mrs. Griffin's TV. It gave the little kids horrors and Lamar the creeps, but it just seemed to grin at Corbitt in a strange friendly way as if its shadowy orbits saw into his soul and smiled upon all the terrible secrets he kept there. Sometimes Corbitt could swear that it winked, as if what he'd been hiding over the years . . . his first cigarette, a beer with his brothers, and that new discovery in Toby's big bed . . . wasn't a fart in the breeze next to tales *it* could tell. Skulls could see things from both sides, Mrs. Griffin had said. Nobody knew from where it had come or how long she'd had it, but Corbitt suspected several generations of Bridge-end children had seen it in their dreams. Toby thought it was cool, even after it had come to him once in the night. Lamar stayed as far away from the thing as possible, even when tempted into the cabin by Mrs. Griffin's baking. One time he'd called it a gris-gris, and gotten his mouth washed out at the speed of light.

Corbitt turned toward the bridge where yellow-green fire-flies wove and danced through the black iron skeleton. He smelled the earth and the river, and the fields and the trees, and for a moment again he was happy. Then he caught another pair of scents, and heard the soft pad of bare feet as Lamar and Toby appeared from the darkness with their fishing poles over their shoulders. Lamar had a plastic breadbag of cheese bait knotted through a belt loop of his cutoffs, and Toby carried a big slice of peach pie on a palm. "Brung y'all some dessert, Prince Cheetah."

Corbitt smiled and took the pie slice. "Thanks, Tiger-bro. This yours?"

"Course not," growled Lamar. "He done eat his, best believe. I whop this fool longside the head, he gimme any shit over that."

"He be a fool not to eat it," said Corbitt around a mouthful. "Your mom bake most ever bit as good as Miz Griffin."

"Damn right," agreed Lamar. "An she do it the ole-fashioned hard way too, out usin no magic an fancy-ass gris-gris fixins."

Toby snickered. "Boy, you gettin yourself a whole headful of hoodoo-creepers! Next you gonna be seein duppys neath the trees or somethin." He rolled his eyes and peered around. "I *do* believe in spooks, I *do* believe in spooks, I do, I do, I do, I DO!"

Lamar gave the blond boy a poke. "Shut your goddamn mouth, fool! Y'all don't go talkin bout them kinda things with a full moon comin on!"

Corbitt swallowed the last bite of pie and grinned. "Hell, full moon only bring out the werewoofs, man. You seen enough fright-night TV."

"Yeah," agreed Toby. "An what you want chasin you, dodo, some rotten ole zombie movin bout the speed of somebody's gramma, or some slick werewoof dude sittin on a tombstone, tyin up his Nikes, and tellin you go for it niggaboy, I spot you a mile?"

"*Both* you fools shut up!" growled Lamar. He shivered a moment until a new thought seemed to enter his head. "Sherry's shade weren't all the way down when we come passin by."

Corbitt's grin faded. "You tellin me you look in on her? That weren't right!"

"Oh, *course* we didn't look," said Toby. "No more'n by accident anyways. But, best you believe it awful hard not to!"

"Y'all know Sherry sleep in nuthin?" said Lamar.

Corbitt stiffened. "You *did* look!"

"Naw," said Toby. "She tell me one time."

"She TOLE you?"

Toby shrugged. "I ask. So what?"

"Yeah," added Lamar. "So what? Why you gettin all offensive, man?"

"DE-fensive. An I ain't. What Sherry sleep in just . . . well, it just never come to my mind. That all."

"Oh, *sho* it never," said Toby. "An donkeys fly!"

"That case, y'all be cleared for takin off, then!" said Corbitt. He gave Lamar a quick searching look. "Um . . . Y'all gots rubbers at your house, man?"

"Huh?"

Toby giggled. "We gots enough at the store for a whole whorehouse."

"Shush, Tobe," said Corbitt. "I weren't talkin to you."

Lamar was looking puzzled. "Well, course, dodo. Think we gots the room or the money for another Sampson kid? Daddy keep 'em in the top dresser drawer. So, why you askin?"

Corbitt forced a shrug. "Just curious. Your daddy a smart man."

Lamar beamed. "Why sho he be. Fact is, me an him had one of them talks not two months back bout that sorta stuff. He even show me where them things kept. I might just start carryin one in my wallet."

Corbitt nodded. "Mmm. That be a right smart idea, Lionbro."

Toby was studying Corbitt. "Swimmin with Sherry today got you thinkin bout that sorta stuff, huh?"

Corbitt faced the bridge. "Never went swimmin. Bates was watchin cross the water."

Toby scowled. "God damn that dogfuckin ole peckerwood bastard!"

"Mmm," said Corbitt. "An then some, brother." He took his fishing pole off the porch rail. "Well, best we get to it. Night ain't gettin no younger."

"Bates a evil ole thing," Lamar mused as they walked to the bridge. "Times I get to wonderin bout all what the Bible an the preacher-man say . . . I mean, there be Bates with all that good land, an money to burn. Don't seem right. Like God ain't payin enough attention to His job. Why not He strike that evil thing down?"

"Spect Bates be headed for hell in a handbasket anyways," said Toby. "Even but half them things people sayin bout him be true."

Lamar snorted. "So? What good that do *us*, man? Or Corbitt? *Now?* I wish Bates in hell right this minute, an go fuck the handbasket!"

"Shush," said Corbitt. "Never wish nobody in hell, man. Even they deserve it."

"Why not?" asked Toby.

Corbitt looked across the bridge toward Bates's tangled woods on the opposite shore, remembering his hatred of a few hours before. He had been wishing Bates in hell. The faded black letters on the plank seemed to waver in the growing moonlight. "Cause, wishin be playin with power, not knowin. Them kinda wishes like a stick of overripe dynamite . . . just as likely to blow up in your own face as do y'all any good."

Lamar was glaring over at Bates's land. "Guess I just can't help it." Then he shrugged and smiled again, untying the breadbag from his belt loop. "Hey, Corbitt, guess what I gots us to go with our J.D. tonight?"

"Pizza."

"Almost as good," said Toby.

Proudly, Lamar pulled an unopened pack of Kools from the bag. "Daddy come home with a whole goddamn carton! Say Mr. Rudd just up an give it him, no logical reason! Hell, Daddy ain't gonna miss one little ole pack. Even he do, it worth hearin him holler just seein your eyes light up right now."

"Yeah," added Toby. "Shit, we can't pull down one of them stars you always talkin bout. Guess a new pack of smokes an that bottle of J.D. gots to do ya."

Corbitt was thinking he knew the reason behind Mr. Rudd's generosity, but kept the frown off his face and made a smile. "Swear I gots me the two best jungle-cat brothers in all creation."

The boys went down under the bridge and stripped off their clothes on the mudflat beneath. Toby recovered the Jack Daniel's from its hiding place while Lamar tied up the cigarettes and Corbitt's Bic in the breadbag. He knotted it to his pole, then all three boys clamped their poles in their teeth, waded into the water, and swam away from the shore. The bridge's midstream pier was a tower of rust-streaked concrete, tapering from a broad base to the iron girders it supported above. Its bottom was surrounded by a ledge about two feet wide that in summer stood a foot above the waterline. Downstream, a deep pool had been cut by the current and fish gathered there. The river flowed slowly, and it took little effort to reach the pier, even for Toby swimming one-handed while holding the bottle in the other. The boys climbed onto the ledge and moved around to the downstream side. Working in silence, they baited their hooks and dropped their lines and cork bobbers into the pool. They settled comfortably together with their backs against the concrete and their poles between their knees. Corbitt got the honor of opening the virgin pack of Kools. The bottle was passed and the whiskey sipped slow. A whole peaceful night stretched ahead. Behind them the moon had cleared the hills, but the boys sat in shadow, invisible except for their cigarette embers.

One by one the lights winked out along the cabin row, and the murmur of TVs stilled. The children's voices were the last sounds to fade, asking for a drink of water or announcing a trip to the outhouse where a small bulb burned the whole night through to guide the little ones. For a short while longer an occasional kid-curse or giggle was heard when an elbow poked ribs, but these sounds also soon faded to silence. Hunting owls hooted among the trees and bats flicked low over the water, their tiny squeaks echoing as they skimmed for moths. Sometimes a shift in the air would carry the shivery whine of eighteen big tires as a truck rolled the distant highway. The river made only a soft liquid chuckle past the bridge pier. The moon climbed higher and its light grew silvery blue, etching the bridge's ironwork in sharp riblike shadows over the pool. The bobbers floated untroubled on the water's smooth surface.

The boys had patience learned from years of such fishing, but Corbitt knew that in the previous weeks, with money so scarce, he'd caught about all this pool had to offer. Lamar soon fell asleep with his head on Toby's shoulder, though he'd be awake in an instant at a tug on his line. Corbitt and Toby smoked and passed the bottle in the comfortable silence of brothers.

Corbitt several times noticed the blond boy's eyes shift down-river toward the tree-shadowed pool where the glistening water turned west. Maybe an hour had passed before Toby spoke.

"Ain't nobody can own a river, can they, Corbitt?"

Corbitt gazed toward the bend. "No. But they can control the land longside it."

Toby took a sip from the bottle and considered. "Mean like, if we was to build us a raft, we could float on down there an there wouldn't be a goddamn thing Bates could do bout it?"

Corbitt flipped his cigarette away. It made a soft hiss in the water. "Mmm. Thought of that my ownself a few times, man."

"Figured you would. You smarter than me, thinkin up new stuff."

Corbitt glanced at Toby. "You ain't just sayin that?"

"Huh?"

"Nuthin."

"Well? Could we, Corbitt?"

"Mmm. Maybe by law. But what the law say an what it really *mean* for our kind be two different things."

Toby said nothing for a time, then took a swallow of whiskey and turned to Corbitt. "Why do so many of them hate us?"

"I don't know. Mr. Rudd tell me we make 'em feel stupid an foolish sometimes."

"Mr. Rudd tole you that?"

Corbitt slipped the bottle from Toby's hand and drank. "He also say, be goddamn careful who you ask that to."

"Well, I gonna ask you somethin else, Corbitt. But you don't gots to answer me if it hurtful to you. What happen today at the truckstop? Y'all just ain't been the same since comin back. Somethin changed, man. Lamar ain't seen it yet, but he will. Lamar sees a lot of things if you just give him time." Toby hesitated, searching Corbitt's face. "We, um, we is still brothers, ain't we? For real?"

Corbitt touched Toby's arm. "Course we is, man. They can't never change that." Then he sighed and looked back downriver. "I was wrong today, Tobe. I know why your folks don't like Mr. Rudd."

"I just a white-trash to him," said Toby.

Corbitt turned to the blond boy. "You *knew* that?"

Toby shrugged. "Do I gots a sign on my ass sayin I stupid or somethin?"

Corbitt glanced quickly at Lamar, but the big boy was still sleeping.

Toby shrugged again. "Lamar ain't thought bout it enough to figure it out. Yet."

Corbitt's mouth was suddenly dry. He took another drink. Had Toby known the whole secret about Mr. Rudd all the time? If so, didn't that make Mr. Rudd right . . . that a black mind wasn't as smart?

But, Toby went on, "I figure it's cause we come from the north, man. It like Mr. Rudd don't think I good enough for folks round here."

"Oh." Corbitt chose his words carefully. "Don't that bother you?"

Toby smiled. "Why should it? Don't I gots me the two best jungle-cat bros in creation?"

Corbitt felt a strange sense of relief. "You gots to ask, then you just fishin for compliments, nigga."

Toby giggled. "Look like bout all I gonna be catchin tonight, too." He took the bottle and sipped. "Know? I been thinkin on what you said today, there in the road . . . bout me havin a option. I think you wrong, man. I mean, fo sho I could go an *pretend* to be white . . . an you know what I sayin. But I can't never be *that* kinda white. Not like they are. Is that logical?"

"To me it is, cause I know you. But it prob'ly ain't to a lot of people, man. An, maybe it gonna be hard for you later on. I never thought much bout that stuff. Um . . . how you feel when them whiteboys beat you up?"

"Scared an pissed . . . scared, mostly."

"That all?"

"Well hell, Corbitt. What be goin through *your* head when a half-dozen assholes kickin the shit out you?"

"Mmm. Well, it never happen to me, man."

Toby smiled a little. "It wouldn't."

"Huh? Why you say that?"

"Cause . . . well, cause there just somethin bout you, man." Toby glanced up at the stars for a moment, seeming to search for words. Finally he shrugged and grinned. "Like, nobody mess with the cheetah prince, brother."

"Oh, bullshit, Tobe."

"Well, if you was askin me if I felt like some ole freedom-rider goin home all covered in shoe polish, then you a fool, man. Like you always sayin, don't go givin names to things, it make 'em somethin they ain't." Toby passed the bottle back to Corbitt. "Member when Miz Griffin's lucky-skull come to me? It never try an scare me, an best you believe it *could* have! Know what I think? I figure it come to see somethin."

Corbitt smiled. "Figure it like what it see, Tiger-man?"

"Ask it. You the one with the power."

Corbitt shook his head. "No thanks. I figure, it gots somethin to tell me, it say so a long time ago. Lamar ain't but half wrong bout leavin ole bones rest in peace."

"Um, Corbitt? Was that like a duppy?"

"Mmm. Well, there be all sorta duppys, Tobe. Mostly they be spirits come back to trouble the livin or collect on somethin they figure they owed."

"But why they do that, Corbitt? Revenge an stuff?"

"Sometimes . . . like if they got done wrong in life. But like I sayin, man, there be all kinds of duppys. There kid-spirit duppys what don't even know they dead . . . like that story Miz Griffin tell us one time bout the jungle hunter keep hearin this little baby cry. Then, there duppys what died with some secret an can't go on to wherever they sposed to go till the secret get told." Corbitt took another drink and gazed into the moon-silvered water. "Kinda like not gettin their rightful next-things."

Toby shifted his pole. "Y'all figure some of them kid-spirits get pissed-off cause they die so young an never get no next-thing?"

"Mmm. Spose so. But, like I sayin, man, there all kinda spirits . . . spect cause there all kinda people. But, it prob'ly best not to be messin with none of 'em."

"Bet Miz Griffin could, man."

"That different, Tobe. She gots the power."

"You ever think you get the power, Corbitt?"

Corbitt shrugged. "I don't know. Maybe it somethin you born with. Like Miz Griffin talkin bout veils." He frowned a little. "But, seem like to me I gots enough trouble right in the here an the now, out messin with no ole-time magic stuff."

Toby reclaimed the bottle and took a big gulp. "Um, Corbitt? This comin year at school . . . there gonna be dances, y'know? I might be wantin to take a . . . girl."

Corbitt thought of jokes he could make, but this wasn't the time. "Mmm. Yeah, I hear what you sayin, man. That kinda stuff ain't gonna be easy. For none of us."

Toby pulled another cigarette from the pack and took a long time tapping it on the concrete before slipping it into his mouth. Corbitt fired his Bic. The flame flickered low but gave enough light to startle Corbitt at the blueness of Toby's eyes. It was so easy to forget.

Toby sucked smoke and looked suddenly determined. "What if I was to ask Sherry?"

Corbitt took his own time shaking a Kool from the pack. This was a next-thing he *had* been expecting . . . expecting for months since that day in the river with Sherry. The funny part was that he'd also been expecting it from Lamar with an equal kind of dread. He had to spark the lighter several times before it finally fired. For a second he was afraid he wouldn't be able to find the right words, but they came with an evenness that surprised him. "I spect Sherry make up her own mind bout that. It be one of her own next-things."

Toby's hand gripped Corbitt's. "I wish I could say I love you, out soundin like one of them homos, brother."

Corbitt smiled. "Brothers can always say that to each other. Hell, ain't no s'prise to me Miz Griffin's ole lucky-skull like what it see."

Toby smiled back. "It a black skull, y'know."

Corbitt's face turned thoughtful. "Funny. Everbody just sorta cept that fact without never sayin it. Spose it the occipital bone."

Toby grinned. "Naw, man. Hey, that skull fit right inside *your* head." Toby's grin faded as he saw a strange expression come over Corbitt's face. "Um . . . did I say somethin wrong, brother?"

Corbitt shivered, but shook his head slowly. "No. It . . . well, you just give me a real creepy feelin for a minute there, is all."

Then came Lamar's low rumble. "Ask me, was a goddamn creepy thing to go sayin."

"Shit," said Toby. "So, how long you been awake, Lion-bro?"

"Well, it was a good thing wakin up to y'all tellin Corbitt you love him. Fact is, I love you both, an I sure as hell ain't no goddamn homo." Lamar yawned and stretched. "Spose you two boneheads done drank up all the J.D.?"

Toby passed Lamar the bottle. The big boy took a long pull. "The three jungle cats."

"Forever," said Corbitt.

Toby smiled. "An that a long, long time. Know? I wish tonight was my whole life. Spose y'all gonna go an tell me I shouldn't said that?"

"Well, I spect it never hurt to go wishin for good things."

"Spose, if I die right now I come back a duppy?"

"Shush!" said Lamar. "Any fool know givin names to things call 'em up!" He glanced overhead to a gap in the bridge deck where the moon beamed through. At last he relaxed and stretched. "I wish us some fish."

Toby's eyes shifted to the water where the trio of bobbers floated quietly, then moved on downriver. "Well, Miz Griffin also say there times when you gots to go an give luck a good kick in the behind. Like a jump-start."

Lamar's forehead furrowed. He looked toward the river-bend. "Oh, what the hell. Don't take no magic to know what you two be thinkin. I sho ain't scared of no livin breathin Bates, an I spose Corbitt gots enough magic power to run off a few dancin bones. C'mon, cat-bros, lets go an do us some real ole-fashioned fishin."

The boys brought in their lines, then slipped into the river and swam to the mudflat. Toby reached for his shorts, then stopped and stared as Corbitt came out of the water. He grabbed Lamar's shoulder. "Look at Corbitt, man! He *silver*-black!"

Lamar turned, his eyes widening for a moment. Corbitt stood, ankle-deep, and glanced down at himself. "Now, what you two starin at like a couple loony lizards?"

Lamar blinked. "It just the moon doin it, Tobe. Cause he all wet."

Corbitt picked up his own jeans. "Times I think you ain't half dry 'hind the ears your ownself, boy."

Toby eyed Corbitt a long time, but then finally nodded. "Yeah. Spect you right, Lamar. But I never seen that color before in my life."

Lamar slipped into his cutoffs. "Well, be just like him to think up a new one!"

The boys dressed, then climbed the bank and started across the bridge.

Lactameon laid the empty forty-ouncer on top of the other two empties beside him on the couch and dipped his hand into the big KFC bucket that he'd found in Hobbes's fridge. It was empty now, and he scraped up a handful of crispy crust as white-on-black letters spelled out THE END on the huge TV screen. Licking his fingers, Lactameon aimed the remote and thumbed rewind. *They Drive by Night* wasn't what the title suggested, and he'd never seen that one on the movies-till-dawn show. The truck had looked something like the faded graphic on Hobbes's house. Then Lactameon stared at the VCR clock. 5:44. Shit, where was Hobbes?

Lactameon looked over to the bed. Sebastian was still asleep. The J.D. bottle stood almost empty on the floor, but the golden boy was probably more burned from the beating than drunk. He'd bitched for a while, but had finally chilled down and drifted off to sleep when he'd seen that Lactameon wasn't having any and was loading a flick. Lactameon sighed, stroking his stomach and wishing every summer day could be like this . . . off the goddamn street, out of the heat, with plenty to eat. Shit, who had time for gangstuhs and crack if everybody could get down with this? The tape finished rewinding and stuck itself out like a big ugly tongue. Lactameon glanced at the clock again. Where *was* Hobbes? Shit, it would be dinnertime soon, and then he had to cruise to Beamer's and then get his ass to the clubhouse by nine. Mom wouldn't worry too much if he missed dinner, knowing he was probably getting it somewhere else. And, Hobbes's fridge was still well stocked with Mickeys, packed with all sorts of *good* microwave food, and there was even a big box of Twinkies; though you wouldn't figure Hobbes the Twinkie type. But then you wouldn't picture him down with a book or an old movie, either.

The orange-shaded sunlight of late afternoon came slanting through the sooty windows, making the quiet body on the bed all the more beautiful. In sleep, Sebastian's face was almost a child's. Lactameon got to his feet and crossed the small room to the bed. The floorboards creaked under his weight, but Sebastian didn't stir. His solid chest rose and fell gently. Lactameon supposed he could have used a fresh ice pack, but no way in hell did you touch a sleeping dude's dick. Besides, Sebastian could probably use all the peace he could get, and Lactameon wasn't up for any more bitching.

So, where in hell was Hobbes? Lactameon stood, letting the AC's coolness wash over his body. It felt all the more wonderful because the street temperature was probably close to ninety. Hobbes's building faced an empty lot where stumps of ancient foundation stuck up like fangs through dry, straggly weeds. Two toasted car-corpses lay upside down in one corner. Battered old stoves and refrigerators were scattered among heaps of garbage and trash. Nobody had taken the fridge doors off like the TV always warned about, but then black kids weren't stupid. Four half-naked, sweat-sheened, dirty little dudes were playing there now. They all carried mop handles sharpened like spears. Lactameon noticed the spear points were blackened. He wondered how they'd learned to harden them in fire like that. They seemed to be doing a Ninja Turtle number. A splintery plank had been laid from a stove to a knocked-over refrigerator like a bridge, and the program seemed to be battling your way across. Three of the dudes clustered on top of the fridge, while the other, slightly older, tried to fight his way over. They were the same little kids Lactameon had seen in the park that morning, and the small warrior against the odds was the thin Rasta boy. His dreads flew wild, and he didn't have much of a butt to keep his jeans on. The swings and jabs of those spears were savage.

Hadn't their parents ever warned them about poking each other's eyes out? It was a good thing they were just playing.

Lactameon stood in the comfortable coolness and watched the little suckers fighting in the heat. Was this part of Hobbes's idea of whitey's new video game? Lactameon studied the skinny, brass-colored kid . . . the one Beamer felt sorry for because he was going to die soon. His stomach was concave below his rib cage, sucked in even tighter because of the fight. He might have been hungry, but he was a strong little sucker, his moves fierce and sure, dreads whipping, teeth flashing, as he beat back the three smaller warriors. In his mind, Lactameon urged him on . . . halfway there, two-thirds . . . Hobbes probably would have bet on him.

Suddenly, one of the smaller kids darted sideways and swung his spear double-handed at the Rasta boy's ribs. It was a sloppy move, badly timed, and the little Rasta should have seen it coming a block away. Yet the wooden shaft whacked so savagely into his side that Lactameon winced. The boy's mouth opened with what could have been a cry but was more likely a curse, and he tumbled off the plank bridge into the weeds. The smaller kids shouted and danced, thrusting their spears skyward about the way you'd expect them to do.

"Jeeze," muttered Lactameon. "Little sucker gots to be half-blind not to see that shit comin!"

"Huh?" Sebastian stirred, his steel eyes dull for a moment then slitting in sudden suspicion. "Yo! What you doin, man, standin by me when I sleepin!"

Lactameon still watched the small kids. "Just thinkin how easy it been to slam a couch cushion over your face. Shit, all my *blubber* behind it, you history, man."

"Oh, too funny, cocksucka!" Sitting up carefully, Sebastian flexed his muscled arms, then brushed dried blood off his body. "Shit, I'm all stiff an sore, man!" He cautiously lifted the remains of the ice pack. "Well, got to say that seem to work. They still swelled some, but not near as bad. See? Don't hurt so much now, neither."

"Mmm. I so happy to hear that, man."

Across the street, the Rasta boy had gotten to his feet and was ripping some of the stickers out of his hair. His movements

showed that he hurt. The other dudes crowded around him.
Little hands touched his side with surprising gentleness . . . an
Oaktown owie. Maybe it wasn't exactly brotherly love, but it
was probably as close as they could get on instinct.

"Shit! I gots to piss, Tam. Help me get up."

Taking the golden boy's arm, Lactameon eased him to his
feet, steadying his shoulder until he got his balance. "You walk
okay, Sa . . . Akeem?"

"Akeem! Yeah, I think so. Little buzzed from the J.D. is
all."

"Well, scope for blood when you piss, man."

"*What?*"

"Check if it come out pink. Might mean there somethin
wrong inside you."

"Shit! What if it does, man? What I do then?"

"Mmm. Guess we get your ass to 'mergency some way."

"Shit! Swear to God I *hate* you dudes, man! Shit! Help me
to the goddamn bathroom!"

Lactameon walked with Sebastian to the bathroom door,
then waited while he yanked the light string and stumbled to
the toilet. "Ow! Shit! Well . . . it hurt, man, but it all golden
showers. C'mon, Tam, check it out!"

"I don't need seein it, man. If it yellow, it mellow. Seen
enough of my own."

Sebastian turned, holding his dick like a precious thing.
"Um, I like to take me a shower, Tam. You figure soap gonna
sting?"

"Maybe a little. But you prob'ly feel a lot better after."
Lactameon walked to the fridge, considered the Twinkies, but
snagged another Mickeys instead. Water-sound came from the
bathroom as he went back to the window. The four small boys
had propped up the fridge door with two spears and now sat
together in the small patch of shade. It was a shitty place to
chill, but where else could they go and not be somebody's prey?
One dude produced what looked like a Marlboro pack, and all
selected cigarettes in that delicate way little kids handled treasures. Lactameon glanced at the cold green bottle still unopened
in his hand. So, what was stopping him from grabbing an armful
of food and forty-ouncers and just taking it the fuck down there

to those kids? *Happy Kwanzaa, my children!* Was it the goddamn heat, or the motherfucking ordeal of those stairs? Hell, he could open a window and word them. They'd fly up warp-seven . . . why be scared of strangers when everybody was strange? Maybe he just didn't give a good shit? *I got mine, sucka, you get yours.* And, no fucking bonus points for feeding dirty little niggaboys, even if one was a *mulatto.* Self-cleaning oven.

"Yo, Tam! Where the fuck Hobbes?"

Lactameon turned. Sebastian stood tense in the bathroom doorway. Wisps of shower steam curled out around him. He looked scared again.

"Shit, I dunno, he been gone almost four hours now."

"Shit! Maybe you cocksuckas finally got him!"

Lactameon saw Sebastian's eyes flick to the top of the fridge. "Yo, Sabby! Get real! My dudes takin Hobbes? With that .44 of his? I don't think so, man."

The golden boy's gaze aimed out the windows. "Shit, Tam! Maybe the Leopards done him! You an them dudes on terms, man! I seen their whiteboy hangin with you!"

Lactameon puffed out air, then uncapped the Mickeys and drank. "Maybe he just said the hell with this great big sorry-ass motherfuckin donkey show an bought a ticket to Jamaica, mon. Shit, just like my mom say, don't go borrowin trouble."

Sebastian looked doubtful for a moment, but finally nodded. "Yeah. Shit, he be back soon. Prob'ly seein bout new stock to keep Lizard an Beamer busy or somethin. Yeah. Hobbes be late for his own cocksuckin funeral sometimes, man . . . special when he gots somethin on his mind. Um . . . so, you gonna hang with me, huh?"

"Well . . . I can stay a nuther hour or so, but then I gots shit to do. Miss my dinner."

Sebastian's face brightened. "Aw, fuck, man, just drive-by the fridge all you want. Hobbes ain't gonna care. Lotta that shit been in there too long anyways. Um . . . bring me my jacket, huh? An . . . an, my jeans. Okay?"

"Sure." Lactameon got the things. Sebastian took them and shut the door. There was the click of a small lock. Lactameon shook his head and returned to the window. Who the fuck did that sucker think he was fooling? Silver had done that same shit:

keeping it a secret from the other dudes until he didn't care anymore. But then Silver didn't have any bonus points to lose. Sebastian had changed a lot in two months.

The sun was lower now. Lactameon shaded his eyes. The four little boys were still stretched out beneath the fridge door. Somehow they looked like they should have been naked, but a pig would have popped them for that, or maybe he'd have rolled the fridge over, stuffed them all inside, slammed the door and walked away? Then he'd spend his evening coaching a P.A.L. project. Lactameon took another gulp from the bottle. So, why the fuck didn't he just open that window and call them all in for a good old-fashioned African feast? No missionaries on the menu?

Soft footsteps stopped outside the hallway door. Lactameon froze with the bottle to his lips. Somebody seemed to be trying the locks. Lactameon's eyes flicked to the top of the fridge. Beamer or Lizard would have knocked for sure, and Lactameon couldn't imagine Hobbes ever losing his keys. Steam drifted out around the bathroom door, but the shower drummed too steadily for anyone to have been in it. Sebastian wasn't going to be any goddamn help! Lactameon dropped the bottle and moved fast, the floorboards popping as he ran to the fridge and grabbed the big pistol. It was already cocked, and he shoved the select-fire switch all the way forward to A. The door locks clicked, but clumsily, like somebody using an unfamiliar key. Dropping to a crouch, Lactameon aimed double-handed at the opening door.

Hobbes saw Lactameon first thing. He only grinned. "Whoa, bro, I come back an haunt the shit out ya, man." He balanced three big pizza boxes and a paper bag on his bandana-wrapped arm, and held the keys and his board in the other hand.

Lactameon let out air and lowered the gun, then stood and yanked up his jeans. "Shit, Hobbes, where you been, man? We was startin to freak."

Hobbes banged the door shut with his foot and laughed while his muddy eyes scanned the room and missed nothing. "Mmm. Nice to be needed, man. Y'all musta done a good job on Sabby . . . see he washin his pretty self up for supper. So, he okay, huh?"

Returning the fire-switch to S, Lactameon put the pistol back on the fridge. "Yeah. I sure he feelin a lot better now."

Hobbes dropped his board on the couch. "Give y'all much

shit, man? Some of them things he sayin bout your . . . weight
. . . seem sorta nasty."

"Just say fat, man, it save time. An, I hear 'em all before.
Um, so was my hand steady, Hobbes? I wasn't payin no attention."

Hobbes laughed again, coming to the counter and setting
down the boxes and bag. "Was till y'all seen it me, man. Word!"
He ripped back a box lid. "Yo, check this out. *That* be pizza,
brother-mine! Hot's a Leopard bitch after Collector cock! Oh,
an that bag fulla cotton an gauze an that sorta shit for Sabby."
Hobbes glanced at the bathroom door, but then slipped off his
jacket, tossed the .44 on the chair, and snagged a forty-ounce
from the fridge. "Let's eat while they still hot, man . . . soon's
Sabby get his yellow ass out here."

Lactameon's eyes shifted to the bathroom door. Why should
he give a shit? What would probably happen in a minute might
even be fun to watch. The pizza was getting cold. He glanced
at Hobbes, who had crossed to the windows and was adjusting
the AC. Sighing, Lactameon stepped to the bathroom door and
twisted the knob. He felt the little privacy-bolt give slightly.
Glancing again at Hobbes's brown back, he swung his body
sideways for momentum and bashed his bulk belly-first into the
door panel. There was only a soft whump and a rip of old wood,
and Lactameon followed the door into a cotton-wool world. Shut-
ting it quickly behind him, he scanned around in the swirling
white steam. The bathroom was tiny, but now seemed like infinite space, lost in a misty-soft void and soothed by rushing
rain-sound. Between time and Timbuktu. The sharp scent of
rock smoke was the only suggestion that all things weren't right
in this universe. Squatting, Lactameon made out the golden
boy's shape slumped against the far wall between the toilet and
shower curtain. The gray eyes were glazed, but widened when
they saw Lactameon's dark face materialize in the mist. Then
the hard body stiffened, and the eyes went to steel-colored slits.
Sebastian whipped the pipe from his mouth, almost trying to
hide it behind him like a little kid caught with his first cigarette.

"You cocksucker, man!"

Lactameon grabbed the golden boy's shoulders and shook
him like a child. "Yo! Shut the fuck up, asshole! Hobbes back!
Shit, why I waste my time!" Lactameon jerked him to his feet.

Sebastian struggled clumsily, but the fury faded fast from his eyes. "Oh, shit, Tam! My eyes, man! He see my eyes!"

Lactameon glanced around in the white fog. Something green on the sink . . . Snatching the tube of shampoo, he ripped off the cap and squished it all over Sebastian's brown-tinted flattop. The shower was too hot. Cranking the cold faucet full-on, he jammed his hand under the jutting muscle of Sebastian's chest and shoved him into the stall, then whipped up a froth of lather with his fingers in the boy's hair.

"Ow! Shit, man! It in my fuckin eyes!"

"Ain't that a bitch, Frosty."

Lactameon stepped back and shook water from his own hair. Now what? Grabbing the hot pipe off the floor, he stuck it back in Sebastian's jacket. A spray can of Lysol stood on a shelf. That smell would kill anything. He sprayed it around, then eased out the door and closed it behind him. It was like teleporting from one universe to another. AC breath chilled his damp skin. Hobbes was at the counter slicing pizza with a box knife. *From Kalamazoo to Timbuktu is a long way down the track. From Timbuktu to Kalamazoo, it's just as far to come back.* Lactameon walked over to the counter, jerking up his jeans and pretending to button them.

Hobbes smiled and offered a slice. "Sabby gonna shrink, he stay in that water much longer."

Lactameon took a bite of pure pleasure. "Shit, I never did. Aw, now he bitchin cause he gots shampoo in his eyes."

"Mmm. Look like he had y'all scrubbin his back. Wouldn't s'prise me none. He likely want some nigga shakin his dick for him after he piss."

"Well, he still a little drunk, man. An, like you sayin, he been through some changes today."

Hobbes swallowed a hunk of pizza, then gulped from his Mickeys. "Aw, don't you cover his ass, Tam."

"Huh?"

"Shit. Times he get under my skin too . . . specially when he start up his *black thang.* Guess there ain't nuthin wrong with a zebra takin pride in his black side, but times it get to wearin. Me, I just wanna make the most out what I gots to work with. Like, whitey give me just enough to survive in this sorry moth-erfucka. But that ain't livin, man. Tell y'all this; if my black ass been any use at all to me it been for camouflage, man. Only thing whitey been trained to see is my outsides. Shit, he be watchin my shadow on his wall while I struttin right past him!"

The bathroom door opened and Sebastian came out, golden and gleaming. He wore his ebony jeans and carried his midnight-black jacket. He rubbed soap-reddened eyes and walked a little unsteadily over to lean on the back of the couch. "Yo, Hobbes. So, what happen to ya, man? Shit, I was worried!"

"I get to it, man. Up for some pizza?"

"Um, in a minute."

"Well, then put on some sound . . . an I don't wanna hear none of that cocksuckin, gangbangin bullshit, neither. My ass fall in some real sweet-smellin stuff today, man. Make y'all just forget all bout your owies." Hobbes glanced at Lactameon. "Could be some rub off on you, too. Here, Tam, one these Leopard bitches hot for your ass alone. Score yourself another Green an sit down. Naw, forget that one, man. Let the little sucka lay there an bleed."

Lactameon stopped, about to pick up the bottle he'd dropped by the bed. The sunlight was slanting into the room with the ruddy tint of evening. Looking out the windows, Lactameon saw the four little boys coming diagonally across the street, still carrying their spears. Remembering what Beamer had said about the Rasta kid having the right kind of eyes, Lactameon moved closer to look. The thin, brass-colored boy glanced up as if he felt watched, but the sun was in Lactameon's eyes and he couldn't see the little dude's face. The boys reached the sidewalk and moved out of sight. Lactameon had a feeling he'd lost something, but didn't know what.

"Yo, Tam! Ain't nuthin out there worth your time, man. Bring your ass to the party."

Sebastian had slipped a disc into the deck; N 2 Deep's *Back to the Hotel*, which was probably as close to cocksucking and gangbanging as he could get without pissing Hobbes off. The title track had one of those beats that got down in your bones. Silver had that album on cassette, and could dance to it in a way that made everybody want to join him no matter how clumsy you were. Lactameon had even felt Silver's strange pull, though he'd never danced in his life and knew better than to try.

Sebastian was sitting cross-legged in a corner of the couch

with a Mickeys and a big pizza slice. Hobbes might not have noticed, but Lactameon could see he was only eating because he knew it was expected. Hobbes settled into the chair while Lactameon took the rest of the couch. The VCR clock showed 6:37, but a whole Leopard pizza was worth missing two dinners at home, and besides, he didn't have to wash the dishes. Hobbes took a big gulp of malt.

"Hooked up with this dude today . . . turn me on to a max-security house, man! Killer location just two blocks over, an a door on that motherfucka make a tank change its mind! Only one way in, an even Beamer hold off a army from up on the roof with my carbine. Shit, I talkin bout your New Jack City in single-servin size!"

Sebastian scowled. "Yo, man! You figure *he* oughta be hearin this?"

Hobbes bit off more pizza and strung out the cheese. "Tam here gots a lot more goin on than stayin a mascot till some little snot-nose with my-first-gun kick his ass. Fact is, Tam gots him six out seven already." Hobbes gave Lactameon a grin. "Even he don't know it yet." Hobbes took another swallow of Green. "Seem like I do my best thinkin when I cruisin. Done me a lot today, for a fact. Whitey be after them little niggas, guess I gots to get with the program. So, what them little suckas want? Cheap product? Shit, everbody gots that! Naw, they wantin 'em some-place cool . . . out them hot streets. Someplace safe, where they ain't gonna get slapped around. Maybe some sounds . . . an a whole fuckin lotta respect. Shit, y'all wanna go to some house where the management don't treat your ass no better'n the pigs? Hell, Beamer be good with 'em . . . shit, he still *one* of 'em! Lizard might need some retrainin . . ." Hobbes studied Sebastian a moment. "An *you* gonna need a major 'tude adjustment, man."

Hobbes washed down more pizza. "So, I put me in a AC. Score some rugs for the floor from the Salvation Army. Give them little suckas atmosphere. Shit, it be flyer'n that kid-center place, man . . . can't suck no rock there on a hot afternoon."

Hobbes turned to Lactameon. "You be good with kids, man. Dude your shape, like a great big ole teddy bear . . . y'all take that rag off your head. Build me a sellin room. Stick your friendly ole ass 'hind the window. Shit, man, use that head of yours for somethin sides flyin one of whitey's flags. Y'all be kicked-back

in there, big ole chair, cool flowin all round. An, y'all just snap
your fingers an my little runner off like a three-five-seven for
pizza or King or KFC or whatever come to your mind, man.
Anytime. All the time. *That* the way y'all gonna make it through
the summer. Shit, sit there an read, you want. Lizard or Sabby
here handle enforcement."

Lactameon put down his last slice. "Jeeze, Hobbes. I can't
do that!"

Sebastian snorted. "Shit! He get so goddamn fat he can't
walk in a month, man!"

Hobbes raised a palm. "Peace, brothers. Yo, Tam, all I sayin
is turn the motherfucka over in that mind I know y'all gots.
Scope the sucka four different ways. Beamer be good for the
job . . . cept he can't hardly count. Hell, maybe Stacy up for
it?"

Lactameon frowned. "I don't think so."

Hobbes raised his other palm. "Stay chill, Kinté. All I doin
here is offerin y'all a option, man. An you know for a fact ain't
many of them floatin round this hood. House a short-term thing
anyways. Month, maybe two, least till school start again an the
pigs get con-cerned bout them little suckas not gettin their
proper education." Hobbes's eyes went far away for a moment.
"Shit, likely y'all ain't even gonna see my ass in eighth grade,
man. Anyways, Tam, y'all just think bout playin the game with
me. For a change."

Lactameon drained his bottle and got up. "I gots to bail."

Hobbes rose too, crossing to the counter and snagging the
third pizza box. "That cool, Tam. Y'all just take this one for
the road." He reached in his pocket and pulled out a wad of
bills. "An, here, man. This for all that witchdoctor work on my
boy."

Lactameon hesitated, but then took the fifty and the pizza.
That just about covered putting up with Sebastian's bullshit all
afternoon. And, since he couldn't put it in the treasury without
lying to the dudes, it was all his to keep. "Mmm. Thanks,
Hobbes. But, don't hold your breath bout me workin for you.
There a lotta shit I like about you, man. Funny, you never change
at all."

Sebastian had been listening carefully. He hadn't eaten
much, but had finished his forty-ounce. Now he got up, stiff

and a little unsteady. "Um, yo, Hobbes. I think I walk some with Tam. Might do me good. Nuthin bleeding no more anyways." He shifted his eyes to Lactameon. "Huh, man? A walk do me good?"

Lot more good than what you really goin out for! You balanced on the blade too, sucka! "Yeah. Guess it would, Akeem."

Sebastian's eyes turned almost friendly for a second. Lactameon jerked up his jeans, checked that the book and tank-top were still in the back pockets, then waited at the door while Sebastian dressed himself in black. Sebastian glanced at his board, but let it lie, going instead to the fridge and slipping the Uzi inside his leather jacket. Lactameon flicked an uncertain glance at Hobbes, but Hobbes only grinned and winked. Lactameon followed Sebastian into the hall, which felt like an oven after the cool apartment. A big black fly was beating itself to death against the small window facing the street. Sebastian went first down the steep, narrow treads, saying nothing as Lactameon felt his way after. Sebastian kept one hand in his jacket, scanning the shadows at every landing. His bruised face was set in hard lines. He stayed silent all the way down, then paused in the entrance as Lactameon descended the last steps.

"Must be a bitch when you can't see your feet, man."

"Not less I don't know the stairs."

"So, you gonna know these?"

Lactameon sighed, reaching the bottom. "Shit, I don't know, man."

Sebastian got out his Kools and offered them. "So, you gonna tell?"

Lactameon waited for the golden boy to fire his lighter. "Don't mean jack to me, man."

Sebastian hesitated a few seconds before lighting his own Kool. "Some dudes might think so."

"Huh? Oh. Guess you don't know me very good, man." Lactameon blew smoke. "Sides, you could kick me right here. Hobbes might be a little pissed, that all."

"Naw. He likes you, Tam. Um . . . look, man, I'm really sorry bout all that shit I said. Okay?"

Lactameon smiled. "What shit?"

Sebastian smiled a little too. "Um . . . don't go takin this wrong, man, but you be a better black dude if you maybe lost some weight."

"Well, how you figure that? Like, I be more of a black dude by bein less of one?"

"Well . . ." Sebastian shrugged. "Forget it, man. I shouldn't said that. I think I'm a lot more fucked-up than I feel."

"S'cool. Most dudes gots your kinda muscles say shit like that. It don't bother me none. Sides, I wouldn't be me if I look like you."

Sebastian's eyes narrowed. "So, what you sayin, man?"

Lactameon sighed again. "What I sayin is, I prob'ly be just like any other sucker out there. Bein fat give me lots of time to think, man. I can look at shit four different ways."

"Oh. Well, you just got that last thing from Hobbes. He's always tellin dudes that. Course, most of 'em don't know what he's talkin bout."

"Do you?"

"Sometimes."

The air had cooled a little, but the sidewalk still radiated the day's leftover heat. The lowering sun threw long shadows of streetlamps and power poles, and turned deep-set doorways into dark caves. This time of day was the quietest, especially on Sunday. A few cars cruised the street, some with gangstuh music booming deep. Sebastian eyed them because he was a crack dealer's bodyguard, and Lactameon watched them because he wore a bandana. He carried the pizza box, still warm, under one arm . . . he'd give it to Beamer. That dude hardly got anything good to eat, though he'd done a lot better for himself since he'd been old enough not to have to depend on his dad to feed him. Sebastian stayed at Lactameon's side, a little impatient with the fat boy's slow steps like most dudes were. They crossed to the next block of shops and garages, all closed and barred. Sebastian fell back a pace, then stopped. Lactameon wasn't surprised. The nearby doorway was deep, and hidden in shadow.

"Um . . . Tam. You know now . . . so, it don't bother you?"

"Naw. S'cool, man. See ya round."

"Um . . . that ain't what I meant. I mean . . . I really wanna hang with you a little more. Um, can you wait, man?"

Lactameon glanced at the fading sky, then flipped his cigarette into the gutter. "Sure. I watch for you."

"No. I didn't mean that, neither. Um, this shit don't change me."

"Sure, Akeem."

Sebastian slipped into the shadows and sat down. Lactameon leaned against the entrance, watching but not watching while the golden boy got out his pipe and loaded it.

"Um, Tam? You ever done it?"

"Yeah. Once . . . no, a couple times. Maybe three."

Sebastian got out his lighter, then looked up. "Um . . . didn't you like it, man?"

"Mmm. Maybe. Kinda." Then Lactameon smiled. "Be a good way to lose some weight, huh?"

"Oh." Sebastian fired and sucked.

"See, if I wasn't me, I wanna be doin what you doin just cause you doin it."

"Huh?" Sebastian breathed out smoke. "But, you drink, man. A lot."

"All kids do. You gots to do somethin or you go crazy. But that fill me up. Shit, I don't hardly even get drunk no more. Just full."

Sebastian sucked another hit. "It don't last, man."

"I don't guess nuthin does."

A shadow swooped low overhead. Lactameon looked up. Maybe it had only been a seagull searching for something to eat. That reminded him of something, but he couldn't remember what. A few minutes later the boys were walking once more.

"Um . . . why Akeem?"

"Huh?"

"Why you change your name, man?"

"Lots of black dudes take African names. Why? You figure it funny or somethin, man?"

"No. But, you musta figured it was important."

"Well . . . it is. To me. Cause . . . cause of how I look. What I sayin is, I *feel* black, man. Shit, my mom's black as you. An . . . an, that cocksuckin whiteman married her been gone for a year! That's why we had to move down here. Shit, we used to live in a way cool hood, man! Over East. Near the mall. Um, you ever been there?"

"Couple times. With my mom. It pretty cool. Like, we gots us a real mall for our own."

"Yeah. Course, some white people come there. Maybe the cool ones. I mean, they don't gotta."

"Yeah. Gots to be a few of 'em down with us, or we all be dead." Lactameon smiled. "Shit, man, there *you* for proof."

Sebastian stopped. "So, now what you sayin?"

"Jeeze, Akeem. That gots to be the major thing I don't like about that shit. Silver the only dude I ever seen never get all pissed-off . . . never take shit wrong when he smokin . . . never wanna kick nobody's ass over somethin he *think* they sayin when they ain't."

Sebastian looked unsure, but finally shrugged. "Well, all I sayin is, it been goddamn bullshit havin to move from where there was a lotta mixin . . . an dudes like me . . . an where everybody was chillin with it, down to this sorry-ass mother-fucka, man." Sebastian shoved his hands in his jacket pockets. "Shit, I hadn't hooked up with Hobbes right off, I be dead, man. For a fact!"

Minefield! Beware, you stupid nigga! "Um . . . but, don't you think sometimes it might be what you doin? Workin for Hobbes, I mean."

"Huh?"

"Well, what I sayin is, it gots to be pretty goddamn hard to chill with somebody's bodyguard . . . no matter what color they are. Shit, man, Winfield get along."

"Shit! Winfield get along cause he the Leopards' cocksuckin mascot! An . . . an, nobody kicks *your* fat ass cause you're the Collectors'!" Then, Sebastian's shoulders sagged under expensive black leather. "Aw . . . shit!" He stopped to lean, head down, against the bars of a storefront window. Peeling gold-colored decal letters behind dusty glass spelled THE PAMPERED POOCH: DOGWASH PET SUPPLIES. "It just somethin you can't understand, man. Don't try. It waste your time an pisses me off." Sebastian stayed that way a minute, but then raised his head again. "Um . . . your mom do spells an shit, huh, Tam? Like . . . stickin pins in dolls an that sorta stuff?"

"Don't need no dolls, man. Don't need no pins, neither. But, yeah, she do spells. Sometimes they even work."

Moving away from the window, Sebastian came close to the

fat boy. "Um . . . don't some of them people ever come to her
wantin to be . . . white?"

"Mmm. Well, none I ever know about. Seem like, most
them kinda people wouldn't be comin to her anyways, man.
Like, they go to Pay-Less an buy them kinda lotions an potions.
Dye their hair. Shit, go see a doctor, they gots the money for
it."

Sebastian considered that a long time. "Mmm. Yeah. Guess
that figure, huh? An, if they really had the green, they do 'em
a Michael Jackson."

Lactameon nodded. "I guess so."

Sebastian glanced around, then lowered his voice. "Um, I
read this book once, Tam. Bout this white dude changes himself
to black an lives with us awhile."

"Oh. Well, I read that book too, man. But he done it cause
he tryin to get down with what is. But, it wasn't no done-thing
forever. He was just sorta tryin on our skin. Maybe it done some
good, maybe it just make him some money, but it never really
mean much to me cause it wasn't forever. Like, he always had
him a option. It like . . . well, one of them homos go an get his
dick chopped off, you be pretty goddamn sure he *want* to be
somethin else."

Sebastian winced. "Shit, I guess so, man! Yo. You figure
Michael Jackson's forever?"

"Mmm. Guess he could be. Course, with his kinda green,
he be any fuckin thing he want."

Sebastian sighed. "Yeah. It only take green. That what give
your ass options. C'mon, Tam. I walk you to the corner. Gimme
some time for thinkin when I go back. Um . . . Tam? You figure
your mom do some kinda spell for me . . . if I pay her, course?"

"Um . . . you sayin you wanna be white, Akeem?"

Sebastian stopped dead. His eyes went to slits. "No! You
stupid nigger! I wanna be like YOU! The fuck you figure I been
talkin about, asshole?"

"Well . . . um . . . shit, man, you darker'n Ice T already
. . . an, an, a lot better-lookin."

"SHIT! All you stupid cocksuckas down here nuthin but
fools, man! Fools an suckas an cocksuckin stupid niggas eatin
each other! Shit! Only six of anything *you* gots is a hundred

pounds of cocksuckin blubber! *I'm* the only goddamn *black* dude in this whole sorry-ass motherfucka!"

"Oh, uh-huh, man! An, Ice T a nigga! Shit, why I waste my time talkin to some fucked-up motherfucker anyways!"

Sebastian's gun hand whipped from his pocket and dove inside his jacket. Lactameon shifted the pizza box and moved back a pace. *Dance in a minefield long enough an you step on one, fool!*

There was movement in a shadowed doorway. Sebastian's big black Uzi came out of his jacket in his hard golden hand, but the muzzle swung past Lactameon to aim at the darkness. Lactameon turned, seeing three small shadows and a little larger one. A flick of his eyes to Sebastian showed a rock-steady grip on the gun. "Sabby! Chill out, man!"

Gray eyes slid past ebony for a second, flashing a sign that Lactameon couldn't read. And, only the glitter of eyes shone from the doorway, more watchful and wary than scared. Something was wrong with that picture, but Lactameon didn't have time to find Waldo. The kids still carried their spears, but because of the gun were careful where they pointed them. *Sharp objects.* The three smaller boys seemed to be edging behind the bigger one. The little brass-colored Rasta looked a frail and reluctant leader. Lactameon wondered why he hadn't smelled those kids before he'd seen them. Their scent burned his nostrils now: an acid mix of little-boy sweat, unwashed crotches, ropy hair, dirty jeans, and half-rotted Nikes that hadn't been off for days.

Sebastian's nose wrinkled. "Shit!" The gun muzzle swung in a slow arc, covering the kids one by one and then moving back the other way. Lactameon understood that look now . . . Sebastian had decided he couldn't shoot him and was searching for·a substitute.

"Sabby! Leave them kids alone, man! They *mine*! Swear to God I kick you myself, you go an do one!"

Strangely, the golden boy smiled. "Yo, animals! Get the fuck out here! Now!"

Slowly, carefully, the little boys moved into the light. The littler ones bunched even tighter behind the thin Rasta, and seemed to be purposely keeping the smallest between them.

Sebastian's lips curled in something that wasn't a smile. The gun gave a jab toward the smallest boy, Hershey-bar brown and maybe six. "*That* one a Leopard!"

The Rasta's tight chest expanded. "No he not!" Two of the other boys echoed denials. Lactameon watched the smallest one. Black-coffee eyes widened in fear, but he stayed silent. Then, Lactameon saw the Rasta boy's face.

He almost screamed. He caught the sound in his throat, and a jolt like electricity slammed through his body. The boy had a beautiful face. Even grimy and framed by those long, dirty dreadlocks it belonged in a Bible. Except that there was only a dark empty hole where one eye should have been.

Lactameon remembered the boy's battle on the bridge . . . *blind-sided!* What a fucking sick joke! His own eyes shied from what wasn't there. Sebastian hadn't missed Lactameon's reaction.

"Yo! Thought they was *yours*, cocksucka? Mean you never seen him? That's Ethan . . . Ethan the animal. Ethan the cock-suckin animal!"

The little Rasta looked fierce, lips pulling back to bare his own teeth in a snarl that wasn't childish. Brass-colored fists clenched tight at his sides, small knuckles paling on the hand that clutched the spear. Sebastian's eyes flicked to Lactameon's for a second.

"He bites, man. But he won't bite me! Huh, little Ethan? *Nice* Ethan. *Pretty* Ethan." Sebastian's free hand dropped to his crotch. The rip of the zipper seemed loud. "Come here, Ethan. Suck my dick like you do for all them white cocksuckas at the bus station!"

The single eye seemed to search for escape, but found none. It was tawny, tawny and fierce like a tiger's . . . not afraid, only trapped. Lactameon stared now at the beautiful, damaged face. The eye was no animal's. It shifted from the golden boy, whose hand had slipped into his jeans to ready himself. *T.K. hadn't kicked the bastard near enough!* Then the tiger eye lifted to Lactameon's, held a moment, and rose a little higher. *My kids!*

Slowly, deliberately, as only a fat boy could, Lactameon stepped between Sebastian and the smaller boys, shielding them all with his bulk. For a long, scary second he could feel the Uzi aimed at his back.

Sebastian raged. "You stupid cocksuckin nigger! *All* you stupid cocksuckin niggers!"

The little Rasta's chest came about even with the bulge of Lactameon's belly. The one eye searched Lactameon's, maybe grateful, or maybe just waiting for whatever came next. Lactameon felt movement behind him. He tensed for the bullet, wondering what it would feel like.

"Aw . . . shit, Tam! I wouldn't really hurt 'em."

Sebastian eased around Lactameon's side, so close that black leather brushed soot-colored skin. The gun was still in his hand, but half-pointed down at the sidewalk. Bilal would have grabbed for it. Silver would have already had it. But Lactameon knew he wasn't fast enough. This was still Sebastian's game.

"Yo, Ethan! Little homeboy! What happen to your eye, poor little guy?"

Animals showed only mindless fury. Ethan's face twisted in calculating hate. The single eye swung to lock on Sebastian's. "You know what!"

"Yeah. But this sucka don't. Tell him!"

The little boy stuck out his lip. "No!"

The gun muzzle gestured. "Fat boy ain't gonna be around all the time, man, an I know where you live, little cocksucka!"

The tiger eye calculated. Ethan knew the game, and that Lactameon had done all he could until Sebastian got bored with playing it. "It . . . got poked out."

"Shit!" bawled Sebastian. "Any asshole with *two* eyes see that! Tell him *who* fucked you over!"

Ethan dropped his head. Beaten. But not before Lactameon saw tears on both cheeks. The empty place still remembered how to cry. The boy's forehead sank into Lactameon's belly. The words came husky and choked. "My . . . dad."

Sebastian snickered. "Well, ain't that a bitch!"

Behind the little Rasta, six other eyes, black and brown, aimed hate at Sebastian. Small hands curled tighter on mop-handle spears.

"An, what color's your dad, pretty Ethan? Tell him, cock-sucka!"

The little boy buried his face in Lactameon's soft blackness, muffling the word. "No!"

"Yo, Tam. His dad white! *White* cocksucka done that!"

Lactameon almost gathered the boy against him. Instead, he glanced at Sebastian. "That sposed to prove somethin, asshole? Like, it sposed to be some sorta lesson? Like, now they go hunt down Winfield an kick his ass cause *your* dad fuck you over? I don't think so."

Sebastian stiffened. The little Leopard suddenly giggled . . . or, a giggle got out. The gun jerked up. Lactameon spun, his bulk bashing Ethan into the other boys, while all of his weight backed up his fist. Soot-colored knuckles smashed into the golden boy's face. Sebastian staggered backward, arms flying wide for balance. Lactameon didn't try for the gun, just going with his momentum and throwing his shoulder against the other boy's chest. Sebastian crashed down on his back in the gutter. Lactameon almost fell too, stumbling to recover against his own mass. Sebastian's eyes glazed for a second as his head hit the pavement, but jerked up his gun arm to aim.

Four little blurs shot past Lactameon. Four flame-blackened spear-points stabbed straight for Sebastian's throat.

"NO!" Lactameon was almost amazed that the kids obeyed him. Sebastian froze, the gun half-raised, the spears only inches from his face. Lactameon didn't have to look twice to see where Ethan's was aimed. Lactameon got his balance, then stared down at Sebastian. Blood leaked from the boy's nose. "Get your fuckin ass outa here, Sabby! Shit! I can't think of *nuthin* I like about you!" Lactameon discovered he was still holding the pizza box. For a second he wanted to fling it in Sebastian's face. But that would be a waste. Then, he felt a weight in his pocket. That's what he'd forgotten. Jerking out the gold chain, he dropped it on the golden boy's black leather chest. "Don't waste no more of my time, you fucked-up motherfucka! Game over!" He glanced at the Rasta kid. The spear stayed as steady as if in the hands of a little brass statue. "Yo, Ethan. Snag his gun, man. Um, you know how to take out the clip?"

"Shit yeah!" Ethan gave his spear to Lactameon. The three other boys stayed poised. Somehow, Lactameon didn't feel stupid holding the mop handle. Ethan crouched and snatched the Uzi from Sebastian's hand. Expertly, he thumbed the magazine release and pulled the clip, then jacked the chambered round out on the sidewalk. The tiger eye met Lactameon's as an equal. "Now what, man?"

"Um . . ." *A good leader keeps one step ahead of his followers, fool!* "Unload the bullets. Put 'em in your pocket or somethin." Lactameon gestured with the spear as if he'd been carrying one all his life. "Rest of you dudes, let the sucker up."

Slowly and painfully Sebastian got to his feet as the three small kids backed away. Blood dripped from his chin. He touched his nose gently with the back of one hand. "Shit! I think you busted it, fucker!"

"Ain't that a bitch."

Hard eyes seemed to search Lactameon's softness for the solid thing that had hit him. "You gonna be sorry, niggerboy!" Sebastian shoved the gold chain into his pocket.

Lactameon snorted. "Yeah, sweetheart, just one more sorry motherfucka in this great big sorry-ass motherfucker. Go an get some more word on what is from *your* hero, man. Least Bogart *knew* he was actin! Yo, Ethan. Give Puddin Pop back his toy for the hood."

The little boy offered the Uzi on both palms, empty clip on top. "Here, *pretty* Sabby." The other kids snickered, standing their spears upright.

Lactameon handed the mop handle to Ethan. "Yo, Sabby. You can tell Hobbes to bill me for the bullets . . . cept I don't figure you gonna say nuthin bout this little ole donkey show."

Sebastian muttered a curse, then spun around and walked back down the sidewalk, shoulders hunched as if against cold.

"Um," added Lactameon. "I cruised your board today, Sabby. Maybe I put a crack in it."

Giggling and maxing, Ethan and two of the smaller boys clustered around Lactameon. "Maaan!" said one, staring up. "Your ass somethin *else*, man!" "Fuck yeah!" said the other. "Maaan, wish I get me that size!" Ethan prodded Lactameon's belly with a palm, making it wobble. "Shit yeah! I *gonna* get that size! Word!"

Lactameon smiled a moment, then saw the little Leopard hanging back. The boy looked unsure, but stood his ground as Lactameon stepped up to him. Ethan and the other two went silent, watching. For sure the little Leopard could have run, but he didn't. Lactameon had a funny picture of the dude hauling back and burying a little chocolate fist in his blubber . . . a fist with a box knife in it.

"I didn't see you, man. What it is. I didn't see you. That all."

The boy didn't move or even nod. How could he when he wasn't there. Lactameon glanced at the evening sky. "Kay, dudes. You done good. Just take care." He turned to Ethan. "Yo. You oughta wear a patch over that, man."

"Why?"

"Huh? Well . . . keep the dirt out, I guess."

Ethan crossed his arms over his chest and looked sulky. "It cool like it is, man."

One of the other boys giggled. "Yo! One time he stick a marble in there! Shit, didn't fool nobody!"

Ethan gave the dude a shove. "Shut up, cocksucka!"

Lactameon sighed, then glanced at the pizza box. "Here, man." He handed it to Ethan. "You share."

"Shit yeah!"

Turning away, Lactameon started up the street. Ethan's voice called after him. "Thanks." The word sounded rusty. Lactameon glanced back and saw the little Leopard whispering something to Ethan. Ethan ran to catch up with Lactameon.

"Um, he say to tell ya, he not see no pizza box, neither."

13

What little remained of the old highway across Bates's land wasn't much more than a few crumbling patches of pavement hugging the riverbank down to the bend. Corbitt, Toby, and Lamar halted on the far side of the bridge and stood for a time, hesitant to take those last steps off the rotted deck planking and onto the leaf-covered concrete beyond. Since passing the bridge's midpoint, Corbitt had felt a kind of invisible wind, like a force field on *Star Trek*, that grew ever stronger the closer they came to Bates's bank. He remembered feeling a similar thing when he'd faced Bates on the bridge that afternoon with Sherry. He wondered now if the old man's aura of evil could have even seeped into the ground. He shivered and turned to the other boys. Neither said a thing, but Corbitt noted that both seemed to be leaning into the strange ghostly wind. Corbitt turned again to face the darkness ahead. A few feet farther on, past the tree where Bates had stood only hours before, the roadway curved right and was swallowed by vine-tangled blackness. While Corbitt knew it was only a strip of bushes and trees shrouding the remains of the road between the river shore and Bates's untended fields, tonight it looked to be endless forest that stretched away forever. He recalled a picture in a book showing an old-time map of Africa: most of the continent featureless black with the word UNEXPLORED standing out in stark white. Corbitt sucked a breath and stepped onto Bates's land.

It was as if he had broken through the force field. Surprised, he stopped so suddenly that Toby and Lamar slammed into him. The night had turned totally silent, so that Toby's whisper sounded loud enough to wake the dead.

"What was it, Corbitt?"

"Yeah," added Lamar, whose deep voice wasn't designed for whispering. "I feel it too! Some sorta magic?"

Corbitt swallowed and tried to sound confident. "Don't right know. But, whatever it was, it ain't there no more."

The boys stood at the edge of the moonlight in what looked like the mouth of a leafy black tunnel. At Corbitt's feet, between the buckled slabs where the tree had grown through, was the double-O impression of Bates's shotgun muzzle. A ten-gauge left big holes. Nearby, a crumpled Lucky Strike butt lay on the leaves.

Toby's eyes followed Corbitt's down to it. "Forget him, man," Toby murmured. "Anyways, he gotta be home in bed an dead to the world at this hour."

"Yeah," agreed Lamar, pressing close to the other boys. "Just too goddamn bad he ain't dead forever."

Corbitt gazed ahead into the jungle-like gloom. "Mmm. I hear some folks sayin there times when his light burn all night long."

Toby patted Corbitt's shoulder. "Aw, maybe he gots himself bladder trouble to go with his sick ole head."

Lamar laughed, and somehow the moon got a little bit brighter. Then an owl hooted somewhere close by and it almost seemed a normal summer night once again. Toby moved forward past Corbitt and into the shadow.

"No," said Corbitt, louder than he'd meant. "I go first."

Corbitt found a narrow trail and felt his way along, helped by stray moonbeams sifting through from above. The strip of trees was tortured and tangled with undergrowth and twisted vines as if all the plants here were in some sort of rage to reclaim this land for their own. The way was not made, Corbitt knew; Bates had no need of it, and the last Bridge-end kids to venture this far had been the three jungle cats on their final raid to the riverbend pool. What passed for a path was only the old road's last feeble defiance before being buried. Corbitt pushed through claw-like brambles into even deeper darkness. The soft swearing of Toby and Lamar as they followed was a lot more reassuring than any lucky charm. Corbitt tried to recall the lay of these woods; how they'd looked in daylight last year when lit by a green glow as if underwater. He remembered too how heavy the air had seemed, and that there had been this same sort of sensation as if something waited and watched.

He shoved through more briars that raked at his skin like skeleton fingers. Then sudden moonlight dazzled his eyes. He stopped, squinting and blinking, as the other boys came through behind him. He heard them suck startled breaths. A clear strip of roadway had somehow survived here. It stretched ahead, forming a strange concrete clearing amid the vine-tangled wilderness. A trace of white line still showed down the center, leading straight toward a tunnel of blackness beyond. It seemed wrong; like finding the relics of two different times. Corbitt thought of cities entombed in trackless jungle. The pavement was tilted at all crazy angles and felt icy cold under Corbitt's bare feet. He wondered why it wasn't layered with leaves like the rest of the road. "I don't member this part," he whispered.

"I don't neither," Toby whispered back. "We musta come another way."

Lamar's voice was an uncertain growl. "I don't like the look of this shit."

Toby giggled suddenly. "White bwana on safari in the Congo. Camped for the night in the jungle. All of a sudden these drums start up. Bwana turns to his best-boy, say, I sure don't like the sound of them drums. Then, this voice come out the darkness. Yeah, well, it ain't our regular drummer."

Corbitt chuckled. Lamar considered a moment, then shrugged and smiled. "Well, spose we can't be lost anyways. River gots to be no more'n ten feet to the right, an this here road run right longside it."

Toby peered around, then nudged Corbitt forward. "Well, then let's us run with it. Lamar's creepers is catchin. I don't like it here, neither."

The boys shifted their poles so they carried them now like spears. His eyes on the faded white line, Corbitt started quickly across the open space for what seemed like the safety of shadow ahead. Toby, with Lamar's bulk at his back, was following so closely that his toes brushed Corbitt's heels.

"Jeeze, Lamar," muttered Toby, "any goddamn closer an y'all be inside my skin!"

The broken road slabs made treacherous footing. Toby's voice quavered a little. "Almost like somethin tryin to bust out from down there."

"Tree roots, fool!" hissed Corbitt. "Next you two burrheads be seein a goddamn duppy eatin a sandwich!"

Then Corbitt looked up . . .

And stopped stock-still in horror.

The other boys crashed into him, but Corbitt hardly noticed. He was frozen, staring, his eyes wide and his mouth dropping open while his heart pounded inside his chest. Far down the forgotten old road a set of dim yellow headlights seemed to rush toward them!

"What the f . . . ," began Toby. Then he must have seen them too. His fingers locked on Corbitt's arm. That doubled Corbitt's terror: it could only mean that those half-dead headlights *were* real! He heard Lamar's gasp, but a scream was trying to tear from his own throat even though his lungs couldn't seem to get the air for it. His mind beat about in his skull like a bee in a jar. He was trapped! Pinned in the middle of the road like an animal by those oncoming headlights! Jumbled visions shot through his brain; of rust-rotted trucks rolling this forgotten route, rumbling down the remains of the road, rattling across those bare bones of a bridge, and then clashing their spur-toothed transmissions as they geared-up past his *home* each night! There was a grisly logic in that . . . those long-dead drivers couldn't know this wasn't the way anymore!

The breath seemed to cling in Corbitt's chest, thick and clotted like something decayed. He knew he should run, but still just stood helplessly as the ghost of a truck bore down on him in silence.

The yellow headlights blinked. A sign? Corbitt imagined the skeletal driver, his moldering cap festooned with a gris-gris of grave-tarnished badges, his bony fingers reaching for the air horn's rusted chain. But, how could anyone hear a warning from the past?

And then the headlights blinked again . . .

And became nothing more than the golden stare of an owl on a branch with the moon in its eyes.

"Oh," was all Corbitt could say.

"Shit," added Toby.

"Mutha . . . *fucker!*" Lamar sighed out.

Corbitt found his knees weak and shaking. Still, he managed a smile as he turned to Lamar. "That the first time ever I hear you say that word."

Lamar swallowed, his big body sheened in sweat like the other boys'. "It was time for a next-thing, I spose."

"Gots that right!" agreed Toby.

Corbitt felt suddenly flooded with shame. What would Mrs. Griffin think of him now . . . scared shitless of imaginary eighteen-wheeled duppys! He wiped cold sweat from his forehead and tried to steady his voice. "W-what y'all figure that was?"

"Headlights . . . I guess," said Toby, now staring at the owl.

"Maybe Bates in that ole Jeep of his," added Lamar.

"For true?" Toby demanded.

"Well . . . maybe not at first." Lamar gave the owl a cautious glance, then looked back at Corbitt. "So, what *you* figure it was, man?"

"Um . . ." Corbitt turned back to face the owl. "It . . . it ain't 'portant. Not now. Anyways, best not be givin no names to night-things."

"Oh, suuure," said Toby. "Hey, that the biggest sonofabitchin owl I ever seen!"

Corbitt faced the huge bird, then stood his pole upright and bowed to it. Toby exchanged glances with Lamar, then both other boys did the same. The owl seemed to nod in the solemn way of its kind, then spread a startling wingspan and lifted silently into the night.

"Um, was that some sorta magic?" asked Toby.

Corbitt shrugged. "Don't right know fo sho. Still, it best to keep careful bout them kinda things."

Lamar glanced over his shoulder. "Well, y'all best be believin *this* nigga had him bout all the goddamn magic he want for one night! Better goddamn well be some fish in that pool after puttin me through all this shit!"

Toby snickered a little, then took a deep breath and looked around. "Hey, Corbitt, seem like the air sorta *feel* better now, don't it? Shit, for a minute there I coulda swore I smell somethin dead."

"Shut up, fool!" growled Lamar. "Else what be smellin be *you*!"

Corbitt smiled again and scanned the concrete clearing . . . just a strip of abandoned roadway buckled by tree roots. But, as Toby had said, the air did seem fresh and living again. The usual sounds of a hot summer night came clear once more: crickets, sleepy bird calls, and the boom of a bullfrog down by the riverbank. Corbitt glanced over his shoulder. "Lamar right, man. Figure we us had a 'bundance of magic back there, but we busted the spell cause we face it together. Best we go get what we come for."

Crossing the clearing, the boys passed beneath the low branch where the owl had been sitting and entered a tunnel of shadows once more. It felt good to be together and moving through the night woods. They followed a twisted path of pavement thickly covered with leaves. The brambles and underbrush no longer clutched, and the image of Bates seemed no more a menace than a bogeyman story to scare little kids. A few minutes later the boys slipped through a curtain of vine-tangled willow and emerged on the shore by the riverbend pool.

Toby strutted into the moonlight. "Hell, I knew we all make it! Gots Corbitt the magic cheetah to fight the sooper-natural, and Lamar the lion to stomp the natural."

"Well, I ain't seen much *natural* since we come cross the bridge," muttered Lamar. "Spose that mean we put all our trust in Corbitt."

Toby grinned and knelt at Corbitt's feet. "My cheetah-prince."

Corbitt frowned a little. "Don't start that shit, man."

The westward-curving river cut deeper into Bates's lower field with every springtime flood, stealing away the earth and leaving behind huge rocks and a few tumbled tree trunks. Together, the boys climbed atop a water-worn boulder and gazed down the watery moonpath. Farther along, the trees thinned away so that open fields bordered the banks. Three miles distant, a few lights glimmered gold in New Crossing. A mile to the north glowed the island-like loom of the truckstop's Sinclair dinosaur sign, soft green and white against the purple-blue brilliance of a half-dozen mercury lamps. A shift in the air brought the whine of big wheels as a truck followed the moon toward the hills.

Corbitt felt a new tightening in his chest; not of fear but of sadness he couldn't quite name. "I never seen how small this valley was before," he murmured.

Lamar looked around. "Same size it always was, look like to me."

Toby glanced at Corbitt, then put a hand on his shoulder. "Bridge-end a *good* place, brother. It like . . . like you can feel it in your bones."

Corbitt nodded. "Mmm. Spose I know that, Tobe. But, dammit, times lately it just don't seem enough somehow. Even Sherry tell me today that Bridge-end fo sho ain't the world."

Lamar cocked his head. "Well, why you want the world, Corbitt?"

Corbitt shrugged. "It funny, what it is, like . . . like you don't want a thing till it look like you can't never get it."

Lamar and Toby exchanged glances and moved back slightly, leaving Corbitt alone on the tip of the rock. The air was cooler now, as if the land was finally catching its breath after the day's smothering heat. The moon looked like some huge lucky-charm as it sank toward the hills. But the hour was still more late than early, and the eastern sky was still velvet-black.

"I wish Bridge-end was my real home," said Toby.

Lamar only nodded, but Corbitt turned to the blond boy. "Why?"

"Cause . . . well . . . just cause."

"Course you do," said Lamar.

Corbitt looked at Lamar for a moment, hesitated, then faced Toby once more. "Did . . . did y'all ever wish you was black?"

Lamar seemed puzzled, but Toby looked relieved. "Oh, fo sho, Corbitt. Lots of times."

"Spose that logical," said Lamar.

"Is it?" asked Corbitt. "Why, Tobe?"

"Well . . . just seem like it make things easier. For me . . . an for all us."

Lamar shrugged. "Not no more, man. It don't matter now." His forehead creased in thought. "Well," he added. "Might still matter to some . . ."

"Like your parents?" asked Toby. "Like the special places at supper an all?"

"Mmm," said Lamar. "I hear what you sayin now. Funny, it kinda like Corbitt say a minute ago . . . like I never seen it afore. But, hell, Tobe, they . . . well, they *older* folks, know what I mean?"

Corbitt asked softly. "You don't wish that no more, Tobe?"

"Sometimes I still do. But you an Lamar make it so's it don't seem 'portant no more." Toby lowered his eyes and smiled shyly. "When I first met you brothers I used to wish every night that I wake up black in the mornin. I guess you call that prayin, huh?"

"Well, Jesus, Tobe," said Lamar. "You give your parents a fit, that happen!"

Toby smiled again and touched the big boy's shoulder. "Know what, man? One time I even went an ask Miz Griffin if she could do some kinda spell for me."

Lamar seemed to study the blond boy with new eyes. "What she say?"

"To come back an see her bout it in a few more years."

"Mmm," said Lamar. "Spose she want you to think on it some. Are you gonna?"

"Would we be better brothers if I did?"

Corbitt smiled. "It wouldn't matter none to us. Just to the world."

"Might matter to Tobe's folks," said Lamar.

"Why?" asked Toby. "Couldn't they love me as much if I was black?"

"Well, *course* they would! I mean . . . well . . . you still be *you*!" Lamar raised his eyes to Corbitt. "Wouldn't he?"

Corbitt gazed at both boys for a moment, then nodded. "Bet your ass he would, man!"

Lamar nodded. "Well, glad that settled! Now maybe we can catch us some goddamn fish!"

Two massive tree trunks, all mush and moss with age, angled into the river, forming a V at the waterline where one lay across the other. The boys descended, their toes gripping the matted moss and crushing a tangy fragrance from it. The forked logs made a perfect fishing perch, and the moss was thick and soft to sit on. The boys settled close together, baited their hooks, and cast lines and bobbers into the pool. Almost immediately Lamar's eyelids began to droop, and his head sank down on Toby's shoulder. Toby eased back a little to make him more comfortable, then touched Corbitt's arm and pointed upward. "Tell me one of them star stories, man. Like that one where you arc to Arcturus an curve over to what's-his-name."

Corbitt's eyes narrowed slightly. "Corvus. Corvus the crow." Corbitt made a momentary face, then sighed and aimed a long finger toward the stars. "Ain't the best time of night for catchin him. Mmm, there he be, I think. Right next the golden cup . . . the cup he ain't never sposed to get."

Toby pressed closer to Corbitt. "Why?"

Corbitt lowered his outstretched arm and shifted his pole. "Was a god . . . some white god . . . send Corvus down to the river to fetch him a cup of water. Musta been a long, long ways cause Corvus get tired an stop to rest. Come back late with the god's water. That god, he get all pissed-off bout it, so he curse Corvus an stick him up there in the sky, make him real thirsty, an put a big golden cup of water so's it always just out of Corvus's reach. 'Cordin to the story Corvus condemned to go on tryin to get that cup for all eternity."

Toby was silent for a time after Corbitt finished, staring upward. Finally he sighed and spat into the river. "Only a white god do somethin that shitty. Poor Corvus!"

Corbitt looked upward again. "Maybe Corvus just ain't thirsty enough yet."

Toby yawned. "Spect that why crows down here always wantin pretty stuff?"

Corbitt shrugged. "Mmm. Could be."

Toby settled against Lamar and closed his eyes. Corbitt studied his brothers for a few minutes, their faces peaceful in the soft moonlight, then eased himself down closer to Toby. Soon he too was asleep. Around the boys the riverlife slowly resumed its normal rhythms as the birds and animals came to accept their presence. The water flowed silently past their feet and swirled gently through the pool before turning west. A drop of blood from a bramble scratch on Corbitt's arm sank into the depths. A wood rat crept down and regarded the three sleeping figures for a time, then went about its business. A water moccasin sensed their warmth and came gliding close with questing tongue, but feeling their peace, lowered its head and slipped away once more. The Earth turned toward morning.

And then Corbitt woke . . .

At least he thought he was awake because he found himself standing in the road at Bridge-end with the sky glowing rose to the east, though he had no memory of coming back across the bridge. There was a haziness to the landscape and a floating feeling in his mind as if he really walked in that border-world between consciousness and sleep. And then he discovered he carried a string of catfish over his shoulder and that they were the biggest he'd ever seen. This *had* to be a dream: he couldn't have forgotten catching whoppers like these! It was too bad Toby and Lamar weren't there to see. Corbitt smiled and hoped nobody would roll off the log.

Yet he wasn't completely convinced he was dreaming until he looked up and saw a light bulb burning above the motor court sign. Those wires had been down since before he'd been born. The dawn was growing and the countryside coming into focus like the opening scene of a movie. Corbitt studied the cabin row: the roofpeaks stood straight, the paint wasn't too aged, and raked gravel spread out to the road. He looked down: the concrete was weathered but unbroken, and a solid white line divided it. Yeah, this was definitely a dream. He frowned then, noting that he still wore his same ragged old overall-jeans. Well, it was only a niggaboy's dream, what could you expect?

With a shrug he raised his head and looked around again as the sky brightened to blue above. A law of magic said you had to learn to control and direct your dreams. He'd even read that some African tribes believed your dream life was every bit as real and important as your waking one. Corbitt nodded to himself, satisfied that he knew who he was in this place and would be prepared for whatever happened. He turned toward the cabins once more and stared in sudden wonder. In front was parked a perfect old-time semi-truck. He dashed up the road, hoping it wouldn't just disappear before he could reach it the way things often did in dreams. It was a Corbitt . . . *the* Corbitt! Its green paint gleamed and the stainless-steel Fruehauf trailer shone like a mirror in the new-morning sunlight. Clutching his string of fish, Corbitt ran to the truck, first inspecting all the bright permit stickers on the door and then walking around front to check out the license plates. There were seven, including a yellow-and-black one from California. The chrome CORBITT on the radiator flashed silver fire as the sun cleared the river trees. Corbitt reached a tentative finger to touch the letters; cool from the night but solid and real. He noticed now how the air seemed different, cleaner and fresher then he'd ever remembered it being before. It made the truck's iron and oil and rubber scents stand out sharp. He *had* to see the inside of the cab! Darting back, he started to climb the running board. Its diamond pattern of ridges was rough underfoot, not worn down smooth where he'd sat yesterday morning with Mr. Rudd. Or, he wondered, was that where he *would* be sitting one day many years in the future? Dream logic wasn't the easiest stuff to figure out.

"BOY!"

Startled, Corbitt stared over his shoulder, one hand poised on the door handle. The voice was sharp and shrill and used to being obeyed. Corbitt saw a fat white woman in a dress the size of a small tent standing on the porch of Number One. He also noted that the railing was bare of vines and that there were no flowers in cans atop it. A small sign hung in one window: OF-FICE, VACANCY. Well, he thought, things seemed to follow a consistent time frame in this place, though he sure didn't care for the fat woman's tone or the look she was giving him.

"BOY!" she bellowed again. "Just what in creation you think y'all doin up there? Get your fool self down off that vehicle right this here minute!"

Disappointed and a little confused, Corbitt jumped to the ground. The fresh gravel bit even his tough feet. Cool special-effects, he thought.

The woman waddled to the top step of the porch and made a commanding gesture. "Boy! Y'all come here to me! Now!"

With a wistful backward glance at the truck, Corbitt walked over to the porch steps. The gravel crunched under his feet, painfully real. The woman dropped her hands to her hips and looked annoyed. "Don't dawdle, boy!"

In your ear! thought Corbitt. His very own dream, and now he was being ordered around in it! The fat woman didn't look like a duppy, but Corbitt would have almost preferred one, or even a werewolf in new Nikes spotting him a mile to the grave-yard instead of this bowlegged sow bawling commands.

The woman eyed him suspiciously at first, but then her doughy face took on the same sort of resigned expression the school coach often wore when Corbitt chose to walk laps around the track with the fat kids instead of shooting hoops. "Boy," she said as he neared, "ain't you got a thought in that woolly little head of yours? Foolin with white folks' property! Gettin your dirty feet all over Mr. Rudd's truck!" She shook her head. "Swear, I just don't know what comin over you people. Seem like y'all just gettin more an more irresponsible every blessed day." She heaved a sigh, then glanced momentarily at a big scruffy crow that came flapping down onto the motor court sign. The bird croaked nastily. The woman shot it a disgusted glare, and her expression didn't change much when she turned back to Corbitt. "Who you belong to, boy?"

Corbitt's eyes widened. *That* for sure wasn't consistent with the time frame! He said the first thing that came to mind, even though it sounded stupid. "I . . . I been freed."

The fat woman flushed. "Boy! Are you givin me sass?"

"Um . . . no."

"Then stop talkin nonsense! An, no, *what*, boy?"

"Um . . . no, I ain't."

The crow on the sign muttered to itself.

The woman glared. "Ain't, *what*, boy?"

Corbitt could feel the crow watching him. He wished it would go away. Finally, he realized what the woman wanted. "Ma'am," he added.

The fat lady crossed her arms and looked like she'd just scored bonus points on Space Invaders. "That's better, boy. Now, who's your people? Y'all got considerable more color than the Sampson family."

Corbitt smiled. "Y'all be knowin the Sampsons?"

"Course I know 'em! They a credit to your race. Never catch their boy, Lionel, doin a foolish thing like you just done. He properly respectful, what he is."

Corbitt wondered what Lamar would think, being told that his grandfather had been "properly respectful" to dimwitted old cows. He took a breath, holding back his anger by reminding himself that it was only a dream. You couldn't control things by losing your temper. The crow lifted a wing as if hiding a snicker. Corbitt wanted to shag a pebble at the little black bastard. The woman heaved another sigh, this one of twice-tried patience, and shook her head.

"Boy, I just don't know what they teachin in that there school of yours nowadays. Seem to me like you colored children just losin all respect for your betters. You'll live to regret it, y'all ain't careful!"

Corbitt's hands clenched to delicate fists. He wondered how to start controlling this dream so he could get this fat bitch the hell out of it and return to the truck before he woke up. Maybe if he ignored her she'd just disappear? He looked down at his feet, but the woman stayed right where she was.

"That's better, boy. You don't go starin back at white folks."

Corbitt's head jerked up, but the woman had noticed the fish. A look of speculation crossed her face.

"Some fair-size cats you got yourself there, boy. Where you catch 'em?"

Corbitt almost answered, in the river, which was logical but would probably sound like sass. Instead, he pointed toward the bridge. "Down there a ways."

The fat woman frowned. "Down there a ways, *what*, boy?"

Corbitt sucked another breath and held it. He willed the woman away with all his might.

The woman puffed like a hoptoad. "Stop makin them fool faces, boy! I ask a colored child a question, I spect me a civil answer!"

Corbitt's own chest puffed. His long back straightened and he glared full into the fat woman's baby-blue eyes. "Down the river, DAMMIT, *that* what! Where in hell else you catch catfish? Figure . . . figure they come driftin down from heaven all done up in Saran Wrap or somethin? An . . . an, WHAT you doin whattin me for anyhow? What give you the right to be talkin to me so? I been FREED, goddammit! An that be a big fat joke just like you, cause it somethin you got no right takin from me in the first place! An . . . an . . . why I go an snap my fingers an pop you right back to bogeyman-land where you come from! THAT what!"

The crow did a little dance on the sign, then flew off laughing crow laughs just like the Disney bird. The fat woman's mouth fell open and worked frantically like a fresh-landed catfish's herself. Her eyes rolled up like she was going to faint or pitch a fit.

Corbitt tensed; if she was going to turn into something unnatural, now was the time!

But a figure appeared around the side of the cabin and the fat lady spun to it in relief. "Oh, Lucianne! Thank GOD!" She straight-armed a finger at Corbitt. "Here's the most IMPU-DENT little . . . little *colored* boy, you ever saw in your life, Lucianne! Come struttin right in out of nowhere . . . *upped* himself right on Mr. Rudd's truck just as bold as all brass, an just now sassed me up and down like I don't know what! Lu-cianne, I never saw such a thing! You know for a fact I never, *ever*, use THAT word, but here's one standin right on my own front porch in broad daylight, lippin me just like I'd strayed into Jackson darktown! Lucianne, I won't have it! I got me a good mind to ring up the sheriff!"

Corbitt, meantime, had been studying Lucianne. She was a slim, pert-looking young woman in a faded print dress, long apron, and red bandana, like a youthful Aunt Jemima. She seemed somehow familiar.

Lucianne clucked sympathy to the fat woman, then turned a withering scowl on Corbitt. And yet he caught a twinkle in her cocoa-brown eyes. And then *his* mouth fell open.

"Miz Griffin!"

The fat lady frowned. "Lucianne! You mean to tell me you *know* this here . . . *boy?*"

Calmly, Lucianne returned the white woman's stare. "Yes-sum, spect I does." She flashed another twinkle to Corbitt. "Tho there been times I catch myself wishin I don't."

"Oh." The white lady eyed Corbitt with some uncertainty, then lowered her voice. "Well, is there . . . somethin *wrong* with him, Lucianne? He ain't been actin quite right in the head . . . keep on tellin me he been *freed!*"

Lucianne coughed to hide a sudden smile. "Lord above! Jus no tellin what chilluns gonna up an say these days, ma'am. Truth be, there been times I wonder if he rowin with both oars my ownself. But the way of it is, he just visitin here from . . . someplace else. I awful sorry he been frettin you, Miz Tate, but spect he ain't bein purposeful lippy. Mo like he jus don't know the ways round these parts. I sho nuff take the boy in hand." Turning once more to Corbitt, Lucianne made a fierce face with laughing eyes. "That so, boy? Found yourself someplace where

you don't know your head from your tailbone, huh? *Freed!* Now
what kinda talk that be? *Course* you been freed! This be 1951,
boy! You gots yourself all the freedom 'lowed by law! Now you
jus go an tell nice Miz Tate here how sorry you be for sassin her
back."

Corbitt looked long at Lucianne before finally forcing a
bright Buckwheat smile and bowing to the fat woman. "Oh,
yessum, ma'am! I be sorry somethin awful!"

Mrs. Tate's expression went puzzled. "You got yourself a
right odd way of talkin, boy. You down from the north?"

Corbitt caught a tiny shake of Lucianne's head. "Um . . .
oh no, ma'am. I down from . . . Starkville." He'd almost said
he was from New Crossing, but couldn't recall if it had still been
called Bates Ferry in 1951. And why, he wondered, was Mrs.
Griffin playing Auntie to this fat white bitch? It was only a dream;
he was asleep on a log beside Toby and Lamar, and likely as not
Mrs. Tate was long dead like the old dinosaur she was.

Mrs. Tate mulled Corbitt's words. "Well, I never recollect
the negroes in Starkville bein let to backtalk like that. But then
I don't get up there much anymore. Times I think this here ole
world be movin too fast for me. Lord, Lucianne, I never in my
life laid eyes on a child so dark! Will it fade, do you think?"

"I spect not," said Lucianne, dryly.

Mrs. Tate shook her head. "Poor child. You could almost
forgive him for the burden he got to bear. Well, I was just about
to offer him a whole dollar for his fish. Before he up an give me
sass. Mr. Tate was remarkin only yesterday how much he love
your catfish fry."

Corbitt remembered now; Mrs. Griffin telling him that a
white couple named Tate had owned the motor court, but they'd
sold out a year after the new highway went through. They had
tried putting up a new sign at the crossroads but not many
travelers turned off. And since nobody else wanted an outdated
motel on a crumbling old road to nowhere, Mrs. Griffin herself
had been able to buy it. She'd come into some money long about
then, but Corbitt couldn't recall her telling him how.

Corbitt suddenly grinned: a "whole dollar," when any fool
knew that catfish went for $2.65 a pound in town; and tasteless,
flabby, farm-raised at that!

But Lucianne beamed at Mrs. Tate. "Why, jus you see how

happy that boy lookin now, ma'am! Ain't no wonder folks always remarkin what a good, fair woman you be!"

The fat woman puffed with pleasure.

"Lordy!" Lucianne went on. "That there boy be jus a shinin with happiness! Take only the simplest little things to please him. I clean me them fish right this here minute, you like? Maybe fix up a bite fo the boy. Look like to me he been awake the whole night through." She gave Corbitt a knowing smile. "An he gots himself a *long* journey home again." She crooked a finger. "Jus you be comin with me, boy. Our guests be risin soon, don't need to be seein no raggedy little ole colored chile first thing in the mornin." Both she and Mrs. Tate laughed.

Corbitt started to follow Lucianne, but paused to give Mrs. Tate another little bow. "Thank you, ma'am, I so happy I could die."

Majestically, Mrs. Tate descended the creaking steps and patted Corbitt's head. "Well, boy, you just study up your place a bit better an you get along just fine while you here. We don't never have no trouble with you people round these parts."

Corbitt hurried after Lucianne. Around the side of the office he jammed a finger down his throat and made a throw-up noise. "My ASS!" He caught up with Lucianne at the doorway of what was now a tiny cabin but would be a chicken coop when he woke. "Shi . . . SHOOT!" he hissed. "Hey, Miz Griffin, if that ole warthog figure nee-groes rate less'n nuthin, how come she puff fit to bust when a black lady be givin her butter-mouth?"

Lucianne chuckled. "Whitefolks never get enough of bein told how good they are to us." She took Corbitt's fish and went inside.

"Shuckin an jivin, all that is!" snorted Corbitt. "Any fool see through that!"

Lucianne turned. "Boy, ain't you learned that most folks only be hearin what they want to hear? An, case you forgot, this be Mississippi, 1951. Your school be teachin you how to get along."

Corbitt spread his palms. "Oh, I get it! Miz Griffin? You be figurin I somebody else, huh? From *here*."

Lucianne busted out laughing as she spread the fish on the sinkboard. She was beautiful, Corbitt thought, almost a girl, though she must have been at least twenty. Too old for him,

even now . . . Sherry might look like that in a few years . . .
He smiled; a *lot* more years!

"Corbitt Wainwright! How on God's green earth could I
ever mistake *you* for any other boy?" Still laughing, Lucianne
sank into a chair at the little table and wiped happy tears with
the corner of her apron. "Oh, Lord, boy . . . driftin down from
heaven in Saran Wrap! Pop you back to bogeyman-land!" She
gazed at Corbitt a moment, then broke out anew. "Will it
FADE, do you think!"

Corbitt scowled and swung around to face the office. "Well,
what right she got gettin so uppity with me for? Hey, this may
be 1951, but it my goddamn *dream* 1951!"

Chuckling, Lucianne rose and pulled a knife from a drawer.
Her eyes took on a sly little sparkle as she started on the fish.
"Now, y'all *sure* this a dream, Corbitt?"

"Why . . . what else it be?" Corbitt crossed the small room
to stand beside Lucianne. He found he wasn't as fearfully respectful of this young woman as he was of the "real" Mrs. Griffin.
"Hey, you ain't gonna go an try tellin me I doin some kinda
time travel, like in them *Back to the Future* movies? Or . . .
or, this ain't one of your magic lessons?"

Lucianne sliced fish bellies. "No, son. Best you believe this
ain't no doin of mine. Onliest thing I can figure, you be so mighty
unhappy where you are that y'all gone off looking for somewheres
better. But I don't think you gonna find it here."

"Um . . . so, this what you call a dream-quest, Miz Griffin?
I read me bout one of them in a H. P. Lovecraft book."

"Mmm. Don't much matter what you call it, son. You sho
nuff in it."

Corbitt considered that, then poked a fat fish with his finger.
"Now, why y'all be cleanin them silly things for? Just soon's I
wake up, ole Miz Tate be poppin right back to hell."

"Corbitt Wainwright! I got me a nice new batch of yellow
soap ain't never been tasted by a smarty-mouth yet!"

"But . . . but she belong there if that how she treated us!"

Lucianne went on cleaning fish for a minute. At last she
sighed. "Corbitt, there a lot of things bout these times you ain't
gonna find in no books. Miz Tate was bout as good a person as
this place let her be. Oh I know it prob'ly don't seem that way
to you, but what you got to realize is that whitefolks like her

was just as trapped in the ways as us. When I was a little girl, she come over to my gramma's the week I had the typhoid fever. Always brung soup or somethin. Paid for the doctor right out of her own pocket, yes she did. Sat by my bedside the whole night through so's Gramma could get her some sleep. An she still come back here at nights sometimes. We sit right at that table an talk bout lots of things. She know in her heart there somethin wrong with the way things be."

"Mmm," said Corbitt. "Spect she went to her own kinda school, huh?"

Lucianne wiped a hand on her apron and chucked Corbitt under the chin. "Yes, son. It awful hard to bust down ideas you taught as a child. There a lot of good white people, even here an now. An a lot of 'em just as scared an confused an mad bout the way things be as us. I always figure God take that into account."

Corbitt glanced toward the office again, still looking a little doubtful.

Lucianne smiled. "Ain't everbody can be a warrior, son."

"Mmm. Spose I never think on it like that afore."

"Ain't many folks ever do. It so easy to forget all the ordinary people what never get put in the books." Lucianne chuckled. "An, some warrior *you* be! Come here questin out so much as a shield! Figure all you got to do is snap them fingers an make all the duppys go poof?" She slipped the little ebony crow feather from behind Corbitt's ear, studied it a moment, then put it back. "Mmm. Well, long's you here, best go an make yourself to home. I got to get these cats clean an then I fix y'all some breakfast."

"Huh?"

"Well, it *is* your dream. If y'all ain't hungry in it, that your concern I spose."

"But, what be the laws here, Miz Griffin? The magic ones . . . the *real* ones?"

"Well, since it your dream, I spect you in charge of that."

"You mean, like I brung you back here my ownself to sorta save me from ole Miz Tate?"

"If you did, I be right flattered, son. An proud of you too. A good warrior know when he gonna need help. Any fool can get himself into a bad situation. Any fool can die. It livin that hard to keep on with sometimes."

"What if Miz Tate went an called up that sheriff?"

Lucianne shrugged. "Well, she didn't, so there ain't no need to speculate on it."

"Mmm. Spose that logical. Um, spect I could eat me somethin fore I go, if y'all be wantin to take the trouble."

"No trouble, son. Been many long years since I got myself invited to some young warrior's dream-quest."

Corbitt scanned the room, surprised that a chicken coop could be made so clean and comfortable . . . even if it wasn't one yet. He noticed there weren't as many magic things as Mrs. Griffin would have in the future, and that what charms and trinkets there were could pass for just ordinary stuff, unless you knew their true meanings. But even in this time she had owned all kinds of books. Naturally there was no TV. There was no lucky-skull either. Besides the small table and two straight-backed chairs, there was a big brass bed and an ancient rocker—the same rocker that was now out on Number One's porch. A little Emerson radio sat on top of a chest of drawers next to a framed picture of Lucianne and a young man in an Army uniform. Both the soldier and the girl looked very happy. Corbitt knew that picture though it had faded a lot over the years. It still sat on that selfsame chest, now in Number One, flanked in the future by those of President Kennedy and Martin Luther King, and surrounded by others of her favorite Bridgeend kids including himself, Lamar, and Toby and Sherry playing together on the riverbank. Corbitt walked to it across the oval of rag carpet.

Lucianne watched him. "Michael's in Korea now, but he gonna be home for Christmas."

Corbitt felt a chill. Michael Griffin had never come home from that war! Corbitt remembered his dad talking about how hard it had been for blacks in the military then. They couldn't just be as good as whites, they always had to be better, as if fighting for the privilege to fight and die for a country that treated them like picture negatives. Corbitt noted the sergeant's stripes on Michael's shoulder, recalling his dad saying how hard-won they had to have been in those days. His nose went crinkly in sadness. Then confusion followed: Lucianne had just said that Michael would be coming home. Did that mean she didn't know what was going to happen? And yet, if she didn't know that, how was she able to recognize him here in the past? If he was really making up the laws of this place he wasn't doing a very good job of it. He suddenly realized where the money must have come from that had enabled Mrs. Griffin to buy the motor court from the Tates. If Michael Griffin hadn't been killed, there would never have been a Bridge-end. Turning to Lucianne, Corbitt said softly, "I spect you miss him a lot."

Lucianne smiled as she worked on the fish. "A lot, son."

"I . . . I dream him back if I could."

"I know you would, Corbitt. An thank you." She looked up at a feed-store calendar thumbtacked above the sink. Corbitt saw that the month was July. Lucianne smiled again. "But it a long time till Christmas, son."

Corbitt touched the face of the picture. "Do all things happen for a reason, Miz Griffin?"

"That be goin mighty deep, son. I always just kinda figure all things be connected in some way. Things happen an cause other things to happen. Like throwin a pebble into the river. Ripples spread out in all directions. If there a reason for it, spect only God know."

"But, Miz Griffin, if I doin all this in my own mind, then maybe all that niggerboy stuff Miz Tate pull on me just come out some ole book I read?"

"Well, you got her down to a tee, son. An, far as I know, nobody never put her in no book."

Corbitt moved to the cabin's back window and stared across the river. Bates's lower field lay fallow. "Then I oughta be able to change some wrong things. Make 'em so they never was."

Lucianne paused with a fish in her hand and regarded Corbitt seriously. "Don't y'all go givin yourself airs of power, little negro. You forgettin what I been tryin to teach you bout messin with stuff, not knowin. Just cause you don't set out to make magic on purpose don't mean you can't accidentally stir up a spell or two. Ripples in the river, son. Throw enough things in a pot an there a good chance you gonna brew *somethin*. Onliest trouble with that is you never know how it gonna taste." Setting down the fish, she came to Corbitt and turned him gently from the window. "I know what inside that skull of yours now, boy. You listen to me good. You ain't got nowhere near the power nor experience to try takin on evil like that! Bates be the reason

even good whitefolks got trouble sleepin at night round here.
Take you another look at that calendar, boy. Bates catch y'all
fishin his pool today, best you believe there be a lot more'n rock
salt in that ole shotgun!"

Corbitt looked into the young woman's eyes. They seemed
to have aged years. Beyond the window, the opposite shore
seemed to darken as if a cloud had passed across the sun. Corbitt
shivered. "I . . . I believe you." He tried to put all thoughts
of the man out of his mind. Maybe, one day, when he was
ready . . .

"Um, so how you know where I catch me them fish?"

Lucianne studied Corbitt's face a moment more, then seeming satisfied, smiled and returned to the sink. "Onliest pool for
miles where the cats grow this size. Spect a lot of stuff drift
down to that bend. An Bates never let nobody near it."

Corbitt shook his head. "Some things never gonna change!"

Lucianne sliced a fish from throat to tail. "Things always
change, son. When enough people get together an change 'em.
Corbitt, you got to understand we talkin life an death over us
in these times. Folks *disappeared*, son, even a few good whites.
An *children*, Corbitt! An weren't nobody gonna ask no questions!
You seen Bates comin in them days, not only you step far aside,
you run an hid an pray to God he never took no notice of you!"

Corbitt's eyes narrowed to slits. "That BASTARD! Does
God take him into account too?"

"Yes, son. He does. But that ain't gonna do you much good
while you walkin this earth as flesh an blood."

"An just what color be God, Miz Griffin?"

Lucianne looked to the sunlit doorway. "I always think myself He be like a kind of clear light. A color what ain't of this
Earth. Maybe like silver-black."

"*White* light, you meanin!"

"Mmm. Now wasn't you the one explained to me once how
white light really made up from all the colors of the rainbow? A
scientific fact. Me, I always figure everthing in this world be
exactly the color it oughta."

Corbitt went to the door and stood in the sunlight. The
countryside stretched bright and clear to the west. He could see
details of the distant hills he'd never noticed before. Out on the
road a battered old Studebaker stake truck rattled past. Over-

alled black men and a few boys, some younger than himself,
were packed in the back. They already looked tired. Corbitt
watched the truck slow for the bridge, headed for a long, hot
day in some field downriver. He wondered if those people ever
thought of their next-things. His eyes shifted back to the big
Corbitt parked on the gravel. "Spose I could see Mr. Rudd fore
I go home? I never heard his truck run afore, an I know now I
ain't never gonna for real."

Lucianne was rinsing the fish under the sink's single faucet.
"Spect y'all could, if that what you want. He treat you nice.
Always was that way."

"Yeah. Prob'ly pat my woolly head an let me shine his
reflectors."

"Might give you a ride up the road a ways. Hear tell he
headed clear out for California today."

Corbitt's throat tightened as he gazed at the big gleaming
truck. Then he sighed. "It ain't worth it. Not now, when I know."

"Mmm. He hurt you bad, didn't he, son?"

"Yeah. An the funny part be he believe in his heart he doin
me a kindness."

"But you know that now, Corbitt. An you ain't never gonna
be fooled by his kind again. Gettin your dreams stepped on an
your trust betrayed gotta be the most hurtinest thing in this life,
son. But you can't never stop dreamin nor givin your trust where
you believe. Stop dreamin an tryin to trust, an you start hatin.
First it the whites cause you figure you can't never trust none
of 'em. But, pretty soon, you start hatin your own color folks
cause you figure they lettin you down somehow . . . not tryin
hard enough, an makin you look no-account right along with
'em. An then come the time when you begin hatin your ownself,
cause you only born a nigger so what the use in dreamin."

Corbitt nodded. "Yeah. I sho nuff been thinkin bout that.
But, goddammit, it *do* seem so hard to trust 'em."

Lucianne's eyes crinkled at the corners. "Even Toby?"

"Huh? Oh, *that* a 'tirely nuther thing."

"Mmm. Find yourself a silver crow, did you, son?"

"Spose. I *know* where Toby be comin from."

"He prove himself to your satisfaction, did he, boy? Maybe
when he got beat up a few dozen times, or covered in shoe polish
defendin your little African honor?"

Corbitt frowned. "No, dammit! That ain't what I sayin! Toby never had to prove nuthin to me! He just . . . well . . . he just IS, that all!" Corbitt stared at the truck. "Even when I shove him yesterday, an call him names, I knowed inside I was wrong, but it was like Mr. Rudd set me against him . . . 'gainst my own brother!"

Lucianne spread the fish on a big platter and covered them with a cloth. "Little warrior, I think y'all found what you come for."

Corbitt turned and looked around the room once more. "So, all this *was* true, huh? Spose if I went up to Starkville I gots to ride the back of the bus?"

Lucianne nodded. "An sit in the back of the movie-house, an go to the back of every line with whitefolks in it, or step aside for 'em even you been standin in that selfsame line for hours. An forget bout the ice cream shop. Come to think on it, I can't think of noplace you could go in an sit down for a soda, tho most business be happy to serve you out the back door."

"Yeah. Spose money gots no color."

"Here it does. All the money you could dream yourself up right now wouldn't buy you a single night's rest in one of them cabins out there."

"But you just tellin me Miz Tate a good white person."

"I said, as good as she *can* be, Corbitt. Special with Bates just cross the river."

"Well, if Toby was here now, best you believe he go right to the back of them lines with me an Lamar an Sherry. Yes he would!"

Lucianne smiled sadly and shook her head. "Toby just couldn't exist here an now, Corbitt. It like you tellin me bout other planets . . . the air just couldn't support a life like his, no more'n you could live an breathe underwater. This be one dream you two could never share. Here an now you can't even go to the same school."

"It was like they never want us to know each other."

"Well, give that boy a cee-gar. It easy to make you hate people you can't never get to know. So you see, some things do change, son. But there still a lot of them tryin to keep you an Toby apart. An don't never go forgettin that some black minds be thinkin that way too."

"I spect that make Toby a warrior."

"Well, how many more dragons he got to slay to prove that to you?"

Corbitt smiled. "Seem like he done killed a passel more dragons than me already. Maybe that make him more African than me."

"Mmm. Well, you still got your share ahead of you, boy. But, like it or not, 'African' take on a whole new meanin in a age of jet planes an space shuttles an 'puters."

Corbitt's smile faded. "Don't seem like knowin bout all that stuff gonna do me much good round here . . . or forty years from here."

"Well, it a big world, Corbitt. An y'all been freed."

"Would you be tellin me that if this wasn't a dream?"

"Ask me that when you wide awake with your eyes open, boy." Lucianne took a big frying pan down from the wall. "Now, bout that breakfast?"

Corbitt stayed in the doorway. "Thanks, Miz Griffin. But I spect I should be gettin back an doin me some real-life fishin. Maybe there still some of them big cats left."

"Best you remember ole Bates still got a few teeth left. You three little Africans get your butts full of rock salt, don't come cryin to me to magic it out." Lucianne set the pan on the stove and rubbed in a finger of bacon grease. "Ain't you gonna wait round for your dollar?"

Corbitt grinned. "Naw. You take it, Miz Griffin. Spect a whole dollar still buy considerable much these days."

"Mmm. But not near what it used to."

Corbitt was about to step out the door. Suddenly he froze in amazement. He pointed. "Miz Griffin! Look! That . . . that ME!"

Lucianne laughed as she came up behind Corbitt and stood watching with him as a willowy midnight-black boy clad only in faded overalls walked around the front of the truck. And there was Mr. Rudd, just as he looked in his old picture, swinging a canvas satchel into the cab. The man smiled and said something to the slender boy, who beamed with pleasure at Mr. Rudd's friendliness. The man patted the boy's head.

Corbitt scowled. "I *knowed* he was gonna go an do that! Prob'ly give me a goddamn quarter now too. Or a nickel. Or whatever he give good little niggerboys back then. Shit, I was stupid!"

Lucianne laid a hand on Corbitt's shoulder. "Ain't nobody born to the tricks of this world, son. Fool me once, shame on you, fool me twice, shame on *me*." She touched the little black feather behind Corbitt's ear, then turned to glance at the calendar. "But that ain't you, Corbitt, tho I can't deny he was so much like you. His name was Weylen. Don't know why I still recollect the date, but it was today, in 1951, when he show up here long bout this mornin hour."

Corbitt watched, fascinated, as Weylen came ambling toward Mrs. Griffin's cabin as if he knew his next-thing was going to be breakfast. But then Corbitt realized that naturally he would expect blackfolks to be living behind the whites. Despite what Mrs. Griffin had said, it wasn't until the boy got closer that Corbitt was satisfied he wasn't seeing himself. For one thing Weylen packed more muscle, even on his slender frame. He'd been used to real work. And maybe he had a trifle more confidence in his walk, as if he'd seen a lot of life and knew how to stay in his place while still enjoying it. There was a foxiness behind his features, like he'd risk a raid on Bates's pool even today. He knew he'd been freed. A warrior. Corbitt knew he'd be able to recognize them the rest of his life.

Then Corbitt turned to Lucianne. "How this be my doin? Miz Tate I hear bout afore . . . be in my subconscious mind. But I never know bout Weylen, so how could I be dreamin him up?"

Lucianne regarded Corbitt a moment, then shook her head. "Mmm. You got me on that one, boy." Her eyes saddened. "He wasn't round here long. Wandered in, had him some breakfast, an I spose just went wanderin on again when the mood take him. All them homeless an unwanted children they gonna be talkin bout in the future ain't nuthin new neath the sun of this world."

Corbitt watched the boy approach. Sure enough, he was flipping a coin in his palm. Corbitt murmured, "Maybe he was on a quest?"

Lucianne gripped Corbitt's shoulder before returning to the stove. "Maybe he was. Funny how I still think bout him so much . . . more lately for some reason." She shook the grate to stir up the coals. There was a wistful note in her voice when she spoke again. "Corbitt? You spect you could stay just a little bit longer?"

Weylen was halfway across the yard now, still flipping the coin Mr. Rudd had given him and whistling happily like a treeful of songbirds. Corbitt had to smile: it was clear Weylen never gave a thought to the next-things in life. "Truth be, Miz Griffin, I got me no idea how to go home anyways. Tappin my heels together three times just don't seem very logical."

Squinting into the sun, Weylen caught sight of Corbitt in the doorway. He stopped, hooked his thumbs in his overall straps, and sized Corbitt up and down. "Mornin, brother," he said.

"Um, hi, man," answered Corbitt.

Weylen cocked his head and grinned. "Well, hi your own-self . . . man. That cat talk. Y'all hep?"

"Huh? Oh. Like hip. I never pay no 'tention to that stuff."

Weylen studied Corbitt's ragged jeans. "Don't spose y'all spare nuthin to eat? I gots me a nickel, or I can work fo it."

Corbitt smiled. "Miz Griffin just fixin some breakfast right now, man. We, um, we see y'all comin."

Weylen grinned. "I jus *knowed* this was a good place, man. Feel it in my bones."

Corbitt stepped into the yard. "Maybe you stay on awhile? Spect Miz Griffin find some work for you."

"I Weylen," said the boy, offering his hand. "Any fish in that river? Maybe you an me can catch us some?"

Corbitt reached for Weylen's hand. "I wish we could, brother, but I gots to be findin my own way home." Their hands clasped.

The Earth dropped out from under Corbitt's feet. Someone called his name from far away, and then he plunged into cold nothingness as empty as space.

14

Beamer's building was like a bad dream. It stood in the center of a half-block of rubble left over from the big earthquake. The crumbling corpses of two other buildings sagged against either side and were probably holding it up. The late-evening light was a dull, ruddy orange, and the buildings were silhouetted against it like some haunted castle crawling with ghosts. In this part of Oaktown it probably was. About the only sign of air-breathing life in the place were dim lights showing in second- and third-floor windows. The ones on the ground were all boarded up, except for a single small slit at sidewalk level with wire-backed glass so grimy you had to look close to see its pale glow. Beamer lived with his dad in the basement . . . if that was called living.

Broken brick steps led up to the door. Lactameon cursed them and climbed them, digging in his pocket for the two keys strung on a piece of purple Nike laces. The first door was a rusty gate of pipe-frame covered with chain-link mesh. The lock swallowed his key and clamped on like a rat bite, refusing to turn or let go. Lactameon cursed and twisted, but then dropped his hands and stood back to chill before he broke the goddamn thing off and got Beamer in shit. There was no real secret to that lock . . . no consistency, no pattern you could ever repeat to get by it. Sometimes it opened instantly, and once he'd stood in the cold winter rain jacking the thing off for fifteen minutes. Beamer didn't have any better luck with his keys, and it was best to get your ass out of town when Beamer's dad tried to unlock it . . .

though once, coming over after school, Lactameon had seen the man sitting on the steps and crying while his son comforted him. Silver was the only one the lock never fought.

Lactameon glanced at the sky once more. It was close to eight now and Beamer was expecting him, so if the goddamn thing gave any more shit he'd go back down and beat on the basement window. The air was still fairly warm, but there was a breeze stirring from the Bay that promised a cold night ahead. The tank-top he still had in his jeans pocket covered almost nothing, and gave even less defense against cold. He mainly carried it for those stupid shoes-and-shirts-required situations at Burger King or KFC. Fat kids weren't supposed to feel cold. Yeah, right! And black kids weren't supposed to feel pain when the pigs twisted their necks or beat their woolly little heads with clubs! He probably should have drive-byed home and snagged his jacket because it would probably be chilly from Beamer's to the clubhouse. But then, after the party, he probably wouldn't give a shit walking home. Moving back to the gate, he tried the lock again. It opened at his touch . . . sneaky little cocksucker! The inside lock didn't put up much of a fight either, and Lactameon made his way up the trash-clogged hall to the basement door.

Shadows and steam surrounded him as he carefully descended the old rotten stairs, keeping his weight close to the wall and wincing as each tread sagged underfoot. Beamer's plan to keep him forever in the basement might really come true someday. The basement had been Beamer's playground when he was little . . . The Neitherworld, they'd called it. Lactameon had seen his first dead body dumped down here: an older boy. But then, when you were six, almost any dude rated as an older boy. Only one pale bulb burned in the darkness, making it hard to see the slimy brick walls. A huge black monster squatted in the middle of the echoing space. A single amber eye stared at Lactameon, and a flicker of flame showed behind sinister teeth. The boiler's piping groped out and upward at all crazy angles like a leftover prop from *Poltergeist*. Its hissing seemed to shift a note, as if it was aware of Lactameon. Sullen flame flared a little brighter behind its toothy fire-door. The amber pilot lamp on the gauge panel seemed to search him out in the shadows. Lactameon never knew if that was a welcome or a warning. He'd always been scared of the thing. He'd supposed he would lose that fear as he grew older, but he hadn't. Still, he forced himself to go through the motions of cool, crossing over to the hot creaking creature to prove something he wasn't sure of. His mom would have called it a ritual. He didn't call it anything, but he always did it anyhow.

The gauge glasses were dim with dust as if nobody ever paid much attention to what they had to say. And what did it mean that those slender needles, spear-tipped on one end and crescent-mooned on the other, always quivered at levels about halfway around the dials? Lactameon had had more than one dream of those needles creeping upward where the black numbers ended and the red ones began. He usually woke sweat-sheened and shaking. He stood now a moment, denying the monster and studying its cobwebby control panel. The numbers on the gauge faces were styled like those of an ancient steam locomotive he'd seen at a park. He would have felt better if they'd had one less zero. The needles twitched, always trying to rise, but something held them down. A few times when Lactameon was little the safety valve had let off with a blast that filled the whole basement with steam. It hadn't done that in a long time now. He hoped it still worked. There was a boiler permit in a grimy-glassed frame. It was recently dated but looked too much like something cut off the back of a Cocoa Puffs box for Lactameon's liking. If someone really did come from uptown once a year to check out the thing he'd never seen them. Beamer's dad was the super. That wasn't a hell of a lot to chill with.

"Yo, Tam!"

Lactameon almost jumped. He spun around, dust swirling from under his Nikes and making him sneeze. Beamer wore only his cutoffs, padding barefoot and panther-silent across the concrete, his little-boy face lit with joy that always made Lactameon feel glad he'd come despite the long walk, shitty hood, and those stairs.

"S'the 411, Beam?"

Beamer's grin faded as he remembered something. "Um . . . I gots to show you this, Tam. Like, you gimme some word."

"Your dad ain't sick again, is he?"

"Naw. He okay. C'mon, man."

Lactameon glanced toward the fan of yellow light spreading

from the doorway of a partitioned-off section at the back of the basement. "Um, so how is your dad?"

"S'cool. He chillin. C'mon."

"So, um, Beamer. How you rate your dad, man? Know what I sayin . . . three out seven, five out seven?"

"Um . . . mean like, always?"

"Yeah."

"Mmm." Beamer fingered his jaw, thinking hard. "Um . . . mean, TV dad, or for-real dad?"

"For real, man. Like, how you rate Stacy's dad?"

"Oh, he a seven for sure."

"Okay. So, how you rate yours?"

"Mmm . . . bout . . . um . . . five. So, what you rate him, Tam?"

Lactameon looked up at the spidery, soot-blackened beams overhead. "I sorta hooked with your little homey today, man. Ethan. When he lose his eye?"

Beamer looked sad. "It fore he come here. He won't talk none bout it." Beamer brightened a little. "But, he savin back for a new one."

"Huh? Jeeze, I didn't know they could do that, man. Shit, bet it gonna cost!"

"Um . . . so how *you* rate my dad, Tam?"

"Six."

Beamer considered that awhile. Finally, he nodded. "Yeah. Maybe you right. Um . . . but, I rate your dad a eight, man. Um . . . sorry what happen."

Lactameon shrugged. "It been a long time ago, man. I don't hardly even think bout him no more. S'cool."

Ruddy flame flared behind the boiler's iron fangs. Old seams squeaked, straining rusty rivets, and the sullen hiss rose to a rumble. Lactameon looked back at the gauge panel where nervous black needles jerked rapidly upward. "Shit, Beamer! It ain't gonna blow that valve again, is it? Fuck, I *hate* when that happens!"

Beamer raised a solemn palm. "Chill, homes." Stepping to the panel, he stood on tiptoes, pushing something, pulling something, and twisting something else. The fire flickered down, and the floor-shaking rumble subsided to a sulky hiss once again.

The needles quit climbing, hesitated, then started to drop. Lac-tameon shook his head.

"Shit, you just bout seen some world-class stair-climbin, man!"

Beamer grinned. "Most been worth it, just seein you run."

"Shit, I ain't tried to run in so long I fuckin forgot how."

Beamer's grin disappeared. "That woulda woke up my dad, an . . . Well, just c'mon." He took Lactameon's arm.

The apartment floor was the same sort of rough, dirty con-crete as the rest of the basement, but hidden here and there by threadbare throw-rugs and ragged pieces of carpet. The inside wall was unpainted plywood and two-by-four studs. The back and side walls were the same ancient brick as the rest of the basement. There was all sorts of furniture; way too much, but nothing that matched, and everything beaten to hell. It had all been salvaged through the years from apartments above. There were even three fridges, though Beamer barely managed to keep one stocked. The air was heavy with Kool smoke and Night Train, backed up by the smells of a boy and his dad. Two sofas sat in the center of the room, both covered by shit-colored Army blan-kets, facing a fairly new Hitachi TV that was tuned low to some black-and-white show with Model A's doing drive-bys with Thompsons. Prehistoric gangbangers. Three coffee tables stood in a row, all piled with crumpled Kool packs, butt-filled ashtrays, magazines, Train bottles, and microwave dinner plates crusted with food. Cockroaches feasted freely, and a trail of ants had set up a permanent route from the wall that nobody ever disturbed. Beamer's dad sprawled snoring on one of the couches. Lacta-meon had never seen the man wear anything but dirty denim coveralls or yellowed boxer shorts. He wasn't in coveralls tonight.

Beamer went to one of the fridges and returned with a twin-pack of Twinkies. "Here, Tam. I score these for you."

"Jeeze, Beamer, you don't gotta do that."

"But, you like 'em, man. Anyways, c'mon."

Lactameon saw a rat's tail sticking out from under one of the couches, but decided not to step on it. Beamer's own tiny room was partitioned in the corner with more splintery plywood. It had a dusty old quilt for a door that Beamer held aside for

Lactameon to enter. As always, Lactameon was surprised at how clean Beamer kept his own den . . . considering. The concrete floor was bare, and swept of dirt and dust-bunnies, leaving nowhere for roaches to hide. Rock and rap posters were taped to the wall, with Stop the Violence stickers stuck here and there. Color pictures cut from magazines took up the remaining wall space; most were of African animals or wild-country scenes. A narrow, iron-framed cot was covered by an ancient but real indian blanket, and there was a funky old chest of drawers that someone had painted shocking pink and which held Beamer's few extra clothes and special things. The glow of a gold-shaded floorlamp made the place almost inviting. A big new blaster— courtesy of some careless uptown kid—and a stack of tapes held an honored place atop the chest. It had been nearly a month since Lactameon had been here, and something new had been added. Against the back wall, below the slit of a high and heavily barred window, stood a battered old baby crib . . . a ghetto-special that had a strip of sheet-metal nailed all around to keep rats from climbing in. Nearby, but beyond rodent range, was a wobbly-legged card table that held an economy-sized pack of Pampers, baby powder and oil, cans of condensed milk, and a Big Bird baby bottle. There was also a book with a colorful cover, but Lactameon didn't stop to scope it, going straight to the crib to see what lay there, armored in tin. Gripping the top rail, he stared down in wonder at a little chocolate-brown boy who seemed peacefully asleep.

At least he supposed it was a boy; the blanket was blue, and it had slid down to show a round tummy and chub-padded chest that looked strong and male. The shoulders and arms seemed to hint at a muscular program. Beamer came up beside Lactameon.

"Um . . . he look okay, huh, Tam? Um . . . maybe seven out seven for a baby-dude?"

"Huh? Oh. Well, shit, man. I don't know much bout babies, but a lotta new moms bring theirs in for readins. Um, this one of the . . . the coolest I ever seen."

Beamer looked relieved. "Shit, thanks, Tam. I was scared he gonna be like me."

"Well, why . . . Shit, Beamer! You sayin he *yours*, man?"

Beamer's finger shot to his lips. "Shhhhh, goddammit!"

"Oh, yeah. Sorry."

"So, you sayin he look okay, huh? Seven out seven . . . for babies?"

"Well, jeeze, man, what I sposed to say? I mean, he look strong an healthy . . . an *clean.*"

"*Course* I keep his ass clean, Tam. An change his Pampers. An feed him reg'lar." Beamer smiled. "He a little fat too, huh? Fat good for babies. An, I burp him, bet your ass!"

"But . . . how you know all that shit, Beamer?"

Beamer pointed to the table. "It all in the book. Ever fuckin thing you wanna know be in books. Just like you say."

Lactameon looked at the big, new glossy-bound book. Its cover showed a blond, blue-eyed mother with smiling child to match. Maybe Winfield had looked like that once. "But you can't read, man!"

"Shush, dammit. S'cool. Gots pitchers of everthin . . . burpin, an Pamper-changin." Beamer grinned. "Never show how them little suckers squirt, man! Find that shit out myself!"

"Um . . . yeah. I seen 'em do that too." Then Lactameon looked back down at the sleeping child. "But, shit, there gots to be a b'zillion things go wrong with babies, man."

Beamer's eyes widened. "Word? Um . . . Maybe you check his ass out?"

Lactameon studied the little boy, afraid to touch. "Well . . . I can't see nuthin wrong with him, man. Fact is, I can't member seein a cooler-lookin kid." He glanced around Beamer's tiny room. "Black kids grow up in Africa in a lot deeper shit than this."

"They do in Oaktown too, man. Even when they crack babies."

"Oh, don't start that shit, man!" Lactameon studied the child once more, then frowned a little. "So, whose baby is it, man? What I sayin is, you didn't find him in a dumpster or nuthin?"

Beamer looked disgusted. "Shit, I just tell ya, Tam! He *mine!*"

Lactameon turned to stare at the lanky, dirty boy, then flicked his eyes back and forth between Beamer and the baby.

Both faces seemed almost identical in their childlike innocence
. . . except one was almost fourteen. Lactameon swallowed. "Oh,
shit. But . . . well, who his mother, man?"

"It not cool for tellin, Tam. Even you."

"Mmm. Well, guess that mean she don't want him, huh?"

Beamer seemed to search his files to find the right words.
"Um . . . more like she . . . she just can't keep him, Tam. Can't
'ford him, what I sayin. I mean . . . she *try*, but it just not
workin out." Beamer looked down at the floor. "See, that what
I tryin tell ya today, man. Bout rubbers . . . an fuckin some
serious shit." Then he lifted his head and set his jaw. "But, he
ain't no little black bastard, man! He gots him a dad!"

Lactameon made himself smile, and touched Beamer's arm.
"Yeah, man. He does. Just like you."

"An, I gonna make him a seven out seven dad, man!"

Lactameon glanced toward the quilt-covered doorway. "So,
how your dad chillin with this, man?"

"Well . . . first I figure he gonna get mega-pissed. But, he
only just look sorta sad . . . shake his head . . . gimme that ole
niggers-won't-have-you thing. Y'know?" Beamer turned toward
the curtain too. "Times he almost a seven, man. It been hard
for him . . . raisin up a goddamn crack baby."

Lactameon sighed. "Yeah. An, he never threw your ass
out." He looked back at the baby. "So, what his name?"

"Last name Brown, course. Like me. But . . . um, I can't
think up no good first name for him. Um, what you figure, Tam?"

"Well, jeeze, Beamer, you gots to name him somethin
pretty soon."

"Um . . . maybe you think of one, Tam? You good at
thinkin."

"This serious shit, Beamer. What I sayin is, you just ain't
namin some dog here, man. This little dude gonna wear it all
his life. A name . . . well, it goddamn 'portant to a dude . . .
specially here. Name don't fit right, other dudes gonna pick
another one. I mean, yours cool, man. You used to bust into
white people's cars. But, then there Lizard, cause of his mouth.
T.K.'s cool . . . Terrance Kinté . . . an he for sure ain't no Terry,
but then there that stupid sucker, Gilligan."

"Um . . . so you sayin, not like a slave name, Tam?"

"Forget that shit, man. I almost did some partyin with Sabby today! That dude could be black as Silver an not rate no African name!"

"Um . . . well, maybe you think on it some, Tam? An, an, maybe you come over soon an read me some of that baby book?" Beamer's forehead creased. "Um . . . you not figure he catch what I gots?"

"Huh? Oh." Lactameon moved from the crib and sat carefully down on Beamer's rickety bed. He wondered if this could have been where the baby was made . . . and then what sort of girl would have wanted to share it with Beamer. He scanned Beamer, almost surprised to find him good-looking despite all the dirt and the unfinished face. Still, it was hard to believe that a girl might have actually loved him . . . not just fucked, but really loved. Well, why in hell not? Beamer had ten toes, ten fingers, nice eyes, and a smile that showed all of him. There was a whole heart in that body, even if something was missing from his mind. So, what happened when crack babies had babies? Maybe it was too soon to tell. Or, was that part of the self-cleaning oven?

"I don't think it catchin, Beamer. Um, *she* didn't do nuthin, did she?"

"Shit, Tam, she not even smoke Kools!"

"Mmm. Well, even sleepin he look smart, man. Maybe he learn how to scope shit four ways."

"Huh?"

"Did she . . . um . . . love you, man?"

Beamer's eyes saddened a little. "I think . . . I think she think she did. Um . . . that sound stupid, man? That a cool girl could love me?"

Lactameon smiled. "Shit, what you talkin bout, sucka? Get out my face."

Gunshots and sirens sounded faintly, but it was hard to tell if they were on TV or in the hood. The little boy stirred beneath his blanket and made baby noises. Lactameon watched, not surprised now at how gently and expertly Beamer took up the boy and comforted him. There would be pictures in the book. It seemed almost natural to see Beamer pick up the bottle and a can of milk. Lactameon followed him out to the kitchen.

"Um, Tam? You figure you hold him for me, man? I gots to open this an then nuke the bottle."

"Huh? Well . . ."

"S'cool, Tam. Here, man, take him like this. He chill when he cuddled."

Before Lactameon knew it Beamer had handed him the baby. Lactameon held it the way he handled the golden-haired china doll his mom kept on her dresser. It had belonged to his great-grandmother in a time when the only storebought dolls for little black girls had been white. Beamer smiled from the sink counter as he punched holes in the milk can and poured it into the Big Bird bottle. "Shit, Tam. He black. You ain't gonna break him that easy."

Lactameon relaxed a little and sat down on the arm of the empty couch. His belly spread like a soft, sooty pillow to rest the chocolate-brown baby on. The little boy wiggled with a strength that surprised him, then went for one of his breasts. Lactameon felt his face flush. "Oh . . . *jeeze*, Beamer! Look what he doin! How I pry him off, man?"

Beamer punched buttons on the microwave, then turned, grinning. "Shit, Tam, he gots no teeth. Can't hurt you none. Sides, he stay quiet that way an not wake my dad. Um, good thing yours go in, stead of out."

Lactameon glanced at the sleeping man on the other couch. "Well, shit! One feel like it gonna be out when he through! Hurry the fuck up!" Then, he turned to study the man. Maybe he wasn't much to look at now, but he'd stayed by his own son. There were lots of men in the hood, but not many you could get close to, and even fewer who touched or really talked to you like you were there and had feelings too. For sure this man had slapped Beamer around a lot, but maybe he *had* really been trying to slap some brains into his son. A long time ago, before Beamer, he'd worked on some big dam in Arizona. That was where Beamer's indian blanket had come from. Sometimes he'd tell stories about the desert, though not much anymore.

The man moved a little, but didn't open his eyes. "Calvin?"

"I here, Dad. Just a minute."

Embarrassed by the baby, Lactameon got up and went back by the sink. The microwave beeped and Beamer took out the warm bottle, then got a cold one of Train for his dad.

15

Falling. Darkness and cold, no air to breathe. Corbitt spiraled downward in eerie slow-motion. His eyes were open, but there was no light to guide him. His outstretched hands found nothing to grasp. Panic chilled him: he'd messed with magic, not knowing, and now he was lost! Then his fingers plunged into soft sliminess and clutched what felt like a bundle of twigs.

River bottom!

The panic disappeared. *You fell off the log, you dumb nigga!* Grinning now, Corbitt pulled his hands from the mud, twisted around, and kicked for the surface. The pressure in his ears told him the pool was deep; deeper than he'd ever imagined. But this was his own friendly old river, and Bridge-end was near. The darkness softened as he rose. Dawn wasn't far off. He broke into swirling silver feathers of early-morning mist and sucked a huge breath of the fresh new day.

"Corbitt! Help!"

Corbitt spun to face the shore, then busted out laughing. Toby and Lamar seemed to be dancing on the log, locked in battle with what had to be the great grandaddy of all catfish, judging from the way Toby's pole bent and bowed. The line whipped savagely to and fro, singing as it sliced the water. Both boys wore frantic expressions and looked more like they were fighting each other than the fish. But a cat that size would mean a fine meal, and Corbitt reached the log with a few strong strokes and scrambled from the river. "Play him, fools! Let him run! He bust the line!"

Toby jabbed Lamar in the ribs with his elbow. "Goddammit! What you think I been tryin to tell this burrhead while y'all taking a motherfuckin bath, man! Lamar! Goddammit! Quit yankin so hard!"

Lamar's face showed only determination. He knew he was stronger than any goddamn fish. Trouble was, Corbitt thought, he would naturally forget about the fragile old line. The pole arced dangerously, and the line twanged like a banjo string. Toby fought to keep Lamar from jerking back on it. "COR-BITT!" he bawled, "DO somethin, dammit!"

Corbitt tried to shove between the two boys, almost knocking everybody into the river. "Don't let him go deep! There stuff on the bottom! He tangle the line!"

"What the fuck you figure I tryin to do?" roared Lamar. "This fool fightin *me!*" He reared back with the pole as the fish tried to dart under the log. Mist sheened his solid brown body.

Corbitt could almost see the old line stretch. "Not that much, man!"

Toby's pale hair hung lank over his shoulders. He tried to shove Lamar's arms down to ease the strain. "CORBITT!"

Corbitt gripped the big boy's shoulder. "Lamar! You gonna bust Toby's arm again!"

That worked like magic. Lamar all but dropped the pole. Corbitt managed to squeeze between the other boys and get a grip too. Once more the pole bowed as the fish dove for the bottom. Corbitt dropped to his knees to give slack, and the other boys followed his lead. Six hands on one pole was awkward, but somehow it seemed natural. The boys leaned forward until the pole's tip dipped under the water. "Shit!" said Lamar. "Can't be *that* goddamn deep!"

"Best believe!" Corbitt muttered, noting his own muddy fingers. "I just shake hands with that bottom!"

The line slacked slightly. "Oh shit!" yelled Toby, "now he gone an tangled in somethin down there!"

"Okay," said Corbitt. "We try an bring the bastard up . . . but slow an careful-like."

Cautiously, the boys raised the pole once more. Again it

bent to a dangerous arc, but then jerked almost straight. "It comin!" cried Toby. "Feel it bust loose!"

Lamar nodded, calmer now. "Yeah. Ole fool gone an outsmart his ownself. Likely tangle in his own trap."

"We ain't won yet, brothers," Corbitt warned. "Together now, but *careful*. Use your goddamn heads!"

Concentrating on the fish, Corbitt hardly noticed the growing rose glow of dawn. Somewhere, not far away, came the sound of an engine, but it barely registered in his mind . . . maybe Lucas starting the White to warm it up. Working together now, the boys brought in the line hand over hand. The mist swirled above the river like ghostly smoke, lapping at their feet. They peered into the dark water as the line shortened. A pale patterned shape began to materialize. Lamar's powerful hands suddenly loosened their grip. His voice cracked. "It that ole bone-cage again!"

"Fuck that!" yelled Toby. "Our fish caught inside 'em! Shit, man, after what we go through last night, y'all ain't gonna let a few ole sheep bones frost your dick!"

Lamar's fingers tightened once more. "Course not!"

Corbitt watched the ribs rise and break surface, but had little interest in the mossy old bones. The huge catfish was struggling inside them like a big black heart. It was even bigger than his dream catch had been! He wondered if Weylen had ever fished here and won such a fight. "You two handle the pole now! Careful-like!" Corbitt lunged forward. "Got him!"

Corbitt snatched the fish from its mossy prison and held it aloft in triumph. "We won, brothers!"

Tangled in line, the bones slipped away to hang suspended just under the surface, but even Lamar ignored them now, gazing and grinning with Toby at the struggling fish in Corbitt's grasp. "Bet your black ass we won, boy!" laughed Lamar.

Then, through the glow of his happiness, Corbitt heard the engine-sound again. His own laughter died in his throat. He froze, clutching the fish cold and slimy and squirming to his chest and seeing the other boys tense too. Corbitt knew that motor . . . an old low-compression four-cylinder with loose rods that rattled. Bates's Jeep! It was idling now just beyond the fringe of riverbank trees! Fear clamped on Corbitt's heart as underbrush crackled. He saw his brothers' eyes go identically wide, but then Toby's slitted in sudden hate.

"Stay cool!" Toby hissed. "We . . . we below the high-water mark, or whatever it called by the law! Ain't nuthin Bates can do to us!"

Lamar's gentle eyes turned hard. "Toby right, man!"

Logic said that too, but Corbitt's own fear seemed to double, as if multiplying itself by years. The mist felt like cottonwool ice on his body. "Them things got no meanin for us! Jump in the river! Swim away!"

"Hold it right there, you little black bastards!"

Toby and Lamar stared up the bank. Slowly, Corbitt turned around. Ten feet away stood Bates's battered brown boots. Corbitt raised his eyes to meet the twin black holes of the shotgun muzzle, and he realized with a shiver that he'd never been so close to the man in his life. A child's panic shot through him, like nightmares from a thousand whispered stories, but nobody dreamed up a bogeyman in broad daylight. Yesterday on the bridge, angry and hurt, Corbitt could have attacked the man with just his bare hands. But now he'd been caught in Bates's world, a place where he had no power.

The gun was a Parker, a century old, crafted when wild geese and turkey were hunted for food. Bates often bragged of its value, but this close Corbitt saw it had been too neglected to be worth much anymore. He remembered his dream, and what Mrs. Griffin had warned, but fought back his fear by reminding himself that Bates could only use rock salt today. Yet, at this range, even salt would be deadly, and both the gun's hammers were cocked.

Above the gun's rusty barrels, Bates's face looked as leathery and creased as his boots. Beneath gray-tufted brows were eyes of the same faded blue as bottles left lying for years in the sun. The old voice was ragged and raspy but sure of its power. "Let it go, boy. Fine fish like that. Ain't fittin it end on some nigra's table."

The catfish was still fighting in Corbitt's grasp, though its struggles grew weaker as it smothered in alien atmosphere. Bates's voice seemed to send echoes through Corbitt's mind, compelling as well as commanding. Corbitt's long fingers loosened.

"No!" There was power in Toby's voice too, even if sounding new-found and uncertain. But it broke Bates's spell. Corbitt's grip tightened again on the fish. He saw the man's eyes flick to the blond boy like some old dragon who sensed a new challenge. They measured Toby a moment, not liking what they saw, then passed over Lamar and peered into Corbitt's again. The raspy old voice came surprisingly gentle.

"You two been freed a long time, boy, but you see how *he* still your master." The faded eyes locked on Lamar, somehow seeming sad. "*That* one born your master, boy. Just like you born to serve him. Don't never go thinkin *he* don't know that."

Hate still glazed the gentle brown eyes, but Lamar's forehead furrowed in thought. Corbitt murmured. "Lamar, you know that ain't so."

"Course I do," came Lamar's quiet rumble. "My folks raise no fools!"

Bates's eyes returned to Corbitt's. They seemed to draw him in as if to share a secret. "Ahh. The smart one. I know all bout you, boy. Top of your class in school. Good-lookin too, spite all that color. But I was never one to believe that ole truck bout color an intelligence. Hell, any fool can see you more'n a field-nigra."

Corbitt's eyes narrowed. "Yeah. In them ole days I be in the house."

There was almost approval in Bates's tone. "Course you would, boy. Likely be a companion for your own master's son." The voice changed then, almost inviting Corbitt to join in contempt. "Y'all ever stop to consider that still what you are?"

For just a second, Corbitt glanced at the blond boy. Bates had *that* much power! But then he spat into the pool and pulled the fish tighter to his chest. "No."

Bates gave a single sad shake of his head, then regarded Lamar. "Hell, boy, I'd think even *you* could see that."

Lamar only snorted.

Bates was silent a moment, then looked back at Corbitt. "Know what happen in them ole days when some master's son went an got too attached to his little black playmate? His daddy put a whip in his hand an made him beat that poor little nigra to a inch of his life. 'Minded both 'em their places in this world. An that exactly what this one gonna do to you someday."

The old voice seemed so sad for Corbitt, wise in the ways of the world, and weary with its wisdom. It conjured a vision in Corbitt's mind, not of being beaten, but of Sherry Cooper, her skin a delicate dusk on the snowy white sheets of Toby's big bed.

Lamar's hands, strong and scarred, had hung loose at his sides. Now they clenched to fists. "Liar!" he roared. "You god-damn ole . . . SNAKE!" He moved forward a step but the gun warned him back.

The vision faded from Corbitt's mind. Sherry too had been freed. She had a right to choose from her options. Behind Bates, the sun cleared the trees. Corbitt blinked in the new golden glow.

"Snake!" Toby echoed, then seemed to consider. "*Lizard!*" he added.

The shotgun had lowered a little. It took a lot of strength to keep such a heavy weapon aimed. But now Bates brought it back up, and his finger curled tighter around the rear trigger while his eyes shifted to Toby in new speculation.

"Maybe I judge you wrong, son. Could be you just a little confused. Spect it weren't easy comin down from the North . . . not knowin the ways round here. Maybe it was just hard for you to make the right kinda friends."

Toby moved close to Lamar. "Weren't hard a'tall, ole fool!"

Bates's face turned ruddy, and his voice shrank to the tone of an old man who cursed crows. "Boy, can't you see it natural these nigras want you with 'em? You like some kinda symbol . . . some kinda god!"

Toby's mouth dropped open. But then he gripped Lamar's shoulder and burst into laughter. "Hey, bro, y'all know you busted *God's* arm?"

For a moment, Lamar looked like somebody had tickled him in church. His cheeks puffed, but then his own laugh boomed out. Lion laughter. Tiger laughter. And Corbitt joined in. The three jungle cats once again. The sound seemed like magic, sharper than spears. Bates flinched back as if slapped. The shotgun jerked straight, but Corbitt only chuckled. "Ole fool, y'all just lost it. Trash-talk like that don't work on real brothers."

Bates's eyes slitted beneath their gray brows. His finger

twitched on the trigger. "All you done is prove me right! Ain't but three little smart-mouth niggraboys standin here! An not all you together worth the price of spit to me! Y'all just dirt! I *walk* on dirt!" He stamped a foot. "Dirt don't rise up an trouble me!" He glanced down. "An, this here *my* dirt, an you little black bastards trespassin it!"

Corbitt's gaze drifted across Bates's empty field. Long after slavery that land had still been tended by blacks. Over forty years under Bates's power, and it had produced nothing. Corbitt saw the finger still tight on the trigger. Bates *wanted* to kill them. Forty years ago he would have. Maybe some things *had* changed, even if damn few and too slowly. Corbitt looked upstream. The mist still hid the cabins, and the bridge's iron skeleton was only half visible through it. The men would have already left for their work. The women would be inside doing breakfast dishes while the children watched cartoons. What would Sherry be doing? *Not important now!* Lucas would be getting ready to leave, wondering where his son was. Likely he'd walk out on the bridge to call Lamar any time now. Corbitt's eyes turned back to Bates and the gun. How much power did the old man have left? The law? Trespassing? Bates had never even posted his property, always confident in his aura of fear.

Seconds slipped past as Corbitt scanned those faded blue eyes. Was there a flicker of uncertainty? Maybe the real question was what did Bates *think* he could do? For all Corbitt's life the man had been a figure of fear to the Bridge-end children, but now he seemed just a stupid old fool who had hidden for years behind a curtain while his puffed-up image threatened from a big-screen TV. The man would have to be crazy to think he could kill them. This wasn't 1951 anymore.

The mist was thinning beneath the new sun, but even if Lucas had been on the bridge it was too thick to see what was happening here. Corbitt's mind searched for options: he and his brothers could jump in the river. Bates would probably fire the rock salt . . . pride would make him do that. But he would wait until the range was safe. Corbitt's mind focused on fine points . . . all were strong swimmers, they might even make the opposite shore underwater . . . and would the man even dare shooting Lamar so soon after what happened with Guppy? Corbitt could almost feel the salt blast into his own back, cutting deep to burn and leave scars. Bates would likely shoot Toby, too. But, logic said that would be about all the power left in him. Corbitt felt the fish quiver against his chest. With luck he might even keep it, and the three jungle cats would have won!

Bates noticed the fish, and a new expression came over his face as if he'd also been counting his options. "Right smart bunch of niggraboys here."

Lamar spat in the pool. "You stop callin us that, ole man!"

But Bates only gave the big boy a glance. "Best *you* shut your mouth, boy. You forgettin I know your daddy well, just like I knowed your grandaddy before him. Never had no trouble with you Sampsons, an I spect your folks want to keep it that way."

Bates's voice had dropped low, but somehow that made it more menacing. His words slipped past Corbitt's shoulder like little snake tongues. When Corbitt turned to Lamar he saw only a boy and not a man-child. Then the voice took a new tone, seeking Corbitt's frequency.

"Ah, the *smart* one. Don't think I don't know what goin through that skull of yours, boy. Y'all thinkin you clever. Y'all figurin you learnin our rules, gonna beat us someday. Trouble is, you forgettin who *make* the rules, boy. An them that make 'em can change 'em!"

Corbitt's eyes flicked upriver. How much longer before Lucas came looking for his son?

Bates shifted his own gaze to the bridge for a second. "I think I gettin to know you a lot better, boy. You the kind end up hurtin your own people more'n we could ever hope to do."

Corbitt's body stiffened. The man showed long yellow teeth in what passed for a smile. "An I bet you ain't even figured out why!"

Corbitt faced the old man, somehow fascinated. His voice broke. "W . . . what you sayin?"

Bates's smile widened. Cradling the gun in one arm, he lifted his free hand and touched a finger to his forehead. "You carry the past with you, boy. There somethin you keepin alive in your bones . . . somethin dead an forgot by your people a long time ago. They don't know what it is no more, but they'll see it in you. They'll want to follow, but you don't know how to lead . . . ain't fit to lead . . . cause whatever you was, you'll never be again."

Corbitt shook his head. Was it possible that Bates had said this thing? But Toby reached past Lamar to grip Corbitt's shoulder. "Don't listen to him, man! It just crazy talk! C'mon! Let's go! He can't stop us!"

Bates gripped the gun two-handed once more. "Shut up, yella fool! Think *you* got it all figured out? Maybe trespassin don't carry the punishment it warrant no more, but tell me how the law gonna look on you three big bucks gangin up on a poor ole white man? Seem like that all you hear bout nowadays, nigraboys gangin together."

"What?" Toby cried. "Nobody believe such a lie!"

Bates's lips curled back. "Won't they, boy? You sayin nobody believe Lamar Sampson don't harbor a grudge cause I had to protect myself from his wild little brother? You sayin nobody believe Corbitt Wainwright ain't out for 'vengin his daddy?"

Bates was watching Toby's face. The man had forgotten Lamar. He *knew* Lamar. But lions didn't always roar before attacking. Suddenly, Lamar charged past Corbitt, ducked under the long gun, and drove his solid bulk into Bates, locking his arms around the man and slamming him backwards. Lamar's toes dug deep in the earth as he struggled to bring the man down. Bates staggered back, fighting for balance, throwing his arms up so the shotgun aimed skyward. Time seemed almost to freeze.

Corbitt heard Toby yell a curse or a challenge. His own muscles tensed for attack. Other voices seemed to echo in his mind, screaming in fury and rage. But he couldn't move! Toby shoved past him, blue eyes narrowed to thunder-sky slits, teeth bared in a snarl and blond hair blazing in the sun. Then Corbitt flung the fish in the river and leaped for the bank behind Toby. Cheetahs were faster than tigers!

But seconds had been lost. Alone against Bates, even Lamar's strength wasn't enough. Corbitt was at Toby's side, almost on the man, when Bates slammed the iron-shod gun butt down on Lamar's skull. Lamar made a sound like a sigh, and slid to the ground at Bates's feet.

Bates snapped the gun straight, stopping the other two boys

a foot from the muzzles. Corbitt saw real fear in the faded old eyes. Bates backed away, safe beyond reach of Lamar's hands, even though they lay quiet now on the carpet of leaves. Blood seeped through Lamar's bushy hair. Fury flamed in Corbitt, all the more intense because he was helpless once again. He gleamed with sweat, but the fire seemed to sear his own bones, now that he could do nothing. Toby trembled beside him. Corbitt could feel the blond boy's rage radiate outward. *We were all Africans, once!*

Corbitt couldn't hear the voices anymore. The only sounds in the universe seemed to be Toby's panting and Bates's wheezy gasps. Corbitt's rage began to cool. A new thought chilled the fire inside him . . . *one second sooner and they might have won! Cheetahs were born to be fast. The cheetah-prince had frozen in his first real battle!*

Corbitt's eyes flicked to Toby, but the blond boy was staring down at Lamar. Then, together, both boys started to kneel beside him. Corbitt saw movement in Lamar's broad back . . . not much, but he seemed to be breathing steadily, even with his face buried in leaves. Corbitt reached to lift Lamar's head, but Bates had caught his own breath.

"Get back!" Bates rasped. The shotgun threatened. Slowly, Corbitt and Toby rose to their feet and moved backward toward the river. The shotgun jabbed the air, forcing them on to the edge of the shore. Only then did Bates come forward, cautiously. He glanced down, nudging Lamar's shoulder with the toe of his boot. Maybe the boy stirred slightly, Corbitt wasn't sure, but Bates seemed satisfied and moved away.

"All your skulls thick as cement," said Bates. "Everyone know they can't hurt you there." He studied Toby and Corbitt with new speculation. "I was you, I wouldn't be worryin bout him. Not now. Seem like the truth don't got to be stretched at all no more. Does it?"

Corbitt turned to Toby, half expecting to see an accusing look in his eyes, but the sunlight shone in them and he could read nothing there. Corbitt turned farther, seeing something through the river mist. Below the angled logs, the big catfish floated belly-up on the pool's quiet surface. Unlike Lamar, whose ribs expanded for breath now and then, there was no movement.

The big fish's black-and-white body was borne in slow circles by the current flowing through the pool.

Bates lowered the gun and spoke Corbitt's name. It seemed wrong for the man to say it, like it was giving him more power. "The smart one. The book-reader. Leader of niggers long dead! An now he gone an turn wild, just like his daddy!"

Bates showed his grisly smile once again. "An *you*, little yella fool! Seem like to me you got a touch of that ole tar brush somewhere inside you." Bates's eyes found the fish. "Now ain't that a waste? Tell me, Corbitt Wainwright . . . *boy* . . . how y'all gonna keep stealin food for your mammy when you up for a spell in the county boys' farm?" Bates glanced down at Lamar. "Sure gonna break ole Lucas's heart, with his big fine first son right in there with you. An, Toby, nigger-lovin, Barlow. Spect your own folks won't be feelin so high an mighty no more when you hoein the rows right longside your 'friends'! Fact is, I spect y'all gonna make yourself a whole passel of new 'friends' on that farm, boy . . . niggers what ain't had 'em no pale-haired pets before. Might just find they got a whole different kind of hankerin after white meat!" Bates wet his lips with his tongue. "Wouldn't mind watchin what they likely do to you after lights-out, boy. Give a whole new meanin to 'brotherly love.' "

Confident again in his power, the old man let down the gun and leaned on it casually. The muzzle sank into the leaves. The faded eyes shifted to the fish for a moment, and a different expression crossed the leathery face. "Spect it just now startin to sink in . . . all the trouble gonna rise from this. Almost seem a goddamn shame, don't it? All that trouble over one ole catfish."

Corbitt sensed something . . . a next-thing feeling. He saw new uncertainty in Toby's eyes, too. Bates seemed to be watching them carefully. Corbitt felt the man's gaze slip over his body, and thought again of snake tongues. When Bates spoke there was a strange huskiness in his tone.

"Yeah, boys, a whole world of trouble over one little ole fish." The man seemed to consider. "Course . . . might be . . . just might be we could work us somethin out. Might be, Lamar Sampson here just go on home in a while with a little ole headache . . . seem that poor boy take enough punishment for you all, an I spect he learn his lesson. An, you two . . . just might not be no need for botherin the sheriff over some silly little mistake any big healthy boys could make." Bates smiled. "Fact is, boys your age of bout any color sometimes get feelins inside 'em an just go a little wild. Times they do things without thinkin. Secret things sometimes . . . things what never get told."

The sun was clearing the trees at Bates's back, but Corbitt felt little warmth in it. The sweat on his body had chilled. Even his bones felt cold. A new evil faced him. The cheetah-prince had already failed his first test.

Corbitt's voice came from low in his throat. "What the deal, ole man?"

Toby spoke, "The selfsame deal he try on Guppy!"

Bates only smiled. "Now didn't I say you was smart ones? Corbitt, boy, just y'all go back down there an hook yourself that fish. No use in lettin good things go to waste."

Corbitt turned back to the pool. Was there a movement? He watched. Seconds passed. Yes! The long body quivered.

"Best hurry, boy!" Bates warned. "Look like he wakin up!"

Toby started to move to the log, but Corbitt gripped his shoulder. "No, brother."

Bates cocked his head. "Pride a awful foolish thing for a nigra to have, boy."

Suddenly, the big fish flipped itself over and disappeared downward. Corbitt tightened his hand on Toby's shoulder. "I couldn't give such a thing to my mom. Not now."

Toby nodded, then his chubby face hardened. "I go with Bates. Do what he want, man. That best for Bridge-end."

"Toby the tiger," Corbitt murmured. Then he shook his head. "No, brother. I gots to do this."

"Corbitt, why? Ain't we still the three jungle cats? No matter what happen?"

"Course. An that why I got to do it." Turning away before Toby could answer, Corbitt faced the man. "I go with you. Just me. Let Toby stay with Lamar."

Bates scowled. "Y'all ain't in no position to bargain, boy."

Corbitt's slim chest expanded. His long back straightened. His voice came with a strength that surprised him. "Then, best you go call up the sheriff, ole man. You reachin the end of your power." Without waiting, Corbitt turned once more to Toby. "Get our poles, man. Help Lamar home. Figure up somethin to say to his daddy." *Another goddamn secret!*

Bates lifted the gun, but stayed silent as Toby descended the log. Lamar stirred slightly on the ground, and the old man edged farther away from him. Both Bates and Corbitt watched as Toby knelt down and pulled up the bones to untangle the line.

Toby cried out. Corbitt froze in horror. Stark in the sunlight it was instantly clear what the moss-covered bones were! Something made Corbitt lift his eyes to Bates's lower field . . . unplowed and forgotten for the last forty years. Mrs. Griffin's words echoed in his mind . . . *folks disappeared. An, children!*

As in Corbitt's dream, the sunlight seemed to fade over Bates's field. Corbitt stared back at the dripping bones. How long had they lain there, waiting for this next-thing? Their structure was small, slender and fine: they could have been Corbitt's own. Then, a new thought, even more terrible . . . *Weylen!* Corbitt tried to imagine the torture, lying unburied for all those years in the darkness and cold while other children laughed and played and sent their ripples of life through the water.

Bates's voice cut the silence, edged with fear and something else Corbitt couldn't name. "You! Bring that! Both of you! Get over here with it!"

The mist had all but vanished now, and Bates cast an uneasy glance toward the bridge. Toby reached the bank with the bones, staring at them, eyes wide. Corbitt slipped the rib cage from Toby's unresisting fingers. The bones seemed icy cold, but Corbitt held them close to his own chest.

Bates shifted nervously, cradling the gun in one arm while feeling in the pocket of his old Carhart coat where he likely carried more shells. He glanced down at Lamar again. Corbitt saw that the man was afraid. Bates stayed clear of Lamar's reach while moving around and backing the other two boys toward the curtain of willows that shrouded the road. Only when they were all standing in leafy shadow did the old man relax slightly. "Smart ones!" he muttered. "Too goddamn clever by half!"

Bates threw a glance over his shoulder to make sure Lamar hadn't moved. "Well, you ain't beat us in all these years, an y'all so far behind now you ain't never gonna!" The old man's lips twitched in another grisly smile. "That's one of the secrets, boys. We always keepin watch on you! We take out you smart ones, like takin out culls. We even got you doin it for us these days! More an more, case you don't follow the news!" Bates laughed, dry and raspy. The faded eyes focused on Corbitt. "Shame you can't keep on livin, boy. You the kind do our best work for us! Your kind give out hope when there ain't none . . . hope that only turn to hate in the end. You leave a trail of dead niggers wherever you go, boy, not even knowin you do it! Just like you doin it now!"

The broken concrete felt cold under Corbitt's feet as he and Toby edged ever backward. It was almost as if they moved backward in time. Corbitt found he was clutching the bones as if they could shield him.

Toby's voice quavered on the border of breaking. "You . . . you crazy, ole man!"

Strangely, Corbitt was no longer afraid. He felt only sorrow to have failed once again. His voice sounded toneless, uncaring, even in his own ears. "Course he crazy. All them secrets." Corbitt leveled his eyes at the man; pride was a foolish thing for a nigger to have, but what did that matter anymore. "Spect even *you* don't dare this ground after dark. You hear 'em, don't you?"

Bates's eyes widened for an instant. "You got no power over me in life, boy. Why be afraid of you dead?" He made a jab with the gun, grinning when Corbitt jumped back and slammed into a tree. Corbitt still held the bones to his chest, and Bates laughed again.

"Oh, I member that one, boy. He coulda been you!" Bates looked around. "Was right here in this road I kill him. Same mornin hour. An he doin the same thing as you . . . stealin what rightfully mine . . . just like you an your kind steal it all if we let you! Weren't no time to bury him proper . . . with the others. These here trees wasn't so thick then, an this road still in use. So I put him in the river. We done that, boy . . . sent your bodies floatin down past the fields an towns to show there was a power keepin watch!" Again, Bates laughed. "Oh, he coulda been you!"

Corbitt didn't know where the words came from. They weren't even the right ones because the real words were in a language that was stolen from him long ago. "He *is* me! I'm him! Goddamn you to hell!"

Fear showed again in Bates's eyes. He jerked the gun to his shoulder. "He curse me that same way, boy! But it done him no good, just like it do you no good!"

Toby took Corbitt's hand, gripping it tight. Corbitt whispered, "I sorry, brother." He stared into the shotgun bores. Suddenly, he saw a chance!

"Run, Tobe!"

The shotgun roared. Corbitt was blinded by a huge flash of fire. Something smashed into his chest. His head cracked back against the tree trunk.

Darkness.

16

The gunshot woke him. Lactameon's eyes snapped open to moon-silvered city-glow seeping through the sweaty window glass of his room. Echoes of the blast seemed to linger in his mind. It had been close; maybe right down in the alley below, and the way his ears still seemed to be ringing, had been loud enough to wake the dead. Pigs liked using their shotguns in the hood . . . a nice quick kick for some niggaboy, and no stories told later on. Nobody around here paid much attention to gunfire in the night, but a blast like that should have woken the whole goddamn building.

Lactameon lay there a moment, expecting to hear his mom get up and come down the hallway past his door to look out at the bathroom window. At least she still tried to help people. Lactameon waited. Nothing. She wasn't exactly a light sleeper, but a blast like that should have carried clear over to Emeryville.

Lactameon sat up before he remembered he was drunk. Well, not that drunk, at least anymore. Funny, that for the first half-minute after waking his mind had been as clear as KSOL on new blaster batteries, but now he felt as righteously fucked as he should be after drinking for most of the night. He glanced at the crimson numbers of his clock: 3:37. He rubbed his eyes, then wiped steam from the window and peered out. The building across the alley was silent and dark. Was everybody fucking deaf, or had the gun-blast been all in his head? He listened hard, but there were no other sounds except the scream of a distant siren, headed away.

Lactameon lay down and pillowed his head on his arms. He couldn't remember what time it had been when he'd gotten back from the gang party, but then he barely remembered leaving the party, much less walking home. He discovered he was still wearing his bandana. He left it on. He'd for sure earned the right to wear it any goddamn time he wanted. It was a part of him now and a part of what made this summer so different from the past ones. Things changed; some changes you saw right away, and some came slinking up on you. He fingered the sweat-stiffened cotton around his head. It was funny that he couldn't tell his brothers how he'd been ready to die instead of taking it off. For sure Hobbes wouldn't have shot him but he hadn't *known* that, so it came down to the same thing.

He switched on his bedside lamp and gazed up at the pattern of light cast by the shade on the ceiling above. He wasn't sleepy at all now. Maybe it was the moon? His mom always said that a full moon stirred unburied bones and brought visions to those who could see. But maybe that was just a bunch of spooky talk for the customers. The moon's pull did make tides in the Bay, he knew, and it probably pulled on a forty-ouncer too, except that effect would be too small to see. He'd read that a human body was supposed to be about ninety percent water, so why shouldn't the moon pull on people too? Pushing down the blankets, he patted his belly and watched it ripple. A lot there to pull. He glanced at the clock again. It was a long time yet till morning.

Shoving the blankets all the way off, Lactameon eased from the bed and cautiously stood up. Yeah, he was still pretty fucked, but it was the good kind. Going to the door, he opened it a crack and peered out. He remembered watching Toni this way when she'd come in for a reading just after school ended. That memory seemed to be clearer each time he pictured it; her full-figured profile on that chair over there, leaning forward with her elbows on the table while his mom rolled the bones. Toni always wore those huge Cross Colours T-shirts that covered too much of what you wanted to see, but the big, rounded shapes of her breasts had suggested a lot of good things that day. He recalled how the candle-glow had flickered over her dusky face and the tiny gold sparkles in her curly, sheened hair.

Familiar warmth spread through his loins. Sooty Jimmy couldn't sleep either. Buried by blackness, he struggled to rise. Well, that was his problem. Lactameon wasn't having any of that shit right now. The small living room was dark, and no light shone from under the door to his mom's room across it. Maybe there really hadn't been a shotgun blast? Years of practice had mapped the squeaky board floor like a minefield, and Lactameon knew just where to step. His mom didn't really mind a midnight drive-by on the Kenmore, but she'd come out of her room with a baseball bat if she heard any noise. She was big, and Lactameon was prouder than hell of his mother, but he didn't want to meet her right now. He'd scoped Sooty Jimmy enough in the mirror for two years to know how his head would be poking from under the twin moons of blubber that usually hid him from sight. If there was a brain in that head, it had a one-track mind. Nobody but Beamer knew Jimmy's name, but then it was Beamer who'd named him. The dudes all knew him from occasional appearances at clubhouse parties when rooftop temperatures and forty-ouncers made clothing uncool, but then they kept no secrets either. It was funny that the only other person who'd seen Sooty Jimmy goin on had been the Leopards' whiteboy, Winfield.

Lactameon and Winfield had been buzzed by a sixer of Big Mouths last summer, and had taken their chill to the pool. Someone had left the padlock open on the filter-pump shed for the first time in history. Slipping inside to scope the place out seemed the natural thing to do. There hadn't been much: a rough concrete floor, a murmuring gray machine, and the strong scent of chlorine. The tin walls were hot from the sun, but both boys were still soaked from a swim, and the dim-lit interior seemed almost cool after stark white cement and eye-stabbing glare off the water. Lactameon remembered sunbeams slanting through cracks and spotlighting drifting dust motes. Outside was laughter and splashing and shouts, but somehow they seemed far away. Neither of them had really been drunk, so that couldn't have been an excuse. But Lactameon was sure that neither had known what they were going to do. Maybe it had just been because a couple of city kids had discovered one of those few places where they could be alone, and had to do *something* there? If they'd had cigarettes they might have just kicked-back and smoked. Sometimes Lactameon wished they'd just smoked, and sometimes he was glad that they hadn't, and sometimes he didn't give a good shit either way. If a first move was made, it was Lactameon's cutoffs slipping down to his ankles. For sure, Winfield couldn't have been curious about black dudes, yet he'd grinned and slid his off too. But, Lactameon *could* have pulled his up again. On the other hand, Winfield was one of the few whiteboys Lactameon had ever talked to in his life, and the only one he'd ever touched. He recalled everything perfectly, but somehow those sunbeams and the sound of water had become the clearest images.

Anyway, what had they done that was supposed to be buried? Winfield was skinny and white; technically tan, but white all the same. And, he had a white dick . . . a dick about like any other dude's, except it was white. If Winfield had ever been one-up on Lactameon, they were even now. That left only two dudes from about the same hood, with deuce working dicks that needed regular service or they drove you fucking crazy. Maybe it had just been the heat or the danger or two bodies slippery wet? There'd been some touching, some clumsy hugging and stroking, and one try at a *real* kiss that got both of them snickering before their lips even met. Winfield had wasted some time on Lactameon's tits, but then Lactameon was used to dudes copping a feel. The only thing that really bothered him about having his breasts stroked and squeezed was knowing it wasn't *his* breasts Winfield wanted. Holding a warm, willing body tight to his own was a new experience for Lactameon, but then it really wasn't Winfield he was holding. Black fist on white weapon, white fist on Sooty Jimmy, some panting, some sweating, a lot of imagining, and then two hot bursts of gunfire and the scent of it mingling with chlorine. Then, cold cutoffs concealing smoking guns, they'd walked out in sunlight, heads up in defiance of anyone watching, and jumped in the pool to cool off. No crime had been committed, but the evidence vanished anyway.

They'd never done it again; maybe because it would never just *happen* again. They'd both gotten something they'd wanted for a long time, and maybe that made them luckier than a lot of dudes. Like the skateboard sticker said: don't die wondering.

The pale wedge shape of a dog skull grinned at Lactameon from the table . . . did the moon stir unburied dog-bones too? Lactameon gave it a second glance as he crossed to the kitchen. Shielding the light with his body, he opened the fridge door and scoped out the options. There were two full sixers of Bud, showing his mom had been to the market about the same time he'd been chilling Sebastian. His mom was cool for one can a day, and he drank it with dinner or after he'd done his home-work. Two rated for good report cards or anything else that got most moms off. Any more was cruising somebody else's turf in your colors. She had offered open-house for his last birthday, but he'd sipped only three, and the third really to show he was down with her heart, though he could have slammed the whole sixer and still balanced a peanut on his nose.

He twisted two cans from the plastic, not sure he really wanted both, but it would save time if he did. So, what had he missed for home-cookin tonight? Mmm, there was a big bowl of leftover spaghetti. Three minutes in the reactor, watch the time, and open the door before the beeper sounded to *win your prize, you lucky little nigga!*

Three and a half minutes later, Lactameon was back in his room. There was a little wooden desk in one corner that his mom had bought him years ago at the Salvation Army thrift store. It was a kid's desk, and he could hardly get under it anymore, but he still did his homework and a lot of good thinking at it. Setting the Buds and the steaming bowl of spaghetti on the desktop, he switched on the lamp. It was a chipped plaster hula girl who was anatomically correct everywhere but beneath her plastic grass skirt. He'd really wanted it last year, and his mom had probably paid way too goddamn much for it at the pawnshop. Every dude who had ever been in his room had scoped under her skirt first thing. Beamer had kept on checking up until last summer; and now Lactameon had the 411 why he'd stopped.

A cloudy old mirror was mounted on the closet door, and Lactameon caught sight of himself as he was about to sit down. Stepping over, he studied the huge sooty boy in the glass. There had been a change today, and it wasn't the bandana. Coming close, he scanned his face. It was his eyes. Eyes changed in a slinky sort of way, and you might not notice unless you watched

every day. Dudes you hadn't seen all summer would come back
to school with changed eyes; some changed only a little, some
a lot. Beamer's eyes had never changed. T.K.'s had changed
overnight.

Returning to the desk, he sat carefully down in the creaky
little chair. Popping a Bud, he sucked an icy swallow that
spooked some hovering shadow from his mind. He opened a
drawer and searched inside for one of those plastic spoon/fork
things from KFC he kept by for times like this. It was a surprise
to find so much kid-crap he'd collected over the years. There
were those stupid Cracker Jack prizes, a few ancient Garbage
Pail Kids cards, and a handful of cartridge casings, all calibers,
he'd picked up on the streets. All the dudes traded those back
and forth until everybody had a complete set.

A bubble-gum comic caught his eye: Bazooka Joe and His
Gang. Joe was chilling with one of his homeys: *Yo, Pud, word
y'all scope out the circus come to town, man. Shit yeah, bra,
had 'em this bitch what jump on a donkey, swing underneath,
an blow that muthafucka off, man! Well, shit, fool, your sister
done that to every nigga in Oaktown!*

Lactameon blinked, staring at the little square of wax paper.
What the fuck, it didn't say any such thing! Crumpling it in his
fist, he flung it into the wastebasket, then slammed down the
Bud. He finally found a fork. Thumbing his little blaster on low,
he hooked over the bowl of spaghetti. The words of an old Bobby
Brown song drifted softly around the room saying things about
not being cruel.

TICK!

Something hit the window glass. Dropping the first forkful
of spaghetti before it even touched his lips, Lactameon tensed
and swung around. What the fuck? Sounded like somebody had
thrown a pebble. One of the walking-dead with a joke left in
him? Or maybe one of the dudes? Lactameon's hand went to
his bandana. Or . . . maybe somebody else's dudes!

"Shit!" he whispered. Moving fast, he switched off both
lamps, then eased onto the bed and crawled cautiously to the
window.

TICK!

Keeping low, he raised his face just far enough above the
sill to see out. The moon shone down from straight overhead,

bathing the alley in soft blacks and silvers. Lactameon scanned the passage, searching the shadows among the dumpsters and cans. From what he recalled of the party, it was hard to imagine any of his dudes up for anything until long after the sun. Silver? Maybe. Crack and Colt did strange things to a dude, and this wouldn't have been the first time he'd cruised by at some weird hour wanting to talk until his batteries were dead and then fallen asleep beside Lactameon. Yeah, it *had* to be Silver.

There was movement next to a dumpster against the far wall. Lactameon's eyes locked on target, but he felt a chill flash through his body. There was somebody there, but it sure as shit wasn't Silver! Jerking away from the glass, Lactameon pressed himself back against the wall. He could feel his own heart. The figure below was too small to be Silver, but seemed hooded and cloaked in full gangstuh gear! The room was warm, but Lactameon shivered, squirming away from the square of moonlight on the blankets as if touching it was death. He shut his eyes for a second, and whispered, "Make it be Stacy, *pleeeze!*"

That was bullshit, and he knew it. Stacy had both his parents, both of them worked, and they loved his fat ass off. He might have stayed at the clubhouse, drunk, or he might be safe home in bed, but he'd never be cruising at four in the morning. Lactameon shivered again, wanting to scream for his mom. But what the fuck good would that do? If somebody was after his ass with a gun, all of her love and a baseball bat wouldn't signify a goddamn thing! But who the fuck was it out there? For sure, somebody who knew where he cribbed. The Collectors were on terms with the Leopards, but none of those dudes would come cruising to meet with a mascot. Winfield had balls, but he sure wasn't a fool, and would never cruise the hood alone at this hour. Shit, maybe Hobbes had realized he *was* supposed to kick him! *Oh yeah, he'd looked it up in the rule book, right!* No, not Hobbes . . . but maybe Sebastian? Especially after what had come down on the corner with those little suckers. But, that wasn't Sabby out there; he was a little bigger than Bilal. Some dude he'd sent? Maybe Lizard? Lizard was small, only twelve, and Lactameon didn't know him because he'd moved into the hood less than a month ago and gone right to work for Hobbes. Previous experience, word said, from over East. Came with his own little Smith & Wesson.

TICK!

"Shit!" *Okay, Tam, chill on this! You fuckin figured your ass was kicked once already today, didn't ya? Shit, an you wasn't even drunk then!* Gritting his teeth, Lactameon forced himself to look back out of the window, half expecting a bullet between his eyes any second. The small shape was still there, but that wasn't the latest gangstuh look at all; it was just some little sucker in a goddamn blanket! Well, little suckers had guns too . . .

Don't die wondering.

Sucking a breath, Lactameon flipped up the latch and cranked open the window. Chill, salt-scented air and garbage stink filled his nostrils. The little figure below threw back its hood and stared up. Long, matted dreadlocks spilled everywhere. One eye glittered under the moonlight in the damaged angel face, Ethan. The strange moon-shadows made him look like a kid who'd been buried in the *Pet Sematary*. Even his voice sounded like it came from a crypt. "Yo, Tam."

For a moment Lactameon was as pissed as he'd been at Hobbes for scaring him shitless that day, but maybe Ethan was running a message. Shivering now because the real-world cold was invading his room, Lactameon leaned from the window. "Yeah. S'up, man?"

Ethan's grin flickered out like a candle in the wind. "Nuthin." He clutched the blanket tighter around his small body. Lactameon saw he was shivering too. The little boy looked like he'd raised up a spirit but didn't know what to ask it for. Spirits got really pissed-off when that happened.

"Um . . . I just seed your light, man . . . an figure you wake. Dat all."

Lactameon felt the warmth of his room being sucked out the window. "Oh. Well, so what you doin down there anyways, man? Yo! Was that somebody shootin at you bout a half hour ago?"

"Huh?"

Shit, little sucka, you deaf besides bein half-blind? "Jeeze, mean you didn't hear nuthin, man?"

"Nuh-uh, Tam. An I been here since you get home." The boy smiled a little. "Shit, man, was you ever drunk on *your* ass!"

Lactameon frowned. "Well, so what you followin me for

anyways, man? An, why the fuck you still hangin here? Um
. . . I didn't fall down or nuthin?"

"Naw. But you piss right in da middle of da motherfuckin
street, man!" Ethan giggled. "Lucky for your ass no pigs come
cruisin by!"

"Mmm. Well, ain't pigs I worry bout. An, yo, how you
know my name anyways?"

"Beamer tell me. Say, you coolest motherfucka in da hood,
man!"

"Oh yeah. I forgot. You live in his buildin, don't ya?"

Ethan kicked a toe on the garbage-slimed concrete. "Well
. . . my folks does. But, Beamer let me sleep by da boiler in da
basement."

"Mmm. Well, you gots big balls, man. Fuck *I* ever sleep
next that spooky ole thing! But, so why you here now?"

"Um . . . I lose my motherfuckin key, Tam. Shit, my folks
kill me for dat! An I scared knockin Beamer's window, man.
Wake up his baby, den *he* kick my ass!"

"Mmm. He wouldn't, man. Course, his dad prob'ly kick
his. Jeeze, seem like everybody in the hood know he gots a
baby."

"Nuh-uh, Tam! It a secret, man! Beamer trusses me."

"Mmm. Guess he would. You gots the right kinda eyes."

"Huh?"

"Nuthin. But, why you ghost me, man? An why you cribbin
down there for?"

"Well . . . like I sayin, you way past drunk, Tam. I seed
ya come out da Collectors' clubhouse buildin. I . . . sorta wanna
see you get your ass home okay. Know?"

*Yeah. Just what the fuck I need, an eight-year-old body-
guard!* "But, why you stay?"

Ethan shrugged. "Cause you dere. Ain't far. Know?"

Lactameon sighed. *An I give your ass some food, an act
like I give a shit for two minutes!* "Yeah, man, I know. Well, so
why don't you cruise your ass over to that kid-center place? Shit,
it just a few blocks, an they gots beds there, an they feed ya."

"Yeah. I down with dat place, Tam. But, you hang dere too
much and da motherfuckin pigs scope your ass, man! An, dem
goddamn stupid social motherfuckas too! Start drillin ya, man
. . . wanna know bout your folks an shit, man. An bout da . . ."

da accident with my stupid eye, man." Ethan came across the
alley and stared straight up. "Dey wanna take me *away*, man!"

Lactameon shivered once more, the temperature in his
room about equal to the real world. *Away from what?* More
like, *to* what. His mom had a saying: *better the frying pan you
know than the fire you don't.* He lifted his eyes to the moon,
suddenly hating that pale white face smiling so stupidly from so
far away. He glanced back at his desk, where the big bowl still
steamed and the second Bud waited, then looked down at the
little boy again.

"Yo, Ethan. Bail your ass round to the door. Don't push no
buttons. I be down in a minute."

"Huh? Um . . . for sure, man." Ethan's little blanket-
wrapped ghost-shape disappeared down the alley at a run.

Pulling his jeans on, Lactameon eased into the living room.
The dog skull still grinned like it had all seven on everybody's
probs. Crossing to the hallway door, Lactameon listened a moment, checked the peeper, then opened it a crack on its chain
and peered out. This was what passed for a security building,
which in this hood meant you stood a fifty-fifty chance of not
meeting a Neitherworld refugee in the hall after dark. Then he
cursed softly and dropped the chain, remembering how he'd
probably come crawling up those stairs easy prey for anything
only hours ago.

Lactameon eased his bulk carefully down the steep, creaky
staircase and pushed open the door. Ethan stood out in the dark
entryway, wrapped tight in his blanket and panting from the
run, but still shivering. Lactameon had prepared himself, but
seeing the little boy's face up close still sent a chill through him.
He held the door open against its spring, but Ethan hesitated.

"Um . . . I cost, man."

Lactameon made a face. "Oh, get your ass in here!"

Ethan slipped in under Lactameon's arm. Without waiting
to see if he would follow or not, Lactameon started back up the
stairs.

"Um, yo, Tam! Wait up, man! It fuckin spooky in here!"

A minute or so later, Lactameon was back at his hallway
door with Ethan behind him. He checked inside, then put a
finger to his lips. "Follow me, man. An stay chill. You wake up
my mom, an I fuckin kick ya!" He let Ethan enter, then followed

and softly shut the door, locking all the locks. Ethan stood still, head up, sniffing the air.

"Shit!" he whispered. "Somethin smell *good*, man!"

"Shush, dammit!" Lactameon hissed. "Over here! C'mon!"

Almost shoving the little boy into his room, Lactameon pushed the door closed and fastened the wire hook, which wouldn't have stopped a determined two-year-old but got respect from his mom. Then he snapped on the switch for the overhead bulb. Ethan blinked, which looked horrible, scoped the whole room in a three-sixty, then let the blanket slip in a heap on the floor just like he was home. His tiger eye widened in wonder.

"Way cool, Tam! Dis *all* fuckin yours?"

Lactameon shrugged. "Guess I just lucky, man."

Ethan had put on a shirt since Lactameon had last seen him; a big, dirty tee in three faded stripes of red, yellow, and green. A thin shoulder showed through a hole. The kid-center had given those out years ago when the people supporting it still had enough money to care. Lactameon hadn't seen one in almost two summers. For the first time up close and in light, he saw that the kid was so totally dirty he looked made up as a Dungle-boy for trick or treat. And here in Lactameon's own room with its familiar scents, the little kid's smell overpowered his looks. His jeans were so rotten and black that they looked like leather instead of Levi's. His Nikes were in sadder shape; holes showing soot-colored feet, and one torn to reveal toes with long, jagged nails. His shirt had been sweated in until it seemed starched.

"Jeeze, Ethan. You know they give away clothes at that center?"

"Oh, shit yeah, Tam! I sell 'em to dat junkshop dude! Same's dese blankets."

"Oh."

Ethan's nose dragged him straight to the spaghetti bowl. He stood gazing at it with that same little quiver of yearning like a moth on a window lusts for the light bulb. He swallowed before he could drool. "Um . . . fuuuuck, man. You eat any motherfuckin time you want!"

Lactameon sighed. "Just do it."

The little boy almost leaped, but held back a second. "*All*
it, man?"

"Jeeze, Ethan, you *can't* eat all that."

"Shit yeah!"

Ethan didn't bother sitting down at the desk about his size.
And he didn't use the fork. Lactameon watched for a moment,
feeling sick and fascinated, then sat down on his bed and fired
a Kool. "Take the Bud too, man."

Ethan didn't look back, or nod. He just collared the can
and ripped the tab. Lactameon glanced at the clock. 4:23. A
long time yet till morning. Ethan was done with the spaghetti
. . . all of it . . . before Lactameon had finished his Kool. He
watched the little boy gulp down the Bud. Now what? Another
few hours of sleep seemed like a good move. The bed was a
double, and plenty big even with Lactameon in it; Stacy had
spent a few nights and it still hadn't been too crowded.

"Yo, Ethan, you gots lice, man?"

The little boy put down the beer can. "Nuh-uh."

"Mmm. Come here."

Instantly, Ethan was at the bedside, bowing his head. Lactameon dug around in the matted dreads. They were dirty and
oily but nothing seemed to be moving. At least somebody gave
that much of a shit about him, or maybe he'd just been lucky
so far. "Take off your clothes, man."

Ethan was naked in seconds. "Ta da! Um, you change your
mind, Tam? S'cool. I not charge ya nuthin."

Lactameon frowned. The boy's feet were the worst, but the
rest of him wasn't much cleaner. "You take baths, man?"

"Shit yeah . . . sometimes."

Sighing, Lactameon got up and crossed to the door. "C'mon,
man. Stay quiet."

Ethan padded after him down the short hall to the bathroom. "Yo, Tam. What if your mom hear da water?"

"Mmm. She prob'ly figure I had a wet dream."

17

So this was death, thought Corbitt; a drifting awareness after the light was gone. It wasn't peaceful because there was pain. He wondered why he *could* still feel, and then why he could even wonder. That conjured up a horrible thought . . . that he'd be able to feel the dirt cover him as Bates filled one more lonely grave in his forgotten field. *Lonely?* Maybe not. Toby and Lamar would likely be with him, the three jungle cats for eternity!

Unless . . .

Could Toby have seen that chance for escape? Corbitt hoped that he had. Then his own death might have meant something after all. Maybe it was better this way, not to have gone on living, if people believed he was something he wasn't? Corbitt let himself drift, like a body downriver. In a way, Weylen had defied the old man from beyond death by never leaving this place. But the silence of a grave had to be better than looking up at the sunlit surface and feeling the ripples of life all around when it was forever beyond your reach. Maybe that was what being black in this world really meant?

Corbitt's chest ached as he struggled for breath. *Why?* Was it just some kind of primitive reflex, the way a lizard's tail kept twitching after it was cut from its body? Or was it some alien atmosphere in some other universe where he'd have to learn breathing all over again? Maybe he was being reborn into a future where there was no black and white but only shades of gold? Words from a Sunday School song came to mind: *and in*

His word I'm told, I'll walk the streets of gold. Funny: he'd always thought that meant the pavement, but maybe it really described the people? After all, who in heaven would care what they walked on?

Corbitt tried to let go of the past; to move on in new hope to the next-thing ahead. Maybe that was the secret to stop the pain? But, wasn't there supposed to be a clear light to guide him? So, where in hell was it? *Best watch your mouth, nigga!*

Then, a voice called his name, sounding far away but familiar. Weylen? But it seemed to come from the wrong direction . . . Corbitt didn't want to go back to the past! That road only led to a bridge going nowhere. The voice called again, and like the fish, Corbitt felt something slender and unseen pulling him upward. Colors began to swirl in his eyes; all of the rainbow that made up clear light. He seemed to slip into a body . . . his, maybe Weylen's, but at least it fit right. He touched a hand to his chest. His fingers found warm, sticky wetness: blood . . . and dirt!

Just one more cruel joke! He wasn't even dead yet and Bates was already filling his grave! Corbitt fought now, toward the light and the voice. Colors merged and formed shapes. He opened his eyes and found himself looking into the face of a warrior. "Toby the tiger," he murmured.

"What?" Toby shook Corbitt's shoulders. "Corbitt! C'mon, brother, wake up! Please! We gotta get outa here, man!"

The grave? Corbitt wondered. That was logical enough. Then he felt leaf-covered concrete under his back. And then, through the echoes in his ears and Toby's frantic pleas, came a strange mewling sound. Corbitt saw Toby flick a terrified glance in that direction, but he didn't want to look for long at whatever lay there.

"C'mon, Corbitt! *Please!*" Locking his arms around Corbitt's body, Toby lifted him up.

The strange sounds came again. Corbitt tried to look, but Toby pressed his face against his chest. "No, Corbitt!"

Then, Corbitt remembered . . . what he'd seen in that last second, staring into the shotgun barrels as Bates pulled the trigger . . . *both bores blocked by riverbank dirt!*

Corbitt pulled away from Toby and stared toward the sounds. His mind almost shut down in darkness again. His stomach twisted. Sickness rose in his throat. He clutched Toby tight and fought it back.

Bates lay face-up on the carpet of leaves, half-tangled in willow and vines. Patches of pavement had been bared by his struggles. Corbitt couldn't seem to look away. Fascinated, he watched the man's hands grope at a face that was no longer there!

The wet, whimpering sounds came again. The hands fell back. Bloody white fingers clutched at willow wands. A new kind of mist seemed to close around Corbitt, thicker than any he'd seen on the river. He pressed close to Toby until the fog cleared, but his eyes wouldn't leave the man-shape on the ground. No duppy he'd ever imagined could have looked worse. What was left of the gun lay on Bates's upper body, both breeches blown open into jagged steel shards. The first barrel exploding must have dropped the second hammer. Corbitt's knees almost gave, but Toby held him. Finally, Corbitt managed to pull his eyes off the man and looked down at himself. His chest was clotted with blood and warm dirt, and was pocked in places with rock-salt chunks that stung like fire. He brushed at his skin, wincing a little, his fingers finding a few bird-shot pellets though none had cut deep. Clenching his teeth, he dug them out. Something else seemed mixed with the bloody dirt, like bits of soft chalk. Corbitt looked down at the shattered remains of Weylen's rib cage. It hadn't been much of a shield, but maybe it had helped. Corbitt noted blood and salt pocks on Toby's shoulder and arm.

There was a low moan, but it couldn't have come from that blood-spattered thing on the ground. Corbitt turned toward the river. Lamar was struggling up on his elbows. His head was still down, and he shook it in painful slow-motion. Corbitt's senses sharpened . . . something had to be done, even if he wasn't sure what. He moved toward Lamar. "Tobe! We can't let him see this!"

Toby followed. Corbitt was almost past Bates when the man made more sounds. Corbitt stopped, his eyes drawn against his will. It didn't seem possible that the faceless thing could make words, yet Corbitt was certain he heard them . . . *help me . . . please!*

Corbitt hesitated, then pulled Toby past him and pointed. "Help Lamar!"

Toby's eyes darted from Bates to the big boy. "How?"

"Hold him! Hide his face an get him down to the river, man! Don't let him see this!"

Toby dashed to Lamar, dropping to his knees and gathering the bigger boy against him to hide what lay beyond. Corbitt sucked a deep breath, feeling his own battered ribs creak inside him. It took all his courage to make himself kneel beside the man. Setting his jaw, Corbitt looked at Bates's face; seeing peeled, blackened flesh, pale splinters of bone, and tiny steel spears. Somehow, there were still eyelids. They were squeezed shut, and Corbitt prayed they wouldn't open, sickened by the thought of what might not be there. Despite his determination he almost leaped away when a bloody white hand found and clutched tight on his arm. Corbitt swallowed. It hardly seemed possible for the man to be alive. Something old whispered in Corbitt's mind. His eyes went to Weylen's bones. Beneath them was a block of root-broken roadway. As if in a dream, Corbitt saw himself raise the block overhead and smash it down on Bates's head.

Corbitt blinked. The wrinkled old hand still clutched his arm. The concrete block lay unmoved. Near the water, Toby held Lamar's face to his chest, man-child comforting man-child. Corbitt glanced upriver, seeing the bridge's rusty red skeleton bared in the sun. A crow called nearby, and maybe another, and then Corbitt heard Lucas roar Lamar's name from the cabin row. Corbitt's ears had cleared and he heard other sounds . . . the ragged lope of Bates's Jeep still idling beyond the fringe of trees, a child's laughter, maybe Guppy's, drifting down from Bridge-end. Corbitt's nostrils were filled with the scents of gunpowder, hot metal, and blood. Yet he swore he caught the faint fragrance of bacon and eggs. Toby had gotten Lamar on his feet. Draping one arm over his shoulders, Toby led him toward the river. The big boy stumbled, head down as if drunk. Corbitt heard Lucas's truck fire up. In a few minutes more Lucas would come out on the bridge, figuring his son and the other boys were asleep underneath from fishing all night.

Again, Corbitt felt the man's hand clinging to him. How could Bates still be alive! Weylen was dead, and how many black bodies lay under that field, and still this old devil lived on! Toby and Lamar disappeared from sight down the bank. Corbitt's eyes returned to the bones and what lay beneath them.

Then, the old man made a different kind of sound. The wrinkled white hand trembled a moment before slipping off Corbitt's ebony arm. Slowly, Corbitt rose to his feet. The air was growing warm, steamy and thick for what would be another hot day of Mississippi July. Sunlight sparkled on green river water. Flies were gathering, adding their sleepy drone to the other morning sounds. Pale gold gleamed as Toby peered over the bank. "Corbitt?"

"He dead, Tobe."

The blue eyes went wide for an instant, then narrowed to icy slits. "*Good!* That mean we win!"

Did it? Corbitt wondered. *Too little, too late.* And even this might prove a last victory for Bates! How could anything but trouble rise up out of this? Bates's death wouldn't set Corbitt's dad free, and the whispers and rumors would only bring more trouble for Bridge-end! Corbitt shook his head in sadness. "How Lamar?"

"Startin to wake up."

Corbitt's thoughts seemed to cool and condense. Again, the cheetah-prince had failed! Corbitt lifted his eyes to the silent field. He saw Toby look too, but the blond boy said nothing. *Just one more secret.* How could digging up the past ever help anyone? Corbitt stood, waiting for the cries of betrayal to echo in his mind. Nothing. Not even a breeze stirred the dry weeds. Bates had been right. What good was a prince from the past? Africans were obsolete! Even the ghosts had exiled him!

Corbitt looked around. No one would know Bates hadn't died here alone. He'd been shooting at crows and his rusty old gun had blown up. Corbitt felt Toby's eyes on him . . . a warrior waiting for commands. What a joke! Still, Corbitt said, "Get the poles. We swim Lamar across an figure out somethin to tell him . . . an somethin to say to our folks . . . so this thing stay a secret."

Silently, Corbitt gathered up Weylen's bones and carried them back to the river.

PART TWO

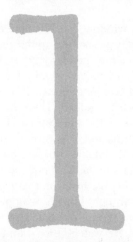

1

A Greyhound is silver and gleaming and going somewhere.

At least that's how they seemed when you stood with your toes in the roadside dirt and watched while one passed you by. From there nothing showed behind silver-black glass, but inside looking out was a different thing.

Corbitt had never known that a person could be too tired to sleep. His eyelids drooped, but only sandpapered his eyes when he closed them. His throat was dry, and his tongue tasted tinny from condenser-cooled air that was always the same temperature, and somehow the wrong temperature. Strong disinfectant burned his nostrils, but could never quite cover old cigarette smoke and new plastic. Most of the people aboard were probably a lot cleaner than he was, but used too much deodorant or perfume. Even the homey scent of diesel fumes bothered him, and the engine-sound made his head ache. The motor moaned fiercely now, wound tight to its governor as the bus pulled a long grade north of Los Angeles. Of course it wasn't the same bus Corbitt had flagged down at the Bridge-end crossroads . . . in fact it had been a surprise to find that the sleek silver Scenicruisers crossing his valley were just old rural rattletraps compared to the new coach he'd boarded in Jackson. Like the freeways they ran, these Greyhounds all seemed the same, differing only by number, destination sign, and the color of their seats as they carried Corbitt west for two nights and

days. But this would be the last: the sign in the windshield read
OAKLAND.

Turning to the window, Corbitt noticed the remains of an
ancient concrete highway snaking up through the canyon below.
He could almost imagine the shiny green Corbitt toiling along
with its stack pouring smoke. *Before I die and turn to rust,
please let me pass a Greyhound bus.* But those days were long
past, and the past was long dead. Then, he caught sight of a big
black bird circling over the emptiness. He felt a chill: so they
had crows in California too. He turned from the window and
pulled a book from his satchel, but was too tired to read.

*. . . had a nigger's baby. Nice girl too. Never held her head
up in that town again. We never did catch that coon . . .*

Corbitt sat up straight. In the window glass he could see
the reflection of two skinny old crackers across the aisle, one
row back from him. He watched for a minute, but it was clear
that they weren't talking that way for his benefit. Likely they
hadn't even noticed him . . . or didn't care. Old fools!

At first, Corbitt had tried to believe he was on some kind
of quest, so this thing could have a meaning. Now he just wished
he wasn't so tired; wished he could still find some interest in
the new things around him, and wished that his feet didn't hurt
in the shoes he was wearing. The first day he'd been too fascinated to feel tired. He'd watched as the countryside changed
from the soft greens and browns of Mississippi into the thicker
lush tangle of Louisiana, and then grew leaner through East
Texas until night fell and there was nothing more to see. The
next morning showed little but rocks and rusty red plains through
New Mexico and Arizona, and then he'd seen sand dunes and
a movie-set desert. He'd been amazed to learn that he was now
in California, until he recalled his schoolbooks. But northern
California would be green, with trees, he reminded himself.
Why else would they call it Oakland?

He'd spent most of the night in Los Angeles, suffering
through another layover from hell until the Oakland bus left. It
hadn't taken him long to discover that the big city terminals,
where he usually had to wait and change buses, were strange
and savage places for a kid on his own. The conditioned air was
always cool, but barely fit for breathing. The floors were always
polished, but strewn with trash and cigarette butts. There were

always the same rows of slippery plastic chairs that hated being
sat on, and stony-eyed people behind the counters, with faces
set in perpetual disgust, who made every word sound like a
curse. Everyone else seemed either worried or hurried, or crazy
or mad, no matter what color they were, and Corbitt soon
learned that a smile only made them suspicious.

Of course Corbitt had seen movies about cities, and listened
to truckers' talk; but he'd never imagined it could really be true,
or that once he got off the buses he'd be nothing but prey. It
hadn't taken long to realize that no one would help him, and
that nobody could be trusted no matter what color. Anyone who
acted friendly probably wasn't, and it seemed like the only good
people were the ones who ignored you. Boys his own age were
the greatest danger; with their offers of drugs, their threats, or
their constant begging for smokes and spare change . . . as if he
looked like he could spare anything! They tried to steal his satchel
the second he sat down. In El Paso there had been a sad-eyed
little brown boy who couldn't have been more than six. Corbitt
had given him fifty cents . . . twice what he'd asked for . . . and
then the little bastard had tried to pick his pocket on the way
to the bathroom.

Those motherfucking bathrooms! Tile-lined caves lit by fluorescent lights, with the stink of shit and piss always overpower-
ing some pine-cleaner strong enough to melt out your eyes, and
where boys and men of all ages and races whispered things
Corbitt only half understood and never hoped to. They would
watch with strange smiles if he tried to use the urinals, then
laugh or wink when they saw he was too scared to piss. The
toilets cost money, except for the one that always had somebody
in it. Corbitt tried to use the bus bathrooms whenever he could,
and suffered in misery during layovers.

Even out in the huge main rooms among hundreds of people
Corbitt felt hunted and alone. Ragged old men shuffled after
him whining for quarters. Other boys would surround him or
try to cut him into a corner. Whiteboys called him nigger. Black
ones called him *stupid* nigger. Scowling security guards would
turn away when he was threatened, but constantly demanded
to see his ticket, and usually looked disappointed that he had
one. There was no escape from this torture until the next bus.

Still, Corbitt learned . . . to avoid all eyes and never smile, and to keep his head up and walk as if ready to fight. He supposed that was called being cool, but felt like Guppy trying to strut. He suspected he looked older than thirteen because of his height, and that his very blackness was another small advantage. But it felt wrong to have to act this way, playing a part that didn't fit him. If you played a part long enough would you begin to believe it yourself? Would Oakland be different because it was a black city? Maybe when black people were all together they wouldn't be cruel to each other? That at least seemed logical.

Now, Corbitt shoved the book back into his satchel. He hadn't had a chance to really read much on the way, but sometimes people left you alone if you pretended to. He sighed and tried to relax in the seat. The people on this bus seemed to be of all races. And, except for those two dried-up old crackers lost in the past, maybe that was a good sign. Corbitt tried to rest. His butt was sore from so much sitting, and the salt pocks itched on his chest. But his feet hurt worse. Never in his life had he worn shoes for so long. He looked down at the big black-and-white B.K.s, wishing they were at least one size bigger. He glanced out the window again and saw the crow still circling, then slumped back and forced his eyes shut. His mind drifted.

Swimming . . . he and Toby, with Lamar between them . . . *away from the past.* Once in the river Lamar's senses seemed to sharpen and the glassiness cleared from his eyes. Halfway across he stopped to tread water and gingerly touch the back of his head. He winced, then turned to face Bates's land. *"Bastard!"*

Corbitt spun himself around, his eyes scanning carefully, but the old man's body lay out of sight in the curtain of willow.

"Shut up, man!" said Toby. "Hey, your dad been callin. Best we hurry. Um, you okay, brother?"

Lamar frowned, swimming on, his strokes now strong and sure. "Spose I is, no thanks to that ole cocksucka. So, what happen?"

"Bates hit you with his gun," said Corbitt.

"Shit, man! Take no logic for figurin that out! What I askin is, what he do to you an Tobe? An . . . what he *gonna* do, catchin us on his land? Spect he gonna go an call up the sheriff?"

Toby and Corbitt exchanged glances. "No," said Corbitt.

"I . . . don't spect Bates gonna be makin us no more trouble."

"No more'n he already done," added Toby.

Reaching the shallows, the boys stood up, waist-deep. Lamar touched his head once more, scowled at the blood on his
fingers, then turned to stare at the other two boys.

"Shit! That ole muthafucka shoot you!"

Corbitt looked down at himself. The river had washed off
the dirt and blood and cleansed the salt from his wounds. Toby
glanced at his own shoulder, then shrugged. "Hell, Lamar. Don't
signify nuthin, man."

Lamar scowled. "What you tellin me? Hell it don't! That
ole bastard shoot you brothers! He can't go doin that to niggas
no more!"

Corbitt grabbed Lamar's arm. "Listen to me, man! This
thing be over an done with now! All what we *don't* be needin
is bringin home more trouble to Bridge-end!"

"Corbitt right," said Toby. "An, y'all know for a fact your
daddy go an blow his top, he hear bout this. Member what you
say your ownself right there under that bridge yesterday? So, it
be best for all Bridge-end not tellin nuthin to nobody."

Lamar's scowl faded a little. "Mmm. Spose that logical . . .
even it suck."

Corbitt let go of the big boy's arm. An ebony flicker caught
his eye. A half-dozen crows were circling over the riverbend
pool. Several more rose from the weeds of Bates's field. Corbitt
shivered. Then Lucas Sampson called his son's name from the
bridge.

Lamar turned and raised a palm to his father. The man on
the bridge waved back. Lamar waded to shore and pushed
through the trees. "Daddy ain't gonna be too awful mad. He
know I been fishin for Corbitt's mom." Lamar stopped and
turned around, seeing the poles Toby carried. "Shit! Spose that
ole cocksucka stole our fish too?"

"It got away," said Corbitt. "The big ones always do."

A few minutes later the boys had stopped in the leafy shade
by the bridge entrance. Lucas was walking toward the idling
White, carrying paper-bag lunches for himself and his son.

"Y'all gonna be okay now, Lamar?" asked Toby.

"Mmm. Spect I live, man." Then the big boy grinned. "Best
I get a move on fore it my own daddy whackin me upside the

head." He broke into a trot, heading for the Sampson cabin to change into his work clothes. "See you jungle cats tonight!"

"Lamar the lion," murmured Toby, watching the big boy leap his porch steps. "This gots to be the first time ever the three jungle cats keep a secret from each other."

Corbitt frowned. "Well, maybe it be bout time we all stop playin little-children games. That stuff all in the past. Sides, y'all be knowin goddamn well it for Lamar's own good, man."

Toby sighed. "Yeah. Spose I do. It just . . . well . . . it just like somethin change last night, man. Change us all."

"Mmm. It just we growin up, Tobe, what it is. Maybe it take somethin like what happen back there for showin we ain't little kids no more. Mmm. See the Coopers' pickup gone. Mom prob'ly ride in to see Miz Rudd again. C'mon, man. I make us some coffee, then you an me sit down an do us some figurin bout this thing."

The boys walked to Corbitt's cabin. Lucas had turned the White around, and now Lamar ran out to it, clad in his jeans and Pumas with a ragged red bandana tied around his head. He swung himself into the cab and the truck rumbled off trailing dust. Toby leaned on the porch rail, watching. "Nuthin hurt Lamar, man. Wish I be half that strong."

"Ain't much hurt his outsides anyways. It be up to us to keep his insides strong."

The sounds of the *Teenage Mutant Ninja Turtles* carried from the Sampson cabin. They had the biggest color set, so all the other children would be gathered there with Hayes and Guppy until the cartoons were over and Mrs. Sampson ran them out. Corbitt wondered what Sherry was doing.

Toby glanced at him. "Sherry gonna see somethin changed, man."

Corbitt pulled open the door. "Times I wonder if you an me ain't twins, Tobe. C'mon. We gots us some talkin to do."

Toby entered the cabin and Corbitt followed, closing and latching the door. The ancient bolt was stiff and rusty from not being used. "Pull them shades, Tobe."

Toby obeyed, and Corbitt went to the sink. He filled the big enamel pot from the faucet, spooned in coffee, then fired the stove with a match and set the pot on to boil. The small room grew shadowy as Toby pulled down the last shade. Corbitt reached for the bulb that dangled on wires over the table, but then left it off and took a candle from a drawer and lit it instead. He placed it in a holder in the center of the table as Toby came over and sat. Then Corbitt went to his mattress, pulled a Top pouch from underneath, and rolled cigarettes while the coffee boiled. Finally, he poured two cups and sat down across from Toby. For a minute or two the boys smoked in silence and watched the candle flame.

"Corbitt? So, what y'all figure gonna happen now?"

"Mmm. Bates be missed . . . 'ventually. Likely be the mailman see somethin wrong first."

Toby sipped coffee. "Well, my mom say one time he don't get that much mail."

"Still happen. Maybe few weeks, maybe more. Then the deputy come. Look around. See Bates's Jeep way down in the field."

Toby lifted his eyes from the flame. "But, what it even matter if somebody find him *today*, man? It was a accident."

"Never no accident when a whiteman die an there blackfolks around. There another lesson for you, brother." Corbitt met the blond boy's eyes over the flame. "You love Bridge-end, then y'all know for a fact we can't us say nuthin. Lamar went an 'tack Bates. Don't never forget that."

"But, who cept *us* know that, Corbitt? Sides, that got nuthin to do with the ole bastard blowin hisself to hell."

Corbitt's ebony hand closed tight over Toby's tanned one. "Listen, brother. Y'all know Lamar ever bit good as me. Pitcher him in your mind, locked up in some little room, gettin throwed all kinda fast questions by the sheriff. Shit, be no time at all till he tellin what he done. Then, best you believe, all what some white jury gonna hear be big strong Lamar Sampson 'tack a poor ole whiteman, an now that whiteman be dead." Corbitt's grip tightened even more. "Y'all wish to be black, Tobe. Well, it come true."

Toby put his free hand on top of Corbitt's. "An I proud, brother! It like that thing you say, fore you curse Bates to hell, I you, an you me."

Corbitt tensed. "I didn't mean it that way!" He squeezed Toby's hand. "But course we's brothers, man. Always was. But y'all be seein why we gots to keep this a secret from Lamar.

Maybe . . . maybe after Bates found an buried we won't be holdin no secrets from each other no more."

Toby nodded, but then seemed to consider a new thought. "Corbitt? Ain't there some sorta scientific way they gots of findin out how long a body been dead? What I sayin is, even Lamar gonna wonder if it come out that Bates die the same day we was there."

Corbitt's eyes returned to the flame. "Mmm. Spect that one bridge we can't cross till we come to it, man."

"Yeah. Spose so." Then Toby touched Corbitt's arm. "Listen, brother. What happen to Bates was a rightful thing. We *all* of us wish for that! So, maybe it rightful what you an me doin now. But, like Miz Griffin say, the truth gonna rise sooner or later, man. Day gonna come."

"Well, maybe it just ain't the time for that next-thing yet."

Toby picked up his cup, but suddenly froze with it halfway to his lips. "Corbitt? What we gonna do bout the *other* secret, man? The people in that field?"

Corbitt's head jerked up. Toby shot glances around the darkened room. "Corbitt? What you hearin, man?"

Corbitt leaped from the chair and dashed to the window that faced downriver. Lifting a corner of the shade, he peered out. Toby came over, mouth open, eyes wide. Corbitt dropped the shade and faced the blond boy.

"Nuthin, man! I be hearin nuthin!"

Toby's eyes shifted from the shaded window to Corbitt's face. "But . . . is that a rightful thing for us to be doin, Corbitt? Leavin all them people forgot?"

Corbitt grabbed Toby's shoulders, his long fingers clenching on the raw shot wounds. "Goddammit, Tobe, they ain't *people* no more! They only ole bones! Like . . . Weylen."

Toby winced from Corbitt's grip, but then his eyes widened once more. "Corbitt? How you know his name?"

"I don't know! Shut up! Listen to me, Tobe! Maybe . . . maybe it ain't a rightful thing to be forgettin them people . . . them *bones*. But, y'all figure it bring pride for Bridge-end . . . an, an our little ones, to go an dig all that up? All them people, man . . . an children too. They buried there for no reason other cept they was black! *Listen*, goddammit! *We* let it happen back then! I don't know why, but we did! Shit, Miz

Griffin was a maid . . . right here! Butter-mouthin whitefolks an washin their goddamn sheets! Lamar's grandfather was a goddamn ole Uncle Tom . . . properly respectful! Tobe, what I be sayin is, *we* never got together an stood up an try an stop what was goin on back then. An, an what we doin now? Here my own daddy be in prison for standin up to that ole power, an where in hell was all us niggas when the whiteman put him on that bus?" Corbitt fell silent, staring into Toby's eyes. Then something like fear crept into his own. "No, man! Don't you go an do that to me, too! Don't you go puttin that on me!"

Toby searched Corbitt's face. "Huh? What you sayin, man? Put what on you?"

Corbitt dropped his hands and turned away. "You still doin it, Tobe. Why y'all be waitin on me for tellin you what to do?"

Toby spread his hands. "Cause you always *know* what to do!"

"DAMN!" Corbitt threw back his head, clenching his fists, the fine muscles in his body all standing out stark. He squeezed his eyes shut for a moment, but then opened them again and slowly relaxed. He scanned the small room but seemed to find nothing familiar in it any longer. Sighing, he took Toby's shoulders once more, gently now. "Listen, Tobe. Please. There be one more secret y'all gots to be keepin, brother. But it be just a little, no-account one, an only for me. But it still gonna be best for Bridge-end. Hear me?"

Toby pulled away. "No! I don't hear you, goddammit! You ain't makin no sense! There too goddamn fuckin many secrets already an we never had none before!"

Corbitt let go of Toby, the blond boy's blood on his fingers. Going to his parents' bed, he pulled the cardboard box of his good clothes out from underneath. Shucking his old overall-jeans, he slipped into his best 501s; even these were faded and thin at the knees. Toby came over, almost warily, stepping like a tiger cub with wet feet.

"Corbitt? What y'all doin, brother?"

Corbitt found his father's old Army satchel and started to pack . . . another pair of jeans, some T-shirts and socks. "I be doin what best for Bridge-end. Y'all gonna see that, Tobe, an that why you gonna be keepin this secret too."

"*What?* Shit, Corbitt, look more like to me you be runnin away!"

"Don't go givin names to things, Tobe. It make 'em somethin they ain't." Corbitt's eyes flicked to the window. "An it go callin up things what shouldn't be called." He went to the cabin's tiny closet and took out his blanket-lined denim jacket. "I ain't *runnin* nowheres, Tobe. I be *goin* somewheres."

Toby watched, looking helpless, as Corbitt folded the jacket into the satchel and then sat on the floor to brush mud from his feet and slip on his socks. "Corbitt? So, *where* you gonna be goin, man? Goddammit, I your *brother!* An . . . an, what bout your mom?"

Corbitt glanced up. "My mom be a lot better off out me around. Specially now."

Toby dropped to his knees beside Corbitt. "But . . . but, what bout your *idea*, man? Workin at the truckstop? That *help* your mom!"

"No it won't! That just be hurtin her . . . an hurtin all us, in a different kinda way." Corbitt reached under the bed for his Nikes, but Toby took his hand.

"Corbitt. Listen to me. I know why you thinkin y'all gots to leave. It cause of what Bates say to you! That . . . that bullshit! That cocksuckin motherfuckin liar!"

Corbitt shook his head. "No, brother. Miz Griffin say, even the devil himself tell the truth when it be suitin his purpose." Corbitt sighed, drawing up his legs and dropping his arms atop them. "It be like . . . like I wake up from a dream this mornin an see everthin all clear. For the first time. It be like I been a little child playin . . . like I been messin with magic, not knowin. Tobe, we *all* us coulda been killed back there . . . cause of me!" Corbitt looked around the room, his eyes seeming big in the dimness. "All this I gots . . . my mom, an you, an Lamar . . . Sherry an Miz Griffin too. But it be like that wasn't enough. It be like . . . like I weren't satisfied with all that livin around me so's I went lookin in dark places for things what weren't livin . . . or not livin no more . . ."

"Corbitt!"

But, Corbitt only lifted a hand. "Listen, brother! It be like that ole African story Miz Griffin tell, bout that ghost in the forest what come to lost hunters . . . give 'em hope, but then only go leadin 'em further off the trail. Weylen was one of them things . . . maybe he didn't know it neither, but he was."

Toby shook his head stubbornly. "Corbitt! You can't know that!"

Corbitt took the blond boy's hand. "I be one of 'em too, Tobe. You heard it your ownself, even a whiteman like Bates see it. I don't belong here, Tobe. Maybe I don't belong nowheres no more. But what I be doin now be the rightful thing." He reached again for his shoes.

Toby kept hold of his hand. "How that the rightful thing, Corbitt? What be the logic in leavin us when all this new trouble tryin to rise up?"

"Ain't no *new* trouble, Tobe. What I tryin to tell you. It be *ole* trouble . . . ole, ole trouble I stir up with my foolishness. Out me round, it lie back down an sleep again." Corbitt slipped on one of his shoes.

Toby stood up. "Miz Griffin could make it lay down! Miz Griffin could kick its bony ole ass!"

Corbitt shook his head. "There stuff even Miz Griffin don't know. I find that out last night."

Toby stayed silent, watching Corbitt for a few moments as if trying to see some change in the slender boy. Finally, he sighed. "Wait, brother." Going to Corbitt's mattress, he picked up his B.K.s and offered them. "Wherever you goin, I be proud y'all wearin these."

Corbitt regarded the shoes for a time, then raised his eyes to Toby's. "An I be prouder'n hell to be wearin 'em, brother." He put them on, then stood and zipped the satchel shut.

"I know you wrong, Corbitt," said Toby. "But it like I can't logic out *why* you wrong. Not yet. Maybe I be like Lamar that way, gots to do me some lotta thinkin. But I trust you cause you be my brother, an I keep this secret, but only cause of that, an cause of I know for a fact y'all gonna be comin back when you logic this out for your ownself." Toby considered. "Corbitt? Hey, for all you know Weylen was on *his* way home cause of the same thing."

Corbitt hesitated, his eyes meeting Toby's again. But then he shrugged. "Don't *you* go an start diggin now, brother. You be ever bit as African as me, an member how Miz Griffin's lucky-skull come to you once already." Corbitt held Toby's eyes a moment more. "Um, spect y'all could go down neath the bridge an dig up my secret money? I best write a note for my mom."

Toby started to speak, but seemed to have run out of arguments. Finally he nodded. "Yeah. Sho."

Toby went out. Corbitt got his school binder from a bookshelf and pulled out a sheet of paper. Getting a pencil, he sat at the table. There was so much he wanted to say, but almost nothing that *could* be said. He finally just wrote *Mom and Dad, I love you.* He folded the paper and left it under his mother's pillow, then blew out the candle, picked up the satchel, and went to the door, pausing a moment to glance at the bookshelves. It didn't really matter what book he took along because he'd already read everything there at least twice. He grabbed the first paperback that came to hand, then stepped out onto the porch and pulled the door shut behind him. Maybe it was the shoes, but the worn boards no longer felt familiar underfoot. The sounds of cartoons still carried from the Sampson cabin, but no one else was outside yet, and Sherry was likely still helping her mother with chores. Now was the best time for slipping away unseen.

Toby returned on the run with the Prince Albert can. "Shit, y'all ain't goin far on thirty dollars, man!"

Corbitt folded the bills carefully into his pocket. "Spect you be right. This ain't 1951 no more."

"Well, listen, brother. I gots that money of mine home."

"No time, Tobe. That Greyhound gonna be passin the crossroads in less'n a hour. That be the best way to clear out this valley fast."

"Well . . . listen, Corbitt! I ride my bike home, get my money, an meet you up there. Twenty more dollars got to help some."

"But, I don't know how I ever pay you back, Tobe."

"Shit!" Grabbing his bike, Toby pedaled hard for the field path.

Corbitt gazed after Toby for a few seconds, then went out to the old highway and started up past the row of cabins. It was funny to think that this crumbling old road led to anywhere in the world. He hoped Sherry wouldn't see him. He was almost past Number One when he glanced up at the rusty motor court sign. A crow sat atop it, staring down at him with fierce golden eyes. Corbitt spat in the dust. "Satisfied? Shit, go off an polish your ownself, little black bastard!"

The bird took wing and soared away downriver. Despite himself, Corbitt stopped to watch. He stiffened suddenly, almost dropping the satchel. Down at the riverbend the air seemed black with crows!

"Corbitt!"

New sweat broke out on Corbitt's body as he turned to face the voice that had called him. Mrs. Griffin's chuckle came from Number One's shady porch. "Well, what we got here? Look to me like some fine young warrior settin out on a quest."

"Yo, Tam! Shit, wait da fuck up, man!"

Lactameon stopped by a gang-marked mailbox, scowling because the Leopards had sprayed their sign over the Collectors' again. That joke was starting to wear. He wasn't sure whether to be pissed-off at Ethan or not, because it was his own goddamn fault the little kid was sticking to him like shit to a shoe. He turned around, yanking up his jeans, as Ethan came running from back on the corner. The little boy dodged between two bad-looking dudes, leaped over the legs of a winehead, and caused an old lady to clutch at her purse like she was going to be bitten. The kid looked wild enough to take a finger off, especially with that empty eye-socket and his waist-length dreads flying every which way, but Lactameon thought he could see a slight change in the boy. For sure, he was still fairly clean, which wasn't surprising considering the layers of dirt that had come off in Lactameon's bathtub two days ago. His yellow-brown locks had fluffed like a Rasta explosion, and his jeans and Nikes had somehow survived the washing machine in Lactameon's base-ment that even ate clothes which weren't half-rotten. Lactameon had spent some of Hobbes's money on scoring the boy a brand-new big Cross Colours T-shirt, and most of the rest had gone for feeding the kid. And, shit, did he eat!

Lactameon couldn't figure if Ethan loved food more than anything else in the world, or if he was using his mouth as a weapon to kill anything that came near it. Lactameon had seen some strange shit done to kids, but he'd never imagined any child living to be eight years old in the America they showed on TV and not being taught to use silverware . . . not just to hold it right, but to use it at all. What should have been spooned, he drank. What should have been forked, he grabbed with his fingers. And it didn't take much imagination to figure what he did with anything that should have been cut with a knife. He had a rusty box knife but that wasn't for eating. And he ate anything given to him: leftover broccoli vanished as fast as factory-fresh Twinkies.

He wouldn't talk about his parents, except to say they were sick . . . word and a half on that! Beamer didn't know a hell of a lot about them either, only that they stayed in their apartment, paid their rent, and had a lot of product delivered that was way out of Hobbes's class. Beamer's dad called them trash that even the niggers wouldn't have, and Lactameon didn't figure it was because Ethan's dad was white. Lactameon wondered if they'd raised Ethan like an animal on purpose; not really to be cruel but more so they wouldn't have to care for him like a kid.

He'd almost gotten used to the boy's missing eye, or maybe he'd just trained himself to look into the remaining one. It seemed to show twice the expression of most people's eyes, but then it was working two jobs. Still, Lactameon wondered if he'd ever be able to stand the sight of Ethan winking. He'd taken the boy to Pay-Less Drugs yesterday to scope out eye patches. They were only a few dollars, but no way in hell could he convince the kid to wear one. Ethan's only explanation was that he was saving to buy a new eye. Then he'd winked like little kids do when they had something goin on, and Lactameon decided to let it slide before Ethan did it again.

Maybe it wasn't cool to think that way, but Ethan had really given Lactameon something to do with his own days. His mom was chilling with his new "little friend," and even the amount Ethan ate didn't seem like a hell of a lot to her after having fed Lactameon for thirteen years. For sure she was cool, but Lactameon could tell she was curious too . . . wondering why they always ate in Lactameon's room, and occasionally asking about Ethan's parents. Being a mom in the hood put her down with a lot, and it wasn't the first time Lactameon had a friend staying over because of some serious shit. Beamer once stayed a week, and Silver almost two, but Ethan was a *little* kid, and any good mom could melt a goddamn iceberg. Lactameon could picture her taking the chilly little Rasta up on her lap, smiling when he winked, and getting all seven in five minutes. Then she'd likely leave him milk and Twinkies before cruising over to see Ethan's parents with her baseball bat. Or maybe she'd light the candles and sit down with the bones. That might take a little longer than the baseball bat.

"S'up, Tam?" demanded Ethan, skidding to a stop like a cartoon puppy.

Lactameon started walking again. It was early afternoon and another hot day. He stripped off his tank-top and stuffed it into his pocket. "Not much, man. Spent a couple hours helpin Beamer read his baby book. So, you go home this mornin after breakfast?"

"Shit no. I scopin for a half buck, Tam." Ethan pulled off his own shirt and tied it around his waist, then strutted along beside Lactameon like a miniature bodyguard, eyeing everyone and everything.

"Well, shit, Ethan. That three nights now you been cribbin with me. What I sayin is, my mom gonna want the 411 pretty soon."

"Why?"

"Cause she a mom."

"Oh."

"Jeeze, Ethan, don't your folks give any sorta shit about you?"

Ethan shoved his hands in his pockets. "Yo, Tam. I come back all fuckin clean like dis, wearin dis way-killer shirt you buy my ass, dey figure I gots myself some buck, man! Oh yeah! Or, I been to da Center, tellin shit bout 'em. Dey figure I gots me some green, gonna want it. Dey figure I tellin shit, nuther . . . accident gonna happen."

Lactameon frowned. "Mmm. Well, that suck hard, man." Then he glanced at the boy. "Yo. If your mom been . . . sick, then who done your dreads?"

Ethan's face brightened. "Oh. Da dogwasher lady done 'em, man. She wanna cut some, but I not havin dat shit. She kill all da cocksuckin creeper-crawlers with dog-poo."

"Don't say that, man."

"Dog-poo?"

"No. Cocksucker. Make me think of Sabby, an that a total waste of my time. Yeah, that dogwash lady kinda cool. She friends with my mom."

"Shit yeah! She be a way cool mom, I thinkin, man! Fat moms always cool, huh?"

Lactameon smiled. "Seem that way, now you sayin it."

Pulling a hand from his pocket, Ethan stuck out his tummy and patted it. "Shit, check me out, Tam. I gettin fat or what?"

Lactameon smiled again. After two solid days of stuffing himself about the only change in Ethan's thin body was a flat stomach instead of a hollow one. You could still see several ribs. "Well, you movin on it, man."

"Shit! I gonna get *real* fat, man! Den I never be hungry no more!"

"Well, I still get hungry, man."

"Naw. Listen up! I gonna get me so motherfuckin fat I gots tits out to here, man! Big ole watermelons! Shit, I gonna get so goddamn fat my belly hang down to my *knees* . . . down to da motherfuckin *ground,* man! Yo! I gonna have to *shove* that great big ole motherfucka down the goddamn sidewalk! Shit, an den I gonna get so goddamn motherfuckin fat I can't *even* walk, man! An, suckas gonna come from all over da whole motherfuckin world to scope me out! An dey gonna *pay* to see me, man! Cause I gonna be da fattest fuckin kid in da world! An den I ain't never gonna be hungry no more!"

"Well, there this man live over in Leopard ground. Word say he weigh close to eight hundred pounds. Gots him six kids too."

Ethan looked up. "Yeah? So, people come an pay to see him, huh?"

"Naw. He drive a forklift at the shipyard."

"Oh."

"Y'know, it sorta funny, man. What I sayin is, me an the dudes go cruisin uptown an the pigs an all them rich white-ass motherfuckers be givin us hate stares cause we poor black ghetto-boys. But me an Stacy get second-helpins cause we poor black *fat* ghetto-boys. I used to figure dudes like Bilal an T.K. an Silver scared 'em cause they was big or hard-lookin. But me an Stacy freak 'em too. Maybe they figure we all sposed to be skinny an starved on what they let us have?" Lactameon glanced down at the thin little Rasta. "Rats the best survivors in the world, man, an they eat garbage nobody else want."

Ethan considered. "Shit yeah! Mean, who da fuck ever seen a starvin rat, man?"

"Mmm. Think four things about rats."

"Huh?"

"Just think. You don't gots to tell me. Fact is, maybe it better sometimes not to go tellin everybody what you thinkin."

"Um, cept your homeys?"

"Yeah. Only just be goddamn sure they really your forever-homeys, man. People change sometimes when you ain't lookin."

Ethan slipped a finger into his empty eye-socket. Lactameon had learned that was something he did when he was thinking hard. Like his wink, it was almost impossible to watch.

"Um, Tam? You ever gonna change, man?"

"Mmm. Times I figure I already gone through all the changes I wanna."

"Um . . . den, why you gonna work for Hobbes?"

Lactameon stopped. "What? Where you hear that, man?"

"Well, dat where you goin, ain't it? Hobbeses's place?"

"Mmm." Lactameon jerked at his jeans and started walking once more. Maybe Ethan could see out of that hole . . . like a window right to his mind? "Yo. Hobbes pay dudes for other shit, sides movin product, man. Like, that half buck in your belly come for babysittin his boy the other day. For sure I ain't up for that again, but I don't want you hangin at the goddamn bus station doin . . . what you do, man."

"But, I need me a half buck, Tam."

"Well, why? I mean, spose I can go on feedin your ass awhile. What you need money for, man?"

"I *tole* ya!"

"What?"

They reached the corner. Ethan looked up the cross street. "Um . . . c'mon, Tam. I wanna show you somethin, man. Kay?"

Lactameon glanced up the blocks ahead, where Hobbes's apartment was. Dammit, he should have taken the bus so Ethan wouldn't have tagged him. No wonder some of the dudes bitched about their little brothers!

"Tam. I done what you say, man. I thought four things bout you. Um, it not far. C'mon, man. Please?"

"Mmm. That was sposed to be rats, man."

"Give a shit bout no motherfuckin rats!"

The place was the same dirty little pawnshop where Lactameon had begged his mom for his hula girl lamp, and where he would have sold Sebastian's gold chain. It was also where the Collectors had scored their .38. The shop's one dusty window was cracked, held together by bolted plywood patches, and displaying the usual collection of tarnished trumpets, Taiwanese blades, and rusty hand tools. There was also an ancient flat-deck Variflex skateboard still fitted with ACS trucks and Kryptonic Red wheels. It should have been in a museum. The guns and cheap jewelry were kept way in the back of the shop, under glass. The shop's interior was dark and dank and smelled like bad dreams. The owner seemed almost a part of the shadows behind the barred cashier's cage. He looked like an evil old shaman in some story book, but the word *reptilian* always crossed Lactameon's mind. Lactameon was surprised when the man saw Ethan and actually smiled. He felt reptile eyes scope him for a second, but figured the old man had already scented him with his tongue. Maybe snake eyes could never show warmth, but these seemed to soften when returning to Ethan. And, maybe even rattlesnakes buzzed gently to their young.

"What shakin, little man?"

Ethan went confidently to the high counter, leaning way back to stare up. "Dis my homey."

Once more Lactameon felt the gaze of something cold-blooded. "Mmm," the voice buzzed. "Find the secret of the lamp yet, my man?"

Lactameon frowned. "There ain't none."

Rattlesnake laughter. "Maybe that was the secret."

"Um," said Ethan. "I wanna show him my eye."

A shiver rippled Lactameon's body. Ethan couldn't have said *that*!

But the wrinkled old wizard just gave what passed for a smile and slipped away into deeper shadow. A moment later he materialized once more and slid an ancient El Producto cigar box through the bars and into Ethan's eager hands. Lactameon had a feeling he wasn't going to like what he saw, but moved closer as the little boy held out the box and reverently opened the lid. Lactameon almost yelled. The goddamn thing was full of eyes! They lay all over on rotted red velvet, reminding him of grisly church relics he'd seen on TV. None of them matched. It took Lactameon a second to realize that made sense. Most were shades of brown. A few were black, and two were amber, and all seemed crusted with decades of dust.

Except one.

Ethan's little fingers closed over it carefully. Then he held it toward Lactameon on his small brassy palm. Lactameon had to look twice in the dim light to be sure. Then he had to swallow to make his voice work. "But . . . but, it *blue!*"

Ethan just nodded sadly. "Just like my first one."

"Shit! You mean . . ." Lactameon began. Then, "Oh. Um, guess that happen sometimes." He shut his mouth, feeling the snake eyes laugh. He swallowed again and tried to chill with it. "But . . . will it fit you, man?"

The little boy turned his tiger eye to the man. There was a nod from the shadows, and the dry voice buzzed gently. "Member how I show you, son."

Seeming suddenly shy for the first time since Lactameon met him, Ethan turned away and bent his head. Lactameon watched, fascinated, as the boy did something. He didn't know what in hell to expect, but it looked like a miracle when Ethan faced him again.

The little boy grinned. "Ta da!"

Ethan's face was perfect! That the eyes didn't match only seemed to make it more beautiful. Still staring at the small Rasta angel, Lactameon asked, "How much?" He could have sworn he saw wonder in both Ethan's eyes.

"For him? Fifty bucks."

Lactameon scowled. "*What?*"

A shadowy shrug. "Ain't chargin him tax. Lots of stuff the whiteman got no right taxin us for. That's one of 'em."

Lactameon glanced at the battered old box full of grimy glass stares. "Yo, man! Any fool see you had all them things a b'zillion years!"

Laughter. "Just like your lamp, big boy. Best y'all go truckin uptown an price the merchandise new, my man. If they even

let you in to look. Got me a livin to make." The reptile eyes
went thoughtful. "Sides, way you little fools doin the whiteman's
work these days, the demand for spare parts just might go on
the rise. Goddamn shame I ain't got me no boxful of brains."

"But," said Lactameon, before he realized how stupid it
sounded. "That a *blue* one, goddammit!"

"Well, hang on to anything long enough, y'all find a buyer.
Even hula girl lamps."

Lactameon felt his fury heating the air around him, but he
said nothing. Ethan had taken out his eye and now laid it back
with the others. It seemed all the more wrong to see him without
it. Lactameon wanted to grab the thing and run: but he couldn't
run. He just stood and watched in helpless rage as Ethan stood
on tiptoes to hand back the box.

"That his, an you know it!"

The old man shrugged. "An it be right here waitin when
he come back with the money to buy it."

"Yeah? Some things black people gots no right denyin each
other!"

The old man only chuckled. "This ain't Africa, boy. It the
whiteman's bills we payin here. Blood or money, we all his
collectors, little negro."

Out on the street, Lactameon grabbed Ethan's shoulders
and squatted in front of the boy. "Yo, sucker! Why didn't you
snag your eye an bail, man! Shit, bet you roust anythin ain't
nailed down!"

Ethan cocked his head. "Not my own eye, Tam! Yo, it gots
to be bought. With a real ceet so's nobody never say it ain't
mine."

"With a what? Oh." Lactameon sighed and nodded. "Mmm.
Guess you right, man." He got up and glanced down the street.
"Listen. You gonna get your eye, man. Word. Here my last two
dollars an some chrome. Score yourself somethin to eat. Maybe
hang awhile an play some games, then cruise on back to my
place bout dinnertime."

"I can't play dem games too good, man."

"Huh? Oh. Yeah. Cause you gots no depth perception."

"Huh?"

"Nuthin. Look, man. Just go an find somethin safe to do
somewheres. An, keep a eye out for Sabby!"

Leaving the little boy, Lactameon started down the block. Reaching the corner, he glanced back in time to see Ethan crossing the upper street. Goddammit, that stupid little sucker was going to the bus station anyway, even after all the ragging Lactameon had done. Didn't Ethan trust him? Lactameon glanced in the direction of Hobbes's apartment. Why should he give a shit about Ethan anyway?

A bus hissed to a halt at the stop. Lactameon checked its number. Maybe that was a sign? He hurried to get on.

Corbitt pushed through the station doors with the other passengers, too exhausted for much more than putting one foot in front of the other to somehow keep moving. His feet felt on fire, and he limped. Quest's end: Oakland, California, City of the Black. He'd been asleep when the bus pulled in, and the driver, black, fat, and grumpy, might have kicked him awake for all Corbitt knew. The man had looked at Corbitt like he figured he was drunk, and told him to move his black ass. Well, bus stations were all the same, and it wasn't logical to have expected a welcome, but Corbitt wondered why he felt nothing . . . no accomplishment, not even a sense of relief. Vaguely, he realized he'd let the door swing shut behind him in the face of an old lady struggling with two heavy suitcases. Two days ago he would have offered to carry the goddamned things! He didn't look back, and couldn't even remember if she was black or white.

The terminal wasn't even half as big as he had expected. Maybe Oakland was smaller than he'd thought? But it was just another station, except that now there was no escape as simple as boarding a bus. His tired eyes burned in the smoky air, and he wiped at his nose with the back of a hand. People's faces all looked the same, no matter what color, and all were indifferent to him.

The flow from the bus had almost carried him across the little room and out the front doors before he realized he couldn't face that yet. He stumbled aside to let people pass, bumped somebody, mumbled an excuse-me, and got what sounded like a curse in return. It took effort to focus his eyes. To his left was the waiting area with its all-too-familiar rows of butt-biting seats. A security guard, black and bored-looking, leaned on the ticket counter talking to a black lady clerk and occasionally scanning the room. Corbitt gazed longingly toward the chairs . . . god-dammit, he'd just spent a lot of money, surely Greyhound wouldn't grudge him an hour to sit and think?

But he knew better. He'd already watched that scene a million times; the demand for a ticket and, without one, the jerk of a thumb toward the doors. Maybe it happened faster to blacks, but it always happened eventually. Corbitt's ticket was all used up and he felt the same way. He saw the guard scan the room again, and knew he was conspicuous just standing there. To Corbitt's right, in the usual place by the bathroom door, stood a thin black boy, maybe fourteen, wearing a big gold chain. Like the guards, these boys seemed standard-issue for bus stations. Closer to Corbitt's right was a little restaurant. The smell of meat made Corbitt's empty stomach growl. He hadn't eaten much on the journey, figuring he didn't need the energy for just sitting on buses, and that restaurant food was so damned expensive. But coffee might clear the fog from his mind, and he could sit in peace for a while and decide his next-thing.

Corbitt entered the restaurant and ordered a large coffee from a pretty black girl at the counter. She looked tired too, but managed a smile anyhow. Corbitt took the cup to a tiny table in the farthest corner and slid his satchel underneath where he could sit with his feet on it. His stomach didn't much care for the hot coffee, but it did seem to wake up his mind a little. He wished he had a watch so he could glance at it from time to time to at least give the impression that someone was coming to meet him. There had to be someplace nearby where he could clean up and get a good night's sleep, even if it meant a sizable chunk of the nearly thirty dollars he had left. He felt dirty and sweaty and sticky, the salt and shot pocks itched on his chest, and he could smell himself. Finding a job would be the next-thing, and who would want to hire him in this sort of shape? The way his feet felt he wasn't even sure how far he could walk. Elbows on the tabletop, Corbitt dropped his face to his hands and stared down into his cup. The steam curling up reminded him of the mist on the river that last morning in Bridge-end. He suddenly felt scared and alone, the same way he had when Mrs. Griffin called his name.

Corbitt had frozen, pinned in the middle of the road by the old woman's questioning eyes. He'd never lied to Mrs. Griffin before, not even as a child, and he wasn't sure it was possible now. He swallowed, and his voice came out husky. "G . . . goin over to Toby's, Miz Griffin." It sounded like a lie in his own ears.

But, the old lady only chuckled again, making her sound like the girl, Lucianne. "Mmm. Way you walking this mornin make me think how Cain musta looked on his way to the land of Nod."

Corbitt lowered his eyes and swallowed again. He'd never understood that story . . . nothing Cain had ever done had pleased anybody, including God. Was it any wonder Cain had finally blown his top?

"Spect a young warrior might spare a minute to help a ole woman?" Mrs. Griffin asked with a smile. "I needin me that big ole chest of drawers moved so's I can dust back there. Really a job for a lion or tiger, but I spect a cheetah do just as well if he set his mind to it."

Or a houseboy? Corbitt's eyes flicked downriver to the black cloud of crows. He felt trapped. "Um . . . sho, Miz Griffin." He came down from the road and walked to the old office, watching the woman's expression as he neared. Her eyes were warm, like Lucianne's had been . . . or still were . . . and even her magic couldn't see everything. Then he remembered his chest, and cursed himself for not putting on a shirt, even if it would have been sweat-soaked by the time he reached the crossroads. He saw her eyes rest on the satchel a moment and then show concern as they lifted to his body. She came down from the porch. Corbitt stopped. "I . . . fall off the skateboard."

Another lie, and a stupid one! Corbitt knew for a fact that Mrs. Griffin could see what the wounds really were. Then, to Corbitt's horror, the woman turned to look downriver. A shadow crossed her face. "Best you come inside, Corbitt. Got me some salve to help them hurts."

Number One boasted two rooms, the largest in front, twice

the size of Corbitt's cabin, and the bedroom in back. Still, the main room seemed small, cluttered as it was with tables and trunks and dark old furniture from a long time ago. Except for the books and magazines and the little TV, Corbitt could have been stepping back into 1951. All seemed peaceful here. Morning sun sifted through the thick vines draping the porch and lit the room with a cool green glow like being underwater. The small skull sat atop the chest of drawers. Corbitt's eyes shied from it, but found the framed photo of the smiling young woman and soldier. It was dim and faded again.

Mrs. Griffin was studying Corbitt. She pointed to a chair at the kitchen table. "Sit down, son. There a long road ahead from thirteen, best you learn to rest whenever you can."

Corbitt thought of the bus, somewhere up the valley and coming for him, but pulled out the chair and sat down with the satchel at his feet. He stayed quiet as Mrs. Griffin tended his chest with her yellow sulphur salve. Her touch soothed and took the sting from the wounds. The ripple of children's laughter carried from outside. Then came Hayes's cry, "Look down there! Somethin *dead!*"

Corbitt flinched. Mrs. Griffin drew back her hand. "That hurt, son?"

Corbitt stared at the floor. "No. I . . ." Mrs. Griffin was watching him, but he seemed to feel other eyes from across the room. A sunbeam had found its way in and the small skull seemed to glow.

"I . . . had me this dream last night," said Corbitt.

Mrs. Griffin replaced the lid on the old blue cold-cream jar, then sat down at the table across from Corbitt and wiped her hands with a dish towel. "Mmm. Look like to me that dream of yours turn into somethin mighty real."

Corbitt turned slightly so he wouldn't see the skull from the corner of his eye. "Mean, you don't member?"

Mrs. Griffin's eyes looked past Corbitt, out the screen door, maybe toward the hills in the west. "Mmm. Just bits an pieces, son." She smiled a little. "Don't signify much. I dream a lot bout you."

A strange sort of feeling came over Corbitt . . . disappointment, maybe even betrayal. "Don't you never dream bout Weylen?"

Mrs. Griffin drew a sudden breath. Then her eyes sharpened, searching Corbitt's. "Yes, son. I do. But, how could you know bout him?"

The feeling of betrayal was growing in Corbitt; somehow like talking to Mr. Rudd the day before . . . only he hadn't put a name to it then. He glanced at the feed-store calendar tacked above the sink. "Don't matter how I know. But it was today, in 1951, Weylen come here. Wasn't it? Mr. Rudd was leavin out for California in his truck. He give Weylen a pat on the head an a nickel." Corbitt was watching Mrs. Griffin's face, seeing first wonder and then something else. Corbitt went on. "Miz Tate buy Weylen's catfish . . . fish he catch down at Bates's pool . . . for a dollar. But Weylen never get that dollar, did he? He leave after you feed him bacon an eggs, but he never come back for his dollar. Did he?" Corbitt had risen to a crouch, gripping the edge of the table with both hands, his eyes leveled at the old woman. "An you don't know why. Do you?"

Corbitt wasn't sure what he saw in Mrs. Griffin's eyes now, but it looked a lot like fear. He sank back into the chair and shook his head. "Weylen go down to Bates's pool again. Bates kill him there."

Mrs. Griffin made a frightened sound and lifted a trembling hand to her mouth. Corbitt had never seen her do such a thing. A long minute passed while the woman just stared at Corbitt. Then she got up, moving slowly like an old woman would, crossing to the chest of drawers and taking out a battered tin box. She brought it back to the table and opened it. Corbitt scented musty old paper. With unsteady fingers Mrs. Griffin searched inside. At last she drew out a dollar bill and hesitantly offered it to Corbitt. He noticed the words, *silver certificate,* on the front side, and that the seal was blue instead of green. Then he saw the series date and nodded. He ran a slender fingertip across the soft old paper, then looked up. "Why you been keepin this?"

Mrs. Griffin's eyes shifted away to gaze out the door. "I spose . . . for a while . . . I thought he come back for it. Then . . . well, I spect I just forgot about it."

Corbitt's fist clenched on the bill, crumpling it. "Why you be lyin to me?"

"Corbitt! You got no right . . ."

"What y'all gonna do, Miz Griffin? Wash out my mouth? I

know what a lie sound like, now!" Corbitt raised his fist. "You wasn't keepin this cause you thinkin he come back! This a kinda gris-gris cause you *wishin* him back! The onliest thing you forget be you *was* wishin him back!"

Mrs. Griffin's fingers clutched the edge of the box, rustling yellowed old paper from the past. "Corbitt, it was . . . lonely for me in them days, with Michael gone to Korea. We wanted children, son. Michael would've loved Weylen like his very own."

Corbitt only shrugged. "But Michael never come back. Then you buy Bridge-end with the government money. An there was always children after that. So, you went an forgot Weylen." Corbitt's fist unclenched and he pointed an accusing finger at the woman. "Trouble was, *Weylen* never forget that, one time, one place, somebody want him!"

Corbitt shook his head. "All your power . . . all the stuff you know . . . an you still give a name to a thing an call it back!" Corbitt felt watched again, somehow accused himself. He swung his finger to point at the skull. "Where you get that?"

The old woman seemed confused. She had lifted a letter from the box and was gazing at the faded handwriting. At first Corbitt wasn't sure she'd heard his question, but then she turned to look where he pointed. Her words came out in the same sort of tone she used telling stories to children.

"Back in '57. We had terrible spring floods that year. All of Bates's lower field was underwater . . . almost a foot of it right over this floor . . . an New Crossin sandbagged up to the shop windows. River come up so high it tore all the plankin off the new bridge, but ours stood against it strong as ever. County run a bulldozer up the ole highway cross Bates's land, clearin the way again. Bates raved an swore an waved his shotgun, but them people was Army Engineers an Bates had no power to stop 'em. I member them big green Army trucks rollin through here for days cross our ole bridge, even stoppin sometimes to help us, all them soldiers treatin us like we was every bit as important as them whitefolks in town."

Corbitt had gone to the chest of drawers, standing and looking at the skull while Mrs. Griffin spoke. He could imagine Bates's terror at having a bulldozer in his field.

Mrs. Griffin went on. "I found it downriver, a few days after the flood passed. Didn't seem right to just leave it lyin there."

Corbitt stared into the empty eye-sockets. Had that been Weylen's first try to make the secret known? Corbitt sighed. "So you brung him back after all, Miz Griffin. An you keep him here all them years. An he been watchin an listenin to the children play . . . seein 'em grow up. Musta been like that ole slave story you tell . . . bout how they used to lock them leather masks on us when we was workin the cane fields so's we couldn't eat none."

There was a quaver in the old woman's voice now. "Corbitt! You can't *know* that him!"

Corbitt only shook his head once more. "Just like I can't know bout this dollar?" He unfolded the bill and held it up in front of the skull; a childish thing like teasing a younger brother. "*This* what you been doin to him all these years, not knowin!" He shoved the dollar into his pocket and faced the woman. "Oh, but he a smart one, Miz Griffin . . . just like Bates an Mr. Rudd say *I* be. Weylen, he wait, an he watch all the children growin up. He breathe the magic around him. He try out his power like Lamar flexin his muscles. He even go to Toby. But, *I* be the one he want!"

Some of the fear left Mrs. Griffin's face. Her voice steadied. "Corbitt, you talkin pure nonsense! That ain't no magic, it somethin out one of them Friday-night spook movies."

Corbitt snorted. "So, what you tellin me now, Miz Griffin? There ain't no real magic? You been lyin bout that too?"

"Course there magic, son. You be a fool for denyin it. An we the most magical people on the face of this Earth. But Weylen was a warrior who never got to finish his quest. If his spirit still lingerin here, it cause of what Bates done to him."

The words came out easily. "Bates is dead and Weylen know it."

Nothing showed on Mrs. Griffin's face. She only nodded.

"It was a accident. Bates be tryin to kill us. Toby seen how it happen, but Lamar didn't . . . an it be best for Lamar not knowin." Corbitt glanced down at his chest. "But *you* already know bout Bates. Don't you?"

Mrs. Griffin sighed. "More logic than magic, son. Them

scars on you. All them crows gatherin at the riverbend. But most of all you leavin your home. But it should be Weylen who movin on to his next-thing. Not you."

"I gots a next-thing too, Miz Griffin. My own. An Weylen ain't gone nowhere. Warrior? My ass! He just a selfish little niggaboy! He *use* me for gettin his revenge back on Bates! I know cause I *feel* him tryin to get inside me . . . tellin me things in some language only him an me know. But seein Bates dead ain't enough for him. He wantin to steal me an *be* me for all the life he miss!"

Mrs. Griffin searched Corbitt's eyes, looking deep. "He *is* you, son. An you be him, just like you was the one before an the one before that. We was all Africans once. Even Toby got you in him. That a fact an there no denyin it. But there somethin else to this thing, Corbitt . . . some other secret you keepin back. That why you *feel* Weylen like something what don't belong in you."

"No! Goddammit, Weylen be just a lazy, thievin . . . *crow!*" Corbitt grabbed his satchel and started for the door.

"Corbitt." Mrs. Griffin's voice was gentle, but it stopped him in the doorway. "You part of eternity, son. All the thousands of miles you could put between you and Bridge-end don't signify a thing. You the past, the present, and the future, son. All of us are, an we all know it somewhere deep down inside. Tryin to deny it only make us miserable." Mrs. Griffin studied Corbitt for a moment, then sighed and lifted the lid of the box. "But I see y'all gonna have to find that out your ownself . . . again." She took out a brown envelope and offered it.

Corbitt took the unsealed envelope and looked inside. There were five twenty-dollar bills. He hesitated, but then finally nodded. "Thanks, Miz Griffin. I pay y'all back when I can."

"I know you will, son. Just like I know you gonna recognize yourself one day soon an see all the power an beauty there."

"Rock." It was a statement of fact in a sly whisper. Two days ago Corbitt would have first thought it meant music. He'd been sitting, chin in hands, staring into his coffee cup, but now his head jerked up, alert, as the boy with the gold chain slid into the next seat like he owned the whole station. Corbitt switched on his new face; the one he'd practiced for miles in those bus bathroom mirrors. Also well-practiced were his words. "Fuck off, sucka!"

"Kiss my ass, nigga!" the boy hissed back, standing up.

"Look too much like your face," returned Corbitt.

"Yeah? I fuck your momma *good!*"

Two days ago Corbitt would have flinched. Now he just made a fist in his crotch. "Fuck *this*, cocksucka!"

"Shee-ut!" The boy's hand dropped to his jeans pocket, but he shot a glance over his shoulder and saw the guard coming. "*Boy!*" he spat, spinning on his heel to leave.

"Best part of you run down your daddy's leg," Corbitt added. He watched the boy and guard pointedly ignore each other, remembering an old cartoon where a wolf and a sheepdog punched the same time clock every day. The guard ambled to the door and considered Corbitt a moment, but noted the coffee cup and left. Still, Corbitt knew it wouldn't be long. He thought about getting a burger to buy more time. Then he began to wonder where he was going to spend the night. Cheap hotels always had neon signs flashing through the windows, but he was too tired to care.

"Yo, brother."

What now? Corbitt turned to find a little brass-colored boy at his elbow. Dreadlocks floated in yellow-brown streamers down to the kid's waist. Then Corbitt saw the face and cringed back.

The little boy looked sad and stared at the floor. "I sorry I scare you, brother. But I lost an nobody help me."

Corbitt was almost surprised to find he could still feel pity for someone. The little boy looked up again. Corbitt tried to concentrate on the one tawny eye and ignore the savage empty place. The boy laid a brass-colored hand on Corbitt's ebony arm. "Please be my friend, man."

Corbitt touched the boy's shoulder.

"ETHAN!"

"Well, shit!" the little boy muttered. But, Corbitt's eyes had flicked up to find another boy in the doorway. Then he only stared stupidly. It just wasn't possible for any kid to be that fat! It was almost disgusting—even obscene—and it just didn't seem logical for a boy's skeleton to be supporting all that weight. The kid should have been comical as he came lumbering over, blubber slopping every which way and his faded red tank-top hardly covering any of it. Corbitt stared at those huge bobbing breasts: was it even a boy at all? And that slim little necklace, bone-white and turquoise, looked fragile and girlish above those black masses. But the round, chubby face was man-child furious.

"Get your motherfuckin hands off him, you cocksuckin fag-got nigger!"

Corbitt jerked his hand from the little boy's shoulder. "I . . . I not doin nuthin!"

It sounded like a lie in Corbitt's own ears, and the fat boy's words seemed to echo through the whole goddamn station. Cor-bitt felt blood burn his cheeks. The pretty girl at the food counter gave him a skeptical look. The fat boy grabbed hold of the small kid's shirt collar and yanked him aside like a crane moving scrap. Corbitt suddenly realized how much muscle had to be buried under all that jiggly bulk. The boy was almost a head shorter than Corbitt, but seemed more the size of a runaway truck. His big white teeth were bared in a snarl, and Corbitt found himself scared he was going to be eaten. He shifted way back in the slick plastic seat, almost wishing the guard would come in.

Lactameon kept a fistful grip on Ethan's big shirt. "Ah not dewin nuuuthin! Yeah right, motherfucka! Not till you get him inside a goddamn pay toilet anyways!" Lactameon knew he couldn't fight worth shit, but he wanted to smash a fist into the slender boy's face. The dude was tall, but didn't look any older than he was, and seemed so slim-boned and delicate that Lac-tameon could have thrown him to the floor and crushed his ribs with a kick. Yet, the dude's untamed hair, faded clothes, and big hands and feet gave him a wild kind of look. Lactameon decided that a cool exit would be the smartest next move. Still, he couldn't help scoping the boy a few moments more. It was almost as if he'd seen him before, but, shit, how could he have forgotten anybody *that* black? Lactameon had always considered himself about six out of seven on the African scale, with Beamer a five and Ethan maybe a one and a half. But now he couldn't remember ever seeing a blacker living thing; unless that stupid old crow could be counted. For sure, Silver scored a seven, but if Africa still had Africans this dude had his own area code. Somehow, the slim, fragile boy should have been wearing bones and a loincloth instead of that sweat-stained white T-shirt, jeans,

and B.K.s. Lactameon gazed at the boy for a few seconds more
. . . that's what it was; the dude looked a little like Silver.

Ethan squirmed, and Lactameon glanced down at the kid,
knowing how pitiful he could look when he tried. Maybe the
black dude had really just wanted to help?

Lactameon shrugged. "S'cool, man. Peace." Still holding
Ethan's shirt, he turned for the door.

Corbitt had caught the curiosity in the fat boy's quick eyes.
After two days of nonstop hate stares it was like a gleam of
sunlight through storm clouds. He wondered how kids in the
city could make friends at all if they constantly acted so bad to
each other. For two thousand miles he'd seen tiny tribes in and
around the bus stations, and each little pack was kept equal but
separate by some senseless hate, while the white people hated
them all.

Corbitt sensed some next-thing slipping past as the fat boy
led the small kid toward the door. Somehow they looked like
brothers, and that word came out of Corbitt's mouth as a half-
question.

Lactameon stopped. He couldn't remember ever hearing
the word spoken like that before. It didn't even sound like English, but it couldn't be denied. He turned around slowly, shifting his hand to Ethan's shoulder. "Yeah?"

"Um . . ." Corbitt saw the guard coming. One cup of coffee
just bought so much time for a nigger. Maybe there was a chart
in every bus station office? Corbitt did the logical thing. "Y'all
hungry?"

Lactameon hesitated. So, what did this strange dude want?
Maybe he figured to rent Ethan with food? The slender boy
stood, surprising Lactameon with his tallness. His lean waist was
bared by his shirt and made a stark contrast of white cotton over
ebony skin. Now it was Ethan who grabbed hold of Lactameon,
tugging at his hand.

"Shit yeah, Tam! C'mon!"

Lactameon offered the black dude a cautious smile. "Mmm.
Seem like you know the magic words, man."

Ethan dashed to the table and hopped on a seat by the
slender boy. "What ya gonna get, Tam? C'mon!"

Lactameon came over. Well, if this strange sucker figured

to buy Ethan with a meal he might as well be righteously burned. "Oh, bout four double cheeseburgers, deuce big Cokes, and a couple large fries."

Ethan smacked the tabletop with his palms. "Shit yeah! I have me da same, man!"

Corbitt's eyes widened. They had to be kidding! Well, maybe not the fat boy, though it was still hard to believe. But that skinny little kid? Corbitt looked at the menu above the food counter, noted the prices, and swallowed. "Um . . . sho nuff."

Squirming and twisting, the fat boy forced himself into a seat, his huge breasts flopping onto the tabletop. Corbitt got up and went to the counter, noticing that the guard now stood in the doorway. The man studied the scene for a moment, maybe trying to figure if the fat boy was breaking some law, but then walked away. A minute later Corbitt returned with his arms full of food and his money half gone. The meat scent was driving his own stomach crazy. He set the stuff down and glanced at the guard's back. "Figured he was gonna run us all out."

The little boy giggled, first gulping Coke, then stuffing his mouth full of burger. "Rhun us awwl out!" he echoed after swallowing. "Yo, dude, you sound just like Buckwheat!" He took another huge bite, his cheeks puffing like a chipmunk's as he chewed without closing his mouth.

"Shut up, Ethan," murmured the fat boy, tearing into his first burger almost as messily as the little one had. "He prob'ly from somewheres else, what it is. Shit we in a goddamn bus station, man, an some black people really do go somewheres." He glanced at Corbitt. "Huh?"

"Um . . ." said Corbitt, sipping coffee that boiled in his belly like battery acid. "Yeah, man. That what it is. Sho nuff."

"Shooo, nuff!" echoed Ethan. He reached for his Coke, but would have knocked it into Corbitt's lap except for Corbitt's grabbing it in time. "Shit, I sorry, man," Ethan mumbled around another mouthful of meat. "I gots me dis motherfuckin death recession."

Corbitt handed back the cup. "Huh? Oh." He made himself look at the small, damaged face, trying to get used to it. "Well, I'm thinkin y'all really be meanin you *don't* gots none."

The little boy gulped more Coke, and blasted a burp. "Shit yeah!"

Lactameon cocked an eyebrow at the black boy. "Yo. Mean, you *understand* what he sayin, man?"

Corbitt shifted his butt on hard plastic that seemed to resent his ass. The little kid's face bothered him, though he supposed that was logical, but the fat boy's chest bothered him too, and there shouldn't have been any logic in that. Those were *boy* breasts, goddammit, no matter how big and soft they looked spread out on the table. And they sure as *hell* didn't look like Sherry's! "Huh? Oh. Well, it . . . logical. Spect he gots him a hard time with readin at school."

"Shit no!" said the little boy. "Yo, I can't hardly read a motherfuckin word, man!"

Lactameon popped a fistful of fries into his mouth. "What I sayin is, I only know one dude in the whole world down with shit like 'depth perception,' man. Um, you from Africa?"

"No. I from . . . Mississippi."

Ethan had started on his second burger just as savagely as the first. "Yo! What 'sippi?" he demanded. "Everbody dere look like you, man?"

"Ethan!"

"Well, shit! Ain't dat logical, Tam?"

Despite his misery at smelling the food and watching the other boys stuffing it down while his own stomach raged, Corbitt managed a smile for the little kid. "Course it be, man. That just all the data you gots in your 'puter right now."

"Shit yeah!"

Lactameon noted the slender boy's occasional shy glance at his chest. "You just get out, man?"

"Huh? Uh . . . oh." Corbitt frowned a little. "No. Nuthin like that."

Lactameon slid his hand under one rolly mass. "Wanna feel, man? Get it out your system. Lotta dudes do. I won't scream."

Corbitt dropped his hands to his lap. "Course not! I ain't one of them kind!"

The fat boy grinned. "I know, man, cause ain't no faggot I ever heard of down with fat boys. Maybe we 'mind 'em of what they don't like." He gulped more Coke, then glanced at the slender boy again. "Been a long time, though, huh?"

Corbitt sighed. "Seem like forever, an that be the God's honest truth, brother." He studied the fat kid more openly now.

"Um . . . 'scuse me for askin, but how it feel bein so . . . big?"

Lactameon popped more fries, and shrugged. "Just say fat, man. It save time. Shit, I dunno. So, how it feel bein so skinny?"

Corbitt cocked his head. "Um, 'pared to what?"

"What I sayin, man. I always been this way."

Corbitt nodded slowly. "Mmm. That logical fo sho."

"So, what it like where you come from, man? Say, you gots a 'puter your own?"

"No. See, we all be kinda poor where I comin from."

"Yeah? Well, we all kinda 'po' here too, man. Don't let all this blubber smoke your ass." Lactameon began on his fourth burger. "So, you pick cotton an that sorta shit?"

Corbitt was still trying not to watch the other boys eat. It was cruel to see the little one forcing food into an already full stomach . . . cruel for both him and Corbitt. There really wasn't any way Ethan would finish all that third burger without either throwing up or exploding. And, what would become of the fourth, and those fries, and that second big Coke? Corbitt glanced back at the fat boy, who was munching the last of his fries. He wondered what would happen when all the food was gone. He was suddenly scared of being alone again. "Well, most of that be growin on big ole farms, an machines do the pickin."

Lactameon licked his fingers and sucked down the last swallow of Coke. "Figure. Guess the whole goddamn world gots machines doin the nigger-work now. Till the whitefolks run outa gas anyways."

Corbitt put his elbows on the tabletop and dropped his chin in his hands, his eyes never leaving the little boy's untouched fourth burger. Lactameon pointed.

"Yo. You want that, man? He ain't never gonna kick it."

Ethan stopped struggling with what was still left of his third. "Shit yeah I am!"

Lactameon smiled. "Yo, Ethan. You can't get fat in one day, man. Sides, you go an puke, you lose everythin. That logical, ain't it?"

"Well . . . yeah."

Lactameon turned to the slender boy. "So, you want it, man?"

Corbitt swallowed. "Um . . . no. Go on ahead, brother. I . . . already eat."

The little boy set down his unfinished burger. "Um, I seed dis movie, man. Bout dat 'sippi place. Yo! First dey catch your ass in da jungle, huh? Like, when you out huntin lions an shit. Den dey chain you up an brung you to 'sippi on a ship, huh? An dem white motherfuckas whip your ass a lot, huh? Shit, bet your back hurt, man! Huh?"

"Well, it didn't a'zactly happen yesterday." What did hurt Corbitt were the healing salt pocks on his chest.

The little boy had slumped back in the seat. His legs were spread wide, and his tummy puffed out like a basketball beneath his big shirt. He rested a small hand gently on it, and took careful sips from his Coke as if too big a one would pop him for sure. His eyes were half shut, concealing the empty place. "I mean, when you was a *little* kid, man."

Corbitt's eyes drifted back to the partly eaten burger. He sighed. "Swear, sometime it do seem only yesterday."

The fat boy swallowed the last bite of burger. "Mmm. Well, welcome to Oaktown, brother. I Lactameon, but Tam save time."

"Corbitt," said Corbitt, doing the brother-shake with the fat boy.

The little kid had his eyes completely closed now. He'd slipped one hand under his shirt and was gently stroking his swollen stomach, seeming to balance somewhere between pleasure and pain. He made a small wave with the Coke cup in his other hand. "Ethan," he murmured.

"Um, y'all gonna be eatin what left there, Ethan?"

"I take it with me for later on, man."

"Oh."

Lactameon sipped the last of his Coke. "Yo. I thought you say you was poor, Corbitt. So, how come you buyin us lunch?"

"Well . . . I had me some travelin money, Tam."

Ethan opened one eye. "Gots fifty dollars, Corbitt?"

"Ethan!"

"Well!"

"Um, no," said Corbitt. "Not that much. Not no more."

Lactameon found a stray fry. "Well, guess your folks comin for your ass pretty soon then, huh? So, what part of town they live in, man?"

Corbitt sighed. What was he going to do now? He felt

strangely ashamed. "Well . . . um, I be sorta waitin here hopin to make me some new friends, Tam."

"Huh? Well, shit, brother, you sure the fuck from somewheres else! Ain't nobody make friends in this motherfuckin bus station!"

"Cept homos," added Ethan.

A new voice said, "Shit, I be your friend, man."

"An suckas like *him*," added Lactameon.

Corbitt looked up, seeing the kid with the chain. Ethan gave the dealer-boy a glance, then made a face. "Go home an fuck your momma some more, Gilligan."

The boy's hand whipped to his pocket. "Shut the fuck up, you little cocksucka! I fuckin slice out your other eye an shove it up your asshole!"

Corbitt stood up, a little scared, but clenching his fists. Then, Lactameon spoke, sounding just bored. "Nobody need friends like you, Gilligan. Do a homo an blow . . . *boy*."

Corbitt tensed, but Gilligan's hand stayed out of his pocket. "Fuck you, fat boy!"

Lactameon rolled his eyes. "Oh, *that* original, sucker. S'matter, Gilligan, batteries goin dead already?"

"That ain't my goddamn name, man!"

Ethan snickered, and sipped more Coke. "Oughta be, motherfucka. Ya look just like him. So dere!"

"Bout as bright, too," added Lactameon.

"Shit! Your belly look just like somebody's butt, man!"

"Your *face* look just like somebody's butt, Gilligan." Grunting and squirming again, Lactameon pulled his bandana from his back pocket and twirled it on a chubby finger.

Gilligan glared. "Shit, man, I ain't scared of you pussy cocksuckas!"

Ethan burped, and patted his tummy. "Yo, Gil-i-gan. Word say Hobbes trollin for your ass."

Corbitt saw sudden fear flash in Gilligan's eyes, but the boy only muttered another curse and stomped out the door. Corbitt sat down again, glancing once at the yellow bandana, but deciding to stay cool. Kids who wore those weren't playing Ninja Turtles anymore. "Um, y'all know that . . . sucka . . . Tam?"

The fat boy laid his bandana on the tabletop, and shrugged.

"Since second grade, man. Used to work for a friend of mine. Till he got greedy."

Ethan yawned. "Hobbes gonna kick dat motherfucka! Word!"

"Ethan, shut up."

"Well he *is*! So dere!"

Corbitt wasn't totally sure he understood, but a new thought came. "Um, Tam? This here Hobbes? Y'all sayin he hire . . . dudes . . . to work?"

Lactameon studied the slender boy. This dude was definitely something way new. Lactameon could somehow picture him spearing a lion, but wasn't sure he'd have been up for Gilligan's box knife. "Mmm. Well, I don't figure it really your kinda thing, Corbitt." Lactameon stretched and yawned, then glanced at the clock on the wall. "Anyways, guess you gots the 411 on this sorry-ass motherfucker now. Better go call your folks. Yo, you never did say where you gonna be livin, man."

Corbitt sighed, propping his elbows on the tabletop once more and dropping his face in his hands. "Shit, Tam. Ain't nobody waitin for me. I run away."

Lactameon cocked his head. Ethan sat awkwardly up, both eyelids wide once again.

"The fuck, man," said Lactameon. "Well, Jeeze, Corbitt, you shoulda told us! Yo! Figure runnin away or havin no home somethin you sposed to be shamed of?"

"Shit yeah!" said Ethan, shoving what was left of his burger at Corbitt. "Here, man, you can have dis! I figure me somethin for later!"

The burger was instantly in Corbitt's mouth. It was cold now, and greasy, but nothing had ever tasted so goddamn good! Ethan searched through the wreckage on the tabletop, scraping odd bits of food in a pile, then pushed it over to Corbitt, then poured what remained in all the Coke cups together in one and set it at Corbitt's elbow. Corbitt glanced up once from stuffing his mouth and saw Gilligan in the main terminal getting marched out by the guard. He pointed. "Mmm. Back to his island he go."

Ethan giggled. Lactameon grinned. Corbitt finished the small mound of food, gulped the last of the watery Coke, then licked his fingers. "Know? I always used to wonder over that. What I sayin is, there be all them people stuck on that there island an always inventin all sorta stuff, but ain't none of 'em smart enough to patch them two holes on that boat. Shit, that been the first thing I'd done, best believe!"

Lactameon studied the slender boy again. "Mmm. Yeah. But then, you a African, man."

The afternoon air was lifeless and hot, heavy with exhaust fumes that burned Corbitt's eyes as he followed the other boys out on the sidewalk. Corbitt scented other things: sunbaked concrete, asphalt and oil, strange chemical smells, dry-rotted wood and dusty old brick, and the faint reek of ripening garbage. He almost asked Lactameon if Oakland always smelled this way, but the fat boy sucked a deep breath and sighed. "Shit, I hate the stink of that goddamn bus station, man! Cool gettin out where you can breathe again, huh, Corbitt?"

"Sho nuff," Corbitt murmured, trying not to wrinkle his nose. He looked around, blinking tired eyes in the sun-glare reflected from a thousand windows and the glass of passing cars. Two battered taxis were parked at the curb. The drivers, both black, sat on the hood of one and shared a newspaper. They glanced up as the station door opened, but seeing just the three boys, went back to reading. Corbitt noticed a street sign: Martin Luther King Jr. Way. That seemed reassuring. Then he saw Gilligan on the corner leaning against a lamppost, smoking some sort of small pipe and being casually cautious about it. It took Corbitt a second to realize what it was. It didn't seem right on a street with that name.

Lactameon saw where Corbitt was looking. "Yo, man. Don't pay no attention to that stupid sucker."

"Shit yeah!" said Ethan. "He already dead!"

A shiver traced Corbitt's spine. "What you meanin, dead?"

Lactameon gave the little boy a poke. "He mean that asshole smokin his own profits, man. Shit, Corbitt, for a second you look like you figure he a zombie or somethin."

Corbitt scowled. "I don't go believin in none of that shit."

Lactameon shrugged, like he'd heard that before. He'd slipped the yellow bandana back in his pocket after they'd left the table. Corbitt had expected him to put it on, but supposed there was a reason he hadn't. The fat boy stripped off his tank-top and stuck it in his pocket too. Ethan instantly pulled off his own shirt and tied it around his waist. Corbitt followed the other boys' lead. It was plenty hot enough, but he hadn't been sure about walking around in the city half-naked. He tried not to stare at Lactameon. The fat boy's belly seemed to pour out of his body in a huge wobbly wave. With his back bowed to balance it, he also looked like he was following it, and every change of direction reminded Corbitt of a Caterpillar tractor swinging itself around anything it couldn't climb over or run down. Yet there was nothing really awkward about how he moved, any more than a D-8 clearing a country road. Corbitt thought of Lamar and his huge mass of muscle, but he wouldn't have stood the ghost of a chance against Lactameon in a wrestling match. Corbitt smiled, noticing that Ethan had let his own jeans slip low to cling partway off his brassy little butt, and thrust out his tummy in imitation of Lactameon the way kids always copied anyone they admired. Corbitt glanced down at his own slender frame and flat stomach. He couldn't recall ever seeing one of the Bridge-end children copying his walk. Toby had said he sometimes looked *slinky*. Well, none of the Bridge-end children had ever bleached their hair or taken up weight-lifting, either.

Lactameon yanked at his jeans, then looked at Corbitt. "Well, we better start schemin where you gonna crib tonight, man. Seem like once that covered in your mind it make the rest of the day easier to chill with. Know what I sayin?"

Corbitt unzipped his satchel and stuffed his T-shirt inside. "Mmm. Sound logical to me, Tam. Um . . . you dudes gots homes?"

Ethan frowned slightly. "Shit yeah, man! Course . . . some-time we don't wanna go dere." He looked up at Lactameon. "Huh, Tam?"

"Mmm. Yeah, Ethan. That right."

Ethan toed Corbitt's satchel. "Oughta score you a pack, man."

Lactameon glanced up the street. "Word him later, Ethan. C'mon, we get us a bus over on San Pablo."

Lactameon started for the corner, ignoring Gilligan, who was ignoring him. Ethan followed, pausing once to jerk his jeans further down in front. Glancing back, Lactameon saw the slender boy limping painfully after them. "Yo! S'up, Corbitt? Shit, man, you look like one of them cheetahs with a nail in its paw or somethin."

Corbitt frowned. Was the past going to follow him everywhere? Or did he just look *naturally* slinky? He knelt to loosen his shoelaces a little. "Why you be callin me that?"

Lactameon shrugged. "Shit, man, I didn't mean nuthin. Just sorta come to my mind. Like, we used to play this game when we was little kids . . . jungle cats in the park . . . that sorta shit."

"Mmm. So, which was you, Tam?"

"Well . . . a lion, man. See, lions are big, an they don't climb trees."

Despite the pain in his feet, Corbitt smiled. "Askin me, it still fit you, man."

Ethan poked a thumb to his chest. "I was playin, I be a fuckin saber-tooth tiger!"

"They extinct," said Lactameon.

"Yeah? Well, so do lions, man! I been to dat zoo!"

Corbitt untied one shoe and pulled it off. "I just can't wear these goddamn things no more. They be makin my feet go extinct."

"Shit, man," said Ethan. "Mean, you gonna go barefoot? *Here?*"

"Why not? There some law 'gainst it?"

Lactameon shrugged again. "I don't think so. I just never seen nobody do it before."

Ethan squatted and pressed a palm to the sidewalk. "Shit, Corbitt, you gonna fuckin toast your toes off, man!"

"An there dogshit an busted glass where we goin," added Lactameon.

Corbitt pulled off the other shoe, and then his stiff, sweaty socks. "Well, can't be no worse'n cowflops an scrap iron. Um, yo, they be lettin you on them city buses like this?"

Lactameon snorted. "Shit, man, you gots a pass or some money, they let on a zombie, grave-dirt an everythin." He watched Corbitt unzip the satchel to slip his shoes in. "Yo! I gots that same book, man! Bout them space panthers. Shit, you read too! Ain't that a bitch! Kinda like some sorta sign."

Frowning a little, Corbitt zipped the satchel, and stood. "I say before, man. I don't go believin in none of that supernatural shit."

"Mmm. Well, who say that shit *super*-natural, man? An, you bein . . ."

"An, I ain't no goddamn African neither!"

Gilligan still leaned on the lamppost. He slipped the pipe back in his pocket and shot Lactameon an evil glare as the three boys walked past. Ethan stuck a finger down his throat and looked like he was trying to cross his eyes. Lactameon stepped around the corner of the station building, then froze. Ethan ran into him with a yelp of surprise. An old 70's Camaro, dark blue and dented, came ripping from the shadow of the 980 overpass. Lactameon twisted a look over his shoulder: the stoplight was red but the car wasn't slowing. Turning again, he noted two figures in the car's front seat. The passenger window was open. Then he saw the gun. "DOWN!"

Corbitt was just rounding the corner when he saw the fat boy stop. He heard the roar of an old-time V-8, and saw the Camaro burst from under the freeway bridge. Toby liked that model car. Corbitt noticed blue-black smoke from tarnished sidepipes as the driver floored an engine long overdue for a rebuild. The car's ass-end squatted with torque. Corbitt saw Lactameon's head jerk around, the chubby face suddenly tense. His own eyes followed the fat boy's to the signal light, then logic made him look to see if anyone was in the crosswalk. There wasn't, but a couple of Japanese cars were in the intersection. Then Lactameon yelled.

Ethan flung himself flat on the sidewalk like he wanted a molecular bonding. The fat boy spun around, moving like a roly-poly lion cub. Corbitt just stood stupidly, clutching his satchel. Time seemed to slow, like a movie when too many things were happening too fast for real time to show. Corbitt caught an eye-corner glimpse of the taxi drivers diving for cover between their two cars. The newspaper pages fluttered away like little ghosts. Corbitt saw Gilligan stare up the street at the oncoming car, mouth open, eyes glassy, and movements confused. The Camaro's thunder seemed to shake the pavement under Corbitt's bare feet. The car skidded sideways into the intersection, tires screeching and smoking as the driver recovered by stomping the gas. Both smaller cars cut out of its way and swerved toward each other. Corbitt saw a honey-colored boy, shirtless and muscled with a black cap on backwards, lean from the Camaro's window and aim a big gun. The boy almost looked like Lamar, but had a black bandana covering most of his face, more like an Arab than an outlaw. Orange flame spat from the gun muzzle.

Lactameon had started to drop beside Ethan, but looked up in time to see Corbitt still standing. "Drive-by, asshole!" Somehow he managed to turn his fall into a stumbling charge that brought him slamming into Corbitt like a bulldozer. Corbitt crashed flat on his back with Lactameon on top. The satchel flew from his hand and tumbled across the sidewalk. Screams and bullets sliced the air. The screams must have been Gilligan's, but tires were screaming too. A car horn let out a long, bleating beep. There came a crash and the crumpling crunch of sheet-metal carrying over the gun's chugging clatter. The auto-fire sounded so different from movies, less loud but more deadly. Bullets ripped the air like the hissing of whips. Corbitt's head hit hard on the concrete. Colors exploded behind his eyes, jabbing and rippling to the rhythm of gunfire. Ricochets twanged and whined off the station's steel and brick. Something bit Corbitt's arm. Something else stung his leg. A last scream choked off. The gunfire stopped. Tires tore at pavement as the Camaro roared away.

Down Martin Luther King street. Corbitt struggled for breath, his ribs creaking under Lactameon's weight. He fought the soft blackness smothering him. Lactameon cursed. "Stop it, asshole, that hurts!" He rolled off the slender boy and slammed against the building. Brick chips slid from his back and made dry little clatters on the concrete. Corbitt lay still a moment, trying to suck air. His ribs ached. Then he turned his head toward the street. He found himself looking into Gilligan's eyes.

He remembered when Lucas had shot the old dog; how he and the other children had gathered around the body. The dog's eyes had looked the same way; almost alive but gazing off in some infinite direction no living eye could follow. Gilligan's eyes were clear now, but empty. Two good eyes wasted when Ethan only had one. Gilligan's cheek was pressed to the sidewalk. A cigarette butt lay an inch from his nose. Blood had come out of his mouth, but hadn't spread very far. It was already thickening in the heat. Corbitt scented the little-child smell of piss-wet jeans. His stomach twisted. He scrambled away from the body and slammed into Lactameon, who was struggling to get up.

"Chill, goddammit! Corbitt! Yo! You okay, man? You bleedin."

Corbitt crouched against the wall, fighting not to be sick. Blood dripped from a cut on his arm, and there was another bloody patch on his Levi's where brick chips had hit. "I . . . okay." He looked back at Gilligan. There was nothing movie-like about the sprawled body, and no posing could have made it look any more dead. He realized that only seconds could have passed since the shooting. The taxi drivers were just poking their heads from between the two cabs. The station doors opened a crack, but no one came out. The Camaro's engine-sound was fading away, but distant horns and screeching tires traced its passage along the blocks. The two small cars had collided in the intersection, but their drivers stayed in them, huddled down. A wisp of steam curled from one's grille. Corbitt scented hot antifreeze over the bite of fresh blood and the sour smell of piss and the gunpowder smoke still drifting in the air: Ethan eased warily around the corner of the station, his single eye taking in all.

"Yo! You dudes okay?"

Automatically, Corbitt nodded, still staring at the dead boy. Part of his mind saw the cabdrivers jump in their cars and haul-ass away. Lactameon had made it to his feet, but slumped back against the bullet-pocked wall.

"Yeah," he panted. "But we gots to bail, man. Fast!"

At first, that made no sense to Corbitt. He heard a siren in the distance, then remembered who he was and where he was. He scrambled up beside Lactameon. But, Ethan darted to Gilligan's body and pawed through the dead boy's pockets.

"Ethan, no!" yelled Lactameon.

Ethan snatched out a black nylon wallet and tore the gold chain over Gilligan's head. "Shit, man, he *rat food!*"

Corbitt's stomach lurched again.

"Ethan, goddammit, get away from him!"

The little boy stood, looking fierce. "Well, he *is!*"

Lactameon grabbed Corbitt's arm. "C'mon, man!"

"Huh?"

"*Bail!*"

Numbly, Corbitt let the fat boy jerk him along by the wrist, stumbling around the corner and then breaking into a clumsy run under the freeway bridge. Dimly, he realized that the huge kid *was* actually running. It hardly seemed possible, yet he couldn't seem to keep up.

"Bus!" panted Lactameon. "Next corner! Stoppin! Go for it!"

Corbitt heard the siren coming closer. Another joined it from a different direction. Suddenly, he remembered. "My goddamn satchel!" He tried to stop, but Lactameon clamped on and kept going and it was either run or get dragged. Ethan, loping easily along beside the bigger boys, pointed skyward. "Hammer-copter comin!"

The fat boy was pouring sweat, his jeans soaked and slipping half off his butt. He held them with one hand, pulled Corbitt with the other, and somehow still ran. Diesel smoke swirled. Air brakes hissed. Blood was running down Corbitt's arm and there was a big ruby stain on his leg, but the bus driver only gave Ethan a second glance after seeing Lactameon's pass and taking the money the little boy shoved at him. The man flipped the switch that shut the doors, and swung the bus away from the curb. Lactameon stumbled up the aisle and flopped on the back seat. Ethan hopped up beside him and Corbitt sank down on the other side.

"Dis ain't da right bus," said Ethan.

Lactameon had his eyes closed. Gasping for breath, he just waved a hand at first, but then finally panted. "Better . . . We catch . . . nuther one . . . back. I gots . . . to chill. Shit!"

Ethan pulled the shirt from around his waist and began to mop Lactameon's body. "Shit, man. I never knew you could run!"

"I didn't . . . neither."

"Um," said Corbitt. "Maybe it like that story bout the fox an the rabbit . . . rabbit run faster for his life than the fox for his supper."

Lactameon opened one eye. "Shit. Hope I . . . never gots to run . . . for *my* supper, man! That sposed to be a . . . African story. My mom . . . tell me that."

"I tellin y'all, I ain't no African!"

Lactameon shut his eye again, still gasping. Corbitt hesitated a moment, then bent down and pressed his ear to Lactameon's chest. The fat boy's heartbeat came muffled from deep under his breast with the solid iron thump of an old John Deere.

"I get my ass shot off long before I gots heart probs, man." Lactameon managed a smile as Corbitt sat up, but then it faded. "Shit, man. Sorry bout your bag. Um, there wasn't no I.D. or nuthin in it, huh?"

Corbitt shook his head, taking Ethan's shirt to wipe the blood and sweat from his own body. "Just all my goddamn clothes . . . an my motherfuckin shoes!"

Ethan giggled. "Mah mutherfukkin shues!"

"Ethan!"

"Well!" Ethan held up the gold chain. "Yo, Corbitt! I score your ass some bran new shues, man!"

Lactameon took the chain and gave it a glance. "Mmm. Not with this, dude. It fuckin cheap plated shit. Lucky that pawn sucker give you a nickel on it."

"Aw, motherfuckin Gilligan! Maaaan!" Ethan yanked out the wallet and tore into it. Corbitt watched the little boy in fascination, almost feeling sick again. "But . . . he dead. An, we seen him die."

"Shit," muttered Ethan, concentrating on the wallet. "Aw, nine fuckin dollars! Big motherfuckin wow! Maaaan!"

Lactameon struggled to sit up a little straighter. "Told you he smokin his profits." Then he turned to Corbitt. "Yo, man, I keep forgettin you ain't from here. Guess you never seen nobody get kicked."

Once by a mule. But he didn't need that explained. Corbitt stared down at the dirty floor. "Yeah. I did, sorta. But that a different color horse."

Ethan dropped Gilligan's wallet out the window and looked

interested. "Yo! Mean you kick somebody, man? Dat why you runned away?"

Corbitt clasped his hands between his knees. "Sorta. But, that past now. What I sayin is, Gilligan just a kid. Like us. Um . . . we *is* still called kids here, huh?"

Lactameon shrugged. "Most liquor stores won't sell us beer, guess that still make us kids. But, Gilligan was sellin shit kill other kids, man. Like us. Shit, he woulda kicked your ass in a second for your green, Corbitt. Like, what go round, come round. An that happen way fast here."

Corbitt shook his head and stared out the window. All cities looked the same. "We hear bout this sorta stuff . . . where I come from. See it on TV, an read bout it in the Jackson paper . . . gangs an drugs an killin. Even gots a gang at the New Crossin school . . . course, they be just kids actin out parts. Dude in that car . . . pull the trigger . . . look ever bit like one of my brothers back home. An he same age as me."

Lactameon wiggled his jeans a little more over his butt, then touched Corbitt's arm. "Let him go, man."

"Huh?" Corbitt stiffened. "What you tellin me?"

"I seen it happen lot of times, Corbitt. It like, when you close to somebody who die like that . . . even you don't even know him . . . it like you try an catch his spirit an hold on to it. Shit, maybe his spirit grab you, I don't know. I seen a lotta dudes carryin dead kids around with 'em, man. It don't do no good for neither of 'em. Let him go." Lactameon searched Corbitt's eyes. "I know you hearin me, man. Just do it."

Corbitt turned back to the window. "Lady I know always sayin to think four good things bout somebody, fore y'all decide you don't like 'em."

"Mmm. His name was Bradford. He used to build model airplanes an tell them sorta gross kid-jokes. He always give me his apple in second grade cause he didn't like 'em. Yo, now he gone, man. Ain't your prob worryin where. You gots probs of your own right here."

Corbitt faced the fat boy once more. "Y'all see things, don't you, Tam?"

Lactameon smiled. "My mom say you always know a real African when you see one."

Soft evening sunlight slanted through the bus windows, lending warm tones to the passengers' faces. Ethan's small body seemed to glow almost gold. The bus swung around a corner. It was the last of three since leaving the station, and the half-dozen people on board were all shades of black. Most were dressed for hard work, and looked tired, though none seemed as weary as Mississippi laborers. The flow of their talk seemed as warm as their skins; so different from the second bus which had been mostly white. Fact was, any group of whites Corbitt had seen seemed to more or less deny each other. But then they knew they weren't outnumbered.

Corbitt was starting to get used to how fast people spoke here, and he was surprised to see how many different kinds of black people there were in the world . . . all shapes and sizes, and hairstyles and shades, and speaking with all sorts of accents, though none seemed to look much like him. No wonder Lactameon took him for an African. Corbitt glanced at the fat boy, who was slumped in the seat and seemed to be sleeping. Except for Ethan, most of the kids that Corbitt had seen so far looked fairly well fed. Some were chubby, and a few Corbitt would have called fat . . . if Lactameon hadn't given him a whole new definition of that word.

The bus leaned into the corner and Lactameon rolled sideways, almost burying Ethan against the window. But the little boy only stared out for a moment, then poked Lactameon where another kid's ribs would have been.

"Tam! We goin da wrong way!"

"Huh?" Lactameon opened his eyes. He struggled to sit up, glancing around. Corbitt was almost shoved into the aisle as Lactameon half stood and called to the driver. "Yo!"

The driver glanced in his big mirror, hesitated, then looked disgusted and swung the bus toward the curb. Brakes hissed, and the bus lurched to a stop still half in the street. The man was black, but like most bus drivers Corbitt had seen, he looked like he'd seen everything twice and didn't want to see any more. He flipped the switch that opened the doors, and their sound passed for spitting a curse. His eyes in the mirror added another as Lactameon came down the aisle with Corbitt and Ethan behind.

"S'up?" asked Lactameon. "You wasn't sposed to turn for three more blocks, man."

The driver took a slow breath and drummed his fingers on the wheel. He seemed to be considering replies. He wouldn't say anything about Lactameon's weight: like Ethan's eye and Corbitt's bare feet, that would have been too easy. Corbitt saw the man note the bright bit of yellow showing from the fat boy's pocket.

"Route been changed. Maybe we tired of buyin new windshields. You could read, you know that." The man smiled with one side of his mouth. "You can't get out here, can you, boy? Just like back in the ole days, cept now it ain't whitey you worried about."

Corbitt looked around. The neighborhoods had been getting dirtier and more ramshackle as the bus had rolled toward the lowering sun. Most of the shops and houses had bars on their windows, and several intersections had liquor stores on all four corners. Still, there were kids laughing and playing, and older people walking and talking to each other like everything was normal. At least nobody else had been drive-byed.

Still smiling, the driver reached for the door switch. "Guess you just got to ride all the way back an get yourself a transfer, boy. Bitch, ain't it?"

Lactameon's chubby face hardened. "We get out here." He turned to the others. "C'mon."

The driver laughed. "I send flowers to your momma, boy."

Ethan flipped a finger. "I fuck *your* momma good, cock-sucka!"

The doors snicked shut, snapping at Corbitt's butt as he stepped down in the street behind Ethan. Diesel screaming, the bus bucked ahead and roared off in a black cloud of smoke. Lactameon was already on the sidewalk, heading back to the corner at a lot faster pace than Corbitt would have expected after the energy it must have cost him to run. Ethan was almost trotting beside him. Corbitt caught up easily. The fat boy was puffing hard, but looked determined to get somewhere fast. Ethan kept glancing around as if searching for predators. He pointed. "Yo, Tam. Next block, we can cut cross da tracks past Hobbeses's ole house."

Lactameon nodded. "Yeah. Be longer that way, but maybe we keep our asses."

"Um?" asked Corbitt. "This here one of them bad hoods, Tam?"

" 'Pend on your color, man. Why that motherfuckin driver look like some pig's momma suckin his jimmy."

Corbitt looked around. "But we all be black, so what here we gots to worry over?"

"Leopards!" whispered Ethan. "An, stop lookin all round like dat, fool! Wanna scope, stay chill!"

Corbitt stopped scanning the street like he was on a tour of a foreign land. "Mmm. Spose y'all be tellin me them Leopards the kind with two legs?"

Lactameon snorted. "Give the niggaboy a cee-gar! We Collectors . . . guess that make you one too, less you wanna hang here an try makin some new friends, man."

"Friends too goddamn hard to find, Tam. Make me almost believe a little in signs, meetin up with you an Ethan."

"Yeah? Well, make the sign of the cross till our asses on the other side them tracks there, man. Shit! Mean three more motherfuckin blocks goin that way!"

"Um, I sposed to be lookin for anybody special, Tam?"

"Green bandana. But you prob'ly won't see nobody wearin one."

"Y'all, um . . . be at war with these Leopards, Tam?"

"Naw. Fact is, I know their mascot pretty good . . . um, I

only a mascot too. But, this still their ground an we gots no right cruisin it."

"Um . . ."

Lactameon wiped sweat from his face. "Chill, Corbitt. I don't gots the fuckin breath left for a 411 call! Sides, talk about trouble an you call it up!"

Corbitt sighed. "Ain't that the truth, brother."

They turned down a narrow side street that dead-ended at a double set of railroad tracks on a wide, weed-grown right-of-way passage. Lactameon panted up the ballasted embankment, his Nikes slipping and crunching loud in the gravel, but slowed his pace as they crossed the second set of rails and descended the other side to what seemed a cutoff continuation of the same street. "Shit, I could go for a forty-ounce, man!"

"Shit yeah!" added Ethan.

Corbitt pointed to a small tin building, obviously abandoned, its door hanging open to darkness. "Shit! That there a Fageol on that ole pitcher! Seem I member hearin they was built out here. Course, they don't make 'em no more."

Lactameon glanced at Hobbes's old house. "My hood, all they do is tear shit apart, man. Nobody build nuthin."

It was dusk when the three boys emerged from an alley. Corbitt looked toward the western sky, and then wondered why he cared about direction. Other than knowing he was in Oakland, California, in the U.S.A., on Planet Earth, he had no idea in hell where he was anyway. Lactameon's neighborhood was a lot older and dirtier than any he'd seen so far. Garbage clogged the gutters, paper rustled along the sidewalks in a soot-scented breeze, and broken glass lay everywhere, crunching like the railroad gravel under the fat boy's heavy steps. Ethan seemed fascinated that Corbitt could walk barefoot through it without so much as an owie. The bus benches, storefronts, and walls were layered with spray-painted symbols and words. Corbitt wondered if they all had a meaning. Or, were they more like the knife carvings on the bridge deck back home . . . just kids trying to be remembered? Across the street was a scrapyard filled with mountains of jagged iron. There were two ancient crawler cranes, a Northwest and a Loraine, so rusty and battered it was hard to tell if they moved scrap or were scrap. Just inside the yard's sagging gates was a beat-up old dumptruck. Corbitt's eyes were drawn to it. He squinted in the deepening dusk, then dashed across to the yard and stared through the chain-link mesh. The other boys exchanged glances, then came across too.

"I be goddamned!" muttered Corbitt. "Never figure there another one left in the world!"

Ethan clutched at the gate like a little prisoner and peered through the mesh. "Nuther what?"

"That there truck, little brother. It a Corbitt."

Lactameon glanced at the battered old truck. It was the one with the push bars that shoved scrap around. "You sayin you was named after a *truck*, man?"

"Well, course not. It just kinda . . . cool . . . what it is, findin one here."

"Mmm. Signs an wonders, huh?"

Corbitt frowned. "I tell y'all, I don't believe in none of that shit, man."

"Yeah. You did."

Ethan pointed. "So, what so cool bout dat ole cocksucka, Corbitt?"

"Ethan!"

"Um, sorry. I forgot."

Corbitt sighed, almost wishing he hadn't seen the truck now. It wasn't exactly the same model, being a six-wheeler and a dump instead of a three-axle tractor, but the body was identical, and at first glimpse in the fading daylight the *déjà vu* had been intense. He turned away from the gates. "Signify nuthin, I spose. There one just like it back . . . back in Mississippi."

Lactameon's eyes shifted between the strange slender boy and the battered old truck. "Mmm. Well, seem like it should be in a museum or somethin, stead of gettin the shit beat out it every day."

Corbitt smiled. "Y'all be tellin me it still runnin, Tam?"

"Well, I never pay much attention, but I think it work in there all the time."

Corbitt studied the truck once more. "Mmm. Prob'ly gots it a gas engine, don't see no stack. Maybe a Hercules HXD or HXC."

"Whoa!" said Ethan. "Corbitt gots da 411 on a lotta shit, Tam! Just like you!"

Lactameon smiled. "Most Africans do."

"Um, Tam? You teach me some African shit too? Like you teachin Beamer readin?"

"Mmm. Well, you ain't gonna catch no African sellin his ass at no bus station, man."

Corbitt nodded. "Sho nuff!"

Lactameon smiled. "Don't spose you 'sippi dudes slam a forty-ounce once in a while, man?"

"Well, shit yeah, Tam. How the hell else y'all gonna get peaceful-like with your brothers an talk about whatever come to mind?"

"So, how bout we score us some, Corbitt? An a big bucket of KFC? Shit, I know a real peaceful-like place."

"Fo sho, Tam. But, um, where I gonna be sleepin tonight?"

Lactameon started back across the street. "Aw, we scheme out somethin, man. So, how much travelin green you gots left?"

"Bout twenty dollars."

"An I gots nine!" added Ethan.

"Well, I thought you was savin by for . . . Well, you know."

"Shit. I work dat out tomorrow, Tam . . . Um, some way."

"Mmm. Well, Corbitt, give Ethan five. Ethan, bail on up to KFC. Corbitt an me hook up with ya back of my buildin."

"Shit yeah!" Ethan darted away.

Corbitt followed Lactameon to a corner store with heavily barred windows. An old man in a ragged Army jacket sat against the wall by the doorway.

"That Leon," said Lactameon, as they neared the man. "I talk to him sometimes, even when I don't need nuthin. He was in that ole Viet Nam War. The one nobody wanted to win. That how he lose his leg. Word say he gots some sort of medal. Sometimes I believe that."

The old man had his one leg drawn up and his forehead resting on his knee. Hearing the boys, he came alert but relaxed when he saw it was Lactameon. Corbitt saw that the man's face was creased with what looked like pain lines, and his uncut hair was going gray, but his weary brown eyes warmed a little.

"What them bones tellin tonight, big guy?"

Lactameon grinned. "I see a train in your future." He turned to Corbitt. "Um, give him the green, man."

"Oh. Sho." Corbitt pulled out the last of his money as Leon got up with the help of a shaky aluminum crutch.

"The usual, big guy?"

Lactameon nodded. "All come from the same donkey."

Corbitt asked, "Um, sir? They gots 'em any Top tobacco in there?"

Leon looked at Corbitt with new interest. "Sho do, son."

"Spect y'all could buy me a pack, please . . . if there any that green left over?"

Leon smiled. "Sho, son. Mississippi, right?"

"Um . . . yes, sir."

"Mmm. Well, I ain't gonna ask." The old man hobbled into the store.

Lactameon shook his head. "Jeeze, Corbitt, don't go callin ole wineheads sir."

"Hey. My own dad was in the Army, man. Y'all sposed to be respectin people like that."

Lactameon's face darkened for a moment. "Mmm. So was mine, man. But nobody ever respect him for it."

"Well, leastways he didn't ask if I from goddamn Africa."

"Okay! Chill out, man. But, you ain't in Mississippi no more, neither. An, case you ain't scoped it yet, this street ain't made out yellow bricks. You better start learnin the moves fore the lions an tigers an bears eat your ass all up. I gots me a extra blade home, I give ya."

"Huh? Oh." Corbitt dug in his pocket. "Already gots me a knife. See?"

"The fuck that? Look more like a goddamn can-opener to me!"

"Well . . . it do that too."

"Let's see it. Shit, man, all it gots this pussy-ass three-inch blade! Shit, even a pig let you keep that!"

"Well, it sharp, best believe!"

Lactameon pulled out his box knife. "Not half as sharp as this, man." He put the tip of Corbitt's knife to his chest. "Check this out. An it ain't even no good for stabbin! It more'n three inches to the heart."

Corbitt looked down at his own slender chest for a moment, then took back his knife and folded it. "Um, Tam? Why y'all doin this shit for me?"

"Maybe I like Africans. Anyways, stop askin questions all the time, man. Lotta dudes don't figure that cool."

"But then, how they be learnin stuff, Tam?"

"Shit, the fuck I know, man? Maybe by watchin suckers like Gilligan. An, you doin it again."

"Sorry."

"An, don't say that neither, man. We all in one great big ole sorry-ass motherfucker. Shit, only thing you gots to be sorry over is bein black enough for two dudes."

Lactameon saw Corbitt's surprised look, and touched the slender boy's arm. "Yo, hey, I didn't mean nuthin by that, man. But, shit, Corbitt, what you bring your ass out here hopin to find anyways? Listen up, man. You look bad enough to scare off a lotta concrete cannibals out doin a thing . . . cept you smile too motherfuckin much. Nobody want no friendly African brothers in this hood."

A half hour later, and darkness had settled. The night was warm, even with a breeze that carried the strange yet somehow familiar scent of the sea to Corbitt's nostrils. He sat on buckled old concrete with his back to a dumpster. Ethan and Lactameon were opposite him, across the narrow alley, their backs to a grimy brick wall. This was Lactameon's special place, behind the broken-down old building he lived in. Corbitt had seen some small parks while riding the bus, but Lactameon had said they were mostly for deals and that kids couldn't hang there alone. He made the parks sound like outdoor bus stations with grass.

A small bulb burned inside a wire cage above the building's steel-plated back door. It threw a dim but friendly glow that sparkled in eyes and gave a golden tone to Ethan's brassy skin. Corbitt had just about learned not to see the boy's missing eye, just as his nose was starting to ignore the garbage stink and his ears were already filtering out the siren screams and the occasional gunshot. Neither Ethan or Lactameon paid much attention to the rats, and after what Ethan called the Hammer-copter had clattered over twice, Corbitt ignored that too. In fact, with his belly full of chicken and Colt 45, Corbitt thought Lactameon's special place was almost peaceful.

Most of a forty-ounce had puffed Ethan's tight tummy like a balloon once again. Guppy or Hayes would have been drunk on their asses, but Ethan made sense when he talked; though a few hours ago Corbitt would have thought him retarded or crazy. The little boy had a way of spearing you with his single eye that demanded treatment as an equal, and Corbitt realized the kid was trying to teach him things that would never be written in books. Once, Corbitt caught himself wondering if Weylen would have known some of that stuff.

At first, Ethan had smoked Lactameon's Kools while Corbitt rolled Tops for himself. But the little boy had taken to Corbitt's cigarettes, and now sat concentrating and trying to roll his own. Corbitt supposed that having no depth perception didn't help matters.

"Cock . . . Shit!" muttered Ethan. "Tore another motherfuckin paper! Maaaan!"

Corbitt smiled. "Well, y'all bring your ass over here, little brother. I show you how. Most never enough papers in them packs anyways."

Ethan half scooted, half crawled across the alley and settled beside Corbitt. Corbitt pulled another paper, tapped in some tobacco, and guided Ethan's little fingers through the rolling process. Lactameon smiled too.

"Yo, man. You down with little brothers. Gots some of your own back home?"

"Not by blood. Little brothers need this sorta shit from bigger ones . . . or from their dads. Um, y'all was sayin your dad in the Army, Tam?"

The fat boy frowned a moment, then drained his bottle and sighed. "He dead, man. Since I six. Most the growin-up shit I gots been from the other dudes or come out books."

"Mmm. Sorry, Tam. Y'all get a lotta good shit out books, but sometimes there be things only a growed-up man help you with. Um, he get killed in a war?"

The fat boy reached for the last bottle and twisted the cap. He took a huge gulp, then snorted. "Yeah! What whitey call the war on drugs, man!" He shook up another Kool and fired it, then studied the ember for a minute. "Happen all the time round here, man . . . pigs come to pop some dealer, get the wrong apartment. Shit. That really piss 'em off, man! It like, they *want* it to be you cause they went to all that trouble . . . keep a whole family flat on the floor for hours, man . . . tearin the shit out your place . . . yellin an cussin like fuckin animals, man! Don't fuckin matter if it your mom or your goddamn grandma on that floor!" Lactameon took another long gulp. "Shit. That what them cocksuckin pigs done to us, man! Ripped up my room, rip up my parents' room . . . kitchen, fridge, motherfuckin everthin! Hour of that, an my dad wasn't havin no more. He get up. He a big man . . . gots big bones . . . not like me. Pigs get him in one of them cocksuckin choke holds . . . ain't sposed to be able to hurt niggers that way . . . same's we all sposed to gots thick skulls. Cocksuckas twisted his neck. Busted somethin. Took him two days to die, an all he could move was his eyes, man!" Lactameon tilted up the bottle and gulped it halfway empty. "Pigs say he interferin with a search . . . resisted arrest . . . justifiable . . . *cocksuckas!*"

Ethan had pressed close to Corbitt. Corbitt's hand had gone to the little boy's shoulder. Ethan picked up Corbitt's bottle and drank. "Um . . . so, nuthin happen to them pigs, Tam?"

The fat boy took a long hit off his cigarette, then blew out smoke. "Six of 'em kill my dad. Four of 'em dead now . . . so far. I gots the paper clippins." Lactameon leveled his eyes at Corbitt. "That why I *do* believe in that shit, man." He smiled. "My mom don't need no pins an no dolls. I don't neither. Two of them cocksuckas shot. One kick cause of cancer, an one was chasin some kids through the railroad yards last summer an got 'tween two boxcars a train was slammin together. Took 'em all a *long* time to die, man. I gots the clippins." Lactameon's eyes glittered in the dimness. "Tell me you don't believe in that shit, Africa-boy."

From the alley mouth came the rattle of skateboard wheels and low kid-voices. Lactameon tensed for a moment, listened, then relaxed. "S'cool. They ours."

Corbitt watched the fat boy pull the bandana from his pocket and slip it around his head. Then Corbitt turned as shadowy figures come rattling up the alley. Cigarette points glowed like ruby-red fireflies. The night breeze brought the scents of Kool smoke and kid-sweat and a trace of the sheen Sherry sometimes used. Corbitt tried to take the boys at a casual glance as they passed through the light bulb's dim glow. There were four, and none seemed much older than himself. Lactameon smiled.

"Naw. Don't get up, man. Just be yourself."

"Well," added Ethan. "You can be a *little* cool."

"Yo, Tam!" called the first boy. "S'up, man?"

Corbitt saw that, like the others, he wore big, battered high-tops, loose-fitting Levi's, and a yellow bandana. He didn't pack near Lamar's bulk, but he was beautifully muscled and shirtless to show it. The other boys all wore oversize tees with no graphics, and ranged from one of average size and build to another who looked like a lightweight model of Lactameon, while the last was black as death and willowy slender. All tailed their boards and bunched up behind the first boy. Corbitt saw a silvery glitter, and noted the tiny ring in the black kid's nose. It gave a fierceness to what was a gentle face. Lactameon offered his half-empty bottle to the first boy.

"So, how they hangin, Bilal?"

The chubby boy snickered as the one called Bilal took a gulp from the bottle and passed it back. "Shit, Tam, wonder you walk, way yours got to be hangin, man!"

"Huh?"

Bilal frowned. "One of the little dudes word us he seen you comin cross from Leopard ground, man. You just checkin out your luck, or there somethin goin on?"

Lactameon shrugged, crushing out his Kool. "Motherfuckin bus don't cross the line no more. That all."

"Mmm." Bilal considered a moment, then nodded. "Well, best you watch that sorta shit, man. Gots us enough trouble this summer, out pissin the Leopards off too." Bilal had seen Corbitt right away, but now pointed as if just noticing him. "So, who this dude, man?"

"Friend from outa town. Name Corbitt."

The average-built boy passed the bottle to the chubby one and scanned Corbitt carefully. Corbitt saw he was missing a little finger. "Shit, more like out Africa, you askin me!"

The chubby boy cocked his head. "Yo! Why you barefoot, man?"

Bilal frowned again. "Cause he ain't wearin no shoes, stupid! You. Corbitt. Get vertical."

Corbitt did, and Bilal's frown deepened when he had to look up to meet Corbitt's eyes. "Mmm. Spose you kickin on the court, man?"

"Um, I don't play much," said Corbitt.

"Yeah? Well, I could slam-dunk your skinny ass—no prob, man. Member that."

Corbitt nodded. The chubby boy giggled. "Yeah? Just don't play him in the dark, Bilal."

"Oh, shut up, Stacy." Bilal measured Corbitt a moment more. "So, where you from, man?"

"Mississippi."

The slender boy with the ring moved forward. "Mmm. Walk the roads my forefathers walked, climb the trees my forefathers hung from." He tilted his head slightly. "Swear I seen you before, brother."

Bilal snorted. "Dudes get like you, see anythin, Silver."

Lactameon smiled. "Try lookin in the mirror, man."

"Shit yeah!" piped Ethan, pointing. "Dey most 'zactly alike!"

Bilal swiveled his head back and forth. "Mmm. Close, anyways . . . whatever the fuck that sposed to signify. Or, he a crack-sucker too?"

Lactameon frowned, "Jeeze, Bilal, stop raggin his ass, man. Dude lose all his clothes at the goddamn bus station. Why he got no shoes. Get down with it."

Bilal snorted again. "All that sayin, he goddamn stupid, what it is! Ain't no wonder he Silver's twin brother!"

Lactameon sighed. "He lost 'em in a drive-by. Gilligan got kicked. Right uptown."

The boy with the missing finger scowled. "Shit! Take no 411 call to figure who set that up!" He turned to Bilal. "I *tell* ya we shoulda kicked both them motherfuckas, man! They just gonna open another house!"

Bilal spat. "Just shut up, T.K. Shit, seem like half the dudes we gone to school with out to kick the other half this summer! I sick of it, man!"

T.K. dropped his hands to his hips. "Yeah? So, why you waste all our treasury on that cheap piece of shit for? Goin legit with rat-control, man?"

Lactameon sat up a little straighter. "Now what's up? Yo. Some of that my green too, Bilal. So, what *we* use it for I don't get no seven on?"

Bilal shrugged. "So, where you been, man? Hangin with Beamer? Gettin drive-byed? Cruisin with the Leopards? Shit, what I gots to do, man, score your ass a beeper?" He held out his hand without turning. T.K. reached under his shirt and slipped something big and black from the back of his jeans and passed it to him. Corbitt's eyes widened a little when he saw it was a gun . . . some sort of square pistol with a long magazine. Ethan cocked his head.

"Whoa! Dat a Ten, Bilal?"

T.K. spat. "Shit! In your dreams! Goddamn cheap-shit Cobray . . . an now it jammed! Shit! We had us a chance at a Uzi an a .44, an Bilal blew it all!"

Bilal gave T.K. a shove. The other boy stumbled back, his hand almost going for his pocket.

"I tellin you, shut the fuck up, T.K.! Kickin Sabby woulda done nuthin but bring down the pigs an start 'em stirrin up shit 'tween us an the Leopards. Sides, we coulda got both them guns out kickin nobody, you been down with your brothers, man!"

Silver spoke softly. "Yo. Seem like none of us gettin nuthin with all this shit, man. Now we ain't even gots us a gun that shoot."

Bilal faced the slender boy. "Yeah? Well *you* come away with enough to stay fucked-up a week, man!"

"Everybody shut the fuck up!" yelled Lactameon. "Jeeze, what a motherfuckin sorry-ass donkey show!" He pointed. "So, where *we* get *our* new gun, Bilal?"

Stacy made a face. "Ole cocksucka at the pawnshop, where you think? Shit, I bet only reason he give us a trade-up on our .38 cause he already know that Cobray don't work worth a fuck! Shit, we gonna kick somebody, it oughta be him!"

Ethan scrambled to his feet. "No!"

"You shut up, you dirty little sucka!" bawled Bilal. "Shit! You shouldn't even be hearin all this!"

Lactameon waved the little boy to his side. "Chill, Bilal. Ethan cool. So, you sayin our new gun don't shoot at all, Stacy?"

"We try it. Down by the water. Three shots an the motherfucka jam solid, man!"

T.K. crossed his arms over his chest. "Yeah! So, now who we gonna get to fix it, Bilal? Shit, what a motherfuckin escapade!"

"Um," said Corbitt. "I look at it, y'all be wantin me to."

Bilal turned from T.K. and eyed Corbitt carefully. "Yo. You know guns, man?"

"Well, my dad gots him a shotgun."

"Sawed?" asked T.K. "Shit, *that* what we shoulda got, Bilal! Just like the pigs, man, ain't no niggaboy gonna get up again!"

"Um, no," said Corbitt. "Fact is, used to be taller'n me."

The little ring glittered like a spark as Silver smiled. "That gots to be one *long* motherfucka, brother-mine."

Bilal shrugged. "So, he little once too, man. Signify nuthin." He gave Corbitt another look, then handed over the pistol.

Corbitt studied it in the dim light. "Mmm. Seem like to me a gun ain't nuthin but a little machine. Same's a 'jector-pump or distributor."

"Um . . . yeah," said Bilal. "That what it is, man."

Corbitt turned the gun sideways and peered into the ejection port. "Mmm. Bullet still stuck in the chamber, Bilal. Askin me, y'all be kinda foolish lettin T.K. skate with it like this."

"Shit!" bawled T.K. "You stupid fucka, Bilal!"

"Everybody shut up!" yelled Lactameon. "My mom come down here in a minute an kick all our asses!"

Corbitt knelt, laying the pistol on the pavement and trying to pull back the cocking knob. Finding he needed both hands, he crouched and gripped the gun with his toes.

"Man," said Silver. "I *know* I seen that dude somewheres before."

"In your dreams," muttered Bilal.

"Mmm. Could be."

Ethan moved beside Corbitt and fired his lighter, holding it over the gun. Corbitt bent closer. "Gots to pry out that bullet fore I figure what wrong." He pulled his knife and opened the punch blade.

"Yo. That some sorta gun-fixin tool, man?" asked Stacy.

T.K. cocked his head. "Look more like a goddamn can-opener, you askin me."

Lactameon smiled. "It do that too."

Bilal glanced at the fat boy. "Um, he like a cousin or some-thin, Tam? Like, he gonna be hangin awhile?"

Lactameon shrugged. "Shit, I dunno, man. Maybe he spendin the summer. Don't bother him now."

Silver pulled out his pipe and started to load it. Bilal pointed. "Yo, man! You gonna do that, do it somewheres I don't gotta watch!"

Silver shrugged and walked down toward the alley entrance.

Corbitt got the bullet out and handed it to Bilal, who handed it to Stacy, who gave it to T.K., who scowled and dropped it in a dumpster. Corbitt worked the gun's action a few times, Ethan scampering to pick up the bullets. "Mmm. Look like to me this here pin come loose, is all. What they be callin a roll pin."

Bilal knelt beside him. "So, can you fix it, Corbitt?"

"Sho nuff." Pulling the magazine, Corbitt tapped the pin back into place with the knife handle, then handed the gun back to Bilal. "Should be workin now, man. Best oil it some."

"Um, that 3-in-One shit okay, man? It what we use on our bearins."

"Sho."

Bilal stood, and turned to Lactameon. "So, where he cribbin, man?"

"Guess that was gonna be the next thing we figure, fore you dudes show. My mom been chillin with Ethan for two days now, but it prob'ly startin to wear. You figure Corbitt could crib at the clubhouse tonight?"

Bilal glanced at Corbitt, who had politely turned away. "Mmm. So, how long you know this dude, Tam? What I sayin is, I trust *your* ass with my life, but there some real slick-boys cruisin this summer."

"Well, jeeze, Bilal. *Look* at him, man. I told you he lost everythin but them jeans when we was drive-byed. Sides, he already seen our gun an heard bout Sabby."

Bilal fingered his jaw. "Signify nuthin, man. Everybody gots guns, an Sabby still suckin wind. Fact is, that one of the best ghetto-boy looks I ever seen . . . no showtime dressin the part. An he fix that gun right off, man. Know anybody our age do that?" Bilal turned to Corbitt. "Um, no 'fense, man. But I just gots to chill on you awhile."

Corbitt nodded. "Don't spose y'all gots a shower at your clubhouse anyways."

T.K. and Stacy snickered. Ethan stepped beside Corbitt and grabbed his hand. "Yo! I take him to da Center! I not been dere a week now. S'cool."

Lactameon nodded. "Yeah. That work." He glanced at Bilal, then whispered. "Um, you thinkin what I think you thinkin, man?"

Bilal crouched, and whispered back. "Maybe. Shit, Tam, I

know it cold, but Silver ain't gonna last another month. We get down to four dudes, them Leopards gonna start schemin . . . they ain't already. What we gonna do then, man? Take us on some little kids like Ethan? We the last ones left, Tam. Else we start looking for dudes we don't really know. So, how he handle the drive-by, man?"

"Well, he didn't freak too bad . . . almost like he been shot at before."

"Mmm. So we chill on this awhile. Scope the dude out. It goddamn hard to trust somebody you never grow up with." Bilal stood. "Yo, Corbitt. Thanks for fixin our gun, man. Maybe we see you around." He took Corbitt's hand and guided it through a complicated shake. A dark slender shadow appeared and Corbitt found his hand gripped again, but now by a mirror-image of his own. Silver's eyes shone in the dimness, but didn't have the murky, confused look Gilligan's had.

"Maybe I see you round too, brother-mine. Now an then."

Corbitt watched as the four boys disappeared down the alley. A moment later the rattle of their skate wheels had faded into the background of city sounds. Lactameon yawned and stretched, then began the process of getting to his feet.

"They give you some clothes at the Center, Corbitt. I see you tomorrow." Lactameon glanced down at Ethan. "Meet me in the park. Take good care of our new brother."

Maybe duppys felt like this, thought Corbitt . . . bone-weary, confused, and searching for a life that no longer existed. He carried Ethan on his back. The little boy was a whole lot drunker than Corbitt had guessed, or maybe all the beer had finally beaten the eight-year-old body. For the last three blocks Ethan's chin lay on Corbitt's shoulder and he mumbled sleepy directions in Corbitt's ear. They had ended up here on this silent side street, where the crumbling old buildings seemed to lean over the cracked concrete that passed for sidewalks. Most of the storefronts were abandoned and boarded. Some were just flame-gutted shells. Garbage and trash lay everywhere, and the curbs were lined with crumpled car bodies, their hoods and trunklids gaping like the mouths of dead fish. All the glass was smashed, and sprays of it glittered on the pavement like those little crystals everybody had been shoving at Corbitt for two days. Even with his tough feet he stepped carefully. None of the cars had wheels, and few were even on blocks. Most were stuffed with more garbage, and rats scuttled in and out of them as if the whole row was some sort of rat-transit system like the BART trains Corbitt had seen from the buses. It was dark midway down this block. The only streetlights were on the corners, and one of those was dim and dying. Corbitt moved warily as if through the riverbank woods, scanning every shadow ahead. Yet he found he wasn't afraid. Like a space traveler who had just landed on a new planet, he realized he had no conception of what passed for danger in this alien place. It had been hard to convince Toby to watch out for water moccasins when he'd first come to Bridge-end.

Ethan might have been asleep. The last words he'd spoken had been back on the corner when he'd told Corbitt to go to the light. This was only a glow from the doorway of a two-story brick storefront. So, this place was supposed to be a refuge for children. It took grown-up courage just to find it. Corbitt passed a burned-out car-corpse. Its doors all hung open and a blanket-wrapped figure was sprawled on the charred back seat. Corbitt hoped whoever it was was only sleeping.

The building with the light looked almost abandoned itself. Corbitt wasn't sure what he'd expected a kid-center to look like: a church, a school, or something cold and official like a social-service building. But this place seemed to be falling apart, and its street-level windows were covered by spray-painted planks. The light came from a single bare bulb overhead in the deep-set entryway. The door was sheathed with plywood, rough and splintery but recently painted in three broad stripes of red, yellow, and green. In the middle was a primitive-looking picture of a watchful lion with a child asleep between its paws. The image seemed somehow sad in all this darkness and ruin. Corbitt felt his nose crinkle. He told himself that was stupid; the way a little kid might react. But, you wouldn't have to be able to read to understand the picture's meaning.

To one side of the entry huddled a boy, maybe ten or eleven. He had his knees hugged to his chest and his face buried against them. He wore old Pumas, faded jeans, and a big dirty sweatshirt with the hood pulled over his head. He seemed to be asleep, though his breathing was shallow and fast. Corbitt set Ethan down and knelt beside the other boy.

Ethan rubbed his eyes and looked around. "Well, dis da place," he yawned. Stepping back out on the sidewalk, he scanned the street both ways. "Dead tonight."

Corbitt bent close to the other boy, his nose wrinkling from the kid's sour smell. The boy's breathing didn't sound right: like an overworked air-compressor on a truck with leaky brakes. Corbitt looked up at Ethan. "What you sayin, dead?"

Ethan shrugged. "Nobody fightin for stash. Um, better not fuck with him, man, ya gonna get your ass cut."

Corbitt frowned. "I ain't fuckin with him. But, shouldn't he oughta be inside?"

Ethan looked sad and disgusted at the same time. Pulling Corbitt out of the way, he grabbed one of the boy's hands and spread grimy fingers showing burns. The boy's head jerked up. Ethan jumped back as the boy swung a razor knife in a vicious arc. Corbitt leaped away too, but the boy made no further move, just dropping his head back on his knees once more. "Don't fuck with me, man," he muttered. "I gots nuthin."

Ethan gave Corbitt a shrug. "Tole ya."

Corbitt relaxed a little. The boy might have been shooing away flies with that three-inch razor blade. "Um, do they always get burned?"

"Only when dey get like him."

Corbitt looked around the entryway, once more amazed by all the strange words and symbols. There were plenty of normal dirty words too, and some of the signs he'd already seen, though he still didn't know if they meant anything. "Um, Ethan? Can you read this stuff?"

About to open the door, the little boy turned, yawning again. He pointed. "Dis here da Collectors. We Collectors, only we just belong to 'em cause we live in dere hood. Dis other thing mean dis place cool by Collectors. Dat one da Leopards, an say da same thing to dere dudes. Dese here dudes been gone a long time, but dis place was cool by dem too. Dis one some Collector talkin to a Leopard . . . bet it Tam and Winfield . . . say somethin bout a pizza." Ethan yawned again. "Shit, man, I fuckin sleepy. C'mon."

Ethan tugged on the worn brass handle and pushed open the door. "Don't worry bout dat little sucka, man. Chad know he here."

At first Corbitt thought it was a small room with a ceiling so high it was lost in the shadow above. Another small bulb dangled from wires. Then Corbitt realized that what looked like walls were just plywood sheets partitioning off this space from a larger area beyond. The floor underfoot was black and white asphalt tiles, clean but unpolished, some cracked and curling at the edges. There was a faint reek of puke in the air, just on the edge of being smelled, and mostly covered by cigarette smoke and dirty-kid sweat. From beyond the plywood walls came the low murmur of a TV. Slightly brighter light shone through a doorway-sized gap in the partition, and there was a glimpse of faded carpet and what might have been the corner of a couch. On this side of the opening was an ancient wooden office desk, turned almost sideways, maybe so that the older boy sitting behind it in a beat-up old swivel chair didn't look like anyone official. He wouldn't have anyway, being about seventeen, with a huge mass of yellow-brown dreadlocks even longer and fluffier than Ethan's that almost hid his narrow, high-cheekboned face. He wore a black fishnet tee that showed a smooth boyish body, old 501s, and scruffy Reeboks on big feet. Corbitt couldn't imagine him being in charge of a kid-center.

A small, cocoa-brown boy about Ethan's age was sitting on the desktop, which was piled with papers and pamphlets and magazines. The Rasta boy seemed to be doctoring the smaller kid's mouth. Bloody Q-Tips and cotton balls were scattered over the papers. The small boy had his lips pulled back. A cigarette dangled from the Rasta boy's, and he looked past the little kid's shoulder as Corbitt and Ethan came in, offering a smile that would have been guarded in Bridge-end but was one of the friendliest Corbitt had seen in two days. The boy was a funny kind of light-dark dusky color with differing shades that somehow looked dirty. His eyes were an amber that almost matched Ethan's. *Another "nice girl" had had a nigga's baby.*

"S'up, Ethan?" asked the boy. "Bring a new brother tonight?"

Ethan went to the desk, his walk a little unsteady. "Yeah, Chad. Dis here Corbitt. Don't gots no home. Shit, don't even gots no motherfuckin shoes!"

The small boy on the desk had paid no attention until Ethan had mentioned the shoes. Now, he turned around to look. Corbitt saw it wasn't his lips but his gums that were bleeding. There was a tube of baby teething-pain stuff among the cotton swabs on the desktop. The boy wore old jeans, Nikes, and a big hooded sweatshirt. It seemed to be some sort of uniform. He was thinner than Ethan, and his eyes had that smoked-up look Corbitt had seen too many times already.

Chad scanned Corbitt like a friendly leopard, warmly, but taking in everything. The first glance, Corbitt knew, was not into his eyes, but at them.

"Yo, Corbitt, you doin all right, brother?"

Corbitt liked Chad's eyes. He wondered if Ethan would have looked that way with two. "Sho, Chad. I just be needin me someplace to sleep." He came over beside Ethan, not knowing what to expect now . . . questions, forms to fill out, maybe having to lie. But Chad only smiled and went back to work on the small boy's mouth.

"Mmm. You look some tired, man. You two dudes hungry? Soup pretty good tonight." He winked at Ethan. "Cream of rats-ass, your favorite."

Ethan giggled and winked back, which gave Corbitt a shiver. "Naw. We eat good today, Chad. Just wanna crib."

"Mmm. Hang a second, man." Chad dabbed a little more ointment on the small boy's gums, then dropped the Q-Tip on the desktop with the others and took the little kid's thin shoulders. There was affection in Chad's voice, and some sadness, but his tone hardly went with the words. "Mmm, Christopher, your shit really in a mess, little brother. You dyin, you know that, man?"

Corbitt's eyes widened a little. Christopher only nodded, smiling slightly, as if Chad had told him he was going to be eaten by the bogeyman. Chad lifted the boy into his lap, cradling his head on one arm. Christopher half closed his eyes like he might want to sleep if he thought about it long enough. Chad crushed out his cigarette in an ashtray full of bloody cotton. His voice was casual. "So, how your folks, Ethan?"

Ethan shrugged. "Dey gettin better. Word, Chad. It all be cool soon. Den I don't gots to do dis shit no more."

Chad's eyes came back to Corbitt, as if reconsidering.

"Shit no!" said Ethan. "Corbitt my African brother, man!"

Chad nodded and smiled once again. "Yeah. I see that now. It good to have real brothers." He glanced at Christopher a moment. "Only one bed left tonight. Course, there always the couches an the floor inside." He tilted his head a little. "Don't figure you get much sleep back there."

Corbitt moved closer to the desk. The shadowy alcove behind it seemed to be floored with mattresses and blankets. There were three boys back there, none over twelve. One was lying down but obviously not asleep. The other two sat against the wall in the darkest corner. One was smoking a cigarette as if it was a drug. None looked peaceful. The faint smell of puke was stronger, and there was a trace of piss and diarrhea even though everything looked clean but the kids themselves.

Chad studied Corbitt a moment more. "Yeah, I think you are a African brother. Well, ain't a lotta rules here, but the ones we got make more sense than what pass for law outside that door."

"Yo, Chad!" piped Ethan. "Lemme tell him, man!"

"Sure, little brother."

Ethan turned to Corbitt, his beautiful, damaged face taking an expression of little-kid serious. "Cigarette smokin only, an not upstairs. Got anythin else on ya, chill it outside. No weapons, even just blades. No startin shit . . . y'know, fightin. An, no dealin, or your ass out forever."

Corbitt pulled the Army knife from his pocket. "I gots me this, Chad."

Ethan snickered. "Shit, man, dat only a motherfuckin can-opener!"

"Well," said Chad. "It still slice somebody's throat. I keep it here till you leave, Corbitt. An, yo, Ethan, how bout that box knife you keep on forgettin?"

Ethan grinned like a little kid caught in the cookie jar, and dug in his pocket. Corbitt handed over his knife. Chad shifted Christopher on his knee, then slipped a key on a leather thong from around his neck and locked both blades in a desk drawer. "Oh, an once you in, try an stay in, huh? I mean, we won't try an make you or nuthin, but if you don't figure you can get through the night out havin to go out for somethin, it better to stay here with these dudes. Breakfast at seven." Chad glanced at Corbitt's feet. "I find you some shoes in the mornin, brother. Shit, wonder you ain't sliced 'em to shreds, all that goddamn glass outside."

"Corbitt from somewheres else," said Ethan.

Chad smiled again. "Yeah. I see that too. Yo, Corbitt, you ever just need to talk about somethin, we always here to listen. Don't seem like much else we can do for you. What I sayin is, we can't hide your ass if the pigs or somebody trollin for it. Course, I don't member faces too good."

Ethan snickered again. "Maaaan, what you tellin him, Chad? Who da fuck *ever* forget a face black like his! Yo. How you know he not some cocksuckin slick-boy?"

Chad laughed. "Now, what you tellin *me*, little bro? How one of them suckers ever slide by you? Sides, didn't you just now tell me he your African brother?"

"Shit yeah!"

Chad saw Corbitt's puzzled expression. "See, what it is, sometimes the pigs send somebody in to scope the place. Or they try an plant some rock or a gun. They always out for shuttin us down."

"Shit yeah! It like a motherfuckin war on kids, Corbitt!"

Corbitt nodded. From what he'd seen in the last few days only a fool could think otherwise. He rubbed the salt pocks on his chest. "Um, y'all gots a shower here, Chad? I awful goddamn dirty."

"Sure, brother." Chad got up and gently laid Christopher down on a mattress, bending close for a moment to press his ear against the little boy's chest. Then he came around the desk and walked to the opening in the partition. Corbitt moved beside Chad and touched his arm.

"Um . . . that Christopher? Um . . . he really dyin, Chad?"

Chad sighed. "Yeah, man, he is. Had one little dude die right in my arms there at the desk last month. Lost a lot of brothers an a couple sisters there on them mattresses too."

"But . . . can't you do somethin, Chad?"

There was almost no tone to Chad's voice. "Like, what? They worn-out, man. All their insides. We had a real doctor here for a while, but he couldn't handle it no more. That what he told me . . . ain't nuthin left can be fixed. Some long name for it, but just come down to their hearts finally stop. Believe any fuckin thing you want, man, but crack custom-designed for killin our kids, an we know by who."

"Um . . . there another little one outside, Chad."

"Yeah. I know. He for the mattresses."

The large room beyond was dimly lit, or maybe most of the lights were just turned off because it was late. The place looked like the lobby of a skid-row hotel Corbitt had seen in a movie. Different sizes and shapes and colors of carpet covered the floor like a huge patchwork quilt. Sofas and chairs were scattered all over, not one of them matching another. Several were grouped around a TV, and others were clustered like places to talk, while still others sat off by themselves. There were low coffee tables with stacks of old magazines, comics, and books, along with crayons and pencils and pads of blank paper. One corner of the room was obviously for little kids, judging from the big battered Tonkas and well-worn stuffed animals lying around. Big cans on the floor, filled with sand, bristled with cigarette butts. Off to one side, near a closed door, stood a table with a big coffee urn. Beside the urn were paper cups, a jar of powdered creamer, and a box of sugar cubes. A piece of cardboard taped to the wall read in childish Magic Marker lettering, PLEASE DON'T EAT THE SUGAR. IF YOU ARE HUNGRY, TELL US. There was also a funny little cartoon drawing of a kid popping sugar cubes like peanuts, and a lion holding a big bowl of steaming soup in one paw while making a no-no gesture with the other. Most of the wall space was decorated with rock and rap posters. There were also pictures of Malcolm X, Huey Newton, and Dr. King Jr., and so many hand-drawn kid-pictures it looked like a school on open-house day. There were a few Stop the Violence and anti-drug posters, some drawn by kids, and one that just said WHITEY HATES YOUR BLACK ASS AND WILL KILL YOU WITH CRACK.

About a dozen kids were scattered around on the couches and chairs. Three boys watched the TV, which was showing an ancient *Outer Limits* episode that faded to a commercial of Hammer selling something. The kids in the room ranged in age from about six to mid-teen. Most were doing something; one was asleep in a chair, and another just wandered around and looked like a candidate for the front-room mattresses. There were four girls, all dressed in jeans and tees like the boys. The sleeping kid clutched a small backpack, and most of the other kids kept theirs close to them as well. There were a few skateboards, too. Three of the girls were playing some sort of board game across a coffee table. The oldest girl was about Corbitt's age. She was dark and chubby, and Toby would have described her with a sigh as being squeezably soft. She was reading a Little Golden Book to a small boy. Steam spiraled up from a cup of coffee on the sofa arm beside her. Smoke from other kids' cigarettes drifted in lazy streamers near the ceiling. A couple of kids glanced up as Chad led Corbitt and Ethan toward a staircase on the opposite side of the room. Chad smiled at them and they smiled back. The older girl looked up from her book. Corbitt could feel her curious eyes slip over his body. He felt his face flush as her gaze lowered to his bare feet.

Chad climbed the creaky staircase, Corbitt and Ethan following, and they reached a hallway on top that was also dimly lit. The only light came from two doorways at the far end, marked MEN and WOMEN, and a small gooseneck lamp on a table at the head of the stairs. A big woman with beaded hair sat at the table mending a small pair of Levi's.

"This Miz Davis," said Chad. "You dudes need anything, just ask her. I got to get back to the door. Night, brothers."

The woman smiled as if barefooted boys and one-eyed kids were the most natural things in the world. "I keep sayin I can make you a nice little patch for that."

Ethan managed to look shy and stubborn at the same time. "Naw. Thanks."

"Ma'am?" asked Corbitt. "Chad be sayin there someplace I can take me a shower?"

Ethan giggled. "Yo, Miz Davis, he always talk like dat! Um, I wanna take me one, too!"

Mrs. Davis nodded. "Course, son." She got up and went to a nearby shelf, taking down two folded towels that were threadbare and mismatched. She handed them to the boys, along with two tiny paper-wrapped bars of soap. "Ethan here show you bout the shower. There a pan full of some nasty green guck, but be sure to step in it first, okay?"

"I show him what is, Miz Davis," said Ethan.

The woman nodded again. "We get you a bed when you through cleanin up."

Like the rest of the building, the bathroom was ancient but clean, with that makeshift look of something adapted from one purpose to another with limited resources. Nigger-rigged, thought Corbitt. A world built out of stuff that white people didn't want anymore. This place could have been some kind of office building once, and these bathrooms for employees. There were two old-fashioned sinks, a long urinal, and a pair of high-tank toilets in wooden cubicles. The walls and floor were a checkerboard pattern of small black and white tiles, which were worn in pathways to the fixtures. Everything had that sad look of being scrubbed until all the shine was gone. The shower had been added recently; a simple steel stall in one corner, plumbed with PVC pipe, with a big plastic pan of locker-room footbath slime set in front of it. On the wall nearby were shelves and hooks for clothes. Corbitt shucked his jeans, folded and put them on a shelf, and dutifully waded through the cold green goo. Ethan stripped, flung his stuff in a pile, and followed, jerking shut the shower curtain, which was patterned with smiling dolphins.

Corbitt turned on the faucets and adjusted the temperature. The water smelled like rust and chemicals, but a hot shower seemed a luxury almost sinful. Ethan was looking Corbitt up and down. "Maaan! Are you ever black! Ever-fuckin-where!"

Corbitt smiled, closing his eyes and letting the water run over his face. "I be a couple shades lighter when I done, best believe. Shit, but this feel *good*!"

"Well, fuck, Corbitt. It just a plain ole shower. Everbody in hell gots one!"

"Mmm. I tell you some Mississippi stories sometime . . . dude."

The soap was some sort of flowery-scented stuff that didn't lather worth a damn. The wrapper had the words PROMOTIONAL GIVEAWAY, NOT TO BE RESOLD. Corbitt wished he had some of Mrs. Griffin's, and hoped he didn't end up smelling like a goddamned honeysuckle.

Screwed to the wall was a plastic dispenser full of greenish-yellow slimy stuff. Touching the button, Corbitt got a spurt of it on his finger. It smelled like somebody's infection.

Ethan giggled. "Yo! You gots creeper-crawlers, Corbitt? Dat what it for."

Corbitt hoped not, recalling Ethan's hair tangled in his own when he'd carried the boy. "No."

"You will, man. Everybody in hell get 'em." The shower seemed to have sobered Ethan a little. He was taking a few half-hearted swipes at himself with his own soap, but still seemed fascinated by Corbitt's body. "Um, you ever wish you wasn't so black, Corbitt?"

Corbitt shook the lice-killer from his finger, and shrugged. "First I didn't, then I did. Now it don't seem to matter none. Sides, what good it do to wish for stuff?"

"But, um . . . don't some wishes come true? I mean, if you really, *really* believe?"

"Well . . . yeah. But you gots to be careful what you be wishin for."

Ethan stuck his finger in his empty eye-socket. "Um, is it cool to wish for somethin good for yourself?"

"Sho. If it somethin y'all really be needin. But you gots to be careful that when you wishin a good thing your ownself, you ain't wishin a bad thing on somebody else."

"What you mean?"

"It um . . . well, it kinda complicated, Ethan. Shit, I still ain't figured it yet."

Ethan stuck out his lower lip. "Aw, what you sayin is, I just a stupid little sucka. Never unnerstand nuthin. It sorta like death recession."

Corbitt frowned. "No I ain't! You be no way stupid, man. Don't never go callin your ownself that! Not when the whole goddamn world be happy as hell to do it for you."

Ethan considered that, and finally nodded. "Shit yeah! You sayin, everybody call black kids stupid, den dey get thinkin it true. Huh?"

Corbitt smiled. "Now see? What I tellin you. It take a smart brother for figurin that out. An you done it all by your ownself."

"Shit yeah! An now I gonna think three more things I not stupid bout, neither!"

Corbitt worked up what lather he could from the little soap bar and squeezed it into his hair. Some got in his eyes and he squinted them shut. He felt Ethan move closer to him.

"Um, Corbitt? What it like to come?"

"Huh? Come where?"

"Shit. Anywheres. I come right here if I could!"

"You already here, so's you can't come here."

"Shit, man. I can't come nowheres!"

Corbitt frowned, his eyes still closed, feeling too tired for little-kid logic. "Course you can. Y'all come here with me."

"Yo! You sayin you can make me come, man?"

Corbitt tried to wipe his eyes, but the soap kept stinging

them. "I wouldn't try an make you come nowheres, y'all not wantin to."

"But, I *do* want to, goddammit!"

"Well, then course you can come with me."

"Oh. You sayin, you first. Dat cool. I can make it hard for you anyways."

"Huh?" Corbitt felt Ethan's little hands grasp him. He jerked back, slamming his head against the stall's steel side. "SHIT!" Eyes burning with soap, he shoved Ethan away. "Don't never do that to me!"

Ethan cringed, expecting to be hit. Both hands flew up to protect his eye. When nothing more happened, he looked up for a moment, then stared down at the water gurgling in the drain. "I thought dat what you want, Corbitt."

Corbitt replayed the last minute in his mind. He wasn't sure whether to laugh or cry. Then he knelt, taking Ethan's shoulders and looking into his face as if both eyes were there. "Sorry, little brother. I not understand what you askin me."

"You don't like me nomores, huh? Cause I just a cocksuckin dirty little animal."

"Hush that shit! Course I like you, man."

"Um . . . but could you like me better if I make you feel good?"

"You already make me feel good, Ethan. By takin care of me the way y'all done today, an callin me your brother."

The single tiger eye searched Corbitt's. "Tam dat way too, man. He like me just cause. Maybe you both come from Africa."

Corbitt smiled. "Y'all did too, man. A long time ago."

"Um, Corbitt? Can you all help me wash my hair? With dat stinky-poo. I don't wanna give your ass no creeper-crawlers tonight."

"Mmm. Sho, little brother. Maybe I best do my ownself too." Corbitt rose, and stabbed the dispenser button for a palmful of the stuff, then knelt beside Ethan once more. "Close your eyes, man."

"Um, Corbitt?" asked Ethan, as Corbitt worked his fingers through the boy's tangled dreads. "So, what it like to get hard an come? What I sayin is, it gots to be somethin way past cool cause everbody wanna do it all the time."

Corbitt glanced down at Ethan's brassy little self. "Mmm.

Seem like a lotta goddamn trouble, y'all askin me. Trouble what come along right when y'all gots you enough already."

"But, it gots to be a good thing, Corbitt. Why else people pay for it?"

"Mmm. Maybe it only a good thing when people don't pay for it." Corbitt picked Ethan up and held his head close to the shower nozzle to rinse the shampoo from his hair. "Best y'all be keepin your eyes closed a little while longer."

"I don't unnerstan, man," Ethan spluttered.

Corbitt sighed, setting the boy down and starting on his own hair. "Well, I ain't rightly sure I do neither."

"So, what it like fuckin a bitch, Corbitt?"

Corbitt frowned. "Girls ain't to be called bitches, man. That just same's I tellin y'all bout givin names to your ownself. Givin the wrong names to somethin make 'em what they ain't. Specially people."

"Well, so what it like fuckin a girl, man?"

"Mmm. Shoulda seen that one comin. Fact is I never . . . least, not all the way."

"Mean, all the way in her . . . Um, what da right word for cunt, man?"

What in hell *was* the right word? Maybe you could tell Sherry she had beautiful breasts, but she would have laughed for a month if you said she had a pretty . . . *vagina?* "Um . . . 'pend on how good you be knowin her, man. Not all words be meanin the same things all the time . . . like kick."

Ethan considered that. "Um, are African words better?"

"Mmm. Prob'ly."

"Well, you gots a kickin dick, Corbitt."

"Ethan!"

"Well, hey, if I tole ya you gots a cool face or some bad muscles you wouldn't get all pissed-off or figure I a cocksuckin homo."

"Mmm. Yeah, spect I see what y'all sayin."

"Well, I seen dicks, man, an yours be way bad." Ethan grabbed his own. "Shit, all I gots me this little sorry-ass wiggly thing!"

Corbitt smiled. "It grow, little brother. Just like the rest of you."

"Yeah? Well I want me a *big* dick, man. Out to *here*, man!

Bit . . . girls come from all over da motherfuckin *world* to see me! *Pay* me to shove my great big ole dick up dere . . . whatever da African word is."

Corbitt smiled again. "Well, I don't spect y'all want too big a one, man. Might take all the blood from your head to get it up, an then you can't think cause dicks got no brains."

"Oh."

"Sides, I seen a few dicks my ownself, an look like to me y'all gonna be real happy with your own stock equipment."

Ethan studied himself a moment, then dropped his dick and came close to Corbitt. "Yo. Dere somethin stuck in your hair, man."

"Huh?"

"Not *that* hair. Bend down."

Corbitt leaned over and Ethan pulled something from behind his ear. "Look like a little black feather, all wet."

Corbitt looked at the little ebony thing in Ethan's palm. "Mmm, Ain't no wonder my luck been nuthin but bad."

Ethan looked up. "Yo! How you figure, man? You hook up with me, an Tam, didn't ya?"

An look where I be now! But, Corbitt made a smile. "Yeah. You right, little brother. Well, go an dry yourself off now, an let's you an me get us some sleep while there still some dark left."

A few minutes later, Mrs. Davis led Corbitt and Ethan into a large room that opened off one side of the second-floor hallway. Rows of mattresses covered the floor, each with a small figure lying beneath a blanket. Some faces showed, defenseless in sleep, while others were buried under cover as if denying the world around them. Bags or backpacks were always close by, a few still clutched in small hands. As down in the main room, there were skateboards too. Corbitt was surprised to see a pale arm and a tangle of blond locks. He stared for a moment before realizing how stupid that idea was. Besides, the arm was too thin to be Toby's.

The air was heavy with sleep and kid-smell. There were soft sounds of breathing, an occasional cough or sniffle, and once in a while a murmur. Light from the hall shone soft through the doorway, and a small ruby-red bulb burned above one window over a fire-escape sign.

Mrs. Davis put a finger to her lips and pointed to the one vacant mattress near the window. On top was a pillow and a folded blanket. Ethan now wore only his jeans like Corbitt, his shirt and shoes in a paper bag. He padded along beside Corbitt to the mattress and lay down. Mrs. Davis watched as they spread the blanket, then smiled and left. Corbitt felt good being clean again. And he felt somehow comforted by having Ethan's warmth close. He was asleep a few seconds after his head touched the pillow.

And then, seemingly an instant later, he was jarred awake by hard man-voices, confused kid-murmurs, and overhead lights glaring in his eyes. Morning already? But no; the breath-steamed windows were still black. Ethan was sitting up beside him, alert and wary. He put his palm on Corbitt's chest, and whispered, "Stay chill! It just them cocksuckin pigs again!"

Corbitt pushed off the blanket and sat up too. Across the room were three cops, in uniforms that somehow reminded him of Nazi storm troopers in old movies. Their stark white helmets almost looked like floating skulls. The overhead bulbs caught cold glitters off buckles and badges and the bits of chromed steel on their heavy black belts. Two of the men were white, one of them standing with hands on hips by the doorway, keeping a scowling Mrs. Davis and a furious-looking Chad from entering the room. The other went from mattress to mattress with a big-bellied black cop shaking awake those few kids who weren't already. They wore thin plastic gloves. The black one squatted with a grunt at each bed, jerking up the chin of the boy on it and staring a moment into a sullen or sleepy face. Then he would ask a few questions in a bored tone of voice, look disgusted, and scribble something on an aluminum clipboard. The white cop carried a cheap little camera and took a picture of each kid when the black cop had finished his questions. The whiteman seemed to be enjoying his job, firing the blue-white flash right in the kids' faces and then smiling with one side of his mouth while they rubbed their blinded eyes. One or two of the older boys swore at the cops, but the men either ignored them or casually shoved the boys down before moving on.

"Yo!" whispered Ethan. "Dey trollin for your ass, man? We can bail out dat window if we bust now!"

Corbitt glanced toward the tall, old-fashioned window with the fire-escape sign over it. *Were* they looking for him? Toby might have guessed where he'd gone; but Toby was a brother and would never betray a secret. Besides, with what Corbitt had seen since leaving Bridge-end, it hardly seemed logical that what passed for law in this country would waste much energy searching out one Mississippi blackboy.

"No," Corbitt whispered back. "You?"

"Naw. Only, dem cocksuckas tooked my pitcher two weeks ago, man. Dey do dat again, mean it not safe me hangin here no more."

Five beds away, the black cop shot them a scowl. "You two suckers! Shut up!"

The cops came to the next bed, where a little boy, maybe six, was plainly terrified and wouldn't watch the birdie. The black cop finally grabbed the kid's hair and jerked his head up. "Stop that goddamn cryin, you little shit! We ain't gonna hurt your ass! Be a man, goddammit!"

"Christ, what a goddamn rathole!" muttered the white cop, looking around. "Worse'n that goddamn sanctuary place! At least it's easier to handle 'em when they're this size."

The black cop grunted. "Shit, these little suckers blow you away in a minute an laugh about it after! Just take his fuckin pitcher fore the little bastard bites an I got AIDS to worry over too!"

The little kid screamed and blubbered, struggling to burrow beneath the blanket. In the next bed, the blond boy shook a bony fist. "Leave him alone, you fat-ass cocksucka!"

The black cop chuckled. "Oh, you baaad, white-ass! Shut the fuck up or I bust your fuckin head, *boy!*"

Chad cursed and tried to push past the cop in the doorway. The man slammed him against the wall and jammed his club to his throat. "Easy, jungle-boy. Ain't gonna be any revolutions tonight."

"Shove that stick up your ass an try a few revolutions, dick-breath!"

Several boys snickered and flashed signs. The cop's face reddened. Then, Mrs. Davis pushed past into the room. "Try that with me, whiteboy!"

The man looked confused, his hands full with Chad. Mrs. Davis came over to comfort the small crying kid. She glared at the black cop. "Where's your search warrant, boy?"

The man shook his head. "I told you before, ma'am, we don't need one here. It part of the violence-suppression program."

"Shit, boy, who in hell you think you talkin to? Violent *repression* only thing on your program! Kiss the whiteman's ass an then come down here an slap our children around!"

The cop spread his hands. "Ma'am, I'm black too."

"Oh, you somethin all right, but black sure as hell ain't the word come to my mind!"

The cop shrugged and turned away. He tried to question the blond boy, but the kid wouldn't answer. Corbitt thought of the rules of war: how a prisoner of war wasn't supposed to give any information to the enemy. Wasn't it also a prisoner's duty to escape by all means necessary?

"Boy," the man warned. "You don't talk to me here, you gonna do it downtown. I throw your white ass in with a real bunch of bad niggers!"

"Least they black!" the boy spat back. "Not some white-cocksuckin Oreo dogfucka like you!"

More kids snickered. A couple laughed. The black cop glared around. "All you little bastards! Shut the fuck up!"

The kids quieted a little, but not much. Corbitt sensed a rebellious feeling in the air . . . a lot like the last week of school when teachers' threats began to sound foolish.

The cop turned back to the blond boy. "Maybe I can have your Leopard ass tossed in with some other kinda niggers, boy. We got us a few from that Emeryville gang. Wanna meet 'em . . . *boy?*"

Ethan stood up. "Yo, pig! Toss *your* ass in with some KKKs, dogfucka! You . . . you ain't nuthin but a whiteman's ho!"

Both cops looked startled when they saw the little boy's face. Ethan flashed a finger sign to the white kid, who smiled.

"Stop that shit!" bawled the black cop. "Get back down on that bed, you little bastard!"

Ethan spat, for real, barely missing the cop's shoes. "DIE, PIG!"

"Yeah!" yelled the white kid. "Die, pig, *die!*"

Several other boys began chanting the words. Soon the

whole room took it up. The little boy Mrs. Davis was holding stopped crying and joined in too. The chanting grew louder. Some kids stood and raised their fists in the air in a sign Corbitt had only seen in old pictures. The cops exchanged uncertain glances.

Corbitt scanned the room: maybe twenty kids, and none over fourteen, yet the white cop put down the camera and pulled out his club. Some boys stood up. Others followed. One picked up his skateboard and held it like a weapon. The chanting grew louder. Corbitt caught movement in the doorway: three girls wrapped in blankets had come from their room across the hall. Then, more joined them, and their voices took up the chant. The cop holding Chad let go and backed away from the door as kids from downstairs appeared among the blanket-wrapped girls. One hand went to the walkie-talkie on his belt. He looked to the black cop. "Maybe we should get backup?"

The black cop stood, dropping his hands to his hips and trying to make himself look bigger. "All you! Shut up! NOW!"

A few kids looked uncertain. The blond boy stood. "You gonna shoot us all, pig?"

Chad's voice carried above the chanting. "S'matter, pig? Can't do that yet, can you, cocksucker? Maybe next year!"

Suddenly, Corbitt found himself on his feet. Slender ebony fingers aimed at the black cop, two extended with the thumb, the last two folded against his palm. Words he hadn't imagined came from his mouth. "I see you! Nigger with a gun, nigger with a whip! You help 'em chain us! Kill us! An you still doin it. Day come, fool! Day come!"

The black cop stared at Corbitt. For an instant Corbitt saw real fear in the man's eyes as if *he* had remembered. Then the man grabbed the white cop's arm. "Get a pitcher of *him!* Now!"

But the whiteman was glancing around at the kids. Slowly, a circle was forming. "Forget it! Let's go!"

"Yeah!" called Chad. "Best bail your asses fore somethin happen your masters ain't ready to cover."

The three men moved cautiously toward the door. Some kids spit. The men's hands went to their guns, but they kept moving. Chad snatched the camera off the floor. "Yo! Pig! Forget your new toy? The camera slipped from his fingers and hit the board floor. The loading door popped open and the film roll fell out. Chad shrugged. "Hell, what you spect from a stupid nee-groboy?" Chad recovered the camera and tossed it to the man, the film unrolling as it flew through the air.

Mrs. Davis cleared the doorway of kids to let the cops through. The chanting followed the men down the hall. Ethan tugged Corbitt's hand. "C'mon!"

There was no logical reason to watch the cops leave, but Corbitt was still wondering where those words had come from. He went with Ethan out in the hallway. The dark, chubby girl who had been reading downstairs passed by. The blanket had slipped from one shoulder, baring soft skin and showing the suggestion of a full-rounded breast, but Corbitt hardly noticed. The kids were still chanting and shouting curses at the cops. The men had reached the top of the stairs and were starting down. Corbitt stopped. "No, Ethan. Ain't nuthin more to be done, man. Let's us go back to bed."

Then the black cop pitched forward, but his cry was drowned by the chanting. He must have tripped because no one was near him but the two whitemen. Corbitt heard the fleshy thuds and the clatter of equipment as the man crashed down the staircase. He dashed to the rail at the head of the hall, shoving between the other kids to stare down. The chanting had changed to laughter and shouts, but Corbitt hardly heard them. Below, the other two cops had reached the bottom and were helping the black one to his feet. The man was clutching his arm the way Toby had when Lamar had broken it. Mrs. Davis came to the head of the staircase and watched as the cops moved across the main room toward the door. Her face showed no expression.

Corbitt turned away, walking back to the sleeping-room. Ethan caught up. "Yo! Do people die from busted arms, man?"

Corbitt frowned. "Mmm. Ain't likely nowadays . . . less infection set in."

"Shit, I *wish* it happen, Corbitt! Um, it wrong wishin for dat, man?"

Corbitt shook his head. "Two days ago I say yeah, it wrong. Now I don't know." Then he noticed something small and black in Ethan's hand. "Yo! Why you be keepin that feather?"

"Well, come all da way from 'sippi stuck in your hair, man. Shit, maybe it lucky or somethin. Um, want it back?"

"No. All I want be some goddamn peace."

Despite his weariness Corbitt didn't sleep well for the rest of the night, waking instantly every time a kid coughed or murmured or got up to go to the bathroom. Yet Ethan slumbered peacefully, right up until a tired-looking Chad came in and began gently rousing the boys. Corbitt nudged Ethan, who smiled, stretched, and yawned. "Mornin, little brother."

"Mornin, big brother."

Corbitt sat up and looked around. He noted gray fog beyond the weeping windows. Its paleness made the overhead bulbs golden by contrast, warming the black and brown skins of the kids that surrounded him. That gave him a funny feeling of pride, like something half-remembered. His mind drifted to imagine the girls' room across the hall. He felt his dick tingle, and shifted his thoughts to something else. The blond boy was sitting up on his mattress and seemed to be doing an inventory of his backpack. He looked about twelve, with no muscle to speak of, and a small puckered scar on his side that might have been made by a bullet. But other than his pale hair and blue eyes there was nothing Toby-like about him except the way he seemed so at home surrounded by black kids.

"He the Leopards' mascot," whispered Ethan, seeing where Corbitt was looking. "He pretty cool. Him an Tam prob'ly be homeys, cept for him bein a Leopard. Don't let his color smoke ya, man. He seven out seven with us."

"Huh?"

"He bad."

Corbitt grabbed Ethan's foot and tickled it. "Yeah? All black kids be bad as you, man?"

Ethan giggled and squirmed. "G . . . gots to be. Dey make us dat way."

Corbitt let go. "Mmm. Maybe they do. An we let 'em."

Breakfast downstairs was all happy noise, rowdiness, and cigarette smoke, with paper cups of bluish milk, or coffee if you wanted, and all the oatmeal topped with sugar you could eat. Ethan stuffed down three bowlfuls, and Corbitt decided that topping off the fuel tank whenever possible was a pretty logical idea. There were morning cartoons on TV, the same ones seen in Bridge-end, and though most of the older boys and girls took their blankets and bags and backpacks and headed for the street after eating, a lot of the littler ones sat down to watch. There were also some new kids who were being dropped off by their parents. Others picked up comics or magazines, and one or two started on coloring books. Most of the really young ones zeroed in on the boxful of toys in the corner. One small boy was making picture transfers from a *Brother Man* comic to a sheet of blank paper with Silly Putty. Corbitt noticed the dark, full-bodied girl again. A boy had given her what looked like a letter, and now she was addressing an envelope for him at the front desk. Corbitt watched her leave, noting the confidence in her walk, so like Sherry's, then his eyes came back to the pads of paper on the tables. He smiled a moment, seeing the boy with the Silly Putty now trying to transfer a dollar bill while two others watched critically. Corbitt considered writing a letter to Toby. But no; that wasn't a logical idea. Mrs. Barlow was the New Crossing postmistress. Writing to Lamar or Sherry or sending a reassuring note to his mother wouldn't work either . . . the letter would carry an Oakland, California, postmark. Mrs. Griffin? Likely, Mrs. Barlow would still notice the postmark. Besides, what could he say . . . that he'd been in the City of the Black less than twenty-four hours and gotten shot at, seen a boy killed, fixed a gang's gun, lost everything but his Levi's, and spent all his money on junkfood and beer? He felt in his pocket where Weylen's dollar was still folded carefully in cigarette-pack tinfoil. He wondered how much a silver certificate would be worth. But where could he try and sell it without being afraid of getting cheated?

Corbitt sighed: Bridge-end could have been another planet for all the reality it held for him now. It was frightening to realize that everything he'd learned about life in thirteen years counted for nothing in this place. To survive here he had to rely on an eight-year-old who sold his ass in bus stations and couldn't read or write. Was this the kind of home black people chose and built for themselves when white people didn't care for them?

Corbitt sank into one of the old chairs, noting that Ethan had settled on the floor in front of the TV, giggling along with the other children at a Ninja Turtles commercial. Sewer-spitting Turtles. Guppy had wanted a set of those, but Mrs. Sampson swore she wouldn't have such disgusting things in her house.

Of course the Bridge-end kids still played sewer-spitting down in the river. *When the student is ready, a teacher will appear.* Mrs. Griffin had said that. But who taught these little kids? And how could they even *be* children when they had to go around in armor all the time? Didn't anyone love them? How could people *not* love children? Chad loved them, and Mrs. Davis, but love was like butter that way . . . spread so thin you could hardly taste any. How many of those kids would live to grow up?

Corbitt let his slender body sink deeper into the worn-out old chair. He suddenly felt small and fragile, and alone . . . a baby cheetah lost in panther-land. Pulling out his tobacco, he started rolling a cigarette.

Ethan appeared as if by magic. "Yo! Make me a smoke, big brother!"

Corbitt waved his hand. "Poof, y'all be a smoke."

"Huh? Oh!" Ethan giggled. "Too funny, dude!" Then he glanced over his shoulder and grabbed Corbitt's hand. "Yo! C'mon, man! Chad givin out shit!"

Chad had unlocked the door to a small room under the staircase, and a dozen or so kids had gathered there. Inside were big boxes of used clothes and shoes. Chad seemed to be expert at measuring, handing out T-shirts and jeans after only a glance. While most of the clothes were far from new, they were usually better and a whole lot cleaner than what the kids were wearing to begin with. Chad's smile widened when he saw Corbitt. "Yo, brother, I been savin this back for somebody it fit proper."

He held up an old brown leather jacket, wrinkled and scuffed, its red satin lining worn and stained. To Corbitt, it was a beautiful thing. Amazingly, it fit, right down over his long arms.

"Thanks, Chad," said Corbitt. "I always wanted me one of these."

Ethan studied Corbitt critically. "Shit yeah! Make you da flyest, dude! Word an a half!" He dropped his voice. "I know dis store give you twenty fuckin dollars for dat."

"Shush!" said Corbitt. "I wish me one of these ever since I your size."

"Well, I just wanted you should know, dat all. Sides, you

can't eat da motherfuckin thing!" Ethan shoved another kid aside and went into the room where there was a big box of used shoes, mostly high-tops and a few older-style sneakers, all tied in pairs by their laces. Chad grinned, watching Ethan dig through them. "Seem like he your life-brother now, man."

Corbitt considered that. "It sorta a 'sponsibility."

Chad gave Corbitt a thoughtful look. "Mmm. I like the way you see things, brother."

"Well, I can't rightly say it be a 'sponsibility I was lookin for."

Chad handed a pair of jeans to a little girl. "Responsibility for your brothers an sisters ain't a option, man. Either it's each one teach one, or there ain't no hope for none of us." He sighed and scanned the room. "Only, it ain't workin that way . . . you can see that with your own eyes."

Corbitt nodded. "Yeah. It like, each one tryin to teach a hundred, ain't it?"

Ethan was still burrowing like a badger. Now he gave a whoop and yanked a pair of shoes from the box. "These is *you*, man! An don't gimme no shit, neither!"

Corbitt eyed what Ethan was proudly holding up. Surprisingly, they looked about the right size, though they certainly wouldn't have been the shoes he'd have chosen for himself. They looked something like old-style Converse high-tops, black and white with red striping. But they were leather, and the black was that shiny patent kind. Corbitt took them, not sure he really wanted them, but Ethan looked so eager.

Chad nodded. "Your little brother gots him a eye for style. They ain't made them kinda Cheetahs in years, but you could cruise 'em like tomorrow's news."

Corbitt looked at the label: Cheetahs. Was that a bad sign or a good one? He sighed and knelt to try them on. They seemed to fit right. Just what he needed to slink around in. Maybe the universe liked a good joke once in a while?

Chad handed him a new pair of cheap crew socks and a plain white T-shirt. "Look like this the only one come close to coverin your middle, man. Need a blanket too?"

Corbitt caught Ethan mouthing words that looked like *you can sell it*. Corbitt shook his head, knowing his own jeans were better than what the Center had to give, and the jacket alone almost seemed too much. "No, thanks, Chad. Um, there be somethin I do to help here? I pretty good at fixin stuff."

Chad smiled. "We can't pay you nuthin, cept food. Can you read, like to little kids?"

"Sho!"

But Ethan grabbed Corbitt's arm. "Yo! C'mon, man. Gots no time for readin an shit. We gots to meet somebody. Member?"

Chad's eyes saddened slightly. "Sound like you got somethin important goin on, man."

Corbitt glanced at Ethan, then nodded. "Yeah. I gots to be makin me some money. Don't seem like that a option. But I come back an read to your kids soon's I can."

Chad nodded. "I know you do what right, brother. You got the look. An they *your* kids too."

Ethan had scored a blanket and had it wrapped around him as he led Corbitt out onto the street in the chill morning fog. "Word, Corbitt, dat place be way cool, but you can't go hangin dere too much or da motherfuckin pigs take you away!"

Corbitt glanced back at the ramshackle old building. "But, what about them kids gots no other place to go? You ain't tryin to tell me them cops put you in prison just cause you a black kid nobody want?"

"Shit!" snorted Ethan. "Dey don't call it prison, but your ass locked in so what da fuck da difference? Pretty soon it gonna be special black-kid prisons all over hell! Word!" He peered defiantly around. "Dey never catch *my* ass! Real Africans way too smart for dem motherfuckas! Word!"

"But, that just plain silly, man. I mean . . ." Then Corbitt shut his mouth, recalling Mr. Rudd's words . . . *we should be taking better care of you.*

Corbitt put his hand on Ethan's shoulder. "We should be takin better care of our own African asses."

"Shit yeah, Corbitt! Just like you an me, man!"

Without the darkness the street looked ten times worse. Bridge-end came to Corbitt's mind: the old cabins needing paint, plumbing that needed fixing, and all the other things that didn't work. But fixing those things took time and money, and when you were poor most of your time was spent trying to make the money.

Two boys were sitting on the fender of a garbage-stuffed hulk as Corbitt and Ethan walked past.

"Yo!" called one. "Wanna buy . . ."

Corbitt snorted. "You entirely the wrong color to be selling that shit, sucka."

Lactameon stopped at the top of the last flight of stairs and leaned against the banister to get his breath back. This was only the second time in his life that he'd climbed these steps, but he already knew them a hell of a lot better than he wanted to. Mopping his face with the tail of his tank-top, he glanced down the hallway toward Hobbes's door. He hoped Hobbes was still home. Ethan woke early, even when there was no reason to, and this had been the first morning in three that Lactameon had been able to sleep until nine. It was close to ten now, but his mom had cooked extra, thinking that Ethan had spent another night, so breakfast had taken a little more time. Jerking up his jeans, Lactameon went down the hall and knocked at Hobbes's door. But it was Sebastian's sleepy voice that answered.

"Beamer, if that's you, fuck off for a while!"

Lactameon tensed and looked back toward the stairs. He hadn't expected Sebastian to be here. Now, if he just tried to leave without saying anything, Sebastian would probably come out to check. Lactameon stepped back from the door, just in case.

"It me, Sabby."

There was a moment of silence. Lactameon wasn't sure what to expect, but the golden boy's voice sounded casual. "Oh. Well, hang a minute, man. S'cool."

Next came a murmur, and then what might have been a giggle. Lactameon couldn't imagine either Sebastian or Hobbes doing that. Bedsprings squeaked, and bare feet padded across the floor. Locks clicked, and Sebastian pulled open the door. He was naked, and his gray eyes looked more sleepy than hostile. Most of the bruises had faded from his body and face. It was hard to muss a short flattop, but his came close. He yawned. "So, c'mon in, Tam."

Leaving the door half open, Sebastian walked back to the bed. Lactameon pushed the door wider and stepped in. The small room was gloomy in lead-gray fog-light. The dirty windows were steamed, and dope smoke drifted in sweet-smelling streamers. The stereo was playing a Bobby Brown song. Sebastian was back in bed, his hard body half covered by a rumpled sheet about the same color as the fog. He had a doob between his fingers, and looked almost peaceful for the first time Lactameon could remember. Mulattos in the mist. The big Uzi pistol lay on a little table beside the bed. Lactameon caught another, faintly familiar scent before he saw Toni White beside Sebastian.

Lactameon's cool almost slipped for a second, but he covered by kicking the door shut with his heel. Sebastian slid an arm under his head and yawned out smoke. "Wanna hit?"

"Uh-uh. Thanks." Lactameon tried to think of something cool to do, not sure whether to deny Toni or not. He'd hardly seen her for months, except when she'd come for a reading from his mom, and he'd almost forgotten how pretty she was . . . not pretty by Cosby-kid standards, but then that was Sebastian's department. Toni was dark, her skin like velvety midnight compared to Lactameon's dull, sooty shade. She had bright obsidian eyes and tight curly hair in a short, rounded puff. And, she had a real body, at least what Lactameon had seen of it. Silver had once said that Toni was the kind of girl most African dudes would cherish but most African-American boys had been trained to dis. Lactameon couldn't see much of her now, with the sheet almost up to her neck, and only one arm showing, but her arm looked substantial and real.

Toni's lips opened wide in a smile. "Hi, Tam."

"Um, hi, Toni." Lactameon caught himself before he could add something stupid like, what you been doin? There were two Trojan wrappers on the floor by the bed. *How's tricks, sister?* Bogart could say that, Lactameon couldn't. He pulled out his

Kools and fired one, asking a question while already knowing the answer. "Hobbes here . . . Akeem?"

Sebastian smiled, looking friendly. "Naw. He over at the new house, man. Been there all night again. He tryin to build that sellin room, cept there just ain't no dudes in this hood up for that shit." Sebastian snickered, leaning over to crush out the doob in a tuna can bristling with Kool butts. "Sent Beamer over to that big hardware store yesterday for a saw an a hammer. Retard cruise back with some hacksaw blades an a goddamn ball-peen cause they was on special or somethin! Maaan, don't even ask what kinda donkey show he made out scorin the nails! Shit, Tam, you wouldn't fuckin *believe* how many different kinds of nails there are in the world!"

Lactameon plopped down on the arm of the sofa. "Well, didn't you take wood-shop for 'dustrial arts last year?"

Sebastian snorted. "Shit! Taught us how to make a motherfuckin shoeshine box with dovetail joints! An a cocksuckin kitchen stool! Yo! Who in hell wears shoes that gotta be shined . . . cept pigs! An, what real black kid gonna shine some sucka's shoes anyways? Shit, I seen some cocksucka doin that, I fuckin kick his ass in one, man! Then, my mom bout busted her behind fallin off that goddamn stool!" Sebastian snagged his own Kools off the table and fired one. "Lizard ain't no fuckin help. Fact is, he up an told Hobbes he work in a crack house, not no cocksuckin carpenter shop."

Lactameon smiled. "So, how bout you, man?"

Toni took Sebastian's free hand. "Sabby a bodyguard. He don't go gettin his little golden fingers all splintery."

Lactameon choked on smoke and covered his mouth. Sebastian scowled and jerked his hand away. "Don't do that, bitch! It makes me nervous!"

Lactameon frowned, but asked. "So, why ain't you guardin, sweetheart?"

Sebastian shrugged. "Shit, what's to guard, man? Anyways, Hobbes gets all hyper cause I fucked up a two-by-four cuttin it wrong. Then he sends me on a nail run . . . after your shit-for-brains homey come back with the wrong kind again . . . an when I come cruisin back from the store, some white-ass cocksuckas roll by in one of them jacked-up rice-rockets an start yellin how some nigger fucked my momma good, so's I shot out two of their cocksuckin tires."

"Jeeze!"

Sebastian snickered again. "Shit, man, you shoulda seen them cracker-ass faces! Cocksuckas figure they *safe* up there. An, yo! Them little trucks don't even need no air in their tires! Shoulda seen them cocksuckas bail!"

Toni squeezed Sebastian's arm. "Make a big gold muscle again, Sabby."

"Yo, bitch! We done! An, quit callin me Sabby! I told you what my name is! Anyways, Tam, Hobbes got a little pissed when I told him bout that . . . even if I did get the right kinda nails. Told me to hang my black ass here till bout ten, case Lizard or Beamer run outa product. Maaaan, you wouldn't fuckin *believe* how much plywood an boards an shit like that cost! Hobbes had to hire some old dude with a truck to haul the shit, an then pay him extra to keep his mouth shut."

"So, I guess Hobbes ain't finished with the new place yet?"

"Shit, man, you askin me, he ain't even started!" Sebastian peered over at the VCR clock. "Mmm. Guess I better get my black ass over there an pound nails or somethin."

Toni asked, "Can I use your shower, Sab . . . Sebastian?"

"*Akeem*, bitch!"

"Sorry . . . Akeem."

Sebastian yawned and stretched. "Yeah. Fuck, why not. I don't got time for one."

Toni hesitated, sitting up but holding the sheet over her body.

"Oh." Lactameon stood and headed for the door.

Sebastian snorted again. "Shit, Toni! Who the fuck you figure you foolin? Think Tam don't know you a ho?" Snatching his black jeans from the floor, Sebastian pulled a twenty from a pocket, crumpled the bill in his fist, and dropped it on the sheet. "Buy a life, bitch! An, remember, it coulda been more!"

Lactameon waited in the hall until he heard the bathroom door close before coming back in. Sebastian had his jeans on and was tying his black Cons. The Kool dangled from his lips. "Shit, Tam, what the 411 on bitches anyways?"

Lactameon glanced toward the bathroom, hearing water-sound. "Well, it only polite, man."

"*Polite*, my black ass! Yo, put all your polite in one hand, shit in the other, an check which one fill up first in this sorry-ass motherfucka!" Sebastian saw where Lactameon was looking. "Mmm. Well, maybe you right, man. Shit, she prob'ly wanna get paid for the peek-out!" He studied Lactameon a moment. "Yo. You mean you never fucked her?"

Lactameon frowned. "No."

"Well, shit, man, I figure she done all you Collectors on the group rate."

"Oh, shut up!"

Sebastian only looked surprised. "Hey, Tam. I sorry bout the other day, man. But, shit, you gotta know what it is . . . gettin the shit kicked out me like that. Sides, I was drunk."

"Yeah. I know what it is."

"Well, I just wanna say it cool you chillin with it, man. An, shit, I wouldn't really hurt none of them little kids. An, I woulda paid Ethan. Always do. Ain't seen the little sucka lately."

"He gots somethin else goin on."

Sebastian shrugged. "Well, ain't none of my business, man. But, seem like to me, your gang own them kids, you should be takin better care of 'em."

Lactameon sat back down on the sofa arm. "I just the mascot. My mom give money to the kid-center. Last year I play Santa Claus for 'em."

"So, want some breakfast, Tam? Hobbes don't mind."

"No. I just ate. Fact is, I come to talk to Hobbes."

Sebastian straightened from his shoes and gave Lactameon a long look. "Yeah? Bout that job in the house, man? Kinda figure you would."

Lactameon made a face. "No. I hooked up with this dude yesterday. Just moved here. He needin green."

"So? Who don't?"

"Well, I figure he a dude Hobbes could trust."

Sebastian's eyes narrowed. He pulled the Kool from his mouth and crushed it in the tuna can. "So, what you sayin, man?"

"Chill, Akeem. This dude could never do your job. He ain't gots the ice for it."

Sebastian considered that, then nodded. "So, what you figure we use him for, then? We gots Beamer for the little suckas, an Lizard for the rest, an we already gots us a runner work cheap."

Lactameon got up to drop his Kool in the can. "Well, I was thinkin this dude be way fly with tools. Hobbes need somebody like that right now, don't he?"

"Mmm. Word-up on that! So, how old this sucka, man?"

"Thirteen. But he look a lot older."

"Bigger'n me, what you sayin?"

"Well, taller. But he don't gots muscles like you."

Sebastian glanced down at himself for a second. "Mmm. Well, spose he a slick-boy?"

"I don't think so."

Sebastian reached for his jacket and pulled out his pipe. "So, where he livin now?"

"Crib at the Center last night. He run away."

Sebastian paused in packing his pipe. "To *here?*" He laughed. "So, what the fuck is he, man? Some sorta space-case like Beamer?"

Lactameon got up again. "Yo! I just askin, okay? An, maybe I askin the wrong dude."

Sebastian rose and took Lactameon's arm. "Yo, Tam. Chill. Look, you say he's cool, I go with the program. But, let me run it by Hobbes. He gots too much on his mind right now for shit like that. If the dude worth shit, I see you get paid for your time." Sebastian slipped the pipe into his mouth, but then noticed the clock and jerked it back out. "Shit! Gots no time!"

Lactameon smiled. "Shoulda taken a shower, man."

"Mmm." Sebastian glanced at the pipe, then stuck it in his pocket. "Um, thanks for what you done the other day, Tam. I guess I owe ya. Hobbes ain't no fool . . . least over shit like that. Um, figure you an me could ever be sorta . . . friends, man?"

Lactameon shrugged. "Can't have too many."

"Well, cruise your ass back by here round five, Tam. I give you the 411. Um, you really should lose some weight, man."

"Thanks."

Sebastian picked up the pistol and cocked it. An already chambered round spit from the ejection port and clattered across the floor. "Shit! You see where it go?"

"Under the bed."

"Shit!" Sebastian handed the gun to Lactameon and crouched to peer under the bed. "Tell you this, man. I see a lotta shit Hobbes miss. Fuck, he could be twice as long if he work at it harder. I know what he always sayin bout whitey after the little dudes, but some of them suckas really do listen to all that anti-crack bullshit. I was talkin to this whiteboy uptown the other day. He tellin me bout some new kinda shit, specially for little kids. Kinda bust 'em in easy, what I sayin. But Hobbes ain't havin none. Sometimes I think he just don't gots the ice no more. Yo! You sure it go under here, man?"

"Uh-huh. Well, you go an tell that to Gilligan."

Sebastian started to squirm under the bed, but looked up and grinned. "Yeah! Word come over from Leopard ground bout that, but I didn't know it was Hobbes wrote the program."

"Well, I ain't sayin it was. But, everybody know Hobbes eighty-six Gilligan's ass for smokin on the job."

"So, you sayin it Gilligan give you dudes the password?"

"I ain't sayin nuthin, man. Sides, dude get like Gilligan, piss a lotta people off. Prob'ly run somebody else's boy out the bus station."

"Yeah, well, guess we both know what it is without sayin. There been some word on the Leopard side say Hobbes lost the ice by not payin you dudes back. Maybe he figure kickin Gilligan chill all that. You *sure* it went under here?"

Lactameon sighed. "I seen it. Watch out for ass-kickin dust-bunnies, man. Shit, it only one little bullet."

Sebastian wiggled under the bed. "They special. Rip right through them vests the pigs an major-time gangstuhs wearin. Fuckin 'spensive too. Hobbes counts 'em, swear to God! Shit, I was outa pocket for that clipful you took the other night. Had to score some from that ole pawn-sucka so Hobbes wouldn't know."

Lactameon smiled a little, thinking that Sebastian had probably bought back his own bullets.

Sebastian squirmed a little deeper. "Tell you this, man. *I* runnin a house, I go ahead an make some slick-boy's monthlies. Stay open a fuck a lot longer that way. Found it!"

"Had that happen with a Milk Dud one time. Rat got it. Oh well."

"I hate rats! Cocksuckas! They bite babies an spread disease!" Sebastian stood and dusted himself off, then took back the gun, pulled the magazine, and slipped the bullet in. "Maybe you can get Toni to fix you some breakfast. She might do that much for *free*."

"Thought I sposed to lose weight, man?"

"So, start tomorrow. Fat ain't healthy, an you gots way too goddamn much. Why don't you least wear a shirt that cover you, man?"

Lactameon spread his arms. "Why? I sposed to be shamed of all this or somethin? Like, I stole some baby's food to get this way? Shit, man, when my mom have a bad week I go hungry like anybody else. Sides, seem like we fed every kid in the hood one time or another. I like a walkin free-meal sign."

"Nobody respect a fat dude, man."

"Yeah. Guess it hard to be icy when you look like me."

"Well, don't all that blubber make it hard to fuck?"

"Never had no probs."

"Well, don't go takin this wrong, but I for sure wouldn't wanna be under you."

"I try not an take that wrong, man."

Sebastian slapped the magazine back into place. "Shit, Toni do you. Give you any goddamn thing you want. For a price. Want me to front you a twenty?"

"No. So, she give you what you need, man?"

Sebastian slipped on his black satin T-shirt, then hesitated a moment, looking puzzled. "No. She didn't."

Lactameon frowned, wondering why he'd asked that. He didn't really want the details. Besides, it wasn't hard to figure what Sebastian would have wanted, and the Toni he remembered would have been smart enough to use a rubber for that too.

Sebastian nudged the Trojan wrapper with his toe. "I offer her twice the price if she let me fuck her without one. She wouldn't."

Lactameon took a breath and tried to think of four good reasons not to throw the golden boy through the window. The gun wasn't one of them. "All that show is she smart, an you crazy."

"Yo! What you sayin?"

"Jeeze, Sabby! How you be that motherfuckin stupid?"

"Huh?" Sebastian thought a moment. "Oh. Well, shit, man, *course* I got the 411 on all that AIDS stuff. But, word say Toni never do it without one since she have that baby. So, she gots to be clean, right?"

Lactameon shook his head. "Man, I can't believe this shit! Now I spose you gonna tell me you clean for a fact cause all you do is pay little boys to suck your dick?"

Sebastian scowled. "Yo, Tam! I owe ya, but don't go startin shit with me, man! I try an be your friend . . . try an tell you stuff. But I don't need no niggerboy bullshit, man! Yo! You gots some sucka needin green, maybe I help, but don't fuck with me, man!" Sebastian shot a glare at the bathroom door. "Anyways, who give a cocksuckin fuck what happen to her? I just want me some real black cunt, out no goddamn hat on my dick! Want me them juices, man! She gots what I want an she goddamn well know it, but she ain't givin me none!"

Rage was mounting hot in Lactameon, but now it cooled a little. He kept his voice low. "What. The. Fuck. Are you talkin bout, Sabby?"

"I read it in a book, man! A real cocksuckin book with covers, just like you readin all the time!"

"Read, *what?*"

"Bout *us*, goddammit! Black people! We change melanin durin sex!"

Lactameon's eyes widened for a moment. Then he sighed. "*Ex*-change, an I think that bullshit."

"It in a book, Tam. An the book wrote by a black dude."

"My mom gots a book, wrote by a black dude . . . the *real* High John. Tell how to mix up money-drawin oil. Yo. You figure that true, I be sittin here listenin to *this* bullshit? There a lot of real African magic, man. An there a real lotta black bullshit too."

Scowling, Sebastian glanced at the clock once again. "Well, I gots no more time for *your* bullshit, man. Specially when you already gots ten tons more goddamn melanin in all your goddamn blubber than anybody need!"

"So, eat me, Sabby."

"Oh, fuck you, cocksucker! Yo! We almost even, man. I score some nigger-work for your boy, an that make us one an one." Sebastian shoved the pistol into his jacket and started for the door. "Yo! Make sure that black-ass bitch vacate fore you do!" He stepped out, slamming the door behind him, the locks doing their gunbolt thing.

"Dog-poo," said Lactameon. *That* was one crazy-ass niggerboy, whether he knew it or not. But he was just one in a whole great big crazy-ass motherfucker, so who was going to notice? *Don't you play with that little boy, Tam, he's weird.* Lactameon looked around the empty room. It was still cool because of the fog, but that was thinning and it was going to be another hot summer day in sorry-ass land. Ethan and Corbitt might already be waiting for him in the park, but he had nothing to tell Corbitt yet. Ethan would take care of him . . . like a brother.

The love-scent from the bed made Lactameon restless. He glanced toward the bathroom, where wisps of steam were curling out around the doorframe. *Déjà vu.* Then he got up and went to the fridge. Hobbes had restocked, and there were two sixers of Bud and so many forty-ounce Colts there hardly seemed room for food. Snagging one, Lactameon twisted the cap off and flipped it across the room. He tilted back his head and lifted the bottle to his lips, feeling a shiver of anticipation because there was nothing as good as those first icy swallows. Then, the bathroom door opened partway and Toni peered out through a curtain of mist. Seeing Lactameon, she drew back a little, but smiled.

"Oh. I thought Sabby was still here. Could you get me my clothes please, Tam?"

Lactameon lowered the bottle, his tongue only teased by the taste. "Oh. Um, yeah. Course."

Setting the bottle on the sink counter, he went for the girl's jeans and T-shirt, which lay neatly draped on the back of the couch. He noticed a used rubber nearby on the floor, pictured Sebastian throwing it there, and then wondered why that pissed him off so much. "Um, Toni? You want your shoes an socks too?"

"No thanks, Tam. I put 'em on later."

Toni stood behind the door as Lactameon gave her the things. Steam drifted around her, cottony-white, caressing her darkness. Only her face and shoulder showed, but Lactameon imagined more. In his mind he saw her shadowy shape moving through that misty universe between time and Timbuktu. He tried to keep his eyes where he thought they belonged, but her velvety skin glistened wet and he wanted to see as much as he could. Was that the full-rounded shape of her breast, glimpsed for a second as she reached out her hand? There was the wide, dusky curve of her hip. The door shut softly, puffing girl-scented mist in his face. He stood there, gazing at the peeling old door panel. The lock didn't work anymore: what if the door accidentally swung open? A finger of steam curled from the keyhole like an invitation. Sooty Jimmy rose solid and fast.

Lactameon frowned, jerking at his jeans and wishing he could get one more button to fasten. Either that, or let the goddamn things fall off. He didn't need an invitation; all he needed was twenty dollars and he'd be changed forever. Maybe that would be the last major change in his life? He turned away from the door before he could do something childish or stupid. Funny; he couldn't remember what Toni looked like now. Her image in his mind was a smiling face seen in the street, school hallway, or classroom. Other memories revealed only a dark, chubby girl in a faded pink swimsuit a season too small. He glanced once again at the keyhole, then shifted his jeans to trap his hot dick against his leg. Bastard! He went back to the counter, picked up the bottle, and slammed the whole thing. Somehow he missed the first taste.

"Can I have one, too?"

Startled, Lactameon almost dropped the bottle. Toni had come up beside him, silent on bare feet, and now stood with her shoulder touching his. He could feel the warm dampness still on her skin.

"Um . . . you want one of *these?*"

He felt Toni's smile before her lips even parted. She was so close that her face was almost all he could see of her. It was almost like he remembered; round cheeks with dimples, wide little nose, full lips in a half-smile even at rest, and those black long-lashed eyes.

"Well, I *could,* but I was thinkin more bout one of them Buds. Seem like it ought to taste extra good after that shower."

The scent of her breath was peppermint toothpaste. Whose brush had she used? "Um, oh, for sure, Toni."

Lactameon tore a can from a sixer and gave it to the girl, then cursed himself for not opening it first. What if she broke a fingernail? He looked at her hands, relieved to see that her nails were strong and cut short. Their natural cream tone was polish enough. He moved back a step, wanting to see all of her as she really was now. It was mostly a disappointment because her faded black T-shirt was way oversize and her gray gangstuh jeans were loose-fit and styled with extra pockets at knee-level that made them all baggy. Still, her behind filled them out like the song said it should, and the way her shirt spread and fell in the front promised breasts that lived up to the name. She tilted her head back to sip from the can and Lactameon saw the concave of a tummy-button padded with chubbiness. Her feet were the right size to carry her weight. Her toenails were large, and showed careful trimming on toes that had walked enough without shoes to take a determined stance. Lactameon noticed the tip of a toothbrush peeping from one of her knee pockets. Somehow that made her seem brave in his mind . . . a girl who might grab a rat by the tail and swing it three times before launching it out of a window.

He caught Toni catching him scoping her. She smiled and took another sip from the can. Lactameon's mom maintained that drinking from a can wasn't ladylike, but it was the way Toni was doing it. She set the can on the counter and peered into the fridge. Her nose wrinkled in just the same way Lactameon remembered from math class when old Mrs. Maxwell screeched chalk on the blackboard.

"Yuk! Just you look at all that junkfood. Surprise me how Sebastian manage to keep his muscles, livin on that kinda crap."

"Um . . . well, he prob'ly just gots 'em natural. Like most black dudes."

Toni smiled again, as if Lactameon had said something funny. "Mmm. Well, do I actually see some real eggs in there? An, could that be a honest to God carton of milk? Wonder they still any good?"

Lactameon moved back to the fridge, close to the girl, feeling her warmth through her clothes. Her clean-washed scent filled his nostrils. "Yeah. Some of that shit look like it belong in a museum."

Toni's eyes turned curious. "You ever been to one, Tam?"

"A museum? Sure. Lotsa times."

Toni's eyes lingered on Lactameon's a moment. She touched

his arm, and warmth seemed to flow from her fingers. "Um, you like some of them eggs scrambled?"

Lactameon's hand could have accidentally brushed Toni's hip. It wanted to. Sooty Jimmy was trying to raise all kinds of hell. "Um, sure, Toni. But, you don't gots to . . . I mean, the trouble an all. There some pizza we could nuke. Leopard pizza. We can't get that here."

Toni grinned, a girl's grin, and beautiful. Her hand went to Lactameon's shoulder, then slipped down the strap of his tank-top to lightly slide over his chest. The feel of her fingers was like he imagined mink might be. Her hand came to rest on the roll of his waist.

"I see a whole box of Twinkies in there too, Tam."

"Um, but I thought you say you don't like junkfood?"

"Twinkies too good to be junkfood. Maybe we have 'em for dessert." Lifting her hand, Toni turned again to the fridge and took out the eggs and milk. She gave the milk carton a cautious sniff. "I a little hungry too, Tam. I mean, if that cool?"

Lactameon jerked at his jeans. "Oh, um, course. Hobbes chill with it."

A tiny line creased Toni's smooth forehead. "You, um, workin for Hobbes now?"

Lactameon shifted his legs. "No . . . Well, he offer me a job, but I don't figure I gonna take it. Anyways, I think he really just likes me. For a friend, I mean. Shit, he coulda kicked my ass the other day, but he didn't. Um, I didn't know you knew Sabby."

Toni was searching through cupboards above the sink, stretched up on her determined toes, but her shirt was too long to lift past her jeans. Lactameon gazed at her behind as it strained gray denim. There was muscle beneath those big, round shapes, but then she probably did a lot of walking.

Toni found a big black frying pan and rinsed it out in the sink. "I don't know Sabby. Least, no more'n I want to."

The stove was an ancient O'Keefe & Merrit that had to be lit with matches. Lactameon fired a burner with his Bic. "Yeah. Them was way-shitty names he was callin you, Toni. I shoulda done somethin."

Toni put the pan on the stove. "I hear you tellin him to shut up. That took balls, Tam. Ain't you scared of him?"

"Shit no! I mean, what I sayin is, for sure he could shoot my ass, but that *all* he can do. An, hell, any pig can do that. I mean, just cause somebody can kick you, don't mean you scared of 'em. That why pigs kill us whenever they can. It scare the shit out of 'em when some niggerboy fight harder for his life than they do for their dinner."

Toni smiled. "Mmm. You always did see stuff in ways nobody else does. But, I still be scared of Sabby. Seem like, if there somethin worse he could do sides just killin somebody, he do it. I don't spose there any butter?"

"Huh? Oh." Lactameon pointed. "I see a bottle of Mazola way up there. Um, I get it . . ." *Shit! How the hell you gonna get up there, fool!*

"Just boost me a little, Tam. There, got the sucker."

Reluctantly, Lactameon let go of Toni's hips. She poured some oil into the pan, then shrugged. "Anyways I heard all them names before. Hobbes never call me no names."

Lactameon felt his face flush, like the blood had rushed up from his dick. "Oh. Uh-huh! Yeah, I guess Hobbes pay pretty long too, don't he? Shit, he pay me a whole fuckin half buck for babysittin Sabby's ass the other day!" Yanking open the fridge, Lactameon snatched another Colt, then went to the couch and flung himself down so hard the floorboards creaked. "Shit, I ain't hungry! Fix whatever the hell you want! Take some with you, Hobbes don't mind! I sposed to stay till you leave. No hurry." Twisting off the cap, Lactameon tilted the bottle and took a huge gulp, then slammed it down on the floor and fired a Kool.

Toni cracked eggs in the pan. "Eeeh, wrong. Huh?"

"Sho nuff!"

Toni sighed. "Guess I can't expect you to like me no more."

Lactameon blew smoke at the blank TV screen, took another swallow from the bottle, then shrugged. "Sorry. Shit, maybe it just that I ain't seen you for so long, an then here I come cruisin in, an there you an Sabby. Jeeze!" He turned, dropping an arm over the back of the couch. "What I guess I sayin is, the fuck happen? I mean . . . you a goddamn *nice* girl, Toni!"

Toni poured a little milk into the eggs and started scrambling them with a fork. "Funny, I used to think I a nice girl too . . . not just ghetto-girl nice, but maybe sorta TV nice. Like, My Little Pony, an rockin with Barney, an that kinda bullshit.

Maybe what I sayin is, I sorta felt I was worth somethin. Seem like the whole goddamn universe change since the pool close last year. White people went an show the whole world we ain't shit to them and they gonna keep it that way if they gots to bomb a whole city. Then I went an done somethin feel right an good, an now I ain't even a nice ghetto-girl no more. Kinda like a magic trick."

Lactameon blew smoke. "You can't blame what happen to you on that other bullshit."

"I know. An I try not to. But, seem like for the rest of my life I gonna remember the year they close the pool down."

Lactameon sighed. "Yeah. I done a lot of stuff since then surprise the hell out me too. But, there ain't no such thing as a magic trick. If the magic real, ain't no trick. White people's magic ain't nuthin but tricks, but we wanna believe in it so goddamn *bad!* Toni? I sorry for sayin them things. You *real* nice."

Toni smiled. "You see that in your crystal ball?"

"Gots no crystal ball. My mom use that dog skull for lookin."

"I wonder bout that. Why a dog skull?"

"Why not? Either you see, or you don't. Make no difference what you lookin through, long's you can see past the bullshit."

Toni nodded, stirring the eggs. "Tam? Would it piss you off if I was to say I like you?"

"Well, course not. But, shit, Toni, you had the desk right next to mine in fourth period. An, we had study-hall together. Yo. You an me? We used to talk about all sorta stuff . . . like we was friends, stead of all that stupid-ass boy-an-girl bullshit. An then you stopped comin to school. An then word go round you went an had a baby. But, what I sayin is, if we *was* real friends, how come you never told me?"

"Guess maybe I figure you wouldn't like me no more."

"Jeeze, Toni!" Lactameon crushed out his Kool, then heaved himself up and came around the couch. He spread his palms. "So? The fuck I sposed to do for provin we was friends? Ask you to a dance? What a motherfuckin escapade!"

Toni cocked her head. "Why?"

"Why, what?"

"Why a motherfuckin escapade?"

Lactameon threw his arms wide. "Fuckin *look* at me!"

Toni smiled. "I am. An I like what I seein."

Lactameon glanced down at himself. "Why? You gots a thing for fat boys or somethin?"

"No. Just you." Toni began to fluff the eggs. "Anyways, I don't like to dance. Can't, really. Now, ain't that a motherfuckin escapade. But, you never ask me what sorta stuff I like."

Lactameon sat down on the couch arm. "Well . . . maybe I figure, pretty girl like you, wanna do all that cool shit."

Toni made a face. "Lotta that cool shit nuthin but fool shit. Like tricks pretendin to make magic where there ain't none. Member them godawful jokes you used to tell me in study-hall? Well, you can't make no Disney cartoon out Johnny Fucker-faster."

Lactameon smiled a little. "Maybe a rap."

Toni smiled too. "Seem like that the one thing we good at . . . makin stuff out what white people don't want. Kinda make you wonder what we could do if we had us good shit to work with stead of their garbage. But, see, I like readin, an then talkin to somebody bout what I read. An, I like funny movies, an old ones, stead of all that gangbangin an gangstuh shit they makin for us nowadays. I like walkin in them clean little parks cross town, even if all them white people look pissed or the pigs wanna know what I doin there. I like the zoo, an museums, an I got me a pet rat name Splinter who I raise up myself from a ugly little baby with no hair. He sit right on my shoulder an take carrots an stuff in his little paws, an he never bit nobody."

"Um, so why a rat? How come not a hamster or somethin?"

"Rats are free."

"Oh yeah."

Toni's eyes drifted to the foggy windows. "One time I went to this real ocean beach. I ain't talkin one of them over cross in the city that all full of people. This one was way off by itself, where you could make believe it was your own little island." Toni's eyes returned to Lactameon's. "What I sayin is, ain't none of them things cost a whole lot of money, it just they ain't really no fun less you with somebody who like 'em too."

Toni checked the eggs, then faced Lactameon again. Her smile turned shy. "I used to watch you them summers, swimmin at the pool. You always look so way past cool in the water . . . so big an round an shiny-nice. You always walk like you was goin somewheres for a reason, an even them big kids would get out your way. Sometimes, when you come climbin up the ladder, your cutoffs would go slidin down round your ankles, an I loved you so much I coulda died. I try talkin to you once when we was little there, slinkin over all shy while you was sunnin yourself on the cement. I wanted so goddamn *bad* to touch an cuddle with you. Cept, you wasn't havin none of that silly-ass boy-an-girl bullshit back then. Matter of fact, you made me cry."

"Huh? Shit, I sorry, Toni! Um, what did I do?"

"You tell me the Easter Bunny got rabies."

"Oh, shit! What a stupid-ass thing to say!"

"Well, I stop believin in the Easter Bunny a way long time ago. Sides, our preacher used to say it was a ghastly symbol for a holy day anyhow."

"Yeah, I guess a rabbit nailed to a cross would be kinda gross, even a white one."

Toni made another face. "Tam! Now, that just like them awful jokes you used to tell me! Like, what easier to load, a truck full of feathers, or dead babies?"

"The babies. You can use a pitchfork."

They both giggled for a moment, but then Toni's face saddened. "Tam? I just want you to know, I didn't leave my baby in no dumpster."

"Well, *course* you didn't!" Lactameon watched as Toni scooped the eggs onto old microwave plates. "Um, so you did go an really have a baby, huh . . . I mean, the . . . regular way?"

Toni heaped golden mounds onto the plates, adding pepper and salt and taco sauce. "Yeah. It was a boy. A big, fat, healthy-ass boy. I wanted to keep him, Tam. Swear to God I did. But, shit, with my mom losin her job last year, an the law sayin I too young to get one, there just wasn't no way." Toni found another fork in a drawer, and rinsed it under the faucet. "But, I didn't wanna give him up to get raised by no white people. I seen black kids like that. Uptown. Some of 'em look at you like you was a nigger. Maybe some white people could raise a black kid. But not uptown. I give my baby to somebody love *all* his blackness for the right reasons."

"Winfield's parents raised a white kid."

Toni smiled. "No they didn't."

"Mmm. Yeah. Well, I guess I shouldn't be askin shit like

that anyways. But, you coulda come to me, Toni. I mean, I ain't saying I coulda helped much, but you still coulda come to me, and we coulda talked about stuff like we used to. An, Toni? I be proud to go with you anywheres."

Toni brought the plates to the couch. She ate like someone who was hungry. Lactameon could have taken his plateful in three bites, but ate slowly. "These the best goddamn eggs I ever had, Toni."

Toni grinned. "That bullshit, an you know it, boy."

"Okay. They make me wanna puke. Like Sabby."

Toni shook her head. "Funny with him. He want just the opposite what a lot of us want, even we never come out an say it. Almost seem sorta sick."

"Sabby wantin to be all black?"

"No. Some of us wantin to be white."

"Do you?"

Toni sighed. "I just wanna feel like I worth somethin. Like I used to feel."

Lactameon shrugged. "Whole fuckin world sick, case you ain't noticed. Black kids just the first to get puked on. Seem like the best trick white people ever done was makin us shamed of our color."

"Would you wanna be white, Tam?"

"Nobody respect fat white kids. Ever see one on TV just bein a kid an not gettin no stupid jokes made bout him? Ever read bout a fat kid bein a hero in a book? White people the cruelest cocksuckas on earth. Ain't nuthin bad we ever done rate a one out seven 'pared to them. It like all them stupid cannibal jokes. Shit, read any history book an most of the *real* stuff bout people eatin each other is white people. Course, they all just *know* we used to stew up missionaries in some big iron pot. Like, they just *know* we didn't build no pyramids, an that we stupid an violent an just plain naughty by nature. Course, since we ain't, they gots to write the books an work overtime to prove it. Funny, with all that starvin in Africa an all these wild little niggers runnin round hungry here, ain't none of us eatin each other. Surprised the white people ain't set that up yet."

Toni wrinkled her nose. "Pleeeze, Tam! I tryin to eat!"

Lactameon grinned. "Yeah. Talkin bout white people even fuck up my appetite."

Toni turned to gaze at the empty TV screen for a moment. "I told you bout that beach, like it bein some little island where you can pretend there ain't no white people around to remind you what you are. No niggers neither, tryin to do the same. It like some sorta adventure just gettin there . . . got to take a lotta different buses, an finally end up on a Sam-Trans goin way off by itself along the ocean. There this big ole lighthouse, just like in pitchers." Toni took her last forkful of eggs, then set the plate on the floor and moved closer to Lactameon. "He the only boy in this hood I ever knew who wasn't scared to take his ass out the city where knowin the ghetto games don't score you nuthin. He built us a real fire out real driftwood, right there in the sand, just like he been doin it all his life."

An image came to Lactameon's mind: an empty beach . . . something he'd never seen except in movies or on TV . . . sunlight sparkling on waves as they rushed up onto white sand. He pictured two dark bodies together by the fire, Toni and . . . But the boy's shape was unfocused, unfinished. Of course it wasn't his; not the huge sooty boy who'd searched the mirror three nights ago. Still, he knew the lovemaking would have been gentle. "Um . . . it was the first time, huh? For both you?"

Toni nodded, her eyes going distant. "It wasn't like we went there for that. It just . . . happen. You can't go plannin things like that. An, you can't never do 'em again."

"Yeah. If you ever try an do 'em again, they mean somethin else."

"Maybe that why we never figure nuthin else would happen."

Lactameon set his empty plate on top of Toni's. "Um, you still love him? Or, did he get kicked or somethin?"

"Maybe I do. An, no, he didn't. But, it kinda a love like watchin you at the pool . . . a little-kid sorta thing."

"Um, Toni? Don't take this wrong or nuthin, but you figure sometime you an me could go to that beach? I know it ain't the same thing."

Toni smiled. "Maybe it be a next kinda thing." Her smile turned shy. "Tam? Can I do somethin now?"

"Well, sure, I guess."

Moving close, Toni slipped the tank-top over Lactameon's head and draped it on the back of the sofa. "I still wanna touch an cuddle with you." Her hands slipped down from Lactameon's shoulders and over his chest, then she spread her arms wide and wrapped them around his body, pressing herself tight to him. Slowly, Lactameon's arms went around her. Even separated from him by thin cotton, she felt like he'd always imagined she would.

"Um, Toni? Is it what you expected?"

Toni nuzzled her face against Lactameon's chest, her hands still moving over his body. "Everythin, an more."

"Well, there a lot more now."

"Stop makin jokes."

Lactameon lowered his head, resting his cheek on Toni's soft hair. "I thought about you a lot."

"Tam? Will you take off your clothes for me? I wanna see all of you. Just like when you come climbin out that pool."

Lactameon smiled. "Lotta things change since then, an you just make one of 'em change real fast right now."

"Like I say, I wanna see all of you."

"Um . . . I kinda like to see all of you, too."

They stood up together. Toni reached to pull off her T-shirt, but Lactameon took her hands. "This another one of them things ain't never gonna happen again. It kinda like unwrappin a Christmas present when you only gots one."

Smiling into Lactameon's eyes, Toni lifted her arms as he slipped the T-shirt off her body. It *was* like that, he thought, unwrapping your one present after waiting so long. He stood there a moment, just looking. Toni was full-rounded curves of softest ebony; a female shape that defined the word. Gently, he touched one of her breasts, first stroking, then slipping his hand underneath to cup its soft weight. Her nipples were big buds of pure midnight . . . African centers, the center of the world. Had she held her baby there? It seemed right to imagine she had, just as it seemed right to lower his head and kiss one. Then, he ran his hands down her body, and his fingers found the button of her jeans, even as her fingers went to find his. The Levi's slid down round his ankles. He wished he was barefoot so he could have stepped out of them as easily as Toni did from hers. Feeling awkward, he sat down to take off his shoes. His fingers fumbled the laces while his eyes scanned Toni. There was a lot more of her too . . . a lot more than the shy, chubby girl in the faded pink swimsuit. His dick struggled, then stood out proud when he got to his feet.

They moved to each other. Her lips against his were like a soft-petaled flower. He parted those petals with his tongue to get at the sweetness inside. This too would never just happen again. They kissed long and slow, eyes closed, hands exploring.

"Tam?" Toni whispered. "Will you make love to me? Not fuck, but really make love?"

Lactameon moved back just a little, searching her eyes for a sign he might have missed. "Um . . . but I don't gots no money."

Toni's face took on that same look of amused tolerance it had in study-hall. "Not funny, Tam."

"Oh. Well, then . . ."

Toni smiled and bumped his nose with hers. "I got some."

Lactameon glanced toward the bed, almost seeing Sebastian in it. But, a bed was a bed. Toni kissed him lightly on the lips, then bent down and reached for her jeans.

"Um," said Lactameon. "I gots one. Beamer give it to me." He reached for his own jeans and pulled out his wallet. "It a 'spensive one," he added, before thinking how stupid that sounded.

But, Toni's smile only seemed brighter. "It cool you an him bein homeys." Taking Lactameon's hand, she led him to the bed. They sat down close together. Lactameon carefully opened the Trojan. He'd used rubbers before . . . practice sessions, anyway . . . but sitting wasn't how he could put one on.

Toni tugged at his shoulder. "Lay down, Tam. I do it. I want to."

Lactameon sank back on the bed. A shiver of pleasure ran though him as Toni's warm hands gently and expertly slipped on the sheath. But her touch was almost too much. Lactameon tensed, clenching his fists and holding his breath. Sooty Jimmy hadn't been serviced in way too long. Toni felt what was happening and took her hands away. She lay down alongside of Lactameon. Her hand stroked his chest. He shivered again.

"Please don't do nuthin for a minute, Toni. Okay?"

"Does he have a name?"

"Huh?"

"Some dudes gots names for 'em."

Lactameon closed his eyes for a moment. The pressure seemed to be easing a little. "No. Seem like little-kid shit. Ice T prob'ly gots a name for his."

"I glad Bobby B's on the stereo." Toni kissed Lactameon's cheek. "I like his color. Sorta sooty."

"Bobby B? Oh." Lactameon opened his eyes. "It chillin now. Enough. Um, Toni? Um . . . I never done this before."

Toni smiled again. "Lot of dudes wouldn't have the balls to say that, Tam. Like, it was uncool or somethin."

"Fuck cool. Seem like everybody in the hood waste half their lives tryin to be cool an bad. Neither one gots nuthin to do with bein black. Ain't much ice in Africa."

Toni's hand moved lightly over Lactameon's chest, her fingers touching a nipple. "I love these. I used to have dreams bout puttin the tip of my tongue in there."

"Um, don't do that now. Okay? Um, Toni? I so goddamn big. I mean . . . you know what I sayin. What if I hurt you?"

"That another one of my dreams, Tam. Sorta like that thing bout bein a center smothered in dark chocolate."

"A *sweet* center, what it say."

Carefully, Lactameon moved over the girl. He felt big and clumsy, but her hands went to guide him and he sank down and in. Nothing had ever felt so good. Again, the pressure mounted. Toni sighed. Her arms went around him, pulling him even tighter to her, but he was afraid to move in her soft glove of heat. And then he did move, slowly at first, somehow amazed that what he was doing brought pleasure to Toni as well. His own body wanted this *now*, but it seemed important to hold back for Toni. Then came the surging release, too soon, an instant of ecstasy that thirteen years had led to.

Toni kept her arms around him, smiling up into his eyes. "Just stay a little while like this, Tam."

The room was still cool, yet Lactameon discovered that both their bodies were slippery with sweat. He had read a lot of stories where the dude asked that question, after. But the answer was already in Toni's eyes. It made him feel proud . . . even Beamer could fuck . . . but it still made him proud.

Toni sighed, and invited a kiss. "I got more," she whispered.

"Yeah. So do I."

"You bein cool again, boy?"

"Mmm. Bobby Brown sayin cruel. Sometime seem like it mean the same thing. I never be cool to you, Toni."

They kissed again, and Toni smiled once more. "An, I show you why Twinkies too good to be junkfood."

"Well, I be shamed to say I built me a 'bomination like this!"
Corbitt dropped his hands to his hips and steadily met the other
boys' eyes. Hobbes seemed more curious than anything else,
Lactameon surprised, and Lizard looked definitely hostile. Beamer's face was blank, as if awaiting a cue, and Ethan looked like
he was trying to figure the angle.

Corbitt didn't much care. In the four days since leaving
Bridge-end he could have counted the hours of untroubled sleep
he'd had on the fingers of one hand. The stink and noise of the
city seemed like an endless assault to kill what was left of his
senses, and two kids had tried to steal his new jacket while he'd
been waiting with Ethan in some dirty little park. Lactameon
had finally shown up about mid-afternoon, smelling like cake
and Colt 45 and grinning like a fox in a chicken coop. He said
he'd seen the dude called Hobbes, and that Corbitt now had a
job.

Some job!

"Shit!" spat Lizard. "The fuck you know bout buildin
nuthin, sucka?" He was a short, chocolate-brown boy of twelve,
with a chest about as impressive as Ethan's and a potbellied
posture that made him look like he'd swallowed a basketball.
He seemed to have almost as much trouble keeping his jeans
on as Lactameon. But his hair was carefully razored, his big-
buck B.K.s about half a week old, and he wore two gold earrings
that looked expensive enough to buy Bridge-end twice. The huge

Dogtown skateboard he carried had every accessory but a cel-
lular phone. Corbitt thought of a child playing some city-cool
dress-up game.

"Black-ass sucka couldn't build his way out Lego Land!"
Lizard added.

The top of Lizard's head came up to Corbitt's chest. Corbitt,
hot, sweaty, and in what Mrs. Griffin called a low-cotton mood,
considered picking the kid up and giving him a good healthy
shake. But there was a little gun in back of Lizard's jeans, and
he probably didn't carry it for balance.

Hobbes, who reminded Corbitt of a lanky Buckwheat, ignored Lizard. His muddy eyes shifted from Corbitt to the mess
of plywood and two-by-fours that sectioned off a third of the
room. "So, what y'all tellin me is, you'd tear it all down an start
the fuck over?"

Corbitt shrugged. There was no doubt how badly he needed
the money, but he still hated the idea of working for a crack
dealer, even if it was just a carpentry job. At first, when Lactameon had told him, he hadn't wanted any part of it. But then
Ethan had proceeded to explain some facts about kids, money,
and survival in the city.

Hobbes chewed his lip. "Shit, man, gots me almost two
bills in this . . . 'bomination."

"Yo!" piped Lizard. "Don't go layin that shit on me, Hobbes!
It Beamer been fuckin everthing up!"

"Ain't not!" said Beamer. "Most what wrong come from
Sabby!"

"I gonna tell him you say that!"

"Both you chill out," said Hobbes. "Nobody's shit smellin
like sugar today!" He looked Corbitt up and down while firing
a Kool. "So, y'all gots the 411 what I needin here, sweetheart?"

Corbitt glanced around. The house was a small, brick-
walled, low-roofed room about thirty feet square. It smelled like
ancient engine-oil, and there were rusty rings on the rough
concrete floor showing where barrels had stood. The single big
door of riveted iron faced down a narrow alleyway. Overhead
were wormy beams and boards with tar drooling through the
cracks like mummified licorice whips. Cobwebs clustered everywhere, and spiders lurked in shadowy corners, twitching uneasily whenever a streamer of cigarette smoke ghosted past. Behind

the sloppy new wall was what looked like a trapdoor in the roof with a wooden ladder leading up to it. Corbitt supposed the opening had once been for a swamp-cooler; logical in a place that stored flammables, but now it made an escape hatch. Despite what Hobbes did, Corbitt's respect for the boy climbed a notch. Black kids *could* think; it was just too goddamn bad what the world gave them to think about.

The only other opening was a heavily barred transom above the door that let in little light and even less air. One big bulb glared from a rafter, and with the door shut, the place was like a boiler room. Corbitt was shirtless like the other boys, but had his jacket slung over one shoulder because it seemed like every time he'd set it down that day somebody had tried to steal it.

Hobbes wiped his forehead. "I gonna put me in a AC over the door, there. Soon's I find me somebody to do it. But we gots to keep the place closed up case the pigs come cruisin around. I found me a ole dude with a truck, gonna score me some couches an rugs. This gonna be the flyest house in Oaktown when it open." He jerked a thumb at a rusty refrigerator chugging against the back wall. "Beamer! Snag us all some brew while me an this dude do some figurin."

Beamer trotted to the fridge and returned with a sixer of Bud, passing a can to each of the boys. Hobbes popped his, took a few gulps, then faced Corbitt once more. "So, Corbitt, y'all sayin you can really get this goin on? Word, man, I gettin real sick of bein bullshitted. Course, Tam say you cool, an he ain't never been wrong yet."

Corbitt went over to the flimsy wall and thumped it with a fist. "Well, seem like to me, y'all be needin somethin strong. Shit, I could blow this 'bortion down with a fart." He sipped his beer and examined the wall, recalling how his dad had given estimates. "Mmm. Should oughta be least three-quarter ply. If I had me all the right stuff, I could build what y'all want in bout two days."

Hobbes arched an eyebrow. "By yourself, man? Shit, took us all most three days to get that much up, an we ain't even gots the door on yet."

Corbitt shrugged. "Ain't nuthin to it. Y'all just gots to be keepin a plan in your mind. Ain't gots no plan, y'all end up with nuthin but a nigger-rig like this."

Lizard slammed half his Bud, and burped. "Listen to this shit! I never seen nobody *his* color build nuthin!"

But Hobbes was smiling. "Yeah, Corbitt, you right, man. Don't gots a plan, y'all end up in a sorry-ass motherfucka for sure." He turned to Lizard. "Yo! I never even *seen* nobody his color, but ain't none of you chilly brown boys done much for me lately, or my yellow one, neither." He fingered his jaw and eyed Corbitt again. "So, y'all sayin I gots to buy a whole bunch of new shit now?"

"Well, I take me some measures. Might be I could save you some money by doublin these here half-inch sheets. Y'all gots a tape?"

"Lizard! Get him a tape."

"Um . . . what kinda tape?"

"A measurin tape, raisin-brain!"

"Oh. Well, we don't gots one." Lizard went behind the wall and came back with one of those cheap wooden yardsticks hardware stores gave away. "This gots inches on it. See?"

"That do," said Corbitt. "I can make up a list of what I be needin in bout half a hour."

Hobbes nodded. "Well, print it, don't write it. An use big letters, case I gots to send Super-Lizard to the store for ya. So, how much this costin me, man?"

Corbitt considered. He knew what his dad would have gotten around New Crossing for a simple job like this . . . about thirty dollars. Ethan gulped his beer and strutted over beside Corbitt. "Yo, Hobbes! I gonna be helpin him, an it gots to be worth two bucks! Corbitt from Afrosippi, man. Dey down with all sorta shit back dere!"

Corbitt's mouth almost dropped open. *Two dollars!* Was that supposed to be a joke?

But Hobbes only shrugged. "Mmm. Okay. Long's it done right. Cool by you, Corbitt?"

Ethan nodded. "Done deal, Hobbes!"

"Yo, Hobbes!" said Lizard. "You never pay me an Beamer them kinda bucks, man!"

Hobbes finished his Bud and tossed the can into a corner. "Shit, you all the time bitchin you don't do this kinda work, man. So, get your ass busy doin what you sposed to do! Beamer! You too, man. Both you bail on over my place an score some more stock. Corbitt, you make me that list of what you need. I go find that dude with the truck. This place clean, but y'all keep that door shut an locked. Nobody but me or this posse come in. You needin to chill your ass awhile, book up on the roof. There plenty of brew in the box, an I send Beamer or maybe my little runner back later with some pizza or somethin." Hobbes turned to Lactameon. "Yo. You seen Sabby today, man?"

"Um, yeah. He leave your place a little fore ten. Say he comin here."

Hobbes frowned. "Well, he didn't. So, what he look like when y'all seen him, man? He drinkin or somethin?"

"Um, no."

Hobbes cocked his head. "Somethin I should know, Tam?"

"Um, no. He was just kinda pissed. I, um, come in when he in bed."

Hobbes smiled. "Not alone?"

"Uh-uh."

"Well, that ain't no motherfuckin excuse. Swear to God that dude's shit get shakier ever goddamn day! Um, look, Tam, can you kinda cruise around an find his ass for me? Sometimes he go home to his mom when he pissed-off over somethin. Anyways, give that sucka the 411 I ain't havin no more of his shit. He wanna lay around drinkin an fuckin some ho, he can do it in somebody else's crib!" Hobbes pulled a roll of bills from his pocket and peeled off a twenty. "This cover your time, man." He thought a moment, his eyes resting on the small bit of yellow showing from Lactameon's back pocket. "You dudes still gots probs by me?"

"Ain't nuthin much change, Hobbes."

"Mmm. Well, gots a feelin ain't nuthin much *gonna* in this sorry-ass motherfucka, least till whitey figure out some new way to rattle the cage." Hobbes picked up his skateboard and checked the bearings. "Seem like Silver gettin to be one of my best customers, but then he know I only sell quality product . . . even it gettin harder to come by. Like I say before, man, this hood do a lot worse. Your boy, Corbitt, finish that wall, there always a place behind it for a dude I can trust. I get this house open by the end of the week, might just be a real goin-on summer yet." Hobbes turned to Beamer and Lizard, who were standing by the door with their boards. "Well, what in hell you two waitin on?"

Beamer pulled open the heavy door, then left with Lizard, the rattle of their wheels echoing down the alley. Hobbes slipped on his jacket, checked the .44, then picked up his board again and walked over to Corbitt.

"Tam say y'all on the street, man." Hobbes pointed to a dirty old mattress in a corner. "Crib there, you want. I gonna sleep in my own bed tonight for a change." He went back to the door. "Yo, Tam. Y'all seen that ole Variflex in the pawnshop window? Them things built like tanks, man. Why don't y'all just cruise your ass by an tell the man to put it on my account."

"Jeeze, Hobbes, I never figure that old dude trust nobody."

Hobbes grinned. "Well, he trust me, sweetheart." Decking his board, Hobbes rolled away.

Corbitt watched Lactameon fold the twenty into his pocket. "Um . . . yo, Tam, Hobbes be figurin to pay me the rest in . . . product, or somethin?"

"Huh? Rest of what?"

Corbitt spread his palms. "Two goddamn dollars for all this here work?"

Ethan stared up at Corbitt, then started to giggle. "Two *bucks*, Corbitt! Two *hunners*, dumbo!"

Lactameon laughed. "Yo, man, you goddamn lucky you gots Ethan for a manager. You get your ass eat up, otherwise." He glanced down the alley, seeing heat-ghosts wavering from the dumpster lids. Twenty dollars and a ride. For sure there was nothing stylin about that antique Variflex; it would be heavy and slow, but it just might last out the summer, and with his own ride maybe he could spend a little more time with the dudes. He hoped it wouldn't take long to locate Sebastian. Toni might be at the Center, reading to kids. Hell, he might even give that a run-through himself. He turned toward Corbitt again. "Well, guess I gots to earn my own green. Catch you dudes later."

Ethan came over to close the door behind Lactameon, putting his back to the heavy plates and shoving it shut with a clank, then dropping the bar into place. "Yo, Corbitt! Let's get da fuck busy, man! Um . . . you gonna share some dem bucks with me, huh?"

Corbitt smiled, laying his jacket on top of the fridge and then sitting down to take off his shoes. "Course, little brother."

"I only need a half buck, but it kinda 'portant."

"Well, you gots it, sho nuff." Corbitt picked a pencil off the floor and glanced around. "Need us some paper. Can y'all write letters an numbers?"

"Yeah. An some words too, if I know da right sounds." Ethan found an empty twelve-pack carton and ripped it apart. "Here da paper, man." He took the pencil from Corbitt and sharpened it on the floor. "Ta da! Ready up!"

For the next half hour Corbitt took measurements with the yardstick. Ethan did his own job with deadly seriousness, though he seemed to be drawing the letters instead of printing them, lying on his stomach with his feet in the air and a determined look on his face. Corbitt glanced once at Ethan's list, wincing when he saw "skroos" and "toobyfoors," and supposed he'd have to translate it into English later. Corbitt found a claw hammer, and Ethan helped as he began to tear down the rickety partition. Corbitt was careful to save all the wood that he could. The closed-up room grew miserably hot, and the only thing in the fridge to drink was beer. Corbitt figured that might have been one reason why the wall was so sloppy. Still, they soon had the partition apart and most of the reusable wood separated and stacked.

Corbitt wiped sweat from his face. "Spect we earn usselfs a break, little brother."

"Shit yeah!" Ethan panted. His dreadlocks were dripping and his small body glistened like burnished brass. "Kinda feel good, huh? I mean, doin somethin."

Corbitt looked over what they'd done so far. Despite knowing what the work was for, he still felt a sense of accomplishment. "I hear that. It always feel good when you done somethin real by your ownself. Grab us another beer an we go up on the roof for a smoke. Take five when y'all can, my dad always say, cause there fifty more comin."

Ethan went to the fridge. "Your dad must be pretty cool, Corbitt. So, why y'all runned away?"

Corbitt's smile faded. "My dad in prison, man. For no reason other than bein the wrong color in the wrong time an place."

"Um, so he a African too?"

"Might's well be one, for all the good the law in this country done him."

Climbing the ladder, Corbitt opened the bolt and pushed up the wooden trapdoor. The flat roof was covered with crackly black tarpaper that sent heat waves shimmering skyward, but it still seemed a lot cooler than the closed room below. Three-story buildings surrounded the house, except for the front, which faced down the alley. A four-foot brick parapet ran across there, making the place seem like a castle or fort. A cast-iron vent pipe came up through the house's roof and was bracketed to the wall of the backside building. It would be an easy climb for a kid to escape across the other rooftops, and Corbitt supposed Hobbes had already checked out that option. The late sun slanted from the west, leaving a strip of shade behind the parapet. Corbitt and Ethan sat there awhile, sipping beer and smoking before returning below to finish their work.

Back in the windowless room, with no light but the overhead bulb, it was hard to keep track of time. To Corbitt, it felt like around sunset when they finished. Ethan snagged another beer and flopped down on the old mattress. "Yo! Wonder when Hobbes gonna send us dat motherfuckin pizza, man? I hungry enough for cream-o-rat soup!"

Corbitt sat beside the smaller boy and started rolling cigarettes. "Um, that be only a joke Chad make . . . ain't it?"

"Shit yeah. But I knew dis dude what ate rats." Ethan giggled. "He say, why da fuck not, rats eat *your* ass if they can!"

"Mmm. Spose y'all got hungry enough you could eat just bout anythin. Course, there a sayin go, you be what you eat. Anyways, it long past my suppertime back home."

Ethan fired the cigarette Corbitt handed him. "You mean y'all had you a goddamn regular eatin time, man? Ever fuckin day?"

"Sho. Cept when mom be waitin supper till my dad get home from a job."

Ethan's face turned wistful. "Just like real kids."

"Huh? What y'all sayin, little brother? Hell, you be real enough to rattle."

"Shit, Corbitt, I mean real kids on TV. Like dem fuckin *Cosbys* an *True Colors*. Dey all gots moms an dads an straight-up suppertimes . . . cept for dat Bundy bitch!"

"Oh." Corbitt glanced to the barred transom where the gray glow of twilight shone in. "Course, it be two hours later back home. I keep on forgettin that."

"Yo. What you mean later, man?"

"Time difference. Like, it be different times all over the world."

"Huh? So, y'all sayin, right now it be two more hours in Afrosippi?"

"Yeah. Cause, well, see the world go round, but the sun sorta stay in one place."

"No shit, Corbitt?"

"Sho nuff. An when this here side of the world turn away from the sun, it be nighttime. But the sun still shinin on the other side, so there it be day. So, if everwhere was to be all the same time, then some places it be noon in the middle of the night. See what I sayin?"

Ethan stuck a finger in his eye-socket. "Shit yeah. It be pretty motherfuckin stupid to try an have school in da middle of da goddamn night. Den *nobody* go! Um . . . so, on da other side of da world, like in Africa-land, it mornin right now?"

"Well, I spose."

Ethan cocked his head. "Yo! But dat mean it already tomorrow dere!"

"Well . . . yeah."

Ethan considered that a long time. "Yo! Do African dudes gots newspapers, man?"

"Shit yeah."

"Well, y'all figure dey put some 'merican shit in dem African papers? Like Chad sayin one time bout African kids gettin shot by white pigs?"

"Well, spose that logical."

Ethan sat up straight. "Yo, Corbitt! We gonna be motherfuckin rich, man! Listen up! We call us up some African dude you know an ask him who won da lottery! See, we get him to tell us dem winnin numbers from today . . . cause it already *tomorrow* dere! Den we buy us a ticket an play dem tomorrow numbers today!"

Corbitt smiled and put a hand on Ethan's shoulder. "Well, gots to say that be the most 'riginal idea I ever heard, man.

But Mississippi ain't in Africa, an time don't a'zactly work that way."

Ethan scowled. "Aw, shit! Maaaan, I shoulda knowed! Nuthin in da whole motherfuckin world ever work like you figure it should!" He gulped the last of his beer and flung the can across the room, then flipped his cigarette away and flopped down on his back. "Wake me up when da pizza come . . . *if* da cocksuckin thing ever come!"

Corbitt sighed and picked up the pencil to translate Ethan's list into English. The brick walls still radiated heat like a pizza oven, but it was cooler here on the floor, even if the old mattress stank of kid-sweated cotton. Scattered around were magazines: *The Source*, *Transworld Skateboarding*, some *Ninja Turtles* comics, and what looked like a how-to book titled, *Adding That New Room to Your House*.

So, Hobbes the crack dealer could read. In a way that was logical: from what Corbitt had seen of the dude he did seem smarter than the others around him. Except Lactameon. But then Hobbes was probably considered way cool, while Lactameon was just a big fat kid who couldn't do much. Maybe actions spoke louder than words in this place?

Corbitt finished the list, then picked up the skate magazine. Maybe he'd buy himself a board after Hobbes paid him. He leafed through the pages, scanning the ads and noting the prices. Even a basic board would take most of his money, and he had to send something back to Mrs. Griffin soon. But how? Somebody would see the Oakland postmark. Corbitt sighed again and skimmed through the magazine once more. Toby had sent away for free catalogs and stickers, and still got new ones in the mail now and then . . .

Corbitt suddenly sat up straight. "Well, fuck you, Mr. Rudd," he muttered. "I do believe I gots me a real 'riginal idea after all!"

Somebody thumped on the iron door. A kid-voice called. "Yo! Open up!"

Corbitt tensed. The voice wasn't Lactameon's or any of the crack-house dudes'. Hobbes had said not to let anyone else in. Lactameon had told Corbitt what had happened at Hobbes's other place, and seeing Gilligan killed left little doubt in his mind that kids with guns didn't play. His eyes flicked to the trapdoor in the roof. He shook Ethan's shoulder.

The little boy came instantly awake. "S'up, Corbitt?"

"Somebody outside, wantin in."

"Goddammit!" bawled the voice. "Open this cocksuckin door! I gots your stupid-ass pizza an it's gettin cold, asshole!"

Corbitt glanced at Ethan. "Um, spose it one of them Domino's dudes?"

Ethan spat on the floor. "My ass! It dat weird sucka, Sabby! Hobbeses's bodyguard. Shit! Better let da cocksucka in fore he go an piss all over our pizza."

Corbitt got up and crossed to the door. He had hardly lifted the bar before the door was shoved open and a gold-skinned boy in black Levi's, black Cons, and expensive black leather jacket pushed past. The kid carried a Steadham skateboard and a big pizza box under one arm while keeping the other hand inside his jacket, where Corbitt supposed there was a gun. For a moment the boy stood, scanning the room, then half turned to Corbitt. "Well, close the fuckin . . ."

Corbitt shoved the door shut with a clank, not hearing how the golden boy's voice trailed off or seeing his look of amazement. Corbitt dropped the bar into place, then turned to find the boy staring at him. For an instant Corbitt remembered how Bates had looked at him on the riverbank, as if he was still something that money could buy. But then the boy's steel-colored eyes softened in a strangely wistful way. He suddenly blushed and swallowed. "Um . . . sorry, brother. I didn't know . . . I mean, it, um, ain't been a very good day, what I'm sayin."

Back on the mattress, Ethan let out a big burp. "Way past fly till you come, sucka!"

The golden boy spun to glare at Ethan, his face twisting in fury, but then seemed to remember that Corbitt was watching. "Aw . . . shut up, Ethan. Okay?"

Ethan leveled his tawny gaze at him. "Shut up bout *what*, Sabby? Corbitt my brother. Brothers can tell each other any fuckin ole thing."

Sebastian's eyes shifted from the half-naked little boy on the mattress to Corbitt, barefoot and shirtless. Corbitt caught a glint of speculation in the steel-gray, then something else he couldn't name before the eyes lifted to meet his own once more. There was a huskiness in the boy's voice.

"I'm Akeem, man." Sebastian put out his hand, almost shyly.

Corbitt smiled and shook the way Bilal had showed him. He noticed the boy looking down at their hands together, gold grasping ebony. There was a tenseness in the touch. "Hi, Akeem. I Corbitt."

"Yeah. Um, Hobbes told me when he sent me to score you the pizza." Sebastian seemed to realize he was still holding Corbitt's hand. He let go and coughed to clear his throat. "Um, Hobbes told me to sorta scope what you been doin." He turned to the pile of plywood and two-by-fours. "Hey! Didn't take you no time to tear down everythin we built!"

Ethan had crept over, and now snatched the pizza box from Sebastian. "Dat cause you make nuthin worth shit, Sabby!"

The golden boy stiffened, his free hand clenching into a fist, but Ethan slipped past him and pressed against Corbitt. "Don't pay no 'tention to *him*, big brother. He crazy, what he is. C'mon, let's eat." Grabbing Corbitt's hand, Ethan led him back to the mattress, sitting down and tearing open the pizza box lid. It was a large combination, the kind Lamar could have killed for, and its wonderful smell had Corbitt's mouth watering. Toby had once said a good pizza was better than sex . . . but then how would he know? Corbitt could have eaten it all by himself. Still, he looked back at Sebastian. "Y'all have some, man. There be plenty here for all us."

Again, Corbitt thought he caught a wistful glimmer in steely gray, but the golden boy exchanged hard glances with Ethan and shook his head. "Naw . . . thanks . . . brother. I already ate. You wanna beer to chase that?"

"Sho, man. Don't spose even sex be better'n pizza an beer."

Sebastian seemed to search Corbitt's eyes for a moment. "Word, brother." He went to the fridge and leaned his board against it, then pulled Corbitt's jacket from on top. "Fuck, whose piece of shit is this . . . Beamer's?"

"Dat Corbitt's, asshole!"

Sebastian flushed. "Um, sorry, brother. I, um, forgot you don't got no green."

Corbitt smiled. "That okay. It still a dream come true for me."

"Yo, Sabby! Snag me a beer too . . . *brother!*"

Sebastian shot Ethan another glare, but pulled three Buds from the fridge. His stiff back and jerky motions reminded Corbitt of some sort of toy with its spring wound too tight, and it wasn't hard to figure Ethan had done the winding. Sebastian brought the beers over. "Please don't call me that. My name's Akeem."

"Call you what . . . Sabby, or brother?"

Sebastian gritted his teeth. "Be cool, Ethan. Please?" He handed one can to Corbitt, tensing again when their fingers brushed, then set another can down on the floor in front of the little boy.

"Yo, pop dat for me . . . Akeem. Brother. My little fingers all sticky."

Sebastian ripped the tab and handed the can to Ethan, then opened his own and gulped about half. His eyes kept shifting to Corbitt, watching him eat. He sat down on the dirty floor in front of the slender boy. "Um . . . word say you from Africa, man."

Corbitt sighed around a mouthful of pizza. "Mississippi."

"Oh. But, you come from Africa before, huh?"

Corbitt felt a little uneasy. "Before, what?"

Ethan snickered, winding melted cheese around his finger and slipping it into his mouth in a way that looked somehow obscene. "Everybody from Africa, one time . . . Akeem. *Maybe* even you."

Sebastian's fingers clenched until the beer can crinkled. Corbitt sensed the hate between the two boys, but found it hard to imagine that this beautiful golden kid would ever have used Ethan when he no doubt could get any girl he wanted with those looks and muscles. Maybe it was just little-kid jealousy? All Corbitt wanted to do was eat in peace.

"Hush yourself, Ethan," murmured Corbitt. "Akeem bring us this here pizza, an he be just doin his job for Hobbes. Y'all stop givin him shit, now."

"Maaaan!" Ethan looked sulky but snagged another pizza slice.

Sebastian smiled. "Yeah, Ethan. Just be chilly, little bro. Shit, maybe we can even be homeys."

"My ass!"

Sebastian shifted onto the mattress beside Corbitt. "Little dude need him a sorta big brother like you, man. I mean, a real black brother."

Corbitt sipped beer and smiled. "Well, I be real black, fo sho."

"No, man. I mean, don't take this wrong, but I'm sayin *you're* real . . . like African-real!" Sebastian lay a hand on Corbitt's arm. "Like, you gots all seven on what is an what ain't about bein black."

Corbitt felt uncomfortable with Akeem touching him, yet he didn't want to hurt the boy's feelings by pulling away. It was funny: Toby and Lamar touched him all the time, but that seemed a natural thing; just like sleeping with Ethan cuddled close. Corbitt tried logic . . . maybe it was like he'd wondered about yesterday in the bus station; how kids who acted bad and cool all the time could ever show real affection for each other. Then too, Corbitt supposed he should be grateful that this beautiful golden boy even wanted to be friends. A new thought came, and he turned to Akeem. "Seem like you be the future, man. I just the past."

Sebastian's fingers tightened on Corbitt's arm. "I don't understand, brother."

"Well," Corbitt said, carefully. "Ain't like there no secret to bein black. I mean, y'all can understand the blues, can't you?"

"Um . . . well, sure. That's when you get to feelin like the whole goddamn world hates your ass, an there ain't nuthin you can ever do to change it."

Corbitt nodded. "See? Y'all do know."

Sebastian swallowed once, then reluctantly let go of Corbitt's arm. "But, you're . . . *pure*, man. It's like you gotta know all the old stuff. It's *in* you. Like melanin."

Corbitt shrugged. "That like knowin how to fix a steam engine, or double-clutch a spur-gear transmission. Just ain't no call for that sorta stuff no more." He smiled again. "Seem like to me bout time we put us a coon on the moon."

Sebastian touched Corbitt's shoulder. "We could do that,

brother. We could do us fuckin anything if we just remembered our old magic. Um . . . you done magic. I can tell."

Corbitt smiled a little. "Great white hunter lost in the jungle. Gets captured by us savages. They take him to the great chief. Whiteman figure he get his ass out the mess easy. Pulls out his lighter an fires it. Says, look, chief, *magic*! Ole chief's eyes get big. He say, surely is magic, whiteman, I *never* seen one of them Bics light on the first try."

"Huh?" Sebastian pulled back his hand and stood up. "You shouldn't make jokes about black stuff, man." He looked uncertain. Sweat glistened on his forehead. He wiped it away before shedding his jacket. "I mean, I'm sorry if I say somethin piss you off, brother."

The black satin T-shirt clung to Sebastian's muscled body like a second skin. Corbitt thought the golden boy looked like God's new idea for a man-child for all ages. The big Uzi slung over one shoulder should have completed a warrior's appearance. But something seemed to be missing, and without it he was only a kid with a gun.

"Um?" asked Sebastian. "Wanna get wasted tonight, brother?"

"Shit yeah!" piped Ethan.

Corbitt drank the last of his beer. "Well, we gots us a lotta work ahead of us, little brother."

"Aw," said Sebastian. "That's tomorrow, man. Let's party now."

Ethan gave the golden boy a careful look, but then killed his Bud and threw the can away. "Shit yeah! C'mon, Corbitt."

Sebastian went back to the fridge. "Y'know, I could like you, little bro. I mean, really."

"Um, mean without all dat . . . other shit?"

"Word, homey. Fact is, I was talkin to Hobbes about you."

"No shit? Yo, Hobbes say today he think I cool."

Sebastian nodded. "That's just what I told him, too. I was seein this dude today from my old hood, bout some other stuff Hobbes should be sellin. It a natural kinda thing for little brothers."

Ethan frowned. "Don't smoke me no rock, Sa . . . Akeem."

Sebastian returned and handed out fresh Buds. "Hey, me an Hobbes know that, man. It's why we both figure you way past cool. Besides, you know most of the little suckas in the hood." Sebastian knelt in front of Ethan. "It'd be like a real job for you, man. An you wouldn't never have to do that other shit no more."

Ethan popped his can and took a gulp. "So, what dis new shit you talkin?"

Sebastian reached for his jacket and pulled a baggie from a pocket. It had some dirty-white powder in the bottom. He handed the bag to Ethan, who studied it carefully.

"Dis look like dust, man. Some ole dude gimme dat shit one time an it fuck me up for a week! Homey don't play dat no more!"

Sebastian smiled. "Naw. This shit way past *clean*, little bro. It's so fresh we ain't even figured a name for it yet . . . maybe ice-powder or somethin cool like that. Anyways, it's totally easy to do. Smokin's the best way, but you can even eat it if you can't score no fire."

Corbitt found himself strangely fascinated by the talk. Was this kid-stuff what the great "war on drugs" was all about? "Um, seem like to me I hear that dust stuff be some sorta animal tranquilizer?"

Sebastian waved a careless hand. "Yeah. Like that shit they shoot lions an cheetahs with on *Wild Kingdom* so's they can catch 'em. But, like Ethan say, most kids ain't havin none of that no more."

"But then, why they doin all this crack?"

Ethan frowned. "Cause it da kinda shit always make you *want* more, till you don't want nuthin else. It, um, always gone too fast . . . like some sorta joke."

Sebastian shrugged. "Some dudes can chill with it, man."

"Yeah? Silver can't, an he used to be ass-kickin cool!"

Sebastian shrugged again and took back the baggie. "Yo, what can I say, man? That's just what it is sometimes. Sides, them cocksuckin Collectors ain't nuthin but a pain in the ass for me an Hobbes!"

Ethan glanced at Corbitt. "Well, I gots to do me some thinkin on dat. Okay, Akeem?"

Sebastian frowned and lay the baggie on top of his jacket. "Yeah, well, don't snooze too long, dude. Ain't no shortage of little . . . brothers on them streets wantin a chance at some real

juice. You never goin nowhere sellin cookies." Sebastian snickered and looked at Corbitt. "Y'know, they even tax them little
suckas!"

Corbitt finished the last pizza slice and licked his fingers.
"Mmm. Spose that logical. Them cops prob'ly be needin more
film for they camera."

Ethan giggled. "Shit yeah!"

Corbitt popped his beer, then set it down beside Sebastian's
jacket and stood up. "Best take me a piss if I gonna do me some
serious drinkin with y'all."

"Yeah," said Ethan. "Best take me one, too."

Sebastian settled on the mattress as Ethan followed Corbitt
to the door. "Yo! Turn off the light so's it don't show down the
alley." He pulled a pack of Kools and a Bic lighter from his jacket
as Corbitt lifted the bar and Ethan reached for the switch.

Outside it was night, except for the city glow. A streetlight
shone from the alley entrance. The smells of garbage and rot
seemed like fresh country air compared to the atmosphere inside
the little room. Corbitt lifted his head and scented that *déjà vu*
sea-breeze once more. The boys crossed the alley and faced the
brick wall near a dumpster. Ethan mingled his stream with
Corbitt's, and laughed. "Yo! Maybe I can't come yet, but I can
sho nuff piss further'n you!"

Corbitt smiled. "Gots that right, little brother." Then his
smile faded. "Um, y'all ain't gonna go sellin none of that shit for
Akeem, is you?"

Ethan glanced over his shoulder where the flickering glow
of Sebastian's lighter showed in the doorway. "Um, I don't know,
man. I mean, if I gonna get dat half buck from you, den it cover
six out seven of everthin I ever gonna need." He looked up at
Corbitt again. "Um . . . we is gonna always stay brothers, huh,
Corbitt?"

"Course. Brothers be forever, man. Brothers be like all
seven."

"Well, den you gots to start watchin your ass more better,
Corbitt. Word! I mean, y'all been lucky so far, but dere just so
much motherfuckin shit goin on all da time round here! You
don't start learnin da moves, y'all gonna get you a major dirt-
nap!" Ethan buttoned his jeans and waited for Corbitt to finish.

"Yo. Just like dat Sabby-sucka in dere! Don't y'all go trustin his ass no further'n you can piss, man!"

"Well, seem like to me he be really wantin friends."

"My ass, Corbitt! Oh, he wantin somethin fo sho, but it ain't friends, best believe!"

Corbitt buttoned his jeans. "Can't the leopard change his spots, little brother?"

"Huh? Well, I don't know much bout dem Leopards, Corbitt. But Sabby fo sho missin some spots off his dice!" Ethan dug in his pocket. "Here. Maybe y'all oughta take dis back for 'tection."

Corbitt squinted in the dimness at what Ethan held out. "Oh, hell, why don't y'all just throw that goddamn thing away?"

"Cause! It . . . well, it just fuckin feel good, man! Like magic. But I gots dis feelin you gonna be needin all da Afrosippi magic you can get round here!"

Corbitt started back to the rock house. "Oh, stop bein a goddamn child, man."

Ethan jammed the feather back in his pocket. "Shit! I *wish* I could be a goddamn child for a motherfuckin change!"

Corbitt closed the heavy door and dropped the bar. Ethan snapped on the light switch. Sebastian was sitting on the mattress, just slipping the baggie back into his jacket. He moved close to Corbitt as the other boys sat down, handing them their beers and watching as they drank. Then he sipped from his own and offered Kools. "Um, Corbitt, I can understand if you don't wanna talk about it, but how come you run away? Was it a black thing?"

Corbitt took another swallow, then frowned down at the can.

"Oh. Sorry I ask, brother. That wasn't cool, huh?"

Corbitt shook his head. "It ain't that. I was just thinkin how beer in bottles always taste better." He took another gulp, and shrugged. "Gettin so's what happen back home seem like nuthin much more'n some sorta bad dream."

Sebastian put his hand on Corbitt's arm. "Tell me some of the good stuff, brother. What's it like bein black there?"

Corbitt wasn't sure what he said after that because he seemed to drift into a real dream. *Real dream?* That wasn't a logical idea . . . how could a dream be real? His mind seemed to wander in circles like that, but he must have been making some sort of sense because Sebastian kept smiling and nodding, his touch warm on Corbitt's arm. Corbitt supposed he was drunk, but couldn't recall ever getting this drunk on just beer, except when he'd been a little child. Then he began to feel like a child. It was a safe sort of feeling . . . nothing to be afraid of because someone would always take care of him, just the way someone was now . . . easing him down onto softness, stroking his forehead, and whispering how everything would be all right. It must have been his mother: the murmured words were so gentle. Maybe he had a fever again, like that time years ago when Toby and Lamar had both come to sit on the floor by his mattress to watch over him. He'd woken to find Lamar holding his hand. He felt lips press to his . . . nobody had ever kissed him like that . . . except Sherry. He must be drunk on the riverbank. The sun glared in his eyes from straight overhead and the whole world seemed smothered in cottonwool haze. He felt a flicker of fear . . . Bates would come and see this childishness . . . foolish young crows playing dress-up, too stupid to realize that a shotgun waited and their graves had already been dug. But soothing words calmed him while hands moved lovingly over his body, and it felt so good to give himself up and be cared for. Yet, he wasn't sure that Sherry should be touching him that way. Why would she lick his chest or trace her tongue over his stomach, and down? Heat flowed through his loins and he felt himself harden until he seemed to be the one solid black thing in this marshmallow universe. Where had Sherry learned to do magic like that? It didn't seem right, yet next-thing sensations mounted in Corbitt, spreading outward from his center like ripples on the river. He felt his own power even though someone else was controlling it, trying to steal it from him. He almost tried to fight, but then his own body betrayed him.

Corbitt woke in confusion, his mind seeming to spin in slow circles like a body in Bates's pool. Had it all been a dream, compressed into that one final second before Bates pulled the trigger? But bodies floated face-down, and the sun overhead was hurting his eyes. He squinted, and found only a light bulb where the sun should have been. He seemed to have lost all sense of time. Was it morning or midnight or noon? Grimy brick walls swam into focus, surrounding him. What was this place? What fool would leave a light bulb burning in a tomb? *Think, niggaboy! You CAN think, no matter what Bates and Rudd want you to believe!* Corbitt's mouth tasted like tin. His tongue felt swollen, and dry as a lizard's. Memories flicked through his mind like bats skimming the river, always just on the edge of being seen. Some of them didn't seem to be his . . . strange faces and places all faded and dim like old-time photographs. His mind shied from those. But there was something important he had to do . . . something unfinished. He tried to sit up, but the room rocked and tilted and he fell back on the mattress. A distant scream came to his ears . . . a siren. The city! Then, close by, he heard what sounded like strangled breathing. He moved a hand, touched something warm beside him. A sick, sour smell burned his nostrils. This time he managed to sit up, even though the walls reared and bucked and the floor seemed to drop out underneath.

Ethan was sprawled face-down in a puddle of puke. His small rib cage shuddered with his efforts to breathe. Corbitt tried to reach for him, but his muscles wouldn't obey. Long seconds dragged by and Corbitt could only watch the little boy smother. It was happening again! . . . that *déjà vu* feeling of being frozen in time when all he could do was watch the world moving on without him while he was powerless to change a single thing in it. Then, finally, in clumsy slow-motion, Corbitt took hold of Ethan and lifted him up. The little boy's head lolled back into Corbitt's lap, his brassy skin paled to sickly yellow and his face a slime-covered mask. Corbitt's hand shook as he brushed back the sodden dreadlocks. There was a bluish tint to Ethan's lips. The heart in that thin chest couldn't have been an inch below Corbitt's palm, but he barely felt it beating. Desperately, Corbitt fought back the fog in his mind. There had been a class at school, but not much more than an excuse for children to escape real work. He and Toby had paired off for this, snickering and giggling like fools the whole time. Toby's breath had been scented with Juicy Fruit gum and Kool smoke. Now, Corbitt's stomach twisted in sickness, but he laid Ethan's head on his leg then bent down and sucked out what filled the little boy's mouth.

Ethan choked. A small hand grasped at nothing. Corbitt

spat on the floor, then leaned down again and forced air into Ethan's lungs. Ethan's chest expanded. It was a wonder to feel the heartbeat grow stronger. Ethan retched, but Corbitt spat that out too. Minutes passed. Ethan coughed up his sickness and Corbitt took it into his own mouth to get rid of it until finally the boy was breathing again. Ethan's eyelids fluttered, sending a new shiver through Corbitt because he'd forgotten. Tears came out of the empty place. Corbitt gathered the boy against him and held him while he cried. It seemed almost a surprise to see Ethan cry.

For a time they stayed there, Ethan's face pressed to Corbitt's chest while Corbitt stroked the boy's back. Gradually Ethan's sobbing subsided to that of a little child who only wants to be comforted as long as possible. Sick as he felt himself, Corbitt let the boy go on; crying was another right stolen from him. At last Ethan let go of Corbitt and looked around. Corbitt followed his gaze, seeing the iron door still barred but the silvery glow of pre-dawn sifting down through the open roof cover. Then Ethan wiped savagely at his cheeks, his child-face hardening.

"Dat cocksuckin Sabby! I gonna kill dat motherfucka!"

Corbitt said nothing. Ethan's words might have come in a squally kid-voice, but there was nothing childlike in their meaning. Not in this place. Ethan spat something slimy on the floor, then stared up at Corbitt in new wonder.

"Oh, *shit*, man! Dat GROSS what you done!"

Corbitt wiped his mouth and made a smile he didn't feel. "Spose it ain't no more gross'n them sewer-spittin turtles."

Ethan wiped his face again, then hiccupped a giggle. "Shit, man. Check dis out. Is we a motherfuckin mess, or what!"

Corbitt looked down at himself. "Mmm. Y'all gots that right for a fact." He frowned then because he couldn't remember taking off his jeans, yet they lay in a heap nearby. Had Akeem stripped him naked? Why? He tried to remember, but only blurred images formed in his mind. "Um . . . you member what happen, little brother?"

Ethan was wiping out his eye-socket with a finger. "Sabby put dat shit of his in da beer, man! Some ole white faggot done me dat way. You can't member much what happen. He keep me fucked a week like dat. Den, ta-da, I wake up in dis park way cross town in nuthin but my jeans! It wintertime an rainin, an I don't know where da fuck I am. But you figure dem white suckas help me? Maaaan!" He glanced down, checking that his own jeans were still buttoned, then frowned up at Corbitt. "I . . . member Sabby keep askin you give him somethin. Better check your pockets."

Corbitt grabbed his jeans and searched through them. His knife and the few remaining dollars were still there, along with the tinfoil-wrapped silver certificate. "Don't look like he stole nuthin from me. Sides, what I got he want?"

Ethan's considering gaze was way too aware for an eight-year-old's. "Um . . . maybe y'all member more later on. Sometime you do . . . even you don't wanna."

"Huh? What you sayin?"

Ethan looked uneasy. "Nuthin, Corbitt. Chill out."

But Corbitt grabbed the little boy's shoulders. "Goddammit! Y'all know somethin I don't, you tell me right now! Nobody gonna go stealin a piece of my life!"

Ethan didn't struggle in Corbitt's grip. "You ain't gonna hit me or nuthin?"

"Huh? Well, course not!" Corbitt took his hands away.

"Sabby suck you off, man."

"*What?*"

Ethan shrugged. "So? What da fuck? It sposed to feel good, ain't it? Shit, I say I do it for you da other night, man. Maybe he better at it?"

Before he knew it Corbitt's hand shot out, slapping Ethan hard across the face. Ethan flinched away, covering his eye, then burst into new tears.

"Goddamn you! LIAR! Why you hit me when say you not, motherfucka? Liar! Stupid black nigga! I TELL you dat sucka strange, man! I *tell* you watch your stupid Afrosippi ass!" Ethan jammed a hand into his pocket. "*Here*, motherfucka! I don't wanna be your brother no more!" He flung the little black feather at Corbitt, but it just floated down onto the mattress between them.

Corbitt stayed still a few minutes, feeling sick and helpless again. Ethan had turned his back, but made no move to get up. Corbitt pictured a little child, all packed and ready to run away, but standing at the door waiting for someone to stop him. Corbitt touched the boy gently and gathered him close once more.

"You be right, little brother-mine. I should oughta be listenin to you. Y'all gots to know more'n me cause you be five years closer the source."

Ethan sniffled and wiped his nose. "I don't unnerstand."

"Well, it be the same sorta thing y'all tellin me last night . . . bout how nuthin in the world seem to work the way you figure it should. Maybe you just stop seein that after you get older. Like, losin your depth perception."

Ethan looked up, smiling a little. "Shit yeah."

"I sorry I hit you, little brother."

Ethan shrugged. "S'cool. It sorta maybe like my mom try an tell me after what happen with my eye. She say my dad really try an hit somethin else, cept I got my stupid ass in da way." Ethan picked up the feather, then giggled. "Shit, man, maybe Sabby just tryin to do what you tellin me last night . . . be what he eat."

Corbitt shook his head. "Now, *that* be gross, best believe!" He brushed the sticky locks back from Ethan's face. "Y'all tell me this, man, how in hell we gonna clean usselfs up? Ain't no water here, an I be shamed goin back to that Center lookin like this."

"Well, Chad seed a fuckalot worser, best believe." Ethan looked toward the open trapdoor where the gray light was brightening to rose, then grabbed his shoes and shirt. "C'mon, big brother. Follow da saber-tooth tiger, even if he stink."

Corbitt had to concentrate to make his body obey, but he managed to get up and put on his clothes. Then, carrying his jacket, he followed Ethan up the ladder. The morning air was cool, and Corbitt supposed about as fresh as city air could ever be. It cleared his head some, but he still felt weak and dizzy, watching as Ethan went to the vent pipe and climbed the two stories to the back building's roof. He forced himself to follow, ashamed of his shakiness, and sweating and trembling by the time he pulled himself onto the rough graveled tar above.

"Dat shit totally fuck you up, huh?" asked Ethan.

Corbitt wiped his forehead. "Shit yeah! Most make me want to kill Akeem too."

"Don't call him dat, man. He never be no African! C'mon."
Ethan led Corbitt across several rooftops of different heights,
taking a running leap over a four-foot gap between two buildings,
and finally descending an old wooden ladder to the roof of a
single-story storefront. Its backside faced another narrow alley,
and toward the rear was an ancient swamp-cooler almost rusted
to pieces. Ethan took hold of one side and tilted it back to reveal
an opening about twelve inches square. "Ta-da!"

Corbitt wasn't sure what Ethan had in mind, but before he
could ask the small boy had slipped through. His little fingers
clung to the edge for a moment and then disappeared. There
was a soft thud as he landed somewhere below, then his voice
echoed up as if out of a well. "Yo! Follow da leader! Member?"

Corbitt crouched and peered down. Sunlight striped the
taller building next door, but there seemed only blackness where
Ethan had gone. A strong smell of wet fur drifted up into his
face, mingled with shampoo scents that reminded him of passing
by the beauty shop in Starkville where Sherry had always wanted
to have her hair "technically" done. Corbitt studied the small
opening, not sure if even his slender frame would fit. "Um, yo,
Ethan. How far is it?"

"Not far."

How many pieces of string would it take to reach the moon?
One, if it's long enough. Corbitt dropped his jacket through the
hole, then eased himself in, twisting diagonally so his shoulders
would pass. Letting himself down, he hung by his fingers a
moment until his eyes could adjust to the dimness.

The room was only about half the size of Hobbes's house.
The rear and side walls were bare concrete still showing the
grain of the planks they'd been poured in, and the floor was
unpainted cement glistening here and there with puddles of
water. Toward the front was a plywood partition, and a little
ruddy-orange daylight came filtering through a curtained doorway. About a foot beneath Corbitt's toes was a battered kitchen
table that could have been twin to the one in his cabin back at
Bridge-end. He let go and dropped onto it. Ethan stood nearby,
spreading his arms as if to present a new wonder. "Dis a secret
place, brother."

Corbitt got down from the table. Against one of the room's

side walls crouched a big old-fashioned bathtub on rusty clawed feet. A showerpipe rose from its faucets in a stately gooseneck, but instead of a showerhead had a length of hose clamped on that trailed down into the tub to end in a pistol-grip nozzle which peeked over the rim like a water moccasin seeking escape. Over the tub was a shelf lined with bottles and jars of all different colors.

"What this place?" Corbitt whispered.

"Da Pampered Pooch. Doggie-wash. Yo, you don't gotta whisper, man. Miz Hanna never come in till way later on. She do my dreads."

Corbitt glanced around again, noting a clock on the partition wall that showed a few minutes to six. "Oh. Well, she know y'all come in here like this?"

"Naw. Dat prob'ly give her a litter. But, check dis out, man. We gots us hot water an soap an all sorta shit to wash our asses clean!"

Flecks of Ethan's sickness clung to Corbitt's hands and body, but he felt even dirtier because of what Sebastian had done to him. He wondered if that feeling would ever wash off. Ethan went to the tub, leaning way over to pop in the stopper, then twisted the faucets full-on. The sound of splashing water echoed between the concrete walls and was somehow safe and soothing. Steam curled upward in wisps. Ethan stripped off his clothes, but Corbitt went to the partition and cautiously peeked through the curtain. The front room was set up as a pet supply store. Shelves and counters displayed dog dishes and collars and chains. Cages caught Corbitt's eye, and he saw what he supposed were hamsters. A larger cage held white rats.

Ethan came up beside him and parted the curtain. "Funny, huh, man? I mean, rats all over hell out dere, an some stupid people come here an *buy* dem fuckas!" Ethan strutted into the front room and snagged a can from a shelf. "Dis here da bestest shit, if y'all hungry, man."

Corbitt's stomach lurched when he read the label: Alpo Pure Beef. "Um, well, let's us clean up an then we go to the Center an sco' us some oatmeal. Okay?"

"But dis here real meat, man! Make ya strong! Dat shit at da Center just poor-niggaboy food!"

Corbitt turned back to the bathtub. "Spect I best be gettin used to it, then."

"Um, we still gonna do Hobbeses's wall, ain't we, Corbitt? I *need* dat green, man."

Corbitt sighed, squatting to untie his shoes. "Yeah. Spose there ain't no way other. Sides, my dad always say to finish what you start."

9

"RAT! RAT!"

The cry was a call to battle. All over the Center's main room kids burst into action, leaping over couches and chairs, grabbing plastic bats and balls from the toy box and scrambling in pursuit. The rat scuttled frantically here and there, first darting under a chair that the kids grabbed and tipped over, then diving for cover beneath a couch, where the kids jabbed and prodded it out with their plastic bats. Bright-colored balls were flung, most missing, but one or two scoring a hit and knocking the rat in a furry gray tumble across the floor. Corbitt smiled, ducking a ball as it flew past his head and bounced off the wall. This was the second time today there had been a rat-alert. It was pretty obvious why the toy box was so well-stocked with those cheap plastic bats and balls. He watched Ethan take a golf-club swing as the rat scurried past, and connect hard . . . not bad for a kid with no depth perception. The object wasn't to kill, but to make the game last as long as possible until the exhausted rat was finally chased or batted out the front door. No doubt those white-ass animal rights people would have been furious at the mis-treatment of one of God's creatures. The hunt moved noisily toward the partition doorway. The last rat had tried to take refuge among the mattresses behind Chad's desk. One of the boys there had caught it by the tail and smashed its skull against the wall. Kids on crack didn't have much sense of humor.

Corbitt replaced the access plate on the back of the big

coffee urn, and used the screwdriver blade of his knife to tighten the fasteners. Then he plugged the new cord into the wall socket and checked that the urn's amber light came on. Shouts of triumph echoed from beyond the partition as the rat was launched into the street. Corbitt leaned against the table and started to roll a cigarette.

It had been another long day. After he and Ethan had cleaned up at the dogwash, they had come here for breakfast, then returned to the crack house. Corbitt felt like he'd been mummified, and his mind boiled with rage at what Sebastian had done, but he still managed to build Hobbes a good solid wall with a heavy plank door. Sebastian hadn't come around. That was way cool by Corbitt because he wasn't sure what he'd have done to the golden boy if he'd seen him . . . probably gotten himself shot. Hobbes had come in a few times to check on the progress, and Lizard had given final approval of the job with grudging respect. He'd said that Lactameon would bring the money to Corbitt later.

Both exhausted, Corbitt and Ethan had come back here for some coffee and quiet. But the big urn was cold. Chad said that some city inspectors had shown up to check out an *unsafe* staircase, but couldn't find anything wrong with it, so had discovered a frayed cord on the coffee urn and fined the Center $250. Corbitt had offered to fix it, so Chad had located a Leopard to run over to the hardware store for a $3.98 replacement.

The coffee was warm by the time Corbitt had smoked his cigarette. He drew a cupful, added sugar and creamer, then went to the front desk, where Chad had his feet up and was smoking a Kool. The other kids had returned to the main room, resetting the knocked-over chairs and putting their weapons back in the toy box. Some gathered in front of the TV, others were picking up comics or magazines. One little boy went back to his coloring book.

Corbitt handed his knife to Chad. "It fixed now. Spose y'all still gots to be payin that fine?"

Chad shrugged. "It whitey's game, man. Ain't no justice, there just us."

Corbitt glanced into the shadowy alcove behind the desk. Just one small figure lay slumped against the wall. "Um, Christopher better today, Chad?"

"Dudes like Christopher don't get no better."

"Um . . . can't you keep him from goin out no more?"

Chad sighed smoke. "For how long? Till there ain't no more rock left? Sides, we start lockin kids up for their own good, we ain't no better'n the whiteman." Chad looked over his shoulder. "Oh, for sure there some people I can call, come take him away. He know it, an he know all he gots to do is ask."

"Um, what happen then?"

Chad shrugged again. "Never had a kid come back an tell me. But, I don't figure they get sent to the magic land of Oz." He dropped his feet from the desk and dug through the piles of paper. "Here somethin from one of those places." He handed Corbitt a three-page pamphlet. "Ain't far from here, you ever decide to scope it. Just be goddamn careful what you tell 'em or you might not get out again." He poked among the stuff on the desktop. "We get some of the strangest junkmail here, man. Like nobody sure exactly what we do, but everybody tryin to get a piece of it. Here's a catalog from a prison-industry supply . . . key word there is *industry*. Kinda explains why they won't do nuthin bout schools but they can't build prisons fast enough. Here's somethin from a drug supply . . . shit to keep kids *calm* an help them *cope* with *childhood's imaginary fears!* Got this piece of dogshit from the government last week. They doin a million-dollar study on why our inner-city kids are so *violent*. Some white cocksucker out to prove it in our *genes*." Chad glanced up. "Um, you know what I talkin about, man?"

"Genetics? Sho."

"*Genetics*, my ass! Like anybody with the brains Jah give a rat couldn't figure what happen to *any* color kids livin in a sorry-ass motherfucker like this! Now, some of them white assholes want to catch our kids an *re-program* their little minds. Tell you this, Corbitt, if the idea of white people lockin up your black-ass an messin with your mind don't scare the shit out you, maybe you born the wrong color." Chad glanced over his shoulder once more. "Chris there ain't no fragile little child without no life-experience, man. He seen kids die, an he gots all seven on what that's about. I doin everythin I can for his ass, but I be goddamn to hell if I gonna give him to the whiteman like some little rat to experiment on . . . specially when it whitey who made him like that in the first place." Chad took a last hit off his Kool and crushed it out in an ashtray already half full of new bloody cotton. "Thanks for fixin the coffeepot, Corbitt."

"Sho. Um, y'all spect I can buy me one of them envelopes an stamps?"

Chad smiled. "They free, brother. Shit, we *want* kids to write home if they figure there any hope left. Lots of times home don't seem like such a bad place after a few days down here."

Corbitt shrugged. "Spose that be 'pendin on what y'all gots for comparin it to."

Chad smiled again. "Sorry, man. I forget I was talkin to a brother down with genetics." He pulled a business-sized envelope from a drawer. It already bore a Black History stamp.

"Um, Chad? Spose I be wantin somebody to write me back?"

"No prob." Chad snagged a pencil and printed an address on a piece of paper. "Just put whatever name you wanna use care of this. Pigs ain't sposed to fuck with the mail, but we still get a lot of letters marked *opened in error.*"

Corbitt nodded. "Thanks, Chad. I chill with that."

Returning to the main room, Corbitt picked up a pencil and a sheet of binder paper off a table, then got another cup of coffee and found a quiet corner. He wrote a long letter to Toby, then searched through a stack of books and comics until he found a skate magazine. In it were several ads for Bay Area skate shops. Going to the toy box, he pulled out a plastic egg of Silly Putty. After a few experiments on blank paper, he managed to make a transfer from a skate shop logo to the top of his envelope like a letterhead. Now it would look like just more junkmail for Toby.

Ethan came over from the TV. "Um, can I make me a smoke, Corbitt? Whoa! You doin some magic shit dere?"

Corbitt gave Ethan the pouch of Top. "No magic, little brother, just a trick. Seem like to me it way past time we start fightin back with some tricks of our own." He popped the Silly Putty back into its egg. "Sho nuff hope Tam be comin soon with that money. Gots to be sendin some along with this letter."

Ethan paused in rolling a cigarette. "Um, I still gettin dat half buck, huh?"

"Course. I say it, I be meanin it. Brothers don't lie to each other." Carefully, Corbitt tore an advertisement page from the magazine and folded it over the letter.

"Yo! Why be you sendin your Afrosippi brother dat?"

"Case he open it front of his parents."

"Shit, Corbitt, you be way past smart, man! I wish you my brother for real. Maybe some dat Afrosippi magic rub off on me."

A big shadow darkened the toy box. "Look like a lot rubbin off already, man. I couldn't roll up no cigarette like that."

Corbitt looked up to see Lactameon. "Shit, Tam, y'all sho come slinkin in quiet-like for bein a fat lion."

Lactameon grinned, leaning the old Variflex against the toy box. "Still a lion, I guess." He looked around to make sure no one was watching, then pulled a sweat-wet wad of bills from his pocket. "Hobbes blown-away with what you dudes done. Wants to know if you can 'stall a AC?"

Corbitt took the money and counted off five twenties. "Best you believe I ain't workin for no more drug dealers, man. Not after what I seen out there 'hind Chad's desk! Little brother, no older'n Ethan here, don't even wanna live."

Lactameon spread his hands. "Goddammit, Corbitt, *whitey* doin that to us!"

Corbitt shook his head. "Ain't no doubt in my mind that a fact. But, whitey *always* been doin that to us. What make no goddamn logical sense be, we still *helpin* him do it! Just like we a bunch of little children taught never talk back to the white teacher, or tell the white coach we ain't havin no more of his little-kid games!"

Corbitt folded the bills inside the letter and sealed the envelope. "Ain't only the drugs, Tam. It be shit like some nigger cop the other night treatin us worse'n the whitemen was with him." Corbitt made a sudden move, snatching the bandana from Lactameon's pocket. "An then there be this bullshit. We coulda had coffee here hours ago, cept there wasn't no Leopard could go to the hardware store." He slipped the bandana around his head. "Funny, I *still* feel like a nigger boy."

Lactameon flicked glances around. "Yo! Take that off, Corbitt! You can't wear that in here! You gots no right wearin it anyways!"

Corbitt dodged away as Lactameon made a grab. "Spose the penalty be death by other nigger boys, huh?" He pulled off the bandana and studied it a moment, then handed it back to Lactameon. "Gots me a blue one at home . . . couldn't wear it here, could I? Mornin I leave, one of my brothers wearin a red one. Both of 'em buck seventy-five at the Starkville Wal-Mart. Couldn't wear neither of 'em here cause they stand for two real bad-ass bunches of nigger boys. Sho, I know it ain't the rags we be dyin for. The rags be flags, an look how many people dyin for flags. Did Africans have flags fore whitey come along? I don't think so."

Corbitt considered the bandana in Lactameon's hand, then sighed and shrugged. "That Sister Souljah say one time we oughta take a week off an kill whitefolks. Ain't sayin I think she right about that, but maybe we shoulda least took a day off from killin each other."

Lactameon stuffed the bandana back in his pocket and balanced his butt on the edge of the toy box. "You ain't from here, Corbitt. You ain't gots all seven yet."

Corbitt snorted. "Seem like to me I gots six out them seven, an that all what we need to get by in the hood. It like that ole song go, you never been to the ghetto, don't never come to the ghetto, cause you not *understand* the ghetto. Sound like all seven, till you stop an figure out it be only a bunch of nigger boys spoutin bad-soundin nonsense with no more meanin than a child's storybook rhyme. Wasn't no nonsense built them pyramids. *That* took all seven. That took black *men*. Ain't gonna be no niggerboy nonsense stop what whitey doin to us."

Lactameon sighed. "You still here a week from now, tell me that again, man. It still won't make no sense, but you be too goddamn busy keepin your black ass vertical to pay no attention. Look, maybe I can get somethin else goin on for you, Corbitt. It prob'ly just be nigger-work."

"Long's it *for* niggas an not against 'em, I be your boy, man." Corbitt peeled a fifty from the remaining money and gave it to Ethan. "Here, little brother, an y'all earn ever cent of it. Like a African." Corbitt glanced at the stacks of books on the table. "There be a whole lot of stuff wrote down bout bein black, but I sho don't see no young African's guide to understandin nigger boys."

Ethan stuck the bill in his pocket. "Ta da! Now I can buy me my eye! Um, come with me, Corbitt. Please?"

Corbitt's own eyes widened. "What y'all tellin me, man? You sayin there some sorta operation for fifty dollars?"

Lactameon smiled. "Just go with him, Corbitt. Make sure he don't get his ass cheated. An, tell that ole sucker you want a real ceet."

"Um?" asked Ethan. "Don't y'all wanna come too, Tam? You my other African brother."

"You know I would, Ethan. But I gots to meet somebody here." Lactameon looked across the room to the front desk. "Fact is, she here now."

Corbitt turned to see the same dark chubby girl who had been reading the other night. She was dressed like a street-survivor in baggy gray jeans and big black T-shirt, and held a small blanket-wrapped bundle like a precious thing against her breasts.

Ethan giggled. "Ooooo! I see!"

Picking up his skateboard, Lactameon got to his feet. "C'mon, brothers, meet Toni."

Crossing the room behind the other boys, Corbitt saw Chad standing in front of the desk, shaking his head and looking more unhappy than mad about something. The girl glanced sadly toward the street. Rounding the partition wall, Corbitt saw the lean, dirty boy, Beamer, from the crack house standing uneasily in the open front door. The slanting sun of evening stretched his shadow across the curled black and white floor tiles. He was still clad in just cutoffs and Nikes, and his unfinished face wore the same expression Corbitt had seen on a child watching people eat in a bus station restaurant.

Lactameon's face went through several changes as he moved beside the girl and gazed at the baby cradled in her arms. His eyes lifted to the girl's for a moment, then went to Beamer's. "Well . . . jeeze," he finally whispered.

Beamer stood with one toe over the invisible line. "Um . . . you not pissed, Tam?"

Lactameon scanned the three faces again; Toni's, Beamer's, and the small one haloed by the blue blanket. "Um . . . well, shit no." His hand went to Toni's shoulder, and he smiled. "I mean, I knew it had to be a way cool dude." He glanced toward the main room. "Guess we gots some talkin to do, huh?"

Beamer's chin quivered. "I can't come in, Tam."

Frowning, Lactameon turned to face Chad. "So, what the prob, man?"

Chad sighed. "You know the rules here, brother."

"Jeeze, Chad! It *Beamer*! Shit, how many options you figure he gots?"

Christopher had gotten up when he heard Beamer's voice, and now came around the desk. "Yo, Beam. Need to see ya, man."

For a moment Chad's face hardened, but then he took a breath and let it out slow. "Beamer, get outa here, man. Now. Tam, Toni, you wanna talk to him, take it to the street."

Beamer turned silently and walked away from the door. Toni followed. Lactameon glanced back at Chad for a moment, then left too. Corbitt watched Christopher go out, fighting the urge to stop the little boy, but then sighed and handed the envelope to Chad. Chad met Corbitt's eyes. "Any ideas, brother?"

Corbitt shrugged and shook his head, then lay his hand on Ethan's shoulder. "Don't seem like none of us gots many options."

The days passed by, becoming a week, and then almost another;
it was hard for Corbitt to keep track of time with no structure
to shape it . . . no school or Sundays, and nothing that felt like
a next-thing in the future. Some days were hot, some cloudy,
some scented with *déjà vu* breezes from the unseen sea, but
when Corbitt recalled them at all it was just as the one he'd
spent hungry after cops and inspectors had invaded the Center
and closed it down while looking for "health violations." Or the
day he'd gotten beat up by two big dudes for no special reason
. . . they hadn't even wanted his jacket. So too, the nights were
remembered as simply the one he and Ethan had spent shivering
inside an abandoned storefront, trying to keep watch for each
other against rats, or another endured beneath the sullen city
sky on a rooftop. There had been a couple of good nights: sleeping at the Center, and getting full with the Collectors at their
clubhouse. The only sad thing about that had been Silver, who
smoked rock about as fast as he could reload his pipe.

   Some things weren't worth remembering . . . the taunts
and curses from cars cruising by, and having to dive for cover
whenever guns were aimed out their windows. And it was always
black boys doing that stuff . . . the sort of thing everybody
seemed to think whitemen in sheets did to Mississippi niggers,
except now it was niggers doing it to themselves, like the KKK's
Afro-American auxiliary.

   Corbitt was curbed and questioned by cops a lot, though

their questions just seemed an excuse to shove him around, and the last thing they wanted was logical answers. Corbitt learned to lie fast with the greatest of ease, saying whatever they wanted to hear while playing the part they expected to see. Sullen, smart-mouth niggerboys were tolerated a lot better than smart-minded ones. Usually they slammed him against the nearest wall or over the hoods of their cruisers, searching his body as brutally as possible while assuming he carried nothing in his mind that could hurt them. The pair of whites who had invaded the Center that first night found him one morning and slapped him around. Corbitt wished them in hell or worse.

As time passed, Corbitt felt rage building inside him like a nameless next-thing: a pressure that mounted until sometimes it seemed like his skull would explode. Shadowy images played through his mind like the ghosts on the third TV channel back in Bridge-end that would never quite sharpen to focus. Sometimes he felt like a child on the riverbank, sensing Bates's eyes and stopping his play to search out the evil that watched him unseen. Here it was the same; he couldn't bury the sensation of being on display . . . as if his picture was showing on some Sony Big-Screen in a comfortable living room where bored white people played with remote-control clickers. But the channels they changed shaped the episodes of Corbitt's own life.

Corbitt fought this feeling; tried to reason it away, but it was beginning to color his speech, thought, and actions, and that was all the more frightening because he suspected it was part of their plan.

There were good times too; reading to kids at the Center and seeing them pick up books afterward like someone had been keeping another secret from them. There had been a wonderful supper at Lactameon's, with Ethan using silverware in grim determination. It was no surprise that Lactameon's mom was a lot like a younger Mrs. Griffin. Corbitt also spent hours outside the scrapyard fence just watching the old Corbitt work. But the good was never enough to balance the bad, or to hold back the rage that rose daily within him . . . that feeling of being locked in a cage while those on the outside jabbed him through the bars or waved food in his face, then jerked it away.

You can never be white, boy. We try our damnedest to make you want that, so you're always outside the candy store with

*your African nose pressed to the glass, but you can't come inside.
Maybe, if you do the right tricks, we'll sell you stale somethings
or factory-seconds out back. We control the vertical. We control
the horizontal. And, frankly my dear dusky children, we'd like
to see you all horizontal . . . permanently. So, boys and girls,
pretend to glory in your blackness . . . dress black, talk black,
and dig up your primitive past as if that means anything now.
But you're really just nothing but children who can't play in the
real game, so you make up games of your own. Not very satis-
fying, is it? Like beating off. You're beating off while we're
fucking your mother good. Makes you frustrated and mean, so
you break things and kill . . . your OWN things and each other
. . . because we taught you stupid niggers a long time ago that
you can't touch us.*

In a way it was almost funny: black as space for thirteen
years and Corbitt was only *beginning* to realize what that meant.
Of course this wasn't 1951 anymore, and he had all the freedom
allowed him by law. Technically, he could go anywhere.

Technically.

But it hadn't taken many quests into the better sections of
the city to discover from the hate stares he got on the sidewalks
and the suspicious looks tracking him through stores that he'd
ventured into a world not meant for his kind. The police in those
places were quick to remind him where he belonged and lost
little time in suggesting he get his black ass back down there.
How much had really changed since Weylen walked by the river?
Sunlight might sparkle the surface, but the bottom remained
dark and cold. The big fish were still guarded, and the guards
packed a lot more than rock salt in their guns. If Weylen was
inside him, looking out through his eyes at the future he'd
missed, maybe soon he'd decide he was better off dead and
forgotten like the others in the field.

Ethan had taken Corbitt to another sort of center one night.
It was a bright, clean place run by colorless people of all colors.
Corbitt submitted to a buck-naked physical by a clueless black
woman who dressed like somebody from Kenya and talked like
something from *Wayne's World*, before being turned over to a
white clone who seemed to have taken a course on relating to
black children from other planets. She'd asked Corbitt questions
that should have made her ashamed of herself, but then he was

just a niggerboy-child and shouldn't have cared if she was more interested in what he did with his dick than his mind. Corbitt had about as much use for her counseling as Ethan had for 3-D movies. The food was delicious, the beds had white sheets, and Corbitt couldn't wait to get his black butt out of there before she started telling him Afro-American bedtime tales.

The morning sun was already hot as Corbitt turned the corner and walked up the alley to the dogwash shop's rear entrance. The top half of the steel dutch door stood open and the scents of wet fur and shampoo drifted out, masking the alley reek of shit, piss, and overstuffed dumpsters. Corbitt was early as always, and shucked his jacket and shirt, sitting down by the doorway to roll a cigarette. Ethan was still at the Center waiting to see if a letter from Toby would come today.

Skate wheels rattled at the alley mouth. Corbitt turned, hoping to see Silver, even if the dude had just come begging spare change. Corbitt had become almost as close to his Oaktown twin as he was to Lactameon or Ethan, even though being friends with a crack-sucker was like trying to polish a crow. Corbitt sometimes wondered if the worst thing about crack wasn't that it killed you sooner or later, but how lonely it made you before you died.

Then, Corbitt tensed when he saw it was Sebastian rolling toward him. He hadn't seen the golden boy since that night at the crack house, but Sebastian was still dressed in black head to foot, his face glistening with sweat and the satin T-shirt clinging to his chest plates like paint. Corbitt's eyes went to slits, studying the boy as he neared. Sebastian's expression was a strange mix of shyness and anger. His voice had an uncertain tone. "Hi, Corbitt."

Corbitt blew smoke, wondering why he no longer felt fury at what Sebastian had done to him. But then, being beaten up, bitten by rats, and kicked around by cops, besides suffering the city's other humiliations, didn't leave room for much more than disgust toward Sebastian. Corbitt shrugged. "Lo, Sabby."

The golden boy winced, but tailed his board and stood it against the wall. He slipped off his jacket, revealing the big Uzi pistol slung over one shoulder, then sat down. "Um, can I talk to you, brother?"

Corbitt nodded toward the dogwash door. "Gots to be workin in a few minutes."

Sebastian wrinkled his nose. "Shit, man, what's that old bitch payin you anyways?"

"Five dollars a day, an tips."

"Man, why you doin shit like that for chump-change? That ain't no kinda job for a African."

Corbitt frowned. "Least I ain't killin nobody. Maybe that a African thing, which case y'all wouldn't understand."

Sebastian's eyes slitted for a second, but then he sighed and pulled a pack of Kools from his pocket. He fired one, then stared at the dirty pavement. "Listen to me, brother. Please. I'm sorry about what happened, okay? I never done nuthin like that before. I . . . I was kinda fucked-up myself."

So you try an fuck me? But Corbitt recognized real pain in Sebastian's voice. Adding to it didn't seem very logical. He took a long hit off his own cigarette and let the smoke trickle out through his nose. Finally, he shrugged. "Spose it don't matter a hell of a lot no more. Mind me of a ole joke . . . two dudes see this dog lickin it ownself. One say, 'Times I wish I could do that.' Other dude say, 'Well reckon y'all should pet him first.' "

"Huh?"

"Ain't a'zactly the world's coolest joke." Corbitt blew smoke again. "Sides, y'all did bring me a pizza."

"Um, is that some sorta African sayin, man?"

Corbitt sighed. "Forget it."

"Look. I just want you to know I ain't no goddamn faggot or nuthin, brother. I . . . I just *like* you, man. Um . . . maybe we can just forget it, huh?"

Corbitt shrugged again. "Forget what? Sides, I gots more important things on my mind."

"See? That's what I mean, brother. You're just naturally cool. I wish I could be like you."

"Workin for chump-change?"

"C'mon, Corbitt, you know what I'm sayin. It's like you're the real African everybody wants to be."

Corbitt laughed and shook his head. "Seem more like round here I be the real black butt everbody wantin to kick."

"That's cause them niggers forgot what it means to be black."

"Mmm. Well then, spect y'all gots 'em bowin down at your feet, man."

Sebastian fingered his gun. "That ain't what it is, brother. These dudes got nuthin but a slave fatality."

"I think y'all be meanin, *mentality*."

"Yeah. What I'm sayin is, it's like they figure my mom fucked the master or somethin. They *hate* me, man!"

Corbitt studied the beautiful golden kid for a moment. "Now, that a silly-ass thing to be sayin, Akeem. What I seen so far, ain't nobody wanna be my color no more. Case y'all ain't noticed, them shops an stores round here be sellin the hell out skin *lightener*. Don't seem like no call for dark tannin oil." He sighed out smoke. "I be the color get hated . . . primitive genes from the past, gots no place in the here an the now."

Sebastian crossed his arms over his knees and buried his face against them. "You don't understand."

"Well, I might if y'all try talkin English, man. I don't speak no Swahili."

"It's like these stupid niggers think I betrayed 'em or somethin."

Corbitt hesitated, then put his hand on Sebastian's shoulder. "Mmm. Lately I been gettin the idea that color mean more to us than *them*. Maybe that part of the plan. Lady back . . . home . . . call it dividin an conquerin. Course, y'all ever figure dudes not likin you might gots more to do with what you be doin than the color of your skin?"

Sebastian's shoulders jerked in a helpless shrug. "Hobbes got friends, man. Even Tam likes him."

"Well, Tam just be one of them people what can see the good part in everbody."

"But, *I* got a good part, Corbitt! The black part! Only, nobody can see that!"

"Maybe cause all you been showin 'em be your big-ass black gun?"

Sebastian's head jerked up. There were tears in his eyes. "They'd kill me without it, man! Specially them cocksuckin Collectors!"

"Tam be a Collector."

Sebastian wiped savagely at his eyes. "He don't count, man!

He's just their stupid mascot! A big fat niggerboy joke they can laugh at!"

Corbitt took his hand off Sebastian's shoulder. "I never seen 'em laughin at him. Fact is, anybody be knowin him respect him."

"Aw shit, Corbitt! You can't be that stupid!" Sebastian gripped his gun. "*This* is the only fuckin thing these niggers around here respect!"

Corbitt crushed out his cigarette. "Oh, you be a nigger boy fo sho. Y'all bought the whiteman's plan a long time ago . . . that we all be nuthin but niggers so's it don't matter what we end up doin to each other."

"You don't understand."

Corbitt snorted and got to his feet. "Just cause I don't give a shit bout your stupid-ass ideas don't mean I can't understand 'em. Yo! Gots me a blond, blue-eyed brother back home with more goddamn African blood in his one little finger than you ever have even wearin my skin an lookin out through my eyes, Akeem."

Sebastian seemed confused. "You called me Akeem."

Corbitt shrugged. "A asshole be a asshole by any ole name . . . a asshole what shit on his brothers."

Sebastian leaped up, fists clenching. "Goddammit! I didn't *ask* to be me!"

"Well, I fo goddamn sho don't member askin to be me, neither. But I can't see no logic in spendin the rest of my life hatin my ownself."

Sebastian gripped his gun and aimed it at Corbitt. "Shit! You ain't no different than the rest of those stupid niggers!"

Corbitt supposed he should have been afraid, but he only felt tired. "So, what you gonna do, Sabby? Kill me an eat me like Africans used to eat lion meat to make 'em more like lions? Shit, boy, now there be a ole idea for you! Now, take the fuck off an go polish your ownself, I gots me a job needs doin!"

Corbitt felt the gun track him as he got up and grabbed his jacket and shirt. He turned his back on the golden boy, finding he didn't much care if Sebastian shot him or not. But then he heard the rattle of Sebastian's skate wheels head down the alley. "Yo, Weylen," he murmured. "Get yourself a eyeful of that?"

Then he laughed. "Shit. Hear yourself, boy! Talkin out loud to dead Afrosippians!"

Reaching over and unlatching the door, Corbitt went in. Against the bare concrete wall opposite the tub were several big pens built of unpainted pine and chicken-wire. Above these was a row of smaller cages, one occupied by a patient-looking brown-and-white spaniel who gave Corbitt a dog-smile while wagging its stub of a tail.

Corbitt smiled back. "Yo, Doofus." He had bathed the dog on his first day of work . . . one of the few he'd seen who seemed normal. Most city dogs had weird personalities, which Corbitt supposed was logical.

In one back corner was a tiny bathroom. Corbitt entered, then emerged a minute later clad only in cutoffs made from an old pair of jeans Chad had given him. There were rubber boots and a raincoat on a shelf, but they were hot and uncomfortable to work in. Old Mrs. Hanna called Corbitt her little Nubian.

He caught sight of a pair of suspicious yellow eyes glaring at him from another small cage. He sighed: that was Miss Lavoe's "precious little Fluffy" . . . a dirty-white dustmop with teeth any rat would be proud to own. Corbitt reached in and patted Doofus, then offered his hand to Fluffy. She snapped at his fingers.

"Bitch," Corbitt muttered. He was pretty sure what Miss Lavoe did for a living.

"That you, Corbitt?" called a voice from beyond the partition.

"Shit yea . . . Um, sho nuff, Miz Hanna."

"Shoulda known. You always on time." Mrs. Hanna came through the curtain, struggling against the leaps of a huge Labrador who would have yanked an average-sized woman off her feet. Both the dog and the lady were about the same color. The big dog saw Corbitt and roared, jerking the leash from Mrs. Hanna's hands and lunging for Corbitt.

Corbitt knelt, bracing himself for the crash, then let the dog slobber his face and smother him in hot meaty breath. Doofus watched with envy. Fluffy went insane. Mrs. Hanna ignored Fluffy's squeaky rage, and smiled. "Bageera sure got a thing for you, boy. Miz Rowe just tellin me yesterday how happy he seem after you bathed him last week. Good dogs always know good people."

Corbitt glanced up at Fluffy's cage, wondering what sort of people shit-for-brains dogs liked. He calmed the big Lab, then stood up and wiped his face. "Gots him lion-breath, for a fact."

"Ain't no wonder. Miz Rowe feed him only that Alpo Pure Beef. There folks spendin less on their children. Course, she need a good dog, buildin she live in."

Mrs. Hanna reminded Corbitt of a big beach ball in fluorescent colors of orange and green. She really made stretch pants work for a living. He grabbed for the leash as Bageera bounded to the tub and hooked his huge paws over the rim. Up in her cage, Fluffy frothed.

"Want I should do Baggy first, Miz Hanna?"

Mrs. Hanna went to the cage, scowling when Fluffy tried to bite her finger. "No. Miss Lavoe need Fluffy by noon. Wash, rinse, and comb like you done the last time. An use the herbal scent."

Corbitt wrestled Bageera to a pen and shouldered him inside. "Best use the flea stuff on her, seem like to me."

"Well, you got that right, boy. But Miss Lavoe don't take to the smell of it."

"Mmm. Spose it be bad for business," muttered Corbitt.

"What's that?"

"I say, maybe it give her the sneezes." Corbitt returned to the tub, leaning over to pop in the stopper. "Well, Fluffy gots her more fleas than a possum, an all that there herb stuff do is make her smell like magnolias. Ain't no wonder she gots such a 'tude."

Mrs. Hanna moved to the hot plate on a partition-wall shelf and poured a cup of coffee, then fired one of those long slender cigarettes that came in all colors. "Well, I never been able to convince that woman bout nuthin. Only reason I put up with her nonsense is she spend close to fifty dollars a week on that dog. Oh, an she mention Fluffy a little upset last week. Try an treat her more gentle, boy."

Corbitt twisted the faucets. "Best I clean the tub good when I done with her, then. Don't want Baggy goin home with Miz Fluffy's fleas."

Mrs. Hanna nodded. "You a good boy, Corbitt. Just you

keep yourself away from them drugs an them gangs an you have a real fine future ahead."

"Yeah. I member me that, Miz Hanna." Corbitt reached to the cluttered shelf above the tub. "Spect Fluffy like the red goo or the green?"

"Dogs can't see color, boy, just black an white. Oh, an Miss Lavoe say to feed Fluffy her lunch when you through. Here's her special dish. I already add a can of Alpo to the bill."

Corbitt's stomach growled. He and Ethan had eaten supper last night at the Center: some sort of meat that looked like slimy Spam and the kids called chopped rat. Maybe Ethan would track down something for lunch? The phone rang up front and Mrs. Hanna went to answer it. Corbitt chose a plastic bottle that smelled most like a pimp, then switched on the little blaster that Lactameon had loaned him. The batteries were almost dead so he uncoiled the power cord and plugged it into a nearby socket. Kris Kross filled the room, rapping about showing suckas how it was done. Fluffy started yapping nonstop.

Mrs. Hanna parted the curtain. "Corbitt, I got to run up to the bank. Keep an eye on the front an answer the phone. There's only about ten dollars in the register. Somebody come in an want it, you just let 'em have it. Ain't worth gettin shot over. An don't call the cops, they more trouble than they worth."

"Sho, Miz Hanna."

"Well, I want you to know, ain't many boys I trust like you, Corbitt. But I seen you was special the minute you walk in the door."

That and a gun get me lunch anywhere in this city. Corbitt tested the water temperature in the tub, hearing the front door bell tinkle as Mrs. Hanna left.

"Yo, African bro!"

Corbitt turned to see Silver at the back door. The boy was smiling, but it seemed to take lots of effort. His eyes were dull and his face sheened with sweat. Snot glistened on his lip below the small shiny ring in his nose, making him look like a tired old child. Corbitt came to the door. "Hi, Silver. What up?"

Silver sniffled as if he'd been crying. "Just checkin my lonely homey, man. Look like you the keeper of the zoo, fresh prince of animal-land, schemin a plan."

Corbitt smiled. "Schemin like dreamin, brother of mine,

either a crime or a waste of your time." Silver seemed even thinner, though it had been only two days since Corbitt had last seen him. His long-fingered hand felt like a bundle of twigs when Corbitt shook it, and his face looked like skin stretched over a skull. "Y'all best stop smokin that shit, brother. I need me a bunch more rappin sessions with you."

Silver lowered his eyes. "This gonna be day last, brother. Swear to God. Bilal word me he ain't havin no more of my ass around till it clean. But you know what it is, Corbitt . . . you just can't stop, slam-bam, man. I need to burn me a few to get through. Um . . . spose you could help a bro? I mean, I feel like a fool for askin."

Corbitt sighed. "I don't get paid till Friday, man. Ain't gots nuthin but some change in my own pocket now. Look, couldn't y'all go to the Center? Chad an Miz Davis help you chill."

Silver gripped Corbitt's arm. "I gotta do this my own way, man. My own plan." He looked down at his skateboard. "Pawn-shop sucka say he give a nickel for my ride."

"Oh shit, y'all can't go sellin your board, brother!" Corbitt glanced quickly over his shoulder toward the front of the store . . . ten dollars in the register, and Mrs. Hanna wouldn't doubt he'd been robbed.

Because he was a good boy who could be trusted.

Corbitt sighed again, wondering if he'd ever learn the secret of how to be bad and not give a shit. "I help you, man. Brothers gots to help brothers or none of us goin nowhere." But instead of going to the register, Corbitt went into the bathroom and dug in his jeans pocket, returning with the tinfoil-wrapped bill. "Here. Y'all take this over to that pawnshop dude. It be a ole, special kinda dollar. Even gots your name on it. Don't know what it worth, but I spect he be givin you least a nickel for it." Corbitt smiled. "Your ride be your pride, man. Can't be havin my brother sellin that."

Silver took Corbitt's hand. "This the last fuckin time, man. Swear to God!"

"Mmm. Well, here be a rap I been workin on. Brothers hear the news, crack be government-approved, just the thing for little niggas cause it stop 'em gettin bigger."

Silver wiped sweat from his forehead and stuffed the dollar into his pocket. "Maybe we work on that one together, man.

But I gotta go get my battery charged now." He decked and rolled away.

Corbitt went back to the tub, which was filling slowly because the water pressure was low. The phone rang up front. Corbitt ran to answer it. "Um, Pampered Pooch. Yessum, all sizes. Safe? Well, I ain't drowned one yet. Oh. Well, I don't right know, never seen none of you whitefolks come in here, course I sho ain't gonna eat you. Well, y'all think about it, then. Bye."

Lactameon was grinning over the door when Corbitt returned. "S'up, Corbitt? How ya hangin with this job, man?"

Corbitt flipped the latch to let Lactameon in. "Ain't makin no bucks an a halfs for a few hours work, fo sho, but best y'all believe I been sleepin better." He smiled, seeing the suggestion of a strut in Lactameon's walk. "Toni a real nice girl, Tam. Y'all be lucky as hell findin her."

Lactameon leaned his skateboard against the wall and plopped a paper bag onto the tabletop. "Funny, she was there all the time, I just never got all seven."

"Y'all still readin at the Center?"

"Yeah. It turnin into a regular thing, an some of them kids gettin so's they expect it every day. Course, most of 'em still hang with the TV, but Chad saying there a lot more books gettin cracked lately. Um . . . Christopher die last night, man."

Corbitt nodded. "Mmm. Wasn't nuthin more could be done. Beamer still workin for Hobbes?"

"Yeah. Ain't a lot can be done bout that, neither. Toni helpin out more at the Center these days. Miz Davis even payin her when there extra green, but Beamer still carryin most of the load."

"Mmm. You bout the coolest African dude I ever knowed, Tam."

Lactameon shrugged. "Why? Like, I sposed to be pissed-off or jealous cause my homey an a girl I love went an had a baby fore they knew what the fuck they was doin? Shit, man, you the one always talkin bout logic. Sides, it *our* baby now. The three of us's. Yo. Ain't that a sorta African thing, man? Like, the kids really belong to everybody."

"If it ain't, it oughta be. Still too bad Beamer gots to keep workin for Hobbes."

"Yeah, well, it that option thing again, man. But, there somethin up on that too. Beamer was tellin me business better'n ever for Hobbes, cept it seem like Hobbes cuttin back. He always talk bout gettin his ass out the business, but I never hear of no dealer who really did." Lactameon opened the bag and tossed a package of Twinkies to Corbitt. "Chad score a truckload of these today. Some sorta donation to us poor nigga kids. They a little stale, but what the fuck."

Corbitt tore open the package and ate one. "Stuff like this only make you hungrier."

Lactameon took a pack for himself. "Prob'ly the idea, man. If they couldn't make us want what they got, it be pretty hard tryin to keep us from gettin it. Sometimes I think, stead of havin a Black History month, we oughta have a week where we all ride the butt-end of buses. We just ain't pissed-off at the right people." Lactameon looked at the clock. "Gots to bail, man. Cruise by the Center when you done here. Some little dude was askin me if the Afrosippi brother was gonna come back an tell some more *real* stories."

Corbitt stood by Bageera's pen for a few minutes after Lactameon left. He stroked the big dog's glossy black fur and murmured, "So, where y'all bury your bones in the city?" Then, warily, Corbitt unlocked Fluffy's cage. The little dog growled but let herself be picked up and petted. Bageera gave a sudden eager roar and lunged for Fluffy. The pen's flimsy framework crackled and creaked.

"Stay chilly, blackboy," muttered Corbitt. "Y'all go an eat up this here little white furball, they be wantin to put you to sleep."

Fluffy wiggled in Corbitt's arms, not seeming afraid of Bageera at all. She made soft whining sounds. "Mmm," said Corbitt. "An what go an turn you into a sweet little Twinkie all of a sudden?"

The phone rang again.

"Well, dammit to hell!" Corbitt took the paper bag and put it on a shelf, then set Fluffy on the table. "Y'all stay." He ran up front and grabbed the phone. "Pampered Pooch. Um, no, ma'am. Y'all should be feedin 'em that special rat food. It gots vitamins an minerals an stuff like that. Sho I know what regular rats eat, but these be white ones so's y'all gots to be takin better care of em."

Yaps and barks suddenly erupted from the back room. Wood splintered like gunfire. Corbitt spun to face the curtain. "Oh, shit! Um, no, ma'am, I weren't talkin to you." Then he saw a bright spot of blood on his arm. "Oh, SHIT!" Slamming down the phone, he dashed around the partition. Fluffy was on the floor with her behind pressed to Bageera's pen. The big dog had almost broken out. Doofus looked on from above with interest.

"Well, you little ho!" Corbitt grabbed Fluffy. She snapped at his fingers. "Bitch!" Corbitt flung her into the half-full tub. Bageera burst from his pen. Corbitt got hold of his collar and skidded him to a stop. "Dammit to hell! Y'all quit actin like a animal!"

The front door bell tinkled.

"Just a fu . . . just a minute!"

Corbitt dragged Bageera to another pen and pushed him inside. Fluffy was paddling around the tub in frantic circles but couldn't get out. Corbitt ran back up front where a pretty woman in a purple jogging suit was looking over the pet food display. "Um, can I help y'all, ma'am?"

"You have that new diet cat food?"

From the rear came Bageera's roars, Fluffy's squeaky yaps, and the sounds of splintering wood. Even Doofus started to bark. Corbitt tried to give the woman a reassuring smile. "Yessum. Over there. Top shelf, next the white rats."

The lady was looking toward the curtain, a puzzled expression on her face.

"Um, scuse me, ma'am. I be right back."

Fluffy was waterlogged and panting but still swimming in circles. Bageera had his door half open. Corbitt managed to quiet him a little, jammed the door shut as tight as he could, then ran up front again. The woman was waiting at the counter with four cans of cat food. Corbitt rang them on the register and counted the lady's change backward like the Barlows did in their store.

The woman smiled. "Why, you doin that right in your head, ain't you, son?"

"Um, yessum. See, this here ole thing ain't smart like the ones at McDonald's."

"Well, I just never seen no young man your age do it like that before."

"Um, thank you, ma'am." Corbitt bagged the cans and tried to keep a smile on his face until the lady left the store, even though all hell seemed to be busting loose in the back room. He was just dashing through the curtain when the phone rang again. "SHIT!" He ran back and grabbed it. "Pampered Pooch! WHAT? Hell no! An if you gots any goddamn sense in your head you won't try washin your cat, neither!"

The tub was overflowing. Fluffy was struggling to climb out but Bageera had both big paws on the rim and was slobbering her face with swipes of his tongue, shoving her back into the water each time. Corbitt grabbed for Bageera and slipped on the wet floor, landing on his butt. Bageera forgot Fluffy and tried to play, knocking Corbitt down every time he tried to get up, then slamming into the table and scattering combs and brushes all over the place. Finally, Corbitt got a grip on Bageera's collar and wrestled him into the little bathroom. He shoved the door shut, then darted across to the tub and turned off the water. Fluffy looked like a soggy white rat as she tried to climb out. Corbitt reached for her. "Po little Fluffy. Y'all havin one hell of a day, ain't you?"

Fluffy clamped onto Corbitt's finger like a rat.

"BITCH!"

Corbitt jerked back. Fluffy caught a paw in the blaster's dangling power cord and pulled it off the shelf. Corbitt lunged, catching it a second before it hit the water. Shampoo bottles rained down on his head.

"Goddammit to hell!" Corbitt shoved the blaster back on the shelf, then snatched Fluffy by the collar. She snarled and snapped. Corbitt cursed and plunged her underwater. Guppy could hold his breath almost three minutes. Corbitt glanced over his shoulder at the clock. When he finally pulled Fluffy out again she coughed and spluttered and tried to cuddle against Corbitt's chest. But he held her nose about an inch from his own and stared into her eyes. "Now, bitch! Y'all gonna get a *nice* motherfuckin shampoo an a kick-ass combin an behave your little shit-eatin self, or y'all gonna be the very first housepet in hell!"

Fluffy stayed quiet and cooperative as Corbitt shampooed, rinsed, and carefully toweled her dry. She stood still on the

tabletop as he gathered the combs and brushes off the floor and
groomed her silky, flower-scented coat. Finally, Corbitt tied a
pink ribbon around her neck, then wiped sweat from his forehead
and stepped back. "There. All anybody want in this world be a
little goddamn respect."

"Yo, Corbitt!" Ethan came scrambling over the door, his
brassy skin gleaming and both eyes seeming to shine with equal
eagerness. "Your letter come, man! All da motherfuckin way
from Afrosippi!"

Corbitt caught the little boy under the arms and tossed him
into the air before grabbing him in a Sampson-style hug. Ethan
giggled. "Shit, man, don't go squeezin me too goddamn hard!
Y'all pop my new eye out!"

Corbitt grinned while scanning Ethan's face. It seemed like
real magic how a simple sphere of colored glass could turn horror
into beauty. Maybe it was just a trick of light, but sometimes it
seemed as if the blue eye could actually see. Of course Ethan
swore that it could, and Corbitt would have never tried to tell
him otherwise. Somehow, the fact that the eyes didn't match
only made the blue one seem all that more real. Mrs. Griffin
had once said that dogs with one blue eye could see the wind.

Corbitt lifted Ethan to the table. "Mmm. Seem like to me
y'all puttin on some pounds, little brother."

Ethan slapped his tummy. "Shit yeah! I gettin fatter'n hell,
man! Nuther couple weeks, my goddamn belly be draggin da
ground!"

Corbitt smiled. In another couple *months* Ethan might gain
enough weight to resemble a normal Bridge-end eight-year-old,
but at least his ribs no longer looked like they'd ring like a
xylophone if you ran your finger over them. There was a hint
of roundness to his stomach, and his chest and shoulders were
taking on a shadowy suggestion of muscle. Corbitt's pay from
the dogwash was barely enough to keep hunger a mouthful away,
even supplemented by meals at the Center. Lactameon was
providing the extras.

The phone rang.

"Damn!" Corbitt turned toward the front. "Yo, Ethan. Lock
up Miz Fluffy while I answer me that."

Ethan was back on the table, kicking his legs and eating a
Twinkie when Corbitt returned. Corbitt hopped up beside him

and took the envelope. It was addressed in Toby's big bulky pencil-print and bore a Starkville postmark. That was logical: Toby would have mailed it from there so it wouldn't be seen by his mother, who canceled all the New Crossing mail. It took willpower to put it down unopened, but Corbitt got the mop, cleaned the floor, drained and rinsed the tub, then lined the shampoo bottles back up on the shelf. Ethan went up front and returned with a can of Alpo. "Um, y'all hungry, Corbitt? All dey gots at da Center be more dese here Twinkies."

Corbitt climbed back on the table. "Mmm. Well, spose Miss Fluff-stuff owe me a meal." He tossed Ethan his knife. "Set it on the hot plate awhile, little bro. We gonna be eatin dog food, least let's have it warm." He glanced at the cages. "Yo. Where y'all put Fluffy, man?"

"In da batroom."

"Oh, shit!" Corbitt jumped off the table and ran to the bathroom door. He was about to yank it open, but then heard soft sounds inside. He took his hand off the knob, and smiled. "Miss Lavoe gonna be s'prised at how happy her little pet be today. Spect y'all call that a 'tude adjustment."

Returning to the table, Corbitt carefully opened the envelope. It held several sheets of school binder paper covered on both sides by Toby's writing. To Corbitt's surprise, two bills and a Polaroid picture fell out when he unfolded them. Ethan darted over and snatched up the money. "Whoa! Check dis out, man! A motherfuckin buck an a half! Can I hold 'em for ya?"

"Mmm. Sho, little brother." Corbitt picked up the picture. It showed Toby and Lamar with Sherry between them and the old bridge in the background. Their expressions looked so open and unguarded, and they seemed so young, that Corbitt first thought it must be an old photo. But it still smelled strongly of developing chemicals. Ethan scrambled up beside him and peered at the picture. "Whoa! Dat dere your tiger-bro, huh? Shit, check out dat hair! An your lion-bro! Check dat bod! Maaaan, he smoke some butt! Word an a half! Um, so who da b . . . mink belong to, Corbitt?"

Corbitt smiled, flattening out the letter sheets. "She been freed."

"Yo, dat some sorta park dey playin in?"

"That where we . . . they live."

"No shit? Fuck, I only seed places like dat on TV, man. Y'all musta done somethin way past bad to make you leave dere."

Corbitt sighed. "It be only a pitcher, Ethan. There be a lot of stuff don't show in the daylight. Here, roll us a couple smokes."

"Sho nuff. Um, read me what your tiger-bro write. Okay?"

Scooting back a little on the tabletop, Corbitt spread the sheets of binder paper out on his leg and bent over them. "Dear Corbitt, Cheetah-bro . . ."

Ethan leaned over Corbitt's shoulder. "I *knew* dat what dey call ya! Um, read slow, man, an move your finger past dem words so's I can 'tend I readin too. Okay?"

Corbitt began again, tracing his long slender finger under each word.

Dear Corbitt, Cheetah-bro,
> *It is real good to hear that*
you are ok. Me and Lamar talked it over and decided we
should go and tell Sherry because you know for a fact
she would have figured a lot of stuff out for her ownself
anyway. We all read the letter you sent me and then we
took it to Mrs. Griffin. She read it too and then talked to
us a lot. She has been helping your mom to understand
what you done, some. She would not take the money you
sent but said for me to send it and this here other money
back to you so that you can come home when you are
ready. Please do not worry over my shoes that got lost
because I am still wearing yours even if they are some
too big for me. Your mom is very sad you are gone but
like I said Mrs. Griffin helps her in a lot of ways. Every-
body in Bridge-end misses you and can not figure out
why you up and ran away. But there is good news. The
deputy found Bates's body a few days ago. There was
nothing left but bones because the crows had eaten him
all up. It was in the Starkville paper that they are not
sure when he died but they are saying it was a accident.
Even a lot of white people are not very sad about it if
you know what I mean. The deputy came by special to
tell Mrs. Griffin that the investigation was closed. Of
course nobody told him about you ran away and I am

*still keeping all the other secrets even though I had me
this dream about Weylen for two nights in a row now.
Me and him go across the bridge and into Bates's field.
He looks just like you Corbitt but is very sad and won't
talk at all. I wish you were here so we could dream this
dream together. But I have better stuff to tell you
brother. Bates don't have no kin they can find. The deputy went into his house. There were pictures of boys hidden away in there. Some were taken a long long time
ago. They were of real bad things Bates was doing to
them. You know what I mean. The deputy took them to
the judge who sent your dad to prison and the judge said
that there were some kind of circumstances about this
and is going to set your dad free! But there is even better
news! When your dad was there in that prison he worked
in the motor pool and was so good at teaching the other
prisoners about fixing trucks that the warden asked if he
would come back and teach there. Of course he will not
be locked in and they will pay him. So please come home
brother even if you don't want to tell about that one big
secret. And I am not a homo but I still love you.*

> *Your tiger-bro forever.*
> *Toby*

Ethan leaned over Corbitt's shoulder to stare wide-eyed
into his face. "Crow-birds eat dat ole cocksucka all up?"

Corbitt nodded slowly. "All up. Just like in the storybooks."

"Um, Mrs. Davis read dem kinda stories, but it always
naughty little children get dere asses eaten all up." Ethan's hand
went to his dreads. Mrs. Davis liked helping the Center kids
with their hair and had been so delighted with Ethan's new eye
that she'd spent hours with the boy putting some order into his
locks. She'd also woven in a few colored beads of red, green,
yellow, and black, and Ethan had asked her to attach Corbitt's
"magic" feather. It was braided on with fine silver wire. He
touched it now. "Um, I seed dis great big ole *nasty*-ass black
bird when I come here just now, Corbitt. Um, y'all don't figure
he be pissed cause he seed me wearin dis, huh? Like, he figure
I go an ice his brother or somethin?"

Corbitt glanced toward the back door for a moment, then

smiled. "No. Spect he might even be a little proud. Maybe I ain't been lookin at crows with the right kinda eyes."

"Um, *I* ain't naughty, huh?"

Corbitt took the little boy's shoulders. "No, brother. Y'all just as good as you can be."

"Um . . . so y'all gonna stay long enough we have lunch, Corbitt?"

Corbitt gazed around the small shabby room. He *could* go home! In less than an hour he could be on a bus, prepared now to battle his way back to Bridge-end. More: he could go to the phone right this minute and be talking to his mom, his brothers, Sherry, and maybe even his dad.

Ethan handed Corbitt a cigarette made with childish determination. Corbitt took it, fired, and sighed out smoke while folding the letter sheets back into the envelope along with the picture.

"Course, little brother. Can't be leavin out here with Miz Hanna gone. An, I still gots Baggy and Doofus to wash." Sliding from the table, Corbitt went to the hot plate and dumped the can of Alpo into Fluffy's dish. "Y'all be the keeper of our money, Ethan. Fact is, cruise your ass on up an score us some Burger King lunch."

"Fo-fuckin-sho!" Ethan jumped to the floor and ran to the door, scrambling to climb over instead of opening it . . . a little-kid thing to do. Suddenly, he froze, hanging by his elbows, both eyes wide. *"Corbitt!"*

Corbitt spun around. "What wrong?"

Ethan let himself slowly to his feet, staring down, both hands pressed to his crotch. "Corbitt! C'mere, man! *Fast!*"

Corbitt ran to the boy. "You hurt yourself?"

Ethan ripped open his jeans. "Corbitt! Look! It *hard*! It motherfuckin hard!"

Corbitt knelt in front of the little boy, not sure whether to smile or not. "Mmm. Sho nuff is, man."

"Um . . . put some magic on it, Corbitt! Hurry!"

"Huh? Well, ain't nuthin to worry over, Ethan. It be back."

"Corbitt, please!"

Corbitt thought a moment, then rubbed his palms together hard and fast and pressed them to Ethan's straight little dick.

"Oooo, shit, man! I *feel* dat go in!"

Corbitt stood, smiling now, and ruffled Ethan's dreads. "Best y'all believe it be back any time you want . . . an a whole hell of a lotta times when you don't."

"Um, I better score me some hats, huh, Corbitt?"

"I always knowed you was smart, little brother. Now y'all gots a 'sponsibility to your African sisters."

Ethan carefully buttoned his jeans. "Um, I gots a lotta shit I wanna ask you bout, man. Um, maybe after lunch?"

"Sho, little brother."

Corbitt worked the rest of the day on auto-pilot while most of his mind seemed to wander in space. He was no African and this was no quest. According to the stories a real quest was over only when the warrior found what he was seeking . . . gold, knowledge, or something sacred . . . and returned to share it with his people. He'd found nothing here. For sure there was "gold" . . . pieces of paper printed with pictures of long-dead whitemen, and fought over by ice-cold and uncaring black boys. Forget about anything "sacred"; no one seemed to hold anything holy, even life itself. And the only knowledge Corbitt had won was the realization of what niggers would do to each other to possess those pieces of whitey's paper. Gangs, drugs, and violence. What a motherfucking donkey show, and whitey loved every performance! Corbitt could almost hear Marlin Perkins narrating . . .

By providing a closed environment and restricting contact with other species, it has been found that the American Negro population will control its own numbers, thereby reducing the threat of overgrazing upon the rapidly dwindling resources of the Wild Kingdom.

Home. Maybe he was a fool not to be on a bus right this minute. If his dad was free and now had that job, then maybe neither Corbitt nor his mother would have to work for the Rudds or anyone else like them. Maybe there was a lot of time left to just be a kid.

Free. Corbitt whispered the word while brushing Bageera's ebony coat. Once that must have been a powerful word . . . a magic word. Bates's field was full of people who had died believing that real freedom would come to them someday. But Africans were obsolete now, and the only thing black people fought was each other.

Corbitt tried to picture fishing from the bridge on a starlit summer night. It should have been the easiest vision of all to bring to mind, but it somehow just wouldn't come clear. Across the river would be the silent field full of secrets and, Corbitt realized, he'd always be wondering about Ethan.

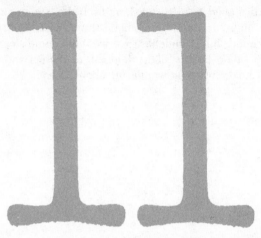

It was close to midnight and the backstreets were almost deserted. There was an occasional carful of party-people moving
uptown to safer territory, and one or two silent vehicles cruising
search-patterns for prey. These slipped slowly through the dark
grid of blocks as if playing some huge Kirby game. But Sebastian
wasn't going to be eaten by niggers. He skated the sidewalks
fast and warily, eyes constantly scanning, one hand gripping his
gun. Hobbes's little runner had come by the apartment nearly
an hour ago with a message that Hobbes wanted him at the
house. Hobbes would probably be pissed because he was late,
but there just wasn't a goddamn thing he could have done about
his eyes. Now the runner knew Sebastian's secret too, but that
snot-nose niggerboy would keep his goddamn mouth shut or
he'd never see fourth grade this fall.

For some reason, Corbitt's words from that morning still
cut like razor blades loose in Sebastian's mind. *Polish your ownself.* Did that really mean anything or was it just another joke
to remind him he wasn't all black? If he was in Mississippi he'd
goddamn well be black! But here even the uptown pigs left him
alone. Maybe that was why these stupid niggers hated his ass
so much?

Kicking into the alley entrance, Sebastian tailed his board
and walked toward the crack house. The yellow rays of a streetlight didn't penetrate far, and Sebastian stepped carefully over
the garbage-slicked pavement, checking the shadows behind

dumpsters and cans for suckers too fucked to have made it away
when Hobbes ran them out. But rats were the only things to be
seen, either ignoring Sebastian or eyeing him with stares too
much like speculation on something yet to be tasted. Nearing
the big iron door he noted the dim glow leaking through the
barred transom where Hobbes and Lizard had mounted a new
AC unit. The work was childishly sloppy: Corbitt could have
done a near-perfect job, but *that* niggerboy figured he was too
cocksucking pure to dirty his ebony fingers on whiteman's green.
What he needed was to have his flat little African nose shoved
in the shit of what is.

Reaching the door, Sebastian stood his board against the
wall and unzipped his jacket. The night was still warm, but the
AC had been turned off . . . just like Hobbes to worry over
every cocksucking penny! Sebastian had often wondered where
Hobbes stashed what had to be some major-time long. Not at
the apartment; Sebastian had gone over every inch of it more
than once, and he doubted if Hobbes would have kept it in a
bank where he'd need his mom as a co-signer. Sebastian fanned
his jacket to dry some of the sweat on his body. Could Hobbes
trust his mom enough to leave all that money with her? Sebastian
had never seen Hobbes's mother, but she lived in what was
probably the best security building in the nicest part of the hood.
Sebastian frowned and fired a Kool, wishing it was something
else. He noticed a Collector warning freshly sprayed on the wall
. . . for all the good it would do. The job was too sloppy for
Lactameon; probably Bilal or Stacy. He scowled: those cocksuckers had a payback coming even if Hobbes didn't have the
ice to do it. Sebastian stroked the Uzi's short barrel with a finger. It wouldn't take much to set up. The Leopards wouldn't
have any, but it wouldn't be hard to find some dudes who
would . . . maybe those niggers who had kicked Gilligan. He
frowned again: that would take green. Shit, he could do it himself; catch the Collectors some night at the clubhouse when they
were drunk. But that would be almost too easy. A real ice-quality
payback should be something you knew was coming but that
you had no power to stop. And that came back to money again.
He fingered the supple black leather of his jacket: almost four
bills. He was spending way too much, especially since he had
to pay the full retail price for rock to keep Hobbes from finding

out he was smoking it. But the stuff helped him think . . . because he *used* it to think with instead of just getting fucked-up like those other suckers. Well, he didn't need any more clothes, and he could let his hair grow a little. If he took a clue from Hobbes and was more careful with his green, maybe in a month he'd have enough to start teaching these niggers what time it was in the hood.

Sebastian flipped away his Kool, then pounded on the door with his fist. Hobbes's voice came faint through the heavy plates.

"Sabby?"

Sebastian scowled again; Hobbes would never learn. "Yeah."

A few moments later came the metallic scrape of the bar being lifted. Hobbes pulled the door open. Sebastian slipped quickly inside, his eyes shying from the other boy's but carefully scoping the room. Old couches and chairs now filled the main area, and the floor was mostly covered with pieces of carpet. Several battered old table lamps had been placed here and there to give a more laid-back light, but they were off now and the big ceiling bulb hurt Sebastian's eyes. The dusty tang of crack smoke hung heavy in the air, along with the bitter scent of kid-sweat and the sour stink of puke. The plank partition door stood open, revealing an old kitchen table and rusty chrome chair. A cigarette smoldered in a Mickeys cap ashtray beside a small pile of money that Hobbes had probably been counting. A forty-ouncer of Colt stood near it. Sebastian took another look at the table. It should have been loaded with bottles and packets of product, but except for a few empty vials, a Kool pack, and a magazine, it was bare.

"Sorry I'm late, man," said Sebastian. He pointed to the selling room. "Musta had a kickin day, huh?"

The house was still warm, and Hobbes had his shirt off. He yawned and stretched and scratched at his armpit. "Kinda like one of them sell-to-the-bare-walls sales. Takin a shower, was ya?"

Sebastian turned quickly, his eyes flicking to Hobbes's but there seemed to be no hidden meaning in the words. Sebastian noted the big .44 tucked in the back of Hobbes's jeans. "Yeah. I didn't hear the little shit knockin."

Sebastian walked into the selling-room, checking the empty

table again, then looking at the stack of money. "This place doin a lot better'n down by the tracks."

Hobbes closed the front door and dropped the bar, then came into the selling-room and sat down in the chair. He laid the .44 on the tabletop and picked up the bottle, taking a couple of swallows and watching while Sebastian counted the wrinkled kid-money.

"All them poor little suckas wantin is some respect, man." Hobbes sighed and set the bottle back on the table. "Don't get none from their folks or their teachers. For sure don't get none from the white world. So, who they gonna call? Ain't that a bitch." Hobbes glanced down at himself, then patted his stomach. "Gettin old, sweetheart. Gettin fat an lazy an sick out the asshole of this whole great big donkey show."

"Huh?" Sebastian laid down the last bill. "Shit, man, you only fourteen."

Hobbes took the Kool from the bottlecap and sucked a big hit, then let the smoke trickle from his nose. "Ain't the years, sweetheart, it the miles. I *feel* old, man." He smiled a little. "I like to be a kid once, fore I die." His smile faded, and he held out a hand. "Let's see the gun, Sabby."

Sebastian hesitated. "Shit, Hobbes, I ain't shot no more of your bullets. Swear to God, man. Don't you fuckin trust nobody?"

Hobbes's smile reappeared for a moment. "That one of the major things you miss, not bein a kid." He crooked a finger on his outstretched hand. "The gun, man."

Reluctantly, Sebastian put the big black pistol into Hobbes's brown palm. Instead of pulling the clip, Hobbes just laid the gun on the table. "Go an snag yourself a forty-dog, Sabby."

Sebastian gave Hobbes a long look, but then went back into the main room and took a bottle from the fridge. Hobbes was kicked-back in the chair when Sebastian returned, one leg crossed over the other, one arm resting on the tabletop, the cigarette held between bony fingers. Sebastian stopped in the doorway. A chill ran through him despite the room's warmth. Hobbes's casual pose was also the gunfighter position, facing the door, his fingers an inch from the big .44, and the gun pointed ready to grab. Then, Sebastian relaxed a little: Hobbes always sat that way.

"Um . . . so, somethin up, Hobbes?"

Hobbes's muddy eyes were half closed. He yawned, looking like a slightly drunk fourteen-year-old. "Chill, homes. I know y'all been smokin. A lot. Figure I just ride into town on a truckload of watermelons or somethin? Beat the shit out me why Tam cover your ass with that ole soap-in-the-eyes bullshit. Hell, I don't give a fuck no more. I just figure you was smarter'n the rest of these suckas."

Sebastian's eyes narrowed. "Why? Cause I'm half-white?"

Hobbes sighed and shook his head. "Shit, man, don't go draggin your goddamn color into ever fuckin thing. My mom tole me this ole Jamaican sayin, one time . . . y'all wouldn't worry so much what other people think of you if you knew how seldom they do."

Carefully, Sebastian uncapped the bottle and took a drink. "I'm gettin way sick of stupid black sayins, man. You got somethin to tell me, do it in English. I don't understand no cocksuckin Swahili."

Hobbes regarded the golden boy a moment, his eyes still half-shut. Then he crushed out his Kool and reached for his old denim jacket, which lay in a heap on the floor. He pulled a small, bright-colored folder from a pocket and held it out to Sebastian. "The whiteman teach y'all readin, man. Time I think if we ever had the balls to do more of it, just might turn into whitey's biggest mistake." He smiled. "Wouldn't that be a bitch?"

Shifting the bottle to his other hand, Sebastian took the folder and lifted the flap with a finger. He'd never seen airplane tickets before, but it wasn't hard to figure them out . . . two, to Jamaica, one way.

Hobbes yawned again, though Sebastian could feel his eyes watching carefully. "My mom got some cousins way back in the hills. Ganja give me headaches, but I figure I make a real good Rastamon anyhow."

Sudden fury shot through Sebastian. He almost crumpled the folder in his hand. But he kept his voice steady and low. "You musta known you was gonna do this a long time ago, man. So, why did you go to all the shit of openin this place?"

Hobbes shrugged. "Let's just say I always knowed I was gonna do it, *someday*. Shit, maybe I just didn't want them Collectors figurin it was them run my ass out the hood." Hobbes sighed again. "Or, maybe business been so fuckin good it startin to make me nervous. Seem like to me the best way to survive a war is to be somewheres else when it start. If that ain't a black sayin, it sure the fuck oughta be."

Sebastian glanced around. "So, what about all this, man?"

Hobbes shrugged once more. "Rent due tomorrow. Three bills." He shifted his hand slightly away from the gun to finger the stack of money. "Had sorta a goin-out-business sale today. Spect y'all could lay in some product yourself."

"I ain't got that kinda green, Hobbes."

"Shoulda been savin by for a rainy day, sweetheart."

"Um . . . could you front me some, Hobbes? Just to get started? Shit, I pay you back . . . send it to you in Jamaica. Shit, they gotta have mail there, even in the jungle."

Hobbes laughed. "Now y'all really makin me feel old, man. Yo. Ain't nobody give *this* nigga no business loan."

"You just don't trust me!"

"Only a fool trust a crack-sucka, an I didn't live this long by bein a fool, Sabby."

Sebastian's eyes flicked to the Uzi near Hobbes's elbow. "Let me keep that, Hobbes! Swear to God I pay you for it! You . . . you can't take guns on a airplane!"

Hobbes grinned. "Figure I give ole Bilal somethin to member me by. Dudes like them Collectors ain't gonna have many options when the war start."

Again, Sebastian almost crumpled the ticket folder, and again he fought to keep his voice low. "You sold out, man."

Hobbes's eyes saddened for a moment. "Yeah. I sold out a long time ago, but I ain't makin no excuses to justify my ass. Funny, could be that poor sucka Corbitt who start me thinkin I just ain't havin no more. Dude like him almost make y'all proud to be black. Wrong sorta 'tude for a crack dealer, sweetheart." Hobbes held out his hand for the tickets.

Sebastian was ready. He whipped up the forty-ounce bottle and swung it with all of his strength. In the movies, bottles always broke over somebody's head. This wasn't a movie. There was a thunk as the big bottle hit the side of Hobbes's skull. Colt spewed in amber foam over Hobbes's lanky brown body as he crashed to the floor. Sebastian dropped the bottle, and it did break then, shattering on the concrete beside Hobbes's head.

Hobbes still moved, moaning a little, one hand reaching to clutch at nothing. Sebastian leaped to the table, grabbing the Uzi and shoving the fire-switch all the way forward to A. Twisting around, he aimed the gun down with both hands, then jerked hard on the trigger.

No gangstuh movie could ever give you the *feel* of a killing. The big gun bucked in Sebastian's hands, wrenching his wrists. The long burst of full-auto fire ripped a ruby trail across Hobbes's muddy-brown chest. Bright blood sprayed upward, spattering hot on Sebastian's face. Hobbes's body twisted and arched in agony as the bullets tore into him. Concrete chips and ricochets sputted and screamed in all directions. Then the gun clacked empty, smoke spiraling up from its muzzle. For a long moment Sebastian stared down at what he'd done. The bitter gunsmoke burned his nostrils and made his eyes water. His mouth went salty with the coppery bite of fresh blood. Hobbes's eyes were open, but their stare went off in some distant direction, even though the strong fourteen-year-old body still quivered and fought to hold on.

The echoes of the gunfire seemed amped inside Sebastian's own skull. His head jerked up. He stared wildly around, suddenly sure that someone had heard. His eyes found the ladder and focused on it. The gun slipped warm from his fingers and clattered on the floor. He had to get out of this place! Leaping over Hobbes's body, feet slipping in the spreading pool of blood, Sebastian scrambled to the ladder and frantically climbed the wooden rungs, slamming the trapdoor open with his shoulder. Once on the roof, he raced to the iron vent pipe and flung himself onto it, clutching and kicking his way up toward escape. His jeans cuff caught on a bracket bolt. He almost screamed, arm muscles standing out stark as he yanked himself upward and tore the cuff loose.

And then he stopped climbing. It seemed a surprise to find himself clinging to cold iron a floor and a half above the crack house. It was more of a surprise to find tears streaming hot down his face. He hung there, panting, sobbing, and shaking, feeling his heart hammering in his chest. Slowly, he became aware of the usual city-night sounds . . . a siren in the distance, but heading away, the dim drone of traffic off toward the Bay Bridge. He looked down. Little wisps of gunsmoke were drifting up through the open trapdoor, wavering in the golden glow from below. Sebastian sniffled, feeling snot running warm over his lips but unable to let go his grip to wipe his nose. Cautiously, he let himself slip downward to the roof, then crossed to the front parapet and peered down the alley. There was nothing going on except what passed for silence in the city. Sweat was drying chill on his body. He wiped his nose with his sleeve and felt the cool stickiness of Hobbes's blood. His tongue ran over his lips, tasting.

Sebastian took one more look down the shadowy alley, then went to the trapdoor and crouched, staring in. What a motherfucking mess! That was almost funny . . . like Hobbes's last joke. Fuck him! "Suck my dick, niggerboy!" Sebastian called. Hobbes didn't move . . . why had he expected him to?

Sitting down with his legs dangling through the opening, Sebastian took out his pipe and loaded it. The shit was gone way too soon, but then it always was. Carefully, he eased onto the ladder. Halfway to the floor he stopped and looked over his shoulder. "You're dead, nigger!"

Descending the rest of the way, Sebastian stood by the ladder and studied the still form on the bloody concrete a long time. There were stories about dead people sitting up in their coffins. Sebastian pulled the pipe from his pocket again, darting glances at Hobbes while he loaded and fired it. The crackle seemed loud in the stillness. Slowly, Sebastian moved to the body and crouched, ready to leap away. Then he eased out a hand and touched Hobbes's shoulder, surprised to find it still warm. Sucking another hit from the pipe, he pressed his palm to Hobbes's chest. Nothing. His fingers came back bloody. He brought them to his lips, tasting. Africans ate lions to make them strong and brave.

Still crouching, Sebastian crossed his arms over his knees and gazed at the dead boy. Hobbes's mother would let him in. All he had to do was say her son had been hurt. Maybe he'd take a little piece along to show her just how bad her son had been hurt.

"So, um, what da next thing, Corbitt?"

Corbitt zipped up his jacket against the cold wind blowing down the street, then turned to Ethan walking beside him. "What you meanin, little brother?"

"Um . . . like, when y'all goin home, man? I mean, fo sho I not wantin ya to, but it been three days since your letter come, an you gots da money now."

Corbitt glanced down into the little boy's eyes; one tiger-tawny, one smoky blue. Both seemed uncertain and sad. Corbitt sighed, cupping his hands around his lighter to fire Ethan's cigarette and then his own. "Onliest next-thing I gots on my mind right now be checkin out that skateboard y'all tell me about. Ain't no better way of gettin round, an it half past time y'all be learnin to ride for your ownself."

Ethan's face brightened in the shadow of his shirt cowl. "Shit yeah! An it be way-easy now I gots my goddamn 'ception back!" He giggled. "Maaaan, y'all been da bestest thing ever happen to me in my whole motherfuckin life, Corbitt! Shit, here I be gettin fatter'n hell, my dick startin to work, an I gots both my eyes again!" He peered up at Corbitt. "But, um, y'all thinkin bout somethin sides dat board, man. Y'all gots dat *look*."

Corbitt blew smoke and pocketed his lighter. "Now, what y'all tellin me, look?"

Ethan grinned. "Yo! Don't try an smoke your own little brother, man. Y'all knows what I be tellin ya. It dat dere selfsame look you get when you be seein somethin what only you or Tam can see. It dat . . . Afrosippi kinda look. Um, y'all figure you could teach me dat too?"

Corbitt slipped his hands into his jacket pockets as he and Ethan rounded a corner and met the wind head-on. "Mmm. I think y'already gots it, little brother. Just maybe y'all ain't had no chance for tryin it out yet." He smiled. "Like comin. But, seem like to me, just bein able to see when I doin it show you gots the selfsame power."

Ethan's sweatshirt was a score from the Center. It would probably have come close to fitting Lactameon. Its tail and sleeves hung below Ethan's knees. Clasping his hands in front of him, trudging along with the hood hiding his head, he looked like either a miniature monk or Death's youngest apprentice. "Shit yeah. Dat logical."

They reached the pawnshop window, and Corbitt pressed his nose to the grime-coated glass. The whole day had been overcast and windy, and now nearing sunset there was little light left. A streetlamp had already come on nearby, and its rays reflecting from the window made it hard to see the cluttered collection of junk inside. Corbitt searched the shadows for the skateboard Ethan had told him about. With the prices the old man charged it hardly seemed likely that it would have already been sold.

Ethan jumped up and pointed. "Dere, man! Way da fuck in da back!"

Corbitt blinked in the deepening dusk, expecting some ancient tank-like antique like the old Variflex Lactameon rode. But he saw a sleek, radical shape somehow defiled by being used to display a green-crusted trumpet. Corbitt studied the deck with a frown, feeling a twinge that might not have been *déjà vu* but was too close to call. "Mmm. Best we go in an find out how much he be wantin for it."

Just a single small bulb burned in the center of the pawnshop's ceiling. Its yellow glow threw weirdly shaped shadows among the shelved and piled merchandise filling the room. Things suspended on strings stirred in the wind as the boys entered. A saxophone's shadow wavered on the wall like a prehistoric lizard-bat. The cashier's cage was shrouded in deeper darkness as if the old man had no use for light except as a courtesy to customers. From behind rusty bars came a dry, raspy chuckle. "What shakin, little man? Come back for a trade-in?"

As he had been when they'd come in to buy Ethan's eye, Corbitt was reluctant to get near the man, but Ethan strutted right back to the high counter and stared up, pointing with a hand hidden in his sleeve. "We wanna scope dat new board y'all gots in da window dere."

Again, the dusty chuckle. "Word go round fast. Just took it in yesterday. Well, come closer, little man. How the world lookin to you these days?"

Corbitt caught himself tensing as a bony pair of claws reached through the bars and turned back Ethan's hood. Yet, there was a curious gentleness in the touch, and Corbitt relaxed. Ethan's expression was an unguarded grin. "I can see now!"

The old man laughed. "In the kingdom of the blind, son, they make you a prince."

Corbitt approached the cage as close as he cared to. "Um, sir? If y'all just take that board in yesterday, don't that mean you can't be sellin it yet?"

Corbitt felt unseen eyes scanning him. Then came a shadowy shrug.

"That nigger ain't comin back. Forty-two years in this business give you a feel for losers. Y'all go have a look, boy. Might be, you on your way up."

Going to the front window, Corbitt set the trumpet aside and picked up the skateboard. It was a hard-ridden Sword and Skull. Boards were probably the most personalized possession a kid could own. Every sticker or decal or hand-drawn design that went under a deck reflected a kid's own ideas and dreams. There were stickers naming the things you hoped for, or at least the stuff you could afford, and stickers for your music and your radio station. If you had the board long enough there would be stickers over stickers as your hopes and dreams were shaped and changed by the world around you. It didn't take any magic to read a kid's life from the underside of his board. Corbitt turned the deck over. The downside was painted totally black.

Ethan appeared at Corbitt's elbow, a small shadow among shadows. "Shit!" Ethan whispered. "Dat Silver's board!"

Gripping the front truck, Corbitt carried the skateboard to the cashier's cage. "How much?"

"Depend. Y'all gonna try an jew me down like you done with your little friend's eye?"

"No."

A grin appeared in the gloom like the storybook cat's. "Fifty dollars. No tax. You buyin a genuine piece of ghetto history there, boy."

Corbitt dug in his pocket and slapped three twenties on old wood worn shiny from the passing of paper. He stepped closer. "I want that dollar back too. Y'all know so much, y'all be knowin which one."

The old man cocked his head for a second, then nodded. "Mmm. We just call that your rightful change."

Ethan stayed quiet as he followed Corbitt out onto the street. Night had come, but the wind still sighed in gusts through the gutters and sent paper scuttering along the sidewalks. A beer can rolled past with a faint hollow clatter. Corbitt turned up his jacket collar. "Most smell like rain. I never figure it do that in California summertime."

Ethan flipped the hood back over his head. "Maybe it cause of all dem stupid white motherfuckas paintin dere houses green."

"What? Oh. Well, maybe that pretty close to the truth, little brother. But, who tell you that?"

"Beamer. He pretty smart for a crack baby, huh?"

"Mmm. Just wish he stop workin for a crack dealer. He be wantin so bad to come into the Center, an y'all can tell how Chad was wantin to let him in. I hear Toni gots her baby back now, an Miz Davis helpin her an Tam with it."

"Yeah. But Beamer be given 'em all da money he can."

"Well, still feel like rain comin on, little brother. Figure we best be cribbin at the Center tonight? Don't want y'all catchin cold."

Ethan tapped his blue eye with his little finger. "Uh-uh. Member how dem cocksuckin pigs scope us dere last night? I seen 'em tryin to get some 411 out Chad. Yo, maybe we motor past Beamer's. Cold night mean he gonna be hangin by da boiler so's his fucked-up dad don't lose his job."

A newspaper page skittered past like a little ghost late for a haunting. Ethan dodged out of its way. "C'mon, Corbitt. Um, ain't y'all gonna cruise your new ride?"

Corbitt slipped one hand into his jacket pocket. "Ain't

rightly mine, little brother. I be givin it back to Silver when I seein him again."

Ethan shook his head. "Maaaan, it gonna take me a b'zillion years fore I unnerstand all dat Afrosippi shit."

Corbitt smiled, tucking the board under his arm so he could get his other hand out of the cold. "Mmm, Maybe Tam write that there book he been talkin bout: *The Young African's Guide to Understandin Nigger Boys*."

"Do me no good, till I learn to read."

The boys walked a block of blustery darkness, then Ethan cut into a trash-choked lot where dry weeds festooned with old paper rippled and hissed in the wind. Corbitt followed Ethan's miniature Grim Reaper shape across a shaky plank bridge over a ditch full of muck, and then through a gap-toothed board fence and down a passage between two burned-out buildings. They emerged on a lightless street that reminded Corbitt of an old black-and-white movie of World War Two London. Most of this block seemed to be nothing more than weed-grown mountains of brick and concrete. They passed a faded old sign that swayed and creaked on its remaining post. About the only words still readable were REDEVELOPMENT PROJECT and something that looked like FEDERAL FUNDS. The rest of the street looked like a scrapyard used for artillery practice. Corbitt stared around, fascinated. "This here make Tam's hood seem like the Emerald City of Oz!"

"I seen dat movie. It where dey gots different-color horses."

Corbitt glanced down at the small hooded figure trudging against the wind. "Um, I know it prob'ly ain't cool to be askin, but don't y'all *never* go home?"

Ethan hesitated, then pointed ahead to a trio of buildings where only the one in the middle showed lights. "Beamer's dere where my mom an dad live. Second floor, front. Dey been . . . sick. Sorta."

Corbitt raised his eyes, slitting them against the dust and grit slicing the air. Two third-story windows showed dim yellow light, and one on the ground floor glowed sickish pink from a fluorescent behind its boards, but the whole second level was dark. Ethan stopped, pulling back his hood and staring up. Corbitt saw something that looked like fear on the little boy's face.

"Um, spect they gone out, Ethan? Maybe to a movie or somethin?"

"Dey never go nowhere!" Ethan broke into a run, dashing up the middle building's crumbling steps and digging in his pocket as he reached the landing on top. The security gate was a nigger-rigged thing of rusty pipe and old wire mesh. Ethan cursed as he wrenched and rattled the key in the lock before it reluctantly opened. The inner door might have once been varnished oak, though now it was sheathed in spray-painted plywood. Again, Ethan fought with the lock before it finally surrendered.

Clutching Silver's board, Corbitt followed Ethan into a stinking hallway where the only light was the pinkish fluorescent seeping through a planked-over transom. He had already seen too many such buildings to pay much attention to the trash or the smell or the free-roaming rats. But he felt fear in the air, and wasn't sure if it came from Ethan or himself. The stairway was treacherous with loose treads and no banister, yet Ethan leaped the steps two at a time toward the blackness that waited above. The sound of the little boy's breath was the only thing that kept Corbitt from crashing into him when he reached the second-floor hall. A small hand, cold and sweaty, gripped his own.

"Stay chill!" Ethan hissed. He pulled out his box knife. "Keep your ass 'hind me!"

Corbitt shivered, feeling a rat scuttle over his feet. Rap music thumped from the third floor above. His eyes were slowly adapting to the darkness, and he noticed a faint glow coming from down toward the front of the building. It wasn't much more than a paler shade of black, but seemed the right size and shape for a doorway.

"What goin on?" whispered Corbitt, digging in his pocket for his own blade.

"Dat my mom and dad's 'partment down dere. Da door open, see? Sometimes dese bad suckas come . . . for da 'lectricity bill. I go first. Keep your hand on my shoulder, okay?"

Army knife ready, Corbitt shifted Silver's skateboard under his arm and grasped Ethan's shoulder with his other hand. He followed the little boy along the narrow path remaining down the middle of the trash-choked hall. Overhead, the rap sounds stopped for a moment then resumed to a different beat as the tape reversed. Corbitt's eyes had adjusted now, and he could see into the apartment's front room as he and Ethan neared the wide-open door. The pale glow came from two curtainless windows and cast a couch's lumpy shadow across a bare floor littered with the kind of household junk always left after a rummage sale. Reaching the doorway, the boys separated in unspoken agreement to flank it and peer in around the frame. Except for the couch and one battered chair there were no other furnishings remaining in the room.

Fear now showed stark on Ethan's face, but he slipped silently inside, clutching the little knife in a way that left no doubt he could and would use it. Cautiously he crossed to another open door and scanned the blackness beyond. Corbitt moved to the couch and looked around, tense and confused by this new next-thing feeling. A kitchen section off to one side showed empty shelves and open drawers. A faucet dripped soundlessly into the sink, and a big patch of pale paint revealed where the fridge had once stood. An empty Night Train bottle lay on the scarred countertop among a scattering of cigarette butts. Over beneath the front windows stood a rusty radiator, its silver paint peeling like kid-scabs. A wisp of sulphur-scented steam ghosted up from one of its fittings. In the room's far corner was a dirty little mattress pad that could have come off a patio lounge. Near it, a small cardboard box lay overturned and had spilled out a fan of more worthless junk. A few sheets of paper and what looked like some magazine pictures had been tacked to the wall above, but they hung limp and curled and Corbitt couldn't tell what they were.

Noting another open door, Corbitt eased to it, the skateboard gripped like a club. Pulling out his lighter, he held it over his head and flicked on the flame. There was only a small filthy bathroom with a clogged-up toilet and a torn shower curtain. Not even a sliver of soap had been left on the sink. The hard midnight face reflected in the cloudy cabinet mirror took a long moment to recognize itself. Something like a cigarette lay on the floor. Corbitt bent down but then straightened quickly when he saw it was a syringe barrel. His breath came out in a sigh. Pocketing the lighter, he turned to see Ethan entering the darkness of the other doorway. Corbitt crossed over, and one glance was enough to take in the empty bedroom with its ancient box-springs and mattress not worth the effort of hauling away. Here was another next-thing he could never have dreamed of.

Ethan walked slowly past Corbitt as if he wasn't there, to stand in the center of the empty apartment and stare around with eyes that seemed wide in wonder. For a second, Corbitt was sure the little boy would throw back his head and scream. A windowpane rattled as wind gusted outside. Small specks of glitter appeared on the glass; more than mist but less than real rain.

"Maybe they leave you a note somewheres."

Ethan's voice sounded worn-out. "Dey know I can't read."

That wasn't totally true, Corbitt knew. Ethan could have recognized the word love, if somebody had bothered to write it. The little boy half turned to face him. An eye glistened, but that was just glass. "It been four days since I seed Beamer. Dey knew we was homeys. If dere was somethin dey wanted me to know, dey woulda told him."

Ethan walked over to the mattress pad in the corner. Kneeling, he gently began pulling the papers off the wall. "Um, Corbitt? Dis my stuff. Wanna see?"

Corbitt came and sat beside the boy.

"Dese here some drawins I done when I was way little, man." Handing them to Corbitt, Ethan began picking up things that had spilled from the box. "Me an Beamer used to look at dese Turtle comics all da time. Maybe it was more fun cause we didn't know what dey was sayin. One time I was gonna collect dese cards, but dey too fuckin 'spensive for my ass. Check dis mini-Tonka truck, man. Shit, I had dat fuckin forever . . ."

One by one, Ethan gave Corbitt his things, each with its own little story, and, feeling like a fool, Corbitt could do nothing more than say something soft and meaningless and watch Ethan return them to the box until all his toys were put away.

"Make me a cigarette, Corbitt."

Corbitt pulled out his Top and rolled two smokes. "Spect we could spend the night here, little brother. Y'all could sleep in your own bed."

Ethan sucked smoke as Corbitt fired the lighter, then blew out a cloud. "I hate dis fuckin place, man. I always hated it.

Sometimes I almost think I didn't, but I did." Getting up, Ethan yanked the sweatshirt hood over his head. "C'mon, Corbitt, let's go down with Beamer."

Corbitt rose as Ethan headed for the door. "Um, don't y'all wanna be takin your stuff?"

"Da fuck for? It just little-kid shit!"

Ethan disappeared into the hallway. Corbitt considered a moment, then took Ethan's drawings from the box and folded them carefully into his pocket along with the wrinkled old dollar. Then he picked up Silver's skateboard and walked back up the hall. Ethan was waiting at the head of the stairs, one eye reflecting the cigarette ember. "Um . . . you figure it cause I didn't pay da 'lectric bill, man?"

Corbitt sighed. "No."

Together, the boys descended the squeaky staircase, then Ethan led Corbitt deeper into the building and finally pushed open a door at the end of the first-floor hallway. Dim light showed steep wooden steps leading down. Steamy wet warmth floated up from below. There were strange creaky sounds and a sinister hissing. Corbitt followed Ethan. At least this hell was warm.

Beamer was barefoot and clad only in the same ragged cutoffs he'd probably outgrown a good year before. He was standing, staring up at a panel of dusty-glassed gauges like some primitive bush boy scoping an airplane, yet his hand was sure as he reached for a valve and made some adjustment on the hissing boiler. There was a floor-shaking rumble like faraway thunder, and yellow flame flared behind long iron teeth. Beamer's face flashed pure happiness as he caught sight of Ethan and Corbitt. A few minutes later all three boys were sitting on a musty double-sized mattress beside the boiler, smoking Corbitt's cigarettes and sharing a bottle of Night Train.

Beamer looked infinitely sad as Ethan told of finding his mom and dad gone. But then he smiled a little and touched Ethan's shoulder. "I figure you gone away with 'em, homey. An I never see you again."

Ethan took a long pull from the bottle. "Dey wasn't never my parents, man. Dey fuckin lied. My real parents be in Africa somewheres."

Beamer nodded, his gentle brown eyes seeming to search

in some distant past. Old iron creaked, expanding with heat. Beamer glanced at the gauges, then a new sort of sadness came over his face. "Somebody kick Hobbes. Nobody seen him for three days, an Sabby been runnin the house like he own it himself. Then, Tam read in the paper this mornin bout some garbage truck driver find Hobbeses's body when he get to the dump. Pigs say Hobbes eat on bad by rats or somethin." Beamer's eyes hardened. "Sabby sayin it Hobbeses's own stupid fault . . . sayin Hobbes never had the ice for bein a dealer."

The rumbling boiler radiated waves of warmth. Corbitt slipped off his jacket and shoes. But now he shivered, staring into the shadows that surrounded the little island of light beneath the overhead bulb. Ice could mean a lot of things, but it didn't sound African. Once, Corbitt might have called Hobbes *street-smart* . . . but that was a term he'd seen only in newspapers or heard on TV; dreamed up by clueless white people to describe something they could never understand. In their world cops carried *batons* instead of clubs, and the beating of black people was done in the name of *violence suppression*. *Street-smart* might translate to niggerboy-smart, but that was only one more dead-end road for black kids to take. Sooner or later you always came to a river, and all the bridges were condemned. Mrs. Griffin had once read something from a book: *those who forget the past are condemned to repeat it*. But it was always white people who were first to preach about burying the past.

Corbitt sipped from the bottle, wondering why Hobbes's death should sadden him. Just fourteen years of some niggerboy's life eaten by rats and hauled to the dump. Even Bates couldn't have thought up a much better plan. Corbitt shivered again, wondering how Weylen liked seeing this future. It wasn't trying to be cool that had killed him; it was just being black in a time when white people could get away with murder by calling it something else. At least in 1951 black kids had known what color the enemy was.

Beamer was saying something about Sebastian buying from a white supplier back in his old neighborhood. Corbitt supposed that was logical; dealing directly with the source. It would have been simple to blame the golden boy's white half, but in the end anybody was only as black as they wanted to be.

A movement at the edge of the light caught Corbitt's eye.

He stiffened as the biggest rat he'd ever seen came strutting right up to Beamer. But Ethan just smiled. "Heeere's Roger!"

Beamer grinned, then made clicking sounds with his tongue, and the huge rat climbed across his bare leg and settled comfortably in his lap. It gave Corbitt a curious look, whiskers quivering as it sampled his scent. Ethan reached over and scratched behind its ears. "Yo! Dis here Roger, Prince of da Neitherworld."

It was good to see Ethan smile again. Cautiously, Corbitt offered his fingers for a sniff, then stroked the rat's gray-brown fur, surprised to find it so soft. "Um, how your baby doin, Beamer?"

"Toni gots it home now. I took her the crib an all the other stuff. Tam score a old buggy somewheres. We all goin to the park tomorrow mornin."

Corbitt pictured the scene in his mind. There was something that should scare the shit out of whitefolks.

"Course," Beamer went on, "we still ain't tagged him with a name yet. Tam say it gots to be somethin strong." Beamer's smile turned shy. "An somethin go good with Brown."

The rat yawned, showing long needle-teeth. *Benjamin* crossed Corbitt's mind, but he shoved it away.

"Calvin!"

Corbitt turned toward the rear of the basement where a section had been walled-off into a separate room. Light shone from a doorway, silhouetting a man-shape clad only in boxer shorts.

"Turn it up!"

Beamer gave the other boys that universal look of apology any kid offered his friends when bothered by parents. "Is up, dad. Way up."

The man-figure swayed in the doorway, grabbing the frame for support. "Goddamn you, boy! Don't smart-mouth me! I say, turn it up!"

"Turn it no higher, fool! It fuckin *blow* up!"

Corbitt tensed as the man stumbled toward them spewing out curses, but Beamer only looked resigned, and Ethan disgusted. The man lurched to a halt at the edge of the light, clutching a half-empty Night Train bottle and glaring down at the boys out of red-rimmed eyes. "What losers you drag in tonight, boy? Shit! Even the niggas won't have you!"

Beamer shrugged. "Go to sleep, Dad."

The man staggered closer. Corbitt's nose wrinkled at his scent. The man shook his head. "Even the niggas won't have you, boy."

Ethan stood up and shoved the dreadlocks away from his face. He might have been reciting an old magic formula. "I gots AIDS, an I gonna bite you." He drew back his lips in a snarl.

The man stumbled back as if slapped, but pointed once more at his son. "Even the niggas won't have you!"

Beamer sighed. "Night, Dad."

Meaningless curses flowed from the man as he returned to the room and slammed the door behind him. Beamer set the rat back on the floor and turned to Corbitt. "Um, sorry, man." He got up and twisted a valve on the boiler. The rumbling subsided and the flames flickered low behind the fire-door. Beamer watched as two gauge needles stopped climbing, and steadied. "Spose to do that by itself, but I guess it forget how."

Then, Corbitt heard a tapping sound. He peered into the shadows at the front of the basement. Someone outside was knocking on the glass of a small barred window. Beamer ran to the wall, jumping up on a box to look out of the high-set slit. "It Silver!"

Leaping down, Beamer dashed across the room and up the staircase. Corbitt glanced at Ethan, then picked up the skateboard. "Maybe that a good sign."

Ethan shrugged, watching the rat disappear into darkness. "Bout motherfuckin time!"

But Corbitt's smile faded as Silver came into the light. Despite the night's cold he wasn't wearing a jacket, and one strap of his dirty tank-top had slipped off his shoulder, revealing stark ridges of ribs below what had once been a tight-plated kid's chest. His midnight skin seemed the color of old truck tires. The shirt was supposed to be oversize anyway, but there was nothing cool in how it hung on him like old scarecrow clothes. The outline of a skull defied any denial behind his face. Beside him, Beamer's own skinny underfed frame looked like an ad for Iron Kids Bread. Silver sank shivering onto the mattress, clutching at the blanket that Beamer draped over his shoulders, and pressing close to the low-growling boiler. Beamer cranked the feed valve wide open again and the flames leaped and danced behind the fire-door.

Silver stayed huddled against the creaking iron for a few minutes. His eyes were the lusterless black of old telephones and seemed reluctant to meet the other boys'. Finally, Corbitt took Silver's cold hand and guided it gently through the motions of a shake, almost afraid to grip it too hard. Silver's teeth chattered when he tried to smile, and the sound sent a shiver along Corbitt's spine. The voice was worse; like the scrape of dead leaves in the wind.

"S . . . so this where the Africans hang?"

Beamer had been hovering near, darting glances at the gauge panel while his hands made helpless little moves. Now he knelt beside Silver and touched the boy's shoulder like a fragile thing. "Um . . . you stay here tonight, brother. Um . . . I make you some soup. Um . . . gots chicken gumbo."

Corbitt almost expected to hear the crackle of bone as Silver managed a smile. "S'cool, Beamer. But I ain't hungry."

Corbitt frowned, pressing the wine bottle, now warm, into Silver's hand. "Well, best y'all get your fool self hungry, brother! An right fuckin now! Shit, want me to walk up to KFC for you?"

The little ring glinted in Silver's nose as he turned to face Corbitt. The tiny spark that Corbitt caught in his eyes might have been only its reflection. A long, slender finger, mirror-image to Corbitt's, pointed to the skateboard. "You could always ride."

Corbitt laid the board in front of the other boy. "Ain't mine to be usin."

Silver stared at the board, lying deck-down and dull black. Finally, he pulled the blanket tighter around him. "Shit, brother, just keep it. I only sell it again. Make me feel even worse, thinkin what that old sucka burn your ass for it."

Corbitt shrugged. "Be my own ass to burn, brother. Sides, how y'all be a Collector, out your ride?"

Silver hunched his shoulders and stared into the flames. "Ain't no Collector no more. What I need that goddamn toy for?" Tilting up the bottle, he sucked down what was left in it.

Beamer had been splitting his attention between Silver and the boiler. Now he rose and turned down the valve once more. "Um . . . I snag us another bottle . . . an put on the soup."

Silver rolled the empty bottle in his palms, still staring into the flames. "I need somethin else, man. Why I come here."

Ethan had been rolling another cigarette. Now he looked up and curled back his lip. "Oh yeah! Don't take no motherfuckin magic to see dat comin!"

"Shush, man," Corbitt murmured.

"Well!"

Beamer shifted from one foot to the other like an uncertain child. "Um . . . I ain't gots no more what Hobbes was sellin, man. Sabby score some new shit. One dude tell me it fuck him up bad."

Silver shrugged, digging his pipe from a pocket. "All come from the same white suckas, don't it? Sides, figure anybody gonna come bustin down Sabby's door for a refund? Shit, he already set up tighter'n that house in *New Jack City!*"

Beamer glanced for a second at Corbitt, then sighed. "Okay. But, I gots to get paid, man. Sabby don't let me slide nobody no more."

Almost, Silver turned to Corbitt, but then raised his head and lifted his hands to his face. Corbitt had always been curious about the little ring, wondering if it had somehow been forged forever through Silver's nose. But there must have been some sort of joining because a few seconds later it lay gleaming in Silver's dark palm.

"You know it real, Beamer. Here."

Feeling miserable, Corbitt started to reach in his own pocket for money, but a small brassy hand clamped onto his wrist. Both Ethan's eyes were cold as he shook his head. Beamer looked unhappy, but took the ring and walked away into the shadows. Silver gave Corbitt a sudden stare of defiance.

"My folks out on the street now, man. No more worry bout the rent or eviction paper sent. Lucky niggas they are, got the freedom of their car. Ass-draggin stationwagon, but it kinda give 'em class, cause they be mobile Africans long as they got gas."

Corbitt stared back at the boy: he looked so different without the ring. Corbitt suddenly realized that he'd only seen two other faces like that in a lifetime . . . one in a dream, and one in a cloudy mirror upstairs. His slender fists clenched. "Goddammit! They love your stupid black ass, don't they?"

Silver shrugged. "I stole a twenty out my mom's coat yesterday. Coulda been her last twenty. Prob'ly was."

"That ain't what I askin you, fool!"

Silver turned away as Beamer came back with a little rock bottle that looked like it had been recycled many times. "Oh, get the fuck real, nigga. It gone."

Corbitt's anger faded. He watched as Silver took the bottle and began to load the pipe. "You . . . member things too, don't you?"

Silver paused with the pipe to his lips. "Not no more." His eyes met Corbitt's for a moment. "There was never enough of us to make no difference." He smiled as he lifted his lighter. "Don't ask me what that signify, cause I forgot a long time ago." Sucking deep, he closed his eyes and slumped back against the boiler. "Tell me that story again, brother . . . the African one . . . bout why crows don't sing."

A shiver ran through Silver's thin body, but his face looked peaceful. Corbitt lowered his eyes and slowly spun a wheel on the skateboard. "Long time ago, crows got their song stole away. Word say it took 'em a hundred years but they finally steal it back. Course, nobody know fo sho, cause crows be terrible liars. Y'all ask any crow today an they tell you they *can* sing, any ole time they be wantin to, cept their song so pretty it might just get stole all over again. Sides, since every crow know down deep in his heart he can sing, then why he be needin to prove it? But, best believe day gonna come when all them other stupid-ass birds wear out their own songs from screamin at each other in the treetops. Maybe then the crows sing for the world like they used to."

Ethan tugged at Corbitt's hand. "Um, but won't dey be ascared dem other sucka-birds try an roust it again?"

Corbitt smiled. "Maybe they be smart enough by then so's that don't happen."

A new scent came to Corbitt's nostrils. He jerked his head around. Silver still lay against the boiler, but his head had fallen back on the hot fire-door and the dead pipe had slipped from his fingers. Leaping to the boy, Corbitt pulled him away from the flames. The long body fell limp on the mattress. For an instant Corbitt could only stare down at his own wasted image. Then, Beamer yelled Silver's name, crouching over him, grabbing his shoulders and shaking him savagely. Beamer slapped Silver's face hard, and then again. Corbitt tore open the blanket and pressed his ear to Silver's chest.

Nothing.

Ethan scrambled to Corbitt's side. "Do dat thing, man! What you done me!"

But you had a heartbeat! Silver was dead; Corbitt knew that for certain without knowing how, and no wish on Earth would jump-start that worn-out body. Still, he went through the motions, stopping just long enough to look up at Beamer. "Call 911 or somethin! Fast!"

Beamer spread helpless hands. "Phone don't work!"

Corbitt closed his mouth over Silver's again and tried to force in life. From the corner of his eye he saw the slim chest expand, but that was only his own leftover life-force. Silver had gone and only a fool would want to call him back. Corbitt wondered, if he'd been watching, would he have seen the boy's spirit rise like in the old stories. Where was Silver now . . . pausing a moment to look down through three floors transparent as glass and laugh at the funny little niggas in the basement?

Corbitt's lips left the dead boy's. Slowly, he moved back and sat down beside the body. He picked up a mirror-image hand and held it.

"Um?" asked Ethan. "Should I cover his face with da blanket?"

Corbitt wiped tears, but smiled a little, looking up to the sooty rafters overhead. "Sho. Spect he like seein y'all do that."

Beamer sank down on the floor, pulling up his legs, burying his face on his arms, and sobbing. "I . . . didn't wanna sell him that shit! I don't wanna sell nobody that shit!"

Corbitt shook his head, laying Silver's hand down as Ethan drew up the blanket with a solemnness that was almost funny. "Options, man. It ain't your fault. I coulda stopped him . . . tonight. But I didn't. He had all seven. Ain't no magic can make you go on livin when you just don't want to no more."

Beamer brushed tears from his own cheeks. "Um . . . we gots to take him away, Corbitt. Pigs come. Slap my dad around. Happen ever time somebody die in this buildin."

Corbitt sighed. "Yeah. But, we can wait awhile." He pulled out his tobacco pouch and began rolling cigarettes. "How much for his ring, Beamer?"

Beamer dug in his pocket. "Um, here, Corbitt. Just take it."

Corbitt held the little circle of silver on his palm. Ethan came close and touched it gently with a fingertip. "Um, y'all gonna get dat put in, man? Miz Davis can do dat. She use ice so's it don't hurt much."

Corbitt glanced upward once more. The ring felt warm in his hand. He pulled out his knife and opened the punch blade. "Here, little brother. Y'all do the diggin for me." Corbitt sat back and lifted his chin as Ethan crouched close with the knife. Beamer winced as Ethan pushed and twisted the sharp-pointed punch through Corbitt's left nostril.

"Um . . . I snag us another bottle of Train. We gots lots."

Corbitt stayed still while Ethan's little brass fingers slipped the silver ring in and locked it in place. Then he wiped blood from his chin and fired a cigarette. "Maybe we best get Tam an the other Collectors."

Ethan cleaned Corbitt's knife on his jeans, then folded the blade and handed it back. "I go find Tam. He know where da other dudes be hangin."

Beamer looked uncertain. "Maybe they not come. He not one of 'em no more."

Corbitt blew smoke. "They come. A brother be more'n some ole K mart rag."

Ethan zipped up his sweatshirt and ran for the stairs. Beamer started for the basement apartment. Corbitt called, "Beamer? Y'all gots any candles?"

"Um . . . yeah. There some left over from Kwanzaa. Red, green, an black ones."

"Bring 'em, man." Corbitt pulled the last twenty from his pocket. "An, bring back enough of that Train for everbody."

While Beamer was gone, Corbitt turned the blanket down to Silver's waist. He picked up the crack pipe, opened the boiler's fire-door and threw it into the flames. Then he crossed Silver's hands on his chest and brushed back the boy's dirty hair with his fingers. A warrior's death deserved a warrior's rites, no matter the time and the place.

Lactameon was the first to come, the stairs creaking under his weight as he followed Ethan down. He wore his bandana over rain-sparkled hair and carried his old Variflex. His bulky black gangstuh coat couldn't be buttoned over his belly. Corbitt looked up from the three candle flames now burning beside Silver's head. His eyes widened slightly, seeing a whiteboy following Lactameon. Corbitt tried not to stare. The only white faces he'd seen in days were cops'. Then he recognized the boy who had been at the Center that first night. He wore Levi's and Nikes and a dirty gray sweatshirt, and carried a splintery Hammerhead. His long blond hair glistened like gold as he passed beneath the light bulb. He knelt with Lactameon at Silver's side.

Lactameon gazed at Silver a long time, then lifted his eyes to Corbitt's, flinching a little when he saw the fresh blood. "Thanks for doin this, man. Um, this Winfield. He a Leopard, but he knew Silver too."

Corbitt's ebony hand took the white one above Silver's body. Then he pointed to the box of bottles Beamer had brought. "Plenty for everybody, brother."

Ethan passed out the bottles and took one for himself. Beamer left for a minute then returned with a blaster and a handful of tapes. "Um . . . Silver like any of these, Tam?"

Lactameon took a swallow of Train, then slipped off his coat and sat down beside Winfield. He checked through the cassettes. "This one, man. Soul II Soul. Wind up the *African Dance* cut."

A short time later the other Collectors came down the stairs. Like Winfield and Lactameon, their hair sparkled with water-drops above wet bandanas and their jackets and jeans were damp from the rain. Bilal glanced once at the whiteboy, but then seemed to decide he wasn't really there. He took off his jacket and picked up a bottle. T.K. and Stacy did too. All flicked glances at Corbitt's bloody nose, but then sat down and fired Kools. Beamer slipped the tape into the deck and found the cut Tam had asked for. A simple African beat with no words throbbed out through the shadowy basement. Minutes went by in silence except for the pulse of the music. The boys sat in a circle around Silver's body. Bottles were lifted and cigarettes smoked. It was a time for coming together, like crows gathering in a tree until they could move with one purpose. Lactameon took another bandana from his pocket.

"Um, Bilal? Should I put this on Silver?"

Bilal considered a moment, then took the yellow cloth. "He don't need it no more." Bilal handed the bandana to Corbitt.

Corbitt hesitated a few seconds, then slipped it on his own head. Winfield glanced once at Bilal, then pulled a green bandana from his jeans and put it on. Bilal gave only a slight nod. T.K. frowned but said nothing. The music played on in a timeless rhythm. The boys drank wine, and smoked, and listened. Fingers tapped bottles, and shoulders moved slightly to the heavy bass beat. At last, Stacy spoke.

"What we do with him, Bilal? What I sayin is, his folks livin in their car. They just gots to give him to the whiteman."

Beamer was sitting a little ways out of the circle, near his blaster. "Um . . . the buildin next door mostly fall down, but there a way into the basement. Dirt floor there. Um . . . I gots two shovels."

Lactameon gazed at Silver's face, somehow peaceful in the candleglow. "Too bad we can't take him somewheres nice . . . with trees an shit."

T.K. shook his head. "Dude wouldn't know what to do in someplace like that."

"Be like buryin him with a bunch of rich white suckas," added Winfield.

Bilal glanced around at the other boys, then nodded. He took a long hit off his Kool. "Somethin gots to be done bout Sabby. Hobbes was one thing, but he only out for the green. Sabby *like* doin the whiteman's work."

Lactameon looked up as Ethan passed out a second round of bottles. "Now ain't the time for plannin more death, man. Tomorrow we figure what we gonna do bout Sabby." His eyes went to Corbitt for a moment, then shifted back to Silver.

The boiler rumbled and hissed. The African music throbbed on. Then, Corbitt got to his feet. If the other boys seemed surprised, he didn't care. He stripped off his T-shirt and slowly began to dance. He'd never danced before. He didn't know the moves, yet every movement he made seemed to fit its proper place. The music's beat was deep in his bones; a recording by

English black people, captured on Japanese tape and played now through Taiwanese speakers. Yet the meaning came clear as if Silver himself were pounding those drums. Corbitt's bare feet moved gracefully over the dusty concrete. The furnace flames flickered on his midnight-black skin. The other boys watched him in silence, their eyes first wide with what might have been wonder, then seeming to go distant in longing that was almost pain. The silver ring caught the firelight's gleam. A new trickle of blood ran down Corbitt's lips and dripped on his chest. His moves were still slow but somehow more confident as if he was remembering them one by one. Lactameon felt the pull; just as when Silver had danced. But, what was the logic in wishing?

Strangely, it was the whiteboy who first followed Corbitt; pulling his shoes off and then his shirt to move pale and slender in Corbitt's ebony shadow. His hair flashed gold fire in the furnace flames' glare. Ethan came next, his small body gleaming like fierce burnished brass, his yellow-brown dreadlocks twisting and flying, somehow more savage than the two bigger boys he danced in between. Then Stacy, awkward at first but learning the steps, and Bilal, all hardness and muscle but blinking back tears. T.K. was moves with a fury, hating what he couldn't name and dancing because he couldn't kill what he hated. Then Beamer, seeming to do what only came natural. The music throbbed on, the beat never changing. A flute joined the drums like an unseen singer. The boys moved faster, freer, their bodies shining with sweat, shifting and sliding between one another but always reforming the circle around Silver. Only Lactameon remained on the mattress, watching the others and sharing their pain with no way to lessen his own.

Corbitt passed near to him, his eyes far away. "It be in you," he murmured. "The next-thing."

Lactameon looked up. "I . . . can't."

Stacy moved by. "Now we know where to stick the knife, brother."

And then the blond boy. "This just never happen again, man."

T.K. "An I figured you had balls!"

And Bilal. "Silver was your brother."

Finally came Ethan. "Dis a magic thing!"

And then Lactameon was on his feet, kicking off his shoes

and stripping off his shirt. Corbitt spun and leaped, tasting blood and sweat that seemed more than his own. The other boys followed him, learning his moves. For only an instant he saw them as the white world would . . . foolish children who would never be tamed. Some would die for their defiance, and all would be punished for something that was no sin in the eyes of God. But, the next-thing would come . . . someday . . . when all niggers became Africans once more.

13

"Peace, brother. Wanna shoot some hoops?"

Corbitt looked up. *You entirely the wrong color to be talkin peace to me, boy!* The kid was about his own age, dressed only in shorts and big Cons. He was pudgy and pale, with so many freckles on his face, chest, and arms that Corbitt wondered why he didn't just take a brown Magic Marker and connect them all together for a Toby-like tan. Except for the fiery mane hanging midway down his back and the Marlboro in his mouth he could have come straight off one of those Norman Rockwell calendars the Starkville drugstore gave away . . . the all-American children who were never, ever black.

So this was the enemy. Corbitt noted the scuffed Wilson basketball balanced on freckle-specked fingers, the clear emerald eyes, and the unguarded smile. Corbitt felt the boy's friendliness. Why not? This kid could afford to be open and innocent and nice to niggers . . . *here.* After all, this was his world; this clean, almost sweet-smelling neighborhood park, with its carefully tended garbage-free grass, gold gravel paths, and a sparkling fountain in a pond that looked clear enough to drink from. There were lots of laughing white children, big and round and butterball-muscled, with nothing more important on their minds than play.

If there was dealing here, Corbitt hadn't seen it going on, though he'd been watching as if through Ethan's experienced eyes. But all he'd noticed so far were the cops in their cruisers watching him back. There would be no spooks haunting *this* park after the sun went down, and Corbitt suspected that the slightest rumor of rock in this neighborhood would bring in a SWAT team armed with tanks and flame-throwers. Still, this white child was right in a way . . . Corbitt had found peace in this place, even if it wasn't meant for him. Sitting on a bench in the afternoon sunlight he was stealing all he could before somebody noticed, like a crow in a songbird sanctuary.

Nearby was a sandbox looking pure as new snow, where little kids played with big Tonkas. Two chubby blond boys had constructed a sandcastle, but were now busy butting it down with a dumptruck. Another round-tummied boy-child, maybe four, had toddled over and stared up at Corbitt a long time before finally demanding to have his shoe tied as if that were the natural order of things. Corbitt had done it without knowing why. The little kid had touched Silver's ring when Corbitt bent down, and said something that sounded like "owie."

That was true enough; but the pain seemed to serve as a reminder of what Corbitt was. He didn't feel much like returning the freckled dude's friendliness, and there had been damn few times in his life when he'd willingly shot hoops with anyone. A new kind of anger flared for a second, and his hand went to the pocket that held Silver's box knife. He had a strange sort of vision . . . of forcing this clueless marshmallow onto a bus and during that all too short ride to an alternate universe telling him every sick, sad, and scary detail of what passed for childhood twenty minutes away. He wondered what emotion those green eyes might show if he told of Hobbes's mother found shot to death, or if he said he was sitting here trying to plan what the white world would call a gang murder because there were no other options.

Likely enough this whiteboy had been peacefully asleep in a bed with clean sheets when Silver's worn-out body was being wrapped in a motheaten old indian blanket and laid in a hole to be buried beneath the filth that passed for dirt in the ghetto. Those images were burned forever in Corbitt's mind: the damp, stinking basement of the half-collapsed building where brick walls wept slime that was probably sewer, the flickering stumps of candles and how their feeble flames reflected in the eyes of the nearly naked boys whose bodies were streaked with Silver's gravedirt. And above all Corbitt could still feel the tremendous crumbling mass of the structure overhead, the awesome rotten *weight* of the thing that brooded over the digging, the childish little ceremony, and the filling of the grave. Only Corbitt had seemed aware that the whole thing was ready to fall any moment and bury them all. Logic said it should have already fallen because he could see nothing solid remaining to hold it up. Yet, he'd forced himself against every instinct to be the last to leave, even stopping once to look back in the darkness where Silver's only headstone was a pile of trash to conceal his crime of living and dying a black boy.

Later, there had been a kind of war council at the Collectors' clubhouse. Rumors in the hood . . . what Corbitt had learned to call word . . . hinted at things Sebastian had done or might be planning to do. Stacy's cousin had seen the golden boy uptown talking to an older white kid in a new four-by-four. Some little Leopard had told Lactameon that Sebastian came cruising through their hood in the back of an old blue Camaro with two gangstuh dudes in serious gear. Even in this place where killing was common and Death worked overtime there was a lot of speculation on what had happened to Hobbes and his mother. Naturally there was no proof, but then in a system where the law could even accuse a camera of lying, how much proof did anyone need? Silver was dead, that was proven beyond the ghost of a doubt. Maybe Sebastian hadn't actually put a gun to his head and pulled the trigger, but the final result was the same. More kids would die, and Sebastian would be six out of seven responsible . . . unless you believed that close only counted in horseshoes and hand-grenades. Was it black-on-black crime when Africans were forced to evolve their own justice? What would have been Bates's punishment under white law for killing Weylen? Something had to be done, but Sebastian had his guns and his soldiers and spent most of his time locked safe behind his big iron door.

Only seconds had passed, and the freckle-face dude was still smiling. Corbitt wondered if this boy could be called one out of seven with Silver's death. He glanced around the pretty little park again: just what *was* holding this whole thing up? But a real smile was like rabies. Corbitt's eyes returned to the white-boy, catching a glint of gold in the dude's left earlobe . . . why would he want to suffer an owie? A rebel without a clue? Corbitt felt his own smile melting his mask. The whiteboy wasn't trying to be politically correct, he just wanted someone to shoot some hoops with. Unfocused rage was nothing but a dead short that drained your batteries while producing no power. A laser beam tightened on target could burn through steel, but that same energy spread wide on everything in sight was as harmless as a flashlight.

The boy had seen Corbitt's hand slip to his pocket. He pulled a Marlboro pack from his shorts. "Here, bro, burn one of mine."

Corbitt nodded and took a cigarette. The whiteboy plopped down beside him and produced a blue Bic. "I'm Troy."

Course you is, an I be Leroy. The voice in Corbitt's mind had been Silver's. His smile took on its V for a moment. "Corbitt."

"That African, man?"

"I don't think so."

"Well, you wanna shoot?"

"Well, I ain't very good at it."

"Shit, man, I ain't either, but it's only a game."

Only a game, but they never explain. Two kids in a park, a light and a dark. The evil art is to keep them apart, cause hate don't rate when they can relate.

"Sho nuff." Corbitt picked up Silver's skateboard and followed the whiteboy toward the courts. It would be cool just being a kid for a while. Passing the sandbox, he noticed again the little boys battering down the sandcastle with their dump-truck. Children didn't know what couldn't be done. Left to themselves all their ideas were original. Troy was pretty piss-poor at basketball, but Corbitt let him win.

14

Corbitt waited behind Bilal, who was checking the street beyond the alley entrance. It was hours past midnight, and fog swirled like a cottonwool river between the buildings, its substance seeming to suck up the smells of garbage and rot and spread them like slime over everything living or dead. The air clung clotted and thick in Corbitt's lungs. It felt like he was trying to breathe maggots.

Despite the damp cold, Bilal wore only a faded black T-shirt. His hard-muscled arms glistened in the dimness. Ethan was draped in his huge hooded sweatshirt, and T.K. and Stacy wore similar shirts. Lactameon was clad in his usual tank-top that hardly covered half of him. With his huge breasts and belly he looked like a pissed-off black Buddha. A sixth figure stood in the fat boy's shadow: Winfield, wearing ragged jeans and threadbare Levi's jacket. Lactameon was no longer the gang mascot. The Collectors had bought Winfield from the Leopards. Corbitt still wasn't sure exactly how you went about buying a kid these days, or what the going rate was, but Ethan had told him the Leopards would be getting monthlies for a long time to come. The blond boy seemed happy with his new owners.

Fog droplets glittered in all the boys' hair, and Winfield's pale mop seemed to glow in the dark. A chill breeze shifted the fog, and Corbitt shivered even in his leather jacket. Stacy pulled a hardpack of Kools from his pocket and passed them around while Bilal continued scanning the territory ahead. Ethan dug

out his lighter and fired each of the boys' cigarettes like a little
Rasta monk performing a ritual. It was Sunday morning, somewhere close to three, when the city was still and the prowling
pig cruisers scarce. Only hours before, Corbitt had carefully
disassembled and cleaned the Collectors' cheap pistol, oiling
each part with the can of 3-in-One they used on their skate
bearings. The old pawnshop wizard had supplied a strange se-
lection of 9mm rounds for the gun's fifteen-shot clip; from cup-
nosed wadcutters intended for targets and some hollow-points
which would mushroom in flesh and rip out huge holes, to a
half-dozen Army steel-jackets that might even pierce armor
plate. Bilal had bitched about being cheated again, but the old
man had just laughed and asked about options. Bilal now packed
the pistol, slung over one shoulder on a strap that Corbitt had
made from a dog leash. Everyone else had their knives.

Corbitt lifted a hand to touch Silver's bandana. He still
wasn't sure why he was wearing it . . . one of whitey's flags. Did
that make him a mercenary? For who? It was a strange world;
a long, long way from Timbuktu to Kalamazoo, and just as far
to go back. Ethan wore a bandana too: Bilal evidently recognized
a warrior when he saw one. Were they all here tonight doing
the whiteman's work . . . black-on-black crime? Or, was this
just a job only Africans could be trusted to do?

Across the narrow backstreet loomed mountains of jagged
junk behind the scrapyard fence. No lights showed in the place,
but then nothing in there was worth protecting. The city's sullen
overglow and the fog-haloed streetlamp down on the corner
made everything too bright for Corbitt's liking anyhow. He
wished for the deep velvet black of the riverbank woods on a
moonless midnight. Yet Bilal had his own ways of stealth, guiding
his gang through a jungle of junk cars and ruin, along secret
trails of garbage and trash, and down dripping brick canyons
where wet walls wept slime and other eyes watched from the
shadows. The pace had been fast, until now both Stacy and
Lactameon were panting out steam. Corbitt could scent each of
the boys individually. The lighter's flare in Ethan's cupped hands
showed young warrior faces intent on the hunt. Corbitt felt pride
to be with them. Darkness pressed down as the lighter's flame
died, leaving cigarette points glowing like ruby-red fireflies. Bilal

gave Lactameon a critical glance. "Might be some major butt-bailin goin on in the program, man. Figure you up for it?"

Lactameon shrugged and blew smoke. "What it take. Silver my brother too, man. An, we the last ones."

"Mmm. Well, I still figure you better off stayin home an puttin some sorta curse on that cocksucka, man."

Lactameon smiled a little. "I curse him already, but we ain't none of us gots time to wait for it to work."

T.K. moved up beside Bilal. "What a motherfuckin escapade! Just hope no pigs come cruisin by!"

Bilal shook his head. "Shit. Ain't nuthin here worth wastin their time, man."

Corbitt looked to the corner at the wider, better-lit cross-street. They would have to travel it three blocks, along the route he and Bilal had skated earlier that day, before being able to turn off and get back on a darker side street once more. Even now a car went past, fast and frightened like a small animal in a big jungle.

Bilal dropped his cigarette and crushed it under his Nike. "Well, we ain't gots but a few hours more of things bein this dead. We better get busy."

The dimlit street seemed daylight bright to Corbitt after the alley. He was glad when they all reached the jumbled shadows along the junkyard fence. The boys moved quickly up the cracked old sidewalk to the entrance. The gates were bent out of line, and the three-strand straggle of rusty barbed wire sagged loose on top. Corbitt took hold of the upper frame and stuck the toe of one Cheetah into the mesh, preparing to climb. Then he stopped, turning his head in unison with the other boys to stare at Lactameon.

"Shit!" muttered Bilal. "No way in hell he gonna climb that!"

"Yeah!" agreed T.K. "What a motherfuckin escapade! Yo, Corbitt, you sposed to be the man with the plan. The fuck you thinkin bout?"

Ethan, meantime, had managed to squeeze his own small body between the gates and now stood looking out at the older boys. "Yo, T.K. elbow-face! Y'all go an take a motherfuckin piss, ya spect Corbitt be shakin your dick for ya too?"

Stacy smiled. "Silver woulda said somethin like that."

"Mmm," said Bilal. "Times when Corbitt round, I forget Silver gone." He studied the gates, then turned to Lactameon. "So, how much you weigh now anyhow?"

Lactameon shrugged. "My mom's scale only go up to three hundred, an I weigh that much last summer."

Bilal considered. "So, we front you another fifty. How much that divided by five?"

T.K. snickered. "So, what you gonna do, Bilal, cut him in pieces like Ice T done his mother?"

Bilal frowned. "I checkin how much the five of us can lift, stupid!"

"Seventy pounds," said Corbitt.

Bilal flexed a solid arm. "Shit, I can press one-fifty, no prob!"

"Well," said Corbitt. "Liftin people be different from hoistin cotton bales. An this here fence be most six feet high, plus that wire on top. Maybe I best go in an get the truck by my ownself."

Lactameon fingered the huge Master padlock holding the gates shut. "Um, what bout this, man?"

Corbitt peered through the mesh to where the old Corbitt dumptruck sat near a scrapheap about forty feet away. He scanned the big iron bars bolted to the front bumper. "Po ole padlock."

Suddenly, T.K. spun around and pointed to the corner. "Pigs comin!"

Corbitt heard a car only faintly. He wondered how T.K. could tell it was a cop when all sounds were smothered by the fog, but he didn't doubt for a second that the boy would recognize his own version of water moccasins. For an instant everybody froze, but then all the boys burst into action, grabbing hold of Lactameon anywhere they could grip and struggling and cursing to shove him up over the gates. Corbitt winced as Lactameon fought the barbed wire, but the rusty strands snapped beneath his full weight. Ethan dodged as Lactameon crashed to the ground on the other side. Stacy leaped up next, grabbing the top rail and kicking his legs. "Shit! I can't!"

Bilal boosted him over. "The fuck I gots to work with!"

Stacy landed in a heap beside Lactameon, who was struggling to his feet. Lactameon snorted. "Been a lotta Twinkies since *you* try an climb a fence, brother-mine!"

Corbitt and the other boys swarmed over the gates, and

dashed for the old truck's shadow, diving underneath as the police car swung around the corner, its headlights slashing the fog as they swept past the scrapyard entrance.

"Everbody get their asses back!" hissed Bilal. "Far as you fuckin can!"

The boys scrambled deeper underneath the old truck. Bilal twisted around to lie poised on his elbows, gun ready, as the car came angling toward the gates. It stopped, its lights boring bright cones through the mist and seeming to beam straight into Corbitt's face. He noticed a sapphire glitter beside him. "Ethan! Close your eyes!"

"Sucka pop his spook-light, we all gonna be history!" whispered T.K.

Bilal held the gun aimed steadily toward the headlights. "No, man. *He* is."

Corbitt tensed. These city cops wore bulletproof vests, but he'd loaded the steel-jacket rounds last in the magazine so they would be the first up to fire. Strangely, he wasn't sure how he felt about killing a cop . . . not anymore. Maybe those men inside that car were good cops, yet that hardly seemed logical after what he'd seen since leaving Bridge-end. He could hear the crackle of the car's radio, and could even scent leather and polish over the oily scrapyard reek and the sharp sweat-smells of the other boys. He heard two men's voices, sounding somehow familiar. Why had they stopped here? Did they have a key to the yard? Would they come in? If Bilal had to shoot, could he get both of them? The law would call that murder, but what would those people in Bates's field name it? Corbitt remembered the New Crossing deputy leading his father away in chains. Yet that man hadn't been enjoying his job . . . that man would have thrown away his badge before beating a kid, no matter what color.

The car's spotlight remained folded down. Instead, the doors opened and the two men got out. It was the pair who had been enjoying their job at the Center. Maybe their partner still had his arm in a cast? Corbitt was suddenly glad he wasn't holding the gun. Maybe those men weren't really evil; maybe they were only fools. But how many white-law-enforcing fools could black people tolerate?

Both men yawned and stretched and rubbed their lower

backs. One took a Burger King box off the dashboard and tossed it into the gutter before walking with the other to the gates. Corbitt tensed again, his eyes going to the dangling strands of broken barbed wire. Once more he pictured the New Crossing deputy, who would have probably tilted back his straw summer Stetson and looked thoughtful while taking up a strand of rusty wire and noting the shiny new break. Thinking back, Corbitt wondered how the deputy could have found Bates on the riverbank and gone over the area without seeing some sign of the three jungle cats. That man was no fool. Maybe he just knew the difference between law and justice?

But the two cops only unzipped and pissed through the mesh on the evidence. Bilal sighted his gun and whispered, "Bang, bang, motherfuckas." Ethan giggled; Corbitt poked him in the ribs. Then the men fired cigarettes and returned to the car. It made a leisurely U-turn and drove away.

Corbitt glanced at Bilal. "Know? Seem like to me, them cops be the biggest gang of all."

Bilal regarded Corbitt for a moment. "Silver say that once."

The boys crawled out from under the truck, exchanging grins and flipping fingers after the cruiser. Lactameon hoisted himself onto the running board. "Shotgun!"

Bilal snorted, but led the other boys back to the tailgate where they climbed into the bed. Lactameon opened the door and slid into the cab, then leaned from the window as Corbitt popped the hood latches and raised a panel. "Yo! The fuck you doin now, man?"

"Checkin the oil, course."

"Jeeze, Corbitt, you stealin it, not buyin the goddamn thing!"

Corbitt pulled the dipstick. "Be a goddamn shame to go an throw a rod cause we be low on oil. Sides, we not be stealin. Stealin where y'all take their an make it yours. This here be more like borrowin."

"Uh-huh. Well, whitey 'borrowed' Africa, an he left it stripped on blocks, man! An, yo, the fuck you gonna do if it *is* low on oil? Send Ethan on a run to Grand Auto?"

Corbitt slipped the dipstick back in. "Mmm. Gots a point there, brother."

Bilal leaned over the iron headboard. "The fuck he doin, man?"

Lactameon snickered. "Bein a responsible nigga. Like you."

"Huh?"

"He check the oil, you don't go shootin pigs less they deserve it."

"Whatever! Get the fuck busy!"

Ethan had gotten in on the driver's side and now squished himself tight against Lactameon to make room for Corbitt. Corbitt slid behind the big steering wheel and flicked his lighter, scanning the dashboard in the flame-glow. "Mmm. What I be figurin . . . a'zactly the same's the one back home. Cept this gots a gas engine. Hercules HXC, look like. 779 cubic inches."

Lactameon rolled his eyes. "Yeah? Don't see no Alpine." He squeezed against the door to make more room. "For sure gots a tiny little cab for such a goddamn huge motherfucker."

Corbitt shrugged. "That just the way they make trucks back then. Spose they figure it all the space a driver be needin for doin his job."

"Well, you *can* really drive it, can't you? Right now that your job."

"Shit yeah!" said Ethan. "Africans do any fuckin thing!"

Corbitt flipped one of a row of switches and the instrument panel lights came on. "Well, check this out! There be the key right in the ignition!"

Lactameon sighed. "So, why the hell not, man? Not even a stupid nigga gonna want to steal this ole thing! Like, you gonna go trollin for ho with a dumptruck?"

Corbitt turned the key. The ammeter needle quivered and the fuel gauge flicked to half full. Pulling the choke knob, Corbitt pumped the gas pedal a couple of times, trod down the clutch, shifted to neutral and then punched the starter button. The engine turned over once and fired up smoothly.

"Just like Lucas's ole White," Corbitt murmured. "Take the selfsame little ole spell." He eased in the choke and let the engine idle, then pointed to a gauge. "Gots to let the air build up. Take a few minutes."

"Yo?" asked Ethan. "Why y'all needin air?"

"For the brakes, little brother."

"Oh. Like da buses. Shit, I knew dat!"

Corbitt studied the dashboard again. "Mmm. They gots the limiter valve shut down."

Lactameon was watching Corbitt, wondering why the slender boy seemed older now, in his scuffed leather jacket behind the wheel of this ancient machine. Somehow he looked like he was home, just gazing out over the long hood as if there was anything to see but rusty junk. "Um, so what that mean?"

"Huh? Oh. Mean the front brakes turned off. Prob'ly leakin. Them tires sho nuff seen better days. We gonna have to take it careful on them foggy-wet streets." Corbitt handed his Top pouch to Ethan, who began rolling cigarettes.

The big engine's idle was deep-throated and strong. The small cab warmed quickly as the temperature-gauge needle climbed. Lactameon found himself wishing that they were all really going somewhere. Ethan passed out cigarettes, expertly made so they looked just like Luckies. Lactameon eased back in the dusty seat and blew smoke. "Could you drive this thing home, Corbitt?"

Corbitt fingered the big wheel. "Too much law 'tween here and there."

"Well, this time tomorrow you should be on a bus, headed home."

Corbitt flicked ashes out the window. "Y'all be seein that?"

"Well, no. But you should, man. It like you was sayin bout next-things."

Corbitt sighed out a soft silver cloud, the ring in his nose glinting in the dashboard light. "Next-things don't come automatic. Specially, good ones. There be a 'bundance of difference 'tween what people should have an what they end up with if they ain't willin to do more'n what spected of 'em. Times I get to thinkin we all still waitin for whitey to hand us our golden cup an throw in a pat on the woolly head for bein so patient."

The truck rocked slightly as the other boys moved in the bed. Bilal leaned over the headboard by Corbitt's window. "Yo! The fuck we waitin on, man?"

"Bout that time, I spose." Corbitt reached for a switch. "Hope them lights still workin." He flipped the switch and a pair of pale beams tunneled the fog in front of the truck. Pulling himself half out the window, he looked over the roof of the cab. "Mmm. Markers all dead. Ain't s'prised."

"What they for?" asked Lactameon.

"Sposed to show how high an wide a truck be. Spect it don't matter for us, less some pig be payin attention." Corbitt leaned from the window again. "Yo, Bilal! We gots us taillights back there?"

Winfield leaned over the tailgate. "One!"

Corbitt nodded. "Spect that all she born with anyways." He stepped on the clutch, shoved the parking brake lever forward, and shifted into first. The old truck gave a lurch, then growled slowly toward the gates. Ethan bounced on the seat and pointed ahead. "Just like da motherfuckin movies!" He added sound-effects.

But there was nothing showtime about breaking out: Corbitt hit the gates at a walking pace . . . six tons in motion was a hard thing to stop . . . and the big padlock snapped. The gates burst wide with a screech of rusty hinges, clanking back against the fence on either side as the truck rolled through. Corbitt swung the truck down the street and stepped on the brake for the corner stop sign. Air hissed from somewhere underneath. The rear wheels locked and skidded six feet before the truck finally stopped.

Corbitt frowned. "Touchy as a ole momma-cat."

Lactameon scanned the cross street. "Just bail-it, man! Fore them pigs come back to piss again!"

Corbitt let out the clutch and turned right. The street was fairly well lit, but empty of traffic. Corbitt did an expert double-clutch to second gear, then another to third, and finally up to fourth. The transmission howled as the speedometer needle rose in reluctant jerks to hang shakily at 35. Corbitt leaned from the window to wipe muddy mist from the mirror. He saw that Bilal and the other boys were standing up in the bed like soldiers in a troop truck. "Get your black asses down! Ain't no goddamn parade!"

For two blocks the street stayed deserted, except for a few figures large and small huddled in the doorways of barred store-fronts. Most seemed asleep, or what passed for it anyhow, and the others paid little attention to the rusty old dumptruck rumbling by. Then, halfway up the third block, a car came around the far corner. Corbitt hunched over the wheel and squinted through the misted windshield. "Oh, shit! It a motherfuckin pig!"

"Yo!" piped Ethan. "How fast dis go, man?"

Corbitt shook his head. "In your dreams, little brother."

Lactameon grabbed Ethan and yanked him down. "Corbitt! Sit up real straight!"

Corbitt stretched his long back, gazing over the hood and trying to picture an open highway ahead. He hung his elbow casually out the window and let the cigarette stub dangle from his lips. Then the police car was past. Corbitt watched in the mirror. It made a right at the next corner and vanished. "S'cool. They gone."

Lactameon sat up. "Shit, for a minute I figure we was history!"

Corbitt glanced in the mirror again. "Maybe we already is, cept nobody gonna put us in a storybook."

At the next corner, he swung the truck into a narrow side street. Downshifting to third, he eased cautiously through the rows of battered or abandoned cars that lined the curbs. An occasional rat scuttled through the headlight shafts.

Lactameon pointed. "Crack-house alley on the next block, man. Word say Sabby gots some new dude watchin there in the daytime, but he ain't keepin the place open all night, yet."

"Yeah," said Ethan. "But I done me some scopin from da roof yesterday. Seen dis ole mattress up top da rock house like somebody been cribbin dere."

"Mmm," said Lactameon. "That gots to be Beamer, then. Sabby stash his own ass down safe in that room you dudes built."

Corbitt frowned. "Likely I regret buildin that for the rest of my natural life! But, I spect you right, Tam. Sabby be lookin out for his own butt, best believe. Lock himself in with his guns an his money. Crack-puke likely smell like magnolias to him!" Corbitt pulled the truck over to the curb behind the burned-out corpse of a Datsun pickup and switched off the lights. "Maybe we should oughta get Bilal to send one of his dudes to check that roof?"

"Shit, I go!" said Ethan.

Corbitt touched the little boy's shoulder. "I be needin you here with me, little brother. Like, another good pair of eyes."

Bilal and the other boys leaped to the sidewalk as Corbitt brought the truck to a careful halt, the brakes spitting air and the rear wheels skidding the last few inches. The gang boys clustered on the right-side running board. "S'up?" asked Bilal. "Why we stop here?"

"Ethan think there could be a guard on Sabby's roof," said Lactameon.

Bilal considered. "Might just be Beamer. The fuck else Sabby gonna find to sit on some cold roof all night?"

"He gots him a gun?" asked Corbitt.

"Hobbes never trust him with one," said Lactameon.

T.K. snorted. "Hobbes rat food, man! An Sabby give a fuck if Beamer go an shoot somebody by accident!"

Bilal fingered his jaw and glanced up the street. "Well, Sabby ain't stupid, the fuck else he is. Be just like that cocksucka to keep a watcher on the roof. Give him warnin to bail his butt if some serious shit come cruisin his way."

Corbitt looked at Bilal. "So, what bout Beamer, man? An maybe that other dude, Lizard? Y'all ain't gonna just up an kill them too?"

Bilal made a face. "Yo! *My* name ain't Sabby! He the only cocksucka I wanna see dirt-nappin tonight! If them other dudes wanna bail stead of battle it way cool by me!"

"Um," asked Stacy. "So, what if Beamer on the roof but he do gots a gun? Even that retard kick our asses shootin down from up there."

"Yo!" said Winfield. "I scope it."

Bilal smiled slightly. "Shit, can't lose your ass, man, you ain't even paid for yet." He faced T.K. "Yo, book up there an check the place out. If Beamer on the roof, handle it."

T.K. smiled. "What it take, man?"

Lactameon leaned from the window. "Chill! Shit, what you sayin, Bilal? I ain't havin Beamer hurt!"

T.K.'s voice broke. "You don't want *Beamer* hurt? The fuck this shit? Here you all sayin he might gots him a goddamn Uzi up there, an all I gots is my blades! What a motherfuckin escapade!"

"Well," said Bilal. "Can't you just sorta sneak up behind him like they do on TV?"

T.K. spat on the sidewalk. "The fuck comin out your mouth,

man? Shit, TV my ass! Word, you go an try that on some sucka for real, he yell his fuckin head off! It a . . . a . . . a reflex, what it is. Shit, somebody come creepin up on me like that, *I* yell! So, then what I sposed to do? Cut the sucka's throat? Just like on TV? Yo, you figure *that* quiet? I here to tell you it ain't! Dudes don't never die quick that way. They flop around. A lot!"

Corbitt pictured one of Mrs. Griffin's chickens, then glanced at Ethan, who seemed to be adding data to his computer. Lactameon sighed and jerked the door handle. "I go, man. If it Beamer up there, he listen to me."

Bilal looked doubtful. "Yeah, an what if it ain't, man? What if it some strange sucka shoot anythin move? You ain't a'zactly the world's smallest target."

Lactameon shrugged and climbed carefully down to the sidewalk. "I just gonna do a little more'n what spected."

"Yo!" said T.K. "So how you even gonna get your ass up on that roof, man?"

"Yeah," agreed Stacy. "Been a lotta goddamn Twinkies."

Lactameon shrugged again. "Black magic, maybe."

Bilal thought a moment more, but finally nodded. "Well, it your ass, Tam. The fuck you wanna go an risk it for that retard, I never know."

"He one of the last, too, Bilal."

Bilal glanced at his watch. "What it is. Three-twenty-eight now. We wait till four."

Lactameon jerked up his jeans and turned to go, but Ethan jumped from the truck, unwinding the little feather from his hair. "Take dis, Tam! It really work!"

Lactameon took the little ebony feather, then looked up at Corbitt. "You believe in this, man?"

Corbitt nodded. "Gots to believe in somethin. Logical it be a black somethin."

15

Lactameon's body was slick with fog and sweat as he struggled up onto the dogwash shop roof. It was a climb that Corbitt could have made in seconds; from the top of a dumpster to the ledge of a bricked-over window, and then finding toeholds in the crumbling wall to boost him the rest of the way. For Lactameon the ordeal had taken many desperate minutes. Kicking and cursing, he finally managed to drag himself over the edge, then flopped panting onto his back and stared up at the nothingness that passed for a sky. His chest had been ripped by the scrapyard's barbed wire, and the cuts burned like fiery stripes. His breath floated above his face in a cloud, and wisps of steam curled from his skin. The loose rolls of his body channeled rivulets of water that collected in a cold puddle beneath him. He pulled up the front of his shirt and mopped his face. Getting himself into this mix was probably a mistake. Toni had her baby back, and Lactameon had Toni. Who needed Beamer hanging around like a graveyard ghost from the past? *I got mine, you get yours, nigga.* Lactameon scowled at the sky. Corbitt would call that a white idea. Maybe it was. Too many cool *black thangs* turned out to be white ideas when seen through the right kind of eyes, and a picture negative still made the same picture.

Sighing steam, Lactameon struggled to his feet. His wet jeans slid to his knees. Cursing, he yanked them back up, then ripped off his tank-top, threaded it through the belt-loops, and knotted it tightly under his belly. He pulled off his bandana and wiped blood from his chest, then glanced at the wet yellow rag. What options did he have? Wringing it out, he slipped it back on his head.

The roof popped and squeaked as he crossed to the ladder that led one story up to the next building. It was made of planks nailed on two-by-four uprights, and looked as rotten as everything else in the hood. Lactameon couldn't see what held it to the wall, and wasn't sure he wanted to know. Lifting his foot to the first rung, he eased some of his weight onto it. The ancient board cracked in the middle.

"Shit!" Lactameon stared upward. The rest of the ladder looked in no better shape. *So, who said it was gonna be easy, nigga?* Lactameon studied the ladder, trying to see it like Corbitt would; just another technical problem to be solved. Corbitt would have probably sat down and rolled up a cigarette, all the while looking like a sleepy cheetah in a tree listening to antelope telling jungle-cat jokes.

Afrosippi magic? Yeah, right! And Dumbo would just fly his ass up there! Lactameon slipped the little black feather from his pocket and stuck it into his bandana.

Carefully, he put his foot on the outside edge of the plank, as close as he could to the upright. He cautiously eased his weight back onto the ladder and felt the old nails slip a little, but the board didn't break. Rung by rung he hauled himself upward. The old ladder trembled and creaked. His arm muscles were soon aching, but at last he reached the top. Pouring sweat, he crawled painfully onto the roof. It would have been way past wonderful to rest there a minute, but time was slinking by fast. Getting back on his feet, he crossed the roof, then came to a four-foot gap of black emptiness separating him from the next building. From far below came the squeaking of rats. He stood for a moment, staring down. Sometimes there was nothing to build a bridge out of. Pacing back, Lactameon sucked a deep breath and launched himself in the same sort of lumbering leap that the big fat zoo lion made pouncing on its dinner. For one scary second he was soaring over nothing, but then he came crashing down in a rolling sprawl on the far side, skin shredding from elbows and knees on the sharp-graveled tar. Scrambling up, he moved to the far edge of the roof, stepping carefully so the gravel wouldn't crunch. Crouching, he peered downward.

Two stories below was the crack-house roof. The four-foot brick parapet on the alley side would make a kickin place to shoot from behind at anyone approaching. Lactameon squinted in the dimness, trying to make out details in the fog-filtered glow from the streetlight at the alley entrance. The passage looked clear, except that a couple of dumpsters were skewed out from the walls about halfway down. Could Corbitt just ram them aside? Lactameon wasn't sure: they were angled in a V and might jam together. Well, Corbitt would logic that out.

Lactameon shifted his gaze to the roof below. It was flat, black tarpaper, and overshadowed by the taller buildings on three sides. Shading his eyes against the streetlight, Lactameon located the trapdoor in one back corner. It was shut. Behind the parapet stretched a broad band of deeper darkness. Faint silver glints that were probably beer cans shone here and there. Lactameon saw a rectangular shape that looked like a mattress. On it lay a form that could have been a kid curled in blankets. Lactameon let his eyes scan the figure a few times, trying not to focus hard: it was a trick Corbitt said helped you see things better at night. Yeah, that was definitely somebody sleeping down there. Who else but Beamer would take a shitty job like that?

Lactameon considered calling, but the crack-house roof was thin and someone inside might hear. He noticed a cast-iron vent pipe close by. It was about six inches thick and bracketed to the wall about every four feet. Lactameon wiped more blood from his elbows, then took hold of the pipe and tried to wiggle it. The bracket bolts shifted in the ancient brickwork, but seemed strong enough to handle his weight. Maybe there was a safer way to wake Beamer? Lactameon picked up a piece of gravel and bounced it on his palm. But, what if that wasn't Beamer down there? Lactameon felt time ticking by. That big old truck was going to make enough noise to wake the dead when it came up the alley. Whoever was on that roof would hear it and warn the dudes inside long before Corbitt could get past those dumpsters and ram down the door. And, Sebastian and his posse would have a clear field of fire from behind the parapet.

Lactameon let out a sigh and put down the pebble. Rubbing his hands with gravel grit, he squirmed over the edge and onto the fog-slicked pipe. The rusty brackets squeaked. The pipe shifted, creaking, away from the wall. Lactameon froze, his thighs locked to the wet iron, clinging desperately and sure the whole thing was going to rip loose and drop him two stories. The top bracket bolts, level with his nose, had already pulled out over an inch. Brick dust drifted down and made him want to sneeze. Still, after that first sickening lurch, the pipe seemed to be holding. Could he make it back up? No way!

His fingers were already slipping. He began to ease downward. The brackets gouged at his chest and belly. He couldn't see below, and the row of brackets sliding past his face seemed endless in number. The bolts chittered and creaked and the sound seemed to echo for blocks. His fingers had gone numb and were losing their hold. Then, finally, his feet touched tarpaper.

The thin planking sagged under his weight. He shot a glance toward the mattress. The streetlight glimmer coming over the parapet made it hard to see, yet it didn't look like the kid-shape had moved. Figuring that the roof would probably pop like hell if he tried to walk over it, Lactameon kept tight to the wall and eased around to the front of the building. Reaching the parapet, he peered down the alley again: it couldn't be many more minutes until the truck came. The mattress was just ten feet away now. Lactameon could see the slow rise and fall of the fog-silvered blankets. The figure was shrouded head to toe; logical enough on a chilly wet night. Lactameon wished there was some way to scope out the dude before trying to wake him. Crouching in the parapet's shadow, he scanned the bundled shape once more. A rolled-up jacket passed for a pillow. He caught sight of something black and metallic showing from under it . . . Sebastian's Uzi pistol! Had T. K. been right about Sebastian trusting Beamer with a gun? Lactameon hesitated, unsure what to do. Should he just whisper Beamer's name and hope for the best? But, if he could slink over and snag that gun he'd be in total control of whatever came next.

Warily, Lactameon rose and inched forward. Three more steps and he'd have it. Then, from down the block, came the deep-throated cough of the truck starting up! He panicked and lunged for the gun. A beer can crunched underfoot. The blanketed figure exploded into motion. But Lactameon had the pistol! He stumbled back against the parapet and yanked the cocking knob. An already chambered round spit from the ejection port. The select-fire switch was all the way forward, and he clutched the safety lever tight, his finger tense on the trigger as the other boy flung back the blankets and froze in a crouch.

It was Sebastian.

The sweat turned to ice on Lactameon's skin. His heart pounded deep in his chest. For a long half-second the two boys just stared at each other. Sebastian was clad just in jeans and his skintight black T-shirt. His hard golden arms seemed to glow in the darkness. The streetlight glow gave a strange silver shine to his steel-colored eyes. The gun almost forgotten, Lactameon pressed back against the cold brick as Sebastian's eyes, first wide in amazement, now narrowed to slits of rage. His teeth gleamed stark behind curled-back lips, and his words hissed out in a steamy cloud. "You goddamn cocksuckin NIGGER!"

He reached for his jacket.

"No!" The big gun felt like a chunk of ice in Lactameon's hand. A helpless sensation washed over him as he watched Sebastian keep reaching for something. His own voice sounded childish. "Don't, man! Goddammit, Sabby, I kick you, man, I really fuckin will!"

But, Sebastian's lips only drew further back in disgust. He kept his movements slow and deliberate, unwrapping the bundled leather jacket. Lactameon could only look on in foolish fascination. It was like a story Corbitt had told of how a snake could hypnotize a rabbit; he could do nothing but watch. Why couldn't he just shoot Sebastian? The gang was coming to kick him anyway; if he just did it now the whole donkey show would be over and nobody else would get hurt. More: word would go around that he'd earned the whiteman's badge of blackness.

"Don't, Sabby! Goddammit, whatever you doin, stop it, man!" Second warnings were for good cops and bad movies, and he'd given Sebastian three.

But Sebastian pulled a rolled-up paper bag from the folds of his jacket. "Give me that bullshit, man! So, here's what you come for, nigger!" Sebastian opened the bag to reveal bundles of rubber-banded bills. "You ain't gots the balls to shoot nobody, fat boy! Only thing I scared of is you shakin so bad you might do it by accident!"

Lactameon felt his fear draining away. Strength seemed to

seep back into his arms. The gun steadied in his hands, warming in his grasp. His voice lost its little-kid quaver. "There ain't enough green in this whole sorry-ass motherfucka to justify your ass, man!"

Sebastian's eyes shifted in new uncertainty from Lactameon's face to the money. "What you sayin? Yo! You got any idea how much here, fool?"

Lactameon could hear the truck coming nearer; in another few minutes it would be swinging into the alley, but most of his mind was focused on covering Sebastian. Money. Sebastian couldn't have made much more than a grand in the week he'd been running the house, yet ten times that wouldn't have tempted Lactameon now.

"Yeah, sucker! All your motherfuckin money an it your ass cribbin out here in the cold cause you gots no brothers to watch your own back!"

Sebastian's fists clenched on the bag. "I *never* had no brothers, cocksucker! There's nobody here but you stupid niggers!"

Lactameon's eyes were drawn to the alley where the rumble of the truck was beginning to echo. Sebastian's own eyes tracked the fat boy's. He shifted to a different stance, his legs tensing to leap, but Lactameon looked back at him. "You just a goddamn . . . a goddamn *waste* of somethin what coulda been beautiful, all you are!"

Sebastian shot another glance down the alley. "What's that comin?"

The gun felt almost familiar in Lactameon's hand now; almost as if it belonged there. He could sense Sebastian's confusion as it mounted toward what would soon become fear. Nobody had ever been afraid of him before. That was a new kind of power. "Maybe it a garbage truck, Sabby. To haul away shit nobody gots time for no more . . . like the one what haul away Hobbes."

Sebastian's eyes went suddenly wide. "I . . . I didn't *mean* to kill him, Tam! Swear to God I didn't, man! We . . . we was fuckin around, y'know . . . an, an the gun just went off!"

"*What? You* killed Hobbes? You . . . MOTHER-FUCKA!" Lactameon's hand clenched on the gun. He could feel the trigger spring give under his finger.

"It was a *accident*, Tam! Swear to God, man!"

Lactameon flicked a glance to the bulging paper bag. It was too dark to see the bills, but there would be a lot more than a grand inside even if they were only twenties. Somehow he knew they were a lot bigger than twenties. It wasn't right that Hobbes had been going to buy his way out on the backs of his brothers, but it was sickening to realize that all the misery and suffering black kids had gone through amounted to nothing more than a bagful of paper.

The alley fog fluoresced as the truck's headlights swung into the entrance. Lactameon's finger stayed steady and tight on the trigger. If he just pulled it now everything would be over and that paper would be his. It was dirty, but the paper changing hands up in those foothills wasn't any cleaner. Black kids' blood was soaked into all of it . . . all the paper in the country, maybe even the world. Would killing Sebastian wash that blood away? Lactameon sighed and shook his head.

"Listen up, Sabby! My dudes comin to kick you. Get your ass out this hood now an fuckin forever! We gonna burn down this shithouse so's nobody never open it again. You don't wanna burn with it, bail!" Lactameon lowered the gun muzzle a little. "Who down inside?"

Sebastian swallowed. "Beamer . . . Lizard."

Lactameon nodded, then glanced to the alley again. Despite the breeze the fog seemed thicker. He hoped Corbitt would see the dumpsters. Sebastian made a movement, but Lactameon jerked the gun up and he froze. "Shag your ass, white *boy!* An leave the paper. Just maybe somethin good still come out your fucked-up life for somebody."

"Shit, man, least let me put on my goddamn shoes!"

Lactameon scowled. "Yo, sucka! You got your jeans an your life! That all what Corbitt come here with. Shit, Sabby, your homey Ice T could walk barefoot through busted glass, couldn't he? He so baaaad."

Sebastian's face twisted in rage, but he took a step backward. "Okay, okay, Tam. Check me out, I'm goin. Shit, I shoulda figured that showtime African nigger would be in this fuckin mix too!" Sebastian hunched his shoulders and turned his back.

Lactameon's eyes went again to the alley. He heard the hiss of air brakes: Corbitt must have seen the dumpsters. Bilal and the dudes would probably get out and move them. But, there was no need anymore. Lactameon wondered how he could signal the gang that the whole thing was over.

Suddenly, Sebastian spun around and leaped for Lactameon, slamming his body into the fat boy and grabbing for the gun. For Sebastian it was like crashing into a bridge pillar wrapped in foam rubber. Lactameon just grunted in surprise and barely budged. Sebastian clutched Lactameon's wrist and tried to tear the gun out of his hand. It went off, blasting a burst of bullets into the roof. Lactameon dropped it and grabbed the golden boy around the waist. Sebastian twisted and fought, trying to reach the gun. He jerked up a knee for Lactameon's balls but got only belly. Arcing backward, Sebastian smashed a fist into Lactameon's cheek. He felt Lactameon's grip loosen for an instant and tried to hit him again. Lactameon cursed and then, clutching Sebastian against him, fell forward, crashing down with all his weight on top of the other boy. "Eat this, cocksucka!"

The whole roof shook as Sebastian smashed flat on his back under Lactameon's mass. He struggled weakly for a few moments, then managed to tear his arms free and batter Lactameon's sides with his fists. Lactameon heaved himself up and slammed down on Sebastian again. The golden boy went limp, whimpering, "You busted my ribs, man! I can't breathe!"

It was a child's cry. Still pinning Sebastian's legs, Lactameon rose to his knees. Sebastian jerked upward from the waist and spat in Lactameon's eyes. Lactameon raised both hands to wipe it away. Sebastian clawed something from his pocket. There was a click. Silver steel glittered. A golden arm flashed, driving the knife into Lactameon's chest.

Lactameon screamed as the blade ripped into him. He clutched at the knife handle, but Sebastian tore the blade free. It came out with a wet sucking sound. Sebastian scrambled to his feet, jerking back his arm for another stab. But then he stopped, poised and panting steam. Lactameon stayed on his knees, doubled over, seeming to stare at the blood running between his fingers. Sebastian laughed.

"You're already dead, nigger! You just too stupid to know it!"

Sebastian watched the fat boy a moment more, then folded and pocketed the knife. He spat on Lactameon, then turned to get the gun, but stopped and stared down the alley instead. A huge shape loomed behind headlights half smothered in fog. What was that thing? Breeze still stirred the air, promising morning but only thickening the mist. The truck, or whatever it was, had stopped. Faint kid-curses carried up the alley, then came what sounded like a dumpster scraping brick. From below, Sebastian heard the confused shouts of Beamer and Lizard. Those stupid niggers would probably open the door unless he chilled them out fast! Leaving the gun where it lay, Sebastian ran to the trapdoor. The partition was locked from the inside and he'd have to go down there and open it to let the other dudes up on the roof. With three guns and the parapet for protection it wouldn't be hard to stop that truck. No matter how big, it had tires . . . and a driver. It didn't take any cocksucking black magic to figure that Corbitt would be driving!

Flinging back the trapdoor, Sebastian swung himself down the ladder. His ribs stabbed pain with every move. Maybe that fat-ass cocksucker *had* broken one? Sebastian cursed and gritted his teeth as he dropped to the floor: ribs could be fixed, a knife to the heart couldn't!

The other boys were pressed against the heavy mesh selling-window. Beamer looked scared, but Lizard had kept most of his cool and carried the Uzi carbine. "Pigs, Sabby?"

"No!" Sebastian ran over to unlock the door. "It just them cocksuckin Collectors! We can take 'em! They got some kinda big truck out there, but we can kick 'em all from the roof! C'mon!"

Lizard and Beamer had been sleeping. Both were barefoot and wearing just jeans. Beamer dashed to a couch and grabbed the .44. Lizard fingered the Uzi. "Yo, Sabby! They gots guns?"

Sebastian stopped, halfway back to the ladder. He spun around, clutching his side as pain shot through him again. "All they gots that pussy ole Cobray! It jams! Now, c'mon!"

Beamer appeared in the doorway beside Lizard. "Um . . . how you know they not gots somethin else, Sabby?"

"Yeah!" added Lizard. "Yo! They gots a goddamn truck, what else they gots you don't know?"

Sebastian's eyes slitted. "You cocksuckin niggers! You're scared!"

The other boys glanced at each other. "Um," said Beamer. "I just a retard, Sabby. I ain't crazy."

"Yeah!" agreed Lizard. "Collectors can't drive no goddamn truck! So, who the fuck else they gots for backup, man? Spose the Leopards in the mix? Hobbes woulda got least six out seven fore he start givin orders, an I want *all* seven fore I start takin 'em from you!"

Sebastian clenched his fists, his eyes flicking to the product on the loading table. No goddamn time! Finally, he nodded. "Okay, okay! Beamer! Open the front door an spray a few at them headlights! That tell us what they got!"

Lizard glanced at Beamer, then nodded. "Do it, man. Keep low."

Beamer glanced uncertainly down at the gun in his hand. "I . . . don't think I can shoot the Collectors, Sabby."

Sebastian gritted his teeth. "They'll shoot *you*, cocksucker! They hate your ass now! Silver's dead, you fuckin retard! Remember?"

"But . . . Tam still my homey."

"You shit! Tam ain't out there! You figure they bring his fat ass along on somethin like this? Now MOVE, nigger!"

Reluctantly, Beamer went to the front door and lifted the bar. Cautiously, he slipped out into the night. Sebastian and Lizard stayed in the partition doorway, watching. Fingers of fog curled into the room. Then, the .44 fired twice, big movie-gun booms muffled by mist. Seconds later came a short ragged burst of auto-fire, bullets sputting brick, one ricocheting off the iron door, another whizzing in to thunk the fridge in the far corner, spattering a spray of porcelain chips. A jet of vapor hissed from the back of the fridge, and an amber trickle of Colt bled from the bottom of the door gasket. Beamer leaped back into the room, slamming the door and dropping the bar.

Sebastian gave Lizard a shove. "See, asshole? Now, c'mon! Both you cocksuckers!" Still holding one hand to his ribs, Sebastian ran to the ladder and started up. He was almost to the top when the trapdoor slammed down with a bang. A few seconds passed while Sebastian just clung to the rungs and stared upward. Below, the other two boys watched in wonder, the guns hanging loose in their hands.

"SHIT!" Bracing his feet, Sebastian jammed a shoulder to

the plywood panel and shoved with all his strength. Pain ripped through his ribs and hard muscle stood out stark on his frame, but the door stayed solidly shut. From down the alley came the iron clash of gear-teeth and the rumbling thunder of a massive old engine. Cursing, sweat gleaming on his body, Sebastian strained at the panel again, then pounded it with his fist. "Tam! I know it's you, cocksucker! Get the fuck off or I'll shoot through this thing!"

There was no sound from above. Sebastian gave the door a last desperate shove, then climbed down several rungs and reached for Lizard's Uzi. "Gimme that, stupid!"

But Beamer shoved Lizard aside. "What you doin, Sabby? Why Tam up there? You motherfucka! Leave him alone!"

Sebastian leaped from the ladder, slamming Beamer back into the loading table, then snatched the Uzi from Lizard's hands. He whirled back to face Beamer, jamming the gun muzzle into Beamer's chest. "You cocksuckin retard! Tam's *dead!* I stabbed him right in the *heart!*" Sebastian twisted the gun, gashing Beamer's skin. "I kicked that nigger good, *boy!* I fuckin kick you too!"

Beamer's eyes went wide in horror. The pistol slipped from his fingers and clattered on the floor. "No!"

Sebastian jerked back the big carbine and slammed the steel butt-stock into Beamer's head. Blood spurted from the boy's torn ear and he crumpled to the floor. Sebastian yanked up the gun to hit him again, but Lizard grabbed his arm.

"You crazy, man? The fuck wrong with you, fool!"

Sebastian tried to pull away, but Lizard held on. "Why you fightin your own people, fool! Shit, if Tam already dead up there, don't waste no more bullets! Shit, ain't both us strong enough to open that now! Maybe there still time to bail out the front!"

Sebastian twisted free of Lizard's grasp, shoving the smaller boy away. "*Nigger!* Cocksuckin chickenshit niggerboys! Can't trust none of you! *I* kicked Hobbes, an I fuckin kick you! I don't need none of you!" Sebastian swung the Uzi up at the trapdoor.

"You fuckin crazy!" Lizard grabbed the gun, jerking it down just as Sebastian fired. The spray of bullets hit the wall. Brick chips and ricochets twanged and screamed around the small space. Bottles shattered on the table. Lizard yelped and jumped back. He stared down at his chest, expression amazed. One hand went to a wet ruby slice where a brick chip had cut him. For a moment he just studied his bloody fingers in stunned fascination. Finally, he looked up at Sebastian. "Fuck you! Hobbes was right all the time, you fuckin *crazy!*" He glanced down at Beamer, then turned for the partition doorway. "Fuck this shit, cocksucka! I take my chances with the niggas!"

Sebastian just stood for a few seconds, watching Lizard cross the main room and reach for the bar on the door. Then, he felt a vibration beneath his bare feet, and the truck's engine-thunder registered in ears numbed by the gun-blast. He jumped over Beamer and darted to the partition doorway. "Don't open that! They'll kick us all!"

Lizard lifted the bar. "What you mean *us*, whiteboy?"

Sebastian jerked the gun to his shoulder and fired. Again, the Uzi's blast echoed back from the bare brick walls. Lizard screamed as the spray of bullets ripped through his back, tearing from his chest to clatter against the door's iron plates. The boy was slammed against the door by the impact, then his body slid down leaving crimson streaks behind. He twitched a few seconds before going still.

Once more Sebastian felt the numbness in his ears that followed a shooting. Dirty white streamers of smoke curled around, stinging his nostrils. The vibration underfoot was getting stronger, and the gaps around the AC were glowing silver from the headlights of the oncoming truck. Sebastian turned for a second, his eyes flicking first to the trapdoor and then down at Beamer. The lanky boy moved, and his fingers clutched at nothing, like a baby's. *Niggerbaby!* Sebastian almost swung the gun to Beamer, but there were more important things to finish first. Running to the front door, he grabbed Lizard's arm and dragged the dead boy aside. "Want somethin done right, get a whiteman to do it!" Sebastian flung up the blood-spattered bar. "Let's see how good your African magic stop bullets, blackboy!"

16

Corbitt scrambled back into the cab and grabbed the steering wheel. One hand poised ready on the shift lever while he watched in the mirror as the Collectors took cover behind the truck. Corbitt had stopped for a second at the alley entrance to let Ethan out. The little boy would be doing a watcher's job now, which was the coolest way to keep him safe without hurting his pride. There had been a short burst of auto-fire from somewhere up the alley. Bilal's face had looked uneasy in the mirror, but he'd waved Corbitt on. They'd only gotten a little way up the passage before two dumpsters loomed out of the mist. They were cocked at such an angle that ramming them with the truck would only have jammed them tighter together. Maybe Sebastian had planned it that way to delay pigs: no matter, there was no option but to stop and move them by hand. Like all the dumpsters in this part of town they were overflowing with sodden garbage, and the boys had struggled and cursed while wrestling them aside. With the truck's headlights reflecting from the fog, nobody had noticed the glow when the crack-house door opened. Then, two shots had echoed out, one bullet whizzing overhead, the other thunking into the truck's left fender. All the boys dove for cover. Bilal fired a burst from his own gun. Moments later came the sound of the heavy door clanking shut.

Corbitt had crouched on the running board when the first shots were fired. Now, Bilal emerged from behind a dumpster, his face tense. "Shit! They seen us, man! Prob'ly be on that roof in a second!"

T.K. crawled out from under the truck. "What a mother-fuckin escapade!"

"Word up!" said Winfield, peering around the rear set of tires.

Running footsteps approached from the street. Bilal spun to face them, gun ready, but it was only Ethan. "Need backup?" the little boy panted.

"Get the fuck back there an do your own job!"

"Well!" Ethan faded into the mist.

"Yo, Bilal," asked Stacy. "So, what up now?"

Corbitt glanced at the bullet hole in the fender. He could scent the freshly torn steel. He peered up the alley. A breeze was shifting the fog around but didn't seem to be thinning it. "What about Tam?"

Bilal scowled. "Well, what about him, man? Seem like to me whatever he figure he gonna do up there didn't work! Them suckas for sure know we here now!"

Stacy's eyes shifted between Bilal and Corbitt. "Yo! Member them shots we heard before? Maybe that was Tam takin out the guard?"

T.K. snorted. "Ask me, it the guard takin out Tam, what that was!"

"Shut up!" hissed Bilal. "He our man, an he gots balls, whatever happen!"

"Carve that on his stone."

Corbitt squinted into the mist. "Well, y'all askin me, if them rock-house dudes *was* up on the roof, then why they risk openin that door? Don't seem logical."

Bilal nodded, glaring at T.K. "Goddamn right, man!"

"Yeah!" agreed Winfield. "An, if they was up there, how come they ain't shootin now?"

Bilal nodded again. "So, maybe Tam did make it to the roof an get it goin on. Shit, maybe he even gots Beamer helpin him. So, that leave Sabby an Lizard an any other suckas stuck down inside . . . maybe." He turned to Corbitt. "That logical, man?"

Corbitt smiled a little. "Shit yeah."

The old truck idled patiently, turning over with the easy rhythm of a long-stroke engine spinning a heavy flywheel. The boys panted steam. Bilal met Corbitt's eyes again. "So, gots any ideas, man?"

"Seem like it best we just go on ahead with our 'riginal plan. Y'all keep down low 'hind the truck." Corbitt climbed back into the cab, watched in the mirror while the other boys took their positions, then released the parking brake and shoved the shift lever into first. He let out the clutch gently, but the alley pavement was slick with old oil and wet garbage and the bald tires spun before getting a bite. The truck bucked forward. Corbitt left it in low: six tons moving at ten miles an hour was plenty of power to ram down the door. He stared ahead through the misted windshield, half expecting the yellow-orange flash of gunfire to lick down from the rock-house roof any second, despite what he'd said to Bilal. He pushed his foot down harder on the gas pedal, hoping the Collectors could keep up without slipping in the trash. The Corbitt's cab rattled as the RPMs rose and the big engine shook in its mounts with a booming bass roar. Then, from ahead, came the sound of more shots, fainter and muffled from inside the house. For an instant Corbitt's foot came off the gas, but then he stomped it down again . . . Prince Cheetah wasn't going to puss-out this time! His slender fingers gripped the big wheel. He stared grimly ahead, trying not to wonder what those shots from inside might mean. The zookeepers were all insane and driving the animals crazy.

The truck lurched over a heap of wet garbage. Slime spurted from under the tires. The rear end fishtailed slightly. Corbitt wrestled the steering wheel straight and pushed even harder on the gas, wincing as the tachometer needle jerked past the red line. The cab doors rattled loose locks and red-hot rust flakes blew from the exhaust pipe to scatter on the pavement behind. Corbitt aimed the radiator cap straight for the center of the crack-house door.

Suddenly, the door swung open. Light burst bright from the big inside bulb. Blinded for a second, Corbitt caught just the blur of a figure charging toward the truck. Then, muzzle-flame flared and the alley walls amped back the stutter of full-auto fire. The mirror exploded, spraying glass splinters against Corbitt's face. Bullets twanged off the truck's iron headboard, ricochets slicing and screaming in all directions while the muzzle-flame swung in a search-pattern. Corbitt kept his foot down, knowing he was the target. Sebastian came on, the big gun bucking in his hands, running straight for the truck, gold-skinned kid-death caught in the headlight beams.

A bullet whined off the mirror frame. More glass shards flew. Corbitt acted on reflex, ducking away from the window and wrenching at the wheel while his foot found the brake pedal and rammed it down.

The carbine clattered hot in Sebastian's hands as he raced for the oncoming truck. His lips pulled back in a snarl of triumph when he heard glass shatter and saw the rear wheels lock up and skid. *Eat it, nigger!* The truck was just a huge shape behind its lights, but the muzzle-flame had licked straight for the driver's seat. Sebastian's finger came off the trigger . . . he'd save the last shots to make sure! Something whizzed past his shoulder, but Sebastian didn't care: he'd pay back *those* niggerboys later! But, something was wrong! The big dual wheels were locked solid but the truck was still moving! Sebastian dodged as the massive front bumper swung toward him. He whipped up the gun to fire again. Then his bare feet slipped in wet trash.

Sebastian fell. His finger jerked the trigger as he screamed and went down. The Uzi's last rounds raked the wall across the alley. Rear wheels still locked, the big truck slid on in a slow-motion skid. It hardly even jolted as one front tire rolled over Sebastian's back. Corbitt heard the sickening snap a second before the truck finally stopped, six feet from the rock-house door. The engine stalled. The headlights dimmed. Sudden silence settled, broken only by the hiss of a leaking brake line.

Then, Corbitt jerked his foot off the pedal. Released air spat, and brake shoes creaked back from drums. The truck rolled ahead a couple more inches. Corbitt pulled the parking brake lever, and its ratcheting rasp sounded loud. Automatically, he switched off the ignition so the points wouldn't burn. Low kid-murmurs came to his ears as the Collectors eased warily up alongside the cab. Bilal glanced at Corbitt, then, gun gripped ready, darted to the rock-house doorway and peered cautiously in. Corbitt saw him stiffen for a second before easing his head past the half-open door and scanning the rest of the room. Finally, he faced the other boys who were waiting tensely by the truck's front fender. "Lizard dead."

"Shit!" cried Stacy, pointing. "Winfield hit!"

"The fuck!" bawled Bilal, dashing back.

Corbitt pushed open the cab door. Its hinges squealed and bits of glass fell from the shattered mirror to scatter on the pavement with musical sounds. He jumped to the ground. Stacy had the blond boy's jacket open and his T-shirt pulled up. Corbitt moved close, and gently probed the bloody place on Winfield's side.

"Mmm. Just graze a rib. Y'all be lucky, brother. Take off your shirt an hold it tight till the bleedin stop."

T.K. shook his head. "Maybe we can get us a refund."

Winfield grinned. "You busted me, you bought me, brothers."

Corbitt's hand went to his own cheek. His fingers came away bloody where the mirror glass had gashed him. Bilal returned to the house. T.K. crouched to stare beneath the truck.

"Shit!" he breathed.

Corbitt turned, about to look, but Winfield grabbed his arm. "Don't, brother."

Corbitt looked anyhow, then straightened quickly and turned away. "What a motherfuckin waste."

The early-morning breeze was growing stronger, swirling the mist and carrying that *déjà vu* sea-smell to Corbitt's nostrils. Above the soft hiss of escaping air he could hear the ticking and clicks of the engine cooling down. T.K. scrambled under the truck to emerge a moment later with the Uzi carbine. "Least you didn't waste this, man."

Corbitt sighed, wondering why he could feel only sadness. "Wonder what his next-thing gonna be?"

T.K. was checking out the gun. "Hell, if you askin me, man."

Corbitt shook his head. "Then don't be s'prised y'all be meetin him again real soon."

Blood was seeping from under the truck, spreading in a glistening pool across the pavement. Corbitt watched as it touched the toe of his Cheetah. Stacy's voice came husky.

"Well, he wasn't no shot, for sure."

"Yeah," agreed Winfield, holding his wadded T-shirt to his ribs. "Full-fuckin-auto an all he hit was that mirror . . . um, not countin my ass."

Corbitt glanced up at the truck. "Weren't no marker lights

for showin the cab. He shoot the right place for a modern-day truck." Corbitt turned, lifting his face toward the freshening breeze. Something small and fragile and blacker than the night floated down to land in the blood-pool. Corbitt's eyes narrowed, flicking up toward the roof. "Tam!"

Dashing through the rock-house doorway, Corbitt almost tripped over another body. He stopped for a moment, blinking in the big bulb's glare, but then ran for the partition. *Just another loser in the whiteman's game.* Entering the smaller room, he saw Bilal helping Beamer to sit up. Beamer was sobbing like a child. Blood covered one side of his face, but otherwise he seemed unhurt. Bilal shook him. "Stop it, fool! Get your ass outa here!"

The other boys appeared behind Corbitt. Bilal looked up. "Take Beamer outside! Give him all seven an then get his ass movin! We gots work to do!"

T.K. pointed. "What about Lizard?"

"Drag him cross the alley. Cover him up with one of them rugs so's the rats don't eat him! Bail!"

Corbitt helped Bilal get Beamer on his feet. Stacy led the lanky boy away. Then, Corbitt climbed quickly up the ladder and shoved the trapdoor with his shoulder. It opened easily and dropped back on the roof. Warily, Corbitt raised his head above the frame. "Tam!"

For a few seconds he could see nothing, but the scent of fresh blood carried strong in the breeze. Then, against the glow of the headlights coming over the parapet, he saw Lactameon's big rolly shape sitting hunched-over on what looked like a mattress. *"Tam!"*

The fat boy's voice sounded tired. "Don't gots to scream, man. I ain't gone up to dat big riverboat in de sky. Yet."

Corbitt ran across the roof and dropped to his knees beside the fat boy. Lactameon had both hands pressed to his chest. Blood glistened in the dimness. He looked up and took his hands away. "Ta da! Just a flesh wound, sweetheart." Corbitt studied the stab wound in the floppy mass of one breast. There was only a trickle of blood seeping from it. Corbitt patted Lactameon's shoulder. "Seem like Sabby knowed what he was goin for, Tam. Just forgot it a long ways to get there."

"Well, I ain't sayin it don't hurt."

"Um, y'all make it down that ladder, Tam?"

"Well, help me get up an I try."

Draping one of Lactameon's arms over his shoulders, Corbitt braced his knees and strained upward with all his strength. Gasping and struggling, he somehow got the fat boy on his feet, then stood, gripping him tight. "Please don't fall down, Tam. Swear I can't do that again!"

"I okay," Lactameon panted. "Just gimme a fuckin minute. Shit, I *hate* ladders!"

"I get Bilal an the dudes."

"Wait." Lactameon pointed to a rolled-up paper bag. Snag that. Stash it inside your jacket!"

Still steadying the fat boy, Corbitt reached carefully for the bag. "What this?"

"Twinkies."

"*What?*"

"Just trust me, man."

A few minutes later Lactameon was standing in the crack house's main room, one arm over Corbitt and the other over Winfield. Bilal had refused to let him sit down on one of the couches because they'd never be able to lift him again. T.K. bent close to Lactameon's chest, checking the wound with an expert eye.

"Mmm. Motherfuckin lucky it a lot more'n three inches to your heart, man. That cocksucka *know* what he aimin for!"

Winfield grinned. "Always figure they was good for somethin."

Lactameon made a face. "Good for a lot more'n you ever got out 'em, for sure!"

Bilal glanced around. "Yo. We finish up here, then help your ass home."

Lactameon shook his head. "No, man. I go to the Center. Chad an Miz Davis used to dealin with shit like this. Winfield, you best go to my mom to get that bullet hole fixed. Never can tell when them pigs gonna show up. Might get your ass drilled."

T.K. glanced toward the door. "Well, it a long motherfuckin walk to the Center from here. You up for it, Tam?"

Corbitt looked out the door too. The truck's headlights shone in. "I drive him. Ain't far, an them streets be all quiet."

Bilal nodded. He picked up Beamer's pistol and the Uzi

he'd brought down from the roof and handed them to T.K. "Well, best bail then, brothers. Things gonna start cookin here real soon!"

Corbitt helped Lactameon out the door. Behind them, the Collectors began shoving the couches and chairs and anything else that would burn over against the partition wall. The crack-house roof was dry as dust and slathered with tar. Likely the whole thing would be gone before any fire trucks could get there, and the empty brick shell would stay that way in this part of town.

It took all of Corbitt's strength to boost Lactameon up on the running board and into the cab. Then he dashed around to the driver's side. Rats were already ripping at Sebastian's body, but Corbitt didn't look. Brushing glass from the seat, he slid into the cab and fired up the engine. He cranked the steering wheel sharply so the front tire wouldn't roll back over the dead boy. Maybe that wasn't logical, but Corbitt didn't care.

Stacy appeared in the crack-house doorway. "Yo! Bilal say take Ethan with you!"

Corbitt flashed a thumb out the window, then shifted into reverse. It wasn't easy backing the big truck down the alley with only one mirror, but not that much harder than getting Lucas Sampson's White out of a tight spot on some narrow country road. Corbitt eased the truck between the two dumpsters with inches to spare on each side. A small dreadlocked figure hopped onto the running board.

"S'up, big brother? Game over, huh?"

Corbitt stopped the truck and opened the door, waiting until Ethan clambered across his lap to take his place in the middle of the seat. "My dad always be tellin me a good soldier fight a battle, never a war. Maybe we went an won us this here little round, but the game sho ain't over by a long shot." Letting out the clutch once more, Corbitt backed the rest of the way into the street.

Lactameon dabbed at his chest with the bloody bandana. "So, you gonna come back an teach us all to fight barefoot, man?"

Corbitt shifted into first and headed the truck into the fog. "Y'all be up for that ever bit as good as me, Tam."

"So, what you gonna do with this thing after you drop me off?"

Corbitt handed Ethan his tobacco pouch. "Mmm, spect I leave it back by that scrapyard. Let it go on earnin a livin."

Ethan pressed close to Lactameon. "Oh, fuck, man! Your poor tit!"

"Ethan!"

"Well!" Ethan yanked off his own bandana. "Here, Tam, let me do dat." He wiped at the blood on Lactameon's chest. "Shit, bet dat one motherfuckin owie an a half! Yo, Corbitt, some cocksucka stab *you* like dis, da motherfuckin blade be pokin out your back! Uh-huh!"

Corbitt smiled and glanced down at his own slender frame while double-clutching to second. Then he pulled the paper bag from inside his jacket. "So, what be so all 'portant you gots in here, Tam?"

Lactameon relaxed back in the seat, letting Ethan tend his chest. "Show you when we get to the Center. They can always use a few extra Twinkies. Seem like you could do with a couple yourself."

Corbitt upshifted to third, then glanced again at the bag. "Mmm. Don't take no magic to figure there a whole lot more'n Twinkies in there." He raised his eyes to Lactameon's. "That be a real rightful thing y'all doin, Tam. But, ain't you gonna be keepin back none for Toni an you? Raisin up babies be a 'spensive proposition, an seem like to me Beamer gonna be needin a few of them Twinkies too."

Lactameon gazed ahead through the windshield as Corbitt made a final shift to fourth. "I keep what we need, man. Let Toni handle it. Then I pay the Leopards for Winfield, an put some in our treasury. Shit, what else I need that paper for?"

"Well, y'all ain't plannin to give up eatin?"

Lactameon smiled and fired the cigarette Ethan gave him, then patted his belly. "Shit, I work *hard* gettin this fat, man. Yo, I had me enough green to lay around on my ass eatin all day, out havin to worry where my next meal comin from, I wouldn't be no better'n them fat whiteboys up in those hills. Ain't no wonder they shamed to take off their shirts." He ruffled Ethan's dreads. "Sides, this dude gonna be the fattest kid in the world."

Ethan grinned. "Shit yeah!"

Corbitt smiled for a moment, but then his face turned

thoughtful. "Mmm. Seem like to me that another next-thing, Tam."

Lactameon's eyes saddened as they met Corbitt's over Ethan's head. "Yeah. I guess it is, huh?" He sighed and looked away. "Shit, an here me an Toni an Beam ain't even gots a solid name goin on for our own son yet."

Corbitt gazed out over the long hood. A scattering of stars shone dimly through the city's glow above the eastern hills. Glancing down, he thought he saw their sparkle for an instant in Ethan's new eye. But that wasn't logical: streetlights were the only stars Ethan would ever see. Buried and forgotten; because no one would do any more than just what was expected of them. Corbitt slipped an arm around the little boy's shoulders, then turned to Lactameon. "So, what y'all think of Weylen?"

17

The rattle of planks woke him. Corbitt sat up and looked out the window as the Greyhound rumbled over the New Crossing bridge. Inside it was cool, bathed in the same filtered air he'd been breathing for two thousand miles; an artificial atmosphere that was never a part of the land he passed through. Outside, the little valley shimmered and steamed under the afternoon sun. Rubbing tired eyes, Corbitt straightened his back and stretched. A few minutes more and the bus would be pulling into the truckstop station. He saw the tree where he'd sat one morning and watched another kind of bus take his father on a sideslip in time. It seemed like centuries had passed since then. A crow perched now in the shaded tree fork. Its molten-gold eyes seemed to find Corbitt's even through the black glass. Corbitt had decided that he wouldn't get off at the truckstop. He'd ride on to the junction instead and walk home down Bridge-end Road. Maybe that wasn't the most logical thing to do, but it made its own sort of sense. He felt as impatient as the fast-idling engine while the bus waited outside the truckstop build-ing. No dark, slender African boy ran to wash its windshield. The familiar scents of home drifted to Corbitt's nostrils through the open door. In the seat beside him another tired traveler slept right on though the five-minute pause. Then the driver returned with a Pepsi and sealed out the real world once more.

They were waiting at the crossroads. Corbitt supposed he shouldn't have been surprised: maybe all Africans were tuned to the same frequency, and maybe someday the right words sung by the right singer would bring all the scattered little tribes together. The big silver bus slowed as the black driver saw Corbitt rise and come forward. The man smiled.

"I seen 'em ever day this whole last week waitin out there in that hot ole sun. I be proud, I was you, havin me friends like that."

Corbitt carried the only possessions he wasn't wearing; his shabby old jacket and Silver's skateboard. The figures of Toby, Lamar, and Sherry blurred for a moment as brown dust swirled from beneath the bus wheels. Corbitt blinked, suddenly sure he saw another boy with them; willowy slender and black as midnight. That was logical: Weylen would walk home with them before moving on to his own next-thing. Corbitt felt in his pocket for the wrinkled old dollar. He would drop it from the bridge. Maybe it would sink in the riverbend pool, or maybe it would drift down past the fields and towns for another child to find.

The driver brought the bus to a smooth, sighing stop, then turned to study Corbitt. "Y'all ain't from round here, are you, son?"

Corbitt smiled. He'd washed this man's windshield at least a hundred times. Maybe it was just Silver's ring that made him look like he belonged somewhere else? "Spect it be bout the closest I ever gonna get to bein home, sir."

Behind Corbitt, the other traveler woke. "Yo! We dere yet? Shit, man, I gots to piss like a motherfuckin racehorse! An I hungry, goddammit! So, where dat fuckin ole river anyways? I wanna learn me some swimmin . . . an catch me a cocksuckin catfish!"

The bus driver's mouth fell open as Ethan came down the aisle. Corbitt grinned. The little boy carried his huge black sweatshirt and a paper bag that bulged with junkfood, Twinkies, and the drawings Corbitt had rescued from the empty apartment. Lactameon's shell necklace glowed bone-white against Ethan's brassy bare chest, adding to the savagery of his long, beaded dreadlocks. He wore a faded red tank-top and patched 501s scored from the Center. The layovers had mostly been spent in the bus station restaurants . . . Lactameon had given Corbitt enough money to make the return trip in almost sinful luxury, with plenty left over for paying his debts. Even after two days of feasting Ethan had a long way to go before being the fattest kid in the world, but he now boasted the normal round tummy of a Bridge-end kid. Mrs. Griffin's baking would add to his mass, but likely the riverbank life would soon fill out his body in more solid ways.

The little boy rubbed his eyes and stared out at the roadside. "Yo! Dat dere *gots* to be Lamar da lion! Shit, he be one baaaad-looking motherfucka, fo sho! An dere Toby da tiger . . . an, an maaan, dat Sherry Cooper a seven out seven an a goddamn half!" Ethan blinked, then tapped his blue eye with a finger and gazed up at Corbitt. "Yo! Y'all be seein somethin, man. I can tell. Da fuck is it?"

Corbitt took hold of Ethan's hand. "Lots of yellow soap in your future, little brother-mine."

ABOUT THE AUTHOR

Jess Mowry was born in Mississippi in 1960
and raised in Oakland, where he was educated through the eighth grade. In 1988 he
bought a used typewriter for ten dollars and
started writing. He is also the author of *Way
Past Cool*, *Children of the Night,* and *Rats
in the Trees.* He lives in Oakland.